The Journals and Miscellaneous Notebooks
of
RALPH WALDO EMERSON

⤷ GENERAL EDITORS ⤶

WILLIAM H. GILMAN   ALFRED R. FERGUSON

MERRELL R. DAVIS

MERTON M. SEALTS, JR.   HARRISON HAYFORD

The Journals and Miscellaneous Notebooks

of

RALPH WALDO EMERSON

VOLUME V

1835–1838

EDITED BY

MERTON M. SEALTS, JR.

THE BELKNAP PRESS
OF HARVARD UNIVERSITY PRESS

Cambridge, Massachusetts

1 9 6 5

Preface

The General Editors note with sadness the passing of Professor William A. Jackson, Director of the Houghton Library and Secretary of the Ralph Waldo Emerson Memorial Association, a friend and counselor to us all. He did much over the years to make this edition possible.

The editor of this volume wishes to thank a number of institutions and persons for help of various kinds.

The Ralph Waldo Emerson Memorial Association has continued to provide regular grants-in-aid which have been indispensable to the progress of the edition generally. For work on the present volume, the John Simon Guggenheim Memorial Foundation awarded a research fellowship and Lawrence College — now Lawrence University — provided a research leave and a humanities research grant.

Grateful acknowledgment for their assistance and encouragement is made to Mr. David Emerson; to the late Professor Jackson, Miss Carolyn Jakeman, and the staff of the Houghton Library; to Mr. Robert Haynes, Mr. Foster Palmer, and the staff of the Widener Library; to Miss Margaret Hackett of the Boston Athenaeum; to Mrs. Howard Kent and Mrs. John Dempsey of the Concord Antiquarian Society and the Emerson House in Concord; to Presidents Douglas M. Knight and Howard F. Lowry; to Professors Harry Hayden Clark, Leon Howard, Herbert Spiegelberg, Willard Thorp, and Arlin Turner; and to other students of Emerson, notably Ralph H. Orth and the editors of Emerson's early lectures: Robert E. Spiller, Wallace E. Williams, and the late Stephen E. Whicher. Miss Millicent Kalaf and Mrs. Fred Alexander typed the body of the manuscript; Mrs. Merton Sealts, Jr. helped in every stage of its preparation, including copyreading, annotation, indexing, and proofreading.

Unless otherwise noted, translations of classical quotations are from the Loeb Classical Library and are reprinted by permission of the Harvard University Press and the Loeb Classical Library. The letters, journals, and manuscripts of A. Bronson Alcott deposited in the Houghton Library by Mrs. F. Wolsey Pratt have been used by permission of Professor Jackson.

Mr. Sealts has been the editor responsible for preparation of this volume; the other surviving General Editors have actively contributed in various ways.

W.H.G.   M.M.S.
A.R.F.   H.H.

Contents

Illustrations

Foreword to Volume V

On September 17, 1836, Emerson wrote to Thomas Carlyle: "I send you a little book I have just now published, as an entering wedge, I hope, for something more worthy and significant. This is only a naming of topics on which I would gladly speak and gladlier hear." The appearance of *Nature*, Emerson's first book, and his orientation toward the future as shown by his words to Carlyle are signs of the happier direction his life had taken since the dark days of 1831, when Ellen Tucker Emerson had died, and 1832, when he had made the painful decision to resign his Boston pastorate. During his ensuing European trip, which did much to restore his severely impaired health and troubled spirit, he had apparently conceived the idea of a book, and he may even have drafted some of its earliest passages while waiting to sail for home in September of 1833. "I like my book about nature," he wrote on shipboard, "& wish I knew where & how I ought to live. God will show me." Between 1833 and the spring of 1836 the "book about nature" began to take substantial form, much of it in his journals and lectures as Emerson turned experimentally toward his new secular career as speaker and writer. In 1834 he moved to Concord and in 1835 married again and brought his second wife, Lydia Jackson of Plymouth, to a house on the edge of Concord village christened "Coolidge Castle" after its former owner. There he completed *Nature* in the summer of 1836, and there in October the birth of his first child, Waldo, crowned the happiness of his new way of life.

Carlyle, acknowledging receipt of the "little azure-coloured *Nature*" in a letter of February 13, 1837, and noting that his friend had described it as "the first chapter of something greater," wrote of the book as "the Foundation and Ground-plan on which you may build whatsoever of great and true has been given you to build."

Actually, *Nature* is both prospective and retrospective. It does in fact name many of the topics on which Emerson was soon to speak: in "The American Scholar" and "Literary Ethics," in his Address on Education in Providence and his Divinity School Address in Cambridge, and in his courses of lectures during the next two winters — on the philosophy of history and on human culture — which in turn anticipate the *Essays* [*First Series*] of 1841. But in taking its brave stand for spiritualism, in asserting the fundamental unity of man and nature, and in calling confidently for "an original relation to the universe" Emerson's book was looking to the future while bringing into sharp focus what he had been learning to see and say all through the early 1830's in his experience, in his journals, and in his apprentice lecturing on popular science, travel, biography, and literature.

The continuity of Emerson's development is evident not only in the gradual emergence of his guiding ideas but also in the reappearance, in the first journals of the Concord years, of names associated with antecedent periods of his life: Dr. Gamaliel Bradford, Abel Adams, George Ripley, Frederic Henry Hedge, and George Partridge Bradford, to mention but a few. Among his various relatives, the most prominent figures in these pages are "the wise aunt," Mary Moody Emerson; the venerable stepgrandfather, Dr. Ezra Ripley; and the brilliant younger brother Charles, by 1835 also settled in Concord, engaged to marry Elizabeth Hoar, and practicing law in the office of her father, Hon. Samuel Hoar, who for one term (1835–1837) served in the lower house of Congress. The relation between such stimulating associates and the growth of his own mind is acknowledged repeatedly in passages of Emerson's journals; for example, seven "benefactors" who set his thoughts in action through their "manners or unconscious talk" are named in an entry for October 3, 1837: his aunt, his brother Charles, his cousin Orville Dewey, the two Bradfords, Hedge, and his newer friend Bronson Alcott. Loss of the beloved Charles in May of 1836 — to tuberculosis, the same disease that had taken Ellen from him in 1831 and another brother, Edward, in 1834 — had been a heavy blow. Writing out of his immediate grief on May 16, 1836, he set down something of what the companionship of Charles had meant to him: "It was pleasant to unfold my thought to so wise a hearer. It opened itself genially to his warm & bright light, and borrowed color & sometimes form from him. Besides my direct debt to him of how many valued thoughts, — through what orbits of speculation have we not travelled together, so that it would not be possible for either of us to say, This is my thought, That is yours."

Perhaps Bronson Alcott came closest to filling the particular void left in Emerson's life after the death of Charles. Before their friendship developed, Alcott was described to Emerson by George Bradford in July of 1835 as "a consistent spiritualist"; after his stay at Coolidge Castle in October he seemed to Emerson himself "A wise man, simple, superior to display." Later, Emerson visited Alcott's Temple School in Boston, read his private manuscripts with the increasing conviction that he was a better talker than a writer, and regretted his own inability to strike a stronger blow in his friend's defense when Alcott and the school came under newspaper attack early in 1837. By May 19 of that year he was ready to declare Alcott "the most extraordinary man and the highest genius of the time." How readily their thought sometimes blended is suggested by a notation of June 22, 1836: "Mr Alcott has been here with his Olympian dreams. . . . He made here some majestic utterances but so inspired me that even I forgot the words often." Following closely after this entry in the journal is a draft of the passage ascribed to "a certain poet" in chapter VIII of *Nature* — the juxtaposition leading several interpreters to propose the Transcendental schoolmaster as the original of that "Orphic" figure. Considering Emerson's acknowledgments to his "benefactors" generally, however, it might be better to say of Alcott as of Charles Emerson, that Emerson "borrowed color & sometimes form from him."

Among other new friendships of the Concord years two must be singled out: those with Margaret Fuller and the young Henry Thoreau. If Emerson is the "he" of the entry opening Thoreau's journal, the two had already met by October 22, 1837, when Thoreau wrote: " 'What are you doing now?' he asked,' Do you keep a journal?' — So I make my first entry to-day." The earliest mention of Thoreau in Emerson's own journal, made in the following February, notes his "simplicity and clear perception," adding: "Every thing that boy says makes merry with society though nothing can be graver than his meaning." As for Miss Fuller, who had long sought Emerson's acquaintance, when she first came to Concord as the Emersons' house-guest in July and August of 1836, Emerson was experiencing diffi-culty in finishing *Nature* and evidently felt apprehensive over the coming visit. "The worst guest is Asmodeus," he wrote in a journal entry for July 21, the day of her expected arrival, "who comes into the quiet house sometimes in breeches sometimes in petticoats and demands of his entertainer not shelter & food, but to find him in work, and every body is on pins until some rope of sand is found for the monster to twist." By August 12, noting her departure, he was more generous, calling her "a very accomplished & very intelligent person," though on the next day he also remarked that from "egotism of place & time & blood" she was "by no means so free with all her superiority" as the more "impersonal" Sarah Bradford Ripley.

Although Emerson's ambivalence toward Margaret Fuller never entirely disappeared, the friendship was an important one to both. In the journals of this period she is seen lending him various German books and even giving him lessons in German pronunciation during one of her visits to Coolidge Castle; later the two collaborated as successive editors of *The Dial*, the Transcendentalist organ that com-menced publication in 1840. The idea of publishing such a journal originated with a group of congenial friends in the Boston area who began meeting in September of 1836 for occasional afternoons of discussion whenever their organizing spirit, Frederic Henry Hedge, returned from his pastorate in Bangor, Maine. Consisting initially of Hedge, Emerson, Alcott, George Ripley, Convers Francis, James Freeman Clarke, and Orestes Brownson, the enlarging group — which Emerson refers to in the journals as "Hedge's Club" and "The Aesthetic Club" — later became known as the Transcendental Club. The founding members, Alcott excepted, were all ordained Unitarian ministers of a liberal persuasion whose "rule of admision," as Emer-son recorded it, was simply that "Whoever by his admission excludes any topic from our debate shall be excluded" — a rule broad enough to admit Margaret Fuller, Elizabeth Palmer Peabody, Sarah Clarke, Elizabeth Hoar, and Mrs. Samuel Ripley to the early meetings which his journals describe.

As important to Emerson as the stimulus of his friends was the continuing influence of books, especially during the pivotal years 1835 and 1836 when *Nature* was approaching completion. "When shall I be tired of reading?" he asks in an entry of July 31, 1835. "When the moon is tired of waxing & waning, when the sea is tired of ebbing & flowing, when the grass is weary of growing, when the planets are tired of going." Before the death of Charles the brothers were reading Sophocles in Greek and discussing such old favorites as Shakespeare, Milton, and Scott, who are as freely quoted in these journals as they had been in earlier years. Here too Emerson habitually leavens his writing with phrases from the Bible and the classics and draws heavily on a few works to which he returned again and again, like Plutarch's *Morals* and *Lives*, the essays of Bacon and Montaigne, and the writings of Swedenborg. Other familiar names include his English contemporaries Wordsworth and Coleridge, Landor and Carlyle, and such Europeans as Madame de Staël and Goethe. In March of 1836 he was translating Goethe — helped, it would seem, by referring to Carlyle's versions — and entering numerous selected passages in his journal; in August, having acquired fifteen volumes of Goethe's *Nachgelassene Werke* in a Boston bookstore, he reported to his brother William that he was reading "little else than his books lately." Among the entries of 1835 and 1836 there are further extracts of some length from the English theologian John Norris; the French Swedenborgian Oegger, whose *True Messiah*, which Emerson read in a manuscript translation, yielded phrasing for *Nature*; and from the sayings of Confucius as translated by Joshua Marshman. Emerson also mentions with approval Elizabeth Peabody's *Record of a School*, dealing with Alcott's work in Boston, and Alcott's own *Conversations with Children on the Gospels*, part of which he heard or himself read in manuscript in 1836 along with Alcott's journal and further unpublished material submitted for his criticism. Other authors given particular attention include the religious writers Ralph Cudworth and Jakob Böhme, the historian Johannes von Müller, and the English poet Henry Taylor, whose recent verse drama *Philip van Artevelde* provoked a variety of Emersonian comments.

Much of the journalizing for 1837 and 1838 is associated rather directly with Emerson's concurrent lecturing and occasional addresses.

There are fewer references during these years to books and authors generally, but there is more original composition and a greater concern for contemporary events: the hard times of 1837; current political developments; Emerson's own reluctant involvement in controversy over the government's arbitrary treatment of the Cherokee Indians. His reading was largely in the quarterly reviews, books of popular science and exploration, and especially works of history and biography that might yield illustrative material for the lectures. Notes and usable extracts are set down from lives of Pym and Hampden, Boswell's Johnson, the conversation and letters of Goethe and his circle (which Emerson was translating), and detailed accounts of Napoleon at St. Helena written by two members of his retinue, Count Las Cases and the Irish surgeon Barry O'Meara. Emerson's evident fascination with Napoleon immediately reveals itself through allusions in both the Divinity School Address and "Literary Ethics" (1838); in later years "Spiritual Laws" and other essays of the 1841 collection and ultimately *Representative Men* (1850) also use material on Napoleon — though little on Goethe — recorded in the journal at this time. Conspicuous among the entries are long extracts from one old favorite, Plutarch's *Morals*, and from a contemporary work by an English writer, William Gardner, called *The Music of Nature*, plus an extensive list of Carlyle's publications to date: Emerson in 1837 arranged for a Boston edition of *The French Revolution* and in early 1838 was planning a selection of the early periodical articles, only to be anticipated by a parallel enterprise to which he deferred.

The Address on Education delivered in Providence on June 10, 1837, reflects some of Emerson's anxieties of the late winter and spring already visible in the journal, which reveals him as gloomy, ill, worried about his own finances and those of his brother William in New York: striking images of fracture and upheaval, which mark his observations on the current financial panic, carry over into the address. "Almost one month lost to study by bodily weakness & disease," he noted on June 29. By late summer, with the Tucker estate at last settled and his health improved, he resumed the optative mood, as seen in the confident exhortations of "The American Scholar," his Harvard Phi Beta Kappa oration of August 31, 1837.

This address and the lectures on human culture of the following winter won a gratifying reception, particularly among the young, generating further opportunities to speak in the summer of 1838 to the senior class at the Divinity School in Cambridge and before two literary societies at Dartmouth College.

As early as August of 1835 Emerson had thought of writing "a chapter on Literary Ethics," his topic at Dartmouth, but in 1838 the subject must have proved difficult to enlarge upon once more after the dynamic Phi Beta Kappa oration of the previous year, which had set forth his conception of "the Duty & Discipline of a Scholar" — his alternative title for the "chapter." Of more immediate concern was the old issue of religion and the church, looked at in relation to his central doctrine of the mid-1830's: that there is "one soul which animates all men," in the words of "The American Scholar." As corollaries to this idea, his "old thrum," as he called it, Emerson had now come to believe that God, or the One, is not personal but impersonal, that evil is not absolute but merely privative, and that the moral constitution of man rather than historical Christianity must provide the basis for a modern religion. Holding such ideas, he moved even farther away from his remaining institutional affiliations. In February of 1838 he discontinued his agreement to supply a pulpit in East Lexington, where he had done occasional preaching since 1835; in March, regretting that his winter lecturing had not specifically identified "the great error of modern Society in respect to religion," he meditated "a discourse to the American clergy showing them the ugliness & unprofitableness of theology & churches at this day & the glory & sweetness of the Moral Nature out of whose pale they are almost wholly shut." The invitation to speak at Cambridge in July provided the occasion for just such a discourse; the present volume closes with Emerson at work drafting materials for this engagement and the oration at Dartmouth.

As he might well have foreseen, Emerson's challenge to institutional religion in the Divinity School Address was to provoke more controversy than anything else he had said, in *Nature* or in his earlier addresses and lectures, since resigning his pastorate in 1832. Yet his fundamental position in 1838 represented no sudden shift in thinking: "In all my lectures," he wrote retrospectively in his journal in April,

1840, "I have taught one doctrine, namely, the infinitude of the private man. This the people accept readily enough, and even with loud commendation, as long as I call the lecture Art, or Politics, or Literature, or the Household; but the moment I call it Religion, they are shocked, though it be only the application of the same truth which they receive everywhere else, to a new class of facts." And in the journals from 1835 to 1838, where this "same truth" first found expression, Emerson's optimistic faith in man's "infinitude," though not unchallenged by events, is seen at its peak.

Volume V consists of three regular journals covering a span of nearly three and a half years. Two of them are made up of largely consecutive entries, Journal B running from January of 1835 through December of 1836, Journal C from January of 1837 through June 7 of 1838. The much shorter third journal, which Emerson dated "June 1835" and designated RO, the editors have titled "RO Mind" to distinguish the entries of 1835 from a later RO sequence of 1855–1856. RO Mind, opening with observations on "the First Philosophy" adapted from passages of B written earlier in 1835, incorporates additional materials taken both from B and from two of the journals printed in volume IV: Q (August 1832) and A (April–August 1834). Other writing of the period 1835–1838 such as quotation books, lecture outlines, and further miscellaneous composition outside the scope of the regular journals will appear in volume VI and later volumes.

Editorial technique. The editorial process followed here continues the policies outlined in volume I and the slight modifications introduced in subsequent volumes of this edition, since the journals of each period of Emerson's career naturally present somewhat different problems. By 1835, as Emerson turned from the pulpit to the lecture platform, his journals were becoming more and more a repository for the substance of future lectures, which he drew "chiefly out of the materials already collected in this Journal," as he remarked of his series on human culture (1837–1838). Most of the journal passages so used are identified in the notes with reference to title and page of *The Early Lectures of Ralph Waldo Emerson*; most of the passages used in *Nature*, the occasional addresses of 1836–

1838, and the later essays are identified with reference to title and page of the Centenary Edition of Emerson's works.

Annotation in this volume draws upon the previous editorial labors of Edward W. Emerson and the findings of such scholars as Edmund G. Berry, Kenneth W. Cameron, Joseph Slater, Charles L. Young, and the editors of the early lectures: Robert E. Spiller, Wallace E. Williams, and the late Stephen E. Whicher. Many of the passages of Journals B and C used in the lectures through 1838 were identified by the lecture editors, others are noted here, and still others employed in later lectures will be specified when volume III of *The Early Lectures* appears. As Emerson prepared his collection of *Essays [First Series]* (1841), he not only incorporated material from various lectures but he also went back directly to the journals as well, so that for study of the provenience of these essays one must work with the texts of both journals and lectures. Here, as in volumes III and IV, Emerson's use marks are fully described in the notes since they afford potential clues to studies of his habits of composition, but not every journal passage used in his other writings has been traced nor do the notes show precisely what modifications took place in passages so employed. Usually, though not always, Emerson marked in pencil the passages he used in lectures; his marks in ink commonly designate passages used elsewhere. Some entries bear marks in both pencil and ink, but others used one or more times carry no marks at all. The definitive pronouncement on Emerson's methods of composing must await the publication of additional evidence, including index materials and outlines scheduled for future volumes.

CHRONOLOGY 1835–1838

1835: January, Emerson becomes engaged to Lydia Jackson; January–March, he gives in Boston his first extended course of lectures, on biographies of great men; February 11, he defends the French Revolution in a debate before the Concord Lyceum; August 15, he buys a house in Concord from John T. Coolidge for $3500; August 20, he lectures in Boston on inspiring a correct taste in English literature; September 12, he delivers the address of the day at

Concord's second centennial celebration; September 14, he is married to Lydia Jackson; October 17–18, he first entertains Amos Bronson Alcott; November, he undertakes to supply the pulpit in East Lexington; November 5, he begins a course of ten lectures in Boston, on English literature.

1836: January, Emerson concludes his lectures in Boston and opens a series on biography at Salem; April, he begins a second course of lectures at Salem on English biography and literature, but interrupts the series to accompany his brother Charles to New York; May 9, Charles Emerson dies in New York; June, Emerson prepares to complete *Nature*; July 21 or 22, Margaret Fuller first visits the Emersons; September 9 or 10, publication of *Nature*; September 19, preliminary meeting of "Hedge's Club," later the Symposium, or Transcendental Club; October 30, birth of Waldo Emerson; December 8, Emerson begins in Boston a course of twelve lectures on the philosophy of history.

1837: March 2, Emerson concludes his lectures in Boston; March–April, he replies to attacks on Bronson Alcott and his school; April, William Emerson requests his brother's financial help; June 10, despite poor health, Emerson speaks in Providence at the dedication of the Greene Street school; July, he receives the final installment of his share of the Tucker estate; August 31, he delivers the Phi Beta Kappa address at Harvard, "The American Scholar"; November 8, he begins in Lowell a course of ten lectures, on human culture; December 6, he opens the same series of lectures in Boston.

1838: February 7, Emerson completes the Boston lectures, which he repeats in Framingham, Cambridge, and Concord during the winter and spring; February 11, first mention of Henry Thoreau in Emerson's journals; February 18, he relinquishes the pulpit at East Lexington — his final separation from the church; March 12, Emerson lectures in Boston on war and peace; April 23, he addresses a letter to President Van Buren protesting treatment of the Cherokee Indians; May, he arranges to borrow money in behalf of his brother William; June, he gathers materials for addresses in July: that to the senior class at the Divinity School, Cambridge, and "Literary Ethics," before two literary societies at Dartmouth College.

SYMBOLS AND ABBREVIATIONS

⟨　⟩　　　Cancellation
↑　↓　　　Insertion
/　/　　　Variant
‖ . . . ‖　　Unrecovered matter, normally unannotated. Three dots, one to five words; four dots, six to fifteen words; five dots, sixteen to thirty words. Matter lost by accidental mutilation but recovered conjecturally is inserted between the parallels.
⟨‖ . . . ‖⟩　Unrecovered cancelled matter
‖msm‖　　Manuscript accidentally mutilated
[　]　　　Editorial insertion
[. . .]　　Editorial omission
[　]　　　Emerson's square brackets
⌐　⌐　　　Marginal matter inserted in text
[　]　　　Page numbers of original manuscript
ⁿ　　　　See Textual Notes
∧　　　　Emerson's symbol for intended insertion
[R.W.E.]　Editorial substitution for Emerson's symbol of original authorship. See volume I, plate VII.
*　　　　Emerson's note
epw　　　Erased pencil writing
☞
☜　　　　Hands pointing
☝

ABBREVIATIONS AND SHORT TITLES IN FOOTNOTES

E t E　　Kenneth W. Cameron. *Emerson the Essayist*. Raleigh, N.C.: The Thistle Press, 1945. 2 vols.

J　　　*Journals of Ralph Waldo Emerson*. Edited by Edward Waldo Emerson and Waldo Emerson Forbes. Boston and New York: Houghton Mifflin Co., 1909–1914. 10 vols.

JMN　　*The Journals and Miscellaneous Notebooks of Ralph Waldo Emerson*. Edited by William H. Gilman, Alfred R. Ferguson, Merrell R. Davis, Merton M. Sealts, Jr., and Harrison Hayford (Volume I edited by William H. Gilman, Alfred R. Ferguson, George P. Clark, and Merrell R. Davis). Cambridge: Harvard University Press, 1960–

L   *The Letters of Ralph Waldo Emerson*. Edited by Ralph L. Rusk. New York: Columbia University Press, 1939. 6 vols.

Lectures   *The Early Lectures of Ralph Waldo Emerson*. Volume I, 1833–1836, edited by Stephen E. Whicher and Robert E. Spiller; volume II, 1836–1838, edited by Stephen E. Whicher, Robert E. Spiller, and Wallace E. Williams. Cambridge: Harvard University Press, 1959–

Life   Ralph L. Rusk. *The Life of Ralph Waldo Emerson*. New York: Charles Scribner's Sons, 1949.

W   *The Complete Works of Ralph Waldo Emerson*. With a Biographical Introduction and Notes, by Edward Waldo Emerson. Centenary Edition. Boston and New York: Houghton Mifflin Co., 1903–1904. 12 vols. I — *Nature Addresses and Lectures*; II — *Essays, First Series*; III — *Essays, Second Series*; IV — *Representative Men*; V — *English Traits*; VI — *Conduct of Life*; VII — *Society and Solitude*; VIII — *Letters and Social Aims*; IX — *Poems*; X — *Lectures and Biographical Sketches*; XI — *Miscellanies*; XII — *Natural History of Intellect*.

YES   *Young Emerson Speaks*. Edited by Arthur C. McGiffert, Jr. Boston: Houghton Mifflin Co., 1938.

The Journals

B

1835–1836

Journal B, a regular journal, opens with the date "1 January, 1835." Its dated entries run from January 6 of that year through December 10, 1836. A few passages are copied from earlier journals; others are incorporated in Journal RO Mind, where in June of 1835 Emerson brought together his observations on "the First Philosophy."

Journal B is written in a hard-covered copybook, rebacked, larger than that used for Journal A in 1833–1834. The leaves, faintly ruled, measure approximately 20 x 25.8 cm. Including flyleaves, there are 348 pages in all; following 6 unnumbered pages (designated i through vi) is Emerson's sequential pagination in ink, 1–335, extending from the first dated entry through the first of 4 pages of index material at the end of the journal. The unnumbered pages designated 337–338 and 339–340, comprising index material inscribed on unlined leaves, are tipped in. Exclusive of 2 marbled flyleaf pages (i, 342), there are 18 blank pages: ii, iv–vi, 173, 193–197, 247, 266–267, 270, 323, 325, 338, and 340.

[front cover]   B
                  1835

[front cover verso] [blank]

[i]–[ii] [blank]

[iii]   B   R. Waldo Emerson.

                —

                —

                Journal.
                1835–6

                —

                —

"To think is to act." [1]

—

—

[Index material omitted]

[iv]–[vi] [blank]

[1]   Concord, 1 January, 1835.
[January] 6th. No doubt we owe most valuable knowledge to our conversation even with the frivolous, yet when I return as just now from more than usual opportunities of hearing & seeing, it seems to me that one good day here, is worth more than three gadding days in town. Sunday I went for the first time to the Swedenborg Chapel. The sermon was in its style severely simple & in method & manner had much the style of a problem in geometry wholly uncoloured & unimpassioned. Yet was it, as I told Sampson Reed,[2] one that with the exception of a single passage might have been preached without exciting surprise in any church. At the opposite pole, say rather in another Zone from this hard truist was Taylor[3] in the afternoon wishing his sons a happy new year praying God for his servants of the brine, to favor commerce, to bless the bleached sail, the white foam & through commerce to christianize the Universe. "May every deck," he said, "be stamped by the hallowed feet of godly captains, & the first watch, & the second watch be watchful for the Divine light." He thanked God he had not been in Heaven for the last twenty five years, — then indeed had he been a dwarf in grace, but now he had his redeemed souls around him.

    And so he went on, — this Poet of the Sailor & of Ann street — fusing all the rude hearts of his auditory with the heat of his own

---

    [1] A quotation or perhaps a restatement by Emerson — e.g., of Carlyle, "Characteristics," *The Edinburgh Review*, LIV (Dec. 1831), 370; see *JMN*, III, 298, n. 85; used in "Spiritual Laws," *W*, II, 163.
    [2] Emerson had known Sampson Reed, his "Swedenborgian druggist," since his college days, when he had copied Reed's Commencement oration on genius.
    [3] Edward Thompson Taylor (1793–1871), a self-educated Methodist minister known as "Father Taylor," was pastor of the Seamen's Bethel established in 1830 at Boston and located in Ann Street.

love & making the abstractions of philosophers accessible & effectual to them also. He is a fine study to the metaphysician or the life philosopher. He is profuse of himself[;] he never remembers the lookingglass. They are foolish who fear that notice will spoil him. They never made him & such as they cannot unmake him; he is a real man of strong nature & noblest richest lines [2] on his countenance. He is a work of the same hand that made ↑Demosthenes &↓ Shakspear & Burns & is guided by instincts diviner than rules. His whole discourse is a string of audacious felicities harmonized by a spirit of joyful love. Every body is cheered & exalted by him. He is a living man & explains at once what Whitefield & Fox & Father Moody[4] were to their audiences, by the total infusion of his own soul into his assembly, & consequent absolute dominion over them. How puny, how cowardly, other preachers look by the side of this preaching. He shows us what a man can do. As I sat last Sunday in my country pew, I thought this Sunday I would see two living chapels, the Swedenborg & the Seamen's, and I was not deceived.

7th January. Bitter cold days, yet I read of that inward fervor which ran as fire from heart to heart through England in George Fox's time. How precisely parallel are the biographies of religious enthusiasts. Swedenborg, Guyon, Fox, Luther & perhaps Bohmen. Each owes all to the discovery that God must be sought within, not without. That is the discovery of Jesus. Each perceives the worthlessness of all instruction, & the infinity of wisdom that issues from meditation. Each perceives the nullity of all conditions but one, innocence; & the absolute submission which attends it. All become simple[,] plain in word & act. Swedenborg & the Quakers have much to say of a new Name that shall be given in heaven.

[3][5] The most original writer feels in every sentence the influence of the great writers who have established the conventions of composition; & the ⟨Moral⟩ religious Revolution effected by Jesus Christ insensibly or avowedly models each of these succeeding reforms. The

[4] George Whitefield and George Fox; Samuel Moody, minister of York, Maine, Emerson's great-great-grandfather.

[5] Emerson indexed the entry on this page under "Theoptics" — i.e., "Vision of God"; see *JMN*, III, 263, n. 109.

boldest vision of the prophet communing with God only, is confined & coloured & expressed according to the resistless example of the Jewish.

Luther's jocularity & learning give him the most reputation for sanity. The Quaker casts himself down a passive instrument of the Supreme Reason & will not risque silencing it by venturing the co-operation of his Understanding. He therefore enacts his first thought however violent or ludicrous nor stays to consider whether the purport of his Vision may not be expressed in more seemly & accustomed forms.

[January] 8. There is an elevation of thought from which things venerable become less, because we are in the presence of their Source. When we catch one clear glimpse of the moral harmonies which accomplish themselves throughout the Everlasting Now & throughout the omnipresent Here how impertinent seem the controversies of theologians. God is before us & they are wrangling about dead gods. What matters it whether the inspiration was plenary or secondary; whether this or that was intended by the Prophet; whether Jesus worked a miracle or no; if we have access inwardly to the Almighty & all wise One, Inspirer of all Prophecy, Container of all Truth & Sole Cause of Causes? All the Godhead that was in either of those ages in either of those men was the perception of those resplendent laws which [4] at this very moment draw me at the same time that they outrun & overwhelm my faculties. The Teacher that I look for & await shall enunciate with more precision & universality, with piercing poetic insight those beautiful yet severe compensations that give to moral nature an aspect of mathematical science. He will not occupy himself in laboriously reanimating a historical religion but in bringing men to God by showing them that he IS, not was, & speaks not spoke.[6]

[January] 9. The only true economy of time is to rely without interval on your own judgment. Keep the eye & ear ⟨always⟩ open to all impressions, but deepen no impression by effort, but take the opinion of the Genius within, what ought to be retained by you & what rejected by

[6] "The Teacher . . . spoke." is used in the Divinity School Address, _W_, I, 144.

you. Keep, that is, the upright position.[7] Resign yourself to your thoughts, & then every object will make that mark, that modification of your character which it ought. This were better advice to a traveller than Sir Henry Wotton's, 'il viso sciolto, i pensieri stretti.' All your time will be lived; the journey, the dinner, the waiting, will not need to be subtracted.[8]

"The spirit of prophecy is the witness of Jesus." [9]
Madame Guyon's incapability to speak before the captious is Swedenborg's inability to utter what is not believed, "though they folded their lips to indignation." [10]
Prayer is, — is it not? — the forcible subjugation for the time of the Understanding to the Reason.

[5] (De)Jan. [10? 11?] I wrote in my last Blotting Book (p. 144) [11] that we need a theory or interpretation of Mythology. How true a picture is Prometheus. There is a state of mind but too familiar in man that feels a discontent that there is any God & regards the obligation of reverence onerous. It would steal if it could the fire of the Creator & live apart from him & independent of him. This is the idea of Prometheus.[12] ↑Antaeus. Admetus p. 11↓

---

[7] With what Emerson called the "philosophy of the erect position" (*JMN*, IV, 333) cf. Milton, *Paradise Lost*, VII, 507–510: Adam,
                              "endu'd
          With Sanctitie of Reason, might erect
          His Stature, and upright with Front serene
          Govern the rest, self-knowing . . . ."
See *The Works of John Milton*, ed. F. A. Patterson, 18 vols. in 21 (New York, 1931–1938), 11, pt. 1, 229.

[8] In "Ben Jonson, Herrick, Herbert, Wotton," *Lectures*, I, 354, Emerson renders Wotton's phrase "Thoughts close the countenance loose"; cf. Sir Henry Wotton, *Reliquiae Wottonianae or a Collection of Lives, Letters, Poems*, 4th ed. (London, 1685), p. 356. Except for the fifth sentence, the entry to this point is used in "Ethics," *Lectures*, II, 146.

[9] Cf. Rev. 19:10: "the testimony of Jesus is the spirit of prophecy." The passage is cited by Emanuel Swedenborg in *The Apocalypse Revealed*, 3 vols. (Boston, 1836), I, 284.

[10] See *The Apocalypse Revealed*, 1836, I, 255; *JMN*, IV, 343.

[11] See *JMN*, IV, 374–375.

[12] "Mythology . . . idea of Prometheus.", struck through in ink with a vertical use mark, is used in "History," *W*, II, 31.

There are some occult facts in human nature that are natural magic. The chief of these is, the glance (oeillade). The mysterious communication that is established across a house between two entire strangers, by this means, moves all the springs of wonder. It happened once that a youth & a maid beheld each other in a public assembly for the first time. The youth gazed with great delight upon the beautiful face ⟨|| . . . ||⟩ ↑until he↓ caught the maiden's eye. She presently became aware of his attention & something like correspondence immediately takes place. The maid depressed her eyes that the man might gaze upon her face. Then the man looked away, that the maiden might gratify her curiosity. Presently their eyes met in a full, front, searching, not to be mistaken glance. It is wonderful how much it made them acquainted. The man thought that they had come nearer together than they could by any other intercourse in months. But he felt that by that glance he had been strangely baulked. The beautiful face was strangely transformed. He felt the stirring of owls, & bats, & horned hoofs, within him. The face which was really beautiful seemed to him to have been usurped by a low devil, and an innocent maiden, for so she still seemed to him, to be possessed. And that glance was the confession of the devil to his inquiry. Very sorry for the poor maiden was the man, & when the assembly separated, & she passed him as a stranger in [6] the crowd, her form & feet had the strangest resemblance to those of some brute animal.

It is remarkable too that the spirit that appears at the windows of the house does at once in a manner invest itself in a new form of its own to the mind of the beholder.[13]

———

Jan. 12. Truth is beautiful. Without doubt; and so are lies. I have no fairer page in my life's album than the delicious memory of some passages at Concord on the Merrimack when affection contrived to give a witchcraft surpassing even the deep attraction of its own truth to a parcel of accidental & insignificant circumstances. Those coach wheels that ⟨passed⟩ rolled into the mist & darkness of the July Morning. The little piazza, a piece of silk, the almshouse, the Davison girl & such other things, which were not the charm, have more reality

[13] This and the preceding paragraph are used in "Behavior," *W*, VI, 179.

to this groping memory than the charm itself which illuminated them.[14]

   ↑— — "passing sweet
  Are the domains of tender memory."↓ [15]
    [Wordsworth, "Ode to Lycoris," ll. 50–51]

Be assured. There is as deep a wisdom in embroidered coats & blue & pink ribbons, as is in truth & righteousness.

———

Is it not the stupendous riches of man's nature that gives an additional delight to every new truth? When I read a problem, I would be a geometer; poetry a poet; history, a historian; sermons, a preacher; when I see paintings I would paint; sculpture, carve; & so with all things, the manifold soul in me indicates its acquaintance with all these things. Similar delight we have in the admirable artist's, soldier's or sailor's life. We individuate ourselves with him & ⟨become him⟩ judge of his work. What is this but our first ride round our estate to take possession, promising ourselves withal after a few visits more, to have an [7] insight & give a ⟨direction⟩ personal direction to all the affairs that go on within our domain, which is the All.

  13 Jan. "Our very signboards show there has been a Titian in the world." [16] Do you think that Aristotle benefits him only who reads the Ethics & the Rhetoric? Or Bacon or Shakspear or the Schools those only who converse in them? Far otherwise[;] these men acted directly upon the common speech of men & made distinctions which as they were seen to be just by all who understood them, were rigidly observed as rules in their conversation & writing; & so were diffused gradually as improvements in the vernacular language. Thus the language *thinks* for us as Coleridge said.[17]

 [14] Emerson is recalling a visit to Concord, N. H., in the summer of 1829 during his engagement to Ellen Louisa Tucker, who became his first wife; this page is indexed under "E.L.T." in his Index Minor [A], p. [121] (second index). "I have no . . . illuminated them.", struck through in ink with two vertical use marks, is used in "Love," *W*, II, 174–175.

 [15] See *JMN*, III, 38.

 [16] Cf. Samuel Taylor Coleridge, *Biographia Literaria* (New York and Boston, 1834), p. 111, and *JMN*, III, 296: "Signboards speak of Titian . . . ."

 [17] Possibly a reference to the complaint in *Biographia Literaria*, 1834, p. 29, that because of its stereotyped language, modern literature "spares the reader the

Also Simeon the Stylite is not quite useless to me nor Danton, nor Robespierre, nor Rabelais, nor Aretin. And the merest speculatist Plotinus & Dante act most intensely on me. Fine sketch of the life of Descartes in Cousin[.] [18]

The student at his first course of philosophical lectures looks wistfully at every knob & ball & glass rod or cylinder as menacing him with the occult energies which they are about to disclose to their compeller[.]

I think I will read for a Lyceum Lecture the three deaths of Phocion, Socrates & Sir Thomas More. Perhaps the martyrdom of Sir John Cobham in Southey's Book of the Church might serve as a fourth.[19]

My friend Mr W[ilder?].[20] will be a good minister
    "When it shall please the Lord
    To make his people out of board."

[8] It is a great happiness when two good minds ↑meet↓ both culti-vated & with such difference of learning as to excite each the other's curiosity & such similarity as to understand each other['s] allusions in the Touch-&-go of conversation. They make each other ⟨very⟩ strong & confident. Display, every where permitted, is then the mark of weakness. The delight of measuring one's own strength & ascertain-ing what are his own real peculiarities, how my aim & bearing diverges from yours, is great, & cannot be ⟨enjoyed⟩ experienced but in such society. This is real measurement. They [21] are ashamed of untruth. Untruth ⟨kills society⟩ whether ⟨it appear⟩ in the shape of complaisance or of display ↑kills society↓. The unspoken part of this conversation is the most valuable. How many secrets that have puzzled us for

_____

trouble of thinking." See "English Literature: Introductory," *Lectures*, I, 229–230, for Emerson's development of the thought of this passage.

[18] Victor Cousin, *Introduction to the History of Philosophy*, trans. H. G. Linberg (Boston, 1832), pp. 51–53.

[19] Sir John Oldcastle, Lord Cobham; see Robert Southey, *The Book of the Church*, 2 vols. (London, 1825), I, 369–394.

[20] Reverend John Wilder was "our orthodox minister" in Concord, 1833–1839 (*L*, II, 28).

[21] "The delight . . . measurement. They", struck through in pencil with two diagonal use marks, is used in "Society," *Lectures*, II, 104.

years are then told, & with most unexpected issues. You may find for example that the reason of your friend's superiority in power arises strangely enough ⟨from⟩ not from a defect but a superfluity in your constitution. Far very far from envy is this free communication. A mutual respect rejoices them both. Cooperation & not exclusiveness is the ⟨resul⟩ fruit.

———

All misery is comparative. The debtor thinks a dun much; but in Constantinople the⟨y⟩ ↑citizen↓ think↑s↓ not much an order for money, when ⟨they⟩ ↑he↓ may expect an order for ⟨a⟩ ↑his↓ head.

[9] The great value of Biography consists in the perfect sympathy that exists between like minds. Space & time are an absolute nullity to this principle. An action of Luther's that I heartily approve I do adopt also. We are imprisoned in life in the company of persons painfully unlike us or so little congenial to our highest tendencies & so congenial to our lowest that their influence is noxious & only now & then comes by us some commissioned spirit that speaks as with the word of a prophet to the languishing nigh dead faith in the bottom of the heart & passes by & we forget what manner of men we are. It may be that there are very few persons at any one time in the world who can address with any effect the higher wants of men. This defect is compensated by the recorded teaching & acting of this class of men. Socrates, St Paul, Antoninus, Luther, Milton have lived for us as much as for their contemporaries if by books or by tradition their life & words come to my ear. ⟨They fortify by the strict likeness⟩ We recognize with delight a strict likeness between their noblest impulses & our own. We are tried in their trial. By our ⟨strong⟩ cordial approval we conquer in their victory. We participate in their act by our thorough understanding of it.

And thus we become acquainted with a fact which we could not have learned from our fellows[,] that the faintest sentiments which we have shunned to indulge from the fear of singularity are older than the oldest institutions, — are eternal in man; that we can find ourselves, our ↑private↓ thoughts, our preferences, & aversions, & our moral judgments perhaps more truly matched in an ancient Lombard, or Saxon, or Greek, than in our own family.

[10]²² It is a beautiful fact in human nature that the roar of separating oceans no nor the roar of rising & falling empires cannot hinder the ear from hearing the music of the most distant voices; that the trumpet of Homer's poetry yet shrills in the closet of the retired scholar across three thousand years; that the reproof of Socrates stings us like the bite of a serpent, as it did Alcibiades.²³

These affinities atone to us for the narrowness of our society, & the prison of our single lot, by making the human race our society, & the vast variety of human fortune the arena of actions on which we, by passing judgment, take part.

History taken together is as severely moral in its teaching as the straitest religious sect.²⁴   And thus we are fortified in our moral sentiments by a most intimate presence of sages & heroes.

Pythagoras is said (falsely I suppose) to have declared that he remembered himself to have existed before under the name of Euphorbus at the Siege of Troy.²⁵ Which of us who is much addicted to reading but recognizes his own saying or thinking in his favorite authors[?]

[11] 14 Jan. Apollo kept the flocks of Admetus, said the poets; another significant fable. Every man is an angel in disguise, a god playing the fool. It seems as if Heaven had sent its insane angels into our world as an asylum & here they will break out into rare music & utter at intervals the words they have heard in Heaven & then the mad fit returns & they mope & wallow like dogs. ↑When the gods come among men they are not known. Jesus was not. Socrates & Shakspear were not.↓ ²⁶

²² At the bottom of the page are traces of erased pencil writing, the substance of which is incorporated in the paragraph on p. [11] concerning Emerson's grandfather.

²³ Cf. Plato, *Symposium*, 217c–218a.

²⁴ "The great value [p. [9]] . . . religious sect." is struck through in ink with diagonal use marks. These paragraphs may have been used in the introductory lecture of Emerson's series on Biography, which he was to deliver in Boston on January 29; the manuscript itself has disappeared (*Lectures*, I, 97).

²⁵ Diogenes Laertius, "Pythagoras," *Lives of Eminent Philosophers*, VIII, 4–5; cf. "Apologie for Raimond de Sebonde" in *The Essays of Michael Seigneur de Montaigne*, trans. Charles Cotton, 3 vols. (London, 1700), II, 367. Emerson owned this edition of vol. 2 of the Cotton translation; his copies of vols. 1 and 3 were in the edition of 1693.

²⁶ This paragraph, struck through in ink with a vertical use mark, is used in "History," *W*, II, 31.

My thoughts tame me. Proud may the bard be among his fellow men, but when he sits waiting his inspiration he is a child, humble, reverent, watching for the thoughts as they flow to him from their unknown source. The moment of inspiration I am its reverent slave. I watch & watch & hail its Aurora from afar.[27]

[January] 15. Saw the morn rise from the hilltop but could not wait for the sun. Those long slender bars of cloud swim like fishes in the sea of crimson light. ["]Nor am I ashamed to be A lover of that silent sea.["] How does Nature deify us with a few cheap elements. Give me health and a Day & I possess more magnificence than emperors covet. The Morning sky before sunrise is my Assyria; the sunset my Paphos & unimaginable realms of Faerie[;] the night is my Germany.[28]

My Grandfather William Emerson left his parish & joined the Northern Army in the strong hope of having great influence on the men. He was bitterly disappointed in finding that the best men at home became the worst in the camp, vied with each other in profanity, drunkenness & every vice, & degenerated as fast as the days succeeded each other & instead of much influence he found he had none. This so affected him that when he became sick with the prevalent distemper he insisted on taking a dismission not a furlough, & as he died on his return his family lost, it is said, a major's pension.

[12] We are all glad of warm days they are so economical & in the country in winter the back is always cold.

[January] 16. The whole of heraldry is in courtesy. A man of fine manners can pronounce your ⟨own⟩ name in his conversation with all the charm that ever "My Lord" or "Your Highness" or "Your grace" could have had to your ear[.] [29]

---

[27] Written in pencil beneath "hail . . . from" is "Dr Parker's Church". With the substance of this paragraph compare "The Poet," *W*, IX, 313: "I snuff the breath of my morning afar".
    [28] "Those long slender . . . Germany.", struck through in ink with two wavy diagonal use marks, is used in *Nature*, *W*, I, 17; cf. also "Sunrise," *W*, IX, 345–346.
    [29] This paragraph is used in "History," *W*, II, 18.

23 January. Home again from Plymouth, with most agreeable recollections.[30]

Some thoughts lost. The Coles & Briggses[31] can finish their sermon[,] the man of genius cannot because they write words & pages which are finite things & can be numbered & ended at pleasure; He writes after Nature which is endless, His work therefore when it is best concluded he sees to be only begun. ☞[32] Mr H[oar].[33] in the coach said of Judge Marshall "that if his intellects failed, he could ⟨spare⟩ ↑lose↓ as much as would furnish brains to half a dozen common men, before common men would find it out."

It is one of the laws of composition that let the preparation have been how elaborate, how extended soever[,] the moment of *casting* is yet not less critical[,] nor the less all important moment on which the whole success depends.[34]

Ichabod Morton[35] at Plymouth said that he did not in dealing with his brother look very sharply to his own interest or mind the loss of a few dollars. He wished to treat all men in the same way.

24 January, Saturday.
28 January Wednesday
30 January I spent at Plymouth with Lydia Jackson[.]

[13][36] ☜

May I say without presumption that like Michel Angelo I only block my statues.[37]

---

[30] Emerson had become engaged to Lydia Jackson, of Plymouth.

[31] Probably Charles Briggs, the Unitarian minister at Lexington, whose pulpit Emerson had filled in March and April of 1828; "Cole" has not been identified.

[32] The hand sign points to the single sentence written opposite this passage on p. [13]. "Some thoughts . . . only begun." is struck through in pencil with a wavy diagonal use mark.

[33] Samuel Hoar, lawyer, and congressman from Massachusetts, 1835–1837; Charles Emerson, engaged to his daughter Elizabeth, was associated with his law office in Concord.

[34] This paragraph is struck through in pencil with a wavy diagonal use mark.

[35] Later described by Emerson as "a plain man . . . engaged through many years in the fisheries with success, eccentric, — with a persevering interest in education, and of a very democratic religion" (*W*, X, 361–362).

[36] The single sentence is centered on the page, opposite the ☞ on p. [12].

[37] See "Michel Angelo Buonaroti," *Lectures*, I, 110.

[14] 2 February. Let Christianity speak ever for the poor & the low. Though the voice of society should demand a defence of slavery from all its organs that service can never be expected from me. My opinion is of no worth, but I have not a syllable of all the language I have learned, to utter for the planter. If by opposing slavery I go to undermine institutions I confess I do not wish to live in a nation where slavery exists. The life of this world has but a limited worth in my eyes & really is not worth such a price as the toleration of slavery. Therefore though I may be so far restrained by unwillingness to cut the planter's throat as that I should refrain from ⟨shouting 'Down with the slaver.'⟩ ↑denouncing him↓[,] yet I pray God that not even in my dream or in madness may I ever incur the disgrace of articulating one word of apology for the slave trader or slave-holder.

Yesterday had I been born & bred a Quaker, I should have risen & protested against the preacher's words. I would have said that in the light of Christianity is no such thing as slavery. The only bondage it recognizes is that of Sin.

9 Feb. To the Indian's wigwam came the white man having a pencil in one pocket, a watch in another & paper money in a third.

Clytemnestra in Sophocles thinks herself too violently reproved by her daughter. Electra answers

> " 'Tis you that say it, not I; you do the deeds,
> And your ungodly deeds find me the words."
>   [*Electra*, ll. 624–625]

[15]   ————— "The childhood shows the man,
             As morning shows the day."
                          [Milton,] *Paradise Regained*. [IV, 220–221]
"Nothing great was ever achieved without enthusiasm[.]" [38]

[February] 11. It needs to say something, they tell me, of the French Revolution.[39] Why, yes, I believe that it has been advantageous on

---

[38] Coleridge, *The Statesman's Manual; . . . A Lay Sermon, Addressed to the Higher Classes of Society* (Burlington, Vt., 1832), p. 30. The quotation, struck through in ink with a vertical use mark, is used in "Circles," *W*, II, 321.

[39] Defended by Emerson in a debate before the Concord Lyceum on this date. See Kenneth W. Cameron, *Transcendental Climate*, 3 vols. (Hartford, 1963), III, 678.

the whole. I very readily seek & find reasons for any such proposition because whilst I believe that evil is to be hated & resisted & punished [or] at least forcibly hindered, yet offences must needs come & out of them comes good as naturally & inevitably as the beautiful flower & the ⟨rich⟩ ↑nourishing↓ fruit out of the dark ground. I believe that the tendency of all thought is to Optimism[.]

Now for the French Revolution. I believe in the first place that it would be an advantage though we were not able to point out a single benefit that had flowed thence & were able to show many calamities. I should still incline to think that we were too near to judge, like a soldier in the ranks ⟨of⟩ who is quite unable amid the ⟨dust⟩ ↑din↓ & smoke to judge how goes the day or guess at the plan of the engagement[.]

⟨But in the⟩ If I could see no direct good which it had occasioned I should still say see what great lessons it has taught the governor & the subject. It has taught men ⟨terribly⟩ how surely the relaxing of the moral bands of society ⟨goes⟩ is followed by ⟨diabolical licentiousness⟩ ↑cruelty↓. It taught men that there was a limit beyond which the ⟨powers⟩ ↑terrors↓ of a standing army & of loyal association could not avail; that there was a limit beyond which the patience[,] the fears of a down trodden people could not go[.]

[16] 14 Feb. Grand is that word of Milton in his letter to Diodati excusing his friend for not writing to him, "for though you have not written, your probity writes to me in your stead." [40]

Well said the wise aunt today "Elizabeth grows on one; she is capable of humility; her manners to the obscure are without fault." [41]

16 Feb. If Milton, if Burns, if Bryant, is in the world we have more tolerance & more love for the changing sky, the mist, the rain, the bleak overcast day, the indescribable sunrise & the immortal stars. If we believed no poet survived on the planet, nature would be tedious. [42]

[40] Cf. John Milton, letter to Charles Diodati, September 23, 1637; see *Works*, 1931–1938, XII, 25. See *L*, II, 121.

[41] Mary Moody Emerson ("MME"), speaking of Elizabeth Hoar, fiancée of Emerson's brother, Charles Chauncy Emerson.

[42] "If Milton . . . tedious." is struck through in pencil with a wavy diagonal use mark and two vertical use marks.

25 Feb. On Visits. If I had any thing to say to you, you would find me in your house pretty quick.[43]

––––

                    I looked upon trades, politics, & domestic life, as games to keep men amused & hinder them from asking *cui bono*,[44] until their eyes & minds are grown. Then came Edward's tragic verses [45] & I thought we ⟨th⟩ give full leave to the poor man and to the parting man to feel bitterness, but not less bitter, (though we give them no allowance,) are the sad farewells of the realist amidst home, friends & wealth.[46]

––––

                        March.
                      SOCIETY.

17 ⟨Feb.⟩March. I come back to my rare book scarce a journal. There is nothing so easy as to form friendships & connexions.ⁿ Yet lies there unseen a gulf between every man & woman, & a Tragedy is the protection of what seemed so helpless. So thought I today, when I heard the details of M's danger.

Many days give me marine recollections as today. It is because when the wind is loud & the air clear, the great masses of cloud move so fast as to suggest immediately their vicinity to the sea. ↑The wind blowing from the west↓ theyⁿ must reach the coast, & shade the sea in an hour. Instantly therefore comes up before the eye [17] the cold blue sea gathered up into waves all ⟨w⟩rippled & ⟨& lined⟩ scored over with ⟨lines of⟩ wind ↑lines↓ & a few sail ⟨over the⟩ scudding on their several tracks though scarce seen to move over the broad black circle. But nature is a picture frame which fits equally well a comic ⟨piece⟩ or a ⟨funeral sketch⟩ ↑mourning↓ piece.[47]

        Taylor in ↑the preface to↓ this healthful poem, "Van Artevelde," says that Sense must be the basis of all consummate poetry.[48] It is

[43] "If I . . . quick." is struck through in pencil with a wavy diagonal use mark.
[44] "Who benefits from it?" (Ed.).
[45] "The Last Farewell" by Edward Emerson, included in *W*, IX, 258.
[46] This paragraph is struck through in pencil with a wavy diagonal use mark.
[47] "I come back . . . mourning piece." is struck through in pencil with wavy diagonal use marks; "black circle . . . mourning piece." is struck through in ink with a vertical use mark. The final sentence in this paragraph is used in *Nature*, *W*, I, 9.
[48] Henry Taylor, Preface to *Philip van Artevelde; a Dramatic Romance, in Two Parts*, 2 vols. in 1 (Cambridge and Boston, 1835), p. x. "Poetry of which sense is not

well & truly said. We have almost a theory of Shakspear, — the wonder of Shakspear is almost diminished when we say, Strong Sense is the staple of his verse. Because what is to be accounted for, is, the extent of the man, that he could create not one or two, but so manifold classes & individuals & each perfect. But we are quite familiar with the expertness & power of men of sense in every new condition, & this experience supplies us with a just analogy.

———

[March] 18. 'Beauty with the ancients was the tongue on the balance of expression,' said Win[c]kelmann.[49] What meant he?

↑Answer. "Beauty no other thing is than a beam

Flashed out between the middle & extreme."

Herrick↓ [50]

———

"Hunc solem et stellas et decedentia certis
Tempora momentis, sunt qui formidine nulla
Imbuti spectant."

Horace. [*Epistles*, I, vi, 3–5] [51]

[March] 19. As I walked in the woods I felt what I often feel that nothing can befal me in life, no calamity, no disgrace, (leaving me my eyes) to which Nature will not offer a sweet consolation. Standing on the bare ground with my head bathed by the blithe air, & uplifted into the infinite space, I become happy in my universal relations. The name of the nearest friend sounds then foreign & accidental. I am the heir of uncontained beauty & power. And if then I walk with a companion, he should speak from his Reason to my Reason; that is,

the basis . . . may move the feelings and charm the fancy," according to Taylor; "but failing to satisfy the understanding, it will not take permanent possession of the strong-holds of fame." His example is the work of Byron.

[49] Augustus William Schlegel, *A Course of Lectures on Dramatic Art and Literature*, trans. John Black (Philadelphia, 1833), p. 50. The quotation, struck through in ink with a vertical use mark, is used in "History," *W*, II, 15.

[50] Cf. "The Definition of Beauty," in *The Poetical Works of Robert Herrick*, 2 vols. (London, 1825), I, 44.

[51] "Yon sun, the stars and seasons that pass in fixed courses — some can gaze upon these with no strain of fear." (The Loeb text reads "spectent" where Emerson has "spectant".) "Sense must be . . . *Horace*.", struck through in pencil with a wavy diagonal use mark, is used in "Ben Jonson, Herrick, Herbert, Wotton," *Lectures*, I, 348.

both from God. To be brothers, to be acquaintances, master or servant, is then [18] a trifle too insignificant for remembrance.[52] O keep this humor, (which in your lifetime may not come to you twice,) as the apple of your eye. Set a lamp before it in your memory which shall never be extinguished.

———

I think Taylor's poem[53] is the best light we have ever had upon the genius of Shakspear. We have made a miracle of Shakspear, a haze of light instead of a guiding torch by accepting unquestioned all the tavern stories about his want of education, & total unconsciousness. The interval evidence all the time is irresistible that he was no such person. He was a man like this Taylor of strong sense & of great cultivation; an excellent Latin Scholar, & of extensive & select reading so as to have formed his theories of many historical characters with as much clearness as Gibbon or Niebuhr or Goethe. He wrote for intelligent persons, & wrote with intention. He had Taylor's[n] strong good sense, & added to it his own wonderful facility of execution which aerates & sublimes all language the moment he uses it, or, more truly, animates every word.

[19] I ought to have said in my wood-thoughts just now, that there the mind integrates itself again. The attention which had been distracted into parts, is reunited, reinsphered. The whole of Nature addresses itself to the whole man. We are reassured. It is more than a medicine. It is health.

In talking weeks ago with M[ary]. M[oody]. E[merson]. I was ready to say that a severest truth would forbid me to say that ever I had made a sacrifice. That ↑which↓ we are, in healthy times seems so great that nothing can be taken from us that seems much.[54] I loved Ellen, & love her with an affection that would ask nothing but its indulgence to make me blessed. Yet when she was taken from me, the

[52] "As I walked . . . for remembrance." is struck through in ink with two wavy diagonal use marks, p. [17], and a vertical use mark, p. [18]. This passage is used in *Nature, W,* I, 10.
[53] *Philip van Artevelde.*
[54] "In talking . . . seems much." is struck through in ink with a vertical use mark.

air was still sweet, the sun was not taken down from my firmament, & however sore was that particular loss, I still felt that it was particular, that the Universe remained to us both, that the Universe abode in its light & in its power to replenish the heart with hope. Distress never, trifles never abate my trust.[55] Only this Lethean stream that washes through us, that gives sometimes a film or haze of unreality, a suggestion that, as C[harles]. said of Concord society, 'we are on the way back to Annihilation', only this threatens my Trust. But not that would certify me that I had ever suffered. Praise! Praise & Wonder! And oft we feel so wistful & babe-like that we cannot help thinking that a correspondent sentiment of paternal pleasantry must exist ⟨in⟩ over us in the bosom of God.

[20] 19[?] March.

> "Spare the poor emmet rich in hoarded grain;
> He lives with pleasure, & he dies with pain." [56]

———

At Waltham, they have 11000 spindles; at Lowell, 200,000.

———

"The road that luxury levels for the coach, industry may travel with his cart." E.B.E.[57]

> "Through Nature's ample range in thought to stroll
> And start at man the single mourner there."
> *Young.* [*Night Thoughts,* "Night VII," ll. 700–701]
> "Heaven kindly gives our blood a moral flow." [58]
>
> [*Ibid.,* l. 347]

Lines written on the Arch erected ⟨i⟩on Boston Neck, 1825
> "The fathers in glory sleep
> That gathered with thee to the fight;
> But the sons shall eternally keep
> The tablet of gratitude bright:

---

[55] "however sore . . . my trust." is struck through in ink with a vertical use mark.

[56] Misquoted from Walter Savage Landor, Conversation IX, "Duke de Richelieu, Sir Fire Coats, and Lady Glengrin," in *Imaginary Conversations of Literary Men and Statesmen,* first series, 3 vols. (London, 1828), III, 202.

[57] The quotation, presumably from Edward Bliss Emerson, is struck through in ink with a vertical use mark.

[58] The quotation, struck through in ink with two vertical use marks, is used in "Worship," *W*, VI, 202.

We bow not the neck, & we bend not the knee,
But our hearts, Lafayette, we surrender to thee."

probable [59]

[21] Landor writes that "no man ever argued so fairly as he might have done." [60] And in a reflecting highly cultivated society it seems as if no man could ever be in a passion, or act with a negligent selfforgetting greatness. Can Webster in the American Senate for ⟨one⟩ any conceivable public outrage, scream with real passion? The reporters say he did the other day. They did not think so when they wrote it, & nobody believes it was any thing else than a fine wise oratorical scream.

Nor can Dr R[ipley]. "eat sponge cake without a ramrod." [61]

But Landor pleased me better when he spoke of the ⟨reverence⟩ ↑respect↓ with which even Napoleon treated the good Grand duke [Ferdinand] of Tuscany.[62] Virtue is not to be mistaken & will inspire respect into the damned.ⁿ [63] Never utter the truism, but live it among men & by your fireside.

If no man ever argued so fairly as he might, ⟨s⟩ neither did any ever state his griefs ⟨his doings⟩ as lightly. Allow for exaggeration in the most ⟨indefatigable⟩ ↑patient↓ & most sorely ridden hack that ever was driven. For it is only the finite that has wrought & suffered, the infinite lies stretched even laughing in utter repose.[64]

This rebellious Understanding is the ⟨most⟩ incorrigible liar.ⁿ

---

[59] The word is written in pencil.

[60] Conversation IX, "Duke de Richelieu, Sir Fire Coats, and Lady Glengrin," *Imaginary Conversations*, 1828, III, 226.

[61] This sentence is written in pencil. Dr. Ezra Ripley, Emerson's stepgrandfather, was a minister at Concord; Emerson, his brother Charles, and their mother were living with him at the Old Manse.

[62] Conversation XIV, "Landor, English Visitor, and Florentine Visitor," *Imaginary Conversations*, 1828, III, 410.

[63] This sentence is struck through in ink with two vertical use marks.

[64] This paragraph, struck through in pencil with a diagonal use mark, is used in "Ethics," *Lectures*, II, 144–145.

Convict him of perfidy, and he answers you with a new f⟨alse⟩ib. No man speaks the truth or lives a true life two minutes together.

"Wrath is not worth carrying home, though a man should ride." Landor.

[March] 23d. There is no greater lie than a voluptuous book like Boccac[c]io. For it represents the pleasures of appetite which only at ⟨select &⟩ rare intervals a few times in a lifetime are intense, & to whose acme continence is essential, as frequent, habitual, & belonging to the incontinent. Let a young man imagine that women were [22] made for pleasure & are quite defenceless, & ⟨p⟩ act on that opinion, he will find the weakest of them garrisoned by troops of pains & sorrows which he who touches her, instantly participates. He who approaches a woman unlawfully thinks he has overcome her. It is a bitter jest of nature. He will shortly discover that he has put himself wholly in the power of that worthless slut. Montaigne, coarse as he is, is yet true.

———

Settle it in your mind that you must choose between your own suffrage & other people's.[n] I used to think, all men use[d] to think that you can have both, but you cannot. Secure your own, ⟨&⟩↑& you↓ shall be assured of others, twenty years hence, but you must part with them so long. Before this Reason with bright eternal eyes, even merits that seem pure & saintlike compared with practices & reputations of the mob, ⟨be⟩ are seen to be vulgar & vile.[65] There are merits calculated on shorter & longer periods; ⟨those⟩ better than those of the hour are the Benthamite & the Calvinist who keep the law all their life for pay; but these dwindle before the incalculable ⟨periods⟩ eternity which the lover of virtue embraces in the present moment.

The virtue of the intellect consists in preferring work to trade. Brougham, Canning, Everett, ⟨turn⟩ ↑convert↓ their genius into a shop, & turn every faculty upside down that they may sell well. Allston, Wordsworth, Carlyle, are smit with the divine desire of Creation, & scorn the auctioneers. Now what you do for the Shop is so much taken from science.

[65] After "vile" the letters "S H" [Samuel Hoar?] are written in ink above the line.

Ingratitude from a friend is snow in summer[.] [66]
⟨‖ . . . ‖⟩R cannot eat sponge cake without a ramrod.[67]

[23] There is almost no earnest conversation, so much of display enters into it. Put two people of good condition together, the talk on one or both parts will probably be merely defensive; that is, they are not thinking ⟨that⟩ how they may learn something, but how they may come off well. Change your parties & perhaps you excite the ambition of each speaker to say something brilliant, to leave a good opinion of himself[.]

Ordinarily men do not exchange thoughts & converse in method[;] that is, advancing. One goes east, the other west. The preacher goes among his people, the professor among his scholars and finds an universal admiration of his sermons or lessons but the first word they speak on the general subject shows him that these discourses never penetrated farther than the ears. They have a sort of instinctive respect for his train of thought & the profession which belongs to it but they live in another train of thought that *in particulars* flatly contradicts his. And when he thinks a perfect understanding is obtained he finds the whole battle remains to be fought. Did you ever take part in a conversation which advanced? Commonly it is merely pastime. They circulate round point-no-point. Each remains fast in his own aura & not once do they communicate.

Dr H., Mr B., Mr S., Mr I. the most powerful men in our community have no theory of business that can stand scrutiny but only bubble built on bubble without end. They skate so fast over a film of ice that it does not break under them. It seems when you see their dexterity ⟨at⟩ in particulars as if you could not overestimate the resources of good sense & when you find how utterly ⟨de⟩void they are of all remote aims, as if you could not underestimate their philosophy.[68]

[66] This sentence is written in pencil. See p. [31] below. The phrase "snow in summer" is used in "Prudence," *Lectures*, II, 314.

[67] See p. [21] above.

[68] The material of this paragraph is incorporated in RO Mind, pp. [11]–[12], and used in "The Senses and the Soul," *The Dial*, II (Jan. 1842), 378–379. See also "General Views," *Lectures*, II, 362–363. Of the "powerful men" Emerson refers to, "Dr H." may be either the wealthy Dr. Isaac Hurd or Dr. Abiel Heywood, Concord's town clerk from 1796 to 1834; "Mr B." is probably Nathan Brooks,

[24] Cannot a man contemplate his true good so steadily as to be willing to renounce all thirst for display, & make all his doings tentative, imperfect, because aiming ever at truth & perfection lying out of himself; instead of tricking ⟨up⟩ ↑out↓ ⟨the⟩ what trifles he has picked up & disposing them to advantage in little popular poems or conversations or books? I think he had better live in the country, & ⟨s⟩ see little society, & make himself of no reputation.[68a]

Sects fatten on each other's faults. How many people get a living in New England by calling the Unitarians prayerless, or by showing the Calvinists to be bigots. Hallet feeds on the Masons, & McGavin on the Catholics.[69] The poor man that only sees faults in himself will die, in his sins.

———

Charles thinks the Unitarians pursue a low conservative policy.

———

The high, the generous, the selfdevoted sect will always instruct & command mankind.

Is it ⟨that⟩ ↑because↓ I am such a bigot to my own whims, that I distrust the ability of a man who insists much on the advantage to be derived from literary *conversazioni?* Alone is wisdom. Alone is happiness. Society nowadays makes us lowspirited, hopeless. Alone is heaven.[70]

In the Marquesas Islands on the way from Cape Horn to the Sandwich Islands 9° S. of the Equator they eat men in 1833.

↑1833 p. 120.↓[71]
March 26. The wild delight runs through the man in spite of

---

lawyer, banker, and in 1835 a state senator; "Mr S." may be William Shepherd, proprietor from 1829 to 1839 of a well-regarded hotel purchased from Dr. Hurd. "Mr I." has not been identified.   [68a] Cf. Philemon 2:7.

[69] Benjamin Franklin Hallett (1797–1862), editor of the Boston *Daily Advocate* and leader of radical antimasonry; possibly William McGavin (1773–1832), author of *The Protestant. Essays on the Principal Points of Controversy Between the Church of Rome and the Reformed* (London, 1825–1827; reprinted in Scotland and the United States), though Emerson appears to be thinking of a living New Englander.

[70] The word "Solitude" is written in ink diagonally across this paragraph.

[71] This circled insertion refers to a paragraph on "wild poetic delight" in *JMN,* IV, 355, that resembles the entry which follows here.

real sorrows. ⟨The⟩ Nature says he is my creature & spite of all his impertinent griefs he shall be glad with me. Almost I fear to think how glad I am.[72]

———

I went by him in the night. Who can tell ⟨when⟩ the moment when the pine outgrew the whortleberry that shaded its first sprout? It went by in the night.[73]

[25] [March] 27. He who writes should seek not to say what may be said but what has not been said that is yet true. I will read & write. Why not? All the snow is shovelled away, all the corn planted & the children & the creatures ↑on the planet↓ taken care of without my help. But if I do not read nobody will. Yet am I not without my own fears. Capt Franklin after 6 weeks travelling ↑⟨no⟩to the N. Pole↓ on the ice found himself 200 miles south of the spot he set out from; [n] the ice had floated. And I sometimes start to think I am looking out the same vocables in the Dictionary, spelling out the same sentences, solving the same problems. — My ice may float also.[74]

"It is something to have an influence on the fortunes of mankind; it is greatly more to have an influence on their intellects. Such is the difference between men of office & men of genius." Landor.[75]

[March] 28. If life were long enough among my thousand & one works should be a book of Nature whereof 'Howitt's Seasons' [76] should be not so much the model as the parody. It should contain the Natural history of the woods ⟨for⟩ around my shifting camp for every month in the year. It should tie their astronomy, botany, physiology, meteorology, picturesque, & poetry together. No bird, no bug, no bud should be forgotten on his day & hour. Today the chicadees, the

[72] This paragraph, struck through in ink with two wavy diagonal use marks, is used in *Nature*, *W*, I, 9.

[73] This paragraph is struck through in ink with a diagonal use mark.

[74] The anecdote concerning Sir John Franklin, the English explorer of the Arctic, is used in "The Senses and the Soul," *The Dial*, II (Jan. 1842), 379. See also "General Views," *Lectures*, II, 363.

[75] Landor, Conversation VII, "William Penn and Lord Peterborough," *Imaginary Conversations*, second series, 2 vols. (London, 1829), II, 405. The word "Genius" is written in ink diagonally across this paragraph.

[76] William Howitt, *The Book of the Seasons, or The Calendar of Nature* (London, 1831).

robins, bluebirds, & songsparrows sang to me. I dissected the buds of the birch & the oak, in every one of the last is a star. The crows sat above as idle as I below. The river flowed brimful & I philosophised upon this composite collective beauty which refuses to be analysed. Nothing is beautiful alone. Nothing but is beautiful in the Whole.[77] Learn the history of a craneberry. Mark the day when the pine cones & acorns fall[.]

A wonderful sight is the inverted landscape. Look at the prospect from a high hill through your legs & it gives the world a most pictorial appearance.[78]

[26] Saturn, they say, devoured his children, thereby presignifying the man who thought & instantly turned round to see how his thoughts were made. The hen that eats the egg[.]

29 March. Certainly a man would be glad to do his country service but he cannot cram his service down its throat. It is time enough if he come when he is called. It is enough for him that he has eyes to see that he is infinite spectator without hurrying uncalled to be infinite doer. Let him brood on his immortality "for every gift of noble origin is breathed upon by hope's perpetual breath."[79] He cannot look to work directly on men but obliquely. Few men bring more than one or two points into contact with society at once, they must be content to influence it thereby. Hereafter they may find more purchase.

We live & grow by use. If you sit down to write with weak eyes & awaken your imagination to the topic you will find your eyes strong. ⟨& all pain vanished.⟩

[March] 31. The tree is a congeries of living vegetables so it often seems as if man was a congeries of living spirits according to

[77] With "Nothing is beautiful . . . the Whole." cf. Nature, W, I, 24; "Each and All," W, IX, 4, ll. 11–12: "All are needed by each one; / Nothing is fair or good alone."

[78] See JMN, IV, 323. This paragraph, struck through in ink with three diagonal use marks, is used in "English Literature: Introductory," Lectures, I, 227, and Nature, W, I, 51.

[79] Cf. Wordsworth, "These times strike monied worldlings with dismay," ll. 10–11, slightly misquoted, in Poems Dedicated to National Independence and Liberty, pt. I, Sonnet 20, 1803. See JMN, IV, 251.

Goethe's monadism. One of them looks to see what another does. Many dissimilar things are done with like earnestness.

———

The robin hops about in the field as if he was waiting for somebody — hop, hop, hop — & then stops again.

[27] The dreams of an idealist have a poetic integrity & truth. Their extravagance from nature is yet within a higher nature & terrible hints are ⟨f⟩thrown to him out of a quite unknown intelligence. I have been startled two or three times by the justice as well as the significance of the intimations of this phantasmagoria. Once or twice the conscious fetters of the Spirit have been unlocked & a freer utterance seemed attained.

10 April. I fretted the other night at the Hotel at the stranger who broke into my chamber after midnight claiming to share it. But after his lamp had smoked the chamber full & I had turned round to the wall in despair the man blew out his lamp, knelt down at his bedside & made in low whisper a long earnest prayer. Then was the relation entirely changed between us. I fretted no more but respected & liked him.

———

Coleridge said ⟨no⟩ it was no decisive mark of poetic genius that a man should write well ⟨of⟩ concerning himself.

Is it not because the true genius the Shakspear & Goethe sees the tree & sky & man as they are, enters into them whilst the inferior writer dwells evermore with himself "twinkling restlessly"[?][80]

A man is seldom in the upright position two moments together, but when he is, let him record his observations & they shall be fit for "the Spiritual Inquirer." [81]

[80] Cf. *Biographia Literaria*, 1834, p. 32: "it is no less an essential mark of true genius, that its sensibility is excited by any other cause more powerfully than by its own personal interests. . ."; "twinkling restlessly" is from Wordsworth, *The Excursion*, IV, 994.

[81] Writing to Thomas Carlyle on April 30, 1835, Emerson mentioned a projected journal "to be called *The Transcendentalist*, or *The Spiritual Inquirer*, or the like," which Carlyle might edit. See *The Correspondence of Emerson and Carlyle*, ed. Joseph Slater (New York and London, 1964), p. 125.

Le Baron Russell has visited me & shown me the stars. Hither came G. as usual appearing as if ↑best↓ridden by a restless and invisible rider[.] [82]

[April] 11. Glad to hear music in the village last evening under the fine yellow moon: it sounds like cultivation[,] domestication. In America where all are on wheels one is glad to meet with a sign of adorning our own town. It is a consecra[ted] [28] beautifying of our place. A bugle, clarionet, & flute are to us a momentary Homer & Milton. Music is ⟨practical⟩ ↑sensuous↓ poetry.

To sit in a jail & smell his thumbs. ——

[April] 12. The gods make those men very bad who talk much about them, says Landor's Cyrus.[83] It must be owned that the Idea of God in the human mind is a very changing luminary. Sometimes seen; never quite unremembered; often quite hidden, to the degree, that the Spirit asks, Is there any? But the moral sentiments are immutable. Was there ever a moment in your life when you doubted the existence of the Divine Person? Yes. Was there ever a moment in your life when you doubted the duty of speaking the truth? No. Then is one mutable, the other immutable.

In the dark hours our existence seems to be a defensive war, a struggle against the enc⟨h⟩roaching All which threatens with certainty to engulf us soon, & seems impatient of our little reprieve. How slender is the possession that yet remains to us; how faint the animation; how the Spirit seems already to contract its domain, to retire within narrower walls by the loss of memory, leaving what were its planted fields to ⟨utter⟩ erasure & annihilation. Already our own thoughts & words, have an alien sound. ⟨To⟩ Projects that once we laughed & leaped to execute find us now sleepy & preparing to lie down in the snow.

---

[82] Russell was a doctor then living in Plymouth; "G." may be George Partridge Bradford, like Russell, a lifelong friend.

[83] Conversation XIII, "Xenophon and Cyrus the Younger," *Imaginary Conversations*, 1828, III, 358.

The cotemporaneous ⟨loss⟩ diminution of Hope & of Memory is the Tragedy of Man.[84]

A man feels that his time is too precious[,] the objects within reach of his spirit too beautiful than that his attention should stoop to such disfigurements as Antimasonry or Convent Riots or General Jackson & the Globe.[85] Yet welcome would be to him the principle out of which these proceed, for all the laws of his being are beautiful. This Translation the wise is ever making.

[29] I should be glad of a Catalogue of Ideas; objects of the Reason, as Conceptions are objects of the Understanding. Mr. Coleridge names a Point, a Line, a Circle, as Ideas in Mathematics. God, Free will, Justice, Holiness, as Ideas in Morals.[86]

[30] "Already my opinion has gained infinitely in force when another mind has adopted it."[87] This is the reason why a writer appears ever to so much more advantage in the pages of another man's book than in his own. Coleridge, Wordsworth, Schelling are conclusive when Channing or Carlyle or Everett quote them, but if you take up their own books then instantly they become not lawgivers but modest peccable candidates for your approbation.

Language of Nature

No man ever grew so learned as to exhaust the significance of any part of nature. Nature never became a toy to a wise spirit. The flowers, the animals, the mountains reflected all the wisdom of his best hour as much as they had delighted the simplicity of his child-

---

[84] "In the dark hours . . . of Man.", struck through in pencil and in ink with two vertical use marks, is used in "The Tragic," *W*, XII, 405.

[85] On August 11, 1834, the Ursuline convent in Charlestown was burned by an anti-Catholic mob; the Washington *Globe* had been set up in 1830 as a Jacksonian organ, subsidized by awards of government printing. Emerson recurs in Journal C to this "foolish" paper and its "lie for each new emergency" (pp. [9], [282]).

[86] In a footnote setting forth his distinction between *sense, understanding,* and *reason,* in *The Friend: A Series of Essays,* 3 vols. (London, 1818), I, 306; "God" is Emerson's addition.

[87] Cf. Carlyle, "Characteristics," *The Edinburgh Review,* LIV (Dec. 1831), 359; see *JMN*, IV, 15, and "Society," *Lectures*, II, 101.

hood.[88] The Germans believe in th⟨is⟩e necessary Trinity of God, —
the ↑In↓finite; the finite; & the passage from Inf. into Fin.; or, the
Creation. It is typified in the act of thinking. Whilst we contemplate
we are infinite; the thought we express is partial & finite; the expression is the third part & is equivalent to the act of Creation. Unity says
⟨Boehmen⟩ Schelling is barren. Duality is necessary to the existence
of the World. Shall I say then that the galvanic action of metals fore-
shows from afar the God head, the zinc the metal & the acid; or the
marriage of plants the pollen, the ovary, & the junction? [n]

[31] 1⟨3⟩4 April. "Ne[c] te, &c." [89] Every Man is a wonder until
you learn his studies, his associates, his early acts & the floating
opinions of his times, & then he developes himself as naturally from
a point as a river is made from rills. Burke's orations are but the
combination of the Annual Register which he edited with the Inquiry on the Sublime & Beautiful which he wrote at the same time.
Swedenborg is unriddled by learning ⟨the⟩ the theology & philosophy
of Continental Europe in his youth. Each great doctrine is then received by the mind as a tally of an Idea in its own reason & not as
news.

Rev. Dr F↑reeman↓. consoled my father on his deathbed by
telling him he had not outlived his teeth, &c. & bid my mother expect
now to be neglected by society.

You cannot show a head of Dante or Rousseau or Laplace ⟨in⟩to
a company but ⟨it sha⟩ one spectator shall see an exact resemblance to
Deacon Bumstead, or Mr Kuhn, or Uncle Barrett; for common people
will not make the effort to raise themselves to the great mind whose
effigy is set before them, but must ever degrade that to the pinched
circle of their habitual experience.

> Hath not the little fly his Italy
> His sphere of the Romantic & the Rare
>
> [by Emerson?]

[88] "No man . . . childhood.", struck through in ink with three wavy diagonal
use marks, is used in *Nature*, *W*, I, 8.

[89] "Nec te quaesiveris extra." — "Look to no one outside yourself." Persius,
Satires, I, 7; the original and a translation occur in Montaigne, "Of Glory," *Essays*,
1700, II, 484. See *JMN*, IV, 318; p. [253] below; "Self-Reliance," *W*, II, 43.

16 April. This 'snow in summer' which falls so fast today is like a wound from a friend.[90] Dr R. calls it 'robin snow.'

Why must always the philosopher mince his words & fatigue us with explanation? He speaks from the Reason & being of course contradicted word for word by the Understanding[91] he stops like a cogwheel at every notch to explain. Let him say, *I idealize*, & let that be once for all; or *I sensualize*, & then the Rationalist may stop his ears. Empedocles said bravely "I am God; I am immortal; I contemn human affairs"; & all men hated him.[92] Yet every one of the same men had had his religious hour when he said the same thing.

[32][93] Fable avoids the difficulty, is at once exoteric & esoteric, & is clapped by both sides. Plato & Jesus used it. And History is such a fable.

Plato had a secret doctrine, — had he? What secret can he conceal from the eyes of Montaigne, of Bacon, of Kant? [94]

"That's indications of intemperance," said my fair stage companion to her friend.

Let the imaginative man deny himself & stick by facts. As a man must not bring his children into company naked, & must not bring more children into the world than he can clothe, so the idealist must retain his thoughts until they embody themselves in fit outward illustrations[.] [95]

[33] A courthouse is a good place to learn the limits of man. The best counsel are not orators, but very slovenly speakers: to use Mr Warren's fine apology for Baylies, "they spread their ability over the whole argument, & have not strong points." The interminable

[90] See p. [22] above.
[91] Cf. Friedrich Heinrich Jacobi as quoted by Thomas Carlyle, "Novalis," *Foreign Review*, IV (July 1829), 117; see *JMN*, IV, 320, n. 195.
[92] Cf. Diogenes Laertius, "Empedocles," *Lives of Eminent Philosophers*, VIII, 66.
[93] The first two paragraphs on this page are written in ink over erased pencil writing, unrecovered.
[94] This paragraph, struck through in ink with a vertical use mark, is used in "Ethics," *Lectures*, II, 149, and "Spiritual Laws," *W*, II, 146.
[95] This passage is written in pencil.

sentences of Mr H[oar]., clause growing out of clause "like the prickly pear," as Charles said, reminded me of nothing so much as certain vestry praelections. But in the courthouse the worth of a man is guaged.

An advantage ⟨of this slavery question⟩ shines ⟨evermore⟩ on the abolition side that these philanthropists really feel no clog, no check from authority, no discord, no sore place in their own body which they must keep out of sight or tenderly touch. People just out of the village or the shop reason & plead like practised orators, such scope the subject gives them, & such stimulus to their affections. The Reason is glad to find a question which is not, like Religion or Politics, bound around with so many traditions & usages that every man is forced to argue unfairly, but one on which he may exhaust his whole love of truth, — his heart & his mind. This is one of those causes which will make a man.

Never is a good cause in facts long at loss for an ideal equipment[.]

It was alarming to see the lines of sloth in so many faces in the courthouse. The flame of life burns very dim. The most active lives have so much routine as to preclude progress almost equally with the most ⟨recluse.⟩ inactive.

[34] "Je défie un coeur comme le vôtre d'oser mal penser du mien," writes Rousseau to Diderot.[96]

19 April. It is a happy talent to know how to play. Some men must always work if they would be respectable; for the moment they trifle, they are silly. Others show most talent when they trifle. Be it said of W that his excess of reverence made it impossible for him to realize ever that he was a man; he never assumed equality with strangers ⟨as⟩ but still esteemed them older than himself though they were of his own age or younger. He went through life postponing his maturity & died in his error. The scratch-cradle. The smelling bottle.

22 April. I have made no record of Everett's fine Eulogy at Lexington on the 20th. But he is all art & I find in him nowadays maugre all

[96] Letter, [Oct. 19, 1797?]; see *Correspondance générale de J.-J. Rousseau*, ed. Théophile Dufour, 20 vols. (Paris, 1924–1934), III, 135.

his gifts & great merits more to blame than praise. He is not content to be Edward Everett, but would be Daniel Webster. This is his mortal distemper. Why should such a genius waste itself? Have we any to spare? Why should Everett make grimaces? He will not deliver himself up to dear Nature, but insists on making postures & sounds after his own taste, & like those he has heard of, & now he does not know there is any Nature *for him*. Neither has he any *faith*. Charles proposed to read a sentence from the Phaedo, conceding that the N. Testament was unfashionable.[97] When he ⟨look⟩ addressed the Relics in the ⟨sarcophagus⟩ wooden box, he manifestly did not know what to do with his eyes & looked out sideways at last to see how people took it, so far has he got in his Lie, & so much of its fruit may a man reap without yet suspecting it. Daniel Webster, Nature's own child sat there all day & drew all eyes. Poor Everett! for this was it that you left your own work, your exceeding great & peculiar vocation, the desire [35] of all eyes, the gratitude of all ingenuous scholars — to stray away hither & mimic this Man, that here & everywhere in your best & (for work) unsurpassed exertions, you might still be mere secondary & satellite to him, & for him hold a candle? ⁿ

Webster spoke at the Table few & simple words but from the old immoveable basis of simplicity & common natural emotion to which he instinctively & consciously adheres.

['We only row we're steered by fate.'[98]   The involuntary education is all. See how we are mastered. With the ⟨intense⟩ desire of dogmatizing, here we sit chatting. With ⟨intense⟩ desire of poetic reputation, we still prose. We would be Teachers but in spite of us we are kept out of the pulpit, & thrust into the pew. Who doth it? No man: only Lethe, only Time; only negatives; indisposition; delay; nothing.][99]

On the same auspicious morning I received a letter from Carlyle the wise, the brave, and his intimations of a visit to America, which purpose may God prosper & consummate.
Better a great deal have friends full grown before they are made

[97] "Neither . . . unfashionable." is struck through in ink with two diagonal use marks. "Charles" is Emerson's brother, Charles Chauncy Emerson.

[98] Cf. Samuel Butler, *Hudibras*, Pt. I, i, 882; see "Holiness," *Lectures*, II, 343.

[99] " 'We only row . . . nothing." is written in ink over an erased pencil version of substantially the same material.

acquainted[;] like Moody & Webster they have the pleasant surprise
of the bare result; a man meets a man. What fact is more valuable
than the difference of our power alone & with others. The scholar
sits down to write & all his years of Meditation do not furnish him
with one good thought or happy expression but it is necessary to write
a letter to his friend & forthwith troops of gentle thoughts embody
themselves ⟨all⟩ on every hand in chosen ⟨expressi⟩ words. Blessed
be the friend.[100]

———

They say here that to succeed as a farmer 'you must either hold
the plough, or drive.'
Concord people are slack.

[36] 23 April. The order of things consents to virtue. Such
scenes as luxurious poets & novelists often paint, where temptation
has a quite overcoming force, never or very rarely occur in real life.

It is very hard to know what to do if you have great desires for
benefitting mankind. But a very plain thing is your duty. It may be
suspected then that the depth of wisdom & the height of glory is
there. Self-Union, — never risk that. Neither lie nor steal nor betray,
for you violate Consciousness. Nothing is selfevident but the commandments of Consciousness.

"The limbs of my buried ones," &c.[101] I dislike the bad taste of almost
every thing I have read of Jean Paul; this scrap for instance; Shakspear never said these hard artificial things.

We think we are approaching a star. I fear it is a nebula. At
least individual aims are very nebulous.

———

Received Cudworth & Herrick & Carlyle.[102]

[100] "The scholar . . . the friend.", struck through in ink with a vertical use
mark, is used in "Friendship," *W*, II, 191–192.

[101] Emerson's reference is to a passage in Carlyle's letter of February 3, 1835,
received on the previous day: "In still nights, as Jean Paul says, 'the limbs of my
Buried Ones touched cold on my soul, and drove away its blots, as dead hands heal
eruptions of the skin.'" The allusion is to Jean Paul Friedrich Richter, *The Life of
Quintus Fixlein*, translated in Carlyle's *German Romance* (1827). See *The Correspondence of Emerson and Carlyle*, 1964, p. 113.

[102] Ralph Cudworth, *The True Intellectual System of the Universe* . . . , ed.

1 May. Cloudy & cold: is not May Morning sure to be?

9 May. Spin out your web to the end of your yarn. Ten rivers stream from your fingers' ends.   A frost this morn.
If what you have read in Newspapers you had read in good books, how much would you know? ⟨a friend⟩

11 May. A foolish German fairy tale,[n] "the short Mantle" which I read in English ↑long↓ years ago, made my cheeks glow again and almost the gracious drops fall at the triumph of the chaste & gentle Genelas. Very docile we are to such pretty tales, but to verify them in our own chaste life & simple spiritual excellence very slow indeed.
It is a fine flattery to tell your friend he is a singular mind an incalculable person.[103]
Quite a piece of nature is my new acquaintance Mr Robbins [n] ↑of Lexington.↓ A Man of genuine public spirit & profuse liberality yet out of his mouth runs [37] ever this puddle of vitriol of spite "at the other village." ⟨Nobleness of sentiment⟩ The low⟨ness of his⟩ slang which seasons all his conversation contrasts oddly enough with the nobleness of his sentiments. "They softsoaped me," &c. Whilst he plays the Man of Ross, he says he does every thing "to please himself, that's all;" he doesn't care for liking or disliking, "he likes fair-weather," & "to see people work," & ⟨al⟩ "to have all sort of 'amusements,'" by which he means churches, schools, lyceums, &c. ⟨He⟩It makes him sick to death to sit in the house, he goes every day to Boston, he pays $10,000. a year for labor in the town of Lexington,[n] — And his fine grounds he has laid out for the public, & filled with pears & peaches & grapes for the boys, "enough for them & me

---

Thomas Birsh, 4 vols. (London, 1820), and possibly Robert Herrick, *The Poetical Works*, 1825, both in Emerson's library. The "Carlyle" may be an unidentified book or other gift sent in the "parcel" accompanying Carlyle's letter of February 3 (*The Correspondence of Emerson and Carlyle*, 1964, p. 118, n. 20).
[103] The entry for May 11 to this point is struck through in ink with a diagonal use mark; "A foolish . . . slow indeed.", also struck through in ink with a vertical use mark, is used in "The Age of Fable," *Lectures*, I, 260, and "History," *W*, II, 35. The tale of Genelas or Venelas ("History," *W*, II, 35; "Domestic Life," *W*, VII, 123) is known under various titles, including "The Boy and the Mantle" (p. [98] below).

too." & built the Hall, & put up clock & bell, & paid for singing & filled the punch pitcher, &c, &c, &c, but hates joint stock companies, & will do all himself, & 'to please himself.' He goes to Campmeeting "to see what the world is made on", & thinks a man may give away $100, & get no thanks or praise, but if he is guilty of a nine penny trick, — then is it proclaimed everywhere. Aunt M. asks if a star could be any thing to him & Herschel's mighty facts. I answer certainly if it were only possible to get his attention once to the facts, but the Pestalozzi is not born that could do this by art.

10 [12?] May. Visited R.B.E.[104] at Chelmsford with a 'Permit.' 'The apple does not fall far from the stem.'
⟨9.00 to RH & REH⟩ [105]

"America", Coleridge said, "was England seen in a solar microscope." "A Gothic Church was a petrified religion." Chivalry is a petrified courtesy.[106]

I am disqualified by hearing this strife concerning Goethe from judging truly of his genius. He is that which the intelligent hermit supposes him to be & can neither be talked up nor talked down[.]

[38] We are all wise for other people, none for himself. That wise Fessenden told me never to have two related ideas without putting them on paper. G.R.[107] I think never had such.

[104] Robert Bulkeley Emerson, a brother whose mind remained undeveloped, was in an asylum at Chelmsford.

[105] Probably Ralph and Rebecca Emerson Haskins, Emerson's uncle and aunt. There is no corresponding entry in Emerson's Account Book (1828–1835).

[106] Cf. Specimens of the Table Talk of the Late Samuel Taylor Coleridge, 2 vols. in 1 (New York, 1835), II, 78–79, on the "possible destiny" of America, which might become an "England viewed through a solar microscope; Great Britain in a state of glorious magnification!" In his Lecture I (1818), Coleridge had termed a Gothic cathedral "the petrifaction of our religion"; see The Complete Works of Samuel Taylor Coleridge, ed. W. G. T. Shedd, 7 vols. (New York, 1854), IV, 233–234. On p. [12] above, Emerson had observed that "The whole of heraldry is in courtesy."

[107] Probably George Ripley, whom Emerson had known since his college days; see JMN, II, 185. "That wise Fessenden" may be either Benjamin or John Fessenden, listed among theological students in the 1820 Harvard catalogue (E t E, I, 430), or perhaps the satirist Thomas Green Fessenden, editor, 1822–1837, of the New England Farmer.

↑Anschauung↓ Truth first. Genius seems to consist merely in trueness of sight in using such words as show that the man was an eye-witness and not a ⟨teller⟩ ↑repeater↓ of what was told. Thus the girl who said "the earth was a-gee;" Lord Bacon when he speaks of exploding gunpowder as "a fiery wind blowing with that expansive force, &c" [108] [—] these are poets. ↑Aristotle↓

Hard Times. In this contradictory world of Truth the hard times come when the good times are in the world of commerce; namely, sleep, fulleating, plenty of money, care of it, & leisure; these are the hard times. Nothing is doing & we lose every day.

The young preacher is discouraged by learning the motives that brought his great congregation to church. Scarcely ten came to hear his sermon. But singing or a new pelisse or cousin William or the Sunday School or a proprietors' meeting after church or the merest anility in Hanover st were the ⟨goads⟩ ↑beadles↓ that ⟨spurred⟩ ↑brought↓ and the bolts that hold his silent assembly in the Church. Never mind how they came my friend[;] never mind who or what brought them any more than you do who or what set you down in Boston in 1835. Here they are real men & women, fools I grant but potentially divine every one of them convertible. Every ear is yours to gain. Every heart will be glad & proud & thankful for a master. There where you are, serve them & they must serve you. They care nothing for you but be to them a Plato be to them a Christ & they shall all be Platos & all be Christs.
                    The instrument of Writing [109]

[39] 13 May. Do believe so far in your doctrine of Compensation as to trust that greatness cannot be cheaply procured. Selfdenial & persisting selfrespect can alone ⟨pr⟩ secure their proper fruits. Act naturally, act from within, not once or twice, but from month to month, without misgiving, without deviation, from year to year, & you shall reap the costly advantages of moral accomplishments. Make haste to

---

[108] Bacon refers to gunpowder as a "fiery wind" in *Natural History*, Cent. I, par. 30, in *The Works of Francis Bacon*, 10 vols. (London, 1824), I, 258; Latin equivalents occur in both *Novum Organum*, Lib. II, Aph. xxxvi (*The Works*, VIII, 152), and *Historia Densi et Rari* (*ibid.*, IX, 18).

[109] This phrase is written in pencil.

reconcile you to yourself & the whole world shall leap & run to be of your opinion. Imprison that stammering tongue within its white fence until you have a necessary sentiment or a useful fact to utter, & that said, be dumb again. Then your words will weigh something, — two tons, like St John's.[110]

What a benefit if a rule could be given whereby the mind could at any moment *east* itself, & find the sun. But long after we have thought we were recovered & sane, light breaks in upon us ⟨for a moment⟩ & we find we have yet had no sane moment. Another morn rises on mid noon.[111]

Who is capable of a manly friendship? Very few. Charles thinks he can count five persons of *character*. & that Shakspear & the ⟨first-rate⟩ writers of the first class infused their character into their works & hence their rank. We feel an interest in a robust healthful mind, an Alfred, Chaucer, Dante, which Goethe never inspires.

The truest state of mind, rested in, becomes false. Thought is the manna which cannot be stored. It will be sour if kept, & tomorrow must be gathered anew. Perpetually must we East ourselves, or we get into irrecoverable error, ⟨or⟩ starting from the plainest truth & keeping as we think the straightest road of logic. It is by magnifying God, that men become Pantheists; it is by piously personifying him, that they become idolaters.

⟨As the world signified with the Greek, Beauty, so Skepticism, alas! signifies Sight.⟩ Not in his goals but in his transition man is great[.][112]

---

[110] I.e., as in the Fourth Gospel, where every word, said Luther, "weigheth two Tons." Cf. *Colloquia Mensalia: or, Dr. Martin Luther's Divine Discourses at his Table . . .* , trans. H. Bell (London, 1652), p. 368; see *JMN*, IV, 349, and "Martin Luther," *Lectures*, I, 121.

[111] Cf. Coleridge, *The Friend*, 1818, III, 222: "that preparatory process, which the French language so happily expresses by *s'orienter*, i.e. to find out the east for one's self." A variation of the passage occurs in Coleridge's "General Introduction; or, A Preliminary Treatise on Method," *Encyclopædia Metropolitana*, 25 vols. (London, 1829–1845), I, 4–5. "Another . . . noon.": Milton, *Paradise Lost*, V, 310–311; see *JMN*, IV, 361, and "Circles," *W*, II, 301. "What a benefit . . . mid noon." is copied in RO Mind, pp. [15]–[16].

[112] "The truest state . . . signifies Sight.)" is struck through in ink with a vertical use mark. "The truest state . . . road of logic." is used in "Religion," *Lectures*, II, 93; "The truest state . . . becomes false." and "Not in his . . . man is great" are used in "The Present Age," *Lectures*, II, 158.

[40] See the second Aphorism of the Novum Organon that neither the hand nor the mind of man can accomplish much without tools, &c. &c. "nec intellectus sibi permissus, multum valet." [113] This is the defence of written or premeditated preaching, of the written book, of the composed poem. ⟨Th⟩ No human wit unaided is equal to the production at one time of such a result as the Hamlet or Lear, but by a multitude of trials & a thousand rejections & ⟨many⟩ the ⟨per⟩ using & perusing of what was already written, one of those tragedies is at last completed — a poem made that shall thrill the world by the mere juxtaposition & inter-action of lines & sentences that singly would have been of little worth & short date. Rightly is this art named composition & the composition has manifold the effect of the component parts. The orator is nowise equal to the evoking on a new subject of this brilliant chain of sentiments, facts, illustrations whereby he now fires himself & you. Every link in this living chain he found separate; one, ten years ago; one, last week; some of them he found in his father's house or at school when a boy; some of them by his losses; some of them by his sickness; some by his sins. The Webster with whom you talk admires the oration almost as much as you do, & knows himself to be nowise equal, unarmed, that is, without this tool of Synthesis to the splendid effect which he is yet well pleased you should impute to him.

No hands ⟨made⟩ could make a watch. The hands brought dry sticks together & struck the flint with iron or rubbed sticks for fire & melted the ore & with stones made crow bar & hammer[;] these again helped to make chisel & file, rasp & saw, piston & boiler, & so the watch & the [41] steam engine are made, which the hands could never have produced & these again are new tools to make still more recondite & prolific instruments.[n] So do the collated thoughts beget more & the artificially combined individuals have in addition to their own a quite new collective power. ⟨E⟩ The main is made up of many islands, the state of many men. The poem of many thoughts each

---

[113] *Novum Organum*, Lib. I, Aph. ii, in Bacon, *The Works*, 1824, VIII, 1. In "Shakspear [second lecture]," *Lectures*, I, 317–318, Emerson freely translates the entire aphorism: "The naked and unassisted hand however strong and true is adapted only to the performance of few and easy works but when assisted by instruments becomes able to perform much more and of much greater difficulty: and the case is exactly the same with the mind."

of which, in its turn, filled the whole sky of the poet was day & Being to him.[114]

↑May↓ 14. There is hardly a surer way to incur the censure of infidelity & irreligion than sincere faith and an entire devotion. For to the common eye, pews, vestries, family prayer, sanctimonious looks & words constitute religion, which the devout man would find hindrances. And so we go, trying always to weld the finite & infinite, the absolute & the seeming, together. ↑On the contrary the manner in which religion is most positively affirmed by men of the world is barefaced skepticism.↓

When I write a book on spiritual things I think I will advertise the reader that I am a very wicked man, & that consistency is nowise to be expected of me.

When will you mend Montaigne? When will you take the hint of nature? Where are your Essays? Can you not express your one conviction that moral laws hold? Have you not thoughts & illustrations that are your own; the parable of geometry & matter; the reason why the atmosphere is transparent; the power of Composition in nature & in man's thoughts; the Uses & uselessness of travelling; the law of Compensation; the transcendant excellence of truth in character, in rhetoric, in things; the sublimity of Self-reliance; and the rewards of perseverance in the best opinion? Have you not a testimony to give for Shakspear, for Milton? one ⟨penny weight⟩ ↑sentence↓ of real praise of Jesus, is worth a century of legendary Christianity. Can you not write as though you wrote to yourself & drop the ⟨seed⟩ token assured that a wise hand will pick it up? [n]

[42] "My entrails I lay open to men's view." I recorded worse things in my Italian Journal than one I omitted; that a lady in Palermo invited me to come & ride out with her in her barouche which I did, though the day was rainy ↑& so the coach was covered.↓ She did not invite me to dine, so I made my obeisance, when on our return I had waited upon her into the house; then I *walked* home through a drenching rain in a city where I was an entire stranger, but not until I had paid her coachman my half dollar who waylaid me

[114] This and the preceding paragraph, struck through in pencil with vertical use marks extending to the bottom of p. [40], are used in "Shakspear [second lecture]," *Lectures*, I, 317–318.

on the stairs. ⟨The ride out in a⟩ To as fat an understanding as mine, I cannot but think it might have occurred, that, to send the guest home or to ⟨control⟩ ↑pay↓ one's servants, would really be a finer compliment. But it is a good specimen of the misery of finery.

Address your Rede to the young American & know that you hook to you all like minds far or near, whether you shall know them or not.

And remember Brutus.

The chapter on Optical Delusions in our lifetime is very large. How many times have we resolved not to be again deceived by one & the same.

"Pherecydes Syr[i]us primus dixit animos hominum esse sempiternos." [115] [Cf.] Cic[ero]. Tusc[ulanae]. Quaest. [i.e., Disputationes] lib. 1, c. 16 [38]

Commerce which vulgarizes great things will never quite degrade for the poet the miracle of the letter which floats round the globe in a pine ship & comes safe to the ⟨hand⟩ ↑eye↓ for which it was writ. To keep our wonder fresh is a principal duty of the wise, until the grand riddle is solved. But there is something higher & better than stupid wonder, namely, to integrate our being across all these distracting forces, & keep a slender human word among the storms, distances, accidents that drive us hither & thither & by persistency make this paltry force of one man reappear to redeem its pledge [43] months years ⟨ago⟩ ↑after↓ by a voice & a hand out of distant climates too. [116]

Good story Squire Adams [117] told here of countryman ⟨seeing the⟩ travelling between day & sunrise, & seeing the locomotive & its train of cars on the rail road. He saw the smoke & the wheels. His horse was frightened, ran, turned over the wagon, & broke it.[n] He crawled to a house for help: They asked him what had happened: He could not well tell what, but that it looked like hell in harness. [118]

---

[115] "Pherecydes of Syros was the first who pronounced the souls of men to be immortal."
[116] This paragraph is used in "Prudence," *Lectures*, II, 317, and "Prudence," *W*, II, 235–236.
[117] Perhaps Abel Adams, Emerson's life-long friend and financial adviser.
[118] See *JMN*, IV, 296.

[44] [May] 15. The thing set down in words is not therefore affirmed. It must affirm itself or no forms of grammar & no verisimilitude can give evidence; & no array of arguments. The sentence[,] the book must also contain its own apology for being writ.[119]

Trifles move us more than laws. Why am I more curious to know the reason ⟨that⟩ ↑why↓ the star form is so oft repeated in botany or ⟨the reason that⟩ ↑why↓ the number five is such a favorite with nature, than to understand the circulation of the sap & the formation of buds? [120] Those two wonders of electromagnetism & ⟨of⟩ the polarisation of light have also a peculiar interest.

———

My niedrig man playing with a beautiful child could think of nothing but to ask the child whether it is careful to keep its head clean of creatures. And when it is mentioned that a red cloth ⟨scares the⟩ irritates ⟨cow⟩the cow, 'Yes,' he replies, 'they think of their calf,' forcing on the ladies the allusion to poor Nature's rags of parturition.

[May] 16. Robert Herrick delights in praising Ben Jonson, & has many panegyrical pieces to others, & in one copy of verses praising many, Beaumont & Fletcher & others, yet never drops the name of Shakspear. 'Tis like the want of the statues of Cassius & Brutus in the funeral of Junia, "Eo ipso praefulgebant, quod non visebantur." [121] Herrick's merit is the simplicity & manliness of his utterance & only rarely the weight of ⟨that he would say⟩ ↑his sentence↓. He has & is conscious of having a noble idiomatic use of his English[,] a perfect plain-style from which he can at any time soar to a fine lyric delicacy or descend to the coarsest sarcasms without losing his firm footing. But this power of speech was accompanied by an assurance

[119] This paragraph, struck through in pencil with a vertical use mark, is used in "Ben Jonson, Herrick, Herbert, Wotton," *Lectures*, I, 349; "The Present Age," *Lectures*, II, 163; and "Spiritual Laws," *W*, II, 152–153.

[120] "Why am I . . . of buds?" is struck through in ink with a vertical use mark. Cf. "Woodnotes I," *W*, IX, 43–44, ll. 22–23.

[121] Cf. Bacon, *Of the Advancement of Learning*, Bk. II, in *The Works*, 1824, I, 20: ". . . learned men, forgotten in states, and not living in the eyes of men, are like the images of Cassius and Brutus in the funeral of Junia; of which not being represented, as many others were, Tacitus saith, [they 'shone brighter than all by the very fact that their portraits were unseen' (*Annals*, III, lxxxvi)]."

of fame.[122]   A similar merit is that of the American Hillhouse[123] ↑though no approach to Herrick's wealth↓[.]

[45] Landor thinks that a knowledge of poetry is reserved for some purer state of sensation & existence.[124]

The observation of a mere observer is more unsuspicious than that of a theorist. I ought to have no shame in publishing the records of one who aimed only at the upright position[125] more anxious that the thing should be truly seen tha⟨t⟩n careful what thing it was. As we exercise little election in our landscape but see for the most part what God sets before us, I cannot but think that mere enumeration of the objects would be found to be more than a catalogue; — would be a symmetrical picture not designed by us but by our Maker, as when we first perceive the meaning of a ⟨formula⟩ ↑sentence which↓ we have carried in the memory for years.

24 May. ⟨Certain facts such as⟩ ↑Coincidences↓, dreams, animal magnetism, omens, Sacred lots, ⟨coincidences,⟩
have great interest for some minds. They run into this twilight & say "there's more than is dreamed of in your philosophy."[126] Certainly these facts are interesting, and are not explained: they deserve to be considered. But they are entitled only to a share of our attention & ⟨that⟩ not a large share. Nil magnificum nil generosum sapit.[127] Read a page of Cudworth or Bacon, & we are exhilarated & armed to manly duties. Read Demonology or Colquhon's Report[128] & you are

[122] The passage "Herrick's merit . . . of fame." is used in "Ben Jonson, Herrick, Herbert, Wotton," *Lectures*, I, 349, and "Art and Criticism," *W*, XII, 296–297.

[123] James Abraham Hillhouse (1789–1841), author of *Percy's Masque* (1819) and *Hadad* (1825), dramas in verse.

[124] Conversation IX, "Duke de Richelieu, Sir Fire Coats, and Lady Glengrin," *Imaginary Conversations*, 1828, III, 206. The observation is cited in "Love," *W*, II, 180.

[125] See p. [4] above.

[126] Cf. *Hamlet*, I, v, 167.

[127] "He knows nothing rich, nothing noble" (Ed.); attributed to Cicero in Sir James Mackintosh, *A General View of the Progress of Ethical Philosophy* (Philadelphia, 1832), p. 25, n.; see *JMN*, III, 323.

[128] Sir Walter Scott, *Letters on Demonology and Witchcraft* (London, 1830; New York, 1830); *Report of the Experiments on Animal Magnetism, Made by a Committee of . . . the French Royal Academy of Sciences . . .* trans. John C. Colquhoun (Edinburgh, 1833).

only bewildered & perhaps a little besmirched. We grope. They who prefer these twilights to ⟨t⟩daylight say they are to reveal to us, — a world of unknown unsuspected truths. But suppose a diligent collection & study of these occult facts were made, — they could never do much for us. They are merely physiological[,] ↑semi-medical↓; facts ⟨to throw light⟩ related to the machinery of ⟨our⟩ man, opening to our curiosity how we live, but throwing no light & no aid on *what* we do. Whilst the dilettanti have been prying into the humors & muscles of the eye, simple active men will have helped themselves & the world by using their eyes.[129] ⟨to⟩

[46] In your Rhetoric notice that only once or twice in history can the words "dire" ⟨or⟩& "tremendous" fit.[130]

We tell our charities because we see not how justice can be done us without. It is a capital blunder. For let another mention his, & you feel his mistake. Tell them not, & they will publish themselves by secret spiritual outlets. Fool, you have spoiled your good act by the boast. ↑Hereby we discover that we always make a just impression↓[.][131]

---

29 May. He weakens who means to confirm his speech by vehemence, feminine vehemence.

"A tremendous faculty that of thinking on one's legs — " is a newspaper description of eloquence; & this is a tolerable use of the word noticed above.

We do not think the young will be forsaken. But ⟨the age⟩ ↑he↓ is always approaching the age when the miraculous external protection & leading is withdrawn & he is committed to his own care. The young man takes a leap in the dark, yet finds no harm. Having ventured once, he ventures again. By & by he learns that such risks he can no longer run. He is oppressed by the melancholy discovery ⟨that⟩ not

---

[129] This paragraph is used in "Lord Bacon," *Lectures*, I, 332, and "Demonology," *W*, X, 23–24.

[130] This sentence is struck through in ink with a vertical use mark.

[131] This paragraph, struck through in pencil with a vertical use mark as far as "the boast.", is used in "Heroism," *Lectures*, II, 337, and "Heroism," *W*, II, 261.

that he incurs misfortunes here & there, but that his Genius whose invisible benevolence was tower & shield to him, is not longer present or active.

At the Sunday School Meeting, G[eorge].P.B[radford]. remarked that his measure of a good speech was the desire it imparted to himself to speak & open the suggestions of the man on the floor. Mr Lothrop spoke & the eminent propriety of his manner answered to the audience the same purpose as if he had said something. All people agreed it was a good speech. Yet is not nature cheated, for these men accomplish nothing. Their effect is as merely phenomenal as their work.

C[harles].C[hauncy].E[merson]. affirms on the road, that "you never are tired so long as you can see far enough." [132]

[47] Add to G.P.B.'s remark just now, our frequent experience of receiving intellectual activity from an ⟨living⟩ acting mind. I read, two days since, verses of Elliot the poet,[133] which filled me with desire to write, with faith in the art.

Now he will render a service to his countrymen who in these days will patiently collect the experiences of this kind & so ⟨embody the⟩ write rules for the discipline of the intellect. Could you show me how in every torpid hour I could wake to full belief & earnest labor, o give me the recipe. Better yet; could you point me to the divine page of Cudworth, Plato, Bacon, Herbert, Carlyle, M. Angelo, or of Paul, or of God in Nature, where I could find a timely restoration of my reason under the insanity of passion, do that and the joy of a Saviour shall be yours.   ↑See Transcript p.181↓

        Happy the ↑wit or↓ dunce; but hard
        Is it to be half a bard.[134]

---

[132] See *JMN*, IV, 255; Encyclopedia (to be printed in *JMN*, VI), p. [138]; *Nature*, *W*, I, 16.

[133] Possibly Ebenezer Elliott, author of "The Village Patriarch," quoted in *JMN*, IV, 361, or James Elliot (1775–1839) of Guilford, Vermont, who had published his *Poetical and Miscellaneous Works* in 1798.

[134] Concerning Emerson's Journal T, or Transcript (to be printed in *JMN*, VI), see the entry for June 3 below. As for the two lines of verse, struck through in ink with a vertical use mark, cf. Emerson's letter to Frederic Henry Hedge, March 14, 1836 (*L*, II, 7): "My versification of this ancient lament is
        Happy Bard or Dunce! but hard
        Is it to be half a bard."

[May] 30. There are two reasons why Wealth inspires respect in virtuous men; first, because wealth forms a strong will, which is always respectable. Second; because the rich man's state is a mockery of the true state of man. 'He speaks & it is done; he commands & it stands fast.' [135] He has not fear. He has not shame. He has not meanness. He can be bountiful, & execute the conceptions of the Understanding[,] the fiat of the Reason. The aunt's amusing theory of the blood royal is the theory of the Angel.

The whole of Virtue consists in substituting *being* for *seeming*, & therefore God properly saith *I AM*.

The Ideal philosophy is much more akin to virtue than to vice. When the mountains begin to look unreal, the soul is in a high state, yet in an action of justice or charity things look solid again.

———

[48] I am convinced that we are very much indebted to each other for stimulus, & for such confirmation to our own thoughts that we venture to try them in practice, a step we should have long postponed but for that seconding.

———

1 June. In this age of Seeming nothing ⟨seems⟩ ↑can be↓ more important than the opening & promulgation of the gospel of Compensations to save the land. The men who put manner for matter at our public meetings should learn that they have lost their time. The man who mistakes his profession, the Scholar who takes his subject from dictation & not from his heart, should know that he has lost as much as he seems to have gained. And when the vain speaker has sat down, & the people say 'what a good speech!' it still takes an ounce to ⟨move⟩ ↑balance↓ an ounce. Societies as well as individuals are bubbles. But Nature cannot be cheated. That only profits which is profitable. Life alone can impart life, & though we burst we can only be valued as we make ourselves valuable.[136]

[135] Cf. Ps. 33:9.

[136] "The man . . . valuable.", struck through in ink with a vertical use mark, is used in "Modern Aspects of Letters," *Lectures*, I, 381–382. The phrase "takes an ounce . . . an ounce." occurs also in "Shakspear [second lecture]," *ibid.*, p. 319, and "Politics," *Lectures*, II, 79. For "we can only . . . valuable.", which Emerson had found in Vicesimus Knox, *Elegant Extracts . . . in Prose*, 7th ed., 2 vols. (London, 1797), II, 1028, see *JMN*, IV, 17.

The irresistible conclusion of your chapter on Compensations should be, Therefore, the Devil is an Ass.[137]

Levi Woodbury occupies the ⟨same⟩ position once filled by Alexander Hamilton;[138] Jackson that of Washington; Isaac Hill is a member of the Senate as much as Daniel Webster. But does any one imagine that this equal *nominal* standing makes the standing of these men *identical?* It is perfectly well known both ⟨to Jackson &⟩ to Washington & to Jackson the gulf that is between them; and likewise to Hamilton & to Woodbury; and likewise to Webster & to Hill.

3 June. I have begun at p. 181 of my Transcript to make a collection of such sentences as stimulate the moral sentiments & do defend me from crime[.][139]

———

[49] Mr Alston[140] would build a very plain house & have plain furniture because he would hold out no bribe to any to visit him who had not similar tastes to his own. A good Ascetic.[141]

———

Sir Henry Wotton said of Sidney that "his wit was the measure of congruity."[142]

———

Miss Martineau says that Mr Ware is sanctimonious, Mr Gannett popish, Unitarians in a twilight of bigotry, and that Mr Furness has a genius for religion.[143]

———

The quantity of mind inversely as the quantity of matter[.]

———

[137] Cf. Ben Jonson, *The Devil is an Ass*, IV, iv, 243: "The Devil is an Ass. I do acknowledge it."

[138] Woodbury served as Secretary of the Treasury, once Hamilton's post, from 1834 to 1841.

[139] The collection begins with the heading "Bread."

[140] Washington Allston, the painter.

[141] See *JMN*, IV, 360.

[142] Cf. Izaak Walton, "The Life of Sir Henry Wotton," in *Reliquiae Wottonianae*, 1685, p. 37. See "Ben Jonson, Herrick, Herbert, Wotton," *Lectures*, I, 354.

[143] The references are to Harriet Martineau, then visiting America; Reverend Henry Ware, Jr., and Reverend Ezra Stiles Gannett, Boston Unitarians; and Emerson's old friend William Henry Furness, a Unitarian minister in Philadelphia.

The year is long enough for all that is to be done in it;[144] it is long enough for Nature though not for Man.

_____

If a conversation be prolonged which is not exactly on my key, I become nervous, & need to go out of the room, or to eat.[n] And when my friend is gone, I am unfit for work. ⟨Solitude does not⟩ ↑Society↓ suffocates, as Lidian[145] said, and irritates.

4 June. It seems as if every sentence should be prefixed with the word *True*, or, *Apparent*, to indicate the writer's intention of speaking after that which is, or that which seems. Thus, *truly*, our power increases exactly in the measure that we know how to use it, but *apparently*, Andrew Jackson is more powerful than John Marshall.

⟨In a true⟩ In Heaven, utterance is place enough. Heaven is the name we give to the True State, the World of Reason not of the Understanding, of the Real, not the Apparent. It exists always, whether it is ever to be separated from the Hell or not.[146] It is, as Coleridge said, another world but not to come.[147] The world I describe is that, where ⟨the Mind makes its own laws⟩ only the laws of mind are known, the only economy of time is saying & doing nothing untrue to self.[148]

[50] Skill of analysis may outrun your practical virtue but the impression you make is proportioned to your real virtue.

The true man in every act has the Universe at his back.[n] ↑J. makes a convenience of us.↓

Away with this succumbing & servility forever. I will not be

_____

[144] For earlier variants of this same remark, see *JMN*, IV, 266, n. 52.

[145] Emerson had so renamed his fiancée, Lydia Jackson.

[146] Cf. the Swedenborgian belief that "heaven is not a place, nor is hell. They are states, — conditions of the will and the understanding. He is in heaven, in whom the love of the Lord and of the neighbor are . . . absolute . . . . He is in hell, in whom the love of self and the love of the world . . . exercise entire dominion." "The Spiritual World," *New Jerusalem Magazine*, IX (April 1836), 280.

[147] See the dialogue between Demosius and Mystes in *On the Constitution of Church and State*, ed. H. N. Coleridge (London, 1839), p. 186; *JMN*, IV, 344.

[148] Cf. p. [4] above: "The only true economy of time is to rely without interval on your own judgment."

warned of the sacredness of traditions. I will live wholly from within. You say they may be impulses from below not from above. Maybe so. But if I am the Devil's child I will live from the Devil. I can have no law sacred but that of my nature.[149]

——

Knowledge is hard to get & unsatisfying when ⟨acquired⟩ gained. Knowledge ⟨is provoking⟩ is a pleasing provocation to the mind beforehand & not cumbersome afterwards.

Am I true to myself? Then Nations & ages do guide my pen. Then I perceive my commission to be coeval with the eldest causes[.]

Do Jim take your Mamma's porcelain waterpot, & go water the forests in Maine.

The clouds are our Water carriers, — and do you see that handbreadth of greener grass where the cattle have dropped dung? That was the first lecturer on Agriculture.

The sea is the ring by which the nations are married.[150]

> "The privates of man's heart
> They speaken & sound in his Ear
> As tho they loud Winds were." *Gower*
>   [*Confessio Amantis*, I, 2806–2808][151]

Do what we can, summer will have its flies. If we walk in the woods, we shall be annoyed by musquitoes. If we go a fishing we must expect a wet coat.[152]

[51] ↑10 June↓
Aristotle Platonizes. Cudworth is like a cow in June which breathes of nothing but clover & scent grass. He has fed so entirely on ancient bards & sages that ⟨he is redolent of their thought⟩ all his diction is

---

[149] "You say . . . my nature.", struck through in ink with a vertical use mark, is used in "Self-Reliance," *W*, II, 50.

[150] The sentence, struck through in ink with a diagonal use mark, is used in "Trades and Professions," *Lectures*, II, 116.

[151] The quotation, struck through in ink with a diagonal use mark, is used in "Ethics," *Lectures*, II, 150, and "Poetry and Imagination," *W*, VIII, 9.

[152] This paragraph is used in "Prudence," *Lectures*, II, 313, and "Prudence," *W*, II, 225–226.

redolent of their books. ↑He is a stream of Corinthian brass in which gold & silver & iron are molten together out of anc[ient]. temples↓[.] [153]

⟨It is the mark of all propositions⟩ I endeavor to announce the laws of the First Philosophy.[154] It is the mark of these that their enunciation awakens the feeling of the moral sublime, & great men are they who believe in them. ↑⟨It⟩ Every one of these propositions ⟨is⟩ resembles a great circle in astronomy. No matter in what direction it be drawn it contains the whole sphere. So each of these seems to imply all truth. Compare a page of Bacon with Swift, Chesterfield, Lacon,[155] & see the difference of great & less circles. These are gleams of a world in which we do not live: they astonish the Understanding.↓ [156]

20 June. The advantage in Education is always with those children who slip up into life without being objects of notice. Happy those then who are members of large families.

Literature. I asked in the woods, What I would know of Homer, if ↑the↓ Oedipus were ready to reply. We would know whether in the mind of his age were any radical differences from ours. Whether they had an equivalent for our organized morale? Whether we have lost by Civilization any force, by Christianity any virtue? Machinery encumbers.[157] Homer is to us nothing personal, merely the representative of his time. I believe that to be his sincerest use & worth. The most abstract questions are really operating actively on men, tho' they know it not, & the real interest that effervesces in this love of literary gossip is a wise curiosity in the human soul to know if our fellow is our counterpart. I suppose we would most anxiously know

[153] On the origin of Corinthian brass, see "Why the Pythian Priestess Ceases her Oracles in Verse," *Plutarch's Morals: . . . Translated from the Greek, by Several Hands*, 5th ed., 5 vols. (London, 1718), III, 100. The anecdote is similarly associated with Cudworth in a note in the manuscript of "Ethical Writers" (*Lectures*, I, 365, n. 16).

[154] See *JMN*, IV, 79: "that species of moral truth which I call the first philosophy." Emerson took the term from Bacon's *Advancement of Learning, The Works*, 1824, I, 95 (see *JMN*, III, 360).

[155] Charles Caleb Colton, *Lacon: or Many Things in Few Words* (1820–1822).

[156] With this paragraph compare the opening of RO Mind (dated "June, 1835"), p. [1].

[157] "We would know . . . Machinery encumbers." is used in "The Individual," *Lectures*, II, 174–175; cf. "Self-Reliance," *W*, II, 85.

what is ⟨their⟩ ↑this↓ moral sentiment, & not so curiously inquire, whether ⟨t⟩he⟨y⟩ managed better than we, with our fellow-beings — the sea, & the land, the plants, the animals, fire, & light.

[52] When we read a book in a foreign language we suppose that an English version of it would be a transfusion of it into our own consciousness. But take Coleridge or Bacon or many an English book besides & you immediately feel that the English is ⟨but⟩ a language ↑also↓ & that a book writ in that tongue is yet very far from ↑you↓ being transfused into your own consciousness. There is every degree of remoteness from the line of things in the line of words. By & by comes a word true & closely embracing the thing. That is not Latin nor English nor any language, but *thought*. The aim of the author is not to tell truth — that he cannot do, but to suggest it. He has only approximated it himself, & hence his cumbrous embarrassed speech: he uses many words, hoping that one, if not another, will bring you as near to the fact as he is.

For language itself is young & unformed. In heaven it will be, as Sampson Reed said, "one with things." [158] Now, there are many things that refuse to be recorded, — perhaps the larger half. The unsaid part is the best of every discourse.

The good of publishing one's thoughts is that of hooking to you likeminded men, and of giving to men whom you value, such as Wordsworth or Landor, one hour of stimulated thought. Yet, how few! Who in Concord cares for the first philosophy in a book? The woman whose child is to be suckled? the man at Nine-Acre-Corner who is to cart 60 loads of gravel on his meadow? the stageman? the gunsmith? O No! Who then?

[53] 21 June. Poetry preceded prose as the form of sustained thought, as Reason, whose vehicle poetry is, precedes the Understanding. When you assume the ⟨music⟩ rhythm of verse & the analogy of nature it is making proclamation 'I am now freed from the trammels of the Apparent; I speak from the Mind.'

---

[158] "Oration on Genius" (1821), in *E t E*, II, 10. A manuscript copy of the essay was given Charles Emerson in 1830.

[June] 22. It is unpleasing to meet with those anomalous wits who say brilliant things and yet have no proportioned strength of mind; Chalmers, Edw. Irving, ⟨or⟩ Brougham, Randolph,[159] or, more frequently, talkers who impose upon us by the vivacity or weight of single remarks, and when you better know the speaker, "you wonder how the devil they got there." The more genius, usually, the more conformity there is to the general model. But these seem hybrids.

I wrote L[ydia Jackson]. that this speechmaking seems to turn the man out of doors, to turn his timber into flowers, & make him like unto Apicius who sold his house but kept the balcony to see & be seen in.[160]

Aunt saith, "the finest wits have their sediment."

↑Persons↓

⟨The⟩ ↑Some↓ people in Rhode Island saying to G. Fox that if they had money enough they would hire him to be their Minister, he said, "Then it was time for him to be gone, for if their eye was to him, or to any of them, then would they never come to their own teacher."[161]

[June] 24. "Three silent revolutions in England; first, when the professions fell from the Church. 2. When literature fell from the professions. 3. When the press fell from literature". *Coleridge*[162]

I remembered to C[harles]. tonight the English gentleman whom I saw in the cold hostelrie at Simplon at the top of the moun-

---

[159] The references are probably to Alexander Chalmers (1759–1834), Scottish journalist and biographer; Reverend Edward Irving (1792–1834), Scottish clergyman; Henry Peter Brougham, 1st Baron Brougham and Vaux (1778–1868), Scottish jurist and political leader (see *L*, II, 262); and John Randolph of Roanoke (1773–1833), American congressman and senator.

[160] Samuel Butler, "A Degenerate Noble: or, One that is proud of his Birth," *The Genuine Remains in Verse and Prose of Mr. Samuel Butler*, ed. R. Thyer, 2 vols. (London, 1759), II, 77. See "The Present Age," *Lectures*, II, 163.

[161] Cf. *A Journal or Historical Account of the Life, Travels, Sufferings, Christian Experiences, and Labour of Love . . . of . . . George Fox*, 2 vols. (New York, 1800), II, 151–152.

[162] Cf. *Specimens of the Table Talk of the Late Samuel Taylor Coleridge*, 1835, II, 23–24. This quotation is used in "The Man of Letters," *W*, X, 249.

tain, & whose manners so satisfied my eye. He met there unexpectedly an acquaintance, & conversed with him with great ease & affectionateness, & as if totally unconscious of the presence of any other company, yet with highbred air.

[54] The selfexistency of the gentleman is his best mark. He is to be a man first, with original perceptions of the true & the beautiful, & thence should grow his grace & dignity. Then he is God's gentleman and a new argument to the Stoic.

"When I am purified by the light of heaven my soul will become the mirror of the world, in which I shall discern all abstruse secrets." Warton quotes this, he says, from an ancient Turkish poet. *Hist. Eng. Poetry*, vol. 2, p. 241 [163]

[55] Books are ⟨never⟩ ↑not↓ writ in the style of conversation. One might say they are not addressed to the same beings as gossip & cheat in the street. Neither are speeches, orations, sermons, academic discourses on the same key of thought or addressed to the same beings. The man that just now chatted at your side, of trifles, rises in the assembly to speak, & speaks to them collectively in a tone & with a series of thoughts he would never think of assuming to any one of them alone. Because man's Universal nature is his inmost nature.

I will no longer confer, differ, refer, defer, prefer, ↑or suffer.↓ I renounce the whole family of *Fero*. I embrace absolute life.

Idealism is not so much prejudiced by danger as by inconvenience. ⟨We⟩ In our speculative habits we sometimes expect that the too solid earth will melt.[164] Then we cross the ocean sweltering, seasick, reeling, week after week, with tar, harness-tub, & bilge, and, as an ingenious friend says, It is carrying the joke too far.

16 June. ↑Books↓ Blessed art & blessed instruments of pen, ink, & paper that hold fast the representatives of the related thoughts. Here logic holds & between the major & minor of a syllogism cannot

---

[163] Thomas Warton, *The History of English Poetry, from the Close of the Eleventh to the Commencement of the Eighteenth Century*, 4 vols. (London, 1824).
[164] Cf. *Hamlet*, I, ii, 129.

the mind whisk away because a thrush flies out of a bush or a smart Golden senecio catches the eye, or an elegant lupine lifts its blue spires in the path.

"No noble Virtue ever was alone."   Ben Jonson

↑Memory↓

26 June. If you would know what nobody knows, ⟨read⟩ read what every body reads, just one year afterwards & you shall be a fund of new & unheard of speculations.

The Mystery of Humility is treated of by Jesus, by Dante, by Chaucer in his Grisilda, by Milton & by Sam[p]son Reed.[165] Or listen to the Discourse of a wise man to a crowd in a perfect conviction that nobody hears it but you.

[56] 27 June, I wrote Hedge[166] that good society seemed an optical illusion that ought to be classed with Bacon's Idols of the Cave. Carlyle affirms it has ceased to exist.[167] C.C.E. affirms that it is just begun — Greek & Roman knew it not. To me it seems that it is ⟨by the order of things⟩ so steadily & universally thwarted ⟨that a design to hinder it must be suspected⟩ — by death, sickness, removals, unfitness, ceremony, or what not, that a design to hinder it, must be suspected. Every person is indulged with an opportunity or two of equal & hearty communication enough to show him his potential heaven. But between cultivated minds the first interview is the best, & it is surprizing in how few hours the results of years are exhausted. Besides though it seem ungrateful to friends whom the heart knoweth by name yet the value of the conversation is not ↑measured↓ according to the wisdom of the company but by quite other & indefinable causes[,]

---

[165] Cf. Reed's "Oration on Genius" (1821), in *E t E,* II, 10: when a man "acknowledges that his powers are from God . . . : this is the humility which exalts." "The Mystery . . . Samson Reed." is struck through in ink with two diagonal use marks.

[166] Frederic Henry Hedge, son of Professor Levi Hedge and friend of Emerson since their student days, was a Unitarian minister and writer on German literature. For the complete letter, dated June 25, 1835, see *L,* I, 446–447.

[167] *Sartor Resartus,* Bk. III, ch. V; see *JMN,* IV, 308, for a comparable allusion.

the fortunate moods. I think ↑we owe↓ the most recreation & most memorable thoughts to very unpromising gossips[.]   ↑I copied the above from memory↓

———

[June] 29. ⟨Th⟩ Geo. Fox's chosen expression for the God manifest in the mind is the Seed. He means that seed of which the Beauty of the world is the Flower & ⟨the⟩Goodness is the Fruit.

I replied this morn. to the Committee that I would do what I could to prepare a Historical Discourse for the Town Anniversary.[168] Yet why notice it? Centuries pass unnoticed. The Saxon King was told that man's life was like the swallow that flew in at one window, fluttered around, & flew out at another.[169] So is this population of the spot of God's earth called Concord. For a moment they fish in this river, plow furrows in the banks, build houses on the fields, mow the grass. But hold on to hill or tree never so fast they must disappear in a trice.

The contemplation of nature is all that is fine. Who can tell [57][170] me how many thousand years, every day, the clouds have shaded these fields with their purple awning? The little river by whose banks most of us were born every winter for ages has spread its crust of ice over the ↑great↓ meadows which in ages it had formed. The countless families that follow or precede man keep no jubilee, mark no era, the fly & the moth in burnished armor. ⟨thrush.⟩ These little emigrants travel fast, they have no baggage wagon. All night they creep. The ant has no provision for sleep. The trees that surround us grew up in the days of Peter Bulkeley. This first celebration f⟨or⟩rom ↑the↓ everlasting past. The oaks that were then acorns wave their branches in this morning's wind. The little flower that at this season stars the woods & roadsides with its profuse blooms won the

---

[168] Celebrated on September 12, 1835. Emerson's notes for his address were collected in his notebook L Concord.

[169] This anecdote is given in Sharon Turner, *The History of the Anglo-Saxons*, 2nd ed., 2 vols. (London, 1807), II, 439. See p. [104] below; "Permanent Traits of the English National Genius," *Lectures*, I, 251.

[170] In the center of this page, beneath "the stern pilgrim . . . Heywood", is a diagram in ink, possibly a floor or ground plan.

eye of the stern pilgrim with its humble beauty. The Maple grew red in the early frost over those houseless men burrowing in the sand. The mighty Pine yet untouched towered into the frosty air. And yet another kind of permanence has also been permitted. Here are still the names of the first 50 years. Here is Blood, Willard, Flint, Wood, Barrett, Heywood ↑Hunt, Wheeler, Jones, Buttrick↓[.] And if ↑the name of↓ Bulkeley is wanting ⟨your⟩ the honor you have done me this day shows your kindness for his blood↓[.] [171]

[58] 1 July.[172] A windmill so soon as it is far enough in the landscape to look like a toy, is picturesque[,] nearer it is disagreeable. The robin like the geranium family ⟨have⟩ ↑wear↓ sober colors. ↑C. says that painting the vans red is adding insult to injury↓[.]

"There⟨s⟩ is scarce truth enough alive to make societies secure;" says Shakspear in Measure for Measure[.] [173]

[July] 2. The distincti⟨ve⟩on of Science objective & subjective I find in Norris's Ideal World Vol 1. p. 129.[174]

In the memory of the disembodied soul the days or hours of pure Reason will shine with a steady light as the life of life & all the other days & weeks will appear but as hyphens ⟨whereby these are joined⟩ ↑which served to join these↓.

"The attention of the Mind is the natural prayer which we make to Interiour Truth that she may discover herself to us." "But this sovereign Truth does not always answer our desires because we know not very well how to ask her as we ought[.]"
    Conversat. Chretien p. 7 quoted ap. Norris; [cf. ibid.,] Vol. 1 p 324
"F. Daniel, the Jesuit, one of the finest wits of his age," the Anti Cartesian, said — ["]That which I clearly conceive is true. To be a Deceiver is an

---

[171] Reverend Joseph Emerson of Mendon, great-great-great-grandfather of Emerson, married as his second wife Elizabeth Bulkeley, granddaughter of Peter Bulkeley, one of the founders of Concord and its first minister; there were no Bulkeleys living in the town in 1835. This and the preceding paragraph, struck through in ink with discontinuous vertical use marks beginning with "Yet why notice" on p. [56], are used in "Historical Discourse at Concord," W, XI, 29–30.

[172] An additional entry headed "Writ June, 1835." occurs on p. [155].

[173] Measure for Measure, III, ii, 240–242.

[174] John Norris, An Essay Towards the Theory of the Ideal or Intelligible World, pts. I and II, 2 vols. (London, 1701, 1704).

imperfection["] [175]   or quotes he them from DesCartes. [Cf.] Norris
[*ibid.*,] vol I   [p]p [350–]351
"Can never go out of the sphere of truth whose centre is every where
& whose circumference is nowhere." [176] [Cf.] Norris, [*ibid.*,] p. 389.
Vol I.

Admirable passages quoted from St Augustine De Lib. Arbitrio;
lib. 2 cap. 13, 14, [177]

"And yet as rich as thy furniture is, O city of God! thy gates stand
always open, free to all comers. For thy immovable wealth needs no guard,
the Exchequer of Light & Truth is [59] secure against all thievish attempts,
& the treasures of wisdom tho' common to all can yet be rifled or carried
away by none." Norris. [178] [Cf. *ibid.*, p]p. [430–]431

Norris's first volume was an unexpected delight this P.M. He
fights the battles & affirms the facts I had proposed to myself to do.
But he falls, I so think, into the common error of the first philosophers[,] that of attempting to fight for Reason with the Weapons
of the Understanding. All this ⟨logic⟩ ⟨logomachy⟩ polemics, ⟨&⟩
syllogism, & definition is so much wastepaper & Montaigne is almost
the only man who has never lost sight of ⟨it⟩ this fact.

4 July. Talked last eve. with G.P.B. of Locke who, I maintained,
had given me little. I am much more indebted to persons of far less
name. I believe his service was to popularize metaphysics, allure men
of the world to its study, if that indeed be a service. [179] G. gave a good
account of his friend Alcott who is a consistent spiritualist & so ex-
pects the influence of Christianity into trade, government, literature,
& arts.

[175] The point at issue is whether an omnipotent God can change the essence of
things: e.g., so that "two and three should not have been five."
[176] Cf. "Modern Aspects of Letters," *Lectures*, I, 383; "Progress of Culture," *W*,
VIII, 221. In "Circles," *W*, II, 301, the expression is attributed to St. Augustine, as
in Coleridge's *Aids to Reflection*, ed. James Marsh (Burlington, Vt., 1829), p. 304,
note; see *JMN*, IV, 381–382, n. 373, for discussion of Emerson's image of truth as a
circle.
[177] Norris, *An Essay*, I, 392–394: Augustine's discussion of the community of
truth.
[178] Erroneously attributed to "St. Austin" in "Modern Aspects of Letters," *Lectures*, I, 383.
[179] Cf. "Ethical Writers," *Lectures*, I, 366.

The arts languish now because all their scope is exhibition; when they originated it was to serve the gods. The Catholic Religion has turned them to continual account in its service. Now they are mere flourishes. Is it strange they perish?   Poetry to be sterling must be more than a show[,] must have or be an earnest meaning. Chaucer, Wordsworth[;] per Contra Moore & Byron.

The object of the politician is to get the hurra on our side.

[60] I study the art of solitude. I yield me as gracefully as I can to my destiny. Why cannot one get the good of his doom, & since it is from eternity a settled thing that he & society shall be nothing to each other, why need he blush so, & make wry faces & labor to keep up a poor beginner's place, a freshman's seat in the fine world[?]

Of Truth Norris said something like this that we could not dis-imagine its existence, but always the Mind recovers itself with a strong & invincible spring to its faith.

One of the good effects of hearing the man of genius is that he shows the world of thought to be infinite again which you had sup-posed exhausted.

"That inbred loyalty unto virtue which can serve her without a livery." [by Emerson?]

15 July. Why do I still go to pasture where I never find grass, to these actors without a purpose unless a poor mechanical one, these talkers without ⟨thought⟩ method, & reasoners without an idea? At the Divinity School this morning I heard what was called the best performance but it was founded on nothing & led to nothing & I wondered at the patience of the people. This P.M. the King of the House of Seem spoke & made as if he was in earnest with pathetic tones & gesture, & the most approved expressions, and all about nothing; & he was answered by others with equal apparent earnest-ness & still it was all nothing. The building seemed to grudge its rent if the assembly did not their time. Stetson [180] who jokes, seems the only wise man. It is pity 300 men should meet to make believe or play Debate.

[180] Reverend Caleb Stetson, a classmate of Emerson at Harvard, was noted as a wit.

They are all so ⟨serious⟩ ↑solemn↓ & vehement, that I listen with all my ears & for my life can't find any idea at the foundation of their zeal.

[61] I forgive desultoriness, trifling, vice even in a young man ⟨who⟩ so long as I believe that he has a closet of secret thoughts to which he retires as to his home & which have a sort of parents' interest in him wherever he is. At sight of them he bows. But if he is not in earnest about any thing[,] if all his ⟨ear⟩ interest is good breeding & imitation I had as lief not be as be him.

Great pudder make my philanthropic friends about the children. I should be glad to be convinced they have taught one ⟨single⟩ child ⟨a⟩one ⟨single⟩ thing. Gray & Barnard,[181] no doubt, teach them just as much as the minister did before, not a jot more; for the⟨y⟩ ↑children↓ don't understand any thing they say.

Quotation.

Coleridge loses by Dequincey, but more by his own concealing uncandid acknowledgment of debt to Schelling.[182] Why could not he have said generously like Goethe, I owe all?[183] As soon as one gets so far above pride, as to say all truth that might come from ⟨me⟩ ↑him↓ & that now does come from ⟨me⟩ ↑him↓ as truth & not as ⟨my⟩ ↑his↓ truth, as soon as he acknowledges that all is suggestion, then he may be indebted without shame to all.

Composition

The history of literature is a hist. of few ideas & even of few tales[.][184]

I see that the young men like to speak at public meetings just

[181] Frederick T. Gray and Charles F. Barnard had been ordained in 1834 as "ministers at large in Boston"; see C. A. Bartol, "Ministry for the Poor," *Christian Examiner*, XXI (Jan. 1837), 335–354.

[182] De Quincey's "Samuel Taylor Coleridge," in *Tait's Edinburgh Magazine*, n. s. I (Sept. 1834), 511, makes the charge that in *Biographia Literaria* Coleridge is guilty of "barefaced plagiarism" for including without acknowledgement "a *verbatim* translation from Schelling."

[183] Cf. Sarah Austin, *Characteristics of Goethe from the German of Falk, von Müller, etc. . . .* , 3 vols. (London, 1833), III, 76–77.

[184] This sentence is used in "Being and Seeming," *Lectures*, II, 304.

as they would take exhilarating gas 'tis so pretty an intoxication. O for the days of the Locrian halters again.[185]

[62] The wit of man is more elastic than the air our bodies breathe. A whole nation will subsist for centuries on one thought & then every individual man will be oppressed by the rush of his conceptions & always a plenum with one grain or 60 atmospheres.

Let not the voluptuary dare to judge of literary far less of ⟨moral⟩ philosophical questions. Let him wait until the blindness that belongs to pollution has passed from his eyes.

We all have an instinct that a good man good & wise shall be able to say intuitively i.e. from God what is true & great & beautiful. Never numbers but the simple & wise shall judge. Not the Wartons & Drakes but ⟨the⟩ some divine savage like Webster, Wordsworth, & Reed whom neither the town or the college ever made shall say that we shall all believe. How we thirst for a natural thinker[.]

It is droll enough that when I had been groping for months after the natural process which I felt sure resembled in my experience the freedom with which at a certain height ⟨thots p⟩ of excitement, thoughts pour into the mind, I should at last recognize it in so mean a fact as the passage of bile into the mouth in the retchings of seasickness. Better said Goethe when he spoke of filling the bottle under water than drop by drop. My illustration would be that the ornithologist from the city goes many miles to the woods & follows the bird all day long & cannot get a sight of him. But a farmer's boy passes thro' the wood & sees the whole manners of the bird in the next bush[.] [186]

[63] I find good things in this MSS. of Oegger & I am taken with the design of his work.[187] But it seems as if every body was in-

[185] "The Locrians," Edward Emerson notes (J, III, 504, n. 1), "had halters around the necks of the speakers so that they could shut off their discourse." Edmund G. Berry, *Emerson's Plutarch* (Cambridge, Mass., 1961), p. 306, n. 7, thinks him in error in citing "A story of Plutarch's" as his father's source here.

[186] "My illustration . . . next bush" is struck through in ink with a vertical use mark.

[187] Emerson was reading a manuscript translation of G. Oegger, *Le Vraie Messie*

sane on one side & the Bible makes them as crazy as Bentham or Spurz-heim or politics. The ethical doctrines of these theosophists are true & exalting, but straightway they run upon their Divine Transforma-tion[,] the Death of God &c [188] & become horn mad. To that point they speak reason then they begin to babble. & so this man cries out Wo to them that do not believe &c &c. This obstinate Orientalism that God is a petty Asiatic King & will be very angry if you do not prostrate yourself, they cannot ↑get↓ rid ⟨themselves⟩ of.

But now & then out breaks the sublimity of truth: [n]

"When was an act of goodness & virtue, when was a sentiment of benevo-lence & love not greater than the conquest of the Universe?"

"We shall pass to the future existence as we enter into an agreeable dream: all nature will accompany us there." [189]

[64] Much that is best is hid by being next to us. Who in Chris-tendom knows the beauty & grandeur of the Lord's Prayer?

July 24. Hooker. "In the first age of the world — by reason of the number of their days, their memories served instead of books." [190] There is no book like a Memory & none that hath such a perfect Index & that of every kind, alphabetical, systematic, & ⟨by⟩ arranged by names of persons & all manner of associations.

"I say three persons, ingenuously confessed St Augustine (on the Trinity; v[ol]. 9) not that I may say something but that I may not say nothing." ap. Oegger

Most persons exist to us merely or chiefly in relations of time & space. Those whom we love, whom we venerate, or whom we serve, exist to us independently of these relations.

(Paris, 1829) — probably that made by Elizabeth Peabody, who later published an English version of its introductory sections: *The True Messiah; or The Old and New Testaments, Examined According to The Principles of the Language of Nature* (Bos-ton, 1842), a pamphlet of 27 pages.

[188] See p. [73] below.

[189] These quotations, presumably taken from the manuscript translation of *The True Messiah*, do not appear in the 1842 pamphlet.

[190] Cf. Richard Hooker, *Of the Lawes of Ecclesiastical Politie*, Bk. I, par. 13 (London, 1617), p. 39. (Emerson was charged with this edition by the Harvard Col-lege Library on July 20, 1835.)

O Thou who drawest ⟨benefit⟩ ↑good↓ out of the fury of devils
save me.

[65] Yesterday I visited Jonas Buttrick & Abel Davis the former
aged 70 the latter 79 years. Both were present at Concord fight. Davis
was one of the militia under command of   J.B. remembered
Maj Hosmer & Capt Davis going back & forward often & said of
Capt. Davis that "his face was red as a piece of broad cloth — red as a
beet. He looked very much worried." I asked, 'Worried with fear?'
No. Both agree that Capt. Davis had the right of the companies [n]
but know not why. J.B. thinks that he did not come up from Acton
until after the consultation of the officers & the conclusion to fight
& that he took the right because that was the side on which he most
conveniently joined the troops. A. Davis thinks that Maj.
having given up his company to   Capt. Davis had the right
in virtue of his rank.

The Indians said of the cannon they did not like those loud
speakers.

> So every spirit as it is most pure
> And hath in it the more of heavenly light
> So it the fairer body doth procure
> To habit in and it more fairly dight
> With cheerful grace & amiable sight
> For of the soul the body form doth take
> For soul is form & doth the body make.[191]
>   Spenser's Hymn in honor of Beauty [ll. 127–133]

Dr Palfrey [192] remarked at Cambridge when we talked of the manners of Wordsworth & Coleridge that there seemed to be no such
thing as a conventional manner ⟨f⟩ among the eminent men of England for these people lived in the best society yet each ⟨had⟩ ↑in-
dulged↓ the strongest individual peculiarities.

-----

[191] This extract, struck through in ink with a vertical use mark, is used in "The
Eye and Ear," *Lectures*, II, 264, and "The Poet," *W*, III, 14; the last line is quoted
in "Literature," *W*, V, 242.

[192] John Gorham Palfrey, Unitarian clergyman, editor of the *North American
Review*, 1835–1843.

For literature one is ever struck with the fact that the good once is good always. The average strength is so fixed that among thirty jumpers the longest jump will be likely to be the longest of 300 & a very long jump will remain a very long jump a century afterward.

[66] Richard Hooker wrote good prose in 1580. Here it is good prose in 1835. There have not been forty persons of his nation from that time to this who could write better.[193]

The Quarterly Review toils to prove that there is no selfish aristocracy in America but that every man shakes hands heartily with every other man & the chancellor says "My brother, the grocer[.]" [194]

And to fix this fact will be to stamp us with desired infamy. I earnestly wish it could be proved. I wish it could be shown that no distinctions created by a contemptible pride existed here & none but the natural ones of talent & virtue. But I fear we do not deserve the ↑praise of this↓ Reviewer's ill opinion. ↑The only ambition which truth allows is to be the servant of all. The last shall be first.↓ [195]

I read with great delight the "Record of A School." [196] It aims all the time to show the symbolical character of all things to the children, & it is alleged, ⁿ &, I doubt not, truly, that the children take the thought with delight. It is remarkable that all poets, orators, & philosophers, have been those who could most sharply see & most happily present ⟨thes⟩ emblems, parables, figures. Good writing & brilliant conversation are perpetual allegories.[197] "My fortunes are in the moult" says Philip Van A.[198] Webster is such a poet in every speech. "You cannot keep out of politics more than you can keep

[193] The passage "For literature . . . write better." is used in "Chaucer," *Lectures*, I, 271.

[194] *The Quarterly Review*, LI (April 1835), 297, citing in translation Gustave de Beaumont, *Marie, ou l'Esclave aux Etats-Unis*, 2 vols. (Paris, 1835), I, 385, note.

[195] Cf. Matt. 20:16; Mark 10:31; Luke 13:30.

[196] Elizabeth Palmer Peabody, *Record of a School; Exemplifying the General Principles of Spiritual Culture* (Boston, 1835). Miss Peabody was the assistant of Amos Bronson Alcott at his private school in Boston.

[197] This sentence is used in "English Literature: Introductory" and "Shakspear [first lecture]," *Lectures*, I, 222 and 290, respectively; and in *Nature, W*, I, 31.

[198] Cf. Taylor, *Philip van Artevelde*, 1835, II, 191: "we are in the moult, / And here's a feather fallen" (pt. II, Act V, scene iii). See "English Literature: Introductory," *Lectures*, I, 223.

out of frost," he said to Clifford. "No matter for the baggage so long as the troop is safe" he said when he lost his trunk. "Waves lash the shore," &c Indian's whole speech. "Back of the hand" was Crockett's expression.[199] All the memorable [67] words of the world are these figurative expressions. Light & heat have passed into all speech for knowledge & love. The river is nothing but as it typifies the flux of time. Many of these signs seem very arbitrary & historical. I should gladly know what gave such universal acceptance to Cupid's arrow for the passion of love; & more meanly the horn for the shame of cuckoldom.

———

Ephraim Slow, says the newspaper, "was born on the last day of the year which gave occasion to a parish wit to remark that he came near not being born at all."

———

27 July. "One of those crystal days which are neither hot nor cold." Mrs R[ipley]. cited a well known character to show that trick & pretension impose on nobody but that my friend is reverenced for his liberality[.]

Every body leads two or three lives, has two or three consciousnesses which he nimbly alternates. Here am I daily lending my voice & that with heat often to ⟨views⟩ opinions & practices opposite to my own. Here is M.M.E. ⟨is⟩ always fighting in conversation against the very principles which have governed & govern her.

Very good remark saw I in the very good Record of a School concerning Unity reproduced by the mind out of severed parts. Yes, all men have thoughts, images, facts, by thousands & thousands, but only one of many can crystallize these into a symmetrical one by ⟨using a b⟩ means of the Nucleus of an Idea.

Humphrey Heywood showed me his fine toy cart which his father made for him. I see nothing of the farmer but his plain dealing & hard work; yet there are finer parts which but for this child would remain latent. His love & the taste which makes a fanciful child's wagon for its manifestation.[200]

---

[199] See "English Literature: Introductory," *Lectures*, I, 222. A further reworking of this and the preceding sentences appears in "Poetry and the Imagination," *W*, VIII, 14.

[200] This paragraph is used in "Perpetual Forces," *W*, X, 80–81.

[68] Manners. There are occasions on which it seems not much can be said. Dr R[ipley] says he has been eating an apple of which he sent the graft to Waterford and he would give me a piece but that he has just eat it up.

Revolutions have their seat in "the devouring thirst for justice which nothing seems to have power to allay, in those generous sentiments which revolt against every abuse whether civil or religious; new sentiments upon earth which recoil before no kind of sacrifices which make the learned repulse academic laurels, the courtier reject honors, & the egotist refuse the gold of corruption." By this original prefix to sentences of Oegger I seem to give them value. He adds "Whence can be this treasure of good will if not from Heaven where we were never forgotten & whence the earth will at length be entirely reformed after having been prepared for it for ages?"[201]

A good example of that prosopopoeia I wrote of p.   ⟨is⟩ is Thomson's[202] "Come to nurse our bantling in the cradle of liberty. Yet I do not know whether that is right, Methinks he is grown so great that if we should rock him in Faneuil Hall his feet would dangle out the door."

"We do not rock babies in the cradle of liberty but stout boys that have been fed on pap & nourished up to good size, but little babies just born, before their sex is determined before it is known whether they will live or die, we do not rock." One of the best examples of this sort is Burke's 'shearing the wolf.'[203]

Yesternight it looked like a storm, but there were streaks of gold & silver in the sky.

[201] This sentence, which does not appear in *The True Messiah* (1842), is presumably from the manuscript translation.

[202] George Thompson (1804–1878), the English abolitionist, associated with William Lloyd Garrison in the American anti-slavery movement during 1834 and 1835. Though Emerson may well have heard Thompson speak, they apparently did not meet until October of 1835, when Mary Moody Emerson brought Thompson to her nephew's breakfast table in Concord, much to Emerson's surprise (*Life*, pp. 227–228).

[203] Attacking Lord North's proposal to tax the American colonies, Burke said on November 27, 1781, that "the claim, without the power of enforcing it, was nugatory and idle," as though a man would "shear a Wolf"; see *The Beauties of Fox, North, and Burke* (London, 1784), pp. 61–62, cited by Kenneth W. Cameron, "Notes on the Early Lectures," *Emerson Society Quarterly*, No. 20 (III Quarter, 1960), 71.

[69] ↑G. Oegger's True Messiah or O. & N. Testaments examined acc[ording to]. the principles of the language of nature. Pt. I↓[:]

"People suppose that when God produced our visible world the choice that he made of forms & colours for animals, plants, & minerals was entirely arbitrary on his part. This is false. Man may sometimes act from whim; God never can. The visible creation then cannot must not (if we may use such expressions) be anything but the exterior circumference of the invisible & metaphysical world, & material objects are necessarily kinds of scoriae of the substantial thoughts of the Creator; scoriae which must always preserve an exact relation to their first origin; in other words visible nature must have a spiritual & moral side. For God every thing is; every thing exists; 'create' conveys not the same idea to him as to us. For God to Create is only to Show. The Universe in its minutest details existed for God as really before the creation, as after it; because it existed in him substantially as the statue exists in the block of marble from which the sculptor extracts it.[204] By the creation we only have been enabled to perceive a portion of the ↑infinite↓ riches ⟨burie⟩ eternally buried in the Div[ine]. ⟨mind⟩Essence. The *perfect* especially must have always thus existed in God. The *imperfect* alone can have received a kind of creation by means of man a free agent tho' under the influence of a Providence which never loses sight of him. Neither the form nor the color of any object in nature can have been chosen without a reason. Every thing that we see, touch, smell, every thing from the sun to a grain of sand, from our own body with its admirable organs, to that of the worms; every thing has flowed forth by a supreme reason from that world where all is spirit & life. No fibre in the animal, no blade of grass in the vegetable, no form of crystallization in inanimate matter, is without [70][205] its clear & well determined correspondence in the moral & metaphysical world. And if this is true of colors & forms, it must by a still stronger reason, be true of instincts of animals, & the far more astonishing faculties of man. Consequently, the most imperceptible thoughts & affections which we imagine we have conceived by our own power; the compositions which we consider our own in philosophy & literature; the inventions which we believe we have made in ↑the↓ arts & sciences; the monuments that we think we are erecting; the customs that we fancy we establish in the things which men consider great, as in the most insignificant transactions of civil & animal life, all this existed before us; all this is simply given to us & given with a supreme reason, acc[ording]. to our diff[erent]. wants. An *infinitely little degree of con-*

---

[204] The passage "material objects . . . moral side." is used in *Nature*, *W*, I, 35. The image of the statue extracted from the marble is found also in Emerson's "Sonnet of Michel Angelo Buonarotti," ll. 1–3, and "Boston Hymn," ll. 19–20; see *W*, IX, 298, 201, respectively.

[205] "Oegger" is written above "clear &" at the top of the page.

sent to receive which forms our moral liberty, is the only thing that we have for our own. And merely by an inspection of the objects by which a man is surrounded, or of some of the customs which he has adopted, a superior intelligence can undoubtedly determine the moral worth of his being, for, according as moral beings for whom alone inferior Nature exists, modify themselves, that nature must admit emblems analogous to the new perfections or degradations."

"And indeed but for all these emblems of life which creation offers, there would be no appreciable moral idea or moral sentiment, no possible means, we fear not to say it, for God to communicate a thought, an affection to his creature any more than for one feeling creature to com-municate ⁿ [71]²⁰⁶ it to another. Above all there would be no possible communication between the present state of man & his state of transforma-tion all is annihilated all is broken up in feeling & thinking nature: the most interior life of the intelligent being is effaced & returns to nothing."

"Had there been no *father*, could you know any thing of *tenderness?* Had there never been a *generous man* could you know what is *generosity? love*; maladies; defilements? The persecutions show what is atrocity &c &c. The necessity of indicating moral distinctions alone explains monstrosities & disgusting images unworthy of the Creat⟨ion⟩or which Nature offers to the eye of degraded man. The abyss of our being cannot be revealed but by the appreciable phenomena of life."

"We are created men, God is uncreated Man. It was at the intermediate point between the infinite which is all & the finite which is nothing that God & man met. And this point is life, life manifested, life revealed by emblems."

"Do but take a dictionary of morals & examine the terms in it: you will see that all of them from the first to the last are derived from corporeal & animal life. &c. & but for those emblems furnished by nature herself the moral & metaphysical world would have remained entirely buried in the eternal abyss." ²⁰⁷

"Man & the serpent form the right angle: other animals fill the whole quadrant & any other kind of beings is geometrically impossible."

[72] "The passage from the language of nature to languages of con-vention was made by such insensible degrees that they who made it never thought of tracing the latter back to their source. They knew not the road they had travelled but the distance appeared striking when they became attentive to it. Primitively men could not name objects they must show them; not corporeally it is true but substantially & by the force of thought

²⁰⁶ "Oegger" is written above "[com]municate it" at the top of the page.

²⁰⁷ The passage "& but for . . . abyss." is used in "English Literature: Intro-ductory," *Lectures*, I, 220. Collation of Emerson's extracts to this point with *The True Messiah*, 1842, pp. 5–9, shows that, apart from occasional condensation and paraphrase, he was closely following their common manuscript source.

as those objects exist in God & as we still perceive them in dreams in which there is evidently something more than imagination [See S. Reed's oration on Genius.]

"An immediate communication of thoughts & sentiments is quite as conceivable & even more simple than all those which are made by means more or less distant, & such a communication is so rich, that it suffers no comparison with the poverty of all the others. When that primitive faculty of seeing & showing the immediate object of thought & the natural emblem of sentiments was weakened, then, only, exterior signs came to join it. Thence the language of gestures, xxxx then conventional sounds, hieroglyphics, & writing. At the epoch when the two manners of speaking (that by natural emblems, & that by articulate sounds) were mixed, then resulted the language which is now called prophetic or extatic, in which conventional words are used only to recal the more significant emblems of nature" [208]

"Kreutzer's Symbolics furnishes evidence excluding all doubt, that the ancient pagan religions, with their different mythologies & cosmogonies, generally arose from the lang[uage]. of nature misunderstood, & that consequently the completion of the Xn [Christian] religion, the only true one, will consist in the same language being [73][209] regained & carried to a certain degree of perfection." [210]

"Man is the true hieroglyphic of the Divinity."

"The different metaphysical qualities are made ⟨visible⟩ perceptible even in their least varieties by the infinite hieroglyphics of earthly acquisitions." [211]

"The death of Jehovah as far as he was clothed in flesh or as far as he was the incarnate Word is itself the necessary emblem of those of his unfortunate creatures who have forgotten him & in whose hearts he has indeed found a tomb."

"Psalm 22 The executioners have continued this psalm in action & the history of the regenerated human race will finish it"

"Doctrine of the Trinity a pernicious error tho' there may have been a time when it saved the faith of the Messiah from an entire extinction."

"Jehovah addresses himself to all his intelligent creation & each being finds in his words what is ap⟨plicable⟩↑propriate↓ to himself. The pure spirits who act on the human race must necessarily be always in advance of it in knowledge of the oracles of the Most High the perfect accom-

[208] " 'Man & the serpent . . . emblems of nature' ": cf. *The True Messiah*, 1842, p. 15.

[209] "Oegger" is written above "regained &" at the top of the page.

[210] Cf. *The True Messiah*, p. 16, note.

[211] Cf. *ibid.*, p. 22. The extracts which follow, presumably from material of the manuscript translation, were not printed in the 1842 pamphlet.

plishment of which oracles they concur to produce spite of the united efforts of all degraded Spirits & spite of the liberty left to men over whom the destinies of earth are simply thrown only as immense nets enveloping masses without restraining individuals. This end Heaven attains ⟨by⟩ only by speaking in emblems."

"Every mortal must voluntarily or involuntarily continually furnish in his life & death emblems capable of characterizing the depth of his being which in itself is a kind of inaccessible infinite. True we cannot appreciate all these emblems; but a more practised eye appreciates & determines them."

"Such is the inconsistency of the human mind that those who in the most trifling conversation personify a hundred inanimate objects, & speak incessantly of the genius of empires, the monster of war, the hydra of revolutions,ⁿ [74]²¹² would be scandalized to hear also the term Devil or Serpent applied to that genius of evil which pursues us every where & which in emblematic language would appear really under the form of a monstrous being characterizing the whole society of those bad ⟨s⟩ men whom our world is constantly spewing forth into the world of spirits & who stripped of their material organs still impel men to commit crimes that they cannot commit themselves."

" 'Thy will be done, &c.' It is necessary that every being in the boundless creation renounce his own will: if a single one of them should act from himself, he would destroy the whole harmony of the heavens. So important is it for our own will to be annihilated in that of the Lord! Even the enlightened age in which we live will not easily understand these truths. Yet there is no other means of combining all those myriads of beings to whom the creating power every moment gives birth in that divine unity which should be as entire as that which unites the Father & the Son."

"they who fast in the spring & abstain for some weeks from eggs & fat.

"Do but examine with impartiality the admirable form of man not as terminated by lines & of such or such a Size but in its nature which is that of an intelligent being in correspondence with all others, & as placed out of time & space, it will appear not so unworthy of the divinity as some have thought it; it contains a kind of infinite of which all other possible forms of life are only degradations."

"The moon refused her light by the ignorance which eclipsed the Church & the stars fell from heaven by the successive loss [75]²¹³ of all true principles."

The triple crown of the pope is "a frightful contrast to the crown of thorns of him who refused to be king — an authority truly infernal

---

²¹² "Oegger" is written above "would be scandalized" at the top of the page.
²¹³ "Oegger" is written above "true" at the top of the page.

which more or less with all sects made holy things subservient to ambition to pride." &c

"Let those that are in Judea flee to the mountains. Quit this temple which the Lord has abandoned. Quit a church which is no longer one. Seek the interior Church which is nothing but love."

"We will see how the ten Commandments may also apply to pure spirits. Passing in silence the *first* evidently common beings who know that happiness & the love of God are synonimous is it not evident that by the *second* it may be forbidden to the Angels to attach themselves to any being of the second order in preference to the Creator, whatever may be the number or nature of the perfections with which this being may be enriched, & as they know that whoever believes he can have a thought a sentiment which is not actually from God & to God, breaks thereby with eternal love & truth, they must shun above all making themselves Jehovah, by resting upon or adoring themselves. That by the *third* it may be enjoined on them never to return to the cares of those beings who separate themselves from the Creator & think to find happiness by their own strength, but rather to taste in peace that which God prepares for them & which is their true Sabbath." &c &c &c

The analogons are shown with some minuteness of detail. The Dominical prayer. Stillingfleet's Origines Sacrae[.] [214]

[76] Every man must live upon a principle & move according to its will as in the vehicular state every soul rides upon its ray. I have seen the adoption of a principle transform a proser into an orator. Every transgression that it makes of routine makes man's being something worth[.]

Humility is a great ⟨econ⟩ timesaver. The whole business must wait whenever each individual of the company has some personal recollection[,] some apology or explanation to make. All sit impatiently deferring till his impertinent vanity is adjusted & then go on. I who know the supreme folly of the thing can collect instances not only from last night's conversation but from my own sayings two nights ago at Dr Willard's[.] [215]

[214] Edward Stillingfleet, English scholar and divine, published his *Origines Sacrae* in 1662. Cf. *The True Messiah*, 1842, p. 18, note: "Stillingfleet, who is known to have studied antiquity most profoundly, was convinced, like ourselves, that, originally, the name of a thing signified its essence. Whoever will consult the 'Origines Sacræ,' will find there the confirmation of almost all our ideas."

[215] Presumably Sidney Willard, who had taught at Harvard (*L*, I, 450, n. 71).

[July] 30th. It is affecting to see the old man's ↑T[haddeus]. Blood's↓ memory taxed for facts occurring 60 years ago at Concord fight. "It is hard to bring them up," he says "⟨they⟩ ↑the truth↓ never will be known." The Doctor like a keen hunter unrelenting follows him up & down barricading him with questions. Yet cares little for the facts the man can tell, but much for the confirmation of the printed History.[216] "Leave me, leave me to repose." [217]

Every principle is an eye to see with. Facts in thousands of the most interesting character are slipping by me every day unobserved, for I see not their bearing, I see not their connexion, I see not what they prove. By & by I shall mourn in ashes their irreparable loss.

⟨The only ambition⟩ No distinction in principle can be broader than that taken by the abolitionist against Everett. Everett said that in case of a servile war tho' a man of peace he [77] would buckle on his knapsack to defend the planter. The philanthropist who was here this morning [218] says that he is a man of peace but if forced to fight on either side he should fight for the slave against his tyrant.

I know nothing of ⟨my origin⟩ the source of my being but I will not soil my nest. I know much of it after a high negative way, but nothing after the understanding. God himself contradicts through me & all his creatures the miserable babbl⟨ing⟩e of Kneeland & his crew [219] but if they set me to affirm in propositions his character & providence as I would describe a mountain or an Indian, I am dumb. Oft I have doubted of his person, never that truth is divine.

You affirm that the moral development contains all the intellectual & that Jesus was the perfect man. I bow in reverence unfeigned before that benign man. I ⟨have more hope & ⟨strength⟩ resolution⟩ ↑know more, hope more, am more↓ because he has lived. But if you tell me that in your opinion he has fulfilled all the conditions of man's

[216] Dr. Ripley had written *A History of the Fight at Concord* in 1827; Emerson owned a copy of the second edition (Concord, 1832).

[217] Thomas Gray, "The Descent of Odin," l. 50.

[218] Probably Reverend Samuel J. May (mentioned in the following day's entry), who had spoken in Emerson's pulpit in 1831 (*Life*, p. 153).

[219] Abner Kneeland (1774–1844), a former Universalist clergyman turned atheist, became leader of Boston's First Society of Free Enquirers — the "crew" Emerson has in mind. Charged with blasphemy in 1833, he was tried, convicted, and after successive appeals finally sentenced in 1838 to sixty days of imprisonment.

existence, carried out to the utmost at least by implication, all man's powers, I suspend my assent. I do not see in him cheerfulness: I do not see in him the love of Natural Science: I see in him no kindness for Art; I see in him nothing of Socrates, of Laplace, of Shakspeare. The perfect man should remind us of all great men. Do you ask me if I would rather resemble Jesus than any other man? If I should say Yes, I should suspect myself of superstition.

Ages hence, books that cannot now be written may be possible. For instance a cumulative moral & intellectual science. If I would know something [78] of the elements & process of the Moral sublime where shall I now seek the analysis? If I would know the elementary distinction of spiritual & intellectual where shall I inquire? A sentence showing a tendency is all that a century contributes to psychology. Where shall I find the result of phrenology? of animal magnetism? of extacy?

By & by books of condensed wisdom may be writ by the concentrated lights of thousands of centuries which shall cast Bacon & Aristotle into gloom. ↑As the Am. Encyc. said of Astron. "How many centuries of observation were necessary to make the motion of the earth suspected!"↓ [220]

3⟨0⟩1 July. Every day's doubt is whether to seek for Ideas or to collect facts. For all successful study is the marriage of thoughts & things. A continual reaction of the thought classifying the facts & of facts suggesting the thought.

— If it would please Heaven, if I could all unworthy call down such uncommon effort of mercy I should pray that the tendency to insanity from organic egotism might be removed from ⟨men[?]⟩ but what imports it? Presently we shall be bubbles or gods. When shall I be tired of reading? When the moon is tired of waxing & waning, when the sea is tired of ebbing & flowing, when the grass is weary of growing, when the planets are tired of going.

The act of duty that might have been omitted but that was inserted in a past day pleases in remembering the contingency with a better satisfaction than that with which we see the mail stage roll off

---

[220] Cf. *Encyclopædia Americana*, ed. Francis Lieber, 13 vols. (Philadelphia, 1829–1833), I, 431; XII, 323; cf. also *JMN*, IV, 24.

in its cloud of dust, if breathless with haste we have arrived just in time to get our letter in.

I wrote yesterday that these orators of a principle owed everything to it, & our good friend S.J. May may instruct us in many things. He goes everywhere & sees the leaders of society everywhere, his cause being his ticket of admission, and talks on his topic with no intelligent person [79] who does not furnish some new light, some unturned side, some happy expression or strike off some false view or expression of the philanthropist. In this way his views are enlarged & cleared & he is always attaining to the best expressions. As when he said the Question between the Colonization & the Abolition men was "whether you should remove them (the negroes) from the prejudice or the prejudice from them."

It is, my God! an antidote to every fear, the conviction twice recently forced on me that men reverence virtue never by the appearance but accurately according to its weight. Nothing but an ounce will balance an ounce.[221] Thus alone is the will strong: thus He whose right it is to reign shall reign. Spit at consequences; launch boldly forth into the pure element & that which you think will drown you, shall buoy you up.

If the stars should appear one night in a thousand years, men would believe & adore & for a few generations preserve the remembrance of the city of God which had been shown.[n] ⟨but they would then decline to their appetites, & eat dust.⟩ But every night come out these preachers of beauty, & light the Universe with their admonishing smile.[222]

⟨We read⟩ ⟨We wish⟩ Men believe that some of their fellows are more happily constituted than themselves after the pattern of themselves. They have in fortunate hours had the eye opened whereby the world was newly seen as if then first seen & which seemed to say that all prior life however loud & pretending was but death or sleep. They believe that some men add to this Eye a Tongue to tell their

---

[221] See p. [48] above.

[222] This paragraph, struck through in ink with three diagonal use marks, is used in *Nature*, *W*, I, 7.

vision & a certain degree of control over [80] these faculties, that the spirits of the prophets are subject to the prophets and they wish such men to take the chronicle of their parish or their age & ⟨let the⟩ in the auspicious hour let the facts pass thro' their mind & see if they will not take the form of a picture & song.

When I cast my look inward & look upon God as mine I may well defy the future & looking upon all the rough weather ahead as exercises to try the pith of the combatants I may merrily predict a victory.

The Reason has her victories. $15 000 were subscribed in a very short time in N.Y. by these abolitionists, $2000 at one meeting in Boston & 5000 at another[,] & forthwith paid. So put that against the burning convent & the Julien Hall.[223] My two facts referred to on the last page were the bountiful E.R.[224] & the Christian Sam. May who both pass for that they are in things to praise & things to blame[.]

> "For Christ made no Cathedrals
> Ne with him was no Cardinals." *Chaucer* [225]

Once in a while we meet with poetry which is also music "high & passionate thoughts to their own music chaunted."[226] The following lines of John Barbour (1365) remind me of the music I heard lately.

> "This was in the moneth of May
> When birdis singis in ilk spray
> Melland their notes with seemly soun
> For softness of the sweet seasoun
> And levis of the branchis spred
> And bloomis bright beside them bred
> And fields are strowit with flowris
> Well sawer and of ser colouris."[227]

[223] Emerson is thinking of (1) the anti-Catholic feeling responsible for burning the Charlestown convent (p. [28] above) and (2) the activities of the atheist "Kneeland and his crew" (p. [77] above) — the First Society of Free Enquirers that met at Boston's Julien Hall. See *JMN*, IV, 326.

[224] Ezra Ripley?

[225] The lines are not included in the Chaucer canon. Where Emerson encountered the quotation and attribution is unknown.

[226] Cf. Coleridge, "To William Wordsworth," ll. 46–47.

[227] Misquoted from Warton, *The History of English Poetry*, 1824, II, 157.

[81] ⟨‖ ... ‖⟩ Me it pleases well to skip the minuter designation of the plants & to slight also the chronicles of kings so that I can learn somewhat of the history of Wit in this world of men; to know what have been the entertainments of the human spirit from age to age[,] what are the best things that it hath said & who & what they were who said them. Yet the beauty that drew us to one or another pursuit as botany, medicine, history of Poetry, & the like, is presently lost sight of in the details of the study itself & none less poetical than the herbalist, the doctor, the critic[.]

A systemgrinder hates the truth.[228]
To make a step into the world of thought is given to but few men; to make a second step beyond his first, only one in a country can do; but to carry the thought out to three steps marks a great Teacher. Aladdin's Palace with its one ⟨vacant⟩ unfinished window which all the ⟨jewels⟩ ↑gems↓ in the royal treasury cannot finish in the style of the meanest of the profusion of jewelled windows that were built by the genie in a night, is but too true ⟨an⟩[n] ⟨allegory⟩ a picture of the efforts of Talent to add a scene to Shakspeare's Play or a verse to Shakspear's Songs.[229]

August 1. A sparrow or a deer knows much more of nature's secrets than a man but is less able to utter them. And those men who know the most can say the least.
Jacob Behme is the best helper to a theory of Isaiah & Jeremiah. You were sure he was in earnest & could you get into his point of view the world would be what he describes. He is all imagination.

Aurora i e the Dayspring or dawning of the day in the Orient or Morning Redness in the rising of the sun i e the root or mother of Philosophy, Astrology,[n] [82] & Theology from the true ground &c &c by J. Behme written in Gerlitz in Germany A.C. 1612 Aetatis suae 37 London 1656[:] [230]
"O world where is thy humility where is thy Angelical love. At that very instant when the mouth says 'God save thee'; then, if the heart were

---

[228] The sentence is used in "Lord Bacon," *Lectures*, I, 327.
[229] "A systemgrinder . . . Shakspear's Songs." is struck through in pencil with a diagonal use mark.
[230] Cf. the title page of Jakob Böhme's *Aurora* (London, 1656).

seen, it might be said, Beware, look to thyself, for it bids the Devil take thee." *Behme*. "O thou excellent Angelical Kingdom, how comely dressed & adorned were thou once! how hath the Devil turned thee into a murderous Den. Dost thou suppose thou standest now in the flower of thy beauty & Glory? No! thou standest in the midst of hell. If thine eyes were opened, thou wouldst see it[.]

Or dost thou think that the Spirit is drunken & doth not see thee[?]" [Cf.] J. B[öhme]. [*Aurora*, 1656, p]p. [251–]252

There sits the Sphinx from age to age, in the road Charles says[,] & every wise man ⟨in turn⟩ ↑that comes by↓ has a crack with her.[231] But this Oegger's plan & scope argue great boldness & manhood to depart thus widely from all routine & seek to put his hands ⟨unde⟩ like Atlas under Nature & heave her from her rest. Why the world exists & that it exists for a language or medium whereby God may speak to Man, — this is his query — this his answer.

↑Sat. Evg↓ [August 1, 1835] The distinction of fancy & imagination seems to me a distinction in kind. The fancy aggregates; the Imagination animates.[232]

The Fancy takes the world as it stands & selects pleasing groups by apparent relations. The Imagination is Vision, regards the world as symbolical & pierces the emblem [83] for the real sense,[n] ↑sees all external objects as types.↓ ↑A fine example is in the acct. of the execution of Lord Russell (Anecdotes p. 11)↓[.] [233]

God hides the stars in a deluge of light. That is his chosen curtain. So he hides the great truths in the simplicity of the common consciousness. I am struck with the contrast which I have repeatedly noted before between the positiveness with which we can speak of certain laws[,] an evidence equal to that of consciousness[,] & the depth of obscurity in which the Person of God is hid. From month to

---

[231] The figure is used in "English Literature: Introductory," *Lectures*, I, 224, and *Nature*, *W*, I, 34; cf. "History," *W*, II, 32.

[232] "The distinction . . . animates." is struck through in ink with a curved diagonal use mark.

[233] When William Russell was on his way to be beheaded in 1683, as Emerson wrote in *Nature*, "the multitude imagined they saw liberty and virtue sitting by his side" (*W*, I, 21). The passage in *Nature*, as Cameron has shown (*E t E*, I, 415), apparently derives from *The General Biographical Dictionary*, ed. Alexander Chalmers (London, 1812–1817), XXVI, 493; the reference here to "Anecdotes" is probably to Emerson's notebook "Σ Anecdotes".

month, from year to year I come never nearer to definite speaking of him. He hideth himself. I cannot speak of him without faltering. I unsay as fast as I say my words. He is, for I am. Say rather, He is. But in the depth inaccessible of his being he refuses to be defined or personified.[234]

After thirty a man wakes up sad every morning excepting perhaps five or six until the day of his death.[235]

It was strange after supposing for years that my respected friend [236] was the heart of the county & blended thoroughly with the people to find him wholly isolated, more even than I, walking among them with these "monumental" manners unable to get within gunshot of any neighbor except professionally. Yet the fulness of his respect for every man & his selfrespect at the same time have their reward & after sitting all these years on his plain wooden bench with eternal patience Honor comes & sits down by him.

2 Aug. Charles wonders that I don't become sick at the stomach over my poor journal yet is obdurate habit callous even to contempt. I must scribble on if it were only to say in confirmation of Oegger's doctrine that I believe I never take a step [84] in thought when engaged in conversation without ⟨having⟩ some material symbol of my proposition figuring itself incipiently at the same time. My sentence often ends in babble from a vain effort to represent that picture in words. How much has a figure[,] an illustration availed every sect. As when the reabsorption of the soul into God was figured by a phial of water broken in the sea.[237] This morn. I would have said that a man sees in the gross of the acts of his life the domination of his instincts or genius over all other causes. His Wilfulness may determine the character of moments but his Will determines that of years. ⟨I⟩ While I thus talked I *saw* some crude *symbols* of the thought with the mind's eye, as it were, a mass of grass or weeds in a stream of which

---

[234] "God hides . . . personified.", struck through in pencil with a vertical use mark, is used in "Holiness," *Lectures*, II, 352–353.

[235] This sentence is used in "The Present Age," *Lectures*, II, 169.

[236] "Evidently Hon. Samuel Hoar" (Edward Emerson, *J*, III, 527, n. 1).

[237] For the same figure see *JMN*, III, 98; a note in the manuscript of Sermon 35 (1829), *YES*, p. 245; "English Literature: Introductory," *Lectures*, I, 221; and "Poetry and Imagination," *W*, VIII, 14.

the spears or blades shot out from the mass in every direction but were immediately curved round to float all in one direction. When presently the conversation changed to the subject of Thomas a Kempis's popularity & how Aristotle & Plato come safely down as if God brought them in his hand (tho' at no time are there more than five or six men who read them) & of the Natural Academy by which the exact value of every book is determined maugre all hindrance or furtherance, then saw I as I spoke the old pail in the Summer[n] street kitchen with potatoes swimming in it[,] some at the top, some in the midst, & some lying at the bottom; & ⟨s⟩I spoiled ⟨by⟩ my fine thought by saying that books take their place according to their specific gravity "as surely as potatoes in a tub." [238]   And I suppose that any man who will watch his ⟨pr⟩ intellectual process will find ⟨an image⟩ a material image cotemporaneous[n] [85] with ⟨his⟩ ↑every↓ thought & furnishing the garment of the thought.[239]

It occurred with regard to A Kempis that it is pleasant to have a book come down to us of which the author has, like Homer, lost his individual distinctness, is almost a fabulous personage, so that the book seems to come rather out of the spirit of humanity & to have the sanction of human nature than to totter on the two legs of any poor Ego.

For language of Nature Ichabod Morton uses no other. Peter Hunt, Crockett, & the Vermont drover.[240] So in the 17 Century it appeared in every book. "And to put finger in the eye & to renew their repentance they think this is weakness." Thos Shepard, 1645. N.E. Lamentation.[241]

---

[238] "Aristotle & Plato . . . a tub.' ", struck through in ink with a vertical use mark, is used in "On the Best Mode of Inspiring a Correct Taste in English Literature," *Lectures*, I, 212.

[239] "And I suppose . . . thought.", struck through in ink with vertical use marks, is used in "English Literature: Introductory" and "Shakspear [first lecture]," *Lectures*, I, 221 and 290, respectively; and in *Nature*, W, I, 31.

[240] Benjamin Peter Hunt, one of Emerson's pupils at Chelmsford in 1825, remained a lifelong friend; "Davy" Crockett, the frontiersman, is quoted above, p. [66]; the unidentified "Vermont drover" is possibly James Elliot, whom Emerson had been reading (p. [47] above).

[241] *New Englands Lamentation for Old Englands present errours* (London, 1645), p. 5.

I suspect that Wit, humor, & jests admit a more accurate classification by the light of the distinction of the Reason & the Understanding. Nothing is so cheap as jests of the sort that fill Byron's
Heaven & Earth. They might be manufactured by the thousand.
All the dinner wit that assails Swedenborg & his church is cut off the
same piece.

"He shall be as a god to me" said Plato "who can rightly define
& divide." [242]

Who can make a good sentence can make a good book.[243] Ex
ungue leonum.[244] If you find a good thing in the writing of a mediocre man be sure he stole it.

[86] Edw. Bagshaw wrote (1662) "An answer to all that Roger
L'Estrange intends to write." [245]

We have little control of our ⟨intellectual possessions⟩ thoughts.
We are pensioners upon Ideas. They catch us up for ⟨brief⟩ moments
into their heavens & so fully possess us that we take no thought for
the morrow, gaze like children without an effort to make them our
own. By & by we fall out of that rapture & then bethink us where we
have been & what we have seen & go painfully gleaning up the grains
that have fallen from the sheaf.[246]

When I see the doors by which God entereth into the mind[,]
that there is no sot nor fop nor ruffian nor pedant into whom thoughts

[242] Cf. Bacon, *Novum Organum*, trans. Peter Shaw, 2 vols. (London, 1802), II,
21: ". . . Plato said well, That he is to be held as a God, who knows perfectly how
to define and divide" (cited by K. W. Cameron, *Emerson Society Quarterly*, No. 20,
III Quarter, 1960, 120). The quotation, struck through in ink with a vertical use
mark, is used in "Modern Aspects of Letters," *Lectures*, I, 378, and "Plato; or, the
Philosopher," *W*, IV, 47.
[243] Used in "On the Best Mode of Inspiring a Correct Taste in English Literature" and "Ben Jonson, Herrick, Herbert, Wotton," *Lectures*, I, 214 and 348–349,
respectively.
[244] "(One knows) a lion by its claw" (Ed.). See *JMN*, I, 219.
[245] Edward Bagshaw, *A Second Letter unto a Person of Honor and Quality* . . . .
Together with a brief Answer unto All that One L'S---- intends to write (London,
1662).
[246] This paragraph, struck through in pencil with a vertical use mark, is used in
"Intellect," *W*, II, 328–329. With "take no thought . . . morrow" cf. Matt. 6:34.

do not enter by passages which the individual never left open[,] I can expect any revolution. ⟨A[?]⟩

Aug. 3. One of the poorest employments of the country gentleman is to sit sentinel at his window to watch every cow, baker, or boy that comes in at his gate. Better be asleep.

[86]–[88] [Letter omitted] [247]

Aunt M. writes her merry Critique after this wise.

"15 minutes after 3 o'c this 29 July I begin Michel's biography with a firm resolve not to add my mite to the laudatory things said by the knowing. Whether pride that I can add no leaf fibre small as the gossamer thread, or that pride would have the world pass the biographer to record ⟨in far other colours⟩ in higher places; the genius that should trace in far other colors the great archetype of all genius & art in the natural, moral, & intellectual universe. Not as an amanuensis merely of the spirit of God, who has given those great outlines of all spir. & practical wisdom in this bodily manifestation, but that thro' this faith he should gather a larger fame than the admirers of the portraits of great men can give. It should be when he descries their most central idea like the fabled somebody who touched the earth to renew his ⟨spirits⟩ strength for etherial heights. Yet tho' I read not to praise 'tis to comment. And the first sentence that arrests me is that which affords an analogy to the divine Jesus, who was such a portion of nature that no arbitraryness [n] [89] was manifest in it; he apprehended the whole & emblematised the perfect character of beauty, moral & intellectual, as this famed Artist did by long efforts of material art. If the marble gave these grand & pure & even terrible characters, how incomparably stronger was the effect from a living breathing being, who acted whatever was noble & heroic, without unfolding the mere humanity in its lower qualities. He only would be said to possess beauty, in its largest sense, 'comprehending grandeur as a part, & reaching to goodness as its soul.' [248] But his errand was far higher than to express only beauty[;] 'twas

---

[247] To Elizabeth Palmer Peabody, August 3, 1835, printed in *L*, I, 449–451, from an incomplete copy, with "belongs" for "belong", "sciences" for "the science", "there's" for "there is", "incline" for "incline I suppose", "hate" for "I hate", "Thos. Browne" for "T. Brown", "some exercise" for "exercise", "Bentham's or" for "Bentham's &", "sympathize with" for "like", "merry" for "so merry", and "the intellectual" for "intellectual", plus minor variations in punctuation and paragraphing.

[248] The quotation is used in "Michel Angelo Buonaroti," *Lectures*, I, 100.

to rescue from all the deformities with which sin had marred beauty. He expressed the beautiful without effort, calm as the pure empyrean, but he labored he agonized to express the nature of vice, & rid it from the beautiful which was not a Science but the nature of things originally his own. Were this wonderful Counsellor for man a being abstracted from man & his obedience & faith, how would certain spiritualists consume the light of sun & stars in describing the beauty & magnificence that had been embodied. Anthropomorphism would have exulted in her native power to assemble every power & grace in her favorite form & modern spiritualism adopt the ⟨favorite⟩ characters as its own ideal. Here they would find a man to all the senses, who could fulfil his own imagination of the perfect not by imitating animated forms akin to worms but the eternal forms ideas of moral beauty worth the attributes of infinite."

[90] Ah Homer! Ah Chaucer! ah Shakspear! But we live in the age of Propriety. Their elegance is intrinsic, ours superadded. Their cleanness is sunshine[,] ours painting & gilding[.]

The character of Chatterton, Diderot, Burns, Byron, Voltaire, Hooke (Newton's rival)

———

Classification

———

⟨Our thoughts come single⟩ A thought comes single like a foreign traveller but if you can find out its name you shall find it related to a powerful & numerous family.
Uprose Shower-of-tears[.]

5 August. Our summer, Charles says, is a galloping consumption and the hectic rises as the year approaches its end.

———

Wordsworth's Ode to Duty singeth,

> "There are who ask not if thine eye
> Be on them; who in love & truth,
> Where no misgiving is, rely
> Upon the genial sense of youth;
> Glad hearts! without reproach or blot;
> Who do thy work & know it not."   [ll. 9–14]

Happy they & their counterparts in the intellectual kingdom, who sit down to write & lend themselves to the first thought & are carried whithersoever it ⟨leads⟩ takes them & solve the problem proposed in a way they could not have predicted & are not now conscious of their own action. Merely they held the pen. The problem whilst they pondered it confounded them.[249]

The Battas in Sumatra are cannibals[.]

[91] The birds fly from us & we do not understand their music. The squirrel, the musquash, the insect, have no significance to our blind eyes. Such is now the discord betwixt man & nature.[250] Yet it is strange that all our life is accompanied by Dreams on one side & by the animals on the other as monuments of our ignorance or Hints to set us on the right road of inquiry.

The life of a ⟨true poet⟩ ↑contemplator↓ is that of a reporter. He has three or four books before him & now writes in this now in that other what is ⟨dis⟩ incontinuously said by one or the other of his classes of thought.

It is a good trait of the manners of the times that Thaddeus Blood told me this morning that he (then 20 years old) & Mr Ball (50) were set to guard Lieut. Potter the Brit. Officer taken at Lexington 19 Apr '75 & whilst staying at Reuben Brown's Potter invited them both to dine with him. He, Lt. P. asked a blessing & after dinner asked Mr Ball to dismiss the table "which he did very well for an old farmer;" Lt. P. then poured out a glass of wine to each & they left the table. Presently came by a compy. from Groton, & Lt. P. was alarmed for his own safety. They bolted the doors &c &c. Bateman, he thinks, could not have made the deposition in Dr R.'s[n] History.[251] ⟨He was⟩ A ball passed thro' his cap & he cried A miss is as good as a mile. Immediately another ball struck his ear & passed out at the side of his mouth knocking out two teeth. He lived about 3 weeks & his wounds stunk intolerably. It was probably Carr or Starr's deposition.

[249] The quotation from Wordsworth and the ensuing paragraph are used in "The Present Age," *Lectures*, II, 168.

[250] These three sentences are used, with alterations, in *Nature*, *W*, I, 65.

[251] The deposition of John Bateman, a British soldier, in Ezra Ripley, *A History of the Fight at Concord*, 1832, p. 38.

[92] The powers of the poetical genius seem quite local & to give no ⟨warrant⟩ felicity in any other work transcending the strait limits of that vein. Wordsworth writes ⟨original &⟩ the verses of a great original bard but he writes ill[,] weakly concerning his poetry, talks ill of it, & even writes other poetry that is very poor.

↑True↓ love ⁿ watched every word & gesture of her shepherd & believed in her heart that things he did & thought not of were beautiful. Faint love talked of her affection but cared only for those words & deeds of the swain that respected herself. What else though it were more wise & good, she noted never.

———

If you read ⟨little⟩ ↑much↓ at a time you have a better sight of the plan & connexion of the book but you have less lively attention. If you read little ⟨you read⟩ fine things catch your eye & you read accurately but all proportion & ulterior purpose are at an end.

———

Charles doubts whether all truth is not occasional; not designed to be stored for contemplation but alive only in action.

Make much of your own place. The stars & celestial awning that overhang our simple Concord walks & discourses are as brave as those that were visible to Coleridge as he talked or Dryden or Ben Jonson & Shakspear or Chaucer & Petrarch & Boccac[c]io when they met[.]

↑For the history of Psalm singing in our churches see Warton Hist[ory]. Eng[lish]. Po[etry]. vol 3   p 447↓[–464]

Hurra when next it rains (in the private sky) for Miss Fanny Kemble's Journal & ⟨for Puckler Muskau's Travels⟩ & ⟨for Bubbles from the Brunnens of Nassau⟩. ↑Lyell's Geology↓ [252]

[93] The human mind seems a lens formed to concentrate the

[252] Frances Anne Kemble Butler, *Journal by Frances Anne Butler*, 2 vols. (London, 1835); Prince Hermann Ludwig Heinrich von Pückler-Muskau, *Tour in England, Ireland, and France in the Years 1826, 1827, and 1829 . . . by a German Prince* (Philadelphia, 1833); Sir Francis Bond Head, *Bubbles from the Brunnens of Nassau; by an Old Man* (London, 1834); Charles Lyell, *Principles of Geology*, 2 vols. (London, 1830–1832). From the Boston Athenaeum, Emerson later withdrew the Pückler-Muskau, February 2—March 1, 1836 (see pp. [130–131] below), and the Lyell, October 4—29, 1836 (pp. [280], [284] below).

rays of the Divine laws to a focus which shall be the personality of God. But that focus falls so far into the infinite that the form or person of God is not within the ken of the mind. Yet must that ever be the effort of a good mind because the avowal of ↑our↓ sincere doubts leaves us in a less favorable mood for action & the statement of our best thoughts or those of our convictions that make most for theism induces new courage & force.

6 Aug. I think I may undertake one of these days to write a chapter on Literary Ethics or the Duty & Discipline of a Scholar. The camel & his four stomachs [253] shall be one of his emblems[.]

Mem. to save ↑Gov.↓ McDuffie's Message, & Gen. Jackson's Message about "embarrassments"[.] [254]

In Dunbar of Saltoun's Golden Terge (Warton Hist[ory]. Eng[lish]. Po[etry]. vol 3   p 102) one of the dramatis personae is New-Acquaintance who "embraces him awhile but soon takes her leave & is never seen afterwards."   STRANGER.

I suppose a reason why one man apprehends physical science better than another is that his fancy is stronger so that he can comply with the prescribed conditions of the problem long enough for the full apprehension of the law: as in learning the Precession of the Equinoxes he can keep the picture of the sun where he ought in his mind & figure to himself the nutation of the axis of the Earth &c &c. But I alas write my diagrams in Water.[255]

[94] In 1542 Robt. Wyer printed the "Scole Howse" in which the writer is thus merciless to women. His name is unknown. I fear it was a private revenge.

[253] The figure is attributed to Charles Emerson in *JMN*, IV, 381.

[254] George McDuffie (1790?–1851), formerly a member of Congress and governor of South Carolina in 1834–1836, was a supporter of nullification. A quotation from President Jackson's unidentified "Message" occurs in Emerson's notebook Composition, 1832? ; see *JMN*, IV, 438.

[255] Emerson may have been thinking of Keats's request that on his tomb should be engraved the words, "Here lies one whose name was writ in water."

     Trewely some men there be
       That live alway in great horroure
   And say it goeth by destinye
      To hang or wed both hath one hour
    And whether it be I am well sure
       Hanging is better of the twayne
      Sooner done & shorter payne.
              Warton Hist[ory]. Eng[lish]. Poet[ry].
                 vol 3. p. 426 [misquoted]

    8 August. Yesterday I delighted myself with Michel de Montaigne. With all my heart I embrace the grand old sloven. He pricks & stings the sense of Virtue in me[,] the wild gentile stock I mean[,] for he has no Grace. But his panegyric of Cato & of Socrates in his essay of Cruelty (Vol II) [256] do wind up again for us the spent springs & make virtue possible without the discipline of Christianity or rather do shame her of her eyeservice & put her upon her honor. I read the Essays in Defence of Seneca & Plutarch; on Books; on Drunkenness; & on Cruelty. And at some fortunate line which I cannot now recal ⟨I⟩ the Spirit of some Plutarch hero or sage touched mine with such thrill as the War-trump makes in Talbot's ear & blood.[257]

    15 August. 1835. I bought my house & two acres six rods of land of John T. Coolidge for 3500 dollars.

    [95] I know no truer poetry in modern verse than Scott's line "And sun himself in Ellen's eyes." [258]
    Every fact studied by the Understanding is not only solitary but desart. But if the iron lids of Reason's eye [259] can be once raised, the fact is classified immediately & seen to be related to our ⟨school⟩ nursery reading & our profoundest Science.

    13 Augt. Add to what was said 6 Aug. concerning literary Ethics

[256] Montaigne, *Essays*, 1700, II, 145–151.
[257] Presumably the "warlike and martial Talbot" of *I Henry VI*, quoted below, p. [291].
[258] Sir Walter Scott, *The Lady of the Lake*, VI, xxiv, 18.
[259] Cf. "the iron lids of the mind's eye" and "the iron lids of the Reason" in *Lectures*, I, 285 and 385, respectively; *Lectures*, II, 158; "Art," *W*, VII, 50.

that no doubt another age will have such sermons duly preached and the immortality will be proved from the implication of the intellect. For who can read an analysis of the faculties by any acute psychologist like Coleridge without becoming aware that this is proper study for him & that he must live ages to learn anything of so secular Science[?]

[August] 14. We would call up him who

> left half told
> The story of Cambuscan bold
> [Milton, *Il Penseroso*, ll. 109–110]

but the great contemporary just now laid in the dust ⟨who⟩ no man remembers; no man asks for him who broke off in the first sentences the Analysis of the Imagination on the warning of a friend that the public would not read the chapter.[260] No man asks Where is the Chapter?

Joseph Lyman[261] describes the iron bed at his residence at Farrandsville, Lycoming Co. Pa on the West Branch of the Susquehanna — a bed of iron ore a thousand acres in extent & four feet thick. The Comp[an]y bought it for 1500 dollars. "This whole region is filled with iron & coal. It is equal to the districts of Wales & Lancashire mile for mile but in extent it is larger than the British isles — extending from this place beyond Pittsburg & of the breadth of the Alleganny Mountains." Letter to CCE ⟨May⟩ ↑Apr.↓ 1835[.]

[96] 25 Aug. Visited Miss Harriet Martineau at Cambridge today[,] a pleasant unpretending lady whom it would be agreeable to talk with when tired & at ease but she is too weary of society to shine if ever she does. She betrayed by her facile admiration of books & friends her speedy limits. The ⟨sp⟩ ear trumpet acts as chain as well as medium[,] making Siameses of the two interlocutors. Henry

[260] Coleridge had died in July of 1834; the allusion is to ch. XIII of his *Biographia Literaria*, 1834, p. 170.
[261] The Lymans and Emersons were family friends. In 1827 Emerson had stayed with the senior Joseph Lyman in Deerfield; Joseph Jr., mentioned here, later became an attorney in New York (*L*, I, 215, n. 109; II, 335, n. 372).

Reeve, Henry Taylor, of Manchester, & John S. Mill, ⟨sh⟩ W.J. Fox, she regarded as the ablest young men in England.[262] What pleased me most of her communications was that W.J. Fox though of no nerve, timid as a woman, yet had the greatest moral courage, as Charles said at my commentary, 'Go & be hanged but blush if spoken to on the tumbril.'

Aug. 31. Use of Harvard College to clear the head of much nonsense that gathers in the inferior colleges.

———

    Communicable attributes
It shall be a rule in my Rhetoric Before you urge a duty be sure ⟨that⟩ it is⟨.⟩ ↑one,↓ Try Patriotism, for example.

Edw. Taylor came to see us. Dr R. showed him the battle field. Why put it on this bank? he asked. "You must write on the monument, 'Here is the place where the Yankees made the British show the back seam of their stockings.' " He said he had been fishing at Groton & the fishes were as snappish as the people that he looked to see if the scales were not turned the wrong side &c.

14 September 1835. I was married to Lydia Jackson.

[97] Newton said of [Lord Pembroke] he cares more about a stone doll than anything; (Spence) & spoke with much contempt of Dr Bentley & Bp Hare for squabbling about an old playbook meaning Terence. (Dr Warburton's Pref. Shaks.)
    He refers ↑to↓ Whiston's Life of Clarke 1748 p 113.[263]

[262] In addition to Henry Taylor — presumably the author of *Philip van Artevelde* (p. [17] above) — and John Stuart Mill, the references are to Henry Reeve (1813–1895), journalist and essayist, and William Johnson Fox (1786–1864), Unitarian preacher and politician.
[263] See *JMN*, III, 177. For the allusions in the present passage, see (1) Joseph Spence, *Anecdotes, Observations, and Characters of Books and Men* . . . (London, 1820), p. 325; (2) William Warburton, Preface to *The Works of Shakespear*, 8 vols. (London, 1747), I, xxvii; (3) William Whiston, *Historical Memoirs of the Life and Writings of Dr. Samuel Clarke*, 3rd ed. (London, 1748). "Newton said . . . Terence.", struck through in ink with a vertical use mark, is used in "Art," *W*, II, 364.

↑"That↓ ⟨"⟩ when [n] one's proofs are aptly chosen
Four are as valid as four dozen"   Prior
[*Alma*, I, 515–516, misquoted]

Oct. 2. 1835. The woods are all in a glow.
Charles thinks never was great man quite destitute of imagination[.]

"The fading virtues of later times were a cause of grief to his father
Archidamus who again had listened to the same regrets from his own
venerable sire," said Agis.   Plutarch Apoptheg Lacon 17 [264]

Where is the ballad of Tamlane from which the fine editor of
Warton borrows these lines

"Our Shape & size we can convert
To either large or small;
An old nutshell's the same to us
As is the lofty hall." [265]

These lines, by the way, I would put into the mouth of the Orators,
as parallel to Isocrates' account of eloquence.[266]

5 Oct. I like that poetry which without aiming to be allegorical, is so.
⟨the⟩ Which [n] sticking close to its subject & that perhaps trivial can
yet be applied to the life of man & the government of God & be
found to hold.

"Little was king Laurin but from many a precious gem
His wondrous strength & power & his bold courage came
Tall at times his stature grew with spells of gramarye
Then to the noblest princes fellow might he be."

I take this to be a picture of a child of nature who draws his wisdom
from the whole world & is great only when he has great argument.
quoted by Ed[ito]r. [of] Warton from Little Garden of Roses.[267]

---

[264] Cf. "Laconic Apophthegms," *Plutarch's Morals*, 1718, I, 375–376. The passage is used in "The Present Age," *Lectures*, II, 170.

[265] Editor's Preface to Warton, *The History of English Poetry*, 1824, I, (51).
See "The Age of Fable," *Lectures*, I, 261.

[266] Cf. "The Lives of Ten Orators: Isocrates," *Plutarch's Morals*, 1718, V, 29:
"Being asked what was the Use and Force of Rhetoric, he answer'd, *To make great
Matters appear small, and small great.*"

[267] Editor's Preface to Warton, *The History of English Poetry*, 1824, I, (50),
n. 72; with "great . . . great argument" cf. *Hamlet*, IV, v, 53–56. This paragraph
is used in "The Age of Fable," *Lectures*, I, 261.

[98] I see this moral in every ⟨fable⟩ novel, fable, mythology I read. I see it in all Plutarch & Homer, in Æsop, in the Arabian Nights, in Ravenswo[o]d.ⁿ In Perceforest and Amadis[,] a garland & rose which bloom on the head of her who is faithful & fade upon the brow of the inconstant; & in the Boy & the Mantle which took me so in German lately.[268]

Oct. 8. My friend wishes that always he might have a new thought in his mind. (C.C.E)

[October] 9. Friday Morn: a good resolution:
Never much good comes of black bead eyes[.] MME

There is no gradation in feeble minds: they "laughed so that they thought they should have died," & five minutes after they have a regret or a vexation which they are sure "will kill them." The great mind finds ample spaces, vast plains, yea populous continents, & active worlds moving freely within these elastic limits & indeed never approaches the terminus on either side[.] [269]

Every man, if he lived long enough, would make all his books for himself. He would write his own Universal history, Natural History, Book of Religion, of Economy, of Taste.ⁿ For in every man the facts under these topics are only so far efficient as they are arranged after the law of *his* being. But life forbids it & therefore he uses Bossuet, Buffon, Westminster Catechism as better than nothing[,] at least as memoranda & badges to certify that he belongs to the Universe & not to his own house only and contents himself with arranging some one department of life after his own way. Our will never gave the images in our minds the rank they now take there. Anecdotes I read under the bench in the Latin School assume a

---

[268] On Ravenswood Castle in Scott's *The Bride of Lammermoor* see *JMN*, III, 247. The garland and rose in *Perceforest* and *Amadis de Gaul* are discussed in the Editor's Preface to Warton, *The History of English Poetry*, 1824, I, (60). For "The Boy and the Mantle," see p. [36] above. This paragraph, struck through in ink with a vertical use mark, is used in "The Age of Fable," *Lectures*, I, 260, and "History," *W*, II, 34–35.

[269] " 'laughed . . . side" is struck through in ink with a vertical use mark.

grandeur in the natural perspective of memory which Roman history
& Charles V &c ⟨the⟩ have not.[270]

[99] The powers of poetry. ⟨In Jamieson's Scottish Ballads⟩ It[n]
is said of the harper Glenkindie

> He'd harpit a fish out o' saut water
>   Or water out of a stane
> Or milk out o' a maiden's breast
>   That bairn had never nane.[271]

10 Oct. This morning Mr May & Mr George Thompson break-
fasted with me. I bade them defend their cause as a thing too sacred
to be polluted with any personal feelings. They should adhere reli-
giously to the fact & the principle, & exclude every adverb that went
to colour their mathematical statement. As Josiah Quincy said in the
eve of Revolution, 'the time for declamation is now over; here is
something too serious for aught but simplest words & acts.' So should
they say[,] I said also, what seems true, that if any man's opinion in
the country was valuable to them that opinion would be distinctly
known. If Daniel Webster's or Dr Channing's opinion is not ⟨dis-
tinctly known⟩ frankly told, it is so much deduction from the moral
value of that opinion & I should say moreover that their opinion *is*
known by the very concealment. One opinion seeks darkness. We
know what opinion that is[.]

The oak is magnificent from the acorn up. The whortle berry
no pruning or training can magnify. Who can believe in the perfectibility of this race of man,[n] or in the potency of Education? Yet compare the English nation with the Esquimaux tribe, & who can underestimate the advantages of culture?

Charles thinks there is no Christianity & has not been for some ages.
And esteems Christianity the most wonderful thing in the history
of the world. But for that, he can arrange his theory well enough
of the history of man. It is, according to him, [100] the first exalting
of the bestial nature, the first allaying of clay with the Divine fire

[270] See pp. [104], [276] below.
[271] Jamieson's Scottish Ballads, I, 93, as quoted in the Editor's Preface to Warton, *The History of English Poetry*, 1824, I, (66). Used in "Eloquence," *W*, VII, 71.

which succeeds in a few cases but in far the greater part the spirit is overlaid & expired. A few however under the benevolent aspect of heaven so cooperate with God as to work off the slough of the beast, & give evidence of arriving within the precincts of heaven. But the introduction of Christianity seems to be departure from general laws & interposition. Jesus seems not to be man.[272]

Strange, thinks he, moreover, that so sensible a nation as the English should be content so long to maintain that old withered idolatry of their Church; with the history too of its whole manufacture, piece by piece, all written out[.]

[101] Thompson the Abolitionist is inconvertible: what you say or what might be said ⟨make⟩ would make no impression on him. He belongs I fear to that ⟨class⟩ great class of the Vanity-stricken. An inordinate thirst for notice can not be gratified until it has found in its gropings what is called a Cause that men will bow to; tying him self fast to that, the small man is then at liberty to consider all objections ↑made↓ to him as ⟨indications⟩ ↑proofs↓ of folly & the devil ↑in the objector↓, & under that screen, if he gets a rotten egg or two, yet his name sounds through the world & he is praised & praised.

The minister should be to us a simple absolute man[;] any trick of his face that reminds us of his family is so much deduction, unless it should chance that those related lineaments are associated in our mind with genius & virtue. But the minister in these days, how little he says! Who is the most decorous man? & no longer, who speaks the most truth? Look at the orations of Demosthenes & Burke, & how many irrelevant things [—] sentences, words, letters, [—] are there? Not one. Go into ⟨the⟩ ↑tone of our↓ cool churches, ⟨of⟩ & begin to count the words that might be spared, & in most places, the entire sermon will go ⟨for it⟩. One ⟨thing⟩ sentence kept another in countenance, but not one by its own weight could have justified the saying of it. ↑⟨Pu⟩ 'Tis the age of Parenthesis. You might put all we say in brackets & it would not be missed.↓ [273]

---

[272] "the first exalting . . . be man." is struck through in pencil with a diagonal use mark.

[273] "Who is the most . . . be missed.", struck through in pencil with a diagonal use mark, is used in "The Present Age," *Lectures*, II, 163.

Even Everett has come to speak in stereotyped phrase & scarcely originates one expression to a speech. I hope the time will come when phrases will be gazetted as no longer current and it will be unpardonable to say "the times that tried men's souls" or anything about "a Cause" & so forth. Now literature ⟨has⟩ is nothing but a sum in ↑the↓ arithm. rule↓ Permutation & Combination[.] [274]

[102] A man to thrive in literature must trust himself. The voice of society sometimes & the writings of great geniuses always, are so noble & prolific that it seems justifiable to follow & imitate. But it is better to be an independent ⟨farmer⟩ ↑shoemaker↓ than to be an actor ⟨to⟩ ↑and↓ play a king. In every work of genius you recognize your own rejected thoughts. It is here as in science, that the true chemist collects what every body ↑else↓ throws ⟨a⟩ ↑a↓way. Our own thoughts come back to us in unexpected majesty.[275] See the noble selfreliance of Ben Jonson. Shun manufacture or the introducing an artificial arrangement in your thoughts, it will surely crack & come to nothing[,] but let alone tinkering & wait for the natural arrangement of your treasures; that shall be chemical ⟨arrang⟩ affinity, & is a new & permanent substance added to the world, to be recognized as genuine by every knowing person at sight. "A writer," says *Mme. de Stael*, "who searches only into the immutable nature of man, into those thoughts & sentiments which must enlighten the mind in every age, is independent of events; they can never change the order of those truths, which such a writer unfolds." [276]

⟨It⟩ A meek self reliance I believe to be the law & constitution of good writing. A man is to treat the world like children who must hear & obey the spirit in which he speaks, but which is not his. If he thinks he is to sing to the tune of the times, is to be the decorous sayer of smooth things, to lull the ear of society, & to speak of religion as the great traditional things to be either mutely avoided or

---

[274] " 'the times . . . souls' " is adapted from the opening sentence of Thomas Paine, *The American Crisis*, No. 1 (1776). The final sentence of this paragraph is used in "The Present Age," *Lectures*, II, 163.

[275] "In every work . . . majesty.", struck through in ink with a vertical use mark, is used in "Self-Reliance," *W*, II, 45–46. Concerning "the true chemist" see p. [128] below: the allusion to Glauber.

[276] Mme de Staël, *The Influence of Literature upon Society*, 2 vols. (Boston, 1813), II, 75. The quotation is used in "Ben Jonson, Herrick, Herbert, Wotton," *Lectures*, I, 341.

kept at a distance by civil bows he may make a very good workman for the booksellers but he must lay aside all hope to wield or so much as to touch the bright thunderbolts of truth which it is given to [103] the true scholar to launch & whose light flashes through ages without diminution. He must believe that the world proceeds in order from principles. He must not guess⟨,⟩ but observe, without intermission, without end; and these puissant elements he shall not pry into who comes in fun, or in haste, or for show. The solemn powers of faith, of love, of fear, of custom, of conscience, are no toys to be shoved aside, but the forces which make & change society. They must be seen & known. You might as well trifle with time. They keep on their eternal way grinding all resistance to dust. If you will, you ⟨can⟩ ↑may↓ read nothing but song books & fairy tales, all the year round, but if you would know the literature of any cultivated nation, you must meet the ⟨stern⟩ majestic ideas of God, of Justice, of Freedom, ↑of Necessity↓, of War, & of Intellectual beauty, as the subject & spirit of volumes & eras.[277]

What's a book? Everything or nothing. The eye that sees it is all. What is the heavens' majestical roof fretted with golden fire to one man, but a foul & pestilent congregation of vapors.[278] Well a book is to a paddy ⟨but⟩ a fair page smutted over with black marks; to a boy, a goodly collection of words he can read; to a halfwise man, it is a lesson which he wholly accepts or wholly rejects; but a sage shall see in it secrets yet unrevealed; shall weigh, as he reads, the author's mind; shall see the predominance of ideas which the writer could not extricate himself from, & oversee. The Belfast Town & County Almanack may be read by a sage; &, wasteful as it would be in me to read Antimasonic or Jackson papers, yet whoso pierces through them to the deep Idea they embody, may well read them.

[104] Oct. 13. ⟨Observe⟩ ↑Do you see↓ what we preserve of history; a few anecdotes of a moral quality of some momentary act or word [—] the word of Canute on the seashore; the speech of the Druid to

[277] This paragraph, struck through in pencil with vertical use marks, is used in "English Literature: Introductory," *Lectures*, I, 231.

[278] Cf. *Hamlet*, II, ii, 315.

Edwin; the anecdote of Alfred's learning to read for Judith's gift; the box on the ear by the herdman's wife; the tub of Diogenes; the gold of Croesus, & Solon, & Cyrus; the emerald of Polycrates; these things reckoned insignificant at the age of their occurrence, have floated whilst laws & expeditions & books & kingdoms have sunk & are forgotten. So potent is this simple element of humanity or moral common sense.[279]

There seems sometimes to have been very little intention in history. We impute deep laid farsighted plans to Napoleon & Caesar but without reason. The cement or spine which gave unity to their manifold actions was not their⟨s.⟩ logic, but the concatenation of events. "My son cannot replace me; I could not replace myself; I am the child of circumstances;" said Napoleon. ↑Tradition does more for an ingenious fable than the poet.↓[280]

My will never gave the images in my mind the rank they now take there. The four college years & the three years course of Divinity have not yielded me so many grand facts as some idle books under the bench at Latin School. We form no guess at the time of receiving a thought, of its comparative value.[281]   ↑Copied p 276↓

Man idealizes every portrait. So are the sentiments of every age unconsciously corrected & pure models upheld in the worst times. The canonizing of a good bishop or monk ⟨to⟩ was a useful preaching to several ages. They who did it, would naturally sink the faults & swell the virtues of their friend & so give to virtuous youth an objective god.

----

[279] The anecdotes of Canute, Edwin, and Alfred are related in Sharon Turner, *The History of the Anglo-Saxons*, 1807, I, 437; II, 439 (see p. [56] above); and I, 193–194, 256–257, respectively. Concerning the gold of Croesus, see Plutarch, "The Life of Solon," in *Plutarch's Lives*, trans. John and William Langhorne, 4 vols. (Philadelphia, 1822), I, 157–158; for Polycrates, see Herodotus, *History*, Bk. III, 40–43. This paragraph, struck through in pencil with a diagonal use mark, is used in "Permanent Traits of the English National Genius," *Lectures*, I, 250–251.

[280] This sentence, a quotation from Mme de Staël, was evidently added from the later entry of October 22, p. [109] below; it does not appear in Emerson's copy of the present passage occurring on p. [276] below, but separately on p. [275].

[281] This and the preceding paragraph, struck through in ink with three wavy diagonal use marks, are used in "Spiritual Laws," *W*, II, 134 and 133.

[105]   On Party.

———

The aliases of the father of William the Conqueror who was called Robert the Magnificent, or ↑Robert↓ the Devil, are a good specimen of every man's Janus reputation[.]²⁸²

———
———

Genius can never supply the want of knowledge though even its errors may be valuable. Mme. de Stael tells me in this fine book of the Influence of Literature that the English do not admit much imagination into their prose because ⟨thei⟩ such is the facility of the structure of their blank verse that every one reserves for poetry all such thoughts. ↑p. 56↓ What shall the English of whom only four or five have ever succeeded in blank verse, say to this?

Shakspear, Milton, Young, Thomson, Cowper, Wordsworth.²⁸³

Oct. 15. It does seem in reading the history or the writings of the English in the 11, 12, 13, 14 centuries, that their eyes were holden that they could not see.²⁸⁴ They submit to received views of religion & politics that a child would deride nowadays & exhibit, at the same time, strong common sense in other things. What stuff there is even in Bacon! What a baby house he builds of diet & domestic rules, — & Montaigne even. The right of civil liberty how slowly it opens on the mind. Surely they say well who say that God screens men from premature ideas.

A great bump of nonsense in Bacon & in Brown.²⁸⁵

When we enter upon the domain of LAW, we do indeed come

²⁸² This sentence is used in "Society," *Lectures*, II, 108.

²⁸³ For Mme de Staël's observation, see *The Influence of Literature upon Society*, 1813, II, 12. In "Shakspear [second lecture]," *Lectures*, I, 308, Emerson again cites what he calls her "curious remark" and names the same six English practitioners of blank verse.

²⁸⁴ Cf. Luke 24:16 and Rom. 11:10. See *JMN*, IV, 377; p. [304] below; and "Spiritual Laws," *W*, II, 147.

²⁸⁵ The first of these two paragraphs is drawn upon in "Ethics," *Lectures*, II, 149, and "Spiritual Laws," *W*, II, 147. With the second, cf. the discussion of Bacon and Sir Thomas Browne in "Thoughts on Modern Literature," *The Dial*, I (Oct. 1840), 143–144.

out into light. To him who by God's grace has seen that by being a mere tunnel or pipe through which the divine Will flows,[286] he becomes great, & becomes a Man, — the future ⟨is⟩ wears an eternal smile & the flight of time is no longer dreadful. I assure myself always of needed help, & go to the grave undaunted because I go not to the grave. I am willing also to be as passive to the great forces I acknowledge as is the thermometer or the clock & quite part with all will as superfluous.

[106] Do not expect to find the books of a country written as ↑an Encyclopedia↓ by a society of savans on system to supply certain wants & fill up a circle of subjects. In French literature perhaps is something of this order of a garden where plat corresponds with plat & shrub with shrub. But in the world of living genius all at first seems disorder & incapable of methodical arrangement. Yet is there a higher harmony whereby 'tis set as in Nature the sea balances the land, the mountain, the valley & woods & meadows. ↑See X next page↓

I listened yesterday as always to Dr Ripley's prayer in the mourning house with tenfold the hope[,] a tenfold chance of some touch of nature that should melt us, that I should have felt in the rising of one of the Boston preachers of propriety — the fair house of Seem. These old semi-savages do from the solitude in which they live & their remoteness from artificial society & their inevitable daily comparing man with beast, village with wilderness, their inevitable acquaintance with the outward nature of man, & with his strict dependence on sun & rain & wind & frost; wood, worm, cow, & bird, get an education to the Homeric simplicity which all the libraries of the Reviews & the Commentators in Boston do[n] not countervail.[287]

What a Tantalus cup this life is! The beauty that shimmers on these yellow afternoons who ever could clutch it? Go forth to find

---

[286] For the figure, suggested to Emerson long before by a sermon on Temperance by George Bancroft, see *JMN*, II, 221, 389, and 402; "Pan," *W*, IX, 360.

[287] "some touch of nature . . . countervail.", struck through in pencil with a vertical use mark, is used in "Manners," *Lectures*, II, 136–137.

it, & it is gone; 'tis only a mirage as you look from ⟨your diligent⟩ ↑the↓ windows of diligence[.] [288]

Charles says that to ⟨see⟩ ↑read↓ Carlyle in N[orth] A[merican] Review is like seeing your brother in jail; & A[lexander] Everett is the sheriff that put him in.[289]

[107] Far off no doubt is the perfectibility, so far off as to be ridiculous to all but a few. Yet wrote I once that God keeping a private door to each soul[,] nothing transcends the bounds of reasonable expectation from a man. Now what imperfect tadpoles we are! an arm or a leg[,] an eye or an antenna is unfolded[;] all the rest is yet in the Ch[r]ysalis. Who does not feel in him budding the powers of a Persuasion that by & by will be irresistible? Already how unequally unfolded in two men! Here is a man who can only say yes & no in very slight variety of forms. But to ⟨give⟩ render a reason or to dissuade you by any thing less coarse than interest he cannot & attempts not. But ⟨the pure⟩ Themistocles ⟨shall⟩ goes by & persuades you that ⟨you saw⟩ he whom you saw up was down, & he whom you saw down was up.[290]

X] And as the eye possesses the faculty of rounding & integrating the most disagreeable parts into a pleasing whole[.] [291]

The ancients probably saw the moral significance of nature in

[288] "The beauty . . . diligence", struck through in ink with a wavy diagonal use mark, is used in *Nature, W,* I, 19.

[289] Everett's review of the American edition of *Sartor Resartus* appeared in the *North American Review,* XLI (Oct. 1835), 454 ff.

[290] For God's "private door to each soul", see p. [86] above and "The Head," *Lectures,* II, 250; also comparable is the figure of the "tunnel or pipe through which the divine Will flows", p. [105] above. With the concluding anecdote, cf. "The Life of Pericles," in *Plutarch's Lives,* 1822, I, 263, where Thucydides is asked who is the better wrestler, himself or Pericles (not Themistocles). "When I throw him," Thucydides replies, "he says he was never down, and he persuades the very spectators to believe so." "Who does not feel . . . down was up.", struck through in pencil with a diagonal use mark, is used in "Society," *Lectures,* II, 111, and "Eloquence," *W,* VII, 73; in the latter, "Themistocles" is corrected to "Pericles".

[291] This entry, an addition to the first paragraph on p. [106], is struck through in ink with a diagonal use mark.

the objects without afterthought or effort to separate the object & the expression. They felt no wrong in esteeming the mountain a purple picture whereon Oreads might appear as rightly as moss; & which was the image of stability & whatever other meaning it ⟨su⟩ yielded to the wandering eye, because they were prepared to look on it as children & believed the gods built it & were not far off, & so every tree & flower & chip of stone had a religious lustre, & might mean anything.

But when science had gained & given the impression of the permanence[,] even eternity of nature & of every substance, & when on th⟨is⟩e new views which this habit imparted to the learned, wit, wine, derision arose, the mountain became a pile of stones acted on by bare blind [108] laws of chemistry, & the poetic sense of things was driven to the vulgar and an effort was made to recal the sense, by the educated & so it was faintly uttered ↑by the poet↓ & heard with a smile.

The objective religion of the Middle & after Age is well exemplified in the spite which heightened Luther's piety.[n] "We cannot vex the devil more, said Luther, than when we teach, preach, sing & speak of Jesus & his humanity. Therefore I like it well, when with loud voices & fine[,] long & deliberately, we sing in the church, 'Et homo factus est: et Verbum caro factum est.'[292] The devil cannot endure to hear these words; he flieth away," &c. Table Talk[293]

October, ↑20↓. The hearing man is good. Unhappy is the speaking man. The alternations of speaking & hearing make our education.[294]

[October] 21. Last Saturday night came hither Mr Alcott & spent the Sabbath with me. A wise man, simple, superior to display. & drops the best things as quietly as the least. Every man, he said, is a Revelation, & ought to write his Record. But few with the pen. His book

---

[292] "And He was made man; and the Word was made flesh" (Ed.).

[293] Cf. *Colloquia Mensalia: or, Dr. Martin Luther's Divine Discourses at his Table . . .* , 1652, p. 108. This passage is used in "Martin Luther," *Lectures*, I, 135–136.

[294] This paragraph, struck through in pencil with a diagonal use mark, is used in "The Head," *Lectures*, II, 257, and "Intellect," *W*, II, 342.

is his school in which he writes all his thoughts. The spiritual world should meet men everywhere; & so the government should teach. Our life flows out into our amusements. Need of a drama here: how well to lash the American follies. Every man is a system[,] an institution. Autobiography the best book. He thinks Jesus a pure Deist. & says all children are Deists.

Charles remarks upon the nimbleness & buoyancy which the conversation of a spiritualist awakens; the world begins to dislimn.

[109] It is the comfort I have in taking up those new poems of Wordsworth,[295] that I am sure here to find thoughts in harmony with the great frame of Nature, the placid aspect of the Universe. I may find dulness & flatness, but I shall not find meanness & error[.]

⟨Why th⟩ Whence these oaths that make so many words in English books? The sun, the moon, St Paul, Jesus, & God, are called upon as witness that the speaker speaks truth. I suppose they refer to that conviction suggested by every object that something IS. And signify *If any thing is*, then I did so and so. Yet now they are all obsolete. Except for the court forms, I doubt if ever they would be used. They import something separate from the will of man. "By day & night" "by Jupiter" &c. By St Nicholas, &c i.e. my will which interferes to color & change all things interferes not here. This *is*.[296]

[October] 22. What can be truer than the popular poetic doctrine of a conjunction of stars? How many things must combine to make a good word or event. Most truly said Mme. de Stael, that 'tis tradition more than invention that helps the poet to a good fable[.][297]

---

[295] *Yarrow Revisited, and Other Poems* (Boston, 1835); see p. [182] below; Journal C, p. [82].

[296] This paragraph, struck through in pencil with a vertical use mark, is used in "Being and Seeming," *Lectures*, II, 298.

[297] See *The Influence of Literature upon Society*, 1813, I, 105: the Greek dramatists "wrote all upon the same subject, without giving themselves the trouble of inventing any thing new . . . . The happy conception of extraordinary events is much more the production of tradition than of the poets . . . ." The comment as recorded here is used in "Thoughts on Art," *The Dial*, I (Jan. 1841), 372; "Art,"

What can be truer than the doctrine of inspiration? of fortunate hours? Things sail dim & great through my head. Veins of rich ore are in me, could I only get outlet & pipe to draw them out. How unattainable seem to me these wild pleasantries of Shakspear yet not less so seem to me passages in old letters of my own.

[110] That sarcasm of Lady Ashton in Bride of Lammermoor that the Lord Keeper had been scared by a red cow [298] is a fit illustration of the twofold face every thing can bear.

What platitudes I find in Wordsworth. "I poet bestow my verse on this & this & this." Scarce has he dropped the smallest piece of an egg, when he fills the barnyard with his cackle.

In the hours of clear vision, how slight a thing it is to die. It is so slight that one ought not turn a corner or accept the least disgrace (so much as skulking) to avoid it. The mob may prove as kind & easy a deliverer as a pin or a worm. The mob seems a thing insignificant. It has no character. It is the emblem of unreason; mere muscular & nervous motion, no thought, no spark of spiritual life in it. It is a bad joke to call it a fruit of the love of liberty. It is permitted like earthquakes & freshets & locusts & is to be met like a blind mechanical force.

What of these atrocious ancestors of Englishmen[—]the Briton, Saxon, Northman, Berserkir? Is it not needful to make a strong nation that there should be strong wild will? ↑If man degenerates in gardens he must be grafted again from the wild stock↓[.]

We all know how life is made up; that a door is to be painted; a lock to be repaired; a cord of wood is wanted; ⟨it⟩ ↑the house↓ smokes; or I have a diarrhea; then the tax; & a hopeless visiter; & the stinging recollection of an injurious or a very awkward word. These eat up the hours.[299] How then is any acquisition, how is any great deed or wise & beautiful work possible? Let it enhance the

Lectures, II, 47; and "Art," W, VII, 46; see also p. [104] above and p. [275] below.

[298] Scott, The Bride of Lammermoor, ch. XXII: "the Lord Keeper was scared by a dun cow."

[299] "We all know . . . hours.", struck through in ink with a diagonal use mark, is used in "Prudence," Lectures, II, 313.

praise of Milton, Shakspear, & Laplace. These oppress & spitefully tyrannize over me because I am an Idealist[.]

[111] The mob ought to be treated only with contempt. Phocion[,] even Jesus cannot otherwise regard it in so far as it is mob.[300] It is mere beast[;] of them that compose it their soul is absent from it. It is to consider it too much to respect it[,] too much to speak of its terror in any other way than mere animal & mechanical agents. It has no will; oh no.[301]

Sunday, 25 Oct. Every intellectual acquisition is mainly prospective. And hence the scholar's assurance of eternity quite aloof from his moral convictions.[302]

———

Behind us, as we go, all things assume pleasing forms as clouds do far off. Even the corpse that has lain in our chambers has added a solemn ornament to the house. In this my new house no dead body ⟨has⟩ was ever laid. It ⟨is s⟩ lacks so much sympathy with nature.[303]
↑v[ide]. p. 156↓

———

Mr Goodwin [304] preached a good sermon this P.M. & said "the Almighty never implanted in a human breast the right of doing wrong." As he taught, it seemed pleasant the ⟨cr⟩ tie of principle that holds as brothers all men so that when a stranger comes to me from the other side the globe, Otaheitan or Chinese to buy or sell with me, he shall have that measure from me as shall fill his mind with pleasant conviction that he has dealt with a fellowman in the deepest & dearest sense.

A talk in the morning concerning eyes & their spiritual & incorruptible testimony. When a man speaks the truth in the spirit of truth God aids him by giving him an eye as clear as his own heavens.

[300] Cf. "The Life of Phocion," *Plutarch's Lives*, 1822, III, 292–294.

[301] With this paragraph cf. "Society," *Lectures*, II, 109.

[302] This paragraph is struck through in pencil with a vertical use mark.

[303] This paragraph, struck through in pencil with a diagonal use mark and in ink with a vertical use mark, is used in "Ethics," *Lectures*, II, 144, and "Spiritual Laws," *W*, II, 131.

[304] Reverend Hersey B. Goodwin, colleague of Dr. Ripley.

When he has base ends his eye is as muddy as a horse pond. When you think of a ⟨character⟩ friend's character you think of his eye rather than of form or mouth.[305] Weston's [306] story of the boy that was cross eyed when ever he lied, ⟨when⟩ but ⟨to⟩ the axes of the eyes parallel when he spoke truth[.]

————

[112] "In no man's path malignant stood." Excellent hymn of Cowper concerning "truths which o'er the world rise but never set." [307]

The preacher, thought I in church, must assume that man is the revelation & that if he will reflect he shall ⟨overflow with⟩ find his heart overflowing with a divine light, & ⟨let him talk[?] of⟩ the bible ⟨it⟩ shall be a mirror giving back to him the refulgence of his own mind. Let the preacher speak himself in the same faith that we all, his hearers, are urns of the godhead, & will surely know if any word of our own language is uttered to us, & will accept it but that all of us which is divine must remain forever impasible to anything else. He the preacher let him then acquiesce in being nothing that he may move mountains; let him be the mere tongue of us all; no individual but a universal man, let him leave his nation, his party, his sect, his town-connexion, even his vanity & selflove at home & come hither to say what were equally fit at Paris, at Canton, and at Thebes.

There is no wall like an idea[.] [308]
I used to remark Edward's Greek petulance disclosed in answers like that of Pyrrhus when ⟨summoned⟩ invited to hear one mimic the nightingale. But I have heard the nightingale itself.[309] M.M.E. has made many such speeches. A good one of this sort — the putting down reverend folly by childish reason, is Hannibal's answer to Antiochus' saying 'that the Entrails of the sacrifice forbad the battle';

[305] "A talk in . . . mouth." is struck through in pencil with a diagonal use mark; "When a man . . . mouth." is struck through in ink with a vertical use mark. The second and third sentences are used in "Spiritual Laws," *W*, II, 156.

[306] Probably Ezra Weston, Jr., a Boston attorney and friend of Charles Emerson (see *L*, II, 24, n. 68).

[307] Cf. William Cowper, "The Olney Hymns," XXX: "The Light and Glory of the World," ll. 11–12.

[308] See "English Literature: Introductory," *Lectures*, I, 218.

[309] Related of Agesilaus (not Pyrrhus), who refused the invitation, saying, "I have heard the nightingale herself." "The Life of Agesilaus," *Plutarch's Lives*, 1822, III, 65.

"You are for doing what the flesh of a beast not what the reason of a ⟨man⟩ wise man adviseth."[310] Socrates also.

Man is a heavenly plant &c   Plato says in Plut[arch].[311]

[113] Webster is in a galvanized state when he makes the Hayne speech, & 'tis as easy to say gigantic things to introduce from God on the world "truths which rise but never set"[312] as ⟨to⟩ at another hour to talk nonsense. He is caught up in the spirit & made to utter things not his own. — ↑See too the galvanized nation J 1833[–1834] p 147↓[313]

28 October. Plotinus says of the intuitive knowledge that "it is not lawful to inquire whence it sprang as if it were a thing subject to place & motion for it neither approached hither nor again departs from hence, to some other place, but it either appears to us, or it does not appear."[314] Every man in his moment of reflection sees & records this vision & therefore feels the insufferable impertinence of contradiction from the unthinking as if had uttered a ⟨mere⟩ ↑⟨bare⟩↓ private opinion or caprice & not made himself a ⟨mere⟩ ↑bare↓ pipe for better wisdom to flow through.[315]

The oriental man; Abraham & Heth, Job, &c[.]

Man stands on the point betwixt the inward spirit & the outward matter. He sees that the one explains, translates the other: that the world is the mirror of the soul. He is the priest and interpreter of nature thereby.[316]

---

[310] Cf. "Of Banishment," *Plutarch's Morals*, 1718, III, 63.

[311] "Why the Pythian Priestess Ceases her Oracles in Verse," *Plutarch's Morals*, 1718, III, 111. The sentence, struck through in ink with a diagonal use mark, is used in "The Poet," *W*, III, 31; see also Journal C, p. [131].

[312] See p. [112] above: the allusion to Cowper.

[313] See *JMN*, IV, 377.

[314] Plotinus, *Enneads*, V, v, as quoted in Coleridge, *Biographia Literaria*, 1834, pp. 144–145. With "appears . . . not appear." cf. "English Literature: Introductory," *Lectures*, I, 226, and *Nature*, *W*, I, 34.

[315] See p. [105] above. This paragraph is struck through in pencil with a vertical use mark.

[316] This paragraph is used in "English Literature: Introductory," *Lectures*, I, 224–225.

I read nothing in St John or St Paul concerning the planting of America or the burning of Anthracite coal. Yet as I sit here ↑in America↓ by my anthracite coal fire, I cannot help thinking that there has been somewhere ⟨some⟩ ↑a↓ design that one should be inhabited & the other burned.

'Tis a good thing for man that I am obliged to pick my words of low trades with so much care. In England you may say a sweep, a blacksmith, a scavenger, as synonym for a savage in civil life. But in this country I must look about me. I perhaps speak to persons who occasionally or regularly work at these works & yet do take as they ought their place as Men in places of manly culture & entertainment[.]

———

[114] Wacic the Caliph, who died A.D. 845, ended his life with these words; "O thou, whose ⟨dignity⟩ ↑kingdom↓ never passes away, pity one whose dignity is so transient!" Turner; [History of the] Ang[lo]. S[axons]. Vol 1   p 286[n.] [317]

———

"What of all his (Alfred's) troubles & difficulties he affirmed ⟨with frequent complaint & the deep lamentations of his heart⟩ to have been the greatest, was, that when he had the age ⟨permission,⟩ & ability to learn, he could find no masters." *Asser.* Turner Vol. 1, p. 289. So rare is it to find the commonest desire of a true mind upon a throne!

"Without wisdom," quoth Alfred, "wealth is worth little. Though a man had an hundred & seventy acres sown with gold & all grew like corn yet were all that wealth nothing worth unless that of an enemy one could make it become his friend. For what differs gold from a stone but by discreet using of it?" ——— Turner Vol 1 p 304[n., misquoted]

"Elueredi Veridici" says a writer at the Norman Conquest [Turner, I, 309] [318]

———

[317] Sharon Turner, *The History of the Anglo-Saxons*, 1807.

[318] "Elueredi Veridici" — "The Truth-Teller" (Ed.). "An author who lived at the period of the Norman conquest," says Turner, ". . . names Alfred, with the simple but expressive addition of 'the truth teller.'" In his accompanying note Turner cites "Hermanni miracula Edmundi script. circa 1070. MS. Cotton Library, Tiberius,

"Asser's general statement that he consecrated half his time to God, gives no distinct idea, because we find that his liberal mind in the distribution of his revenue thought that to apportion money for a school, was devoting it to the Supreme."

Turner, [I, 306–]307

He was afflicted all his life with a miserable disease.

[*Ibid.*, I, 330–331]

[115]³¹⁹ 30 October. How hard it is to impute your own best sense to a dead author! The very highest ⟨com⟩ praise we ⟨give⟩ *think* of any writer, or painter, or sculptor, or builder, is, that he actually possessed the thought or feeling with which he has inspired us. We hesitate at doing Spenser so great an honor as to think that he meant by his allegory the sense which we affix to it.

We seem in this to believe that in a former age men could not attain that maturity of consciousness which we have, — & yet I do not know but we have the same infirmity respecting contemporary genius. We fear that Mr Alston did not foresee ⟨the⟩ & design the effect he produces on us.

Familiar as it is to us, the highest merit we ascribe to Homer ⟨to Shakspear to Dante⟩ is that he forsook books & traditions & ⟨learned⟩ wrote not what men but what Homer thought.³²⁰

↑copied —   p. 276↓

⟨We believe it to⟩ Easy to enter into this region: ⟨as that⟩ every man has some moments of it in his years; but very very few men are able to speak & write those thoughts.

B. 2. It follows Abbo's life of this king. . . . P. 21. he says, 'Elueridi Veridici.' " Cf. "Permanent Traits of the English National Genius," *Lectures*, I, 252.

³¹⁹ Partially erased pencil writing appears in the center of the page beneath the second, third, and fourth paragraphs: ‖ . . . . today My lips in . . . move . . . X X X X X Faraway . . . ‖

³²⁰ These three paragraphs, struck through in pencil with discontinuous diagonal use marks and in ink with discontinuous wavy diagonal use marks, are copied below, p. [276], as Emerson notes, though with revisions; they are subsequently used in "Thoughts on Art," *The Dial*, I (Jan. 1841), 372; "Art," *Lectures*, II, 47–48; and "Art," *W*, VII, 46–47.

To the chaste man the white skin of the woman with whom he talks, appears ⟨as⟩ to be distant by some miles.

———

"Mr Canning was always great when he was jocular & always small when he was serious[.]"
Mr Miles[321] found placards pasted upon posts & walls in London with these words, "Of what use are the Lords?"[322]

———

I suppose all the Saxon race at this day[—]Germans, English, Americans — all to a man regard it as an unspeakable misfortune to be born in France. How odious is the far off sound of a French heroic verse.

[116] It will not do for Sharon Turner or any man not of Ideas to make a System. Thus Mr Turner has got into his head the notion that the Mosaic history is a good natural history of the world, reconcileable with geology &c. Very well. You see at once the length & breadth of what you may expect, & ⟨the mind⟩ lose⟨s⟩ all appetite to read. But ⟨Mr⟩ Coleridge sets out to idealize the actual, to ⟨to give⟩ make an epopoe[i]a out of English institutions & it is replete with life.[323]

Nov. 6. Burke's imagery is much of it got from books & so is a secondary formation. Webster's is all primary. Let a man make the woods & fields his books then at the hour of passion his thoughts will invest themselves spontaneously with natural imagery.

Plutarchiana this morn. Verses & words served as Hampers & baskets to convey the oracle's answers from place to place.   . . . . .
Then was it that History alighted from versifying as it were from riding in chariots[,] & on foot distinguish[ed] truth from fable.

---

[321]Probably Solomon P. Miles, active as an officer of the American Institute of Instruction, before which Emerson had lectured on August 20 (*L*, I, 449, n. 69).

[322] The quoted words are used in "Politics," *Lectures*, II, 80–81.

[323] As Cameron suggests (*E t E*, I, 196, 151), Emerson is thinking here of *On the Constitution of Church and State*, which he considered an "invaluable little book" ("Modern Aspects of Letters," *Lectures*, I, 379).

He speaks of the lovers of omens &c as preferring rainbows & haloes to the sun & moon.[324]

[117] Charles says the nap is worn off of the world[.]

7 November. Wrote yesterday to Mr Putnam & enclosed $56. for Asylum[.] [325]

↑"To know that the sky is everywhere blue you need not travel round the world[.]"↓

Advantage of the Spiritual man in the fact of the identity of human nature. Draw your robe ever so chastely round you, the surgeon sees every muscle, every hair, every bone, every gland. He reads you by your counterpart. So I read the history of all men in myself. Give me one single man & uncover for me his pleasures & pains, let me minutely & in the timbers & ground plan study his architecture & you may travel all round the world & visit the Chinese, the Malay, the Esquimaux, & the Arab. I travel faster than you. In my chimney corner I see more, & anticipate all your wonders. Or do you ransack all the histories & learn what has been done & thought, back in time ⟨from⟩ in the 17 century, in the middle age, at the time of the consuls, or in the twilight of history, & I intent upon the principles of this one man will know what you shall say & will say that also which shall be made good ages hence in some far stretching revolution. Of this truth see what is quoted from Mme de Stael above; p. 102[.] [326]

14 November. Melancholy cleaves to the Saxon mind as closely as ⟨it does⟩ to the tones of an Æolian harp.

When yesterday I read Antigone, at some words a very different image of female loveliness rose out of the clouds of the Past &

[324] Cf. "Why the Pythian Priestess Ceases her Oracles in Verse," *Plutarch's Morals*, 1718, III, 128, 127, 134. The first and third figures are used respectively in "The Poet," *W*, III, 34, and "Demonology," *W*, X, 26.

[325] Emerson's brother Bulkeley was in the care of Israel Putnam of Chelmsford.

[326] This paragraph, struck through in pencil with two diagonal use marks, and the preceding sentence are used in "The Individual," *Lectures*, II, 178–179.

the Actual. That poem is just what Win[c]kelmann described the Greek beauty to be — "the tongue on the balance of expression." [327] It is remarkable for nothing so much as the extreme temperance, the abstemiousness which never offends by the superfluous word or degree too much of emotion. How slender the materials[!] how few the incidents! how just the symmetry! C. thinks it as great a work of genius as any. Every word writ in steel. But that other image which it awakened for me [118] brought with it the perception how entirely each rational creature is dowried with all the gifts of God. The Universe, nothing less, is totally given to each new being. It is his potentially. He may divest himself of it[,] he may creep into a corner as most men do, but he is entitled to deity by the Constitution: Only he must come & take it. "The winds & waves," says Gibbon, "are always on the side of the ablest navigators." [328] What is not, I pray? When a noble act is done, perchance in a ⟨beau⟩ scene of great natural beauty, is not the hero entitled to the additional effect of the fine landscape? And when & where does not natural beauty[—]deep & high yea infinite beauty[—]steal in like air & envelope great actions? Nature alway stretcheth out her arms to embrace man; only let his thoughts be of equal grandeur & the *frame* ↑will↓ *suit⟨s⟩ the picture.* A virtuous man is in keeping with the works of nature & makes the central figure in the visible sphere. It is we ↑who↓ by error & crime thrust ourselves aside & make ourselves impertinent & inharmonious things.[329]

But I thought thus yesterday in ⟨relation⟩ regard to the charming beauty which a few years ago shed on me its tender & immortal light. ⟨It⟩ She needed not a historical name nor earthly rank or wealth. She was complete in her own perfections. She took up all things into her & in her single self sufficed the soul.

[119] People think that husbands & wives have no *present time*[,] that they have long already established their mutual con-

---

[327] See p. [17] above.

[328] *The History of the Decline and Fall of the Roman Empire*, ch. 68. See *The Works of Edward Gibbon*, ed. J. B. Bury, 15 vols. (New York, 1907), XII, 30.

[329] "each rational creature . . . things.", struck through in ink with three wavy diagonal use marks, is used in "Modern Aspects of Letters," *Lectures*, I, 384–385, and *Nature*, W, I, 20–22.

nexion, have nothing to learn of one another, & know beforehand each what the other will do. The wise man will discern the fact; viz, that they are chance-joined, little acquainted, & do observe each the other's carriage to the stranger as curiously as he doth.[330]

The way in which Plutarch & the ancients usually quote ⟨poetry⟩ the Poets is quite remarkable as it indicates a deep & universal reverence for poetry[,] indicates a faith in Inspiration. They quote Pindar much as a pious Christian does David or Paul. Where is that reverence now?

Fine walk this P.M. in the woods with C. [—]beautiful Gothic arches yes & cathedral windows as of stained glass formed by the interlaced branches against the grey & gold of the western sky. We came to a little pond in the bosom of the hills, with echoing shores. C. thought much of the domesticity & comfort there is in living with one set of men; to wit, your cotemporaries: & thought it would be misery to shift them, & hence the sadness of growing old. Now, every newspaper has tidings of kenned folk. I projected the discomfort of our playing over again tonight the tragedy of Babes in the Wood. C. rejoiced in the serenity of Saturday Night. It was calm as the Universe.[330a] I told him what a fool he was not to write the record of his thoughts. He said it were an impiety. Yet he meant to, when he was old. I told him when Alcibiades turned author we worthies should be out of countenance. Yet I maintained that the Lycidas was a copy from the poet's mind printed out in the book, notwithstanding all the mechanical difficulties, as clear & wild as it had shone at first in the sky of his own thought. We came out again into the open world & saw the [120] sunset as of a divine Artist & I asked if it were only brute light & aqueous vapor & there was no intent in that celestial smile? Another topic of the talk was that Lyceums, — so that people will let you say what *you* think — are as good a pulpit as any other. But C. thinks that it is only by an effort like a Berserkir a man can work himself up to any interest in any exertion. All active

[330] This paragraph is struck through in pencil with a diagonal use mark.

[330a] Wordsworth, "Flowers on the Top of the Pillars at the Entrance of the Cave [of Staffa]," l. 9; see *JMN*, IV, 223, n. 40.

life seems an amabilis insania.[331] And when he has done anything of importance he repents of it, repents of Virtue as soon as he is alone. Nor can he see any reason why the world should not burn up tonight. The play has been over, some time.

Peace & War. "The wounds inflicted by iron are to be healed by iron, & not by words," said the elder Cancellieri, & ordered the hand of Lore to be cut off[.]"   Muller Vol 3   p 14[332]
↑Friendship or Society↓
The Emperor Charles IV found Petrarch at Mantua & invited him to accompany him to Rome. "It is not sufficient that I am going to see Rome; I wish to see it with your eyes." [333]

Muller [*ibid.*, p. 45]

Magnanimity of Literary men. Argyropulus & Theodore of Gaza[.] Muller Vol III   p 46[334]

Romano Pane[,] a Spanish missionary who discovered tobacco in St Domingo[,] contributed essentially to improve the revenue from this quarter for that weed became not less productive than the gold mines to the Spanish treasury[.]   *Muller* Vol 3   p 150

Luther — "Spectacle of an individual contending victoriously *by such means only as are within the reach of all* against all the gifts of fortune & all the terrors of power[.]"

Muller [*ibid.*, p. 182; italics Emerson's]

[121] Vulgar princes think that the art of governing is the art of dissembling. Alfred did not.

Samson an indulgence monger in his public preachings in Switz-

[331] "Fond illusion." Horace, *Odes*, III, iv, 6.
[332] Johannes von Müller, *An Universal History*, 4 vols. (American Library of Useful Knowledge, vols. 3, 5, 6, 7. Boston, 1831–1832).
[333] This paragraph is used in "Society," *Lectures*, II, 102.
[334] Argyropulus, according to Müller, "destroyed his translation of Plato in order that it might do no injury to that of his friend Theodorus of Gaza, which was not so well executed as his own."

erland ⟨imitated the⟩ entertained the astonished audience with the
sounds which the soul emits, when, its ransom being paid, it flies
up out of purgatory[.] [335] See Muller   III   p 187

Age of chivalry when "the nobility performed pilgrimages to
countries that could never be found in a map & amused themselves
by defying persons unknown to them to ⟨fi⟩ mortal combat for ladies
whom they had never seen." Ap. Muller

In Elizabeth's time the high church was looked upon by intelligent men as "a horse which was still kept always saddled in readiness
for the Pope." See Muller [*Ibid.*, p. 247]

Charles V always dissembled & never was believed.
↑Compensation↓ [336]

December ↑7↓. Last week Mr Alcott spent two days here. The
wise man who talks with you seems of no particular size but like
the sun & moon quite **vague** & indeterminate. His characterizing of
people was very good. Hedge united strangely the old & the new[;]
he had imagination but his intellect seemed ever to contend with an
arid temperament.
G.P.B. was an impersonation of sincerity, simplicity, & humility without servility.

[122] Dec. 7. Carlyle's talent I think lies more in his beautiful
criticism in seizing the idea of the man or the time than in original
speculation. He seems to me most limited in this chapter or speculation in which they regard him as most original & profound — I mean
in his Religion & immortality from the removal of Time & Space.[337]

----

[335] "Samson . . . purgatory" is struck through in pencil with a diagonal use
mark.

[336] See Müller, III, 199: Charles V "could never conceal the dissimulation of his
character: . . . none believed him." "Charles V . . . believed.", struck through in
pencil with a diagonal use mark, is used in "Ethics," *Lectures*, II, 154. "Compensation" is circled in ink.

[337] Presumably "Natural Supernaturalism," *Sartor Resartus*, Bk. III, ch. VIII,
wherein "the Philosophy of Clothes attains to Transcendentalism."

He seems merely to work with a⟨n alien⟩ foreign thought not to live in it himself.

In Shakspear I actually shade my eyes as I read for the splendor of the thoughts.

Dec. 11. Read M'Duffie's message — See it in Transcript p 15.[338]

"If we go no further than this we had as well do nothing." — Message

Superserviceable.

"Look in thy heart & write"   Sidney [339]

12 Dec. I wrote H Ware, Jr. "that his 4th topic[,] The circumstances which show a tendency toward War's abolition, seemed to me the nearest to Mine, for I strongly feel the Inhumanity or unmanlike character of War & should gladly study the outward signs & exponents ⟨wh⟩ of that progress which has brought us to this feeling." [340]

The Arts & Sciences are the only Cosmopolites.
(Scholar)

[123] 26 December. There are two objects ⟨both desireable⟩ between which the mind vibrates like a pendulum; one,[n] the desire of truth; the other, the desire of Repose. He in whom the love of Repose predominates, will accept the first creed he meets, Arianism, Calvinism, Socinianism; he gets rest & reputation; but he shuts the door of Truth. He in whom the love of Truth predominates will keep himself aloof from all moorings & afloat. He will abstain from dogmatism & recognize all the opposite negations between which as walls his being is swung. On one side he will feel that God is impersonal. On the other, that the Universe is his work.

[338] In Transcript, p. [15], is an extract in praise of slavery from Governor McDuffie's message to the legislature of South Carolina, November 24, 1835, quoted from the Charleston *Courier*, November 27, 1835.

[339] "Astrophel and Stella," Sonnet 1, l. 14. The quotation, struck through in ink with two diagonal use marks, is used in "Modern Aspects of Letters," *Lectures*, I, 382; and "Spiritual Laws," *W*, II, 153; see also *JMN*, IV, 434.

[340] As a member of a committee of the Massachusetts Peace Society, Ware had outlined a projected course of lectures on war and peace (*L*, I, 458).

He submits to the inconvenience of suspense & imperfect opinion but he is a candidate for truth & respects the highest law of his being.[341]

1836

16 January. Mr Meriam owns this field, Mr Bacon that, & Mr Butterfield the next, but the poet owns the whole. There is a property in the horizon which no man has but he whose eye can integrate all the parts. And the best part of all these men's farms[,] the ⟨look whi⟩ face which they show to the poet's eye, they do not possess but he. The view of the field & wood at the distance of a quarter of a mile has no property in it.[342]

There are parts of your nature deep & mysterious. I knew a man who stabbed the name & character of another; and at night he saw a murderer's face grinning & gibbering over him.
↑For Demonology see also the extract from Plutarch↓[.] [343]

[124] What can be more clownish than this foolish charging of Miss Martineau with ingratitude for differing in opinion from her southern friends. I take the law of hospitality to be this: I confer on the friend whom I visit the highest compliment, in giving him my time. He gives me shelter & bread. Does he therewith buy my suffrage to his opinions henceforward? No more than by giving him my time, I have bought his. We stand just where we did before. The fact is before we met he was bound to "speak the truth (of me) in love"; [343a] & he is bound to the same now.

On Truth. The story of Capt Ross's company is good example of the policy of honesty. What do the guns speak asked the Esquimaux

[341] This and the preceding paragraph, struck through in pencil with a curved diagonal use mark, are used in "The Head," *Lectures*, II, 256, and "Intellect," *W*, II, 341–342.

[342] This paragraph, struck through in ink with two diagonal use marks, is used in *Nature*, *W*, I, 8.

[343] The "extract" is possibly the "Plutarchiana" of p. [116] above, or perhaps the version of a passage in "A Discourse concerning Socrates's Daemon," *Plutarch's Morals*, 1718, II, 409–410, quoted in the lecture on "Demonology" (1839): see Berry, *Emerson's Plutarch*, 1961, pp. 154–155.

[343a] Cf. Eph. 4:15.

when they saw the English levelling them. The English replied that they told what Esquimaux stole files & iron. Where shall I find seals & musk oxen said the Esquimaux. The English ventured to point where, & the hunter was lucky.

Presently the Esquimaux boy was killed by an accident & the tribe ascribed it to English magic & had almost exterminated the English crew.[344]

Then the saying of G. Fox's father, "Truly I see that if a man will but stand by the truth it will carry him out."[345]

Then the sublimity of keeping one's word across years & seas.[346]

[125] ↑B.C. 317↓

Attica had 720 square miles with a population of 527 000 souls, & nearly four fifths of that number were slaves.

21 Jany. The Spartan is respectable & strong who speaks what must be spoken; but these gay Athenians that go up & down the world making all talk a Recitation, talking for display, disgust.

[January] 22. A man is a method; a progressive arrangement; a selecting principle gathering his like to him wherever he goes.[347] "Half is more than the whole."[348] Yes let the man of taste be the selector & Half is a good deal better than the whole or an infinitesimal part becomes a just representative of the Infinite. A man of taste sent into Italy shall bring me a few objects that shall give me more

---

[344] The anecdote is reported in Sir John Ross, *Narrative of a Second Voyage in Search of a North-West Passage, and of a Residence in the Arctic Regions* (London, 1835), pp. 284, 322, 341–342.

[345] Cf. George Fox, *A Journal* . . . , 1800, I, 166; see "George Fox," *Lectures*, I, 177.

[346] "On Truth . . . & seas." is struck through in pencil with a vertical use mark. The first two paragraphs are used in "Prudence," *Lectures*, II, 318–319.

[347] See *JMN*, III, 299, n. 91a, which cites *The Friend*, 1818, III, 179; "improgressive arrangement is not Method . . . ." The phrase "progressive arrangement," which recurs in Coleridge's "Preliminary Treatise on Method," *Encyclopædia Metropolitana*, 1829–1845, I, 12, is used in *Nature*, W, I, 36. "A man is . . . goes." is used in "Spiritual Laws," W, II, 144.

[348] Cf. "The half is better than the whole," in Thomas Fielding [John Wade], *Select Proverbs of All Nations* (New York, 1825), p. 21.

lively & permanent pleasure than galleries, cities, & mountain chains. ↑A man is a choice.↓ [349]

I think profanity to be as real a violation of nature as any other crime. I have as sensible intimations from within of any profanation as I should have if I stole.[350]

Upham [351] thinks it fatal to the happiness of a young man to set out with ultra conservative notions in this country. He must settle it in his mind that the human race have got possession and though they will make many blunders & do some great wrongs yet on the whole will consult the interest of the Whole.

[126]   "Let not the mouse of my good meaning, Lady,
             Be snapped up in the trap of your suspicion,
             To lose the tail there, either of her truth,
             Or swallowed by the cat of misconstruction"
                            Ben Jonson Tale of a Tub
                                Act IV Scene IV [ll. 25–28]

             "Wherein Minerva had been vanquished
                Had she by it her sacred looms advanced
             And thro' thy subject woven her graphick thread" [351a]
                            Geo Chapman on Sejanus [ll. 25–27]

[127] Swedenborg finely said that in heaven the oldest angels ⟨apt⟩ have the youngest faces; [n]
    that in the spiritual world the monks who tried to pronounce the words of a doctrine which they did not believe twisted & folded their lips to indignation but could not. Apoc[alypse] Rev[ealed, 1836] Vol 1   p 255 [352]
    ⟨the more a man feels himself to be the Lord's the more distinctly he perceives himself to be his own⟩

    [349] This paragraph is struck through in pencil with a vertical use mark.
    [350] This paragraph, struck through in pencil with a vertical use mark, is used in "Holiness," *Lectures*, II, 344.
    [351] Reverend Charles Wentworth Upham of Salem, Harvard classmate and friend of Emerson.
    [351a] See *JMN*, IV, 438, n. 36.
    [352] "Swedenborg finely . . . p 255" is struck through in ink with a vertical use mark. See *JMN*, IV, 342–343; p. [4] above; and "Spiritual Laws," *W*, II, 157.

"That man, in proportion as he is more nearly conjoined to the Lord, in the same proportion appeareth to himself more distinctly to be his own & perceiveth more evidently that he is the Lord's."

He found in the spiritual world disputants in a hut and a window was suddenly made on the ⟨left⟩ right side of it & "then I heard them complain that they were in darkness.[353] These spent all their time in disputation & they were entirely ignorant that the all of faith is truth & the all of charity, good; and that truth without good, is not truth in spirit; and that good without truth, is not good in spirit; & that thus one makes or completes the other. The reason why darkness ensued when a window was made on the right side, is, because light flowing in from heaven on that side affects the will; & the reason why there was light when the window on the right side was shut & another was made on the left, is, because light flowing in from heaven on the left side, affects the understanding, & man may be in the light of heaven as to his understanding provided the will be closed as to its evil." Apoc. Rev. Vol 1 p 345 [misquoted]

"Interiors associate all in the spiritual world." [*Ibid.*,] p 145 [354]
"Satans appear in the light of heaven like dead corpses & some of them black like mummies [355] —— they are all as to their faces & bodies monstrous, yet, in their own light, which is like the light of a coal fire, they appear not as monsters but as men. This is granted them for the sake of consocation[.]" [*Ibid.*, p]p. [145–]146 [356]

[128] The Scholar works with invisible tools to invisible ends. So passes for an idler or worse; brain sick; defenceless to idle carpenters, masons, & merchants, that having done nothing most laboriously all day pounce on him fresh for spoil at night. ↑p. 60. 45↓ Character founded on natural gifts as specific & as rare as military genius; the power to stand *beside* his thoughts, or, to hold off his thoughts at arm's length & give them perspective; to form il piu nell' uno; [357]

---

[353] "He found . . . darkness." is struck through in ink with a vertical use mark.
[354] The quotation is struck through in ink with a vertical use mark.
[355] " 'Satans . . . mummies" is struck through in ink with a vertical use mark.
[356] The extracts from Swedenborg are concluded on p. [192] below.
[357] *Specimens of the Table Talk of the Late Samuel Taylor Coleridge*, 1835, II, 11: "The old definition of beauty in the Roman school of painting was, *il piu nell' uno* — multitude in unity . . . ." The Italian phrase is used in "Michel Angelo

he studies the art of solitude (⟨J 1831⟩ ↑See above↓ p. 60) he is gravelled in every discourse with common people (J 1833[–1834,] p 119).³⁵⁸   He shows thought to be infinite which you had thought exhausted (see above p. 60). There is a real object in nature to which the grocer turns, the intellectual man (J 1833 p 137)[.]³⁵⁹

                    praestantia norat
      Plurima, mentis opes amplas sub pectore servans
      Omnia vestigans sapientum docta reperta.
           Empedoc[les]. de Pythag[oras]. Cudworth II. 271 ³⁶⁰

So Bacon's globe of crystal & globe of matter[.]³⁶¹
The Thinker like Glauber keeps what others throw away[.]
He is aware of God's ⟨met⟩ way of hiding things i.e. in light;
Also he knows all by one (See above p 117)[.]
Set men upon thinking & you have been to them a god.³⁶² All history is poetry; the globe of facts whereon they trample is bullion to the scientific eye. Meanest life a thread of empyrean light. Scholar converts for them the dishonored facts ⟨wherein they know⟩ which they know, into trees of life; their daily routine into a garden of God by suggesting the principle which classifies the facts. We ⟨stand⟩ build the sepulchers of our fathers: can we never behold the Universe as new and ↑feel↓ that we have a stake as much as our predecessors[?]³⁶³

Buonaroti," *Lectures*, I, 101, and *Nature*, *W*, I, 24; an English version is found in "The Eye and Ear," *Lectures*, II, 264.
    ³⁵⁸ See *JMN*, IV, 354.
    ³⁵⁹ Cf. *JMN*, IV, 370.
    ³⁶⁰ "He knew many outstanding things, guarding vast treasures in his heart, investigating all the discovered learned matter of wise men" (Ed.). Cudworth, *The True Intellectual System of the Universe*, 1820, citing "Porphyry, de vit. Pyth."
    ³⁶¹ Cf. *Of the Advancement of Learning*, Bk. II, in *The Works*, 1824, I, 200: "it is the perfect law of inquiry of truth, 'that nothing be in the globe of matter, which should not be likewise in the globe of crystal, or form;' that is, that there be not any thing in being and action, which should not be drawn and collected into contemplation and doctrine." See "Lord Bacon," *Lectures*, I, 327; "The Head," *Lectures*, II, 252.
    ³⁶² (1) Johann Rudolf Glauber (1604–1688) was a German alchemist and physician (*JMN*, IV, 255); Emerson apparently thought of him as a "true chemist" (p. [102] above). (2) See p. [83] above: "God hides the stars in . . . light." (3) See p. [85] above: "He shall be as a god . . . who can rightly define & divide."
    ³⁶³ This sentence is used in *Nature*, *W*, I, 3.

[129]   Shakspeare born in 1564
                              died   1616, aged 52

                         ———

                    Ben Jonson born 1574
                              died   1637, aged 63

                Robert Herrick, born 1591   death unknown

William Shakspeare older than Jonson by ten years
                    and older than Herrick by twenty seven years

John Milton born in Bread st. London, 9th December 1608
                    eight years before the death of Shakspear

[130] 24 Jan. Cudworth is an armory for a poet to furnish himself withal. He should look at every writer in that light & read no poor book. Why should the poet bereave himself of the sweetest as well as grandest thoughts by yielding deference to the miserly indigent unbelief of this age & leaving God & moral nature out of his catalogue of beings? I know my soul is immortal if it were only by the sublime emotion I taste in reading these lines of Swedenborg. "The organical body with which the soul clothes itself is here compared to a garment because a garment invests the body & the soul also puts off the body & casts it away as old clothes (exuviae) when it emigrates by means of death from the natural world into its own spiritual world."

Influx. p 26 [364]

Feb. 8. "The sinner is the savage who hews down the whole tree in order to come at the fruit."

Puckler Muskau describes the English dandy. "His highest triumph is to appear with the most wooden manners as little polished as will suffice to avoid castigation; nay to contrive even his civilities so that they may appear as near as may be to affronts. Instead of a

[364] Cf. Swedenborg, *On the Intercourse between the Soul and the Body, which is supposed to take place either by Physical Influx, or by Spiritual Influx, or by Pre-Established Harmony* (Boston, 1828).

noble high bred ease — to have the courage to offend against every restraint of decorum: to invert the relation in which our sex stands to women so that they appear the attacking & he the passive or defensive party; &c[.]" [365]

Women have less accurate measure of time than men. There is a clock in Adam: none in Eve.

It seems to me that the Creation is, according to the sentiment of Diogenes, [131] a perpetual festival to the wise man.[366] That to the lover of nature is ⟨perpetual⟩ immortal youth and I see not when I am in the woods how I should grow weary in a thousand years.[367]

Taste tyrannizes in England.

"Great poets work like Nature herself. To every man they assume the garb & color of his own mind and thence admit of various interpretations. They are so rich that they distribute their gifts among a thousand poor & yet have abundance in reserve." Puckler M[uskau] p. 221 [368]

↑Autobiography↓

———

My pill is the sun.

———

The body of man is the temple of ⟨g⟩God.[369]

———

Always is love noble & there is no penitence to it. Remember the giving girl with the beaming eye.[370]

———

Strange is this alien ⟨power⟩ ↑despotism↓ of Sleep which takes

[365] Cf. *Tour in England, . . . by a German Prince,* 1833, p. 268. The paragraph is struck through in pencil with a diagonal use mark.
[366] Cf. "Of the Tranquillity of the Mind," *Plutarch's Morals,* 1718, I, 159.
[367] This paragraph, struck through in ink with three wavy diagonal use marks on p. [130] and two on p. [131], is used in *Nature, W,* I, 9–10.
[368] Cf. *Tour in England, . . . by a German Prince,* 1833.
[369] Cf. I Cor. 3:16, 17; 6:19. "Autobiography . . . God." is struck through in pencil with a diagonal use mark. Cf. "the sun your pill," "Prudence," *Lectures,* II, 323.
[370] Possibly a recollection of Ellen Tucker Emerson. This paragraph is struck through in pencil with two diagonal use marks.

two persons lying in each other's arms & separates them leagues, continents, asunder.

———

March 3.

The philosopher, the priest, hesitates to receive money for his instructions, — the author for his works. Instead of this scruple let them make filthy lucre beautiful by its just expenditure.

It becomes the young American to learn the geography of his country in these days as much as it did our fathers to ⟨learn the⟩ know ↑the↓ streets of their town; for steam & rails convert roads into streets & regions into neighborhoods. ↑Steam realizes the story of Aeolus' bag. It carries the 32 winds in the boiler.↓ [371]

[132] *Sentences of Confucius* from Marshman's Confucius

———

Have no friend unlike yourself. [p. 36] [372]

———

Chee is now able to quote the See. "Tell him the past, and he knows what is to come." [p. 66]

———

Chee says, grieve not that men know not you; grieve that you are ignorant of men. [p. 68, misquoted]

———

Chee-yaou enquired respecting filial piety. Chee says, The filial piety of the present day is esteemed merely ability to nourish (a parent.) This care is extended to a dog or a horse. Every domestic animal can obtain food. Beside veneration what is the difference? [p. 94] [373]

———

How can a man remain concealed! How can a man remain concealed! [p. 103] [374]

———

[371] "Steam realizes . . . boiler." is struck through in ink with a diagonal use mark. This figure is used in *Nature*, *W*, I, 13.

[372] *The Works of Confucius; Containing the Original Text, with a Translation . . . by Joshua Marshman*, 1 vol. only (Serampore, 1809), which Emerson borrowed from the Boston Athenaeum, February 16 — March 1, 1836. The first quotation is used in "Society," *Lectures*, II, 104.

[373] This paragraph is struck through in pencil with a diagonal use mark. The comment is used in "The Heart," *Lectures*, II, 282.

[374] In Marshman, both sentences are interrogative; they are so used in "Ethics," *Lectures*, II, 150, and "Spiritual Laws," *W*, II, 159.

Chee entered the great temple. Frequently enquiring about things, one said, Who says that the son of the Chou man understands propriety? In the great temple he is constantly asking questions. Chee heard & replied, "This is propriety." [p. 175]

———

Chee says, If in the morning I hear about the right way, & in the evening die, I can be happy[.] [p. 226]

———

Chee says A man's life (i.e. existence) is properly connected with virtue. The life of the evil man is preserved by mere good fortune[.] [p. 384] [375]

———

Mung-chee-fwan was not a boaster. His troop flying, he placed himself in the rear to repel the pursuing enemy. Yet when entering the gate of the city he beating his horse said, "It was not my management which placed me in the rear. My horse did [133] not move forward." [p. 377]

———

Chee says, A wise & good man was Hooi. A piece of bamboo was his dish; a cocoa nut his cup; & his dwelling was a miserable shed. Men could not sustain the sight of his wretchedness; but Hooi did not change his serenity of mind. A wise & good man was Hooi. [p. 367, misquoted] [376]

———

Chee says, Coarse rice for food, water to drink, and the bended arm for a pillow; happiness may be enjoyed even in these. Without virtue both riches & honor seem to me ⟨a⟩↑like the↓ passing cloud. [p. 456, misquoted] [377]

———

⟨Choo⟩ Koong Chee is a man who through his earnestness in seeking knowledge forgets his food and in his joy for having found it loses all sense of his toil; who thus occupied is unconscious that he has almost arrived at old age. [pp. 462, 464, misquoted] [378]   ↑J[ournal B]. p. 275↓

———

In forming a mountain, were I to stop when one basket of earth is lacking, I actually stop; and in the same manner, were I to add to the

[375] Of these two paragraphs, struck through in pencil with three diagonal use marks, the first is used in "Character," W, X, 117, and the second in "Religion," *Lectures*, II, 88.

[376] This paragraph, struck through in pencil with a diagonal use mark, is used in "Religion," *Lectures*, II, 88.

[377] This paragraph, struck through in pencil with a diagonal use mark, is used in "Religion," *Lectures*, II, 88.

[378] The quotation, struck through in ink with a wavy diagonal use mark, is copied on p. [275] below.

level ground though but one basket of earth daily, I really go forward. [p. 626]

Chee says of Gnan-in I saw him continually advance, but I never saw him stop in the path of knowledge. [p. 629]

The general of a large army may be overcome, but you cannot overcome the determined mind even of a peasant. [p. 637]

[134]

Chee says Yaou is the man who in torn clothes or common apparel sits with those dressed in furred robes without feeling shame. [p. 639]

The flower of the Thong-ti moving, bends itself from side to side: — and does not my heart thus tend towards you? But far distant is your abode. [p. 647]

Chee was in the Chi country for three months hearing Sun's music & knew not the taste of his meat. He said, "I had no idea of music arriving at this degree of perfection." [p. 448]

To worship at a temple not your own is mere flattery. [p. 135]

[135] Feb.

"Nothing is complete until it is enacted. A fact is spirit having completed its mission, attained its end, fully revealed itself." Alcott MS. [p. 135, misquoted] [379]
"The miracles of a religion, the facts of a religion are the illustrations of the spiritual power of that religion. The more of the supernatural the religion embodies, the stronger the evidence in its favor, provided there be no infraction of spiritual laws; no surrender of the supernatural to the natural; no trenching of matter on spirit." *Alcott.* [*Ibid.*, p. 136]

"Her dreams are so vivid & impressive that they are taken for realities

---

[379] "Psyche. Or the Breath of Childhood" (1835–1836), a composition based on Alcott's observations of the growth of his infant daughters. (The unpublished manuscript, Alcott's journals, and other papers were deposited in the Houghton Library by Mrs. Frederic Wolsey Pratt in 1960.) According to Alcott's journal, Wednesday, February 3, 1836, Emerson had taken the manuscript to Concord "for criticizing" on February 1; his comments appear in a letter to Alcott of February 27 (*L*, II, 4–6). He again examined the manuscript, as Alcott revised it, in August of 1836, March of 1837, and June of 1838 (*L*, II, 32, n. 98; 62, 138–141).

of sense, & she refers to them afterwards as facts in her experience. So strong is her faith in them, that no reasoning, not even the faith she places in the assurance of her parents, makes her relinquish the conviction[.]

"Thus unconsciously even to us perchance doth our waking & sleeping life coalesce, & lose their separate forms in our predominating sentiment or idea, & take a common unity in the spirit from whence they sprung into life & shaping." *Alcott.* [*Ibid.*, pp. 167–168]

[136] Feb. 24, 1836. We are idealists whenever we prefer an idea to a sensation, as when we make ⟨sa⟩ personal sacrifices for the sake of freedom or religion. Religion does that for the uncultivated which philosophy does for ⟨Hume⟩ Berkel⟨y⟩ey & Viasa; — makes the mountains dance & smoke & disappear before the steadfast gaze of the Reason. When the eye of Reason is closed the animal eye is very clear & sees outlines & surfaces with preternatural distinctness; when the eye of Reason opens, — to the clear outline & surface is added color & grace not natural but supernatural, the gift of fancy, imagination, affection; as the eye of Reason grows more clear & strong, the outlines & surfaces become so transparent as to be no longer seen & causes & spirits are seen through them.[380]

As character is more to us, ⟨we cease to have r⟩ our fellowmen cease to exist to us in space & time, & we hold them by real ties. ↑V[ide]. p. 64↓

The Idealist regards matter scientifically. The sensualist exclusively.

The physical sciences are only well studied when they are explored for ideas. The moment the law is attained i.e. the Idea, the memory disburthens herself of her Centuries of observation, her[381]

The book is always dear which has made us for moments idealists. ⟨He who⟩ ↑That which↓ can dissipate this block of earth into shining ether is genius.

I have no ⟨hostility⟩ ↑hatred↓ to the round earth & its gray mountains. I see well enough the sand hill opposite my window.

---

[380] "Religion does . . . them.", struck through in ink with five diagonal and three wavy diagonal use marks, is used in *Nature*, *W*, I, 58, 49–50.

[381] This uncompleted paragraph is struck through in ink with one diagonal and one wavy diagonal use mark.

I see with as much pleasure as another a field of corn or a rich pasture, whilst I dispute their absolute [137] being. Their phenomenal being, I no more dispute than I do my own. I do not dispute but point out the just way of viewing them.[382]

Religion makes us idealists. Any strong passion does. The best[,] the happiest moments of life are these delicious awakenings of the higher powers & the reverential withdrawing of nature before its god.[383]

It is remarkable that the greater the material apparatus the more the material disappears, as in Alps & Niagara, in St Peter's & Naples.

We are all aiming to be idealists & covet the society of those who make us so, as, the sweet singer, the orator, the ideal painter. What nimbleness & buoyancy the conversation of the spiritualist produces in us. We tread on air[;] the world begins to dislimn.[384]

For the education of the Understanding the earth & worlds serve. It takes the first steps by geology, astronomy, zoology, to learn that nature's dice are always loaded;[385] that in the most promiscuous heaps & rubbish, an informed eye can find harmonious, inevitable, & beneficial results, and these are premises to the later conclusion that matter flows out from spirit, & does not find its cause in itself.

How calmly & nobly the mind apprehends one after another the laws of physics, how divine emotions dilate the mortal as he enters into the counsels of the Creation, & feels by knowledge the privilege *to be*. ⟨Every⟩ His insight refines him. The beauty of nature shines in his own breast. Man is greater because he can see this, and

---

[382] This paragraph is used in *Nature*, W, I, 59.

[383] This paragraph, struck through in ink with three diagonal use marks, is used in *Nature*, W, I, 50.

[384] "What nimbleness . . . dislimn." is struck through in ink with four wavy diagonal use marks. For the last two sentences, see p. [108] above.

[385] In "Worship," W, VI, 221, is the observation that "the dice are loaded"; in "Compensation," W, II, 102, is this sentence: "Ἀεὶ γὰρ εὖ πίπτουσιν οἱ Διὸς κύβοι, — The dice of God are always loaded." Cf. No. 895 in *The Fragments of Sophocles*, ed. A. C. Pearson, 3 vols. (Cambridge, 1917), III, 84.

the Universe less because time & space relations vanish as laws are known.[386]

[138] Nature ⟨bec⟩ from an immoveable God ⟨by which we were born⟩ on which as reptiles we creep, & to which we must conform our being, becomes an instrument, & serves us with all her kingdoms. Then becomes a spectacle.

To the rude it seems as if Matter had absolute existence, existed from an intrinsic necessity. The first effect of thought is to make us sensible that Spirit exists from an intrinsic necessity, that Matter has a merely phenomenal or accidental being, ⟨ex⟩ being created from Spirit, or being the manifestation of Spirit.

The moment our higher faculties are called into activity we are domesticated, and our awkwardness or torpor or discomfort gives[n] place to natural & agreeable movements.

The first lesson of Religion is, The things that are seen are temporal; the unseen, eternal.[387]

It is easy to solve the problem of individual existence. Why Milton, Shakspear, or Canova should be, there is reason enough. But why the million should exist drunk with the opium of Time & Custom does not appear. If their existence is phenomenal, they serve so valuable a purpose to the education of Milton, that, grant us the Ideal theory, & the Universe ⟨|| . . . ||⟩ solved. Otherwise the moment a man ⟨ascertains⟩ discovers that he has aims which his faculties cannot answer, ⟨&⟩ the world becomes a riddle. Yet Piety restores him to Health.

[139] Feb. 28. Cold bright Sunday morn white with deep snow[.]
C. thinks if a superior being should look into families, he would find natural relations existing, & man a worthy being, but if he followed them into shops, senates, ⟨&⟩ churches, & societies, they would

---

[386] "For the education . . . are known.", struck through in ink with a wavy diagonal use mark, is used in *Nature*, *W*, I, 38–39.
[387] Cf. II Cor. 4:18. This sentence is used in *Nature*, *W*, I, 58.

appear wholly artificial & worthless. Society seems noxious. I believe that against these baleful influences Nature is the antidote. The man comes out of the wrangling of the shop & office, & sees the sky & the woods, & is ⟨himself⟩ ↑a man↓ again. He not only quits the cabal but he finds himself. But how few men can see the sky & the woods!

Good talk today with C. of motives that may be addressed by a wise man to a wise man. 1. Self improvement; & ⟨the⟩ secondly, it were equipollent could he announce that elsewhere companions or a companion were being nourished & disciplined whose virtues & talents might tax all the pupil's faculties in honorable & sweet emulation. C. thinks it a motive also to leave the world richer by some such bequest as the Iliad or Paradise Lost[,] a splendid munificence which must give the man an affection to the race he had benefitted wherever he goes. Another is the Power that virtue & wisdom acquire. The man takes up the world into his proper being. The two oared boat may be swamped in a squall. The vessels of Rothschild every wind blows to port. He insures himself[.]
The Revival that comes next must be preached ⟨on⟩ to man's moral nature, & from a height of principle that subordinates all persons. It must forget historical Christianity and preach God who is, not God who was[.]
[140] ↑Eripitur persona manet res.↓388
It must preach the Eternity of God as a practical doctrine.
God manifest in the flesh of every man is a perfect rule of social life. Justify yourself to an infinite Being in the ostler, and dandy, and stranger, and you shall never repent.
The same view might hinder me from signing a pledge. There is such an immense background to my nature that I must treat my fellow as Empire treats Empire, & God, God. My whole being is to be my pledge & declaration & not a signature of ink.
Distinguish a man's social duties from his personal duties.
That life alone is beautiful which is conformed to an Idea. Let us not live from hand to mouth *now* that we may not *ever*.

388 "The mask is torn off, the man remains." Lucretius, *De Rerum Natura*, III, 57. The original and a translation occur in Montaigne, "That Men are not to judge of our Happiness till after Death," *Essays*, 1693, I, 90.

I would not have a man dainty in his conduct. Let him not be afraid of being besmirched by being advertised in the newspapers, or by going into Atheneums & town meetings, or by making speeches in public. Let his Chapel of private thoughts be so holy that it shall perfume & separate him unto the Lord though he lay in a kennel. Let not a man guard his dignity, but let his dignity guard him.

⟨This⟩ ↑This passing↓ Hour is an edifice
Which the Omnipotent cannot rebuild.[389]

[141] Goethe writes to his friend, 22 Sept. 1787, from Rome, "It is really cheering that these four pretty volumes, the Result of half a life, should seek me out in Rome. I can truly say; there is no word therein which has not been lived, felt, enjoyed, suffered, thought, & they speak to me now all the livelier." Vol 29   p 86.[390]   30 June. "Whilst I of late only things & not as once by & with things see what is not there," — [ibid.,] p. 8[.]

The vessel that carried him from Palermo to Naples was in danger, & the ship's company roared at the master. "The master was silent, & seemed ever to think only of the chance of ⟨rescue⟩ saving the ship; but for me to whom from youth Anarchy was more dreadful than death itself, it was impossible longer to be silent[.]" *Vol.* 28, p. 233.

He writes to Herder "I am ⟨freely⟩ ↑quite↓, as you say, as respects my views, fast nailed to the present, & the more I see the world, the less can I hope that Humanity can be the one wise rational happy Mass. Perhaps there exists among the million worlds one which can boast itself of this privilege. ⟨By⟩ ↑From↓ the constitution of ours

[389] Cf. "Fragments on Nature and Life," *W*, IX, 350.
[390] Emerson is citing Johann Wolfgang von Goethe, *Werke*, 40 vols. (Stuttgart and Tübingen, 1828–1830); in August, 1836, he bought 15 additional volumes of Goethe's *Nachgelassene Werke*, 1832–1833 (*L*, II, 32–33). The latter volumes are numbered both separately (I–XV) and as a continuation of the *Werke* (XLI–LV). Emerson occasionally confused the two series of numbers in later citations (e.g., Journal C, p. [55]), which have been clarified where necessary. Subsequent editorial citations employ the inclusive numbering (I–LV) and dating (*Werke*, 1828–1833) of the entire set.

remains as little for me to hope ↑for it↓, as for Sicily from its constitution." Vol. 28, p. 242.   ↑See what Alva says in Egmont.↓ ³⁹¹

"For the narrow mind, whatever he attempts is still a trade; for the highe⟨st⟩r an art; and the highest, in doing one thing, does all: or, to speak less paradoxically, in the one thing which he does rightly, he sees the likeness of all which is done rightly[.]" ³⁹² Vol. 21   p. 51

Of his resuming the composition of Faust after many years he says, "Whilst I thro' long rest & seclusion am quite restored to the level of my genuine existence, so is it remarkable how much I resemble myself, & how little my inner mind has suffered through years & events." Vol 29. 293.

He says, of the temptation put in his way to buy a statue antique of a muse — "Yea as a proof how much I herein flattered myself [142] the confession may stand, that I esteemed this ⟨even⟩ incident as a wink of the Higher Daemons, who thought to fix me at Rome, & in the most effectual manner to remove all the grounds which influenced me to the resolution to depart." Vol 29. p 337.

"I will no more rest until nothing longer remains to me word and tradition, but lively conception. From youth up, was this my impulse & my torment, and now ⟨that antiquity comes before⟩ ↑whilst age comes upon↓ me will I at least attain the attainable, & do the practicable, whilst I so long deserved or undeserved have borne the fate of Sisyphus & Tantalus." Vol. 29. p. [7]

"In Botany especially have I come upon an εν και παν ³⁹³ which sets me in astonishment. How widely it holds can I even not see. My principle ↑which is↓ to explain works of art and at once to ⟨con-

---

³⁹¹ In Emerson's copy of Goethe's *Werke*, 1828–1833, VIII, 261, there is a marginal line in pencil marking two sentences of Alva's remarks on freedom in Act IV of *Egmont*: "Weit besser ist's sie einzuengen, dass man sie wie Kinder halten, wie Kinder zu ihrem Besten leiten kann. Glaube nur ein Volk wird nicht alt, nicht klug, ein Volk bleibt immer kindisch."

³⁹² This passage occurs in ch. 6 of Goethe's *Wilhelm Meister's Travels*; in *JMN*, IV, 75, Emerson had paraphrased Carlyle's translation of a portion of it. The present version is close enough to Carlyle's rendering to suggest that Emerson may well have consulted his friend's translation as an aid during his own direct grappling with the German text. See *The Works of Thomas Carlyle*, Centenary ed. (London, 1896–1901), XXIV, 228.

³⁹³ "Xenophanes, philosophizing concerning the supreme Deity, was wont to call it ʿεν καὶ πᾶν, one and all — as being one most simple being, that virtually containeth all things" (Cudworth, *The True Intellectual System of the Universe*, 1820, II, 239).

clude that⟩ unriddle that whereon artist & connoisseur have studied
& explored in vain since the Revival of Art. I find ↑it↓ more just at
every application. Truly it is also a Columbus's egg. Without saying
that I possess such a master key, I talk ↑over↓ with artists the parts
so far ↑as↓ is to the purpose, and see how far they are come, what they
have, & what resists it. The door have I open & stand upon the sill,
& would, alas!, go into the temple & then depart. Thus much is certain: the old artists have as great knowledge of Nature and as clear a
conception of what they would represent, & what must be represented,
as Homer. Alas! that the number of works of the first class is so
small. But when we see these, we have nothing to desire but to know
these well, & then go in peace. These great Art-works are, like the
highest works ⟨of⟩ ↑upon↓ Nature of Man, after true & natural laws
executed. ⟨All⟩ Everything arbitrary, fanciful perishes: Where is
Necessity there is God." V. 29. p[p.] 80[-81]   "We must write
as we live[,] first for ourselves then for related beings[.]" 29 Vol.
p III

[143] "The Nature of the Beautiful consists herein that its inner
being ↑wesen↓ lies out of the limits of the cogitative power in its origin
in its own /being./werden./ It is for that reason beautiful, because
the cogitative power, in the presence of the beautiful, can no more
ask, *why is it beautiful*[?]

"Then there lacks to the cogitative power any Standard (point
of comparison) whereby the Beautiful may be considered & estimated.
What is there for a Standard of true Beauty except the entire circuit
of all harmonious relations of the great Whole of Nature, which no
cogitative power can embrace? All particular beauties scattered up
& down in Nature are only so far beautiful as they ⟨in themselves
open⟩ ↑disclose↓ this [Inbegriff] (enclosed space) circuit of all relations of the great Whole more or less, in themselves. There is not a
standard of beauty in the plastic arts even to the degree that a true
imitation of what is beautiful should serve as a model; because the
highest beauty existing in particulars in nature is never sufficiently
beautiful ⟨for the⟩ ↑to be a↓ daring imitation of ⟨of the⟩the great &
majestic ⟨relations⟩ ↑proportions↓ of the all embracing Whole of Nature. The Beautiful therefore can not be understood, it must be *produced* or *felt*.

"And because, in total want of a Standard, the Beautiful is no object of the understanding, — so must we, in so far as we cannot produce it, wholly forego its enjoyment, ⟨had we⟩ ↑whilst at same time we are↓ not ⟨in us ⁿ been⟩ able to find something which came nearer to the beautiful than the Less-beautiful, but for the fact, that, something supplies in us the place of the producing power and comes as near to it as possible [144] without being it, that is, Taste or Susceptibility for the beautiful, which, whilst it remains within its limits, can supply the want of the higher enjoyment, — that, namely, of producing the beautiful, through the undisturbed rest of quiet contemplation.

"When namely the Organ is not ⟨fine enough⟩ close woven enough to present to the in-streaming All of Nature so many points of contact as are necessary in order to re-image in miniature with completeness all her great proportions, and there still is lacking to us a point to the fulfilment of the Circle, then can we, in lieu ⁿ of the Creative, have the Perceiving faculty for the Beautiful. Every experiment to ⟨describe⟩ ↑represent↓ it again, out of us, will miscarry, & make us so much the more dissatisfied with ourselves the nearer our susceptive power borders on the deficient Creative power[.]" Vol 29   p[p.] 311[–313]

The rest is translated in my Goethe Transcript[.] [394]

The expression of the Human Form is much insisted on by Goethe.

"Man is the highest, yea the only object of ⟨the⟩ Plastic Art. In order to understand him; in order to unfold him out of the labyrinth of his Structure is an universal knowledge of organic Nature indispensable." Vol 38 [pp. 10–11]

"Now at last has the Alpha & Omega of all knowables — the manly figure, — laid hold of me, & I of it, and I say; Lord I leave you not until thou blessest me ⟨then⟩, though I should wrestle me lame. At least am I come upon a thought which cheers me much. It were too spacious to detail, and it is better to do [145] than to say.

---

[394] This and the preceding four paragraphs, beginning with " 'The Nature of the Beautiful" on p. [143], are struck through in pencil with vertical use marks. Portions of the third paragraph are used in "Michel Angelo Buonaroti," *Lectures*, I, 101. For the additional translation, see Journal T (Transcript), in *JMN*, VI.

Enough, it ⟨now[?]⟩ amounts to this, —————— that ⟨now⟩ my obstinate study of nature, the care with which I have gone to work in comparative anatomy, now ⟨enable⟩ enable me to see many things in Nature & the Antique, in Whole, which it is difficult for Artists to seek out in ⟨p⟩ detail, and which they, when they at last attain it, only possess for themselves, & cannot impart to others[.]" Vol 29 p 64 [abridged]

"Today I was at the French Academy where ⟨the best statues are ca⟩ stand together casts of the best statues of antiquity. In such presence, man is more than man. We feel that the worthiest object wherewithal to busy us, is the manly form, which we here behold in all its manifold lordliness. Yet who feels not at once at the first view how ⟨unattainable⟩ ↑insufficient↓ ⟨it⟩he is. Though prepared, we stand stupefied. Had I endeavored to unravel for myself in some measure Proportion, Anatomy, Harmony of Motion, yet now ⟨it strongly⟩ I was strongly impressed, that, ↑the↓ Form, at last, comprizes all. ⟨,c⟩Conformity of limbs to the purpose, Proportion, Character, & Beauty." [Vol.] 29   p. 322 [abridged] [395]

"The 21 September was the holiday of St Francis & his blood was carried round the City in a long extended procession of monks & Believers. I was attentive at the passing by of so many monks whose simple clothing draws the eye only to the observation of the head. It struck me that properly hair, & beard belong thereto, in order to make for one's self a conception of the human individual. First with attention, then with astonishment reviewed I the passing train, and was really enraptured to see that a face enclosed by hair & beard in a frame makes quite another figure than the beardless people around. And I could now easily understand that such faces represented in pictures must produce a nameless charm on the beholder." Vol. 29, p[p]. 97 [-98] ——————

[146] Goethe writes from Rome 1787[:] "I have this year given heed among foreigners and found that all efficient intelligent men more or less finer or coarser ⟨thereon stand⟩ hereto come & remain, — that the Moment is everything, and that the privilege of an intelligent man therein ⟨lies⟩ ↑consists↓; so to bear himself that his life

---

[395] This paragraph, struck through in pencil with a diagonal use mark, is used in "The Eye and Ear," *Lectures*, II, 265.

in so far as ⟨it depends on him⟩ ↑in him lies,↓ shall contain the greatest number possible of reasonable happy moments." Vol 29   p 120

"I get very fast a notion of every region, because ⟨I⟩ at the smallest brook I inquire whence it comes and into what river it runs."
Vol 27   p 6

Very much speaks he of the weather[.]

At Trent[:] "And now that it is evening in the mild air little
clouds rest on the mountains; in the sky rather stand than move; and
immediately after sunset the cry of the grasshoppers begins to be
loud, we feel ourselves once more at home in the world, & not as
concealed (geborgt) or in exile. I please myself as if I were here
born & bred, & now returned from a ⟨g⟩Greenland journey, or a
whaling voyage." Vol 27   p 36

It is a favorite work of Goethe to give a theory of every institution, art, art-work, custom which he observes. Thus his explanation
of the Italian Time-measure as growing out of Italian climate; of
the Obelisk of Egypt as growing out of a common natural fracture
in the granite parallelopiped in upper Egypt; of the Doric Architecture and the Gothic; of the Venetian music of the Gondolier originat-
ing in the habit of the fishers' wives of the Lido singing to their husbands on the sea; of the Amphitheatre which is the natural cup that
forms round every sight in the street; of the coloring of Titian &
Paul Veronese, which one may see in daylight in Venice day by day[.]
[147] See Vol 27   p 135; of the Carnival at Rome, of the
domestic rural architecture in Italy Vol 27 p. 190[.]

At Venice. "The Fishmarket & the endless sea products give
me much satisfaction: I go often thither & observe the hapless caught
dwellers of the sea." [XXVI,] p 140

"⟨Today⟩ I go once more with my story to the sea. There today
have I seen the housekeeping of the sea snail, the patellas and ⟨pocket⟩
crabs, & heartily enjoyed the same.

"What a precious noble thing is an animal (lebendig). How
adapted to his place, how true! how being! (seyend). What use I
draw from my slender study of Nature & how I rejoice to continue
it!" [XXVII, 144–145]

"Zoroaster seems first to have ⟨changed⟩ ↑formulated↓ the noble clear /Nature/Natural/-Religion into a circumstantial Cultus. The mental prayer which includes & excludes all Religions, and only in a few God-favored men pervades the whole life's-course, unfolds itself in ⟨the⟩ most men, only as a flaming beatifying feeling of the moment, after whose disappearance, also, the man given back to himself, unsatisfied, unoccupied, ↑lapses↓ into endless ennui." Vol 6. p. 21

13 Aug. Goethe the observer. What sagacity! What[n] industry of observation! What impatience of words! To read Goethe is an economy of time; for you shall find no word that does not stand for a thing, and he is of that comprehension as to see the value of truth. But I am provoked with his Olympian self complacency, "the damned patronizing air" with which ↑he↓ vouchsafes to tolerate the genius & performances of other mortals:[n] the good Hiller, our costly Kant, &c &c.[396] And excellent of this kind is his account of his [148] philosophy in relation to the Kantian, 'that it was an Analogon of that by their confession.'

I read somewhere that "you might find in him sometimes a maxim, but never a sentiment."

I claim for him the praise of truth, of fidelity to his nature. We think when we contemplate the stupendous glory of the world, that it were life enough to one man merely to lift his hands & say Κοσμος! Beauty! Well, this he did. Here is a man who in the feeling that the thing itself was so admirable as to leave all comment behind, merely went up & down, from object to object, lifting the veil from every one & did no more. ⟨His⟩ What he said of Lavater, I may better say of him[,] that "it was fearful to stand in the presence of one before whom all the boundaries within which Nature has circumscribed our being were laid flat ——"[397] His are the "bright & terrible eyes" which meet you in every sacred as in every public enclosure.

---

[396] "But I am . . . Kant, &c &c." is used in "Thoughts on Modern Literature," W, XII, 325.

[397] Cf. JMN, IV, 343. In both allusions Emerson was probably drawing on a secondary source, presumably "Goethe's Posthumous Works," Foreign Quarterly Review, XIV (Aug. 1834), 149, since he did not acquire his set of the Nachgelassene Werke until August, 1836, as noted above.

This is his praise. There is in him nothing heroic. Epaminondas[,] Agis were greater men. Only he is the king of scholars.[398]

Goethe,[n] "whose thoughts acquaint us with our own." [399] "To Göethe there was no trifle." [400]

See what he says of lower & higher powers of the soul. Nachg[elassene]. Werke, Vol. 10 [*Werke*, L], p[p]. 43[–44]

[149] 5 March 1836. A man should stand among his fellow men as one coal lies in the fire it has kindled, radiating heat, but lost in the general flame.[401]

———

Task work is good for idlers, and Man is an idler. Its greatest disadvantage is that when you accept mechanical measures instead of spiritual ones, you are prone to fill up the chasms of your prophecy with prose.

———

The moment we enter into the higher thoughts, fame is no more affecting to the ear than the faint tinkle of the passing sleigh bell[.]

Gradation; that is one of the lessons which human life is appointed to learn. Therefore is space and therefore time, that Man may know things are not huddled & lumped, but sundered & individual: a pump & a plough have each their use & neither can do the office of the other. Water is good to drink, coal to burn, & wool to wear, but wool can not be drunk, nor water spun, nor coal eaten. We never snatch a corkscrew to cut down an oak nor a shoe to sew ↑up↓ a rent in a garment. Yet among men we make analogous blunders without shame. We expect of one, another's talent. We do not separate them & apprehend that each is a system & has ends of his own. The wise man shows his wisdom in separation, in gradation. His scale of creatures & of merits is as wide as nature. The foolish have no range

[398] This and the preceding paragraph are used in "Thoughts on Modern Literature," *W*, XII, 327–328.

[399] Cf. Ebenezer Elliott, "The Village Patriarch," IV, 32: "Wordsworth, 'whose thoughts acquaint us with our own' " — quoted in *JMN*, IV, 361.

[400] Cf. Austin, *Characteristics of Goethe*, 1833, III, 323, and *JMN*, IV, 255.

[401] This sentence, struck through in pencil with a diagonal use mark, is used in "Holiness," *Lectures*, II, 356.

in their scale, but suppose every man is as every other man. What is not good they call the worst,[n] and what is not hateful they call the best.[402]   ↑C thinks that Homer is the first poet, Shakspear the second, and that the third will be greatest of all, the reflective.↓

[150] 5 March. Nature has that congruity that all its parts make a similar impression on one mind; of the beautiful on the poet; of the lucrative on the merchant; &c. In the talk this afternoon I was instructed that every man has certain questions which always he proposes to the Eternal, and that his life & fortune, his ascetic, are so moulded as to constitute the answers, if only he will read his consciousness aright. I ask one question with eagerness: my friend, another. I have no curiosity respecting historical Christianity; respecting persons & miracles: I take the phenomenon as I find it, & let it have its effect on me, careless whether it is a poem or a chronicle. Charles would know whether it covers the dimensions of what is in man; whether the Cross is an idea in the divine mind? I am the practical Idealist in the view mentioned above. The comfort is great of looking out of the straw & rags of our fortune steadfastly to the first Cause, and saying, Whilst I hold my faith, I have the virtue that can turn these cobwebs into majesty, whilst I remain a Watcher for what thought, what Revelation, Thou canst yet impart.[403] For C. fears the degenerating into a vulgar housekeeper.
All cultivation tends steadily to degrade Nature into an organ, ⟨and⟩ a spectacle, an expedient. Man's enchanted dust.[404]

Strange is it to me how man is holden by ⟨the⟩ a curbrein and hindered from knowing, and drop by drop or shade by shade thoughts ↑trickle &↓ loiter ⟨& creep⟩ upon him & no reason under [151] heaven can he give, or get a glimpse of, why he should not grow wiser faster↑, "moving about in worlds not realized[.]"↓[405]

[402] This paragraph through "the best.", struck through in ink with three diagonal use marks, is used in *Nature*, *W*, I, 38.
     [403] "I have no curiosity . . . yet impart." is used in *Nature*, *W*, I, 60.
     [404] The phrase "enchanted dust" is used in "Holiness," *Lectures*, II, 352. Cf. also "The Poet," *W*, IX, 320:
                    "On Nature's wheels there is no rust,
                    Nor less on man's enchanted dust
                    Beauty and Force alight."
     [405] Wordsworth, "Ode: Intimations of Immortality," l. 149.

All things work together for good unto them that love God.[406]
↑No man is the Idealist's Enemy. He accepts all↓[.]

↑see p. 201.↓

———

Last week I went to Salem. At the Lafayette hotel where I
lodged, every five or ten minutes the barkeepers came into the sitting
room to arrange their hair & collars at the looking glass. So many joys
ha⟨ve⟩s the kind God provided for us dear creatures.
⟨Other men wait upon their bowels most of the day.⟩

———

⟨How⟩ March 9. How important is the education of the Understanding may be inferred from the extreme care bestowed upon it.
The care pretermitted in no single case. See this long discipline, day
after day, year after year, never ending, to form the common sense;
this continual reproduction of annoyances, inconveniences, dilemmas;
this rejoicing over us of little men; and all to form the *Hand* of the
Mind,[n] to instruct us that good thoughts are no better than good
dreams unless they be executed.[407]

Godliness. How strange that such a word exists applied to
men! ⟨How came⟩ It was a masterpiece of wisdom to inoculate every
biped crawling round after his bread with this sublime maggot.

March 11. All is in Each. Xenophanes complained in his old
age that all things hastened back to Unity[,] Identity. He was weary
of seeing the same thing in a tedious variety of forms.[408] ↑The Fable
of Proteus has a cordial truth. Every natural↓[409]

[152] The problem which life has to solve is how to exist in

[406] Cf. Rom. 8:28.
[407] Cf. Bacon, "Of Great Place," *The Works*, 1824, II, 276: "For good thoughts
(though God accept them) yet towards men are little better than good dreams, except
they be put in act . . . ." This paragraph, struck through in ink with three wavy
diagonal use marks, is used in *Nature*, W, I, 37. In RO Mind, p. [6], Emerson inserted the phrase "the hand of the mind" in a paragraph treating the Understanding
which is reminiscent of the present passage.
[408] Joseph Marie de Gérando, *Histoire comparée des systèmes de philosophie*, 4
vols. (Paris, 1822–1823), I, 460–461. Cf. *JMN*, III, 266; *JMN*, IV, 298.
[409] Continued on p. [152].

harmonious relation to a certain number of perceptions; ⟨with⟩ such as hunger, thirst, cold, society, self, health, God. It is the problem of three bodies[.] [410]

[411] form to the smallest, a leaf, a sunbeam, a moment of time, a drop, is related to the Whole, & partakes of the beauty of the Whole. This not only where the analogy is very strict, as when we ⟨mark⟩ ↑detect↓ the brother of the human Hand in the fin of the whale & the flipper of the saurus, but ⟨in the widest⟩ between objects where the superficial dissimilarity is striking. Thus "Architecture is frozen music" according to De Stael & Goethe.[412] Haydn's Creation is said to imitate not only movements as the stag's, the snake's, & the elephant's but *colors* as the green grass. More sublimely is this true in man & his action. "The ⟨highest⟩ ↑wise man↓ in doing one thing, does all; or, in the one thing which he does rightly, he sees the likeness of all which is done rightly." [413] Hence I might have said above the value of Proverbs or the ⟨flexibil⟩ significance of every trivial speech as of a blacksmith or teamster concerning his tools or his beasts, Namely, that the same thing is found to hold true throughout Nature. Thus this morning I read in a Treatise on Perspective that "the ⟨object⟩ end of a Picture was to give exclusive prominence to the object represented and to keep out of sight the means whereby it was done." And ⟨mutatis mutandis⟩ [414] change the terms & of what art is not this true? It is an attribute of the Supreme Being so to do & therefore[n] [153] will be met throughout ⟨N⟩Creation. Every primal Truth is alone an expression of all Nature. It is the absolute Ens seen from one side,[415] ⟨There is⟩ and any other truths shall only seem altered expression of this. A leaf is a compend of Nature, and Nature a colossal leaf. An animal is a compend of the World, and the World is an enlargement

[410] This paragraph is struck through in ink with five diagonal use marks.
[411] Continued from p. [151].
[412] See Mme de Staël, *Corinne ou l'Italie*, Bk. IV, ch. 3; cf. *JMN*, IV, 337.
[413] For the quoted sentence see Emerson's translation on p. [141] above of a passage from Goethe, *Werke*, 1828–1833, XXI, 51. Beginning with "All is in Each" on p. [151], the paragraph to this point is struck through in ink with diagonal use marks. The passage is used in *Nature*, W, I, 43–44, 23, and 45, in that order.
[414] "Changing what should be changed" (Ed.).
[415] This clause is used in *Nature*, W, I, 44.

of an animal. There is more family likeness than individuality. Hence Goethe's striving to find the Arch-plant.[416]

21 March. Only last evening I found the following sentence in Goethe, a comment and consent to my speculations on the All in Each in Nature this last week.

"Every existing thing is an analogon of all existing things. Thence appears to us Being ever, at once sundered & connected. If we follow the analogy too far all things confound themselves in identity. If we avoid it, then all things scatter into infinity. In both cases, observation is at a stand, in the one as too lively, in the other as dead." Vol. 22, p. 245

Man is an analogist. And therefore no man loses any time or any means who studies that one thing that is before him, though a log or a snail.

I *waste*, you say, an hour in watching one crab's motions[,] one butterfly's intrigues; I learn therein the whole family of crab & butterfly. I read Man in his remoter symbols.

Only trust yourself, and do the present duty, & God has provided for your access to infinite truths & richest opportunities.

[154] I find an old letter to L[idian]. which may stand here —[417]

Has not life woes enough to drug its children with without their brewing & seething such themselves? Shall they not forget all, renounce all, but the simple purpose to extort as much wit & worth from the departing hour as they jointly can?

It is strange — strangest — this omnipresent riddle of life. Nobody can state it. Speech pants after it in vain. All poetry, all philosophy, in their parts, or entire, never express it, tho' that is still their aim: they only approximate. Nobody can say what every body feels, & what all would

---

[416] See Austin, *Characteristics of Goethe*, 1833, I, 172; *JMN*, IV, 289.

[417] Dated by Rusk "*c.* May? 1835?" (*L*, I, 445) but possibly written in June of that year, like the paragraph that immediately follows on p. [155]. Printed in *J*, IV, 29–30, with alterations in paragraphing, punctuation, and wording: in the opening paragraph, "Shall they" becomes "Should they"; in the final paragraph, "mind" becomes "muse", "of our life" is omitted, and "or malignity" becomes "and malignity". Emerson evidently copied the letter in this context because of its bearing on his recent journal entries concerning Goethe; it is reprinted here for the same reason.

jump to hear, if it should be said, and, moreover, which all have a confused belief *might be* said. Now this open secret, as he called it,[418] is what
our wise but sensual, loved & hated Goethe loved to contemplate, & to
exercise his wits in trying to embody. I have been reading him these two
or three days, & I think him far more lucky than most of his contemporaries at this game.

There sits he at the centre of all visibles & knowables, blowing bubble after bubble so transparent, so round, so coloured, that he thinks &
you think, they are pretty good miniatures of the All. Such attempts are
all his minor poems, proverbs, Xenien Parables. Have you read the Welt
Seele?

The danger of such attempts as this striving to write Universal Poetry
is, — that nothing is so shabby as to fail[.]

You may write an ill romance or play & 'tis no great matter. Better
men have done so, but when what should be greatest [155] truths flat
out into shallow truisms, then are we all sick. But much I fear, that Time,
the serene Judge, will not be able to make out so good a verdict for Goethe
as did & doth Carlyle. I am afraid that under his faith is no-faith, — that
under his love is love-of-ease.[419] However his mind is catholic as ever any
was. x x x x A human soul is an awsome thing, and when this point world,
this something nothing of our life is re-absorbed into the Infinite, let it
be recorded of us that we have not defaced the page of Time with any
voluntary blemish of folly or malignity.

———

Writ June, 1835. It is luxury to live in this beautiful month.
One never dares expect a happy day, but the hardest ascetic may
inhale delighted this breath of June. It is Devil's needle's Day; — I
judge from the millions of sheeny fliers with green body & crape
wing that overhang the grass and water. Then the inertia of my blue
river down there in the grass, is even sublime. Does not this fine
season help to edify your body & spirit[?]

———

[418] Goethe's use of the phrase was familiar to Emerson through its repeated cita-
tion by Carlyle. See *The Works of Thomas Carlyle*, Centenary ed., XXVI, 41, 225;
XXVII, 131, 377; XXVIII, 58; *JMN*, IV, 87, n. 185; 337; "Humanity of Science,"
Lectures, II, 31.

[419] To a family friend, Moncure D. Conway, in 1853, Mrs. Emerson "quoted
verbatim two sentences" from this letter expressing Emerson's "misgivings about
Goethe, beneath whose fine utterances he had found 'no faith.'" See *Autobiography,
Memories and Experiences of Moncure Daniel Conway*, 2 vols. (Boston, 1904), I,
147.

1836. March 14. Misery is superficial and the remedy, when it can be attained, of presenting to the mind Universal Truths, is a perfect one. The wise man, that is, the healthy mind[,] learns that even the corpse has its own beauty; that every event, every pain, every misfortune, seen in the perspective of the past, is beautiful; that we are enbosomed in beauty; and if, in long retrospect, things are yet ugly, it is because the mind is diseased, & the rays [420] [156] are dislocated & not suffered to fall in a focus & so present a just perspective to the Reason. Of course the ⟨obj⟩ aim of the wise physician will then be to repair the general health.   ↑See above p. 111↓

It is a rule of Rhetoric ⟨to use⟩ always to have an eye to the primary sense of the words we use.

↑"The light of the Public Square will best test its merit." *↓ [421]
I cultivate ever ⟨this dogged⟩ my humanity. This I would always propitiate. And judge of a book as a peasant does, not as a book by pedantic & individual measures, but by number & weight, counting the things that are in it. My debt to Plato is a certain number of sentences: the like to Aristotle. A large number, yet still a ⟨certain⟩ ↑finite↓ number, make the ⟨val⟩ worth of Milton & Shakspeare, to me.[422] I would therefore run over what I have written, save ⟨out⟩ the good sentences, & destroy the rest. ↑C. asks if I were condemned to solitude & one book, — which I would choose? We agreed that Milton would have no claims, & that the Bible must be preferred to Shakspear, because the last, one could better supply himself. The first has a higher strain.↓

A miracle is a patch. It is an after thought. The history of Man

↑* M. Angelo Buonaroti↓

[420] The entry to this point is struck through in pencil with a vertical use mark; "even the corpse . . . beauty" is used in *Nature*, *W*, I, 16.
[421] Slightly misquoted from [Thomas Roscoe], "The Life of Michael Angelo Buonaroti," *Lives of Eminent Persons* (London, 1833), p. 72. See *JMN*, IV, 369. The sentence is used in "Spiritual Laws," *W*, II, 155.
[422] " 'The light . . . to me.", struck through in pencil with two diagonal use marks, is used in "Literature," *Lectures*, II, 66.

must be an Idea, a self-existent perfect circle, and admit of no miracle that does not cease to be such, & melt into Nature, when the wise eye is turned upon it.

[157] All things are moral, & thereto is nature thus superfluously magnificent.

For Lect. I Mem. "Shearing the Wolf" [423]
     Matutina & Vespertina Cognitio [424]

Art is a mixture of the human mind with Nature.

17 March. I pitied J[?]. for his ill speaking, until I found him not at all disheartened, not at all curious ⟨of t⟩ concerning the effect of his speech, but ⟨very ready⟩ eager to speak again & speak better on a new matter. Then I see him to be destined to move society.[425]

The Germans as a nation have no taste. ———
The English are the tyrants of taste.
Fine thought was this Chorus of the Greek Drama.[426] It is like the invention of the cipher in Arithmetic; so perfect an aid and so little obvious. An elegant outer conscience to the interlocutors; Charles says it was the Not-Me.

Idealism. Ideas domesticate us.
     Friends become Ideas.
     Virtue, is, subordinating things to thoughts[.]
     In his sensations & perceptions i.e. in Nature, is a

---

[423] See p. [68] above; the expression is used in "English Literature: Introductory," *Lectures*, I, 223.

[424] Cf. notebook Encyclopedia, p. [104]: "The schoolmen said after St Augustine [*De Civitate Dei*, lib. II, ch. 7] that the knowledge of men was Vespertina Cognitio ['an even-tide knowledge'], and that of God Matutina Cognitio ['a knowledge of the morning']. *Norris.*" Cf. Norris, *An Essay Towards the Theory of the Ideal or Intelligible World*, pt. 1, 1701, p. 159. The figure is used in *Nature*, W, I, 73.

[425] "Art is a mixture . . . society." is struck through in pencil with a diagonal use mark. With the first sentence cf. *Nature*, W, I, 5, 24. The paragraph following the first sentence is used in "Being and Seeming," *Lectures*, II, 300.

[426] Emerson and his brother Charles were reading the *Electra*: see Charles's letter of March 18, p. [180] below.

perfect order not violable by him. In himself as much Disorder as Vice. Nature is therefore an everlasting Hint.

Magnanimity consists in scorning Circumstance[.]

"Our country is where we can live as we ought[.]" [427]

Utterance is place enough. [428]

[158] Goethe moralizes on the Roman Carnival, and shows it as an emblem of human life. [429] And so is every feast, & every assembly, and every institution — , and every work, and every spectacle. "Tobacco Spiritualized" was the title of a poem, I read when a child. [430] A nation represents the world; a town the world; a family, the world; a man, the world. εν και παν. A Day is a miniature Eternity; an hour, a moment, is the same. A child's game hints to an intelligent beholder all the attributes of the Supreme Being.

An intelligent painter, for example, cannot give rules for his art, or suggest hints for the correction or direction of his scholar, without saying what is pertinent & true to a far greater extent than the circle of painting. ↑e.g.↓ "No great painter is nice in pencils." "Nulla dies sine linea[.]" [431]

_____

How eagerly men seize on the classification of phrenology which gives them, as they think, an Idea, whereby the most familiar & important facts are arranged. Much more heartily do they open themselves to a true & divine Idea, as that of Freedom or Right. See the Orator, by a few sharp & skilful statements, unite his various audience, & whilst they stand mute & astonished, he touches their hearts as harp strings, ⟨and⟩ until, in the presence of the aroused Reason, Good & Fair become practicable, and the gravest obstacles are swept away like the morning cloud. Under the stupendous domin-

[427] Cf. letter to Peter Heimbach, August 15, 1666, in *The Prose Works of John Milton*, ed. Charles Symmons, 7 vols. (London, 1806), VII, 456.

[428] See p. [49] above: "In Heaven, utterance is place enough." The expression occurs in "Ethics," *Lectures*, II, 147.

[429] See the concluding paragraph of "Das Römische Carneval," *Werke*, 1828–1833, XXIX, 228–276.

[430] Possibly Ralph Erskine's "Smoking Spiritualized"; see his *Gospel Sonnets; or, Spiritual Songs* (Lansingburgh, 1806), pp. 323–324.

[431] "No day without a line." See Pliny, *Natural History*, XXXV, xxxvi, 84, n.

ion of Ideas, individual interests, even personal identity, melt into the swelling surges of the Universal Humanity.[432]   ↑Eloquence is the voice of Virtue & Truth.↓

———

[159] "All which we call invention, discovery, in the higher sense, is the important practice or setting at work of an original perception of truth which long formed in silence, unexpectedly, as with lightning speed, leads to a useful cognition. It is an opening that is made from the Inner to the Outward which lets man anticipate his resemblance to God. It is a synthesis of the World & the Spirit which gives the most blessed assurance of the eternal harmony of Being." Goethe [*Werke*, 1828–1833,] 22 Vol   p[p. 247–]248

"Things must be ↑described as↓ separated, ⟨in order to be described⟩: Physics from mathematics. The former must stand in a discriminate independence and must seek to penetrate with loving venerable pious powers into nature & sacred life itself, quite careless what the Mathematics on its side may do. This on the contrary must explain itself independent of all Externals, go its own great spirit's-way, and clearly form itself as it can when it, as hitherto, deals with the Present, and endeavors to win something or accommodate something to it."   [XXII, 250–251]

"The Poet aims to represent. The highest is attained when he vies with reality; i.e. when his descriptions are lively to that degree that they have on every man the effect of presences. At its summit poetry seems quite external. The more it withdraws itself inward, is it on the decline. Those who describe the inner without embodying it in an outward; or those who describe the outward without making the soul felt through it, are both on the last step from which we pass into common life[.]" Vol. 22, p. 234.[n]

"Literature is the fragment of fragments. The least of what was done or said was written. Of what was written the least part has remained." Id[em]. 235

[432] "See the Orator . . . Humanity.", struck through in pencil with two vertical use marks, is used in "Society," *Lectures*, II, 110.

↑"The question 'whence had the poet this?' refers to the *What* not the *How*." Ib[id].↓

[160] At Spoleto, Goethe saw the Aquaduct which like a bridge leads from one mountain to the other. "The ten arches which reach across the valley stand of brick so quietly for their ⟨thousand years⟩ milleniums and the water flows ever yet into Spoleto into all parts & corners. This is now the third work of the Ancients which I have seen and ever the same great mind. A second nature which acts for municipal purposes, that is their Architecture, so stands the Amphitheatre, the temple, and the Aquaduct." Vol 27   p[p. 192–]193

Edward B. Emerson   C.C.E. writes to M.M.E. Jan. 26, 1833[:]

"Edward *has* a soul in him, — no shadow at all, — though Sarah Alden [433] say it, but a large & glowing soul — lighted up by fits with the flame of an irregular genius, — but always odorous with the perfume of a taintless generosity. He is far greater & more admirable than when he was most admired."

[161] 21 March. How well men know in what churches & individuals the religious principle is found. Yet we think we can convince men, by talking, ⟨of our being⟩ that we are in the right. All the reasons in the world may be piled together, all the solemn words in the language may be repeated, yet if only the Understanding is addressed your cause is not won. But let a graceless and ignorant man arise who is now exercised by the religious sentiment[,] who follows after the beauty of holiness and he out of his heart will speak to yours. His words are loaded. They penetrate into the soul and will call up the deep & divine powers from their long sleep, and the awestruck understanding shall now be still & docile. Let the laws of thought be stated, & people learn that ⟨primary⟩ master rule of Rhetoric, that things go by number & weight and pass for what they be, not by seeming.

I thought yesterday morning of the sweetness of that fragrant piety which is almost departed out of the world, which makes the

[433] Mrs. Samuel Ripley, née Sarah Alden Bradford.

genius of A-Kempis, Scougal, Herbert, Jeremy Taylor. It is a beautiful mean[,] equidistant from the hard sour iron Puritan on one side,
& the empty negation of ↑the↓ Unitarian on the other. It is the spirit
of David & of Paul. Who shall restore to us the odoriferous Sabbaths
which that Sweet Spirit bestowed on human life, and which made the
earth and the humble roof a sanctity? This spirit of course involved
that of Stoicism, as in its turn Stoicism did this. Yet how much more
attractive & true that this Piety should be the Central trait and the
stern virtues follow than that Stoicism should face the Gods & put
Jove on his defence. That sentiment [162] is a refutation of every
skeptical doubt. David is a beauty, and read 3d chapter of Ephesians.

And yet I see not very well how the rose of Sharon could bloom
so freshly in our affection but for these ancient men who like great
gardens with banks of flowers do send out their perfumed breath
across the great tracts of time. How needful is Paul & David, Leighton, A Kempis, & Fenelon to our Idea. Of these writers, of this spirit
that deified them, I will say with Confucius, "If in the morning, I
hear about the right way, & in the evening die, I can be happy[.]" [434]

↑Idealism↓

Life, Action, is perfected Science. Under strong virtuous excitement, we contemn the body.

Without the ideas of God, Freedom, Virtue, Love, in his *head*,
man would be vermin: but put them in his *heart* and he is one with
God.

All is naught without the Idea which is its nucleus & soul: for
this reason no natural fact interests until ⟨set down in a book⟩ connected with man.

[163] [435] 1836

22 March. It is now four months that we have had uninterrupted
sleighing in Concord; and today it snows fast.

I admire specially three advantages of civilization: the post
office, the newspaper, and the road. Hereby the human race ⟨do⟩ ↑run

[434] For the quotation, see p. [132] above. This and the preceding paragraph,
struck through in pencil with a diagonal and a vertical use mark, are used in "Religion," *Lectures*, II, 93–94, and "Boston," *W*, XII, 193–195.

[435] In the center of this page beneath "in the sunshine . . . a bird." is partially
erased pencil writing, circled: "This my Home is an edifice ⟨‖ . . . ‖⟩ cannot rebuild".
See p. [140] above.

on↓ my errands⟨, for me;⟩; the human race read & write of all that happens for me; the human race ↑turn out, every morning, and↓ shovel away the snow and cut a path for me.⁴³⁶

It is a small & mean thing to attempt too hardly to disprove the being of Matter. I have no hostility to oxygen or hydrogen, to the sun or the hyacinth that opened this morning its little censer in his beam. This is not for one of my complexion who do expand like a plant in the sunshine[,] who do really love ⟨nature⟩ ↑the warm day↓ like an Indian or a bird. I only aim to speak for the Great Soul; to speak for the sovereignty of Ideas[.] ⁴³⁷

⟨Classification is⟩ Science immature is arbitrary classification. Science perfect is classification through an Idea.⁴³⁸

27 March. Man is an analogist.⁴³⁹ He cannot help seeing every thing under its relations to all other things & to himself. The most conspicuous example of this habit of his mind is his naming the Deity Father.⁴⁴⁰   The delight that man finds in classification is the first index of his Destiny. He is to put Nature under his feet by a ⟨true Order of⟩ⁿ ↑knowledge of↓ Laws. Phrenology
Ethics again is ⟨the living⟩ ↑to live↓ Ideas[.] ⁴⁴¹
Science to apprehend Nature in Ideas   The moment an idea is introduced among facts the God takes possession. Until then, facts conquer us. The Beast rules Man.

Thus through Nature is there a striving ⟨for⟩ upward. Commodity points to a greater good. Beauty is nought until the spiritual element. Language refers to that which is to be said[.] ⁴⁴²

---

⁴³⁶ This paragraph, struck through in ink with three wavy diagonal use marks, is used in *Nature, W*, I, 14.
⁴³⁷ This paragraph, struck through in ink with four wavy diagonal use marks, is used in *Nature, W*, I, 59.
⁴³⁸ This paragraph is struck through in ink with a wavy diagonal use mark. On "arbitrary classification" cf. "Humanity of Science," *Lectures*, II, 37.
⁴³⁹ See p. [153] above.
⁴⁴⁰ "Man is an . . . Father.", struck through in ink with three wavy diagonal use marks, is used in *Nature, W*, I, 27.
⁴⁴¹ Cf. *Nature, W*, I, 57: religion and ethics "may be fitly called the practice of ideas, or the introduction of ideas into life . . . ."
⁴⁴² "Commodity," "Beauty," "Language," and "Discipline" (p. [165]) became the titles of chapters II, III, IV, and V, respectively, of *Nature*. The phrase "a striving

[164] He only is a good writer who keeps but one eye on his page and with the other sweeps over things. So that every sentence brings us a new contribution of observation.

This is spotless
That is not less.

March 28. "All that frees ⟨the Spirit⟩ ↑Talent↓ without ⟨giving⟩ increasing ⟨its co⟩ self command, is noxious[.]" Thus the fabled ring of Gyges which is realized in a sort by the telescope as used by Schemel is only mischievous.[443] A new language when it serves only low or political purposes; the balloon could it be guided; the steam battery so fatal as to end War by Universal Murder. Nature gives us no sudden advantages. By the time we have acquired great power, we have acquired therewith sufficient wisdom to use it well. Animal magnetism inspires us ⟨with⟩ the prudent ⟨with⟩ and moral with a certain terror. Men are not good enough to be trusted with such power.[444]

See Goethe's superstition in his Demonology Nachgelassene Werke vol 8 [*Werke*, XLVIII,] p 178 which describes Van Buren & Jackson.[445]

[165] Continued from p. 163,

Finally; Nature is a discipline, & points to the pupil & exists for the pupil. Her ⟨nature⟩ being is subordinate; his is superior.[n] Man underlies Ideas. Nature receives them as her god. Man

---

⟨for⟩ upward" anticipates the lines prefixed to the second edition (1849): "And, striving to be man, the worm / Mounts though all the spires of form."

[443] For Gyges and his ring, see Plato, *Republic*, II, 359c; X, 612b; cf. *JMN*, II, 281–282. The name "Schemel" is unlisted in standard reference works. Edward Emerson, in a note to this passage as used in "Demonology" (*W*, X, 20, n. 3), postulates an allusion to Adelbert von Chamisso, *Peter Schlemihls Wunderbare Geschichte* (1814).

[444] "Nature gives us . . . magnetism" is struck through in pencil with a vertical use mark. " 'All that frees . . . such power." is used in "Demonology," *W*, X, 20–21.

[445] The reference is to *Dichtung und Wahrheit*, pt. IV, Bk. XX (*Werke*, 1828–1833, XLVIII, 178–179), where Goethe describes a "Daemonic element," a force running counter to the moral order as warp to woof, manifested in some men as a tremendous energy and power over others.

1 April. Beautiful morn follower of a beautiful moon. Yet lies the snow on the ground. Birds sing, mosses creep, grass grows under the edge of the snow bank.[446] Read yesterday Goethe's Iphigenia.[447] A pleasing, moving, even heroic work yet with the great deduction of being an imitation of the antique. How can a great genius ⟨submit⟩ ↑endure↓ to make paste-jewels? It must always have the effect compared with the great originals of Franklin's or Taylor's apologue of Abraham or Everett's Burdens of the Nations compared with the comforting or alarming words of David & Isaiah. Yet when in the evening we read Sophocles,[448] the shadow of a like criticism fell broad over almost all that is called modern literature. The words of Electra & Orestes are like actions. So live the thoughts of Shakspear. They have a necessary being. They live like men. To such productions it is obviously necessary that they should take that form which is then alive before the poet. The playhouse must have been the daily resort of Shakspear and that profession on which his circumstances had concentrated his attention. That is essential to the production of his plays. It is quite otherwise with Taylor & his Van Arteveldt. His playhouse & Muse is the reading of Shakspear.   Sermons were thus a living form to ⟨Jeremy⟩ Taylor, Barrow, South, & Donne. Novels & parliamentary speeches since Fielding & Burke. The Instauratio was a natural effect of the revival [166] of ancient learning. But thus it always must happen that the true work of genius should proceed out of the wants & deeds of the age as well as the writer, & so be the first form with which his genius combines, as Sculpture was perfect in Phidias's age, because the marble was the first form with which the creative genius combined. Homer is the only true epic. Milton is to him what Michel Angelo is to Phidias. But Shakspear is like Homer or Phidias himself. Do that which lies next you, O Man! [449]

[446] Beneath "ground. Birds . . . snow bank." is partially erased pencil writing: "Last they gave me ‖ . . . ‖ candles & their water tasted of ‖ . . . ‖".

[447] *Iphigenia auf Tauris, Werke,* 1828–1833, IX, 1–98.

[448] The *Electra*; see p. [180] below.

[449] Cf. Carlyle, *Sartor Resartus,* Bk. II, ch. IX: "*Do the Duty which lies nearest thee.*" See *The Works of Thomas Carlyle,* 1896–1901, I, 156. "It must always [p. [165]] . . . O Man!" is struck through in pencil with two vertical use marks on p. [165] and with one diagonal and one wavy diagonal use mark on p. [166]. "The words of . . . Phidias himself." is used in "Literature," *Lectures,* II, 60–61.

April 2. We improve easily up to the point at which our contemporaries & countrymen have arrived. There we stop for months, for years; and very slowly gain anything beyond it.[450]

———

In these Uses of Nature which I explore, the common sense of Man requires that, at last, Nature be referred to the Deity, be viewed in God. This which looks so prosaic on paper is the highest flight of genius, the last conclusion of philosophy, the inspiration of ⟨|| ... ||⟩ all grand character. Shall I say then that a several use of Nature is Worship? [451]

———

In the Ascetic of the man of letters, I see not well how he can avoid a persistent & somewhat rigorous temperance. Saved from so many hurts & griefs, he must impose a discipline on himself. He must out of sympathetic humanity wound his own bosom, bear some part of the load of wo, and ⟨so to⟩ the most convenient & graceful to him is a quiet but unrelaxing self-command. If he accept this & manfully stablish it, it shall stablish him. Then without a blush he shall meet & console the much-enduring sons [167] of toil & narrow

April 8. pd L[ucy] B[rown] 2.00 & 1.00 for L[idian]. E[merson]. Recd 6.00 of CCE[.] [452]
The motto of the discontented man, is, *Anywhere but here.*

Salem. 19 April. The philosopher should explain to us the laws of redeeming the time. The universal fact, says Goethe, is that which takes place once.[453] Well, let us read in the same faith, that the sentence now under the eye is one of universal application, and the volume in our hand is for us the voice of God & Time. Many are the paths that lead to wisdom & honor: nay, every[n] man hath a private

[450] This paragraph is struck through in pencil with a diagonal use mark.
[451] This paragraph is used in *Nature*, W, I, 60, 61.
[452] The three transactions are entered as of April 9 in Emerson's accounts for 1837–1838 (pp. [9], [4]). Income from Lidian Emerson's invested property was devoted to her sister Lucy Jackson Brown (*ibid.*, p. [15]; *Life*, pp. 220–221).
[453] Cf. Austin, *Characteristics of Goethe*, 1833, I, 64. See also *JMN*, IV, 267; "On the Relation of Man to the Globe," *Lectures*, I, 29.

lane thereto from his own door. Raphael paints wisdom, Handel sings it, Phidias carves it, Shakspear writes it, Washington enacts it, Columbus sails it, Wren builds it, Watt mechanizes it, Luther preaches it.[454] Let us take Duty this serving angel for a God in disguise. Without telling us why, he bids us ever do this & that irksomeness. What if it should prove that these very injunctions so galling & unflattering are precisely the redemptions of time for us? These books thrust into our hands are books selected for us, & the persons who take up our time are picked out to accompany us. I at least fully believe that God is in every place, & that, if the mind is excited, it may see him, & in him an infinite wisdom in every object that passes before us.

22 April. I left Boston with Charles for New York where we arrived 26 April. I arrived in Salem again 2 May.

[168] Salem, 4 May. The Marine Railway, the U.S. Bank, the Bunker Hill monument, are perfectly genuine works of the times. So is a speech in Congress, so is a historical discourse, a novel, Channing's Work on Slavery, & the Volume of Revised Statutes. But Taylor's Van Arteveldt, Byron's Sardanapalus, & Joanna Bailey's dramas are futile endeavors to revive a dead form & cannot succeed, nor I think can Greenough's sculpture. You must exercise your genius in some form that has essential life now; do something which is proper to the hour & cannot but be done. But what is once well done, lasts forever. As the gladiator, the Apollo, the Parthenon, the Iliad.[n]

All the devils respect virtue.[455]

[169] Concord, 16 May, 1836. And here I am again at home but I have come alone. My brother, my friend, my ornament, my joy & pride has fallen by the wayside, or rather has risen out of this dust. Charles died at New York Monday afternoon, 9 May. His

[454] "Raphael paints . . . preaches it.", struck through in pencil with a vertical use mark, is used in "Thoughts on Art," *The Dial*, I (Jan. 1841), 375; "Art," *Lectures*, II, 51; and "Art," *W*, VII, 52.

[455] See p. [21] above: "Virtue . . . will inspire respect into the damned."

prayer that he might not be sick was granted him. He was never confined to a bed. He rode out on Monday afternoon with Mother, promised himself to begin his journey with me on my arrival, the next day; on reaching home, he stepped out of the carriage alone, walked up the steps & into the house without assistance[,] sat down on the stairs, fainted, & never recovered. Beautiful without any parallel, in my experience of young men, was his life, happiest his death. Miserable is my own prospect from whom my friend is taken. Clean & Sweet was his life, untempted almost, and his action on others all-healing, uplifting, & fragrant. I read now his pages, I remember all his words & motions without any pang, so healthy & humane a life it was, & not like Edward's, a tragedy of poverty & sickness tearing genius. His virtues were like the victories of Timoleon, & Homer's verses, they were so easy & natural.[456] I cannot understand why his mss. journal should have so bitter a strain of penitence & deprecation. I mourn that in losing him I have lost his all, for he was born an orator, not a writer. His written pages do him no justice, and as he felt the immense disparity between his power of conversation & his blotted paper, it was easy for him to speak with scorn of written composition.

[170] Now commences a new & gloomy epoch of my life. I have used his society so fondly & solidly. It was pleasant to unfold my thought to so wise a hearer. It opened itself genially to his warm & bright light, and borrowed color & sometimes form from him. Besides my direct debt to him of how many valued thoughts, — through what orbits of speculation have we not travelled together, so that it would not be possible for either of us to say, This is my thought, That is yours.

I have felt in him the inestimable advantage, when God allows it, of finding a brother and a friend in one. The ↑mutual↓ understanding is then perfect, because Nature has settled the constitution of the amity on solidest foundations; and so it admits of mercenary usefulness & of unsparing censure; there exists the greatest convenience inasmuch as the same persons & facts are known to each, and an occult

---

[456] For the comparison, see "The Life of Timoleon," *Plutarch's Lives*, 1822, I, 422. Cf. *L.*, I, 365; "John Milton," *Lectures*, I, 154; "Spiritual Laws," *W*, II, 133; "Milton," *W*, XII, 263.

hereditary sympathy underlies all our intercourse & extends farther than we know.

Who can ever supply his place to me? None. I may live long. I may, (tho' 'tis improbable) see many cultivated persons, but his elegance, his wit, his sense, his worship of principles, I shall not find united — I shall not find them separate. The eye is closed that was to see Nature for me, & give me leave to see; the taste & soul which Shakspear satisfied; the soul that loved St John, & St Paul, Isaiah & David; the acute discernment that divided the good from the evil in all objects around him, in society, in politics, in church, in books, in persons; ⁿ the hilarity of thought which awakened [171] good humor wherever it came, and laughter without shame; and the endless endeavor after a life of ideal beauty; — these are all gone from my actual world & will here be no more seen.

I read with some surprise the pages of his journal. They show a nocturnal side which his diurnal aspects never suggested, — they are melancholy, penitential, self accusing; I read them with no pleasure: they are the creepings of an eclipsing temperament over his abiding light of character.

His senses were those of a Greek. I owe to them a thousand observations. To live with him was like living with a great painter. I used to say that I had no leave to see things till he pointed them out, & afterwards I never ceased to see them.

The fine humor of his conversation seemed to make the world he saw. His power of illustration & the facility of his association embroidered his sentences with all his reading & all his seeing. He could not speak but in cheerful figures. When something was said of maritime people, the pilots & fishermen, he said, "they were the fringes of the human race." When Miss Martineau was commended for the energy with which she had clung to society, despite her infirmity, he said "She *had* brushed pretty well thro' that drift of deafness." We complained much of the ugly mill they built over "Sleepy Hollow" in Concord. By & by they painted the vans red; Charles said, "This was adding insult to injury." [457]

I conversed with him one day upon the agreement of so many

[457] See p. [58] above.

thinkers in representing Nature as the symbol of the mind.ⁿ He said
"Yes there sits the Sphynx by the road-side, & every fine genius that
goes by has a crack with her." [458]

"The nap," he said "is worn off of the world." [459]

[172] He said of the unfortunate Mr.———; 'As fast as
Mrs——— rows, Mr——— backs water.'

"It is only by an effort like a Berserkir's," he said, "that a man can
work himself up to an interest in any exertion. All active life seems
an *amabilis insania*. And when I have done anything of importance
I repent of it: I repent of virtue as soon as I am alone; nor can I
see any reason why the world should not burn up tonight: the play
has been over some time." [460]

He said of our Concord Society, that "we seemed to be on the
way back to annihilation."

He said he never spent anything on himself without thinking
he deserved the praise of disinterested benevolence.[460a]

He said, The south wind made every body handsome.

[173] [blank]

[174] Charles said, There were two ways of living in the world,
viz. either to postpone your own ascetic entirely, & live among people
as among aliens; or, to lead a life of endless warfare by forcing your
Ideal into act. In either of these ways the wise man may be blameless.[461]

Charles said, No speculation interested him that could not help him
in action, & so become his daily bread.[462]

Nothing disgusted him more than aimless activity.

---

[458] See p. [82] above.
[459] See p. [117] above.
[460] See p. [120] above.
[460a] See *JMN*, IV, 292, 378.
[461] This paragraph is struck through in pencil with a vertical use mark.
[462] Cf. the observation attributed to Charles Emerson on p. [92] above: truth is
"alive only in action."

Truth of character he worshipped; truth to one's self — & proportionally despised the excessive craving for sympathy & praise, the parasitic life.[n] [463]

He could not bear to think that he should degenerate into a householder & lead the base life.[464]

He held at a very low rate the praise of fashionable people. He held at a very high rate the praise or ⟨s⟩ ⟨opinion⟩ gratitude of plain men whose habits of life, ⟨made⟩ precluded compliment, & made their verdict unquestionable.

A man is sure of nothing, he said, but what he got himself. Let him count every thing else mere good fortune, & expect to lose it any moment.[465]

He thought that Jeremy Taylor's sermons might be preached in an obscure country village with greatest advantage to the hearers; that they would be a sort of University; in themselves an education to those who had no other.

[175] He thought that the religious sentiment was the right of the poor at Church; that any speculations ⟨or⟩ merely ingenious, or literary merits of a discourse did not excuse th⟨is⟩e defect ↑of this;↓ but defrauded the poor of his Christianity.

He thought Christianity the philosophy of suffering; the religion of pain: that its motto was, "Thy Will be done"; [466] and that the print of the bended head of ⟨X⟩Christ with ⟨folded⟩ hands folded on the breast should be the altar-piece & symbol in churches, & not the crucifixion.[467]

[463] "Nothing disgusted . . . parasitic life" is struck through in pencil with a diagonal use mark.

[464] See p. [150] above: "For C. fears the degenerating into a vulgar housekeeper." This paragraph is struck through in pencil with a diagonal use mark.

[465] This paragraph is struck through in pencil with a diagonal use mark.

[466] Matt. 6:10.

[467] This paragraph, struck through in pencil with a vertical use mark, is used in *Nature, W*, I, 61.

He thought it a measure of any man's ability, the value he set upon his time.

beneficence of Milton & Shakspear [468]

He admired Scott's description of Lord Evandale in the mouth of Burley.   Eliot's Temperance. K James's lug [469]

He sympathized wonderfully with all objects & natures, & as by a spiritual ventriloquism threw his mind into them, which appeared in the warm & genial traits by which he again pictured them to the eye. I find him saying to E[lizabeth]. H[oar]. 3 Apr. 1834 "I do not know but one of the ancient metamorphoses will some day happen to me, & I shall shoot into a tree, or flow in a stream. I do so lose my human nature & join myself to that which is without. Today even Goethe would have been satisfied with the temper in which I became identified with what I saw, a part of what was around me!" [470]

[176]   ↑Extracts from CC.E's Letters to E.H.↓

The spirit of Stoicism saith "Be highminded & fear not." Christianity says, "Be not highminded but fear." [471]

Let noise (he writes to E H 8 Apr 1834) & the unmeaning & undelightful society of those who never knew what truth meant make us hug closer our "eternal jewel."

⟨But⟩ "There is so little romance in sleeping in Washington street,

---

[468] This phrase is written in pencil.

[469] "Eliot's . . . lug" is written in pencil; "beneficence . . . lug" is struck through in pencil with a vertical use mark. (1) The "description of Lord Evandale" occurs in Sir Walter Scott, *Old Mortality*, ch. XLIII; Emerson alluded to the passage in "Heroism," *Lectures*, II, 329, and "Heroism," *W*, II, 247, and "often repeated" it to his children, according to Edward Emerson's note to *W*, II, 247. (2) John Eliot, "apostle of the Indians," "drank water; and said of wine, 'it is a noble, generous liquor, and we should be humbly thankful for it, but, as I remember, water was made before it.'" This quotation, from William Allen, *An American Biographical and Historical Dictionary* (Boston, 1832), p. 371, is used in "Heroism," *Lectures*, II, 333, and "Heroism," *W*, II, 254–255. (3) In Sir Walter Scott, *The Fortunes of Nigel*, ch. XXXIII, King James explains that he has had made in the state prison "a lurking-place called the king's *lugg*, or *ear*," where he can "sit undescried and hear the converse of his prisoners."

[470] This paragraph is struck through in pencil with a diagonal use mark.

[471] This paragraph is struck through in ink with four wavy diagonal use marks.

155

& day laboring in Court st., that except I too was of Carlyle's faith, & reverenced as part of the Universe or rather as an Epitome of the Universe & emanation of God, this thinking principle, this mysterious me, I could find in me a dry mirth at the idea of making a story of my Epigaean life."[472]

Each natural event, the finding of the epigaea, of the indigo bird, the cuckow, & of the palm tree, were the epochs of his life.

⚹ Sunday. 11 Apr. 1834. "Yesterday I spent part of the afternoon in some of the warm hollows of Canterbury. The robin, the bluebird, yea, a moist frog with green uniform & gold enamelled eye, were my companions rather than Weston with whom I went out; for we straggled wide apart. I found the saxifrage just urging through moss & leaves its little ⟨ear⟩ ear of buds."

"Oh sometimes I play teacher, but it is only in the forms of things[,] the dress of life, words, motions, manners. Afterward, I am sorry that such outward things swell in my thought. I am out of love, as Prince Hal says, with my greatness,[473] as a child of God, that is, for entertaining these humble considerations."

[177][474] ↑Apr. 24, 1834↓
"Now your mother, would she say, Better leave reading the silly letter? Why then she frets against dear Nature, & would have no violets grow because of them we cannot make a broom.⟨"⟩ But there is more of God in a violet than in a broom."

"A glass of water is on my shelf, & therein are met, drinking sociably together, anemones & hepaticas, yes, & the pearly fair Arbutus, & Crimson Columbine with other green, white, & pink friends from the fields[.]"[475]

["]You ask if I miss you? I do not know that I miss you because you are in Concord, or in Lincoln. I miss you always so far as any thing within us or without us removes from one another. Yes, I miss you, dearest, as I miss the summer whilst it has not yet come, the flower that has not yet opened, the morning that has not yet fully dawned on my waiting

[472] Edward Emerson, J, IV, 45, n. 1, remarks concerning the Epigæa or mayflower: "Charles was perhaps attending the May Session of Court in Boston, or, more likely, used the derivation of the name of the creeping plant (ἔπι and γῆ) for life *on Earth.*"
[473] *II Henry IV*, II, ii, 15.
[474] "C.C.E. to E.H." is centered above "mother . . . say" at the top of the page.
[475] This sentence is struck through in pencil with a diagonal use mark.

eyes; I miss you as I miss the great Future for which I hope, the virtue I have not yet domesticated, the happiness I have not yet deserved.["]

———

April 13, 1836[,] a letter upon imitation of Xt [Christ].

———

May 10, 1834. "Have I said all this before? Well, we are bells that, — pull us when you will, — strike the same note."
["]Do you think I am stony-natured? No, it is not in you, Lizzie, that such glaciers form. It is always summer in your heart.["]

———

The horror of the housekeeper pervades his views of marriage.

"What is it we seek each in the other? — to enter into a community of being, giving & receiving the freedom of each other's immortal part. If the cares & endearments of earthly marriage cause us to [178][476] lose sight of this its highest end, & dull in us the perception of this its purest happiness, let us go mourning, let us live alone on the mountains, & bewail our virginity." [477]

———

May 14, 1834. Martha Day's Death.[478]

———

⟨A forenoon wedding is dread ch‖ . . . ‖⟩

———

May 27, 1834. Manners.

———

"Tomorrow I go to my Sunday School. That ever I should be a shepherd, — I who cry inly as a weak lamb to be folded & fed."
Wednesday Night, ⟨Aug⟩ ↑Sept. 4↓, 1834. The days go & come & go. Here from my window toward the East I shall presently peruse at length large-limbed Orion, my shining chronicler of many a winter. God be thanked who set the stars in the sky! planted their bright watch along

[476] "C.C.E. to E.H." is written above "this its highest" at the top of the page.
[477] This paragraph is struck through in pencil with a vertical and a diagonal use mark.
[478] "Martha Day's Death." is presumably the topic of Charles Emerson's letter of the date given; for analogies, compare the reference on p. [177] to his letter of April 13, 1836: "upon imitation of Xt [Christ].", and the second item below on p. [178]: "May 27, 1834. Manners." The canceled line immediately following "Martha Day's Death." appears to be the beginning of another extract from Charles Emerson's correspondence.

the infinite deep & ordained such fine intelligence betwixt us & them. Yea, God be thanked for all in nature that is the symbol of purity & peace.[479]

↑C.C.E↓

May 27, 1834. "Something has glanced athwart my mind once or twice that I would say about manners. They should be *distinct*, never slurred. Whatever is said or done should be finished, waited on to its conclusion. A well-bred person shuns nothing, dodges no corners, evades no look or word, cuts short no introduction or farewell, but clearly & cheerfully upon the moment does & says what seemeth suitable & kind."

———

The whole of the letter, Nov. 10, 1833, —

———

March 30, 1835. You never blame me. I will not believe you wanting in the angel office which only great & loving spirits can fitly discharge one to another that of rebuke, yea, of indignation which yet is only the surge & foam upheaved [179][480] from the deep sea of affection[.]

Jan. 20, 1835. I am glad the friendship with Aunt Mary is ripening. As by seeing a high tragedy, reading a true poem or novel, like Corinne, — so by society with her, one feels the mind electrified & purged.

She is no statute book of practical commandments, nor orderly digest of any system of philosophy, divine or human; but a Bible, — miscellaneous in its parts, but one in its spirit, wherein are sentences of condemnation, chapters of prophecy, promises & covenants of love, that make foolish the wisdom of the world with the power of God.

As in the world Thought is divorced from Act, so in the Soul Duty is often times divorced from Religion. The mind has its forms, its habits. Let us be humble & accept it as part of human necessity that we give the homage of the life even while the spirit is caught away by distractions, and God in his omniscience discerning the Sources of action however separated from their issues, will join the twain, & accept & reconcile our dis-parted worship.

Dec. 16, 1836 [1835]. I really congratulate your father on being at Washington this winter. — He had worn the track of his domestic & professional life so smooth that there lacked amalgam to excite electricity.

Let us not vail our bonnets to circumstance. If we 'act so, because we are so', if we sin from strong bias of temper & constitution at least we

[479] "The days go . . . peace." is struck through in pencil with a vertical use mark.
[480] "C.C.E. to E.H." is centered above "deep . . . affection" at the top of the page.

158

have in ourselves the measure & ↑the↓ curb of our aberration. But if they who are around us sway us, if we think ourselves [180]⁴⁸¹ incapable of resisting the drawing of the cords with which fathers & mothers & a host of unsuitable expectations & duties, falsely so called, seek to bind us, alas! into what helpless disorder shall we not fall! ⁴⁸²

March 18, 1836. Waldo & I read as we have opportunity in the Electra. It is very charming to me, the severe taste of these Greeks. I am never offended, & there is an aristocratic pleasure in these lofty & removed studies. It is as if you had left the noisy fuming world of mortal men, & taken passage with that grim ferryman whom poets speak of, & the slow styx *novies interfusa* ⁴⁸³ lay between you & all earthly interests.
I write March 18 with lively satisfaction. If I could get along side of the world wheels, if I wouldn't give them a twirl!

April 3, 1836. W[aldo]. & I have finished the Electra, & he is quite enamored of the severe beauty of the Greek tragic muse. Do you not think it sets the action before you with a more real presence than even Shakspeare's drama? Or is it because this is a new story? I was thinking the splendor of the particular passages in Shakspear withdrew you continually from the steadfast contemplation of the action.

Oct. 5, 1834. Do you look at men as I have become accustomed of late to consider them, stronger or feebler utterances of particular thoughts & affections; so that a shrewd Rochefoucault philosophy could calculate the phenomena they would each exhibit with pretty nearly the same precision as the eclipses of Jupiter's moons. [181]⁴⁸⁴ I see a bloodwarm living man in the throng of his engagements, & I say to myself, what is the mission the significancy of this creature, & when, in a few years, friendly hands shall wrap his dead body in graveclothes, what dot or line in picture which is being finished in the world, will he have left engraved? Yet are they not mere 'hands'[,] artisans, for do I not myself feel a common nature in me, whereby I am drawn towards certain points in the boundless sphere wherein we act? &, while busy about these, my back is turned upon a hemisphere, & a great portion of the centimanous Me must lie unexercised. Yet is there a recognition all the while in my soul of the whole. And the curve of the least arc of the circle tells the dimensions of radius & circumference,

⁴⁸¹ "C.C.E. to E.H." is centered above "resisting the" at the top of the page.
⁴⁸² This paragraph is struck through in pencil with vertical use marks.
⁴⁸³ Cf. Virgil, *Georgics*, IV, 480: "noviens Styx interfusa coercet." — "Styx holding them fast within his ninefold circles."
⁴⁸⁴ "C.C.E. to E.H." is centered above "bloodwarm . . . in the" at the top of the page.

& keeps alive the consciousness of unseen relations in them who seem as fast fixed to that differential point as the ephemerides to their leaf or petal.

Feb. 12, 1835. I shall come to Concord. For homesickness — trust me. A rood of earth that is mine, four walls, a lamp, & a book, will kill that vermin.

It is night. Night is a leveller, a restorer, a comforter. Good Night, I desire acquaintance with thee. Things look hard & peaked in the day. One cannot so well be an Idealist, no, nor a stoic. You see your neighbors, & you are cowed by circumstances. But night is like the grave, & buries all distinctions. I am Myself: thanks, Medea, for the word.

"What I have learned is mine, I have my Thought
And me the Muses noble truths have taught" [485]
Will you have me write more, or is the cocoon [486]

[182] Concord, 19 May, 1836. I find myself slowly, after this helpless mourning. I remember states of mind that perhaps I had long lost before this grief, the ↑native↓ mountains whose tops reappear after we have traversed many a mile of weary region from home. Them shall I ever revisit? I refer now to last evening's lively remembrance of the scattered company who have ministered ⟨in the⟩ to my highest wants. Edward Stabler, Peter Hunt, Sampson Reed, my peasant Tarbox, Mary Rotch, Jonathan Phillips, A.B. Alcott — even Murat has a claim [487] — a strange class, plain & wise, whose charm to me is wonderful, how elevating! how far was their voice from the voice of vanity of display, of interest, of tradition! They are to me what ⟨T⟩the Wanderer in the Excursion is to the poet. And Wordsworth's total value is of this kind. They are described in the lines at the end of the Yarrow Revisited. ⟨They make the⟩ Theirs is the true light of all our day.[488] They are the argument for the

[485] Cf. "How a Man may inoffensively praise himself, and without being liable to Envy," *Plutarch's Morals*, 1718, II, 325; ascribed to Crates. See *JMN*, IV, 96.

[486] Continued at the foot of p. [182].

[487] Hunt, Reed, and Alcott have been mentioned earlier; Edward Stabler (sometimes spelled "Stubler" by Emerson) of Alexandria, Va., and Mary Rotch of New Bedford were Quaker friends (*JMN*, III, 185, 266; IV, 96, 263; *Life*, p. 199). Jonathan Phillips, a deacon in William Ellery Channing's church, had been a family benefactor of the Emersons (*L*, I, 251, 429). The Methodist Tarbox had contributed to Emerson's understanding of prayer (*JMN*, II, 388, n. 91). With the "intrepid doubter" Achille Murat, nephew of Napoleon, Emerson had "talked incessantly" during his return from Florida in 1827 (*JMN*, III, 77; *L*, I, 194).

[488] Cf. Wordsworth, (1) *Yarrow Revisited, and Other Poems*, 1835, pp. 243–

spiritual world for the⟨y⟩ir ⟨a⟩ spirit is it. Nothing is impossible since such communion has already been. Whilst we hear them speak, how frivolous are the distinctions of fortune! and the voice of fame is as unaffecting as the tinkle of the passing sleigh bell.[489]

---

[490] quite spun, & shall I, poor grub, go sleep? That's no bad image, Lizzie. For a man's evening reveries are a sort of soft drapery, a silk night gown, which he wraps round his more serious & intenser soul, & this last starts winged from its slumber when the hours of rest are fulfilled.

Here end my Extracts from the letters of my brother Charles.

[183] Every man has his Parnassus somewhere, though in a band of music or the theatre or gazing at a regiment come home from the wars, or a frigate from the main. The mob draws its attraction out of high obscure infinital regions[.] [491]

By the permanence of Nature Minds are trained alike & made intelligible to each other.

The One Mind
A great danger or a strong desire as a war of defence or an enterprize of enthusiasm or even of gain will at any time knit a multitude into one man & whilst it lasts bring every individual into his exact place; one to watch, one to deliberate, one to act, one to speak, & one to record.[492]

The ⟨human⟩ ↑generic↓ soul in each individual is a giant overcome with sleep which locks up almost all his senses, & only leaves him a little superficial animation. Once in an age at ↑hearing↓ some deeper voice, he lifts his iron lids, & his eyes straight pierce through

---

244: a passage extracted from the then unpublished manuscript of *The Prelude*, XII, 224–278; (2) "Ode: Intimations of Immortality," l. 152: "the fountain-light of all our day."

[489] See p. [149] above.
[490] Continued from p. [181].
[491] This paragraph is struck through in pencil with a vertical use mark.
[492] This paragraph, struck through in pencil with a vertical use mark, is used in "Society," *Lectures*, II, 105.

all appearances, & his tongue tells what shall be in the latest times: then is he obeyed like a God, but quickly the lids fall, & sleep returns.

[184]   [Otherism]

↑Sunday, 22 May.↓ We overestimate the conscience of our friend. His goodness seems better than our goodness. His nature finer, his temptation less. Every thing that was his, his name, his form, his dress, his books, fancy enhances. It is the action of the social principle "aiming above the mark that it may hit the mark." ↑Our own expressed thought strikes us as new & of some more weight from the mouth of a friend.↓[493]

↑See also p. 316↓

Persons: the talk of the kitchen & the cottage is exclusively occupied with persons. ⟨The⟩ It is the sickness, crimes, disasters, airs, fortunes of persons; never is the character of the action or the object abstracted. Go into the parlor & into fashionable society. The ⟨manner is refined⟩ ↑persons are more conspicuous↓ but the fact is the same. The conversation still hovers over ⟨over⟩ persons, over political connexions, over events as they related to individuals. — ⟨W⟩ Go at last into the cultivated class who ask ⟨w⟩What is Beauty? How shall I be perfect? To what end exists the world? and you shall find in proportion to their cultivation a studious separation of personal history from their analysis of character & their study of things. Natural History is elegant, astronomy sublime for this reason, their impersonality. And yet when cultivated men speak of God they demand a biography of him as steadily as the kitchen & the bar room demand personalities of men. Absolute goodness, absolute truth must leave their infinity & take form for us. We want fingers & sides & hair. Yet certainly it is more grand & therefore more true to say 'Goodness is its own reward'; 'Be sure your sin will find you out,' [494] than to say, God will give long life to the upright; God will punish the sinner in hell, in any popular sense of these words. But the angels will

---

[493] This paragraph, struck through in pencil with a diagonal use mark and in ink with two vertical use marks, is used in both "Society" and "The Heart," *Lectures*, II, 100–101, 287, respectively, and in "Friendship," *W*, II, 195–196.

[494] Num. 32:23.

worship virtue & truth not gathered into a person but inly seen in the perspective [185] of their own progressive being. They see the dream & the interpretation ⟨in⟩of the world in the faith that God is within them.[495] As a spiritual truth needs no proof but is its own reason, so the Universe needs no outer cause but exists by its own perfection and the sum of it all is this, God is.

Theism must be & the name of God must be because ⟨wh⟩ it is a necessity of the human mind to apprehend the relative as flowing from the absolute & ⟨it⟩ we shall always give the Absolute a name. But a storm of calumny will always pelt him whose view of God is highest & purest.[496]

I heard today a preacher who made me think that the stern Compensations work themselves out in pulpits too, since if a preacher treats the people as children they too will treat him as a child.

It is strange how simple a thing it is to be a great [497] man, so simple that almost all fail by over doing. There is nothing vulgar in Wordsworth's idea of Man. To believe your own thought, that is Genius. To believe that a man intended ⟨the⟩ to produce the emotion we feel ↑before his work↓ is the highest praise, so high that we ever hesitate to give it[.] [498]

[May] 23. Climate is a great impediment to idle persons. I thought I had given up the care of the weather, but still I regard the clouds & the wind.[499]

After reading ⟨is⟩ ↑has↓ become stale & thoughts truisms, the meeting a young man who has a lively interest in your speculations shall revive the faded colors & restore the price of thought. So thought I at Salem. ↑This is the foundation, in Nature, of Education.↓ [500]

[495] Cf. Luke 17:21.
[496] This and the preceding paragraph, struck through in pencil with diagonal use marks, are used in "Holiness," *Lectures*, II, 353–354.
[497] The word "great" is circled in ink.
[498] "To believe your . . . give it" is struck through in pencil with a diagonal use mark. The first of the two sentences is used in "Self-Reliance," *W*, II, 45.
[499] This paragraph is struck through in pencil with a diagonal use mark.
[500] This paragraph, struck through in pencil with a diagonal use mark, is used in "Society," *Lectures*, II, 101.

↑See also p. 35 last line but three.↓ 501
↑See also p. 277↓

[186] 28 May.

> There's a divinity that shapes our ends
> Rough hew them how we will.
>
> [*Hamlet*, V, ii, 10–11] 502

Nothing bizarre[,] nothing whimsical will endure. ⟨The laws of Nature interfere with⟩ Nature is ever interfering with Art.   You cannot build your house or pagoda as you will but as you must.* Gravity, Wind, sun, rain, the size of men & animals, & such other aliens have more to say than the architect. Beneath the almighty necessity therefore I regard ⟨the⟩ what is artificial in man's life & works as petty & insignificant by the side of what is natural.503 Every violation, every suicide, every miracle, every wilfulness however large ⟨they⟩ ↑it↓ may show near us, melts quickly into the All, & ⟨makes no⟩ at a distance is not seen. The outline is as smooth as the curve of the moon.

Landor has too much wilfulness; he will not let his genius speak but must make it all himself. A writer must have *l'abandon,* he must be content to stand aside & let truth & beauty speak for him, or he cannot expect to be heard far.504

30 May. In that ⟨litera⟩ Sermon to Literary Men which I propose to make, be sure to admonish them not to be ashamed of their gospel. The mason, the carpenter hold up their ⟨saw⟩ trowel & saw

* ↑There is a quick bound set to our caprice: The leaning tower can only lean so far. The verandah or the pagoda roof can curve upward only to a certain point.↓

---

501 "Blessed be the friend."

502 See *JMN*, III, 211.

503 "Nothing bizarre, nothing . . . is natural." is struck through in pencil with three diagonal use marks; Emerson's interpolation, added as a note between paragraphs following "curve of the moon.", is struck through in ink with a vertical use mark. The passage as augmented is used in "Thoughts on Art," *The Dial*, I (Jan. 1841), 369; "Art," *Lectures*, II, 44–45; and "Art," *W*, VII, 41–42.

504 Cf. "Thoughts on Art," *The Dial*, I (Jan. 1841), 373; "Art," *Lectures*, II, 49; "Art," *W*, VII, 48–49.

with honest pride[;] the Scholar thrusts his book ⟨out⟩ into his pocket, ⟨&⟩ drops the nose gay he has gathered in his walk into the fields, & in conversation with the grocer & farmer affects to talk of business & farms. [187] Faint heart never won.[505] Other professions thrive because they who drive them do that one thing with a single & entire mind. Feel that fair weather or foul weather, good for grass or bad for grass, scarcity or plenty is all nothing to you; that your plough may go every day; and leave to God the care of the world.

It is a sublime illustration of the Christian doctrine of Humility, — the fact that God is the Servant of the Universe. If there were any being whom he did not Serve, he would not be the God of that being.

There are English words which I never use, and my style is so much the poorer. Here are such[:]   Yean
                                                                drill v.
                                                                brook (v.
                                                                herald
                                                                surcharged
                                                                superserviceable [506]
                                                                pot valiant
                                                                obverse
                                                                horse-play
                                                                glut
                                                                dip of the balance
                                                                gum
                                                                wind egg
                                                                propound

[188] Put in the Sermon to Scholars the brave maxim of the ⟨Veda⟩ Code of Menu; "A teacher of the Veda should rather die with his learning than sow it in sterile soil, even though he be in grievous distress for subsistence."[507] ↑approved by C.C.E.↓

[505] Cf. "Faint heart never won a fair lady," in Fielding, *Select Proverbs*, 1825, p. 27; "Faint heart ne'er won fair lady," in John Ray, *A Complete Collection of English Proverbs* . . . (London, 1817), p. 72.

[506] See p. [122] above.

[507] *Institutes of Hindu Law: or, The Ordinances of Menu* . . . , trans. Sir William Jones (London, 1825), ch. II, no. 113, p. 38.

Please God the curse of the carpenter shall never lie on my roof!

Fine thoughts flowing from an idea perceived by the mind, & fine thoughts wilfully recollected & exhibited, differ as leaves & flowers growing from a branch, & leaves & flowers tied together by a string.

31 May. ⟨When we⟩ All powerful action is by bringing the forces of nature to bear upon our objects. We do not grind corn or lift the loom by our own strength but we build a mill & set the North wind to play upon our instrument or the expansive force of steam or the ebb & flow of the ocean. So in our manipulations, we do few things by muscular force but we place ourselves in such attitudes as to bring the force of gravity, the weight of the planet, that is, to bear upon the ⟨shovel⟩ spade or the axe we wield; in short in all our operations we seek not to use our own but to bring a quite infinite force to bear. In like manner are our intellectual works ⟨achieved⟩ done. We are to hinder our individuality from acting; we are to bring the whole omniscience of Reason upon the subject before us. We are to aim at getting observations without aim,[n] to subject to thought things seen without thought. ↑What is it that ⟨works the axe or the⟩ gives force to the blow of ax or crowbar? Is it the muscles of the man's arm or is it the attraction of the whole globe below it on the ax or bar?↓[n 508]

[189] Yesterday in the wood it seemed to me that the three aspects of Natural Beauty might take this order. 1. The beauty of the world as ⟨an object⟩ a daily delight & luxury —[n] rainbows, moonlight, & perspective; 2. The beauty of the world as it is [—] the drapery of Virtuous actions, Leonidas, Columbus, & Vane, & always the Unconscious Man; 3. The beauty of the World as it becomes an object of the intellect and so the foundation of Art or the voluntary creation of Beauty[.] [509]

[508] "What is it . . . bar" is added in the lower right corner of the page. The entire paragraph, struck through in ink with two vertical use marks, is used in "Thoughts on Art," *The Dial*, I (Jan. 1841), 369–370; "Art," *Lectures*, II, 45, 49; and "Art," *W*, VII, 42, 49; cf. "Civilization," *W*, VII, 27.
[509] This paragraph is struck through in ink with one vertical and four diagonal use marks. The outline suggested here is followed in ch. III of *Nature*, *W*, I, 16–23.

1 June.

Once there was an urn which received water out of a fountain. But sometimes the ⟨water⟩ fountain spouted ⟨too⟩ so far as to fall beyond the lips of the Urn, & sometimes not far enough to ⟨rec⟩ fill it; so that sometimes it was only sprinkled. ⟨& sometimes it was wholly dry.⟩ But the Urn desired to be always full and Nature saw the Urn, & made it alive, so that it could move this way & that to meet the waterfall, and even when the water did not rise out of the spring, it could change its shape, & with a long neck ⟨it⟩ suck up ⟨with⟩ the water from hollows with its lips. Then it began to go far from the fountain, looking ⟨|| . . . ||⟩ in ⟨different⟩ many places for wells, & sometimes when the fountain was full, the Urn was gone, & did not come back until the fountain was a thread; and often, the walking Urn lost its way & came into sands, & was long empty. Moreover though Nature gave it life, she did not give it more body, so that what was spent in making feet & ⟨throat⟩ ↑legs↓ was lost from the belly of the Urn; and in the motion of ⟨trav⟩ going, much water was spilled [190] so that now it was never full as before. So the Urn came to Nature, and besought her to take away its life, & replace it at the old fountain.

2 June. It is another fact to be remembered in the scholar's sermon that hard labor, — for example farm-work, — is not favorable to thought. My friend Mr Wight tells me that it blunts the sensibilit⟨ies⟩y of the upper system so that he sleeps & not thinks in the study. And I have found the same thing true. Therefore he thinks the farm schools will not succeed in making scholars.

———

I cannot deny myself the pleasure of copying a passage from Mr Alcott's MSS Journal.

"Successful preaching implies, I imagine, the utterance of profoundest truth in simple phrase, touching the common sense of every one[—]the child, & the adult, & being, at the same time, a pure model of eloquence both in tho't & expression. The eloquence that bringeth the old men from their corners, & taketh the children, by surprise, from the delights of play, doth at the same time impress & commend itself to the man in the full glory of his powers, whether he be a genius or of ordinary ability. Such is the great problem to be wrought by the subtile forces of thought in the fit images of words. Whoso exerteth this power hath wrought out the

problem, & shall find fit hearers when he openeth his mouth. The apprehending heart shall not belie its trust. For the ear [191] shall hear & the
spirit understand those heavenly words in wh[ich]. the soul's meaning is
given forth. Such minds deal with ↑the↓ realities of our common nature.
Every one feeleth the force of their words and apprehendeth the truths
that these embody, as the child & the artist, the common man & the connoisseur pronounce upon the great works of art or the things of nature
the verdict — the spontaneous heart conviction that *"This is it"*; that the
sense hath found outness & meaning from the deep & faithful heart."   ₵
↑Alcott's↓ Journal [Sunday, December 13,] 1835. p[p]. [499–]501

"Organizations" which are "the graves of the spirit[.]"

Received this day a letter from Carlyle dated 29 Apr[.]

3 June. Shall I not treat all men as gods?

4 June. The painters have driven me from my apartment. What
a droll craft is theirs generically considered! ⟨Whence is⟩ There
certainly is a ridiculous air over much of our life.

[192] Swedenborg (continued from p 127)
Clouds in heaven — explained in Apoc[alypse]. Rev[ealed, 1836].
Vol. 1. p 48

"I have often seen those clouds & it was evident from whence & what they
are."

[193]–[197] [blank]

[198] Here are two or three facts respecting Science. 1. The
tendency to order & classification in the mind. 2. The correspondent
Order actually subsisting in Nature. 3. Hence the humanity of science
or the naturalness of knowing; the perception that the world was
made by mind like ours; the recognition of design like ours[;] the
⟨sigh⟩ seeing in the brutes analogous intelligence to ours. — Otherwise

    Man puts things in a row
    Things belong in a row
      The showing of the true row is Science

History teaches
    1. The presence of Spirit
    2. The antecedence of Spirit
    3. The humanity of Spirit
Corollary
    Science must be studied humanly.[510]

[199] We are always learning that duration & magnitude are of no account to the soul. In the eternity of nature centuries are lost as moments are. In the immensity of matter, there is no great & no small. The grass & foliage that covers the whole globe from the snow that caps the north pole to the snow that caps the south pole, cost no more design or effort, than went to the opening the bell of one lily, or to the germination of a grain of wheat. Time is nothing to laws. ↑The ocean is a large drop; ⟨a⟩A drop is a small ocean.↓ [511]

———

There is one mind. Inspiration is larger reception of it: fanaticism is predominance of the individual. ⟨A man's call⟩ The greater genius the more like all other men, therefore. A man's call to do any particular work as to go super cargo to Calcutta, or missionary to Serampore, or pioneer to the Western country is his fitness to do that thing he proposes. Any thought that he has a personal summons —

signs that mark him extraordinary
& not in the roll of common men [512]

[—] is dreaming[,] is so much insanity. It denotes deficiency of perceiving that there is One Mind in all the individuals.[513] In like

[510] Emerson's lecture "Humanity of Science" (*Lectures*, II, 22–40), first read on December 22, 1836, follows essentially the outline given here and incorporates phrases from it: e.g., "Man puts things . . . belong in a row"; "Science must be studied humanly" (pp. 25, 36). Cf. also the opening passages of ch. VIII of *Nature*, *W*, I, 66–68.

[511] "The ocean . . . small ocean." is used in "The American Scholar," *W*, I, 112. The entire paragraph, struck through in pencil with a diagonal use mark, is used in "The Individual," *Lectures*, II, 185.

[512] Cf. *I Henry IV*, III, i, 41–43.

[513] The paragraph to this point, struck through in pencil with a diagonal use mark, is used in "Ethics," *Lectures*, II, 147–148, and "Spiritual Laws," *W*, II, 141; the remainder of the paragraph may be a later addition.

manner guessing at the modes of divine action as Norton's about electricity, &c betrays ignorance of the truth that all men have access to the divine counsels, for God is the Universal mind.

[200] 5 June 1836. I have read with interest Mr Alcott's Journal in MS for 1835. He has attained at least to a perfectly simple & elegant utterance. There is no inflation & no cramp in his writing. I complained that there did not seem to be quite that facility of association which we expect in the man of genius & which is to ⟨marry⟩ ↑interlace↓ his work ⟨to⟩ ↑with↓ all Nature by its radiating upon all. But the sincerity of his speculation is a better merit. This is no theory of a month's standing; no peg to hang fine things on; no sham enthusiasm; no cant; but his hearty faith & study by night & by day. He writes it in the book, he discourses it in the parlor, he instructs it in the school.
And whatever defects as fine writers such men may have it is because colossal foundations ⟨do⟩ ↑are↓ not for summerhouses but for temples & cities. But come again a hundred years hence & compare Alcott & his little critics.

[June] 6. Last Saturday eve. I had a conversation with E. H. which I cannot recal but of which the theme was that when we deal truly & lay judgment to the line & rule we are no longer permitted to think that the presence or absence of friends is material to our highest states of mind. In those few moments which are the life of our life when we were in the state of clear vision, we were taught that God is here no respecter of persons[,] [514] that into that communion with him which is absolute life, & where names & ceremonies & traditions are no longer known, but the virtues are loved for their loveliness alone, for their conformity to God; — in that communion our dearest friends [201] are strangers. There is no personëity in it.

Yesterday I remembered the saying of Coleridge's friend Moxon [515] that he would go to the Cabinet Ministers to read their faces, for Nature never lies. Also by writing is the character made

[514] Cf. Acts 10:34.
[515] The name is a later addition in a space left for it.

known. And he who is dumb & motionless for fear of betraying his thought does by very silence & inaction tell it. Dum tacet clamat.[516] So irresistibly does human nature ever publish itself.

[June] 7. Many letters from friends who loved or honored Charles. I know not why it is, but a letter is scarcely welcome to me. I expect to be lacerated by it & if I come safe to the end of it, I feel like one escaped.

The Use of Nature is to awaken the feeling of the Absolute. Nature is a perpetual effect. It is the great shadow pointing to an unseen Sun.[517]

Why fret at particular events? For every thing you have missed, you have gained some thing else: And for every thing you gain, you lose something.

> "Wishing good & doing good
> Is laboring Lord with thee
> Charity is gratitude
> And piety best understood
> Is sweet humanity."

[202] The ⟨rank⟩ ↑value↓ of so many persons is like that of an unit in decimal notation which is determined altogether by the *place* of the number.

"Why strew'st thou sugar on this bottled spider[?"][518]

⟨P⟩ Do not fear the multitude of books. They all have their placc. Shakspear, Moses, Cicero, Bacon, A Kempis, Cervantes, Bunyan, dwell together without crowding in the Mind as in Nature there is room for all the succession of herbs & trees, of birds, & beasts. The world is large enough[,] the year is long enough for all that is to be done in it.[519]

[516] "While he is silent he cries out." (Ed.); see *JMN*, IV, 96. Cf. Cicero, *In Catilinam*, I, viii (21): "cum tacent, clamant." — "by their silence they cry aloud."
[517] This paragraph, struck through in ink with four diagonal use marks, is used in *Nature, W*, I, 61.
[518] *Richard III*, I, iii, 242, misquoted.
[519] See p. [49] above.

So you have undertaken to solve the problem of the world. God speed you, fair sir, in your modest attempt. Remember this however, that the greatest reason is always the truest.[520]

You will always find those who think they know what is your duty far better than you know it yourself. To go to the Sunday School if they bid you; there's a good boy.[521]

10 June. We cannot see out of ourselves. How do I know but I seem an ape or a toad to other people?

Certainly children believe in an external world. The belief that it *appears* only, is an afterthought but on the human faculties if cultured this will as surely dawn as did the first faith[.] [522]

I gladly pay the rent of my house because I therewith get the horizon & the woods which I pay no rent for. For day break & evening & [203] night, I pay no tax. I think it is a glorious bargain which I drive with the town.

The pilgrim goes into the woods but he carries with him the beauty which he visits. For the eye is the painter & the Ear the singer.[523] ↑Where is not man is neither color nor sound.↓

The man is the creator of his world. I choose to pursue certain thoughts to enter certain states of mind, & forthwith I seem to walk into woods by known ways & to hear wood birds & see pines & birches. I choose to pursue certain other thoughts, & lo! I seem to visit the wharves & market.

Can a man forget ⟨what⟩ anything which he truly knows? No, for that which he knows, that is he. The more knower, the more man.[524]

The moral influence of nature is that amount of truth which it illustrates to the mind. Who can estimate this? The visible sky ⟨seems

[520] This paragraph is struck through in ink with two diagonal use marks.

[521] This paragraph is struck through in pencil with a vertical use mark.

[522] This paragraph, struck through in ink with two diagonal use marks, is used in *Nature*, W, I, 59.

[523] This sentence is used in *Nature*, W, I, 15.

[524] This paragraph, struck through in pencil with a diagonal use mark, is used in "Ethics," *Lectures*, II, 146.

to be the true type of⟩ in which the ball of earth is buried with its eternal calm & ⟨the⟩ filled with lights seems to be the true type of the Eternal Reason into which we are born & the truths which revolve therein.[525]

Shall I say, what hovers often among the whimsies of the mind, that blows are aimed at him in broad daylight but that protected & defended by a circle of friendly power he passes on in safety?

11 June. William E[merson]. visited us a few hours this day. A pleasing day.

I become querulous, discontented, even garrulous. In that rare society of which I wrote above p. 182, I dilate and am wise, good, & hopeful by sympathy, but in ordinary company & what is not so, (non é nel mondo, se non volgo,) [526] I shrink & patter [204] & apologize. I know not why, but I hate to be asked to preach here in Concord. I never go to the Sunday School Teachers without fear & shame.

I take admonitions from ↑every↓ passenger with the attitude & feeling of a willow. ↑I am like those opium eaters of Constantinople who skulked about all day the most pitifull drivellers, then at even when the bazars were open slunk to the opium shop & became glorious & great.↓[527]

I am afraid that the brilliant writers very rarely feel the deepest interest in truth itself. Even my noble Scotchman, I fancy, feels so strongly his vocation to produce, that he would not listen with half the unfeigned joy to a simple oracle in the woods that Hosmer or Hunt would find. He is certainly dedicated to his book, to the communication & the form of that he knows. Yet he ought to feel more

[525] This paragraph, struck through in ink with a diagonal use mark, is used in *Nature*, *W*, I, 42, 27.
[526] Cf. Machiavelli as quoted by Coleridge, *On the Constitution of Church and State*, 1839, p. 99; *JMN*, IV, 297.
[527] "I am like . . . great.", struck through in pencil with a diagonal use mark, is used in "Prudence," *Lectures*, II, 316, and "Prudence," *W*, II, 233.

curious to know the truth than anxious to exhibit what he knows.
Yet what is any man's book compared with the undiscoverable All?

14 June. What learned I this morning in the woods[,] the oracular woods? Wise are they the ancient nymphs. Pleasing sober melancholy truth say those untameable savages the pines. Under them bend
& reign each in his tiny sphere surrounded by a company of his own
race & family the violets, thesiums, cypripediums &c. The windflower
(rue leaved) is the Bride. But thus they said.

Power is one great lesson which Nature teaches Man. The secret
that he can not only ⟨f⟩ reduce under his will[,] that is, conform to his
character[,] particular events but classes of events & so harmonize all
the outward occurrences with the states of mind, that must he
learn[.] [528]

Worship, must he learn[.] [529]

[205] Is the pretension of the Ideal Theory enormous? Every
possible statement of the connexion between the world & you involves
pretensions as enormous.

Have you been associated with any friend whose charm over you
was ⟨coexistent w⟩ coextensive with your idea ⟨who⟩ that is, was
infinite; who filled your thought on that side ↑as most certainly befals
us↓; & so ⟨was⟩ you was enamoured of the person. ⟨It is easy to see⟩
And from ⟨of the person⟩ that person have you at last by incessant
love & study acquired a new measure of excellence, also a confidence
in the resources of God who ↑thus↓ sends you a real person to outgo
your ideal, you will readily see when you are separated, as you shortly
will be[,] the bud, flower, & fruit of the whole fact. As soon as your
friend has become to you an object of thought, has revealed to you
with great prominence a new nature, & has become a measure whereof
you are fully possessed to guage & test more, ⟨then expect⟩ as ⟨t⟩his
character become solid & sweet wisdom it is already a sign to you that
his office to you is closing[;] expect thenceforward the hour in which
he shall be withdrawn from your sight.[530]

[528] This paragraph is used in *Nature*, *W*, I, 39–40.
[529] Cf. *Nature*, *W*, I, 61: "the lesson of worship."
[530] This paragraph, struck through in ink with three diagonal use marks, is used
in *Nature*, *W*, I, 46. The "friend" is probably Charles Emerson.

⟨He⟩ To you he was manifest in flesh. He is not manifest in flesh. Has that portion of spiritual life which he represented to you any less reality? ⟨That which was⟩ All which was, is now & ever shall be. See then whether you do not overesteem the greatness of your labors & instead of vaunting so loudly your mission to the world look perhaps if the world have not a mission to you.

It were a wise secret inquiry for the bosom to compare point by point especially at eras or remarkable events ⟨the⟩ ↑our own↓ biography ⟨of⟩ with the rise, progress, & practice of Ideas [206] in us[531] [.]

Truth & originality go abreast always.

June 16. Yesterday I went to Mr Alcott's school & heard a conversation upon the Gospel of John. I thought the experiment of engaging young children upon questions of taste & truth successful. A few striking things were said by them. I felt strongly ⟨th⟩ as I watched the gradual dawn of a thought upon the minds of all, that to truth is no age or season. It appears or it does not appear, & when the child perceives it, he is no more a child; ⟨or⟩ age, sex are nothing: we are all alike before the great Whole. Little Josiah Quincy[532] now six years, six months old, is a child having something wonderful & divine in him. He is a youthful prophet[.]

The more abstract, the more practical.[533]

Monsters & aberrations give us glimpses of the higher law; — let us into the secret of Nature, thought Goethe.[534] Well. We fable to conform things better to our higher law, but when by & by we see the true cause, the fable fades & shrivels up. We see then the true higher law. To the wise therefore a fact is true poetry & the most beautiful of fables.[535]

↑See next page, A☞↓

[531] "It were a . . . Ideas" is struck through in ink with four diagonal use marks.
[532] Josiah Phillips Quincy, grandson of President Josiah Quincy of Harvard.
[533] This sentence, struck through in ink with a horizontal line, is used in *Nature*, *W*, I, 4.
[534] Cf. Goethe's quotation from Geoffroy de Sainte-Hilaire, *Principes de philosophie zoologique*, in *Werke*, L, 224, used in "Humanity of Science," *Lectures*, II, 30.
[535] "We fable . . . fables." is used in *Nature*, *W*, I, 75.

The εν και παν is the reason why our education can be carried on & perfected any where & with any bias whatsoever. If I study an ant hill & neglect all business, all history, all conversation yet shall that ant hill humbly & lovingly & unceasingly explored furnish me with ⟨the same⟩ a parallel experience & the same conclusions to which business, history, & conversation [207] would have brought me. So the sculptor, the dragoon, the trader, the shepherd, come to the same conclusions. All is economized. When you are doing, you lose no time from your book, because you still study & still learn. Do what you will you learn[,] so that you have a ⁿ right mind & a right heart. But if not, I think you still learn though all is mislearned. ↑Pains & prayer will do any thing.↓ [536]

Debt makes a large part of our education.[537]

It lies with you to make that thing you do the one thing important. Visit Dr Channing & you feel that his work is a sacred one; Visit Alcott & you look at every thing from the point of Education; Allston, — & Art seems the end of life; Taylor & you apologize for everything but sailors & bethels. Beside a good carpenter one thinks the world is made of wood; talk with a mason & you stand rebuked before the solidity & true level of brick & ⟨ston⟩ lime and with a farmer the earth exists for grass & potatoes. Each in turn puts his stamp upon the hour. This also shows how transparent all things are & show God through every part & angle. ↑But all the same things are done by false men *with an apology.*↓ [538]

↑opposite page↓ **A**   Hence doubtless that secret value we attach to facts that interest us ⟨well⟩ much beyond their seeming importance. We think it frivolous to record them, but a wise man records them & they agree with the experience & feelings of others. ↑They no doubt are points in this curve of the great circle[.]↓

[536] "All is economized . . . any thing." is struck through in pencil with a diagonal use mark. "When you are doing . . . mislearned." is used in "Ethics," *Lectures,* II, 146.

[537] This sentence, struck through in ink with horizontal lines, is used in *Nature, W,* I, 37.

[538] This paragraph is struck through in pencil with a diagonal use mark. All but the last two sentences are used in "Trades and Professions," *Lectures,* II, 125.

To a sailor the land is only *shore* and Mr [Brindley] thought Rivers existed for navigable canals.[539]

[208] Swedenborg I am persuaded will presently become popular. He needs only to be regarded as a poet instead of a sectarian & low religious dogmatist to be read & admired for his verities.

Cheapest say the prudent is the dearest labor. In my garden I find it best to pay a man's price or to buy *good sense applied to gardening*; in the house, good sense applied to painting; good sense applied to building; &c. So do I multiply myself — [540]

↑17 June.↓ A fact is only a fulcrum of the spirit. It is the terminus of a past thought but only a means now to new sallies of the imagination & new progress of wisdom.

What is a farm but a chapter in the bible almost? Pull out the weeds, water the plants; blight, rain, insects, sun, — it is a mere holy emblem from its first process to the last.[541]

A fact we said was the terminus of spirit. A man, I, am the remote circumference, the skirt, the thin suburb or frontier post of God [542] but go inward & I find the ocean; I lose my individuality in its waves. God is Unity, but always works in variety. I go inward until I find Unity universal, that Is before the World was; [n] I come outward to this body a point of variety.

Magnitude is nothing to science.[543]

[539] This sentence, written in pencil and struck through in pencil with a diagonal use mark, is used in "Trades and Professions," *Lectures*, II, 125, where Emerson included the name omitted in the manuscript here: that of James Brindley (1716–1772), an English engineer.

[540] This paragraph, struck through in pencil with a vertical use mark, is used in "Trades and Professions," *Lectures*, II, 127, and "Compensation," *W*, II, 114.

[541] This paragraph, struck through in ink with three diagonal use marks, is used in *Nature*, *W*, I, 42.

[542] Cf. *Nature*, *W*, I, 34–35: "A Fact is the end or last issue of spirit. The visible creation is the terminus or the circumference of the invisible world."

[543] This sentence is written in pencil.

The drop is a small ocean[,] the ocean a large drop. A leaf is a ⟨miniature of Nature Nature a variety of the leaf. m.⟩ ↑simplified world↓[,] the world a ⟨manifold⟩ compound leaf.[544]

[209] Matter is "the frail & weary weed in which God has drest the soul which he has called into time." [545]

22 June. Mr Alcott has been here with his Olympian dreams. He is a world-builder. Ever more he toils to solve the problem, Whence is the World? The point at which he prefers to begin is the Mystery of the Birth of a child. I tell him it is idle for him to affect to feel an interest in the ⟨thoughts⟩ compositions of any one else. ⟨N⟩Particulars, — particular thoughts, sentences, facts even, cannot interest him except as for a moment they take their place as a ray from his orb. The Whole, — Nature proceeding from himself, is what he studies. But he loses like other sovereigns great pleasures by reason of his grandeur. I go to Shakspear, Goethe, Swift, even to Tennyson, submit myself to them, become merely an organ of hearing, & yield to the law of their being. I am paid for thus being nothing by ⟨a new⟩ an entire new mind & thus a Proteus I enjoy the Universe through the powers & organs of a hundred different men. But Alcott cannot delight in Shakspear[,] cannot get near him. And so with all things. What is characteristic also, he cannot recal one word or part of his own conversation or of any one's let the expression be never so happy. He made here some majestic utterances but so inspired me that even I forgot the words often. The grass[,] the ⟨animals⟩ earth seemed to him "the refuse of spirit."

[210] Jesus says, Leave father & mother, house & lands & follow me. And there is no man who hath left all but he receives more.[546] This is as true intellectually as morally. Each new mind we approach seems to require an abdication of all our past & present empire. A new

[544] See, respectively, pp. [199], [153] above.
[545] A rendering of Michelangelo's Sonnet LI, ll. 9–11, used previously in "Michel Angelo Buonaroti," *Lectures*, I, 110; see *Rime di Michelagnolo Buonarroti il vecchio . . .* , ed. G. Biagioli (Paris, 1821), p. 118. This sentence, struck through in ink with three diagonal use marks, is used in *Nature*, W, I, 58.
[546] Cf. Matt. 19:29; Mark 10:29–30; Luke 18:29–30.

doctrine seems at first a subversion of all our opinions, tastes, & manner of living. So did Jesus, so did Kant, so did Swedenborg, so did Cousin, so did Alcott seem. Take thankfully & heartily all they can give, exhaust them, leave father & mother & goods, wrestle with them, let them not go until their blessing be won,[547] & after a short season the dismay will be overpast, the excess of influence will be withdrawn, & they will be no longer an alarming meteor but ⟨and⟩ one more bright star shining ⟨peace⟩ serenely in your heaven & blending its light with all your day.[548]

I love the wood god. I love the mighty PAN.

↑Yesterday I walked in the storm↓. And truly in the fields I am not alone or unacknowledged. They nod to me & I to them. The waving of the boughs of trees in a storm is new to me & old. It takes me by surprize & yet is not unknown. Its effect is like that of a higher thought or a better emotion coming over me when I deemed I was thinking justly or doing right. We distrust & deny inwardly our own sympathy with nature. We own & disown our relation to it. We are like Nebuchadnezzar cast down from our throne bereft of our reason & eating grass like an ox.[549]

[211]   ↑Man is the dwarf of himself↓

Is it not true that spirit in us is dwarfed by clay? that once Man was permeated & dissolved by spirit? He filled Nature with his overflowing currents. Out from him sprang the sun & moon[;] from man the sun[,] from woman the moon. The laws of his mind[,] the periods of his deeds externized themselves into day & night[,] into the year & seasons. But having made for himself this vast shell the waters retired, he no longer fills its veins & veinlets, he is shrunk into a drop. He sees it still fits him but fits him colossally. He adores timidly his

---

[547] Cf. Gen. 32:24–26.

[548] Here, as on p. [182] above, Emerson echoes Wordsworth, "Ode: Intimations of Immortality," l. 152 ("the fountain light of all our day"). This paragraph, struck through in pencil with a diagonal use mark, is used in "The Head," *Lectures*, II, 258, and "Intellect," *W*, II, 343–344.

[549] Cf. Dan. 4:25, 32, 33. This paragraph, struck through in ink with a diagonal use mark, is used in *Nature*, *W*, I, 10–11, 70–71.

own work. Say rather once it fitted him[;] now it corresponds to him from far & ⟨from⟩ on high. Yet now he starts occasionally in his slumber & wonders at himself & his house & muses strangely at the resemblance betwixt him & it. If now he have power[,] "if that his word is sterling yet in England[,]"⁵⁵⁰ he sees that it is unconscious power; power superior to his will; or Instinct[.]

Now all man's power over nature is by the understanding; as by manure, steam, the ↑economic↓ use of the wind & water & needle, coal, filling teeth with gold; making wooden legs; &c, &c. It is a ⟨reascending his throne by⟩ recovering his world an inch at a time & not a ⟨vaulting into his seat by⟩ resumption of power by vaulting at once into his seat. But Animal Magnetism, the Miracles of enthusiasts as Hohenlohe & the Shakers & the Swedenborgian, ↑prayer, eloquence, self healing as weak eyes,↓ the achievements of a principle as in Revolutions & in the abolition of Slave Trade — & the wisdom (often observed) of children — these are the examples of the Reason's momentary grasp of the sceptre. The exertions of a power not in time or in space but an instantaneous in-streaming causing ⁿ power.⁵⁵¹

[212] ↑The kingdom of man over nature shall not come with observation↓[.] ⁵⁵²

To all these wonders, ⟨he returns⟩ to a dominion such as now is beyond his dream of God, ⟨&⟩ ↑he shall return↓ without more wonder than the blind man feels who is gradually restored to perfect sight.⁵⁵³

The sordor & filths of nature the sun shall exhale & the wind dry up.⁵⁵⁴

It is the property of the ⟨true⟩ divine to be reproductive. The harvest is seed. The good sermon becomes a text in the hearer's mind.

---

⁵⁵⁰ Cf. *Richard II*, II, iv, 264.
⁵⁵¹ This and the preceding paragraph, struck through in ink with a curved diagonal use mark, are used in *Nature*, W, I, 71–73.
⁵⁵² Cf. Luke 17:20.
⁵⁵³ This paragraph, struck through in ink with a diagonal use mark, is used on p. [215] below and ultimately in *Nature*, W, I, 77.
⁵⁵⁴ This sentence, struck through in ink with two diagonal use marks, is used on p. [215] below and ultimately in *Nature*, W, I, 76.

That is the good book which sets us at work. The highest science is prophecy. Jesus is but the harbinger & announcer of the Comforter to come, & his continual office is to make himself less to us by making us demand more.

The Understanding, the Usurping Understanding the lieutenant of Reason, ⟨the⟩ ↑this↓ hired man, ⟨&⟩ the moment the Master is gone ⟨he⟩ steps into his place[;] this usher commands, sets himself to finish what He was doing, but instantly proceeds with his own dwarf Architecture & thoroughly cheats us until presently for a moment Reason returns & the slave obeys, & his work shrinks into tatters & cobwebs.

Not whilst the wise are one class & the good another, not whilst the physiologist & the psychologist are twain, can a Man exist, & Messiah come.

[213] A man is a god in ruins. When men are childlike, life ⟨will⟩ ↑may↓ be longer. Now the world would be more monstrous yet, if these disorganizations were more permanent. ⟨Childhood⟩ Infancy is the perpetual messiah which comes into the arms of these lost beings, & pleads with them to return to paradise.[555]

How hard to write the truth. "Let a man rejoice in the truth and not that he has found it," said my early oracle.[556] Well, so soon as I have seen the truth I clap my hands & rejoice & go back to see it & forward to tell men. I am so pleased therewith that presently it vanishes. Then am I submiss & it appears "without observation." I write it down, & it is gone. Yet ⟨for⟩↑tis↓ the benefit of others & their love of receiving truth from me the reason of my interest & effort to obtain it & thus ⟨does[?] God⟩ do I double & treble with God. The Reason refuses to play at couples with Understanding; to subserve the private ends of the Understanding.

[June] 24. I have read with great pleasure[,] sometimes with de-

---

[555] This paragraph, struck through in ink with a diagonal use mark, is used in *Nature*, *W*, I, 71.

[556] Sampson Reed. Cf. his "Oration on Genius" (1821), in *E t E*, II, 9.

light[,] No 5 of Mr Alcott's Record of Conversations in the Gospels.[557] The internal evidence of the genuineness of the thinking on the part of the children is often very strong. Their wisdom is ⟨the⟩ something the less surprizing because of the simplicity of the instrument on which they play these fine airs. It is a harp of two strings, Matter & Spirit, & in whatever combination or contrast or harmony you strike them, always the effect is sublime.

[214] "And no man gave him. He was alone with the swine; himself a swine." [558] Alcott

Is it not plain that prayer is a true study of truth? No man ever prayed heartily without learning something.[559]

⟨Every one has a ⟨charge⟩ trust of power, one talent, ↑men & boys↓ if it be only a jurisdiction⟩ Every one has a trust of power, every man — every boy — a jurisdiction, if it be only over a cow, or a rood of a potato field, or a fleet of ships, or the laws of a state.[560]

Magnitude is nothing to Science. ⟨A⟩The ocean is a large drop; the drop, a small ocean.[561]

[215] It is essential to a true theory of nature & man, that it should contain somewhat progressive, should ascribe freedom to the will, or benevolent designs to the Deity. And the effect of the ideal theory truly seen is this; Nature is not stable but fluid. Spirit alters, moulds, makes it. The immobility or bruteness of nature is the absence of spirit; to pure spirit it is fluid, it is volatile, it is obedient. Believe that the world exists for you. For you is the phenomenon perfect & what we are, that only we see. All that Adam ⟨saw⟩ ↑had,↓

[557] "Annunciation of Spirit to Paternity. Paternal Sentiment," subsequently printed in *Record of Conversations on the Gospels, Held in Mr. Alcott's School; Unfolding the Doctrine and Discipline of Human Culture,* 2 vols. (Boston, 1836–1837), I, 38–46. See p. [309] below.

[558] Cf. Luke 15:15–16.

[559] This paragraph, struck through in ink with three diagonal use marks, is used in *Nature, W,* I, 74.

[560] This passage, struck through in ink with a diagonal use mark, is used in "Education," *W,* X, 128–129.

[561] See pp. [199], [208] above.

all that Caesar could, you have & can do. Adam called it the earth, Caesar called life Rome; you perhaps call it a cob[b]ler's trade, yet line for line & point for point, you have the whole circle. As fast as your spirit quits its earth, disagreeable appearances, prisons, spiders, snakes, pests, madhouses, vanish; ⁿ they are temporary & shall be no more seen. The sordor & filths of nature, the sun shall dry up & the wind ⟨dissipate⟩ exhale. As before the Summer, the snowbanks melt and the face of the earth becomes green so ⟨shall the ⁿ path of P⟩ the spirit shall create its ornaments along its path & carry with it the beauty it visits & the song which enchants it; create ⁿ intelligent faces & warm hearts and sweet discourse ↑[&] heroic acts↓ around its way until evil is no more seen. This kingdom of man over nature which shall not come with observation,ⁿ a dominion such as now is beyond his dream of God[,] he shall enter without more wonder than the blind man feels who is gradually restored to perfect sight.⁵⁶²

[216] Insist upon seeing Nature as a problem to be solved. It is a question addressed to you. What is a child? What is a woman? What is a year or a season? What do they signify & say to ME? ⁵⁶³

Then it occurs as a question. Whether the Ideal Theory is not merely introductory to Spiritual views. It diminishes & degrades matter in order to receive a new view of it, namely this, that the world is the new fruit of Spirit evermore.⁵⁶⁴

———

There is one drop in the number of its drops which makes the ocean greater than any sea.⁵⁶⁵

———

29 June. In this pleasing contrite wood life which God allows me, let me record day by day my honest thoughts, & the record ought to have the interest to a philosopher which the life of a gymnosophist

---

⁵⁶² This paragraph incorporates material previously drafted: see the first three sentences on p. [212] above. Struck through in ink with four curved diagonal use marks (see Plate I), it is used in *Nature*, W, I, 61, 76–77.

⁵⁶³ This paragraph is used in *Nature*, W, I, 74–75.

⁵⁶⁴ This paragraph, struck through in ink with a diagonal use mark, anticipates passages in ch. VI of *Nature*, W, I, 56, 57–58, concerning the "degrading" of material nature and asserting its "dependence on spirit."

⁵⁶⁵ See Emerson's letter to Charles C. Emerson, May 19?, 1827 (L, I, 200).

or stylite had. The book ↑should↓ smell of pines & resound with hum
of insects. I suppose no man can violate his nature. All the sallies of
his will are rounded in by the law of his being as the inequalities of
Andes & Himmaleh are insignificant in the curve of ⟨sp⟩ the sphere.
Nor does it matter how you guage & try him. A character is like a
quincunx or an Alexandrian ⟨crotchet⟩ stanza, — read it forward or
backward or across, it still spells the same thing. So you may judge a
man by his company or by his books, or by his expenditure, by his
craniology, or his physiognomy — he will⟨,⟩ give the same result.[566]

[217] Exoteric & Esoteric doctrines refer to the distinction of
the Reason & Understanding[.]

A man cannot bury his meanings so deep in his book but time &
likeminded men will find them.[567]

Nature is yet far from being exhausted.
Nature is the projection of God. It is the expositor of the Divine
mind. Chateaubriand called it the divine imagination. Say they, that
Geometry is the divine Mind, and is the landscape less so? Yet see
how far man is at discord with nature for ⟨whilst⟩ you ↑cannot at the
same time↓ admire the prospect, ⟨you cannot⟩ ↑&↓ sympathize with
Wyman & Tuttle who are digging in the field.[568]

Beauty & pleasure no doubt are the pilots of the mind, but it
must first be healthy.

July 2. Mrs Ripley expressed a contempt for Boccac[c]io, & we
agreed that in English his was a wholly false reputation.

It often seems that we do not record the true thoughts; we do
not apprehend them: Those that we feel & live, we cannot yet record.

[566] "I suppose . . . the sphere." is used in "The Present Age," Lectures, II, 171.
The entire paragraph, struck through in ink with a vertical use mark, is used in "Self-
Reliance," W, II, 58.
[567] This sentence, struck through in ink with a vertical use mark, is used in
"Ethics," Lectures, II, 149, and "Spiritual Laws," W, II, 146.
[568] This paragraph is used in Nature, W, I, 64–65.

How far often is the thought that rises in the soul from being lived or how remote yet from the hands.[569] The friend, the spouse perceives unfitness in the friend, in the spouse. Yet periods of discipline, revolutions in state must transpire before that chasm which the far lightning of thought revealed, can be bridged over.

[218] Will any say that the Meaning of the world is exhausted when he sees the allegory of a single natural process? [570]
The wheatear that ⟨No⟩ nods so pensively in ⟨the⟩ July ⟨day⟩ is related to the Day and the Day to the wheatear. Have you quite found out why every natural form, the acorn, the claw, the pine cone, the egg, the palm, and every tree & every leaf should be beautiful? [571]

It does not seem as if the race were progressive in time at all, but merely in spirit. Phocion, Socrates, Anaxagoras, Diogenes, present us the lively image of great men. But they leave no churches. He who is really of their church will be wholly his own man. The improvements of our time are merely mechanical & do not at all affect man. We have no greater men than Epaminondas & Agesilaus.[572]

↑July 5↓. It never rains but it pours. If you see pyrola you see nothing else but varieties of pyrola. To that one thing which a man has in his head all nature seems an illustration[,] all men martyrs. Εν και παν[.]

Human Flora
Subgenus, arid lachrymose apologetic adhesive. ↑wiry↓[573]
     Afternoon man
     Wholesale speaker
     Conservative

[569] "It often seems . . . hands." is struck through in pencil with a vertical use mark.
[570] See p. [217] above; cf. *Nature*, *W*, I, 41: "Nothing in nature is exhausted in its first use. . . . It has already been illustrated, that every natural process is a version of a moral sentence."
[571] This sentence, struck through in ink with a vertical use mark, is used in *Nature*, *W*, I, 16.
[572] This paragraph, struck through in ink with a vertical use mark, is used in "The Individual," *Lectures*, II, 175, and "Self-Reliance," *W*, II, 86.
[573] The word "wiry" is added in pencil.

[219] July 9. I have looked over the designs for Dante by Flaxman. Flaxman was a disciple of Swedenborg and the result is accord-
ingly a threefold cord in which each may claim his strand. As wind
& sun play into one another's hands in nature so do human minds.
Several geniuses of the past generations are reproduced for us today
in their pupils. The corn in my garden[,] the child of Today[,] is a
compound cord of which the sun, air, water, carbon, azote,[n] & oxygen,
are the plies[.]

July 21. The worst guest is Asmodeus who comes into the quiet house
sometimes in breeches sometimes in petticoats and demands of his
entertainer not shelter & food, but to find him in work, and every
body is on pins until some rope of sand is found for the monster to
twist.[574]

Respect yourself. You have first an instinct, then an opinion,
then a knowledge, as the plant has root, bud, & fruit. Trust the instinct
to the end, though you cannot tell why or see why. It is vain to hurry
it. By trusting it, ⟨by & by⟩ it shall ripen into thought & truth & you
shall know why you believe[.] [575]

Pleasant it is to see two persons acting habitually & harmoniously
together of entirely different manner & voice; two strong natures
neither of which impairs the other by any direct modification. ↑The
more perfect the Union, ⟨&⟩ the concession at the same time of individual peculiarity being the least, makes the best society.↓

[220] Make your own Bible. ⟨Collect⟩ Select & Collect all those
words & sentences that in all your reading have been to you like the
blast of trumpet out of Shakspear, Seneca, Moses, John, & Paul.[576]

[574] The expression "To twist a rope of sand" occurs in Ray, *A Complete Collection of English Proverbs*, 1817, p. 141; association of Asmodeus with the phrase is
recurrent in Emerson: cf. *Lectures*, II, 156; *W*, II, 119, *W*, VIII, 149, and *W*, IX,
334 ("The Asmodean feat is mine, / To spin my sand-heap into twine"). This paragraph, struck through in pencil with a vertical use mark, is used in "Behavior," *W*,
VI, 173.
[575] "You have first . . . believe", struck through in pencil with a diagonal use
mark, is used in "The Head," *Lectures*, II, 251, and "Intellect," *W*, II, 330.
[576] An ink sketch of a trumpet follows this sentence.

30 July. Man is the point wherein matter & spirit meet & marry. The Idealist says, God paints the world around your soul. The spiritualist saith, Yea, but lo! God is within you.[577] The self of self creates the world through you, & organizations like you.[578] The Universal Central Soul comes to the surface in my body[.]

31 July. The wise man has no secrets. Secrets belong to the individual, local. He strives evermore to sink the individual in the universal. The friend who can bring him into a certain mood has a right to all the privacies that belong to that mood. Moreover, he believes that no secrets can be: that the nature of the man does forever publish itself and that all laborious concealments lose their labor.

6 August. The grey past, the white future.

A year ago I studied Ben Jonson a good deal. You may learn much from so complete records of one mind as his works are. There is something fearful in coming up against the walls of a mind on every side & learning to describe their invisible circumference.

"I know not what you think of me",[n] said my friend. Are you sure? You know all I think of you by those things I say to you. You know all which can be of [221] any use to you. If I, if all your friends should draw your portrait ↑to you↓ — faults & graces, it would mislead you, embarrass you; you[n] must not ask how you please me for curiosity. You must not look in the glass to see how handsome you are but to see if your face is clean. Certainly I know what impression I made on any man, by remembering what communications he made to me[.] [579]

In the scholar's Ethics, I would put down Beharre wo ↑du

---

[577] Cf. Luke 17:21; see p. [185] above.

[578] Cf. *Nature*, *W*, I, 64: spirit "does not act upon us from without, that is, in space and time, but spiritually, or through ourselves: therefore, that spirit, that is, the Supreme Being, does not build up nature around us, but puts it forth through us, as the life of the tree puts forth new branches and leaves through the pores of the old."

[579] "You must not . . . to me" is struck through in pencil with a vertical use mark. The "friend" referred to was probably Margaret Fuller, the Emersons' visitor.

stehst↓.[580] ⟨Stay by⟩ Stick by yourself, and Goethe's practice to publish his book without preface & let it lie unexplained. And further, the sentence in West Ostlichen Divan about *freedom*[.] [581]

12 August. Yesterday Margaret Fuller returned home after making us a visit of three weeks — a very accomplished & very intelligent person.

All our experience helps us very little directly, except in getting bread & doing the work of the world. But if you have learned with years of pain how to treat an annoying relative as a foolish father or wife & you hug yourself at your acquired skill, let that person die or depart & you shall find all your fancied ⟨su⟩ experience useless in the first new relation you enter, as marriage, paternity, or care of ⟨the⟩ ↑an↓ insane, or vicious person.[582] Indeed who can see that by his own contrivance he has acquired any dexterity in ⟨managing⟩ ↑playing↓ such a hard game as the first-named. It was rather a facility of things, a certain adjustment of things themselves than any wisdom of his own. Each new relation finds us, maugre all our experience & all our talent, mere babies. Our progress in the particular never helps us in the particular. There is only out of the particular a general growth of the soul from [583] [222] year to year. And that helps us in every particular because in every relation the magnitude of the soul is always felt and though for moments resisted by artificial or ⟨local⟩ temporary authorities as of age, paternity, wealth &c. yet in the long run always conquers & has the world at its disposal.
Fathers wish to be fathers of the mind as well as of the body of their children. But in my experience they seem to be merely the occasion of new beings coming into the world than parents of their life or seers of their own affection incarnated as Alcott would think.

[580] Goethe, *Werke*, 1828–1833, XXII, 245.

[581] No passages are marked in Emerson's copy of Goethe's *West-östlicher Divan* (*Werke*, 1828–1833, V); marked passages in the accompanying "Noten und Abhandlungen" (*Werke*, VI) do not pertain to "freedom."

[582] "All our experience . . . vicious person.", struck through in pencil with a diagonal use mark, is used in "The Present Age," *Lectures*, II, 158.

[583] "Each new relation . . . of the soul from" is struck through in pencil with a diagonal use mark. The first two sentences marked are used in "The Present Age," *Lectures*, II, 158–159.

At times, as in the wood on Wednesday, it seems as if all the particular life were mere by-play & in ⟨nowise connected by⟩ ↑no way of↓ cause & effect connected with the absolute life.[584]

⟨Every⟩ The reason of the variety & infinity of objects is given in the doctrine that external objects are mere signs of internal essences. Therefore "every object rightly seen unlocks a new faculty of the Soul." [585] That is to say, it becomes a part of the domain of Consciousness; before it was unconscious truth, now is available Knowledge.[586]

I said once that if you go expressly to look at the moon, it becomes tinsel.[587] A party of view hunters will see no divine landscape. There is however in moon gazing something analogous to Newton's fits of easy transmission & reflection.[588] You catch the charm one moment, then it is gone, then it returns to go again. And spoken of it becomes flat enough. Perhaps the "fits" depend on the pulsations of the heart.

[223] The best Service which history renders us is to lead us to prize the present.

I went to Walden Pond this evening a little before sunset, and in the tranquil landscape I behold somewhat as beautiful as my own nature.[589]

↑Aug. 13↓. Some men have a heart & feel the claims of others — Other men have an intellectual heart or a perception of the claims

[584] This paragraph, struck through in pencil with a vertical use mark, is used in "The Present Age," *Lectures*, II, 159.

[585] Cf. Coleridge's observation on the discoveries of scientific men, *Aids to Reflection*, 1829, pp. 150–151; previously paraphrased in *JMN*, III, 283.

[586] This paragraph, struck through in pencil with a diagonal use mark, is used in *Nature*, W, I, 35.

[587] See *JMN*, IV, 288; cf. *Nature*, W, I, 19.

[588] According to David Brewster, *The Life of Sir Isaac Newton* (New York, 1831), p. 78, Newton regarded ether as that medium "by which light is refracted and reflected, and by whose vibrations light . . . is put into fits of easy reflection and transmission." See *JMN*, IV, 87; cf. "The American Scholar," *W*, I, 98.

[589] Cf. *Nature*, W, I, 10: "In the tranquil landscape . . . man beholds somewhat as beautiful as his own nature."

of others. A third class have neither & are neither desired nor approved. W.⟨L.G.⟩ [590] for example.

All education all philosophy lay stress upon the Individual, not upon society. We are confounded by the discord between our theory & the actual world. By myself for myself I can have faith, Ideas, Progress, God; but if I must apply all these to Society as we see it they become Philisterey, as the Germans say.

How rarely can a female mind be impersonal. S[arah]. A[lden]. R[ipley]. is wonderfully free from egotism of place & time & blood. M[argaret]. F[uller]. by no means so free with all her superiority. What shall I say of MME!

[224] 17 August. "Our part in public occasions, says Goethe, is, for the most part, Philisterei". True of commencement & this Cambridge jubilee.[590a]

Criticism has this defence that, like poetry, it is an accomodation of the shows of things to the desires of the mind.[591]

27 August. Today came to me the first proof-sheet of "Nature" to be corrected, like a new coat, full of vexations; with the first sentences of the chapters perched like mottoes aloft in small type! The peace of the author cannot be wounded by such trifles, if he sees that the sentences are still good. A good sentence can never be put out of countenance by any blunder of compositors. It is good in text or note, in poetry or prose, as title or corollary. But a bad sentence shows all his flaws instantly by such dislocation. So that a certain sublime serenity is generated in the soul of the Poet by the annoyances of the press. He sees that the spirit may infuse a subtle ⟨connexion⟩ logic

---

[590] William Lloyd Garrison? Emerson, though he later came to have "moments of admiration" for Garrison, as Rusk remarks, "was not blind to the man's narrowness and imperviousness to other ideas than his own" (*Life*, p. 366).

[590a] Presumably Harvard's bicentennial.

[591] Cf. Bacon, *Of the Advancement of Learning*, Bk. II, in *The Works*, 1824, I, 90: poesy "doth raise and erect the mind, by submitting the shows of things to the desires of the mind; whereas reason doth buckle and bow the mind unto the nature of things." See *JMN*, III, 247; "John Milton," *Lectures*, I, 162; "History," *W*, II, 34.

into the parts of the piece which shall defy all accidents to break
their connexion.

[225] The man of talents who brings his ⟨genius⟩ ↑poetry &
eloquence↓ to market is like the hawk which I have seen wheeling
up to heaven in the face of noon — & all to have a better view of
mice & moles & chickens.[592]

⟨Li⟩ Colors according to Goethe's theory it seems are merely
the different proportions in which light & darkness are mixed. Equally
mixed they make ⟨blue⟩ red[;] with more light, yellow; with more
darkness blue[.] [593]

29 Aug.   En peu d'heure
                     Dieu labeure [594]

                                        God works in moments.

——

History.   A great licentiousness seems to have followed
directly on the heels of the Reformation. Luther even had to lament
the decay of piety in his own household. "Doctor," said his wife to
him one day, "how is it that while subject to papacy, we prayed so
often & with such fervor, while now we pray with the utmost coldness & very seldom?" Remember Luther's wife! [595]

——

With what satisfaction I read last night with G.P.B[radford].
some lines from Milton. In Samson Agonistes & elsewhere ⟨how⟩
with what dignity he felt the office of the bard, the solemn office borne
by the great & grave of every age for the behoof of all men; a call
which never was heard in the frivolous brains of the Moores & Hugos
& Berangers of the day.

[592] Cf. "The Present Age," *Lectures*, II, 161.
[593] Goethe's theory of colors is set forth in his *Farbenlehre* (1810; *Werke*, 1828–
1833, L–LV). This paragraph is struck through in pencil with a vertical use mark.
[594] Goethe, *Dichtung und Wahrheit*, IV, in *Werke*, 1828–1833, XLVIII, 49. Used
in "Prudence," *Lectures*, II, 323.
[595] This passage, struck through in ink with seven wavy diagonal use marks, is
used in "The Individual," *Lectures*, II, 178, and "History," *W*, II, 29.

The "threnes" of Shakspear seem to belong to a "purer state of sensation & existence", to use Landor's word.[596]

Humanity characterises the highest class of genius[:] Homer, Milton, Shakspear. We expect flashes of thought, but this is higher yet. The sorrows of Adam & Eve[.] [597]

[226] Again I hear the melancholy sentence of Pestalozzi that he had learned that no man in God's wide world is either able or willing to help any other man.[598]

How strongly it came to mind the other eve. at the Teachers' Meeting (as oft before) that nothing needs so much to be preached as the law of Compensation out of the nature of things,[n] that the good exalts & the evil degrades us not hereafter but in the moment of the deed[.]

G.P.B. says of Alcott that he destroys too many illusions[.]

At the age ludicrously called the age of discretion every hopeful young man is shipwrecked. The burdensome possession of himself he cannot dispose of. Up to that hour, others have directed him & he has gone triumphantly. Then he begins to direct himself & all hope, wisdom, & power sink flat down. Sleep creeps over him & he lies down in the snow.[599]

One of us is received with favor & of another the world is not worthy.

[227] There is a difference between the waiting of the prophet & the standing still of the fool.

2 September. We see much truth under the glitter & ribbons

[596] See p. [45] above.
[597] This paragraph is struck through in pencil with a vertical use mark. "With what satisfaction . . . & Eve" is used in "Literature," *Lectures*, II, 62.
[598] Quoted from Edward Biber, *Henry Pestalozzi and his Plan of Education* . . . (London, 1831), p. 203; see *JMN*, IV, 12, 20. The sentence, struck through in pencil with a diagonal use mark, is used in "The American Scholar," *W*, I, 113.
[599] This paragraph, struck through in pencil with a curved vertical use mark, is used in "The Present Age," *Lectures*, II, 170.

of a festival like Commencement. Each year the same faces come there, but each elongated or whitened or fallen a little. The courage too, that is felt at presenting your own face before the well known assembly, is not an extempore feeling, but is based on a long memory of studies & actions. An assembly is a sort of Judgment Day, before whose face every soul is tried. Fat & foolish faces, to be sure, there are ⟨as they⟩in the forefront of the crowd, but they are only warnings & the imps & ⟨victims⟩ examples of doom. The scholar looks in at the door, but unwilling to face this ordeal to little purpose, he retreats & walks ⟨s⟩ along solitary streets & lanes, far from the show.

Every principle is a war-note[.]

Sept. 13. I went to the College Jubilee on the 8th instant. A noble & well thought of anniversary. The pathos of the occasion was extreme & not much noted by the speakers. Cambridge at any time is full of ghosts; but on that day the ↑anointed↓ eye ⟨that⟩ saw the crowd of spirits that mingled with the procession in the vacant spaces, year by year, as the classes proceeded; and then the far longer train of ghosts that ⟨preceded⟩ ↑followed↓ the company, of the men that wore before us the college honors & the laurels of the state — the long winding train reaching back ↑⟨forwa⟩↓ into eternity. —— But among the living was more melancholy reflection, namely the identity of all the persons with that which

turn to p. 229

[228] How we live on the outside of the world! Open the Skin, the flesh, ⟨it⟩& enter the Skeleton, touch the heart, liver, or brain of the Man and you have come no nearer to the man than when you were still outside. All this is as strange & foreign to him as to you. You have almost as much property in his body as he has.[600] The babe is formed in the womb of the mother quite outside of her system. It is carefully guarded from any interference with her constitution. So if you go into a family where you supposed a perfect understanding & intimate bonds subsisted, you find with surprise that all

[600] "How we live . . . he has." is struck through in pencil with a diagonal use mark.

193

are ⟨st⟩ in a degree strangers to each other, that father has one interest & you another, that husband & wife observe each other's acts &
words with much of a stranger's curiosity[.]

To unify is the perpetual effort of the mind.[601]

"Dulness of the age." What age was not dull? When were not the
majority wicked? or what progress was ever made by society? Society
is always ⟨the fool⟩ ↑flat & foolish↓. The only progress ever ⟨made⟩
known was of the individual. A great wit is, at any time, great solitude. A barnyard is full of chirping & cackle, but no fowl clap⟨peth⟩s
wings on Chimborazo.

> The rain has spoiled the farmer's day
> Shall sorrow put my books away
> Thereby are two days lost
> Nature will speed her own affairs
> I will attend my proper cares
> Come rain or sun or frost.[602]

[229] they were in youth, in college halls. I found my old friends
the same; the same jokes pleased, the same straws tickled; the manhood & offices they brought hither today seemed masks; underneath,
we were still boys.[602a]

20 Sept. Yesterday despatched a letter to Thomas Carlyle —
P.M. Attended a meeting of friends at Mr ↑G↓ Ripley's house —
present, F. H. Hedge, C. Francis, A. B. Alcott, J. F. Clarke, O. A.
Brownson, G. Ripley.[603] The conversation was earnest & hopeful.

[601] "So if you . . . mind." is struck through in pencil with a vertical use mark.
[602] The verse, struck through in ink with a vertical use mark, was printed as
"Suum Cuique" in Emerson's *Poems* (Boston, 1847), p. 128; the lines were omitted
from *Selected Poems* (1876) and from *W*, IX.
[602a] This sentence is used in "Domestic Life," *W*, VII, 124.
[603] This preliminary meeting of "Hedge's Club," later the so-called "Transcendental Club," had been projected since July (*L*, II, 29, 34). Except for Alcott, the
men present were all young Unitarian ministers, active or inactive. Ripley and Hedge
have appeared in earlier entries; Convers Francis was a pastor at Watertown; James
Freeman Clarke had been preaching since 1833 at Louisville, where he edited *The
Western Messenger*; Orestes Brownson, formerly a Presbyterian and Universalist,
later became a Roman Catholic.

It inspired hope. G. R. said that a man should strive to be an idea & merge all his personalities, in debate. We agreed to bury fear even the fear of man & if Dr C[hanning]. & Mr J[onathan]. P[hillips]. or Dr J[ames]. W[alker].[604] should join us, no man should look at the spout but only ↑at↓ the flowing water. Incidentally we had some character drawing. I said of Mr F.[605] He has a French mind & should have been born at Paris in ↑the↓ era of brilliant conversation with the Diderots, Grimms, Rousseaus, DeStaels. Pit him against a brilliant mate & he will sparkle & star away by the hour together. But he is hopeless. He has no hope for society. The rule suggested for the club was this, that no man should be admitted whose ↑presence↓ excluded any one topic. I said in the beginning of the afternoon present only G R & J.F.C. that 'twas pity that in this Titanic Continent where ⟨brute⟩ Nature is so grand, Genius should be so tame. Not one unchallengeable reputation. I felt towards Allston as Landor said of his picture[:] "I would give 50 guineas to the artist would swear it was a Dominichino." [606] So A. was a beautiful draughtsman but the soul of his picture is *imputed* by the spectator. His merit is like that of Kean's [607] recitation merely outlinear, strictly emptied of all [230] obtrusive individuality, but a vase to receive & not a fountain to impart *character*. So of Bryant's poems, chaste, faultless, beautiful, but uncharacterised. ⟨&⟩ So of Greenough's Sculpture, picturesque but not creative & in the severe style of old art. So of Dr Channing's preaching. They are all *feminine* or receptive & not masculine or creative.

A rail road, State street, Bunker Hill monument are genuine productions of the age but no art[.]

The reason is manifest. They are not wanted. The statue ⟨the⟩

[604] For these and other names of men to be invited, see Alcott's journal entry for September 19, 1836 — reproduced in *The Journals of Bronson Alcott*, selected and edited by Odell Shepard (Boston, 1938), facing p. 78. Walker, Unitarian minister at Charlestown, 1818–1839, and editor of *The Christian Examiner*, 1831–1839, became a professor and later president of Harvard.

[605] Probably Reverend Nathaniel Langdon Frothingham, one of those to be invited to join the group, successor to Emerson's father as minister of the First Church in Boston, 1815–1850.

[606] Emerson is evidently recalling his conversation with Landor on May 18, 1833, in Italy. This remark, though not recorded in his journal at the time, appears in *English Traits* along with other material noted on that day (*W*, V, 9).

[607] Edmund Kean, the late English tragedian, or his son Charles John.

of Jove was to be worshipped. The Virgin of Titian was to be worshipped. Jesus, Luther were reformers; Moses, David did something,
the builders of ⟨Gothic⟩ cathedrals ⟨believed⟩ feared. ↑Love & fear
laid the stones in their own order.↓ 608

What interest has Greenough to make a good statue? Who cares
whether it is good? A few prosperous gentlemen & ladies, but the
Universal Yankee nation roaring in the Capitol to approve or condemn would make his eye & hand & heart go to a new tune.609

⟨⟨Well⟩ ↑⟨It was⟩↓ ↑⟨Well⟩↓ what shall nourish the sense of
beauty now? Speech ⟨is⟩ ↑⟨It was⟩↓ an art of eternal riches & fitness⟩ 610

It was requested that this be the subject of discussion at the next
meeting & I should open the debate.

[231] These things now are merely ornamental. Nothing ⟨is⟩
that is so, can be beautiful. Whatsoever is beautiful must rest on a
basis as broad as man. There can be no handsome↑ness↓ that is not
such of necessity, that does not proceed from the nature of the man
that made it. ↑Poetry, Music, Sculpture, painting, architecture, were
all enlisted in the service of ⟨the arts.⟩ religion.↓ 611 ↑The gayest petal
serves the flower. The finest form in woman is only perfectest health.↓

The steady tendency, I think, of things now, is, to a reduction
of speculation of all sorts, to Science, that is, to a conformity with the
nature of things, (as observed).n

Swedenborg's reform was from dogmas to the nature of things.
He had no ornament, no diction, no ⟨lo⟩ choice of words.n

Fairs — ↑Centennials↓ Jubilees   Apicius & his balcony.612

608 Cf. "The Problem," W, IX, 7, ll. 31–32: "so grew these holy piles, / Whilst
love and terror laid the tiles."

609 This and the two preceding paragraphs, struck through in pencil with a curved
diagonal use mark, are used in "Thoughts on Art," The Dial, I (Jan. 1841), 378;
"Art," Lectures, II, 54; and "Art," W, VII, 56.

610 This paragraph is struck through in ink with horizontal spirals.

611 "These things now . . . religion" is struck through in pencil with a diagonal
use mark.

612 See p. [53] above.

Ornamental speeches, ornamental sermons, lectures, Resolutions, a Trades' strike or a Methodist Class Meeting or a lover's blush or a traveller's exhilaration in Berkshire[.]

Sir Walter Raleigh's conclusion of his Hist[ory]. of the World is sublime only because it closes a history of the world. In a sermon it would not be of much mark[;] the topstone of the pyramid is sublime by position[,] so the sentence admired by Warburton in Milton's History[.]

I think two causes operate against our intellectual performances. 1. Our devotion to property. The love of Liberty in the Revolution made some great men. But now the sentiment of Patriotism can hardly exist in a country so vast. It can be ⟨got⟩ fired in Carolina by contracting the country to Carolina. It might be here by separating Massachusetts from the Union.
[232][612a] However I confess I see nothing in the outward condition of a native of this country which any but a sickly effeminate person can arraign.
2. But the Influence of Europe certainly seems to me prejudicial. Genius is the enemy of genius[.]

Sunday ↑Dec. 10↓.   Rhetoric
    I cannot hear a sermon without being struck by the fact that amid drowsy series of sentences what a sensation a historical fact, a biographical name, a sharply objective illustration makes! Why will not the preacher heed the admonition of the silence momentary of his congregation & ⟨often what is[n] shown him⟩ that this particular sentence is all they carry away? Is he not taught hereby that the synthesis is ⟨always⟩ ↑to all↓ grateful & to most indispensable of abstract thought & concrete body?[n] Principles should be verified by the adducing of facts & sentiments incorporated by their appropriate imagery. Only in a purely scientific composition which by its text & structure addresses itself to philosophers is a writer at liberty to ⟨g⟩ use mere abstractions.
    A preacher should be a live coal to kindle all the church.

[612a] "Religion" is written above "However I confess" at the top of the page.

[233] ↑Dec. 10↓. I wrote elsewhere of Composition. Yet today the old view came back again with new force on seeing & hearing about King's College[,] Cambridge — that it is what is already done that enables the artist to accomplish the wonderful. That ⟨‖ . . . ‖⟩ hall is covered with a profusion of richest fan work in solid stone to which a charming tint is given by the stained glass windows. The artist who has this talent for delicate embellishment & splendid softening tints, has not usually the talent for ⟨Cyclopean⟩ massive masonry & Cyclopean architecture. One man built a church on solid blocks able to uphold a Mountain; another took advantage of this Alpine Mass to spring an airy arch thereon; a third adopted this foundation & superstructure, the fruit of talents not his own, & converted the rigid surface into garlands & lace; and [n] thus is the Chapel a work of the human mind, & altogether transcending the abilities of any one man.

This is my belief of written Composition that it can surpass any unwritten effusions of however profound genius[,] for what is writ is a foundation of a new superstructure & a guide to the eye for new foundation, so that the work rises tower upon tower with ever new & total strength of the builder.[613]

[234][614] ⟨If y⟩ There is one mind, & every man is a porch leading into it. Prayer is an address to it. Religion is the selfrespect of this mind.

But to be its organ is so much that a man should never in any act, least of all in a religious rite[,] have any trick or ↑sneaking↓ apologetic scraping or leering, demure depressing of the eyes, or any hypocritical nonsense. Let him never when perfect beauty & wisdom are addressed in a high act of the abstract soul palter or do aught unmanly, but inspired with a noble daring let him then most feel the majesty of being & though he be a beggar let him behave himself greatly.

Antique

Our admiration of the Antique is not admiration of the Old but

[613] This and the preceding paragraph, struck through in pencil with a diagonal use mark, are used in "Literature," *Lectures*, II, 63–64.

[614] "Ecclesiastical manners" is written above "one mind . . . man is" at the top of the page.

of the Natural. We admire the Greek in an American plough boy often. The Greeks as a nation were not reflective, but perfect in their senses, perfect in their health. The ⟨men a⟩ adults acted with the simplicity & grace of boys. They made vases & tragedies & statues such as healthy senses should, that is, *in good taste.* Such things have continued to be made in all ages & are now wherever a healthy physiology exists, but owing to their decided superiority of eye, ⟨as a class,⟩ they have done better as a class than any others, & their local forms have ⟨obtain⟩ usurped the conventional reverence.[615]

[235] Nothing is more melancholy than to treat men as pawns & ninepins. If I leave out their heart, they take out mine. But speak to the soul, & always the soul will reply.[616] ↑To treat of the nature of things is to show his life in new glory to every man. When he sees he is no sport of circumstances, but that all nature is his friend and he is related to natures so great that if his private selfish good suffer shipwreck[,] he yet must rejoice↓[.]

Yet do you think a dinner brings a man less surely home than would a sheriff or that ⟨thirst⟩ hatred less surely removes him from another than a chain of mountains. A man's wife has more power over him than the State has.

Mr Webster never loses sight of his relation to Nature. The Day is always part of him. "But, Mr President, the shades of evening which close around us, admonish me to conclude," he said at Cambridge.

I notice George Herbert's identification of himself with Jewish genius. "List, you may hear great Aaron's bell" — "Aaron's drest!" & the like.[617] It reminds me of that criticism I heard in Italy of Michel Angelo, viz. that he ⟨in⟩ painted prophets & patriarchs like a Hebrew; that they were not merely old men in robes & beards, but a sanctity

---

[615] This paragraph, struck through in pencil with two diagonal use marks, is used in "Manners," *Lectures,* II, 134, and "History," *W,* II, 25–26.

[616] "Nothing is more . . . reply.", struck through in pencil with a vertical use mark, is used in "Society," *Lectures,* II, 107.

[617] Cf. Herbert, "Decay," l. 10; "Aaron," l. 25.

& the character of the pentateuch & the prophecy was conspicuous in them[.]

Light & Music are analogous in their law[.]
Light is merely arithmetic & geometry painted or diagramma-
tized.
⟨Painter⟩ ↑Musician↓ draws a picture on air. Norris
Vitruvius thought Architect should be a Musician[.]
Architecture "elevates mathematical laws to rules of beauty[.]"
                                    Am. Encyclop. Art[icle]. Architecture [618]

[236] 21 September. ⟨We get a commission of mileage⟩ ↑The ship beating at sea gains a small commission of miles for her true course↓ on every ⟨mile of⟩ tack ⟨in beating at sea.⟩. So in life our profession, our dilettantism gives us ⟨some solid wisdom⟩ with much parade a little solid wisdom. ↑The days & hours of Reason will shine with steady light as the life of life & all the other days & weeks appear as hyphens to join these. p. 58↓

The bird of passage, what does he signify?
⟨There is no time to brutes.⟩ [619]

Nature. She ⟨never sells her patent but⟩ keeps the market stocked with her article at the lowest price, but never sells her ⟨patent⟩ secret.

Concord 23 Sept. "*Should*" says Goethe "was the genius of the Antique drama; *Would* of the Modern, but *should* is always great & stern; *would* is weak & small." [620]

Shall I write on the tendency of modern mind to lop off all super-fluity & tradition & fall back on the Nature of things? Science had much charlatanism once of magic & gowns & methods, now it is re-

---

[618] *Encyclopædia Americana*, 1829–1833, I, 334. See *JMN*, IV, 337.

[619] "The ship beating . . . brutes." is struck through in pencil with a curved diagonal use mark. "The ship beating . . . join these." is used in "Ethics," *Lectures*, II, 146.

[620] Cf. "Shakspeare und kein Ende," *Werke*, 1828–1833, XLV, 45, 47 ("Durch das Sollen wird die Tragedie gross und stark, durch das Wollen schwach und klein.").

duced to strict observation. Its very experiments are simple & cheap
& it ⟨real⟩ perceives the truth that the Universal fact is ⟨the single
case⟩ what happens once. It works too with a certain praise of the
mind towards simplicity[,] unity in ⟨Caus⟩ process & cause.
Davy, Playfair, Decandolle, Black, Cuvier, LaPlace, Arago are its
names[.]

In Literature it is not different. The Romantic ate up the doric
letters & life of the old nations. The middle age delighted in excessive ornament in foreign & fabulous particulars. It was farthest from
the nature of things. It did not voluntarily clothe truth with fable
but any high colored picturesque fiction pleased the savages. Roman
de la Rose, Saracen giant, horse of brass, Arabian Nights, Amadis,
Morte d'Arthur. These were [237] true without knowing it ⟨or
meaning it⟩ and against their will. And all along the Chaucer, the
Spenser, the Shakspear who fell into this taste of the wild & wonderful by divine instinct drew near to man, held fast to the common.
Yet they ↑too↓ exaggerated circumstance, & thought a King as necessary as the Sky to a poem. Bacon at the same time, wrote of States
& Kingdoms & kings & wealth, and Sidney's Arcadia, how far from
truth! Ben Jonson how fantastical & pedantic and, spite of the depth
of their genius & their noble height of spirit & earnestness they are
very tedious writers, the Hookers & Beaumont & Fletchers —
We come to Milton; learning threatened to make him giddy but he
was wise by ancient laws & clave to the piety & principle of his times.
A whole new world of science & reflective thought has since opened
which he knew not. Addison, Pope, & Swift played with trappings &
not with the awful facts of Nature.
There is in all the great writers especially in Dr Johnson &
Burke, occasional perception & representation of the Necessary, the
Plain, the True, the human; ⟨a⟩ intimations ⟨of⟩ ↑that they saw↓ the
Adamant under all the upholstery of which their age made so much.
But the political changes of the time which have unfolded every
day with a rapidity sometimes terrific[,] the democratic element[,]
have shown the nullity of those once highly prized circumstances
& given a hollow sound to the name of king & earl & lord. Vast quan-
tities of the stock literature of the past, the pastoral poems, the Es-

says, the Sermons, the politics, the novels, turning on merely local & phenomenal questions, written from the understanding & vital with no inspiration of Reason is perishing. The French period brought Rousseau & Voltaire into the field & their [238] army of Encyclopedists to speak for the people & protest against the corruptions & tyrannies of monarchy. Pascal uttered amidst his polemics a few thrilling words. Paine & the infidels began with good intentions & the Cobbetts & Malthuses & Benthams have aimed at the same; foolish men, but dominated by a Wisdom of humanity. Franklin popularised[.]

⟨But out of Germany came a⟩ In England however at last arose Coleridge, Southey, & Wordsworth[:] men who ⟨had an⟩ appreciated Man & saw the nullity of circumstances. Smollett, Fielding, & Goldsmith treat only of the life of common sense: the Apparent. These writers perceive the dependence of that on the life of the Reason; or the Real. Their spirit diffuses itself into pulpits & parliaments & magazines & newspapers.

This came deepest & loudest out of Germany where it is not the word of few but of all the wise. The professors of Germany, a secluded race free to think but not ⟨attracted⟩ ↑invited↓ to action, poor & crowded, ⟨acquired⟩ went back into the recesses of consciousness with Kant & whilst his philosophy was popular & by its striking nomenclature had imprinted itself on the memory, as that of phrenology does now, they analysed in its light the history of past & present times which their encyclopediacal study had explored, all geography, all statistics, all philology was read with Reason & Understanding in view, & hence the reflective & penetrating sight of their research. Niebuhr, Humboldt, Muller, Heeren, Herder, Schiller, Fichte, Schlegel,

A portion of their poets & writers are introversive to a ⟨vice⟩ fault & pick every rose to pieces. Tieck & Richter. Wieland writes of real Man & Herder, [239] and above all Goethe. He is the high priest of the age. He is the truest of all writers. His books are all records of what has been lived. & his sentences & words seem to see.

What is good that is said or written now lies nearer to men's business & bosoms [621] than of old. What is good goes now to all.

[621] Cf. Bacon, dedication of *Essays or Counsels Civil and Moral* (1625), in *The Works*, 1824, II, 252.

What was good a century ago is written under the manifest ⟨expectation⟩ belief that it was as safe from the eye of the common people as from the Tartars. The Universal Man is now as real an existence as the Devil was then. Prester John no more shall be heard of. Tamerlane & the Buccaneers vanish before Texas, Oregon territory, the Reform Bill, the abolition of Slavery & of Capital Punishment, questions of Education & the Reading of Reviews; & in these all men take part. The human race have got possession, and it is all questions that pertain to their interest outward or inward, that are now discussed.[622] And many words leap out alive from barrooms, Lyceums, Committee Rooms, that escape out of doors & fill the world with their thunder.

When I spoke or speak of the democratic element I do not mean that ill thing vain & loud which writes lying newspapers, spouts at caucuses, & sells its lies for gold, but that spirit of love for the General good whose name this assumes. There is nothing of the true democratic element in what is called Democracy; it must fall, being wholly commercial. I beg I may not be understood to praise anything which the soul in you does not honor, however grateful may be names to your ear & your pocket.

24 September. I think the same spirit of reform in the same direction by applying itself more truly to the nature of things may be seen in the Religion [240] of this Day. It repudiates the unnecessary traditions & says What have I to do with them, Give me truth. The unbelief of the day proceeds out of the deepest Belief. It is because men see that the personalities of ⟨the⟩ Christendom & its ecclesiastical history are a pile of draff & jackstraws beside the immutable laws of moral Nature, a doctrine about Baptism for example compared with the obligation to veracity and any picture or declamation about the employments & felicities of the good in heaven compared ↑with↓ what Man doth & therefore teacheth by all his organs every day. All the Devils respect Virtue.[623] There is, it has been said, & perhaps we all have seen history enough to prove it, a certain Demoniacal force in some men which without virtue & without eminent

---

[622] The several paragraphs beginning with "In Literature" on p. [236], struck through in pencil with a series of diagonal use marks, are used in "Literature," *Lectures*, II, 66–68.
[623] See p. [168] above.

talents yet makes them strong & prevailing.[624] No equal appears in the field against them. A force goes out from them which draws all men & events into their favor. Lies & truths, crimes & mistakes seem equally to turn to their account. And only Virtue beats them. Their own vice poisons their life, defeats their victory, besmears their glory & unmakes their ⟨life⟩ ↑being↓ so that in a few years their whole fame goes out in unclean smoke. But Virtue or the sentiment of the Right is the immutable Victor of the Universe.

And what is Virtue? It is adherence of actions to the nature of things. It remains to be taught in no words that can be evaded but in words of fate that what a man does that he has; that he is his own Giver of joy & pain; that with God is no paltering or double dealing & all Hope may in front of him be left behind; that a man may regard no good as solid but that which is the fruit of his nature & which must grow out of him as long as he exists.[625]

[241] This is to walk in the light.[625a] Here is no Hope and no Fear but plain Sight.

For Books & Works —   Unitarianism so called is one manifestation of this Reform not in what it has dogmatised but in what it has denied. Swedenborg is a still more striking example.   Combe's constitution of Man [626] & Bentham's Utilitarianism is another. Pestalozzi & Owen.[627]

There is no concealment. There is no truth in the proverb that ↑if↓ you get up your name you may safely play the rogue. Thence the balancing proverb that in every wit is a grain of fool. You are known. The sly sin bedaubs you & weakens all your good impression. Men know not why they do not trust you but they do not trust you. The sin glasses your eye, furrows with vulgarity a celestial cheek, bestifies

---

[624] See "Goethe's superstition," p. [164] and n. 445 above.

[625] The first two sentences of this paragraph are used in "Religion," *Lectures*, II, 95, and "Spiritual Laws," *W*, II, 160. The remaining sentences, struck through in pencil with a diagonal use mark, are used in "Religion," *Lectures*, II, 95, and "Spiritual Laws," *W*, II, 143.   [625a] Cf. Is. 2:5; John 12:35; I John 1:7; Rev. 21:24.

[626] George Combe, *The Constitution of Man Considered in Relation to External Objects* (Boston, 1829).

[627] "Unitarianism . . . Owen." is struck through in pencil with a diagonal use mark.

the back of the head,[n] pinches the nose,[n] & writes o fool! fool! fool!
on the forehead of a king. On the other hand, can you not withhold
the ⟨confess⟩ avowal of a just & brave act for fear it will go unwit-
nessed & unloved? One knows it. Who? Yourself & are pledged by it
to sweetness of peace & to nobleness of aim & will not that be a better
proclamation of it than the relating of the incident? [628] Look into the
stage coach & see the faces! stand in State[n] street & see the heads &
the gait & gesture of the men! They are doomed ghosts going under
Judgment all day long. Brutus dying was the prince of fops.[629]

[242] This is the effervescence & result of all religions. This is
what remains at the core of each when all forms are taken away. This
is the Law of Laws, Vedas, Zoroaster, Koran, Golden Verses of Pythagoras, Bible, Confucius. This is that which is carved in mythology &
the Undersong of Epics[,] & the genius of history & birth & marriage &
war & ⟨pea⟩ trade do only typify this, and the world as it whirls
round its solar centre ⟨and⟩ sings this perpetual hymn & nature writes
it in flaming characters of meteor & orb & system /all throughout the
Temple of Silent Space/on every ↑far &↓ silent wall of the temple
of Space/.[630]

Why do I like the old sculpture? Because it is like the works of
nature made after a high & severe pattern made by ⟨hands⟩ men in
whom the moral law inhered. The Jove, the Apollo, & the Phidian
works are related to Virtue. Gladly, gladly would I come nearer to
the fact, but I must content ⟨themselves⟩ ↑myself↓ with this coarse &
⟨d⟩ remote generality. (See also what is writ in ⟨M⟩my Journal at
Naples on this subject.) [631]

↑27 Sept.↓ Let us continue then the application of our criticism to
Art. What must be the principles ⟨of⟩ after which it can be reformed?

---

[628] "The sly sin . . . incident?", struck through in pencil with two diagonal use
marks, is used in "Religion," *Lectures*, II, 95, and "Spiritual Laws," *W*, II, 159–160.
  [629] See *JMN*, IV, 276: "that fop of a Brutus"; Journal C below, p. [111] and
note.
  [630] This paragraph, struck through in pencil with a diagonal use mark, is used
in "Religion," *Lectures*, II, 95–96.
  [631] See *JMN*, IV, 142.

Art is the Creation of Beauty. But nothing is arbitrary nothing is insulated in beauty. ⟨Th⟩ It depends forever on the necessary & the useful. It is the sign of health & of virtue. The plumage of the bird[,] the plumage of an insect has ⟨the deepest⟩ ↑a↓ reason for its ↑rich↓ colors in the constitution of the animal. Fitness is so essential to Beauty that it has been taken for it. The most perfect form to answer an end is beautiful. This holds true in all animals. Why not in Architecture? [632] The Temple decorated with Sculpture is better [243] for religious worship than one unadorned. I suppose that a painting pleases somewhat as a poem does[;] it is an impersonated action. It is the past restored[;] the fear is taken out of it. It is eviscerated of care[;] it is offered merely for contemplation as a part of the Universe of God. What is addressed to us for contemplation does not threaten us but makes us intellectual beings; & appeals to the Vaticinating Reason & asks whether the object be agreeable to the preexistent harmonies. A work of art is something which the Reason created in spite of the hands; it was the work of inspired moments & now it is presented to the Reason again for judgment. Its charm, its wonder, is heightened by its contrast to the things around & vulgar thoughts, & by its kindred to the works of nature.[633]

28 September. Some kindred pleasure does Architecture give. The cobweb, the bird's nest, the silver counterpane of the stonespider, the cocoon, the honeycomb, the beaver dam are the wild notes of nature: the wigwam, the tent, the mound, are the elements of it in man. Rome, Athens, the Coliseum, the Cathedral of Strasburg, the obelisk are the poems in which he has allowed his higher thought⟨s⟩ on the foundation of the Necessary to fulfil its demands to the last hair. Strasburg Cathedral is a material counterpart of the soul of Ervin of Steinbach. The poet is a poem[,] the shipbuilder a ship. In the man could we lay him open, we should see the sufficient reason for the last flourish & tendril of his work.[634]

[632] "Art is the . . . Architecture?", struck through in pencil with a diagonal use mark, is used in "Thoughts on Art," *The Dial*, I (Jan. 1841), 375; "Art," *Lectures*, II, 51; and "Art," *W*, VII, 52–53.

[633] "I suppose . . . nature.", struck through in pencil with a diagonal use mark, is used in "Literature," *Lectures*, II, 58–59, and in part in "Intellect," *W*, II, 327.

[634] Here follows Emerson's circled note "as in shell below", indicating the place

We feel in seeing a noble building which rhymes well, as we do in reading a perfect song that it is "spiritually Organic," that is, had [244] a necessity in nature for being, was one of the possible forms in the divine Mind & is now only discovered & executed by the Artist not arbitrarily composed by him.

⟨The⟩ Every spine & every tint[n] in the sea shell preexists in the secreting organs of the fish.[635]

How Nature works through man, see p. 188[.]

The breaks of the Granite showed the Obelisk, the projecting veins of harder stone wrote the first hieroglyphics. An Amphitheatre is a cup of men; the pagoda is a tent; the pyramid a mound, the Gothic aisle a festal grove; the Parthenon a cabin; the[n] ⟨hour⟩ ↑time↓ measure of the Italian a climate consequence. Chivalry a petrified Courtesy.[636] An assembly a discovery of the Universal Man. Venetian music of the gondolier, a fisher's custom. The coloring of Titian belongs to the place; the[n] armorial bearings of families & cities[n] & nations were shovels or aprons or other mean things now glorified. The Cross   A coronation   College of Cardinals were parish priests of Rome. In times of civic discord every family must have a tower[:] then was it a point of pride — then of skill to make a ⟨hanging⟩ ↑leaning↓ tower as of Pisa.[637]

[245] These things make our art supplementary to nature[,] not blots but ornaments of the landscape whereon sun & moon & star shall gladly shine as on water & mountain.

---

for later insertion of "Every spine . . . of the fish." on p. [244] when he used this paragraph.

[635] "Strasburg Cathedral . . . of the fish." is struck through in pencil with vertical use marks. "In the man . . . of the fish." is used in "Thoughts on Art," *The Dial*, I (Jan. 1841), 375; "Art," *Lectures*, II, 51; "Art," *W*, VII, 53. "the elements of it . . . of the fish." is used in "History," *W*, II, 17–18.

[636] See pp. [12], [37] above.

[637] "The breaks of . . . Gothic aisle" and "College of Cardinals . . . Pisa." are struck through in pencil with diagonal use marks. See pp. [146]–[147] above. These passages are used in "Thoughts on Art," *The Dial*, I (Jan. 1841), 377; "Art," *Lectures*, II, 53; "Art," *W*, VII, 54–55; and "Thoughts on Modern Literature," *W*, XII, 324–325.

[246] A very good discourse on Marriage might be written by him who would preach the nature of things. Let him teach how fast the frivolous external fancying fades out of the mind. Let him teach both husband & wife to mourn for the rapid ebb of inclination not one moment, to yield it no tear. As this fancy picture, these fata-Morgana, this cloud scenery fades forever the solid mountain chains whereupon the sky rests in the far perspective of the soul begin to appear. The parties discover every day the deep & permanent character each of the other as a rock foundation on which they may safely build their nuptial bower. They learn slowly that all other affection than that which rests upon what they are is superstitions & evanescent, that all concealment[,] all pretension is wholly Vain, that to the amiable & useful & heroic qualities which inhere in the other belong a certain portion of love, of pleasure, of veneration which is as exactly measured as the attraction of a pound of ⟨|| . . . ||⟩ ↑iron↓, that there is no luck nor witchcraft nor destiny nor divinity in marriage that can produce affection but only those qualities that by their nature extort it,[n] that all love is mathematical[.] [638]

[247] [blank]

[248] ⟨It is a feeling⟩ He who seeks self-union is accused of injustice & inhospitality. People stretch out to him their mendicant arms to whom he feels that he does not belong & who do not belong to him. He freezes them with his face of apathy, & they very naturally tax him with selfishness. He knows it is unjust. Send me, he says, cold, despised, & naked, the man who loves what I love, the man whose soul is regulated & great, & he shall share my loaf & my cloak. But people of this class do not approach him, but the most unfit associates hasten to him with joy & confidence that they are the very ones whom his faith & philosophy invites, they mar all his days with their follies & then ↑with↓ their tacit reproaches, so that his fair ideal of domestic life & serene household gods he cannot realize but is afflicted instead with censures from the inmate, censures from the observer, & necessarily if he be of a sympathetic character censures from himself also.

I suppose he must betimes take notice of this fact that the like-

[638] This paragraph, struck through in pencil with a vertical use mark, is used in "Society," *Lectures*, II, 103.

minded shall not be sent him; that Apollo sojourns always with the herd men of Admetus; that he must not be too much a utilitarian with too exact calculation of profit & loss but must cast his odors round broadcast to the Gods heedless if they fall upon the altar or upon the ground for all the world is God's altar. Let his music be heard, let his flowers open, let his light shine believing that invisible [249] spectators & friends environ him & honorable afar is a kindness done to the obscure.[639] Moreover when once he attains a spiritual elevation sufficient to understand his daily life & the ministry to him of this motley crew[,] this galling prose will be poetry.

For hospitality, however, the duties will clear themselves: give cake & lemons to those who come for such & give them nothing else, & account yourself cheaply let off. And if those seek you, whom you do not seek, hold them stiffly to their rightful claims. Give them your conversation; be to them a teacher, utter oracles, but admit them never into any infringement on your hours; keep state: be their priest not their companion, for you cannot further their plans, you cannot counsel them on their affairs, & you have never pledged yourself to do so by confounding your relation to them.

———

[250] Every law will some time or other become a fact.

———

It is all idle talking to discourse of history unless I can persuade you to think reverently of the attributes of your own mind. If you persist in calling a quadrant a crooked stick, & will not sufficiently credit its relation to the sun & the celestial sphere to put it to your eye & to find the sun ⟨I⟩ ↑you↓ can never learn your latitude. But true it is, that ⟨to⟩ the intelligent mind is forever coming into relation with all the objects of nature & time until from a vital point it becomes a great heart from which the blood rolls to the distant channels of things & ⟨from⟩ to which, from those distant channels, it returns.

———

The fine prints & pictures which the dentist hangs in his ante-room have a satirical air to the waiting patient.

———

[639] "I suppose he . . . that invisible" is struck through in pencil with a vertical use mark. The paragraph through "obscure." is used in "Society," *Lectures*, II, 104–105.

Political Economy

Every cent in a dollar covers its worth; perhaps also covers its wo. If you covet the wealth of London; undoubtedly it would be a great power & convenience, but each pound & penny is a representative of so much commodity, — so much corn & labor, — & of necessity also of so much mould & pain, — of so much good certainly, but of necessity also of so much evil. Could your wish transfer out of London a million pounds sterling into your chest so would also against your wish just so massive an ill-will & fear concentrate its ⟨re⟩ black rays upon you. ⟨If you are rich⟩ It follows that whatever property you have must pay its full tax: if it come not out of the head, it comes out of the tail. Pay the state ⟨&⟩ its full dividend & if your means increase [251] pay society its full dividend, by new exertion of your faculty for its service or you must pay a debt to fate to the Eumenides in such doom of loss, degradation, or death as they shall choose.[640]

An able man is as rich as the world. How much water is there? you ask, when the rain begins to fall⟨?⟩. Why all in the planet, if wanted. And an able merchant takes up into his operations first & last all the property of the world; he bases his projects upon it.[641]

[252][642] Why is there no genius in the Fine Arts in this Country?

In sculpture —	Greenough is picturesque
In painting —	Alston
In Poetry	Bryant
In Eloquence —	Channing
In Architecture —	
In Fiction	Irving, Cooper,

In all feminine, no character

1st reason   Influence of Europe mainly of England. All genius fatal to genius.[643] Come not too near. Keep off — Sculpture did not spring up here but imported. Our painter is the most successful imi-

---

[640] This paragraph, struck through in pencil with diagonal use marks, is used in "Politics," *Lectures*, II, 79.

[641] This passage, struck through in pencil with a diagonal use mark, is used in "Trades and Professions," *Lectures*, II, 124.

[642] "I" ["J"?] is written below and to the right of the page number.

[643] See p. [232] above.

tator of the Titianesque. Poetry — Pope & Shakspear destroy all. In England, the same. Van Arteveldt —   Eloquence Canning & Brougham   Architecture

2d reason   They are not called out by the necessity of the people. Poetry, music, Sculpture, painting were all enlisted in the service of Patriotism & Religion. The statue was to be worshipped[,] the picture also. The Poem was a confession of faith. A vital faith built the Cathedrals of Europe. But who cares to see a poem of Bryant's — or a statue of Greenoug[h] or a picture of Alston? The People never see them. The mind of the race has taken another direction[,] Property[.]

Patriotism   none

Religion has no enthusiasm. It is external: prudential:

But these are only statements of a fact that there is no fine Art now; not explanation of it.[644]

[253] I believe the destitution is merely apparent. It is sickly & effeminate to arraign[.]

The sense of Beauty   springs ever new

The sentiment of Good

The idea of Truth

And every age has its own forms for them. The Greek was the age of observation. The Middle Age that of fact and thought. Ours that of Reflection & Ideas[.]

That people are as hungry now as ever is proved by the success of Scott & Byron[.]

What can be done by us

1. Redeem them from imitation

      Jacobinism will

        Ne[c] te quaesiveris extra [645]

2. Preach the Nature of Things[.]

[644] Cf. p. [230] above.
[645] See p. [31] above.

[254] Sept. 26. The young man apologizes for his smoky room
& slender fire & promises himself that after a year or two he shall
have things as he wishes. But the love of display is too strong for him
still. He builds a bigger house than he ought, keeps a better table, &
the third & fourth year still finds him apologizing for an ill contrived
fireplace which he wants means promptly & thoroughly to remedy.
Want is a growing giant & Have could never cut a coat large enough
to cover him.[646]

Very strange & worthy of study is the pleasure we derive from
a description of something we recognize in our past life as when I
read Goethe's ⟨a⟩Account of the feelings of a bridegroom.[647] The
subjective is made objective. That which we had *only* lived[648] & not
thought & not valued, is now seen to have the greatest beauty as picture; and as we value a ⟨picture⟩ Dutch painting of a kitchen or a
frolic of blackguards or a beggar ⟨picki⟩ catching a flea when the scene
itself we should avoid,[n] so we see worth in things we had slighted
these many years. A making it a subject of *thought*, ⟨a⟩ the glance of
the Intellect raises it. We look at it now as a God upraised above care
or fear. It admonishes us instantly of the worth of the present moment. It apprizes us of our wealth, for if that hour & object can be so
valuable, why not every hour & event in our life if passed through the
same process? I learn (such is the inherent dignity of all intellectual
activity) that I am a being of more worth than I knew & ⟨have⟩ all
my acts are enhanced in value[.][649]

The deepest pleasure comes I think from the occult belief that
an unknown meaning & consequence lurk in the common every day
facts & as this panoramic[n] [255] or pictorial beauty can arise from it,
so can a solid wisdom when the Idea shall be seen as such which binds
these gay shadows together. It is the pleasure arising from Classification that makes Calvinism, Popery, Phrenology run & prosper. Cal-

[646] The final sentence of this paragraph, struck through in pencil with a diagonal
use mark, is used in "Trades and Professions," *Lectures*, II, 114.
[647] *Dichtung und Wahrheit*, pt. IV, Bk. XVII, *Werke*, 1828–1833, XLVIII, 62 ff.
[648] Emerson canceled his underlining beneath "lived".
[649] This paragraph is struck through in pencil with paired diagonal use marks.
"That which we . . . care or fear." is used in "Literature," *Lectures*, II, 58; "A
making . . . care or fear." is subsequently taken over in "Intellect," *W*, II, 326, 327.

vinism organizes the best known facts of the world's history into a convenient mythus &, what is best, applied to the individual. We are always at the mercy of a better Classifier than ⟨we⟩ ourselves[.] [650]

↑I read in Sir Christopher Wren —

"Position is necessary for perfecting beauty.↓ ⟨I read in Sir Christopher Wren —⟩ There[n] are only two beautiful positions of straight lines, perpendicular & horizontal — this is from nature & consequently necessity no other than upright being firm. Oblique positions are discord to the eye unless answered in pairs, as in the sides of an equicrural triangle — "

"An architect ought to be jealous of novelties in which fancy blinds the judgment & to think [of] his judges, as well those that are to live five centuries after him as those of his own time. That which is commendable now for novelty will not be a new invention to posterity when his works are often imitated & when it is unknown which was the original but the glory of that which is good of itself is eternal."

"No sort of pinnacle is worthy enough to appear in the air but statue." & no roof but a dome. "For a portico the longer the more beautiful in infi[ni]tum."
"Variet⟨ies⟩y of uniformities makes complete beauty[.]"
[256] "Uniformities are best tempered as rhymes in poetry alternately, or sometimes with more variety as in stanzas." Life of Wren. Lib[rary of] U[seful] K[nowledge] [651]
"the Doric architecture, recording in its Metopes all the eloquence of sculpture" Life [*ibid*.,] p. 4.

All in each

Sept. [27?]. The ⟨actions⟩ movements & forms of all beings in nature except man are beautiful from their consonance to the whole. The world seems to be guarantee for every particular movement. The All finds its bloom or flowering in that act we at the moment observe. The human will is an exception. Human acts are short, shallow, & awkward proceeding out of so shallow a source as the Individuality of each. Those acts which voluntarily or involuntarily take hold on the

[650] This paragraph is struck through in pencil with paired diagonal use marks. The last three sentences, struck through in pencil with an additional diagonal use mark, are used in "Humanity of Science," *Lectures*, II, 25.
[651] Quoted in [H. B. Ker], "Sir Christopher Wren; with Some General Remarks on the History and Progress of Architecture," in *Lives of Eminent Persons*, 1833, p. 30. The fourth quotation is used in "Stonehenge," *W*, V, 286.

Will of the World seem great on the contrary as they fall in to this Divine order as when a man plants a field, or builds a house.

I like that commendation of Cato that he seemed born for that one thing he did — be it what it might,[n 652] because that is the character of every natural action that it seems the end which all things conspire to produce[.]

How curious we are respecting the attainments of another mind in the knowledge of Deity is shown by our desire to know of Calvinism & Swedenborgianism. The man of another church is no nearer to God than you are, yet you feel so far from God as to be curious concerning what each bigot can say. In other words Sectarianism is the ignorance of God. When I am sane & devout, I see well what sort of revelation a good man hath. I see my curiosity concerning revivals & devotees to be vain. I oversee them.

[257] Sept. 28. The world is full of Judgment Days.[653] The event is always modified by the nature of the being on whom it falls. An assembly of men or a wise man do always try us. As a snowflake falling on the ground is white; falling on a man's hand becomes water; falling on the fire becomes steam.

Very disagreeable rencontres are there all the way. To meet those who expect light from you & to be provoked to thwart & discountenance & unsettle them by all you say is pathetical. Again to make an effort to raise the conversation of your company by communicating your recondite thought & to behold it received with patronizing interest by one of the company & with liberal & foolish illustration returned to you, may make you hang your head. My visit to Groton was variously instructive.[654]

Nature ⟨by no⟩ occupies herself in beautiful contraventions of her

[652] Cf. Livy's praise of the elder Cato, as rendered in Montaigne, "Of three Commerces," *Essays*, 1693, III, 49: "This Man's Parts were so convertible to all Uses, that a Man would think he were born only for whatever he did." See "Manners," *Lectures*, II, 140.

[653] This sentence is used in "Being and Seeming," *Lectures*, II, 301.

[654] Emerson had occupied the pulpit of the Reverend Charles Robinson of Groton on Sunday, September 25, 1836 (*L*, II, 37).

own laws. Thus she takes pleasure in annihilating Space[,] for taking an animal she adds a few feathers to each side of his body & thereby makes all the fields of a thousand miles of the earth's surface equally present to him on the same day as the square feet of the barnyard are to the domestic fowl. See the passenger pigeon.[655]

A vicious ornament ⟨affects us⟩ ↑is↓ like those excrescences on plants which ⟨sometimes assume the appearance of⟩ ↑⟨are⟩ the igno- rant may mistake for↓ a flower, but ⟨on inspection are found⟩ ↑which the botanist knows↓ to be a diseased growth around the eggs of a worm.

The house praises the carpenter.

[258] When we ⟨look at⟩ ↑study↓ Architecture every thing seems ⟨su⟩ architectural [—] the forms of animals, the building of the world, clouds, crystals, flowers, trees, skeletons. When we treat of poetry all these things begin to sing. When of Music, Litchfield Cathedral is a tune[.]
World is picturesque to Allston, dramatic to Garrick, symbolical to Swedenborg, Utilitarian to Franklin, a seat of war to Napoleon &c, &c.[n]
I observe that after ↑looking at↓ the print of a cathedral the houseprints & trade illustrations are offensive, but a Greek statue not; animals & plants not; & especially grateful & homogeneous was the print of organic remains of the Elder world *restored*. Certainly in the forest, Architecture finds its analogons in ferns, in spikes of flowers, in locust, in poplar, in oak, in pine, in fir & spruce, and the Cathedral is a flowering of Stone subdued by the insatiable demand of harmony in man. The mountain of granite blooms into an eternal flower with the lightness ⟨& delicate finish & per[?]⟩ as well as aerial proportions & perspective of vegetable beauty.[656]

The study of one man, of one object radically, is like the study

---

[655] This paragraph is struck through in ink with two vertical use marks.

[656] "Certainly in the forest . . . beauty." is struck through in pencil with three diagonal use marks. This passage is used in "Thoughts on Art," *The Dial*, I (Jan. 1841), 376; "Art," *Lectures*, II, 52; and "History," *W*, II, 20–21.

of one book in a foreign language: when he has mastered that one book the learner finds with a joyful surprise that he can read with equal facility in ten thousand books. ↑A half inch of vegetable tissue will tell all that can be known on the subject from all the forests & ⟨a little ani⟩ one skeleton or a fragment of animal fibre is an account of zoology.↓[657]

[259] If I read a poem or see a Temple I desire to make such; as they say in Arabia 'a figtree looking on a figtree becometh fruitful'.[658]

Moral sentiment must act or there is no self respect. The most brilliant achievement of the intellect would not reconcile me to myself or make me feel that there was any stability & worth in human society. But if I command myself & ⟨ai⟩ help others, I believe in & love man. Intellect has its own ethics. Let it work to cheer all & say to all 'Hope in God', & chill no man & no woman. Where it cometh let it smile, that all who see it may feel, good times are coming.[659]

Genius works ever in sport & Goodness hath ever a smile.

Ellen
29 Sept. ⟨I am glad of a day when I know what I am to do in it.⟩ ↑p. 275↓[660]   Ellen
          Ellen

[September] 30. I dislike the gruff ⟨sansculotte⟩ ↑jacobin↓ manners of

[657] This paragraph, struck through in pencil with three diagonal use marks, is used in "Humanity of Science," *Lectures*, II, 26.

[658] Kenneth W. Cameron, "Emerson's Arabian Proverbs," *Emerson Society Quarterly*, No. 13 (IV Quarter, 1958), 50, compares the version in *The Penny Magazine*, II (Aug. 10, 1833), 307, No. 22: "The fig-tree looking on the fig-tree will be made fruitful." Here, "they say in . . . fruitful'." is struck through in ink with a vertical use mark. The proverb is used in "The American Scholar," *W*, I, 91.

[659] This paragraph, struck through in pencil with a diagonal use mark, is used in "Holiness," *Lectures*, II, 344–345.

[660] September 30 was the anniversary of Emerson's marriage to Ellen Tucker in 1829. "I am glad . . . in it." is both lined out in ink and struck through in ink with a wavy diagonal use mark; see *JMN*, IV, 266, n. 52, and p. [275] below.

our village politicians but I reconcile myself to them by the reflection that Genius hurts us by its excessive influence, hurts the freedom & inborn faculty of the individual: &, if Webster, Everett, Channing, yea Plato & Shakspear, found such cordial adorers in the populace as in the scholars, no more Platos & Shakspears could arise. But by this screen of porcupine quills, of bad manners & hatred, is the sacred germ of individual genius concealed & guarded in Secular darkness. After centuries, will it be born a god. Out of Druids & Berserkirs[n] were Alfred & Shakspear made.

[260] Observe how strongly guarded is the Common Sense. If men were left to Contemplation, if the contemplative life were practicable[,] to what subtilties to what dreams & extravagancies would not all run! Laputa, a court of love, a college of Schoolmen, would be the result. How is this hindered? Poverty, Frost, Famine, Rain, Disease are the beadles & guardsmen that hold us to Common Sense.

Antecedence of Spirit
The world did not make God but God made the world. The organs of the skull or the face did not make the character but the character made them. Beautifully shines a spirit through all the toughness of matter. The adamant streams into softest but sharpest form before it. The spirit seeks & utters truth & the eye becomes clear as heaven. The animal contravenes the spiritual law & utters a lie & the eye is muddy & asquint. (p. 111) [661]

[261] Schoolmasters sometimes vex one with the odious word Composuist for a writer of themes. Hardly better, Charles Sprague [662] must use penman for poet or historian.

Does it not seem that the tendency of Science is now from hard figures & marrowless particulars — dead analysis back to synthesis,[n] that now Ideology mixes therewith,[n] that the Education of the people forces the savant to show the people something of his ⟨sk⟩ lore which

[661] This paragraph, struck through in pencil with a diagonal use mark, is used in "Spiritual Laws," W, II, 156.
[662] Cashier of the Globe Bank in Boston, Sprague figures in Emerson's correspondence both as banker and as author.

they can comprehend, & that he looks for what humanity there remains in his science, & calls to mind by finding it valued, much that he had forgotten[.]

↑Geoffroy de Saint Hilaire, Cuvier, Hunter, Everard Home, Davy.↓[663]

Every thing is necessary in its foundation. The oath that is heard in the street & the jargon profanity of boys points not less distinctly than a church at the conviction in man of absolute nature as distinct from apparent & derivative nature. ↑see p. 109↓ [664]

October 6, 1836. I neglected on my return from Boston to record the pleasant impression made by the Monday afternoon Meeting at Mr Alcott's house. Present — Alcott, Bartoll, Brownson, Clarke, Francis, Hedge, Ripley, Emerson.[665] Alcott maintained that every man is a genius, that he looks peculiar, individual, only from the point of view of others,[n] that Genius has two faces, one towards the Infinite God, one towards men. — But I cannot report him. Bartoll too spake very well. And Clarke gave examples from the West of the ⟨good⟩ Genesis of Art; as oratory & painting.

[262] Transcendentalism means, says our accomplished Mrs B[arlow?],[666] with a wave of her hand, *A little beyond.*

Shall I call my subject The Philosophy of modern History, & consider ⟨generally⟩ the action of the same general causes upon Religion, Art, Science, Literature; consider the common principles on which they are based; the present condition of these severally; and the intellectual duties of the present generation & the tendencies of the times inferred from the popular science[?]

[663] "Ideology mixes . . . Davy." is struck through in pencil with a diagonal and a wavy diagonal use mark; "the Education . . . can comprehend," is used in "Humanity of Science," *Lectures*, II, 38.

[664] This paragraph is struck through in pencil with two diagonal use marks; the second sentence is used in "Being and Seeming," *Lectures*, II, 297–298.

[665] The second meeting of the new "club." Cyrus Bartol, an addition to those present on September 20, was a Bowdoin graduate who had been doing apprentice preaching in Cincinnati since taking a theological degree in 1835.

[666] Probably Almira Penniman Barlow, a family friend and correspondent.

[263] 11 October. In the pulpit at Waltham, I felt that the composition of his audience was not of importance to him who possessed true eloquence. Smooth or rugged, good natured or ill natured, religious or scoffers, he takes them all as they come⟨s⟩[,] he proceeds in the faith that all differences are superficial[,] that they all have one fundamental nature which he knows how to address. This is to be eloquent. And having this skill to speak to their pervading soul he can make them smooth or rugged, good-natured or ill natured, saints or scoffers at his will.⁶⁶⁷ ↑Eloquence always tyrannical never complaisant or convertible↓[.]
In earlier days I wrote, "the high prize of eloquence may be mine[,] the joy of uttering what no other can utter & what all must receive." J. 1833[–1834] p. 88 ⁶⁶⁸

[264]   "Give me a spirit that on life's rough sea
          Loves to have his sails filled with a lusty wind
          Even till his sail yards ⟨crack⟩tremble, his masts crack,
          And his rapt ship run on her side so low
          That she drinks water & her keel ploughs air;
          There is no danger to a man that knows
          Where life & death is; there's not any law
          Exceeds his knowledge neither is it ⟨hurtful⟩↑needful↓
          That he should stoop to any other law.
          He goes before them, & commands them all
          That to himself is a law rational."
                          Geo. Chapman's Byron's Conspir[acy,
                          III, i, conclusion, misquoted].⁶⁶⁹

Oct. 13. Observe this invincible tendency of the mind to unify. It is a law of our constitution that we should not contemplate things apart without the effort to arrange them in order with known facts & ascribe them to the same law.⁶⁷⁰ ⟨Hen⟩ I do not choose to say, "God is within me — I do not like your picture of an external God. I suppose there is one spirit, & only one, the selfsame which I behold

⁶⁶⁷ "the composition of . . . will." is struck through in pencil with a vertical use mark. Cf. "Society," *Lectures*, II, 109.
    ⁶⁶⁸ See *JMN*, IV, 324.
    ⁶⁶⁹ The quotation from Chapman is struck through in pencil with a vertical use mark.
    ⁶⁷⁰ This sentence is struck through in pencil with a vertical use mark. Cf. "Humanity of Science," *Lectures*, II, 22, 23.

⟨inwar⟩ inly when I am overcome by an aweful moral sentiment and He made the world." I do not choose to say this. It is said for me by tyrannical instincts.[671]

Hence Goethe beholding the plant in an hour of Reason & seeing a petal in transition from a leaf exclaims Every part of the plant is a leaf; a petal⟨,⟩ is a leaf; a fruit is a leaf; a seed is a leaf; — metamorphosed; and slowpaced experiment makes good this prophetic vision. In like manner, the skull is with him a vertebra of the spine metamorphosed. For seven colors he seeks the simplest mixture, viz. Darkness & Light[.] [672]

[265] Newton sees an apple fall & says 'the Motion of the moon is nothing but an apple-fall[;] the motion of the earth is nothing but a larger apple-fall. I see ⟨why⟩ the law of all nature,'[n] and slow observation makes good this bold word. The Universal law[n] is the single fact[.]

The system of Lamarck is an imperfect result of the same force. It aims to find one monad of organic life ⟨through⟩ which shall be the common element of every animal and becoming an infusory, a poplar-worm, or a man according to circumstances; It says to the cankerworm, "How dost thou, Brother? Please God, you shall yet be a philosopher!" And in the same audacious spirit Our Weimar man would say, the monad is man or plant only according to the element of darkness or light in which it unfolds.[673]

Another demand of this constitution is There shall be no Miracle.

Another is, ⟨a⟩A moment is a concentrated Eternity. All that ever was, is now.

Nature teaches all this herself. The spines of the shell, the layers of the tree, the colors of the blossom,[n] the veins of the marble.

Concord
May

[671] Adapting the phrasing of this paragraph, Emerson develops the same basic idea — the mind's tendency to unify in response to "tyrannical instinct" — in "Humanity of Science," *Lectures*, II, 23. Discussing the subject of classification in "The American Scholar," *W*, I, 85, he similarly observes that "the young mind" is "tyrannized over by its own unifying instinct."

[672] This paragraph, struck through in pencil with a diagonal use mark, is used in "Humanity of Science," *Lectures*, II, 23–24. See pp. [153], [225] above.

[673] This and the preceding paragraph, struck through in pencil with a diagonal use mark, are used in "Humanity of Science," *Lectures*, II, 23, 24.

[266]–[267] [blank]

[268] The savant is unpoetic, the poet is unscientific. I do not remember but a few names of savans who subordinated the details to the law & never lost sight of the law. Kepler, Newton, Davy. But a Chemist[,] what dull lectures he can contrive to make of that charming science! A chemistry is but a catalogue, as dull reading as a ⟨book⟩ ↑manual↓ of law-forms.

"As sure as death & rates." [674]
Death & rates are sure.

15 October. The brilliant & warm day led me out this morn. into the wood & to Goose Pond. Amid the many coloured trees I thought what principles I might lay down as the foundations of this Course of Lectures I shall read to my fellow citizens[.] [675]

1. There is a relation between man & nature so that whatever is in matter is in mind.   **B**

2. It is a necessity of the human nature that it should express itself outwardly & embody its thought.
As all creatures are allured to reproduce themselves, so must the thought be imparted in Speech. The more profound the thought, the more burdensome. What is in will out. Action is as great a pleasure & cannot be forborne[.]   **C**

3. ⟨The next[?]⟩ It is the constant endeavor of the mind to idealize the actual, to accomodate the shows of things to the desires of the mind.[676] Hence architecture & all art.   **D**

[269] 4. It is the constant tendency of the mind to Unify all it beholds, or to reduce the ⟨widest⟩ remotest facts to a single law. Hence all endeavors at classification.   **E**

---

[674] Cf. Benjamin Franklin, letter to Jean Baptiste LeRoy, November 13, 1789. See *The Writings of Benjamin Franklin*, ed. A. H. Smyth, 10 vols. (New York, 1905–1907), X, 69.

[675] Within the outline that follows, items 1 (**B**), 2 (**C**), 4 (**E**), 5 (**F**), 6 (**G**), and 8 (**A**) are struck through in pencil with vertical use marks. The topics anticipate "Humanity of Science"; 2 (**C**) is used in "Thoughts on Art," *The Dial*, I (Jan. 1841), 367; "Art," *Lectures*, II, 42; and "Art," *W*, VII, 37–38.

[676] See p. [224] above.

5. There is a /parallel tendency/corresponding Unity/ in nature which makes this just,ⁿ as in the composition of the compound shell or leaf or animal from few elements.   **F**

6. There is a tendency in the mind to separate particulars & in magnifying them to lose sight of the connexion of ⟨an⟩the object with the Whole. Hence all false views, Sects;   **G**

7. ⟨That⟩[677] ⟨The remedy for all abuses all errors in thought or practice is the conviction that⟩ ⟨u⟩Underneath all Appearances & causing all appearances are certain eternal Laws which we call the Nature of Things.   **H**

⟨7⟩ 8.[678] There is one Mind common to all individual men.   **A**

2. There is a relation between man & nature so that whatever is in matter is in mind.[679]

3. I
[270] [blank]

[271] October 18. When I see a man of genius he always inspires me with a feeling of boundless confidence in my own powers[.]

Yesternight I talked with Mr Alcott of education. He proposes still the old recipe the illustration of humanity in the life of Jesus. I say, No, let us postpone everything historical to the dignity & grandeur of the present hour. Take no thought for "the great mass" and "the evil of being misunderstood" &c, &c, & "what & how ye shall say", *In that hour it shall be given you what ye shall say.*[680]

Say the thing that is fit for this new-born and infinite hour. Come forsake, this once, this balmy time, the historical, & let us go to the Most High & go forth with him now that he is to say, Let there be

---

[677] "That" is canceled in pencil.
[678] Over the canceled "7" Emerson wrote and canceled "1" — the beginning of a new series — without canceling "8".
[679] This sentence is struck through in ink with two vertical use marks.
[680] Cf. Luke 12:11-12.

Light.[681] Propose no methods, prepare no words, select no traditions, but fix your eye on the ⟨fact⟩ audience, & the fit word will utter itself as ⟨the eye⟩ when the eye seeks the person in the remote corner of the house the voice accomodates itself to the area to be filled.

[272] I rejoice in ⟨my⟩ ↑human↓ riches when I see how manifold are the gifts of men. He is the rich man who can see and avail himself of all their faculties.[682] What should I know of the world but that one man is forever rubbing glass, grinding lenses, cutting with diamonds &c; another would always be mixing colors; another is a hunter, & puts his dog's nose into every thicket & knows what the partridge & the musquash are doing; another mines for coal; another makes almanacks; another traverses Iceland; another prints the book; & so I in my country farmhouse for ⟨a couple[?] of thousand⟩ ↑1500↓ dollars can have the good of all.

Oct. 19. As long as the ⟨worl⟩ soul seeks an external God, it never can have peace, it always must be uncertain what may be done & what may become of it. But when it sees the Great God far within its own nature, then it sees that always itself is a party to all that can be, that always it will be informed of that which will happen and therefore it is pervaded with a great Peace[.]   ↑See p. 281 & seq↓[683]

The individual is always dying. The Universal is life. As much truth & goodness as enters into me so much I live. As much error & sin so much death is in me.

Yet Reason never informs us how the world was made. I suppose my friends have some relation to my mind. Perhaps they are its thoughts, taking form ⟨o⟩& outness though in a region above my will & that in that fact, my ⟨dynamic⟩ ↑plastic↓ nature, I have a pledge of their restoration[:] [273] that is again, hereafter, I shall be able to give my thoughts Outness & enjoy ⟨them⟩ myself in persons again.

'Tis very strange how much we owe the perception of the ab-

[681] Gen. 1:3.

[682] The first sentence of this paragraph, struck through in ink with three vertical use marks, anticipates "Trades and Professions," where the second sentence is used, *Lectures*, II, 124.

[683] This paragraph is struck through in ink with a wavy diagonal use mark.

solute solitude of the Spirit to the affections. I sit alone & cannot arouse myself to thought[,] I go & sit with my friend & in the endeavor to explain my thought to him or her, I lay bare the awful mystery to myself as never before & start at the total loneliness & infinity of one man.[684]

20 October. Nature works unique we say through myriad forms so that music, Optics, galvanism, mechanics still ↑are↓ only divers versions of one law. Is it that she pervades the soul of man with the Same Unity that thus he will classify & unify? Are they two facts or one, these —

Man aims ever to reduce compound appearances to one law

The complex appearances are reducible to a few principles as the Hist[ory] of Lit[erature] is one of few ideas & even of few tales[.][685]

[274] Oct. 21. Sounds not this high & far? "Whilst in Science as well as in Reflection no Whole can be perfected because ⟨to⟩ the first ↑lacks↓ the inward, — ⟨to⟩ the last⟨,⟩ ↑lacks↓ the outward, ⟨is lacking,⟩ so must we esteem Science as necessary to us as Art if we expect from it, in any way, a sort of Wholeness. And truly we have not to seek this in Universals, in the exceeding, ⟨the superabundant,⟩ but as Art ever represents itself entire in every single Art work, so should Science also show itself every time entire in every particular ↑that is↓ treated.

"But in order to approach such a demand we must exclude none of the human⟨ly⟩ powers from scientific activity. The abyss of presentiment, a ⟨secu⟩ secure contemplation of the present, mathematical depth, physical exactness, height of reason, sharpness of understanding, nimble passionate phantasy, lovely joy in the sensual, nothing can be forgone to the lively fruitful seizure of the moment through which alone, a work of art, of what form soever, can originate."

Goethe Nachg. Werke, vol. 10 [*Werke*, L], p[p] 85[–86].

---

[684] This paragraph, struck through in pencil with a diagonal use mark, is used in "Society," *Lectures*, II, 105.

[685] "Man aims . . . tales" is struck through in pencil with a vertical use mark. The final clause is used in "Being and Seeming," *Lectures*, II, 304.

As History's best use is ⟨to give Value⟩ to enhance our estimate of the present hour,[686] so the value of such an observer ⟨of⟩as Goethe who draws out of our consciousness some familiar fact & makes it glorious by showing it in the light of thought is this, that he makes us prize all our being by suggesting its inexhaustible wealth; for we feel that all our experience is thus convertible into jewels.[n] He moves our wonder at the mystery of our life.

[275]   On Time.   ⟨Three⟩Four sentences
I am glad of a day when I know what I am to do in it[.]
There is no time to brutes.

"Koong Chee is a man who through his earnestness in seeking knowledge forgets his food, & in his joy for having found it loses all sense of his toil; who thus occupied is unconscious that he has almost arrived at old age."

↑The only economy of time is in every moment to stick by yourself.↓[687]

22 Oct. The Unity in nature never invites us to indolence but to everlasting & joyful labor. You learn as much from Chemistry as from a farm or a shop that to ⟨in⟩ negligence & pleasure things are dark, brutish, & malignant. Chemistry[,] Astronomy surprises all the time and the appointed way of man from infancy to omniscience is through an infinite series of pleasant surprises.[688]

On p. 188, I have spoken of the power of nature as predominant over the human in all human works. It is remarkable that it also paints the best part of the picture, carves the best part of the statue, ⟨gives⟩ speaks the best part of the oration, &, in short, that the Universal lends to the individual ever his best ornament. The cheek of

---

[686] Cf. The Philosophy of History: "Introductory," *Lectures*, II, 16.

[687] The first three "sentences" are copied respectively from pp. [259], [236], and [133] above; the fourth, a later addition, is a variant of statements recurring on pp. [4] and [49] above and in "On the Best Mode of Inspiring a Correct Taste in Literature," *Lectures*, I, 213.

[688] This paragraph is struck through in pencil with a vertical use mark.

the maiden would be pale but for the sun & wind or for the glitter of the lighted & decorated hall filled with other beauty reflecting ↑rays↓ on her.

In like manner Madame de Stael said 'tis "tradition more than invention helps the poet to a good fable".[689] How many things must combine to a good word or event! Webster is in a galvanized state.[690]

[276] The preponderance of Nature over Will in every life is great. There is less intention in history than we ascribe to it. We impute deeplaid farsighted plans to Napoleon & Caesar. The cement or the spine which gave unity to their manifold actions was not their logic but the concatenation of events. "My son cannot replace me. I could not replace myself. I am the child of circumstances." said Napoleon. My will never gave the images in my mind the rank they now take there. The four College years & the three years of Divinity have not yielded me so many grand facts as some idle books under the bench at Latin School. We form no guess at the time of receiving a thought of its comparative value.[691]

It is remarkable also that we find it so hard to impute our own best sense to a dead author. The very highest praise we think of any writer, painter, sculptor, or builder is that he actually possessed the thought or feeling with which he has inspired us. We hesitate at doing Spenser so great an honor as to think that he intended by his allegory the sense which we affix to it. We have this infirmity of respect also to contemporary genius. We fear that Mr Allston did not foresee & design the effect he produces on us. Familiar as freedom of thought may be to us[,] the highest merit we ascribe to Homer, is, that he forsook books & traditions & wrote not what men but what Homer thought[.] [692]

---

[689] See pp. [104], [109] above.

[690] See p. [113] above. This and the preceding paragraph are struck through in pencil with a vertical use mark. "the power of nature . . . the oration," is used in "Art," *Lectures*, II, 48, and "Art," *W*, II, 47.

[691] See p. [104] above. "There is less . . . value.", struck through in ink with a diagonal use mark, is used in "Spiritual Laws," *W*, II, 134, 133.

[692] See p. [115] above. "It is remarkable . . . produces on us." is struck through in pencil with a curved diagonal use mark; "It is remarkable . . . Homer thought" is struck through in pencil and in ink with two diagonal use marks. This paragraph is used in "Thoughts on Art," *The Dial*, I (Jan. 1841), 372; "Art," *Lectures*, II, 47–48; and "Art," *W*, VII, 46–47.

Just as much better as is the real cathedral to its paper plan so much more beauty does it owe to Nature than to the Artist.[693]

[277] [Letter omitted] [694]

———

Oct. 24.[695] The Understanding speaks much; the passions much; the soul seldom. The only friend that can persuade the soul to speak is a good & great Cause — Out it comes, now & then, like the lightning from the cloud, & with an effect as prodigious.   Copied from J. 1832 [696]   ↑See also p. 185 — above↓

———

Malthus revolts us by looking at a man as an animal. So do those views of genius semi-medical which I spit at.[696a]

[278] [Letter omitted] [697]

———————————————————————————

[279] Good has been a term of contempt.
     A man knows no more to any purpose than he practises. "He that despises little things shall perish by little & little." [698]

[280] [699] The man, the nation writes out its character in every thing & action, in every name it gives. Thus the noble puritans of

———

[693] This sentence, struck through in pencil with two diagonal use marks, is used in "Thoughts on Art," *The Dial*, I (Jan. 1841), 371; "Art," *Lectures*, II, 46; and "Art," *W*, VII, 44.

[694] The final paragraph only of Emerson's letter to William Emerson, October 23, 1836, printed complete in *L*, II, 41–43. The printed text reads "It is anything but Civil History whereof I shall treat." for "My Lectures are anything but Civil History." in the manuscript journal and "become" for "grown"; there are minor variations in punctuation.

[695] The entries for this date are written in a space which had been left blank between two letters, both dated October 23.

[696] See *JMN*, IV, 40.   [696a] See *JMN*, IV, 362.

[697] To the Reverend Warren Burton, October 23, 1836, printed in *J*, IV, 124–125, under date of October 25. Rusk, *L*, II, 44, queries but does not correct the error in dating (see n. 695 above).

[698] This sentence is used in "Prudence," *Lectures*, II, 315.

[699] "Civil History." is written above "the nation" at the top of the page; the entries under this index heading continue on p. [300] below.

Massachusetts called the first vessel which they built, ⟨The⟩ Blessing of the Bay.[700]

Solon said, "He that has better iron shall have all this gold." [701] In modern times the nations that are the best manufacturers of iron are the most civilized & run away with all the gold.[702] ↑"And all that cowards have is mine."↓[n]

A great licentiousness seems to have followed directly on the heels of the Reformation. Luther even had to lament the decay of piety in his own household. "Doctor," said his wife to him, one day, "how is it that while subject to papacy we prayed so often & with such fervor, whilst now we pray with the utmost coldness & very seldom?" Remember Luther's wife.[703]

The poor Irishman, a wheelbarrow is his country.

The German is the only nation that addresses the Deity with the appellation Dear; Lieber Gott.[703a]

Pius VII procured in 1818 a repeal of the edicts against Galileo & the Copernican system. He assembled the Congregation & the late Cardinal Toriozzi assessor of the Sacred office proposed that they should wipe off this scandal from the Church. The repeal was carried with the dissentient voice of one Dominican only. V. Lyell Geol. vol 1 p 69 [n.][704]

God screens men from premature ideas.[705]
Neatness & grandeur of experiment in France. "The greatest

---

[700] "The" is canceled in pencil. See *JMN*, III, 265; cf. "Trades and Professions," *Lectures*, II, 128.

[701] Cf. Bacon, "Of the True Greatness of Kingdoms and Estates," *The Works*, 1824, II, 322. See *JMN*, III, 176.

[702] These two sentences, struck through in pencil with a vertical use mark, are used in "Trades and Professions," *Lectures*, II, 118.

[703] See p. [225] above. This passage, struck through in ink with a vertical use mark, is used in "The Individual," *Lectures*, II, 178, and "History," *W*, II, 29.

[703a] For this and the preceding sentence, see *JMN*, IV, 351, 370, respectively.

[704] Charles Lyell, *Principles of Geology*, 1830.

[705] See p. [105] above.

portion of the earth's surface which has ever been seen at once by man was that exposed to the view of M.M. Biot & Gay Lussac in their aeronautic

(turn to p. 300)[706]

[281] It seemed to me last night at the Teachers' Meeting, as so often before, that the mind is now mature enough to offer a consistent simple system of religious faith. What is true, is selfaffirmed. There are two facts, the Individual and the Universal. To this belong the finite, the temporal, ⟨the⟩ ignorance, sin, death; to that belong the infinite, the ⟨immortal⟩ ↑immutable↓, truth, goodness, life. In Man they both consist. The All is in Man. In Man the perpetual progress is from the Individual to the Universal, from that which is human, to that which is divine. "Self dies, & dies perpetually." The circumstances, the persons, the body, the world, the memory are forever perishing as the bark peels off the expanding tree. ⟨I have wholly lost⟩ The[n] facts so familiar to me in infancy, my cradle⟨, my⟩ ↑and↓ porringer, my nurse⟨, my⟩ ↑and↓ nursery, ⟨they⟩ have died out of my world forever. The images of the following period are fading, & will presently be obliterated. Can ⟨a⟩I doubt that the facts & events & persons & personal relations ⟨I remember⟩ that now appertain to me will perish as utterly when the⟨y⟩ ↑soul↓ shall have exhausted their meaning & use? The world is the gymnasium on which the youth of the Universe are trained to strength & skill. When they have become masters of strength & skill, who cares what becomes of the masts & bars & ropes on which they strained their muscle?

And what is God? We cannot say but we see clearly enough. We cannot say, because he is the unspeakable, the immeasureable, the perfect — but we see plain enough in what direction it lies. First we see plainly that the All is in Man;[n] that as the proverb says, "God comes to see us without bell."[707] That is, as there is no screen or ceiling between our heads [282] & the infinity of /Space/=heavens/, so is there no bar or wall in the Soul where man the effect ceases &

[706] The further entries under "Civil History" continue on pp. [300]–[301] below.
[707] Vicesimus Knox, *Elegant Extracts . . . in Prose*, 7th ed., 2 vols. (London, 1797), II, 1035. See *JMN*, IV, 16.

God the cause begins. The walls are taken away; we lie open on one side to all the deeps of spiritual nature, to all the attributes of God. Justice we see and know; that is of God. Truth we see & know, that is of God. Love, Freedom, Power, these are of God.[708] For all these & much more there is a general nature in which they inhere or of which they are phases and this is Spirit. It is essentially vital. The love that is in me, the justice, the truth can never die & that is all of me that will not die. All the rest of me is so much death[—] my ignorance, my vice, my ⟨bodily⟩ ↑corporeal↓ pleasure. But I am nothing else than a capacity for justice, truth, love, freedom, power. I can inhale[,] imbibe them forevermore. They shall be so much to me that I am nothing, they all. Then shall God be all in all. Herein is my Immortality. And the soul affirms with the same assurance I shall live forever, as it affirms, Justice shall be forever. The same absurdity is involved in the contradiction of both.

Again; because the All is in Man we know that nothing arbitrary, nothing alien shall take place in the Universe, nothing contrary to the Nature in us. The soul is a party to every thing that is & therefore to every thing that shall be done. We pronounce therefore with the voice of fate that such & such things must be[,] that such & such other things are impossible.[709] Never need we ask Calvin or Swedenborg, never need we ask Moses or the prophets, if we are in danger or what God will do. There is God in you. Whilst God is external to the soul, it can never be safe or [283] serene, because uncertain what may befal, but having learned to see God far within itself it shall now be informed of all & is pervaded with a great peace. "If our hearts condemn us, God is greater than our hearts, & knoweth all things; if our hearts condemn us not, then have we confidence toward God."[710]

The All is in Man. Ask no idle questions concerning the nature

---

[708] "First we see . . . are of God." is struck through in pencil with vertical use marks; "so is there . . . Freedom, Power," is struck through in ink with a vertical use mark. "First . . . Power," is used in "Religion," *Lectures*, II, 85, and "The Over-Soul," *W*, II, 271–272.

[709] Apparently a reworking of the first entry for October 19 on p. [272] above. "The soul is . . . are impossible." is struck through in pencil with a vertical use mark.

[710] Cf. I John 3:20–21.

or deeds of Christ. See thou do it not. He is thy fellow worshipper and all power belongeth unto God. Seest thou not, dear brother! what joy & peace flows out of this faith?

[284] 27 Oct. Do they not make a bridge somewhere of such construction that the strength of the whole is made to bear the strain on any one plank? Do they not charter banks on the provision that the entire property of all the stockholders is accountable for every dollar of their issue[?]
    Such a bridge, such a bank is a man[.] [711]

"He who calls what has vanished back again into being enjoys a bliss like that of creating."
                                                    Hare & Thirlwall's Niebuhr
                                                        ap. Lyell [712]

    The present age distinguished by the study of organic remains. The ancients studied not but formed them. It is a type of our reflective character. Well, solid learning is got from the fossils & solid wisdom shall be got from the reflexion. Geology teaches in a very impressive manner the value of facts & the laws of our learning from nature. Plain staring facts that have always been under every body's foot, the s⟨tone⟩lab of the pavement, the stone of the wall, the side of a hill, the gravel of the brook, in ⁿ these crypts has Nature deposited her secret & ⟨told⟩ ↑⟨notched⟩ ⟨recorded⟩ notched↓ every day of her thousand thousand milleniums. A woodsawyer may read it. The facts are capable of but one interpretation as the rings on the tree or in the cow's horn record every year of their age. No leaps, no magic, eternal tranquil procession of old familiar laws, the wildest convulsions never overstepping the calculable powers of the agents, the earthquake & geyser as perfect results of known laws as the rosebud & the hatching of a robin's egg. And a perpetual solicitation of man's faculties to read the riddle is made by the prominence & the beauty of the mountains & the streams under the sun [285] & moon meeting him everywhere in his daily walk. Meantime by these archaic calendars of the sun &

---

[711] "Do they not . . . a man", struck through in pencil with a diagonal use mark, is used in "Being and Seeming," *Lectures*, II, 295.

[712] Charles Lyell, *Principles of Geology*, 1830, I, 74, note: "Niehbuhr's History of Rome, vol. i, p. 5. Hare and Thirlwall's translation."

the internal fire, of the wash of rivers & oceans for durations inconceivable; by ⟨these⟩ Chimborazo & Mont Blanc & Himmaleh these monuments of nature & pyramids of the elements —ⁿ by the side of this silent procession of brute ⟨nature⟩ ↑elements↓ is the poem of man's life.

Much of the process she conceals in her secret shop. Her architecture is commenced & perfected in darkness & undersea. Under the ooze of the Atlantic she builds her basalts & pours melted granite like warm ⟨water⟩ ↑wax↓ into fissures of clay & lime and when the deposits of a thousand rivers have strewn the bed of the ocean with every year a new floor of spoils, she blows her furnaces with a gas & lifts the bed of the ocean above the water & man enters from a boat & makes a fire on the new World & worships God thereon, plants a field & builds a school.[713]

29 October. This very plagiarism to which scholars incline, (& it is often hard to acknowledge a debt) arises out of the Community of Mind. There is one mind. The man of genius apprises us not so much of his wealth as of the commonwealth.[714] Are his illustrations happy so ⟨sa⟩ feel we, do our race illustrate their thoughts. 'That's the way they ⟨do⟩ ↑show↓ things in my country.' Are his thoughts profound, so much the less are they his, so much more the property of all.[715]

[286] I have always distinguished Sampson Reed's Oration on Genius, and Collins' ode on the Passions, & all of Shakspear as being works of genius, inasmuch ⟨&⟩ as I read them with extreme pleasure & see no clue to guide me to their origin, whilst ⟨But[?]⟩ Moore's poetry or Scott's was much more comprehensible & subject to me. But as I become acquainted with S. R.'s books & teachers the miracle is somewhat lessened,ⁿ in the same manner as I once found that Burke's was.

---

[713] This and the preceding paragraph, struck through in pencil with a series of diagonal use marks, are used, with rearrangement, in "Humanity of Science," *Lectures*, II, 31–32.

[714] Cf. "The Poet," *W*, III, 5.

[715] "There is one . . . of all.", struck through in pencil with a diagonal use mark, is used in "Society," *Lectures*, II, 99. " 'That's the way . . . of all." is also struck through in pencil with a second diagonal use mark.

As we advance, shall every man of genius turn to us ⟨his ax⟩ the axis of his mind; then shall he be transparent, retaining however always the prerogative of an original mind; that is, the love of truth in God & not the love of truth for the market. We shall exhaust Shakspear.

———

There is one advantage which every man finds in setting himself a literary task as these my lectures, that it gives him the high pleasure of reading ⟨not⟩ which does not in other circumstances attain all its zest. When the mind is braced by the weighty expectations of a pre-pared work, the page of whatever book we read, becomes luminous with manifold allusion. Every sentence is doubly significant & the sense of our author is as broad as the world. There is creative reading as well as creative writing.[716]

[287] If one man gave me a loadstone & another taught me its property of turning to the north when suspended, I think I should owe more to him who showed me its properties, than to him who gave me the mineral ⟨itself.⟩.

[288] The diamond & lampblack it seems are the same substance differently arranged. Let it teach the importance of Composition[.]

Read Chemistry a little, & you will quickly see that its laws & experiments will furnish an alphabet or vocabulary for all your moral observations. Thus very few substances are found pure in nature. There are metals like potassium & sodium that to be kept pure must be kept under naphtha. Such are the decided talents which a culmi nating civilization produces in illuminated theatres, or royal chambers; but [n] those souls that can bear in open day the rough & tumble of the world must be of that mixed earthy & average structure such as iron, & salt, atmospheric air, & water.

Fontenelle, Keats, Allston,

[716] "When the mind . . . world." is struck through in pencil with three diagonal use marks; "There is creative . . . writing." is struck through in ink with a single diagonal use mark. "When . . . writing." is used, with rearrangement, in "The American Scholar," *W*, I, 93.

Heard fine music at Wayland from Mrs Mellen. What wreaths of sound!

———

⟨It seemed ‖ . . . ‖ as if Man were now endeavoring to traverse every purpose of God in the arrangements of society.⟩
Look now at the arrangements of society, at the parties, the education, the manners, the laws & it looks as if Man were endeavoring to traverse every purpose of God.

Education

"I have faith that man may be reformed when I see how much education may be reformed."

Leibnitz [717]

[289] 31 October, 1836, Concord. —

Last night at 11 o'clock, a son was born to me. Blessed child! a lovely wonder to me, and which makes the Universe look friendly to me. How remote from my knowledge, how alien, yet how kind does it make the Cause of Causes appear! The stimulated curiosity of the father sees the graces & instincts which exist, ↑indeed,↓ in every babe, but unnoticed in others; the right to see all, know all, to examine nearly, distinguishes this relation, & endears this sweet child. Otherwise I see nothing in it of mine; I am no ↑conscious↓ party to any feature, any function, any perfection I behold in it. I seem to be merely a brute occasion of its being & nowise attaining to the dignity even of a second cause no more than I taught it to suck the breast.

Please God, that "he, like a tree of generous kind,
                    By living waters set," [718] may draw endless nourishment from the fountains of Wisdom & Virtue!
Now am I Pygmalion.

Every day a child presents a new aspect, Lidian says, ⟨s⟩ as the face of the sky is different every hour, so that we never get tired.

The truth seems to be that every child is infinitely beautiful, but

---

[717] See *JMN*, IV, 327. The quotation is used in Address on Education, *Lectures*, II, 199, and "Education," *W*, X, 133.
[718] Ps. 1:3, as versified by Isaac Watts.

the father alone by position & by duty is led to look near enough to see. He looks with microscope. But what is most beautiful is to see the babe & the mother together, the contrast of size makes the little nestler appear so *cunning*, & its tiny beseeching weakness is compensated so perfectly by the happy patronizing look of the mother, who is a sort of high reposing Providence toward it — that they make a perfect group.

[290] 2 Nov. There would be no sect if there were no Sect. Is this a foolish identical proposition? I mean that the reason why the Universalist appears is because something has been overstated or omitted by the antecedent sect and the human mind feels itself wronged and overstates on the other side as in this. Each of our sects is an extreme statement & therefore obnoxious to contradiction & reproof. But each rests on this strong but obscure instinct of an outraged truth. Each is a cry of pain from the wounded soul. The Universalist comes out of the Uneducated classes where the instinct of right is very strong but the acumen of criticism & power of drawing distinctions very little.[719]

————

The child preaches to us ever the divinity of Nature[,] the shallowness of our Will.
↑Shall I say 'as ungrateful as an infant'?↓

3 November. A list of the theories that have attracted much attention in our time in all the sciences would be a valuable element of modern History.

A man cannot be considered apart from the world. Put Napoleon in some limbo ⟨wh⟩ alone & unfold his faculties[;] with no men he would ⟨be as⟩ ↑seem↓ crazy. Introduce great space, great population, & antagonist ⟨forces⟩ interests & you shall see him unfold his masterful faculties. We should [291] see that the man Napoleon bounded, that is, by such a profile & outline⟨, was⟩ ↑twas not the virtual Napoleon; this^n is↓ but "Talbot's shadow" [—] "his substance is not here" ⟨f⟩ [;]

————

[719] This paragraph, struck through in pencil with a vertical use mark, is used in "Society," *Lectures*, II, 108–109.

"For what you see, is but the smallest part
And least proportion of humanity;
But were the whole frame here,
It is of such a spacious lofty pitch,
Your roof were not sufficient to contain it"

↑1st Pt. K.Henry VI.
Act II.Sc.3↓ [ll. 46, 51–56,
misquoted] [720]

Columbus needs a planet to shape his course upon. Newton & La-place need myriads of ages & thick strown celestial spaces. Indeed one may say that a habitable gravitating Universe is already prophesied in the nature of Newton's mind. Does not the eye of the embryo predict the Light? The ear of Handel predict the magical powers of harmonic sound? The constructive nature of Watt, Fulton, Whittemore, Arkwright, Moody, predict the fusible, hard, & temperable texture of metals, the properties of water & of wood; the lovely attributes of the human female predict the refinements & decorations of civil society[?] [721]

The world is full of happy marriages of faculty to object, of means to end; and all of Man marries all of Nature, & makes it fruitful.   Man may be read therefore, if you choose, in a History of the Arts, or in a history of Sciences. Every tendency in him writes itself out somewhere to its last effort. He is a quincunx, & may be read forward, backward, or across.[721a]

[292] It seemed yesterday morn as the snow fell, that the adult looks more sourly than the child at th⟨is⟩e phenomena of approaching Winter. The child delights in the first snow & sees with it the spruce & hemlock boughs they bring for Christmas with glee. The man sees it all sourly expecting the cold days & inconvenient roads & labors of Winter. But the experience of a thousand years has shown him that his faculties are quite equal to master these inconveniences &

---

[720] Emerson added the citation in the left margin of his journal page, within a large square bracket.

[721] This paragraph, struck through in pencil with diagonal use marks, is used in The Philosophy of History: "Introductory," *Lectures*, II, 17–18, and "History," *W*, II, 36–37.

[721a] See p. [216] above.

despite of them to get his bread & wisdom. Therefore the child is
the wiser of the two.

> "Disasters do the best we can
> Will come to great & small,
> And he is oft the wisest man
> Who is not wise at all."
> [Wordsworth, "The Oak and the Broom,"
> ll. 61–64, misquoted] [722]

———

I remember with joy such aspects of nature as Bartram saw [723]
far from cabinets & cities, on the lonely canebrakes of Florida & the
Mississippi; and such as we see in desart winter morns not on our
pleasant walk peeping out of our warm houses half a mile or so, but
in the deep echoing forest where the pines grow undisturbed from
year to year & the ↑eagle & the↓ crow see⟨s⟩ no intruder; where the
broad cold lowland forms its coat of vapor with the stillness of subter-
ranean crystallization & the traveller amid the repulsive savages
[293] ↑that are native in the swamp,↓ thinks never of views but only
of frozen fingers & distant towns. [724] The moss hanging from cypresses
so thick that a man would be concealed under the shade[.]

This age will be characterized as the era of Trade, for every
thing is made subservient to that ⟨ele⟩ agency. The very savage on
the shores of the N.W. America, holds up his shell & cries 'a dollar!'
Government at home is conducted on such principles. [725] Superstition
gives way; Patriotism; Martial Ardor; Romance in the people; but
avarice does not[.]

Meantime, it is also a social era; the age of associations, the
powers of Combination are discovered. & hence of course the age of

[722] See Emerson's letter to Charles Emerson, January 19, 1832 (*L*, I, 344). This
paragraph is struck through in pencil with a diagonal use mark.

[723] On February 15–16, 1836, Emerson had withdrawn from the Boston Athenaeum William Bartram's *Travels through North and South Carolina, Florida, the
Cherokee Country* . . . , probably in the edition published in Philadelphia, 1791.

[724] "in the deep echoing . . . towns." is struck through in ink with diagonal use
marks.

[725] "This age will . . . principles." is struck through in pencil with a vertical
use mark. The first sentence of this passage is used in "The Present Age," *Lectures*,
II, 160; the second, in "Trades and Professions," *Lectures*, II, 128.

Constitutions, of Universal suffrage, of schools, of revision of laws, abolition of imprisonment, of railroads[.]

It is the age of Humboldt
                Brougham
                O'Connell
                Scott
                Mahomet Ali
                Paganini
                Baring
                Wilberforce

[294] Striking likeness in the mode of government & of trade. The fever of Speculation in Maine & the prairies is matched by the ardor & restlessness of politicians — reckless experiment. A man can ⟨be⟩ make himself believe that a barren sandbank streams with rivers that shall bear his logs[,] which now are blackberry bushes[,] into the Penobscot which is flowing ⟨150⟩ ↑90↓ miles off, quite heedless of his logs or bushes. And a man caucus-wise whose whole political skill ⟨is⟩ ends in managing a newspaper & a county convention can make himself believe that the Currency or the trade or the productions of a country can be altered by a law[.]

↑One of the marks by which an American vessel is known at sea is the quantity of canvas↓[.] [726]

Talleyrand's thousand miles & thousand years [727]

Chateaubriand's popular character of Rom[an] Ch[urch].[728]

On us the most picturesque contrasts are crowded. We have the beautiful costume of the Hindoo & the Turk in our streets. Our labor is done by the African. Here are some present who have seen the Pacific Islands and ⟨we have the Am.⟩ the Chinese

[726] Used in "Trades and Professions," *Lectures*, II, 128.

[727] See *JMN*, II, 232; "Manners," *Lectures*, II, 136.

[728] Emerson was evidently thinking of the popular success of Chateaubriand's *Le Génie du christianisme, ou beautés de la religion chrétienne* (1802).

We have the American Indian squaw at our doors. And all those contrasts which Commerce so fast abolishes are brought within a holiday excursion of the softness & refinement of Syria or Rome. The /Unitarian/Xn/ Rajah

The ⟨establishment⟩ founding of ⟨enormous⟩ cities to which the course of rivers, the richness of soils, & the meridians of climate predict enormous growth, we see laid. We see the camp pitched, & the fire lighted which shall never be extinguished until great natural revolutions [295] set a limit to human empire.[729]

[296] We are come up to Nature's feast. But the careful mother has made long prospective provision for our entertainment. Many thousand years has the land we dwell on been preparing for our habitation. The wood of our fire — the trees were planted many years before most of us were born. The peat or the vegetable had been crystallizing for a thousand years to form the ↑basket of↓ coals which this moment warms us.

⟨Both my brothers⟩
↑"— Ocean is
Of all things the kind genesis." Plut↓ [730]

I ought not to forget in characterising Charles the things he remarked & loved in nature. G[eorge]. B[arrell]. E[merson].[731] truly said We shall think of him when the June birds return. The birds he loved & discriminated & showed them us. So the pleasing effect of the grey oakleaf on the snow pleased him well; next it was he said in liveliness to green & white of pine tree & snow. Like my brother Edward, Charles had a certain severity of Character which did not permit him to be silly — no not for moments, but always self possessed & elegant ⟨even if⟩ ↑whether↓ morose or playful; no funning

[729] This paragraph, struck through in pencil on p. [294] with a diagonal use mark and a wavy diagonal use mark, is used in "The Present Age," *Lectures*, II, 160–161.

[730] The first line of the quotation begins immediately above the final letters of "brothers)"; the second line, immediately below. The extract is quoted from "Those Sentiments concerning Nature with which Philosophers were delighted," *Plutarch's Morals*, 1718, III, 138.

[731] George Emerson, who had tutored Emerson in geometry at Harvard, was a second cousin of the brothers.

for him or for Edward.   It was also remarkable in C. that he contemplated with satisfaction the departure of a day. Another day is gone[,] I am thankful he said. And to E.H. "Put me by the world wheels, & if I wouldn't give them a twirl!" [732]

[297] The sublime enters into every thing even into a baker's score or a school boy's multiplication table, as the Light beams into privies & garrets. I think that the clerk & the Merchant feel this in their Book-keeping. —

Nov. 5.[733] The reality ⟨of⟩ ↑which↓ the Ancient mind attributed to all things equally[,] to the fictions of the poets & to the ⟨observed⟩ facts & observed by their own eyes[,] is most remarkable. "For Neptune though he came last into the assembly

'Sate in the middle seat'

and Minerva seems &c x x x & Pindar plainly says

'She sits ⟨near⟩ ↑just next↓ the thunder-breathing flames,' &c &c"

says Plutarch in describing the etiquette of a feast of his own. See vol. 3, p. 236, *Plut. Morals* [734]
Then they charm me with their ⟨|| . . . ||⟩ taste, their wantonly beautiful superstitions. Thus; "Some that put Borrage into wine or sprinkle the floor with water in which Vervain & maidenhair have been steeped, as good to raise mirth & jollity in the guests," &c ——— [735]
They seem to be no Transcendentalists, — to rest always in the spontaneous consciousness.

[2⟨8⟩98] ↑5 Nov.↓ I find my measures of the value of time differ strangely. At the close of the day, at the close of the week I am quite incompetent to say if it have been well or ill spent.   When I have least to show for my time, no reading in English or German, no writing in Journal, & no work in the world, I have yet philosophised

---

[732] See p. [180] above.

[733] An entry dated November 4, 1836, occurs on p. [320] below.

[734] Emerson's quotation, somewhat abridged, is from "Symposiacs," *Plutarch's Morals*, 1718.

[735] Cf. "Symposiacs," *ibid.*, III, 230.

best, and arrrived at some solid ⟨&⟩conclusions that become conspicuous thoughts in the following months & years.[736]
This day I have been scrambling in the woods & with help of Peter
Howe [737] I have got six hemlock trees to plant in my yard which may
grow whilst my boy is sleeping.

7 November. Sleep for five minutes seems an indispensable
cordial to the ⟨sys⟩ human system. No rest is like the rest of sleep.
All other balm differs from the balm of sleep as mechanical mixture
differs from chemical. For this is the ⟨submission of⟩ abdication of
Will & the accepting a supernatural aid. It is the introduction of the
supernatural into the familiar day.
If I have weak or sore eyes, no looking at green curtains, no shut-
ting them, no cold water, no electuaries are of certain virtue; ⟨but⟩
whatever My will doth, seems tentative, but when at last I wake up
from a sound sleep then I know that he that made the eye has dealt
with it for the time & the wisest physician is He.[738]

[2⟨8⟩99] 8 November. I dislike to hear the patronizing tone in which
the self sufficient young men of the day talk of ministers "adapting
their preaching to the great mass." [739] Was the sermon good? "O
yes, good for you & me, but not understood by the great mass." Don't
you deceive yourself, say I, the great mass understand what's what,
as well as the little mass. The selfconceit of this tone is not more provoking than the profound ignorance it argues is pitiable[.]
    The fit attitude of a man is humble Wonder & gratitude, a meek
watching of the marvels of the Creation to the end that he may know
& do what is fit. But these pert gentlemen assume that the whole
object is to manage "the great mass" & they forsooth are behind the
curtain with the Deity and mean to help manage. They know all &
will now smirk & manoeuvre & condescendingly yield the droppings
of their wisdom to the poor people.

    [736] "I find my . . . years." is struck through in pencil with a diagonal use mark.
The last sentence is used in "Ethics," *Lectures*, II, 146.
    [737] A Concord neighbor who helped Emerson in his gardening.
    [738] "Sleep for five . . . is He.", struck through in pencil with a vertical use
mark, is used in "Prudence," *Lectures*, II, 322–323.
    [739] See p. [271] above; cf. "Literature," *Lectures*, II, 62.

[300]^{740} expedition to the ↑enormous↓ height of 25 000 feet or rather less than five miles." $\dfrac{1}{1600}$ of the earth's surface[.]

Herschel [741]

Romano Pane a Spanish Missionary who discovered tobacco in St Domingo contributed essentially to improve the revenue ⟨in⟩from this quarter, for that weed became not less productive than the gold mines to the Spanish treasury[.]

Muller   Vol 3. p. 150 [742]

So the potato, silk, tea plant, caoutchouc,[743]

In 1804, when the tribunate had proposed that Napoleon should be made emperor, & the senate had confirmed the proposition, Fontanes, the president of the legislative body, carried an address from those members then in Paris, to the First Consul, approving the measure of the tribunate & senate, & said in his speech, "The desire of perfection is the worst disease that can afflict the human mind." [744]

[See Rev of Thibaudeau F[oreign] Q[uarterly]
R[eview, XVII] Ju[l]y 1836 [p. 359]

King John in the year 1215 in revenge for the constrained concessions of Magna Charta, marched through England from Dover to Berwick, with an army of mercenaries devastating all but crown lands, & burning towns & castles.[745]

---

[740] "Civil History. (continued from p. 280)" is written above "to the enormous . . . rather" at the top of the page. The entries under this index heading conclude on p. [301].
[741] Cf. Sir John Frederick William Herschel, *A Treatise on Astronomy* (London, 1833), p. 23; the book is no. 43 in *The Cabinet Cyclopædia*, ed. Dionysius Lardner (London, 1829–1849).
[742] See p. [120] above.
[743] This entry was left unfinished.
[744] This paragraph, struck through in pencil with a diagonal use mark, is used in "Napoleon," *W*, IV, 228.
[745] See David Hume, *The History of England*, 6 vols. (New York, 1850), I, 435–436.

In the year 1215 there were 1115 castles in England.

———

I notice in the N.Y. Com[mercial]. Adv[ertiser]. (Nov 28) that 47 000 bushels of foreign grain have been sold in N.Y. in the last week:ⁿ red German wheat, white Dantzic wheat, wheat from Holland, rye from Trieste & from Prussia.

———

In St Petersburg one of the churches is surrounded by a fence made of captured cannon.

———

[301] Of the French character, some attributes are hospitality, politeness, vanity, falsehood, absence of natural affection, industry, genius for science & for war, early but unpermanent wit,

———

Mr Canning said in [1826], in allusion to the recognition of the independence of the South American states, "I called the New World into existence to redress the balance of the Old." [746]

———

[302] 8 Nov. The man capable of bursts of prodigious eloquence gives no more intimation of his power talking with you in the street than the cannon on which you sit, or which you measure, does of the flash & report of its discharge. And very pleasant stimulus it is to the faculties to meet some ↑great captain as↓ Napoleon or Murat or Claverhouse in the lassitude & elegance of a parlor & from the sleeping lion judge of the aroused lion; ↑as Caesar said that his soldiers were so well trained that though powdered & perfumed they ran like giants to battle.↓ [747]

The Antique.
A man is the prisoner of ideas & must be unconscious. Every man is

[746] In Parliament, December 12, 1826; see *The Speeches of the Right Honorable George Canning* (London, 1828), VI, 111. The sentence, struck through in pencil with a diagonal use mark, is used in "Manners," *Lectures*, II, 138. This is the concluding entry under "Civil History"; at least the last four items were evidently written after "Nov 28".

[747] Cf. Montaigne, "Observations of the means to carry on a War according to Julius Cæsar," *Essays*, 1700, II, 648. This paragraph, struck through in pencil with a diagonal use mark, is used through "its discharge." in "Society," *Lectures*, II, 110, and thereafter in "Manners," *Lectures*, II, 138.

unconscious, let him be as wise as he may, & must always be so until he can ⟨take⟩ ↑lift↓ himself up by his own ears.[748]

I have read in English (for want of thee, dear Charles!) this P.M. the Ajax & the Philoctetes of Sophocles, of which plays the costly charm is that the persons speak simply. A great boy[,] a great girl with good sense is a Greek.[749]

Webster was a Greek when he looked so goodhumoredly at Major Ben Russell at a Caucus once. Beautiful is the love of nature in Philoctetes. But in reading those fine apostrophes to sleep, to the stars, rocks, ⟨&⟩ mountains, & the sea, I feel Time passing away as an ebbing sea, I feel the eternity of man, the identity of the soul in every age. The Greek had, it seems, the same fellow beings as I; the sun & moon[,] water & fire met his eye & heart as they do mine, precisely. Then the vaunted [303] distinctions between Greek & English, between Classic & Romantic schools, seem superfluous & pedantic. When a ⟨sentiment o[?] of⟩ thought of Plato becomes a thought to me, when a truth that fired the soul of Jesus Christ fires mine, Time is no more. When I feel that we two meet in a great truth[,] that our two souls are tinged with the same hue & do as it were run into one.[750]

Under the great & permanent influences of nature all others seem insignificant. I think we make rather too much of the Greek genius. As in old botanical gardens they turn up in the soil every now & then seeds that have lain dormant for ages and as in families they say a feature will sometimes sleep for a hundred years & then reappear in a descendant of the line, so I believe that this Greek genius is ever reappearing in society, & that each of us knows one or more of the class. Aunt Mary is a Greek & I have more in memory. Every child is a Greek.[751]

[748] These two sentences, struck through in pencil with a vertical use mark, are used in "The Present Age," *Lectures*, II, 170.

[749] The first of these two sentences, which are struck through in pencil with a vertical use mark, is used in "Manners," *Lectures*, II, 134, and "History," *W*, II, 25.

[750] This paragraph, struck through in pencil with a vertical use mark from "Beautiful is the" on p. [302] and a diagonal use mark on p. [303], is used in "The Individual," *Lectures*, II, 187, and "History," *W*, II, 26–27.

[751] "I think we . . . Greek.", struck through in pencil with a diagonal use mark, is used in "Manners," *Lectures*, II, 135.

Yet as I looked at some wild tall trees this afternoon I felt that Nature was still inaccessible, that for all the fine poems that have been written the word is not yet spoken that can cover the charm of morning or evening or woods or lakes, & tomorrow something may be uttered better than any strain of Pindar or Shakspear.[n][752]
A wife, a babe, a brother, poverty, & a country, which the Greek had, I have.
See the naiveté[n] of Xenophon's account of horse troops[.]
                    Anabasis   vol p. 95 [III, ii, 17–19 (?)]

[304] Is there not an improvement in modern medicine whereby the physician exhibits a very small portion of the drug with like effect as a large portion formerly? That were a right modern improvement, characteristic of our history.

9 November. Men are imprisoned by Ideas. Their eyes are holden that they cannot see[753] things which are close to them & shall be obvious enough to the next generation. Therefore said Aristotle well of his works "They are published, & not published."[754]

10 Nov. For form's sake or for wantonness I sometimes chaffer with the farmer on the price of a cord of wood but if he said twenty dollars instead of five I should think it cheap when I remember the beautiful botanical wonder — the bough of an oak — which he brings me so freely out of the enchanted forest where the sun & water[,] air & earth & God formed it. In like manner I go joyfully through the mire in a wet day and admire the inconvenience, delighted with the chemistry of a shower. Live in the fields & God will give you lectures on natural philosophy every day. You shall have the snow bunting, the chickadee, the jay, the partridge, the chrysalis & wasp for your neighbors.[755]

---

[752] This paragraph is struck through in pencil with a diagonal use mark.

[753] See, respectively, pp. [302] and [105] above.

[754] For Aristotle's remark see "The Life of Alexander," *Plutarch's Lives*, 1822, V, 195; *JMN*, IV, 337. It is also used in "Spiritual Laws," *W*, II, 146.

[755] This paragraph, struck through in pencil with a vertical use mark, is used in "The Eye and Ear," *Lectures*, II, 275.

[305] Language clothes nature as the air clothes the earth, taking the exact form & pressure of every object. ⟨It⟩ Only words that are new fit exactly the thing, those that are old like old scoriae that have been long exposed to the air & sunshine, have lost the sharpness of their mould & fit loosely. But in new objects & new names one is delighted with the plastic nature of man as much as in picture or sculpture. Thus Humboldt's "volcanic paps" & "magnetic storms" are the very mnemonics of Science & so in general in books of modern science the vocabulary yields this poetic pleasure.[756]   "Veins inosculate[.]"

[306]   [Compensation]
↑11 Nov.↓ Every faculty which is a receiver of pleasure has an equal penalty put on its abuse. It is to answer for its moderation with its life[.] [757]

The Idea is spiritual sight; the idealess research of facts is natural sight. Cannot the natural see better when assisted by the spiritual?

I read the Anabasis in English today with great pleasure. ⟨Has d⟩ Xenophon draws characters like Clarendon. His speeches are excellent[,] none better than that[n] upon *horses*, & that where having seen the Sea, he draws up his line against the opposing barbarians & tells them "that these being all the obstacle that is left, they ought to eat these few alive." He is an ancient hero; — he splits wood[,] he defends himself by his tongue against every man in his army as by his sword against the enemy[.] [758]

I will tell you where there is music in those that cannot sing: in the mother's earnest talk to her baby, shouts of love.

---

[756] See Alexander von Humboldt, *Personal Narrative of Travels to the Equinoctial Regions of the New Continent*, 7 vols. (London, 1814–1819), IV, 43–44; *JMN*, IV, 331. This paragraph appears to have been drafted in accordance with an earlier entry made on p. [320]: see n. 792 below.

[757] This paragraph, struck through in pencil with a diagonal use mark, is used in "Ethics," *Lectures*, II, 153, and "Compensation," *W*, II, 98.

[758] See *Anabasis*, III, ii, 17–19 (?); IV, viii, 14; IV, iv, 12; and *passim*. Cf. "Manners," *Lectures*, II, 134; "History," *W*, II, 25.

"By broad Potomac's silent shore
    Better than Trajan lowly lies
Gilding her green declivities
    With glory now & ⟨n⟩evermore
Art to his fame no aid hath lent
    His country is his monument." [759]

[307] Nov. 12. We scare ourselves by the names we give 'death watch' (ptinus); earwig; deathshead moth; ↑St Anthony's fire[;] St Vitus's Dance[.]↓

How many attractions for us have our passing fellows in the streets both male & female, which our ethics forbid us to express which yet infuse so much pleasure into life. A lovely child, a handsome youth, a beautiful girl, a heroic man, a maternal woman, a venerable old man, charm us though strangers & we cannot say so, or look at them but for a moment[.]

15 November. On Sunday morn, 13th at 4 o'clock A.M. & again at 5 & at 6 o'clock I saw falling stars in unusual numbers & dropping all perpendicular to the horizon. It was a pleasing testimony to the theory of Arago.

Yesterday the election of state & town officers. One must be of a robust temper & much familiar with general views to avoid disgust from seeing the way in which a young fellow with talents for intrigue can come into a peaceful town like this, besot all the ignorant & simple farmers & laborers, & ride on their necks until as yesterday they reject their long honoured townsman who had become a sort of second conscience to them, a Washington in his ⟨place⟩ ↑county↓ [308] & choose in his place an obscure stranger whom they know not & have no right to trust.[760] Yet the philosopher ought to learn hence how greedy man is of fellowship & of guidance. The low can best win the low and all men like to be made much of.

[759] Printed under the title "George Washington," author anonymous, in Emerson's anthology *Parnassus* (Boston, 1876), p. 226.

[760] Samuel Hoar had been defeated for reelection to Congress by William Parmenter (1789–1866), a Democrat of East Cambridge.

When fear enters the heart of a man at hearing the names of candidates & the reading of laws that are proposed, then is the state safe, but when these things are heard without regard as above or below us, then is the commonwealth sick or dead.

When the philosopher comforts himself with general views over particular disasters to the state, let him not feel that he has any right to his solace so long as it is only derived from the diversion of his mind, the mere hiding of his head ostrich-like in sand, not until he sees that his consolation arises out of the evil itself, that the relief which ↑he↓ contemplates is already working, let him dare to give sleep to his eyes or joy to his soul.

Geology, Botany, Astronomy, become ignominious if cowardly sought.

This is the demerit of Germany.[761]

Edmund Hosmer is a little man but he looks up well, — said Cheney senior[.] [762]

——————

I should think you would scarce be able to sustain the intense heat of the lightning bugs.

[309] An acorn is not an oak but an oak-manufactory.

"I soon found that it is too late to look for instruments when the work calls for execution, & that whatever abilities I had brought to ⟨the⟩ my task, with those I must finally perform it." Johnson's Preface to the Dictionary.[763]

↑There is room in the world for all men & all gifts.↑
Nov. 19. Went to see Alcott in town & heard him read his excellent Introduction to the new book he is printing of Recorded Conversa-

[761] "When the philosopher . . . Germany." is struck through in pencil with a vertical use mark. Cf. "The American Scholar," *W*, I, 104.

[762] Hosmer was a neighboring farmer, termed Emerson's "agricultural adviser and executor" by Edward Emerson (*J*, IV, 394, n. 2); Cheney was presumably the father of John Milton Cheney, a college classmate of Emerson who had become cashier of the Concord Bank.

[763] Cf. *The Works of Samuel Johnson*, 12 vols. (London, 1806), II, 56.

tions.[764] An admirable piece full of profound anticipations. I listen with joy. I feel how much greater it is to hear & receive than to speak or do. Every description of Man seems at the moment to cover the whole ground & leave no room for future poets. But it is, as Goethe said, ⟨We have⟩ "Twenty great masters have painted the Madonna & Child, but not one can be spared," & ⟨not one⟩ no two interfere.

We talked of the men of talent & men of genius & spared nobody. I, at least, feel no audacity in measuring any individual be his powers what they may, though I learn ↑that↓ this valuation of my worshipful superiors gives offence. I am & shall continue to be always an observer. I shall always know & say what individual gives me aliment & what one does not. I acknowledge at once the better gifts of this & that friend who yet lack in my judgment the great [310] gift whereby alone they can become of great value to me, namely, the simple sight of Universal truth. These young men, it seems, now go away, & count our little club arrogant & hurtful. Tell me now whether my instinct was sick or sound, which said, These profit you not; & which I ⟨men⟩ wrote of to G.P.B. the other day.[765]

I said to Alcott that I thought that ↑the great↓ Man should occupy the whole space between God and the mob. He must draw from the infinite source on the one side & he must penetrate into the heart & mind of the rabble on the other. From one, he must draw his strength; to the other, he must owe his Aim. Thus did Jesus, dwelling in mind with pure God, & dwelling in social position & hearty love with fishers & women. Thus did Shakspear the great English man, drawing direct from the soul at one end, & piercing into the play going populace at the other. The one yokes him to the real, the other to the apparent; at one pole, is Reason; at the other, common sense. Plotinus united with God is not united with the world; Napoleon,

---

[764] Emerson had previously seen at least a portion of the manuscript (p. [213] above). Alcott's journal, November 17, 1836, notes that "Mr. Emerson passed the afternoon and evening with me . . . . I read him my Preface and Introduction to the 'Conversations,' in which he expressed pleasure, advising me to print the Introduction separate as a worthy view of my principles and views of education." See *The Journals of Bronson Alcott*, 1938, p. 79.

[765] Acknowledged by Bradford, then in Bangor, Maine, on November 23 and 24 (*L*, II, 45).

Rothschild, Falstaff, united with the world have no communion with the ⟨d⟩Divine.[766]

This extent is perfectly natural to the soul for the outward was made after a divine idea & is therefore beautiful when seen aright & a highest endowment of mind will clearest see the charm of facts & things & transfigure pots & kettles.

↑Remember in this connexion the old woman of Moliere the aunt of genius — ↓[767]

[311] The poet, the moralist have not yet rendered us their entire service when they have written & published their books. The book & its direct influence on my mind, are one fact, but a more important fact is the verdict of humanity upon it, a thing not suddenly settled, &, in the case of great works, not for an age. Not until the French Revolution, is the character of Locke's Essay on the Human Understanding finally determined. We form opinions in the first place upon the talents of a writer but the creeping ages bring with their verdict so much knowledge of the nature of Man. Sir Humphrey Davy is not estimable by his contemporaries but ⟨now⟩ having once filled the whole sky of science by his nearness & been to beholders instead of Chemistry, now globes himself into an unit & so he passes. Once he was Chemistry; now he is Davy.

November 21. I read with pleasure this morning Everett's notice of [Richard] Bentley in N[orth]. A[merican]. Review for Oct. 1836. The beautiful facts are that Bentley having published conjectural emendations of Homer, ⟨his nephew finds⟩ in opposition to all known manuscripts, his nephew finds at Rome, sixteen years afterwards, more correct MSS. in which his conjectural readings are exactly confirmed. And Wheeler & Spon two learned travellers having separately copied & published an inscription on an ancient temple of Jupiter at the entrance of the Euxine,[n] Chishull corrected ⟨them⟩ it & published it in his Antiquitates Asiaticae. Bentley undertook[n] [312] to restore the eight lines to their original form. Chishull received

---

[766] This paragraph, struck through in pencil with a diagonal use mark, is used in "Literature," *Lectures*, II, 61–62, and "Literary Ethics," *W*, I, 182.

[767] Cf. *JMN*, IV, 371.

some & rejected ⟨others⟩ ↑some↓ of his emendations. In 1731, the original marble was brought to England & found to coincide precisely with Bentley's conjectural emendations.

He had said he thought himself likely to live to fourscore which was long enough to read every thing that was worth reading,

Et tunc magna mei sub terris ibit imago.[768]

He died 1742 aet. 80.
He compared himself in old age to "an old trunk which, if you let it alone will last a long time, but if you jumble it by moving, will soon fall to pieces."

⟨Here is his epitaph⟩ He had a club which consisted of Sir Christopher Wren, Sir Isaac Newton, Evelyn, John Locke, & himself. Here is his epitaph on Newton.

> Hic quiescunt ossa et pulvis
>   Isaaci Newtoni.
> Si quaeris, quis et qualis fuerit,
>   Abi:
> Sin ex ipso nomine reliqua novisti,
>   Siste paulisper
> Et mortale illud philosophiae numen
>   Gratâ mente venerare.[769]

[313] The philosopher has this consolation in his pursuits that if they do not interest all men now, yet they will, sooner or later. However alone, or in what small minority he may now stand, every single individual will some time do him justice & recall his image with grateful & honorable remembrance[.] [770]

---

[768] "And now in majesty my shade shall pass beneath the earth." Virgil, *Aeneid*, IV, 654. (The Loeb text reads "nunc" and "terras" where Emerson has "tunc" and "terris".)

[769] "Here repose the bones and dust of Isaac Newton. If you wish to know, who and of what sort he was, go away: but if from the name itself you know the rest, linger a little while and worship with thankful mind that famous mortal authority of philosophy" (Ed.). Emerson's discussion here draws from Edward Everett's notice of two works on Richard Bentley, *North American Review*, XLIII (Oct. 1836), 480, 491–492, 472, 486, respectively.

[770] This paragraph, struck through in pencil with a diagonal use mark, is used in "The Poet," *W*, III, 5.

[November] ↑22.↓ Subjects. The marriage relation. The dependence of the scholar on his company to make him a fool or a god. J.B.

24 November. Talking tonight with E. H. I sought to illustrate the sunny side of every man ↑as↓ compared with his sour & pompous side by the two entrances of all our Concord houses. The front door is very fair to see, painted green, with a knocker, but it is always bolted, & you might as well beat on the wall as tap there; but the farmer slides round the house into a quiet back door that admits him at once to his warm fire & loaded table.

———

↑Nothing is useless↓
[November] ↑25.↓ A superstition is a hamper or basket to carry useful lessons in.[771]

———

I told Miss Peabody last night ↑that↓ Mr Coleridge's churchmanship is thought to affect the value of his criticism &c. I do not feel it. It is a harmless freak & sometimes occurs in a wrong place, as when he refuses to translate some alleged blasphemy in Wallenstein. Some men are affected with hemorrhage ⟨i⟩of the nose; it is of no danger but unlucky when it befals where it should not as at a [314] wedding or in the rostrum. But Coleridge's is perfectly separable. I know no such critic. Every opinion he expresses is a canon of criticism that should be writ in steel, & his italics are italics of the mind.

25 Nov. Here are two or three facts plain & clear. That histories are not yet history; that the historian should be a philosopher, for surely he can describe the outward ⟨phenomenon⟩ ↑event↓ better if assisted by the ⟨spiritual⟩ sight⟨,⟩ of the cause; historians are men of talents, & of the market, & not devout, benevolent, with eyes that make walls no walls; that history is written to enhance the present hour;[n] that all history is to be written from man, is all to be explained from individual history or must remain words. We as we read must be Romans, Greeks, Barbarians, priest & king, martyr & executioner, or we shall see nothing, keep nothing, learn nothing. There is nothing but is related to us; nothing that does not interest

[771] An echo of Plutarch: see p. [116] above.

the historian in its relation; tree, horse, iron, that the roots of all things are in man & therefore the philosophy of history is a consideration of science, art, literature, religion, as well as politics.[772]

⟨Tu⟩Sallust, I think, said that men would put down to the account of romance whatever exceeded their own power to perform. A very safe & salutary truth.[773]

[315] "Bonaparte covered treaties with black crape & called all advocates of liberty, ideologists." [774]

Nov. 28, 1836. B.R. very good in serious, anxious occasions but when nothing's the matter, nothing's the mind.

I thought as I rode in the cold pleasant light of Sunday morning how silent & passive nature offers, every morn, her wealth to man; she is immensely rich, he is welcome to her entire goods, but she speaks no word, only leaves all her doors ajar, hall, store room, & cellar.[n] ⟨h⟩He may do as he will: if ⟨she⟩he ⟨learns her secret⟩ takes her hint & uses her goods, she speaks no word; if he blunders & starves, she says nothing.

Only it seems in what we call tempting opportunities, as if the old dumb power did beckon & cough.[775]

In what I call the cyclus of Orphic words, which I find in Bacon, in Cudworth, in Plutarch, in Plato, in that which the New Church [776] would indicate when it speaks of the truths possessed by the primeval church broken up into fragments & floating hither & thither in the corrupt Church, I perceive ⟨an adaptation⟩ myself addressed thor-

---

[772] "historians are men . . . politics." is struck through in both pencil and ink with diagonal use marks. "We as we . . . learn nothing." is used in The Philosophy of History: "Introductory," Lectures, II, 15, and "History," W, II, 5.

[773] Sallust, Bellum Catilinae, III, 2. This paragraph, struck through in pencil with a vertical use mark, is used in The Philosophy of History: "Introductory," Lectures, II, 13.

[774] Cf. the anonymous review of A. C. Thibaudeau, Mémoirs sur le consulat . . . and Le Consulat et l'empire . . . , Foreign Quarterly Review, XVII (July 1836), 338; "Humanity of Science," Lectures, II, 37.

[775] This and the preceding paragraph, struck through in pencil with a vertical use mark, are used in "Doctrine of the Hands," Lectures, II, 235, and "Powers and Laws of Thought," W, XII, 28. Cf. "Days," W, IX, 228.

[776] The Swedenborgian Church of the New Jerusalem.

oughly. They do touch the Intellect & cause a gush of emotion; ⟨to⟩ which we call the moral sublime; they pervade also the moral nature. Now the Universal Man when he comes, must so speak. He must not be one-toned. He must recognize by addressing the whole nature.

[316] 28 Nov. Of these truths Jesus uttered many, such as; God is no respecter of persons; His kingdom cometh without observation. His kingdom is a little child.⁷⁷⁷

Otherism

I see plainly the charm which belongs to Alienation or Otherism. "What wine do you like best, O Diogenes?" "Another's," replied the sage.⁷⁷⁸ What fact, thought, word, like we best? Another's. The very sentiment I expressed yesterday without heed, shall sound memorable to me tomorrow if I hear it from another. My own book I read with new eyes when a stranger has praised it.⁷⁷⁹ It is, (is it not?) all ⟨the⟩ one & the same radical fact which I noticed above, p. 254, that the picture pleases when the original does not, that the subjective must be made objective for us & the soul, body.⁷⁸⁰

Or is the charm wholly in the new method by which it was classified; for, a new mind is a new method. How often we repeat in vain the words or substance without conveying to others the genius of a friend's remark.

↑See also p. 184↓

No man need be perplexed in his speculation. Let him keep his mind healthy, & though very ignorant of books his nature shall keep him free from any intellectual embarrassment. It is quite another thing that he should be able to represent to another his self union & freedom. This requires rare gifts. His progress is always concentrical and he may move now in his first & narrowest rings, & no ray shoot

⁷⁷⁷ Cf. (1) Acts 10:34 (see p. [200] above); (2) Luke 17:20 (see p. [212] above); (3) Luke 18:17 and Mark 10:15.

⁷⁷⁸ Cf. Diogenes Laertius, "Diogenes," *Lives of Eminent Philosophers*, VI, 54.

⁷⁷⁹ "What fact . . . praised it.", struck through in pencil with intersecting diagonal use marks, is used in "Society," *Lectures*, II, 100.

⁷⁸⁰ "the picture pleases . . . soul, body." is struck through in pencil with a diagonal use mark. The last clause is used in "Literature," *Lectures*, II, 57.

out to the far circumferences he shall hereafter attain, yet there need be no obliquity or death in that which he is. "A few [317] strong instincts & a few plain rules" &c [781] suffice us. Some young people suffer from speculations as Original Sin, Origin of Evil, Predestination &c. I was never sick of those mumps or measles or whooping coughs. Yet can I not describe my health or prescribe their cure.[782]

Edward Taylor is a noble work of the divine cunning who suggests the wealth of Nature. If he were not so strong, I should call him lovely. What cheerfulness in his genius & what consciousness of strength. "My voice is thunder," he said in telling me how well he was. And what teeth & eyes & brow & aspect — I study him as a jaguar or an Indian for his untamed physical perfections. He is a work[,] a man not to be predicted. His vision poetic & pathetic; sight of love, is unequalled. How can he transform all those whiskered shaggy untrim tarpaulins into sons of light & hope? By [n] seeing the man within the sailor[,] seeing them to be sons, lovers, brothers, husbands[.]

But hopeless it is to make him that he is not; to try to bring him to account to you or to himself for aught of his inspiration. A creature of instinct, his colors are all opaline & doves'-neck-lustres & can only be seen at a distance. Examine them & they ⟨are not⟩ ↑disappear↓. If you see the ignis fatuus in a swamp, & go to the place, the light vanishes; if you retire to the spot whereon you stood, it reappears. So with Taylor's muse. It is a panorama of images from all nature & art, whereon the sun & stars shine but go up to it & nothing is there. His instinct[,] [318] unconscious instinct is the nucleus or point of view, & this defies science & eludes it. Do not forget Charles's love of him,[n] who said if he were in town he would go & record all his fine sayings.

↑Mem. Tita's house in speaking of C.C.E.↓

Come let us not be an appanage to Alexander, Charles V. or any

[781] Wordsworth, "Alas! What Boots the Long Laborious Quest," l. 11. Emerson alludes to the same line in *JMN*, IV, 291.

[782] This paragraph, struck through in pencil with vertical use marks, is used in "Ethics," *Lectures*, II, 145, and "Spiritual Laws," *W*, II, 132.

of history's heroes. Dead men all! but for me the earth is new today, & the sun is raining light. The doctrine of the amiable Swedenborgian & of the subtle Goethe is, that "we murder to dissect," [783] that nature has told everything once,[784] if only we seek the fact where it is told in Colossal. Therefore are so manifold objects, to present each fact in capitals somewhere. What else is history? We see not the perspective of our own life. We see the ruts, pebbles, & straws of the road where we walk, but cannot see the chart of the land. "We are not sufficiently elevated with respect to ourselves to comprehend ourselves." [785] Our own life we cannot subject to the eye of the intellect. What remedy? Why, history is the remedy. Its volumes vast have but one page[;] it writes in many forms but one record, this human nature of mine[.]

Like the signs of the Zodiac[,] the crab, the goat, the scorpion, the balance, the waterpot have lost all their meanness when hung in the blue spaces of the empyrean from an unrecorded age, so I can see the familiar & sordid attributes of human nature without emotion as objects of pure science when removed into this distant firmament of time. My appetites, my weaknesses, my vices I can see in Alexander, Alcibiades, & Catiline,

turn to p. 322

[319] The most familiar & stale is the most attractive of all things [n] when once we apprehend its spiritual character.[786] The lank haired, the bald-headed, the wooly pated, black, white, & grey — all became interesting when the phrenologist declared his power to show their class in nature. & the Charlestown Bridge question, the Rantouls & Robinsons, & the Julien-hall gentry would interest us if we read their riddle in absolute Nature.[787]

[783] Wordsworth, "The Tables Turned," l. 28.

[784] Another of Emerson's several variations on a theme from Goethe, as on p. [167]: see n. 453 above.

[785] Adapted from a remark of St. Augustine quoted in Mme de Staël, *Germany*, 3 vols. in 2 (New York, 1814), II, 162; see *JMN*, III, 155. Apparently the altered wording in Journal B, which exactly reverses the original point, must be ascribed to Emerson's faulty memory.

[786] This sentence is struck through in pencil with a diagonal use mark.

[787] In 1827 the legislature of Massachusetts had authorized construction of a second toll bridge across the Charles River between Boston and Charlestown; the

Honor is venerable to us because it is no ephemeris. It is always ancient virtue. We worship it today because it is not of today. We love
it & do homage because it is not a trap for our love & homage but is
essentially self dependent, self derived, & therefore of an old immac-
ulate pedigree even if shown in a young person. Those whom society
disesteems do thou serve. Those of whose feelings mannerly gentlemen & ladies [788]

The Child. I think ⟨F[?]⟩Hope should be painted with an infant on
her arm.

[320] Notes for the correction or enlargement of "Nature." [789]
John Eliot would be a noble figure to add to the group on p. 26[.] [790]

When he was alone with the Indians in the wilderness they threatened to do
him a mischief if he did not desist from his labors. He said to them "I am
about the work of the great God & my God is with me so that I neither fear
you nor all the Sachems in the country; I will go on & do you touch me
if you dare." With a body capable of enduring fatigue & a mind as firm
as the mountain oaks which overshadowed his path he went from place
to place relying for protection on the great Head of the Church declaring
the truths of Christ to the tribes.
    He says in a letter, "I have not been dry night or day from the third

---

proprietors of the existing bridge challenged the validity of the authorization. Robert
Rantoul (1805–1852), an opponent of slavery and capital punishment, attacked the
claims of the proprietors; in 1836 Rantoul was a member of the judiciary committee
of the Massachusetts legislature and John Paul Robinson (1799–1864) of Lowell
was representing Middlesex County in the senate. The bridge case, which had been
carried to the Supreme Court of Massachusetts in 1829, was appealed to the United
States Supreme Court in 1837. For Abner Kneeland and "the Julien-hall gentry" see
pp. [77] and [80] above.
    [788] This uncompleted paragraph, struck through in ink with a diagonal use mark,
is used in "Manners," *Lectures*, II, 140, and "Self-Reliance," *W*, II, 60.
    [789] Most if not all of the entries on pp. [320] and [321] appear to fall under
this heading. The date or dates of inscription cannot be established with certainty.
Like the names recorded on p. [330] below of those individuals and firms given
presentation copies of *Nature*, some of this material may have been written soon after
the book was published on September 9, 1836. Although the two pages of notes occur
between journal entries dated November 28 and November 29 (see pp. [316], [326]),
the fifth item below is entered as of "Nov. 4." and the third item is developed in an
entry of November 10, p. [305] above.
    [790] For the "group," which includes Leonidas, Winkelreid, Columbus, Vane, and
Lord Russell, see *Nature*, 1836, p. 26, and *W*, I, 20–21.

day of the week unto the sixth, but so travelled, & at night pull off my boots, wring my stockings, & on with them again, & so continue; but God steps in & helps. I have considered the word of God, 'Endure hardship as a good soldier of ⟨Christ⟩ Jesus Christ.' " —————— Allen.[791]

The sachems & pawaws feared to lose their authority by the introduction of the new religion. [*Ibid.*, p. 370]

To the same connexion belongs I think the paragraph upon Eyes in p. 111 of this Journal.

———

↑See the notice of Humboldt J[ournal] 1833[–1834,] p 96 — for Chap. on Language.↓[792]

———

↑See p 126 J[ournal]. 1833↓[–1834] [793]

———

Nov. 4. A beautiful object at this season in the oak woods, (on the way to Goose Pond) is the carpet formed entirely of oak leaves thickly strown & matted so as entirely to cover the ground. Where snow has fallen the contrast of the colors is still better.
↑See J[ournal] 1835[–1836,] p 16–17↓[794]
Fire is the sweetest of sauces, said Prodicus.[795]
For

[321] It is remarkable that the greater the material apparatus the more the material disappears as in Alps & Niagara[,] in St Peters & Naples.[796]

---

[791] Abridged from Allen, *An American Biographical and Historical Dictionary*, 1832, p. 370.
[792] In *JMN*, IV, 331, Emerson terms phrases from Humboldt the "mnemonics of science"; "Language" is the subject of the fourth chapter of *Nature*. For a paragraph on language incorporating Humboldt's phraseology, see the entry for November 10, 1836, p. [305] above — apparently written after the present entry.
[793] For the entry, which concerns Emerson's response to "Nature in the woods," see *JMN*, IV, 359–360.
[794] A paragraph of "marine recollections," the last sentence of which Emerson had already used in *Nature* (p. [17] above, n. 47).
[795] Attributed to Evenus in "Symposiacs," *Plutarch's Morals*, 1718, III, 391, cited in Journal C below, p. [132]. See *JMN*, IV, 114.
[796] Copied from p. [137] above.

[322] [from p. 318]
without heat & study their laws,[n] without anger or personal pique or contrition. Scythian, Hebrew, & Gaul serve as algebraic exponents in which I can read my own good & evil without pleasure & without pain.[797]

Whilst thus I use the Universal Humanity I see plainly the fact that there is no progress to the race, that the progress is of individuals. One element is predominant in one; another, is carried to perfection in the next; Art in the Greeks; power in the Roman; piety in the Hebrew; letters in the Old English; Commerce in the late English; Empire in Austria; Erudition in Germany; ⟨Mechanics⟩ ↑free institutions↓ in America. But in turn, the whole man is ⟨sl⟩ brought to the light. It is like the revolution of the globe in the ecliptic: each part is brought in turn under the more direct beams of the sun to be illuminated & warmed & to each a summer in turn arrives & the seeds of that soil have their time to be animated & ripened into flowers & fruits.[n] [798]

↑Nature tells every thing Once[.]
Magnitude & duration are of no account.↓ [799]
⟨M⟩W. Colburn [800] told me he did not understand history. The Historian should be a religious man & have knowledge of the real & not alone of the Apparent in man's nature. All histories are memoirs pour servir. History must be rewritten. The fact is the phenomenon in Nature[;] the principle is the fact in Spirit & transcends all limits of space & time. All history is in the mind as thought long before it is executed[.]

[323] [blank]

[797] Beginning on p. [318] with "Come let us", this passage, struck through in both pencil and ink with vertical and diagonal use marks, is used in The Philosophy of History: "Introductory," *Lectures*, II, 11, 16, and in part in "History," *W*, II, 5.

[798] This paragraph, struck through in pencil with a diagonal use mark, is used in The Philosophy of History: "Introductory," *Lectures*, II, 13–14.

[799] A further variation on a theme from Goethe, as on pp. [167] and [318] above; see also p. [199] above: "duration & magnitude are of no account to the soul."

[800] Possibly Warren Colburn (1793–1833), teacher and author of textbooks in mathematics and reading.

[324]   Spiritual laws.

In our club we proposed that the rule of admission should be this

Whoever by his admission excludes any topics from our debate shall be excluded[.] [801]

The Wise man is everywhere at home[.] [802]

Utterance is place enough.[803]

[325] [blank]

[326] 29 November. There is no more chance goes to making towns than to making quadrants. Knowledge of business & the world tends to acquaint a man with values. Every minute of the day of a good workman is worth something in dollars & cents. The novice thinks this & that labor is of quite inappreciable value[,] it is so little like a bushel of corn or so short in time in the doing. So ought men to feel about character & history. The ⟨least⟩ most fugitive deed or word, the mere air of doing a thing, the intimated purpose, expresses character & the remote results of character are civil history & events that shake or settle the world. ↑If you act, you show character: if you sit still, you show it; if you sleep↓[804]

But in analysing history do not be too profound, for often the causes are quite superficial. In the present state of Spain, in the old state of France, & in general in the reigns of Terror, every where, there is no Idea, no Principle. It is all scrambling for bread & ⟨m⟩Money. It is the absence of all profound views; of all principle. It is the triumph of the senses, a total skepticism. They are all down on the floor s⟨ee⟩triving each to pick the pocket or cut the throat that

---

[801] This sentence is struck through in ink by nine short diagonal use marks; the word "printed" is added in ink below.

[802] Cf. *JMN*, IV, 17 ("A good man is ever at home . . . ."); "Self-Reliance," *W*, II, 81.

[803] A repetition; see pp. [49], [157] above.

[804] "The ⟨least⟩ . . . you sleep", struck through in pencil with two diagonal use marks, is completed and used in "Manners," *Lectures*, II, 129–130, and "Spiritual Laws," *W*, II, 156.

he may pick the pocket of the other, & the farthest view the miscreants have is the next tavern or brothel where their plunder may glut them. If presently one among the mob possesses ulterior aims, & these inspire him with skill, he masters all these brutes as oxen & ⟨hors⟩ dogs are mastered by a man & turns them to work for him & his thought.

[327] Nov. 30.

> Thus when the gods are pleased to plague mankind
> To our rash hands our ruin is assigned[.]

Moore's life of Sheridan [805] is a flagrant ⟨instance⟩ example of a book, which damns itself. He writes with the manifest design of securing our sympathies for Sheridan, our tears for his misfortunes & poverty, our admiration for his genius, & our indignation against the king & grandees who befriended that butterfly in his prosperity & forsook him in his jail. He details the life of a mean fraudulent vain quarrelsome play-actor, whose wit lay in cheating tradesmen, whose genius was used in studying jokes & bonmots at home for a dinner or a club, who laid traps for the admiration of coxcombs, who never did anything good & never said anything wise. He came as he deserved to a bad end.

The contrast between him & Burke is very instructive & redounds to the praise of one & the infamy of the other.[806]

Moore involves himself in the ruin & confusion of his culprit.

I heard of a dishclout gentleman yesterday of the Sheridan stamp who thus against his will unmasks himself & being a puppy cannot restrain his paw from doing the deeds of a puppy, & who affecting to keep the company of men & above all others wishing to be esteemed a man writes as on his own forehead every day, 'I am a whelp.'

[328] 2 December, 1836. The present state of the colony at Liberia is a memorable fact. It is found that the black merchants are so ⟨gratified⟩ fond of their lucrative occupations that it is with ⟨great⟩

---

[805] Thomas Moore, *Memoirs of the Life of Richard Brinsley Sheridan* (London, 1825).

[806] This and the preceding paragraph, struck through in pencil with a vertical use mark, are used in "Being and Seeming," *Lectures*, II, 301.

difficulty that any of them can be prevailed upon to take office in the colony. They dislike the trouble of it. Civilized arts are found to be as attractive to the wild negro, as they are disagreeable to the wild Indian.

[December] 3. I have been making war against the superlative degree in the rhetoric of my fair visiter.[807] She has no positive degree in her description of characters & scenes. You would think she had dwelt in a museum where all things were extremes & extraordinary. Her good people are very good, her naughty so naughty that they cannot be eaten. But beside the superlative of her mind she has a superlative of grammar which is suicidal & defeats its end. Her minds are "most perfect" "most exquisite" & "most masculine." I tell her the positive degree is the sinew of speech, the superlative is the fat. "Surely all that is simple is sufficient for all that is good" said Mme. de Stael. And when at a trattoria at Florence I asked the waiter if the cream was good,[n] the man replied 'yes, sir, stupendous': *Si, signore, stupendo.*[808]

[329] 6 December. Look then at history as the illustration by facts of all the spiritual elements. Stand before each of its tablets with the faith, Here is one of my coverings: Under this heavy & odious mask did my Proteus nature hide itself, but look there & see the effort it made to be a god again. See how never is it quite poor. See the divine spirit shaping itself a tabernacle in the worst depravations & mitigating where it cannot heal disease.

It occurs this evening from the Great Spirit (who always offers us truth but does never volunteer to write lectures) that ⟨th⟩ we must not complain of the meagre historians who wrote what they should have omitted & omitted what they should have written. For they & their works are also part of history: these surely manifest the tendency[,] the genius of the time; what ideas usurped the intellect & to what others they were blindfolded. Always history must be written by men & when will men be unbiassed? The explanation of it must come

---

[807] Possibly Elizabeth Palmer Peabody, to whom, on November 15, Emerson had transmitted his wife's invitation for a visit (*L*, II, 46).

[808] Staël, *Germany*, 1814, II, 253; see *JMN*, III, 296. For the Italian incident, see *JMN*, IV, 176.

from the advancing mind of each student, each man. He must sit upon the case & judge it for himself. His own experience is piercing antiquity & commenting on Roman politics & the feudal ⟨system⟩ tenures[.]

But the important suggestion is this. You say the human mind wrote on the world history, that is, did it; and now the same mind must explain it. And because every man is potentially Universal & whenever he is doing right is becoming Universal therefore must every one out of principles [809]

(turn to p. 331)

[330] Presented ⟨c⟩ one copy of *"Nature,"* to [810]

			G[eorge] P Bradford
7 copies			F[rederic] H Hedge
10		four copies to A[bel].	
		Adams	S[usan]. H[aven]. Emerson
5	1	B[enjamin].	Mrs [Josiah] Bartlett
10		B[ussey]. Thatcher	
4		Miss M[ary	Dr [Ezra] Ripley
		Howland]. Russell	
		S[ophia] A.	Mr Sam[ue]l Ripley
		Peabody	

[809] "Look then at history . . . principles", struck through in pencil with a vertical use mark, is used in part in The Philosophy of History: "Introductory," *Lectures,* II, 15–16, 19, 14; "Stand before each . . . hide itself" is also used in "History," *W,* II, 5.

[810] The entries which follow were presumably made about the time *Nature* was published (it had been advertised for sale on September 9, 1836). Although most of the names are written in ink, "Send it . . . H. Miles" in the left column and "Mrs S B Jackson . . . Am Monthly Mag" in the right column are in pencil. In addition to those persons previously identified or easily recognizable, Thatcher was a Boston lawyer and author; Mary Howland Russell a Plymouth friend of Lidian Emerson; Sophia Peabody (the future Mrs. Nathaniel Hawthorne) a sister of Elizabeth; Mrs. Morrell a friend of the Peabodys (*L,* I, 321); Mrs. Robbins (who died in November, 1836) a family friend (*L,* II, 48); Haskins probably Emerson's cousin Thomas Waldo (cf. *L,* VI, 340); Miles an American merchant Emerson had met in Florence; Susan Emerson the wife of his brother William; Samuel Ripley his half uncle; Miss Haskins his aunt; Dr. Jarvis a Concord physician; Russell a Plymouth manufacturer; T. Jackson a correspondent; Bokum an instructor at Harvard; Mrs. Brown Lidian Emerson's sister; Mrs. Joy a family friend in Waltham; Dr. Bradford a mentor since Emerson's Latin School days; and Mrs. Haskins the wife of Emerson's maternal uncle.

2 copies to W[illiam].
    Emerson
1 Mrs Morrell
1 Mrs [Richard] Robbins.
1 E[dmund]. Hosmer
1 T[homas]. W. Haskins

Send it to
  M[ary] M[oody]
      Emerson
  T[homas]. Carlyle
  N.L.F[rothingham].
  A[bel]. Adams
  A. B. Alcott.
  O[restes]. Brownson
  H[oratio]. Greenough

  W[alter]. S[avage]
      Landor
  H[enry]. Miles
  S.

Mr [Convers] Francis
Mr [Warren] Burton
Miss E[lizabeth]. Haskins
Miss E[lizabeth]. Hoar
Miss [Elizabeth] Peabody
Dr E[dward]. Jarvis.
A[ndrew]. Russell
Mr T. Jackson Jr
Miss [Margaret] Fuller

H[ermann]. Bokum
A B Alcott
O. A. Brownson
C[harles]. Sprague
M[ary] M[oody] Emerson
Mrs S[usan] B[ridge]
    Jackson
Mrs L[ucy] C Brown

Mrs H[annah]. Joy
Mr G[eorge] B[arrell]
    Emerson
[New York] Knickerbocker
Dr [John Gorham] Palfrey
Dr [James] Walker
S[idney] Willard
[Boston] Courier
Am[erican] Monthly
    Mag[azine]
N. L. Frothingham
Dr G[amaliel]. Bradford
⟨Mr B B Thatcher⟩
Mrs T[homas] Haskins
T. Carlyle
M.M E.

[331] in his constitution to interpret the Persian invasion, the institution of the Macedonian phalanx, & the Eleusinian mysteries. Very well; Granted. But I add, if there is Unity in the human mind which originated all this wild variety of actions then wild as they seem they must all proceed after a regular & graduated plan. Which will only disclose itself to our future thought[.]

The great fault of History is that it does not portray Man for me. It presents me with an Alaric or a Bourbon[,] with fighters or law makers[,] but it does ↑not↓ satisfy this great ideal we contain or which contains us. But now when so many toiling ages have turned to the sun all sides of man shall we not have pictures that are panoramic[,] shall not the great & noble laws of the human being meet us in representations of him? But when I look for the soul, shall I find a Jackson Caucus? It seems to me that always he is described from a point too low[;] his ⟨all⟩ essential characteristics are not recognized, [—] this stupendous fact of the identity[,] radical identity of all men[;] the one mind which makes each the measure of all, which makes each intelligible to all, [—] & him most so who has striven to cleanse out of his thought every personal parental patrial tinge, & utter the bare thought.

Then that other fitness & /co⟨n⟩nature/co-nature/ with all beings:
& so I hope his relation to all things [—] to science, to Art, to Men, to young & old, to books & churches [—] will be made to appear[.] [811]

[332][812] Dec. 10.[813] Pleasant walk yesterday, the most pleasant of days. At Walden Pond, I found a new musical instrument which I call the ice-harp. A thin coat of ice covered a part of the pond ↑but↓ melted around the edge of the shore. I threw a stone upon the ice

---

[811] The entire entry on p. [331] is struck through in pencil with diagonal use marks. "The great fault . . . to appear" is used in The Philosophy of History: "Introductory," *Lectures*, II, 20.

[812] On this page, reproduced in Plate II, begins a celebrated passage on the nature of evil, used first in Emerson's lecture "Ethics" and later in his Divinity School Address.

[813] See the entries on pp. [232] and [233] above concerning Rhetoric and Composition, each bearing the inserted date "Dec. 10".

which rebounded with a shrill sound, & falling again & again, repeated the note with pleasing modulation. ↑I thought at first it was the 'peep' 'peep' of a bird I had scared.↓ I was so taken with the music that I threw down my stick & spent twenty minutes in throwing stones single or in handfuls on this crystal drum.

At night, with other friends came Shackford [814] with a good heart & inquisitive mind. He broached the question, out of Brownson's book,[815] of the positiveness or entity of moral evil; which I gladly & strenuously denied, — as a corollary to my /last/preceding/ night's discourse on the Unity of Mind.[816] 'There is One mind in many individuals.' I maintained that evil is merely privative not absolute. It is like cold the privation of heat. All evil is death. Benevolence is absolute & real. So much benevolence & justice as a man hath, so much life hath he. For all things proceed out of this same spirit whose attributes are ⟨benevolence⟩ love, justice, & so on & all things conspire with them. Whilst a man seeks these ends he is strong by the whole strength of the Universe. In so far as he roves from these ends, he bereaves himself of power, of auxiliaries; his being shrinks out of all remote channels & ↑the↓ disuniversalises & ⟨in⟩he individualizes himself & becomes all the time less & less — a mote, a point. Until absolute badness [333] is absolute privation. It is ⟨nothing⟩ annihilation. ↑Pure badness therefore could not exist.↓ Do you not see that a man is a bundle of relations, that his entire strength consists not in his properties but in his innumerable relations? If you ⟨de⟩ embrace the cause of right, of your country, of mankind, all things work with & for you, the sun & moon, stocks & stones. The virtuous man & the seeker of truth finds brotherhood & countenance in so far forth, in the stars, the trees, & the waters. All Nature cries to him All Hail! The bad man finds opposition, aversation, death in them all.

All mankind oppose him. No whisper from secret beauty or grandeur cheers him. The world is silent[;] the heaven frowns. What

---

[814] Charles Chauncy Shackford, Harvard '35, who taught at the Concord Academy (*J*, IV, 166, n. 1).

[815] Orestes A. Brownson, *New Views of Christianity, Society, and the Church* (Boston, 1836).

[816] On December 8 Emerson had given in Boston the introductory lecture of his series, "The Philosophy of History."

is that star ↑to him↓ which prompted a heroic sentiment of love in the hero? A white point. And being not in the current of things[,] an outlaw, a stoppage, — the wheels of God must grind him to powder in their very mission of charity.[817]

We talked further of Christianity. I think that the whole modus loquendi [818] about believing Xy is vicious. It has no pertinence to the state of the case. It grows out of the Calvinistic nonsense of a Gospel-Scheme[,] a dogmatic Architecture which one is to admit came from the God of Nature. Or it grows out of the figment that to believe a given miracle is a spiritual merit. Believe Xy. What else can you do? It is not matter of doubt. What is good about it is self affirming. When Jesus says Kingdom of God comes without observation; comes as a little child; is within you; &c [819] these are not propositions[n] [334] upon which you can exercise any election but are philosophical ⟨truths⟩ verities quite independent of any asservation or testimony or abnegation.

Never a magnanimity fell to the ground. Always the heart of man greets it & accepts it unexpectedly.[820]

A thought in the woods was that I cannot marshal & insert in my compositions my genuine thoughts which are in themselves vital & life communicating. The reason is you do not yet take sufficiently noble & capacious views of man & nature whereinto your honest observation would certainly fall as physical phenomena under chemical or physiological laws.

[817] "I maintained that . . . of charity.", struck through in pencil with a diagonal use mark, is used in "Ethics," *Lectures*, II, 155; "I maintained that . . . absolute privation." is used in the Divinity School Address, *W*, I, 124; "Do you not . . . innumerable relations?" is used in Philosophy of History: "Introductory," *Lectures*, II, 17, and "History," *W*, II, 36.

[818] Manner of speaking (Ed.).

[819] Cf. Luke 17:20 (see pp. [212], [316] above); Mark 10:15 and Luke 18:17 (p. [316]); Luke 17:21 (pp. [185], [220]).

[820] This paragraph, struck through in both pencil and ink with vertical use marks, is used in "Religion," *Lectures*, II, 95, and "Spiritual Laws," *W*, II, 158–159; cf. "The Heart," *Lectures*, II, 294.

One mind.

Once more ⟨of⟩. Add to what was said on last page. There is One Mind, & therefore the best minds who love truth for its own sake, think much less of property in truth. Thankfully they accept it everywhere & do not carefully label & ticket it with any man's name for it is theirs long beforehand. It is theirs from eternity.[821]

[335]–[337][822] [Index material omitted]
[338] [blank]
[339] [Index material omitted]
[340][823] [blank]
[341][824]

[821] "Once more . . . eternity." is struck through in ink with a vertical use mark.

[822] Pp. [337]–[338] and [339]–[340] have been mounted on new leaves for binding.

[823] The word "last" is written diagonally in pencil in the upper left corner — probably not by Emerson.

[824] Centered on the page, in pencil, is "13 July Monday" followed in column by a list of the ten succeeding days ("Tuesday . . . Thursday") — evidently written as a table to indicate correspondence of dates with days. The writing is probably not Emerson's.

RO *Mind*

1 8 3 5

In the journal which the editors have designated RO Mind, Emerson drafted a fragmentary discussion of "the First Philosophy, . . . the original laws of the mind"; his opening paragraphs incorporate material already written in Journal B under dates of June 4 and 10, 1835, and subsequent passages draw upon still earlier journal entries ranging in date from August of 1832 to 1834 and the early months of 1835. The discussion follows Emerson's signature and his date of "June, 1835.", occurring on p. [iii] of a hard-covered copybook written in from both ends to make two sequences, of which this is the earlier. The later sequence (to be published in a subsequent volume) is inscribed in the copybook as reversed, following Emerson's signature and his designations "RO" and "1855–6" on p. [i] of that same sequence. Notations apparently written by Edward Emerson as an addition to index material of that sequence include the words "Other end of book is 1835" (p. [i]) and "RO (Reversed) 1835 / 'First Philosophy' 2–16 / Concord Monument Hymn" [not now in the copybook] (p. [ii]); his published reference to the earlier fragment as "probably written in 1833" (*J*, III, 235) is evidently in error.

The RO copybook originally consisted of 86 leaves measuring 11.5 x 18.5 cm; 18 of the leaves were later cut out, apparently with scissors. The body of the earlier sequence, RO Mind, is inscribed on the first 16 of 30 numbered recto leaves; of the 30, those numbered 10 and 16–30 also bear writing from the separately-paged RO sequence of 1855–1856 (which, with reference to the 1835 sequence, reads upside down and back to front). Pp. [ii]–[vi] of RO Mind also carry writing from the later sequence.

[front cover] [blank]

[front cover verso] [blank]

[i]–[ii] [blank in 1835 sequence]

[iii]   R. W. Emerson.
                                              June, 1835.

[iv]–[vi] [blank in 1835 sequence]

[1] ⟨I shall endeavor to announce some of the laws of⟩ ↑By↓ the
First Philosophy, ⟨or⟩ ↑is meant↓ the original laws of the mind.[1]
⟨These laws are never broken.⟩ ↑It is the Science of what *is*, in distinction from what *appears*.↓ It is one mark of them that their enunciation
awakens the feeling of the Moral sublime, and *great men* are they
who believe in them. They resemble great circles in astronomy, each
of which, in what direction soever it be drawn, contains the whole
sphere. So each of these ⟨seems to⟩ impl⟨y⟩↑ies↓[2] all truth.

These laws are Ideas of the Reason, and so are obeyed easier than
expressed. They astonish the Understanding and seem to it gleams
of a world in which we do not live.

[2][3]   ↑Of the Nature of the Mind.↓

As our Earth & its system are found to lie in the deep thicket
of spheres that compose the Milky Way, so the mind finds its place
to be in the region of grandest Nature, ↑namely,↓ in union with the
Supreme Being. Our compound nature differences us from God, but
our Reason is not to be distinguished from the divine Essence. We

[1] The cancellations and insertions in this sentence are in pencil; a superfluous
"By" is also written in pencil above "shall endeavor". Compare Journal B, p. [49]
above: "The world I describe is that, where ⟨the Mind makes its own laws⟩ only the
laws of mind are known" (June 4, 1835), and p. [51] above (June 10, 1835),
which anticipates the remainder of this and the following paragraph.

[2] The cancellation and insertion are in pencil.

[3] For the sequence of 1835 Emerson numbered and used only the recto leaves.
The heading "Of the . . . Mind." is written in pencil.

have yet devised no words to designate the attributes of God which can adequately stand for the Universality & perfection of our own intuitions. To call the Reason 'ours' or 'human', seems an impertinence, so absolute & unconfined it is. The best we can say of God, we mean of the mind as it is known to us.

[3] Thus when you say

> — "the gods approve
> The depth but not the tumult of the soul."
> [Wordsworth, "Laodamia," ll. 74–75]

the sublime in the sentiment is, that, 'to the soul itself, depth not tumult is desireable.' When you say, 'Jupiter prefers integrity to charity,' your finest meaning is 'The soul prefers,' &c.[4] When Jesus saith, 'Who giveth one of these little ones a cup of cold water, shall not lose his reward',[5] — is not the best meaning, *the love at which the giver has arrived*? "Every plant that my Heavenly Father hath not planted shall be rooted up;"[6] equivalent to Every thing is transitory but what hath its life from the interior of the soul. And so on, throughout the New Testament, there is not a [4] volition attributed to ↑God↓ considered as an external cause, but gains in truth & dignity by being referred to the Soul.[7]

⟨That I may not seem to confound what I adore with anything unworthy let me further define & describe⟩[8]

Man is conscious of a twofold nature which manifests itself in perpetual self-contradiction. Our English philosophers to denote this duality, distinguish the Reason and the Understanding.[9] Reason is the superior principle. Its attributes are Eternity & Intuition. We

[4] See *JMN*, IV, 39, n. 98.

[5] Cf. Matt. 10:42; Mark 9:41.

[6] Cf. Matt. 15:13.

[7] This entire paragraph is copied from an entry in Journal Q, August 19, 1832, *JMN*, IV, 39.

[8] This sentence is canceled in pencil and also struck through in pencil with three diagonal lines — possibly use marks.

[9] Cf. Emerson's letter to William Emerson, May 31, 1834, on "the distinction of Milton Coleridge & the Germans between Reason & Understanding" — a passage deriving from Coleridge, *Aids to Reflection*, ed. James Marsh, 1829, pp. xxix and 136 ff (*L*, I, 412).

belong to it, not it to us.[10] Human individuality is an upstart just now added to this Eternal Beatitude.[11]

[5] Time & Space are below its sphere. It considers things according to more intimate properties. It beholds their essence wherein is seen what they can produce. It is in all men, even in the worst, & constitutes them men. In bad men it is dormant; in the good, efficient. But it is perfect and identical in all, underneath the peculiarities, the vices, & the errors of the individual.[12] A man feels that his fortune, friendships, opinions, yea, all the parts of his individual existence, are merely superficial to the principle of Right. Compared with the selfexistence of the laws of Truth & Right whereof he is conscious, his personality [6] is a parasitic deciduous atom.[13] Hence the doctrine of Cosmism, that the Soul which was, shall be, but that our private life which was created, may be dissipated.

The authority of Reason cannot be separated from its vision. They are not two acts, but one. The sight commands, & the command sees.

The Understanding is the executive faculty, ↑the hand of the mind↓.[14] It mediates between the soul & inert matter. It works in time & space, & therefore successively. It divides, compares, reasons, invents. It lives from the Reason, yet disobeys it. It commands the material world, yet often for the pleasure of the sense.

[7] The Ideas of the Reason assume a new appearance as they descend into the Understanding. Invested with space & time they walk in masquerade. It incarnates the Ideas of Reason. Thus the gods of the ancient Greeks are all Ideas (as Cupid, Apollo, the Muse, &c or Love, Poesy, Wisdom, &c) but make an awkward appearance joined with the appetites of beasts. Reason, seeing in objects their

[10] Cf. *Nature*, *W*, I, 27: reason "is not mine, or thine, or his, but we are its . . . ."

[11] In "On Relation of Man to the Globe," *Lectures*, I, 29, Emerson had described Man as being "no upstart in the creation, but . . . prophesied in nature for a thousand thousand ages before he appeared . . . ."

[12] "Our English philosophers . . . individual." is used in "Religion," *Lectures*, II, 83–84.

[13] Written in pencil on the facing page opposite "is . . . atom." is the following: "In looking at a sunset we seem to lose our identity".

[14] The phrase "the hand of the mind" recurs in Journal B, p. [151] (the entry for March 9, 1836), and subsequently in *Nature*, *W*, I, 37.

remote effects, affirms the effect as the permanent character. The Understanding listening to Reason, on one side, which saith *It is*, & to the senses, on the other side, which say *It is not*, takes middle ground & declares, *It will be*. Heaven is the projection [8] of the Ideas of Reason on the plane of the Understanding.[15] The mind reveals that Virtue is happiness; that good spirits associate; that the only Rank is ⟨degrees of wisdom & goodness⟩ ↑Character↓; that Virtue is the key to the secrets of the world. The Understanding accepts the oracle, but, with its short sight not apprehending the truth, declares that in Futurity it is so, & adds all manner of fables of its own.

Jesus Christ was a minister of the pure Reason. The beatitudes of the Sermon on th⟨is⟩↑e↓ mount are all utterances of the Mind contemning the phenomenal world. "Blessed are the righteous poor; for theirs is the kingdom of heaven." The Understanding contradicts both propositions, yet both are true. "Blessed are the [9] pure in heart; for they shall see God." "Blessed are ye when men shall revile you, & persecute you, & say all manner of evil against you, falsely, in the cause of truth. Rejoice, & be exceeding glad, for great is your reward in heaven."[16] The Understanding can make nothing of it. 'Tis all nonsense. The Reason affirms its absolute verity.[17]

Various terms are employed to indicate the counteraction of the Reason & the Understanding, with more or less precision according to the cultivation of the speaker. A clear perception of it, is the key to all theology, and a theory of human life. St Paul marks the distinction by the terms 'Natural Man' & 'Spiritual Man.'[18]

[10] When Novalis says "It is the instinct of the Understanding to contradict the Reason,"[19] he only translates into a scientific formula the sentence of Paul, "The carnal mind is enmity against God."[20]

---

[15] Cf. Journal B, p. [49], the entry for June 4, 1835: "Heaven is the name we give to the True State, the World of Reason not of the Understanding, of the Real, not the Apparent. It exists always . . . ."

[16] Cf. Matt. 5:3, 8, 11–12.

[17] This paragraph is used in "Religion," *Lectures*, II, 90.

[18] Cf. I Cor. 2:14–15, 15:46.

[19] Concerning Emerson's earlier allusions to this same remark, see Journal B, p. [31] and n. 91.

[20] Rom. 8:7.

[11]   ↑Inaction.↓21

The Mind is very wise could it be roused into action. But the life
of most men is aptly signified by the poet's personification 'Death in
life.' 22 We walk about in a sleep. A few moments in the year or in
our lifetime we truly live; we are at the top of our being; we are
pervaded, yea, dissolved by the Mind: but we fall back again presently. Those who are styled 'Practical men' are not awake, for they
do not exercise the reason; yet n their sleep is restless. The most active
lives have so much routine as to preclude progress almost equally
with the most inactive. We bow low to the noted merchants whose
influence is felt not only in their native cities, but in most parts of the
globe; but our respect does them & ourselves great injustice for their
trade is without system, [12] their affairs unfold themselves after no
law of the mind: but are bubble built on bubble without end; a work
of arithmetic not of commerce, much less, of humanity. They add
voyage to voyage, & buy stocks — that they may buy stocks, and no
ulterior purpose is thought of. When you see their dexterity in particulars, you cannot overestimate the resources of good sense, and
when you find how empty they are of all remote aims, you cannot
underestimate their philosophy.
↑[See "Senses & Soul" Dial. vol II↓23

The man of letters puts the same cheat upon us, bestirring himself immensely to keep the secret of his littleness. He spins his most
seeming surface directly before the eye, to conceal the universe of his
[13] ignorance. To what end his languages, his correspondence, his
academic discourses, his printed volumes? Newton said, that, if this
porous world were made solid, it would lie in a nutshell. And if the
amount that Voltaire or Swift or Goethe have added to known truth,
be sharply stated, less than three hundred volumes would hold it.

21 "Inaction." is written in pencil.
22 Coleridge, "Epitaph," l. 6 — an echo of Shakespeare, "The Rape of Lucrece,"
ll. 405–406.
23 "We bow low . . . philosophy." is copied from Journal B, p. [23], entry for
March 23, 1835. "The most active . . . philosophy." is used in "The Senses and
the Soul," *The Dial*, II (Jan. 1842), 378–379. Emerson apparently drew this essay
from part of his concluding lecture of the series on Human Culture (*Lectures*, II,
357); see also "General Views," *Lectures*, II, 362–363 (a reprint of the *Dial* essay).

All our writings are variations of one air. Books, for the most part, are such expedients as his who makes an errand for the sake of exercise. And for the sincere great men, the wisest passages they have writ, the infinite conclusions to which they owe their fame, are only confessions. Throughout their works the good ear hears an undersong of confession & amazement, the apothegm of Socrates, the recantation of Man.[24]

[14] Statesmen are solitary. At no time do they form a class. Governments, for the most part, are carried on by political merchants, quite without principle, & according to the maxims of trade & huckster. What was said of merchants is therefore true of public officers.[25]

Such is the inaction of men. We have an obscure consciousness of our attributes. We stand on the edge of all that is great yet are restrained in inactivity & unacquaintance with our powers like neuters of the hive every one of which is capable of transformation into the Queen bee.[26] We are always on the brink of an ocean into which we do not yet swim. We talk of the powers of apprehending & using truth as our powers but they are prerogatives we are hindered from using. We are always in the precincts, never admitted. There is much preparation — great ado of [15] machinery, plans of life, travelling, studies, profession, solitude, often with little fruit. But suddenly in any place, in the street, in the chamber, will the heaven open, and the regions of wisdom be uncovered, as if to show how thin the veil, how null the circumstances.[27] As quickly, a Lethean stream washes through us and bereaves us of ourselves. After exercising the powers of reflexion for fugitive moments, we move about without them, quite under their sphere, quite unclothed.

What a benefit if a rule could be given whereby the mind ⟨could at any moment⟩ dreaming amidst the gross fogs of matter, could [16] at any moment east itself and find the Sun. But the common life is an

---

[24] "the wisest passages . . . Man." is copied from Journal A, June 20, 1834, *JMN*, IV, 298.

[25] This paragraph is used in "The Senses and the Soul," *The Dial*, II (Jan. 1842), 379; see "General Views," *Lectures*, II, 363.

[26] This sentence is adapted from Journal A, August 14, 1834, *JMN*, IV, 310.

[27] "We are always . . . circumstances." is adapted from Journal A, April 12, 1834, *JMN*, IV, 274.

endless succession of phantasms. And long after we have deemed ourselves recovered & sound, light breaks in upon us & we find we have
yet had no sane hour. Another morn rises on mid-noon.[28]

[17]–[30][29]

[28] This paragraph, with its phrases drawn from Coleridge and Milton, revises
and amplifies a passage in Journal B, p. [39], entry for May 13, 1835.

[29] These pages, so numbered in the 1835 sequence, carry writing only from the
sequence of 1855–1856, in which they are numbered [78]–[104].

C

1 8 3 7 – 1 8 3 8

Journal C, a regular journal, opens with the date "1 January, 1837."
Its dated entries run from January 3 of that year through June 7, 1838,
overlapping by one day the initial entry of Journal D.

Journal C is written in a hard-covered copybook generally similar to that used
for Journal B in 1835–1836 except that the dimensions and binding differ slightly,
the edges of the leaves are stained in green, and the endpapers are plain blue rather
than marbled brown. The leaves, faintly ruled, measure approximately 20.5 x 25
cm. Including flyleaves, there are 364 pages in all; following 4 unnumbered pages
(designated i through iv) is sequential pagination in ink, 1–355, extending from
the first dated entry through the first 4 of 6 pages of index material at the end of
the journal. Exclusive of 2 marbled flyleaf pages (i, 360), there are 10 blank pages:
ii, 20–21, 46, 49, 95, 133, 252, 350–351.

Laid into Journal C is a later newspaper clipping of seven paragraphs headed
"A Characteristic of Napoleon." The material is credited to "one of Fichte's lectures,
delivered in Berlin in the year 1813." Items on the verso carry datelines of "London, August 3, 1867" and St. Louis, August 19.

[front cover]

C
1837

[front cover verso] [blank]

[i]–[ii] [blank]

[iii]

C

R. W. Emerson.

Journal.

1837

277

Ille velut fidis arcana sodalibus olim
Credebat libris, neque si male cesserat, usquam
Decurrens alio, neque si bene. Quo fit ut omnis
Votiva pateat veluti descripta tabella
Vita.[1]

Horace —
Lib. 2 Sat[ire]. 1 [ll. 30–34] —

I write the laws,
Not plead a cause.   [By Emerson?]

[iv] [Index material omitted]

[1] Concord.

1 January, 1837. ↑3d Jan.↓ It occurred last night in groping after the elements of that pleasure we derive from literary compositions, that it is like the pleasure which the prince Le Boo received from seeing himself for the first time in a mirror,[2] — a mysterious & delightful surprise. A poem, a sentence ⟨which⟩ causes us to see ourselves. I be & I see my being, at the same time.

It is not some wild ornithorhynchus nondescript ⟨out of New Holland⟩ that attracts the most attention but it was the *Man* of the New World that concentrated the curiosity of the contemporaries of Columbus. After I got into bed, somewhat else rolled through my head & returned betwixt dreams, which I fear I have lost. It seems as if it were to this purport; that every particular composition takes its fit place in the intellectual sphere, the light & gay a light & fugitive place; the wise a permanent place; but only those ⟨po⟩ works are everlasting which have caught not the ephemeral & local but the

---

[1] "He in olden days would trust his secrets to his books, as if to faithful friends, never turning elsewhere for recourse, whether things went well with him or ill. So it comes that [his] whole life is open to view, as if printed on a votive tablet." The original and a verse translation occur in Montaigne, "Of Presumption," *Essays*, 1700, II, 488.

[2] George Keate, *The History of Prince Lee Boo, Son of Abba Thulle, King of the Pelew Islands* (London, 1823), p. 57. See "Literature," *Lectures*, II, 56.

universal symbols of thought & so written themselves in a language
that needs no translation into the sympathies & intellectual habits of
all men. Homer & Shakspear.

6 January. It occurred to me at midnight with more clearness
than I can now see it, that not in nature but in man was all the beauty
& worth he sees; that the world is very empty & is indebted to this
gilding & exalting soul for all its pride so that Wordsworth might
write Earth fills her lap with splendors not her own for his line,
"Earth fills her lap with pleasures of her own." The vale of Tempe,
Tivoli, & Rome are but earth & water, rocks & sky.[3]

[2] Jan. 7. Received day before yesterday a letter from Thomas
Carlyle dated 5 November; — as ever, — a cordial influence. Strong
he is, upright, noble, & sweet, & makes good how much of our human
nature. Quite in consonance with my delight in his eloquent letters
||⟨...⟩|| I read in Bacon this afternoon this sentence, (of letters)
"And such as are written from wise men are of all the words of man,
in my judgment, the best; for they are more natural than Orations &
⟨speeches⟩ public speeches, & more advised than conferences or present
speeches." Works [1824], Vol. 1. p. 89[4]

Let nothing be lost that is good. Is Chivalry graceful in your imagination? be courteous to every boy & girl in the village, & so keep
its soul alive. Is honor majestic? With the courtesy, be doggedly just,
& speak the truth, & you shall call out the angel everywhere who lurks
under ignorance & cunning. Discourtesy & selfishness are the shortest
sighted owls. Hold all conventions of society light in your reverence
for simple instinct, so shall you revive the age of the Greeks & of
Shakspear. Fear God, & where you go men shall feel as if they walked
in hallowed cathedrals. Make your perceptions accurate & the sound
of your voice or sight of your name shall be useful to men as Insti-

---

[3] This paragraph, struck through in ink with a vertical use mark, is used in
"Spiritual Laws," W, II, 147. The allusion is to Wordsworth, "Ode: Intimations of
Immortality," l. 77.
[4] Of the Advancement of Learning, Bk. II.

tutes & Scientific societies are suggesting the just use of the faculties to great ends. This is the way to be a Universal Man or take the ages up into an hour & one person.[5]

[3] Jan. 8. Can you not show the man of Genius that always genius is situated in the world as it is with him[?]

   Lidian Emerson
   Waldo Emerson
   R. Waldo Emerson

I had come no farther in my query than this when mine Asia[6] came in & wrote her name, her son's & her husband's, to warm my cold page.

Jan. 9. There are limitations set in the nature of man beyond which the folly or ambition of governors cannot go. It is true society always consists of a vast proportion of foolish, ignorant, & young persons capable of being deceived. The ⟨wa⟩ old & wary who have seen through the hypocrisy of courts & statesmen, die & leave no wisdom to their sons. They believe their own newspaper as their father did at their age.[7] Always too a fresh swarm is ⟨coming⟩ alighting in the places of power to suck suddenly all its sweets. And with such guides Rehoboam's young men would discard even the wise, & run riot[8] but that things refuse to be ill administered.[9] Nothing satisfies all men but justice, and especially when time & much debate have[n] accurately ascertained what justice is in respect to any measure. The interests of all classes are so intimately united that although the rivalry in which they are often set, may please one for a short time with the distress of another, yet very quickly they will make common cause against any great offence. The lie often told makes the liar not to be believed.

---

[5] This paragraph, struck through in pencil with a vertical use mark, is used in "The Individual," *Lectures*, II, 186.

[6] Emerson's first recorded use of this term for his wife. For comment on its connotations, see Frederic Ives Carpenter, *Emerson and Asia* (Cambridge, Mass., 1930), pp. 30 ff, and Rusk, *L*, II, 112, n. 28.

[7] "There are limitations . . . age.", struck through in ink with a vertical use mark, is used in "Politics," *W*, III, 204–205.

[8] Cf. I Kings 12:8.

[9] See n. 20 below.

Virtue is continually reproduced in the young & the selfish statesman has some.[10]

[4] Great men arise like Alfred, Washington, Lafayette, & virtue has resistless effect. Nothing is more apparent than that genuine virtue always tells for such. The majesty of these men impresses the people, & the government are forced to defer to it.[11] Corn will not grow unless it is planted & manured; but the farmer will not plant or hoe it unless the chance is a hundred to one that he will cut & harvest it.[12] The eclat of a good code, or a⟨s⟩ domestic improvement, or a commercial treaty, or a⟨n⟩ scientific survey, or expedition is desired, & each of these things stimulates the mind of the people, cultivates them, & so tends to acquaint them with their true interest. The expedition of Alexander, of Caesar, of Napoleon, not without good fruit.[13]

The interest[s] of persons & property are so difficult to separate, that it is very happy that the progress of society tends to reconcile & to identify them by destroying the class of paupers, of slaves, & making every man a proprietor. Then as every penny carries with it some knowledge he becomes fit to distribute it. Thus the Peace & Trade party grows up the lovers of useful knowledge.[14]
"Man has no predilection for absurdity." The law, the polity that endures a thousand years has some fitness to the human constitution. Every law that continues long alive, tallies to some thing in man.

[5] Jan. 14. Lidian's grandmother had a slave Phillis whom she freed. Phillis went to the little colony on the outside of Plymouth which they called New Guinea. Soon after, she visited her old mistress. "Well, Phillis, what did you have for dinner on Thanksgiving

---

[10] This paragraph, struck through in pencil with a diagonal use mark, is used in "Politics," *Lectures*, II, 75.

[11] "resistless effect . . . to it." is struck through in ink with a diagonal use mark.

[12] "Corn will not . . . harvest it.", struck through in ink with a curved diagonal use mark, is used in "Politics," *W*, III, 205.

[13] The entire paragraph, struck through in pencil with a diagonal use mark, is used in "Politics," *Lectures*, II, 75–76. "The eclat . . . fruit." is also struck through in ink with a curved diagonal use mark.

[14] This paragraph, struck through in pencil with a diagonal use mark, is used in "Politics," *Lectures*, II, 76.

Day?" "Fried 'taturs, Missy;" replied Phillis. "And what had you to fry the⟨m⟩ potatoes in?" said Mrs Cotton. "Fried in Water, Missy;" answered the girl. "Well Phillis," said Mrs Cotton, "how can you bear to live up there, so poor, when here you used to have every thing comfortable, & such good dinner at Thanksgiving?" — "Ah Missy, Freedom's sweet," returned Phillis.

———

A poor woman having covered her children in the winter nights with all the rags & bits of cloth ↑and carpet↓ she could find, was accustomed to ↑lay down↓ over all an old door which had come off its hinges. "Ah, dear mother," said her eldest daughter, "how I pity the poor children that haven't got any *door* to cover them." [14a]

———

[6] 16 Jan. How evanescent is the idea of Spirit, how incomprehensible! Strange obstinacy of the human affections to enshrine Wisdom & Virtue in a Person, & no less obstinancy in the Reason ↑not↓ to admit the picture. The mystery is to be explained only by ↑the↓ personability of virtue & wisdom in the seer himself.

But as far as History is concerned, can I not show that in regard to this element of civilization, man underlies the same necessity as in Science, Art, letters, politics? For, always as much Religion as there is, so much appears. All the devils respect virtue.[15] Always the high, heroic, self devoted sect, shall instruct & command mankind. Hypocrisy is a foolish suicide. All virtue consists in substituting Being for seeming, & therefore God ⟨properly⟩ ↑sublimely↓ saith, *I AM*.[16] Yes, Justice is; Love is; and that deep Cause of causes which they as it were outwardly represent; but is God a person? No. That is a contradiction: the *personality* of God. A person is finite personality, is finiteness.

The Universal mind is so far from being measured in any finite numbers, that its verdict would be vitiated ⟨immediately⟩ at once by any reference to numbers, however large. "The multitude is the worst argument," and, in fact, the only way of arriving at this Univer-

[14a] One of Emerson's favorite stories: see *JMN*, IV, 243.

[15] See Journal B, pp. [168], [240].

[16] "But as far . . . *I AM*.", struck through in pencil with a diagonal use mark, is used in "Religion," *Lectures*, II, 94–95, and "Spiritual Laws," *W*, II, 158, 160.

sal mind, is to quit the whole world, & take counsel of the bosom alone.[17]

[7] 21 January. Every change in the physical constitution has its ⟨sign⟩ external sign, although for the most part it is not heeded. Hemorrhage of the lungs or palsy does[n] not suddenly overtake a man, but after long warnings which he ha⟨s⟩d disregarded. Look at the clock: you have only noticed the striking of the hours, but it struck the seconds, & showed the seconds & minutes on the dial, which were making up the hour; but you had no ears & no eyes.[18]

I either read or inferred today in the Westminster Review that Shakspear was not a popular man in his day.[19] How true & wise. He sat alone & walked alone a visionary poet & came with his piece, modest but discerning, to the players, & was too glad to get it received, whilst he was too superior not to see its transcendant claims.

[January] 22. Being a lover of solitude I went ↑to live↓ in⟨to⟩ the country seventeen miles ⟨northwest of⟩ ↑from↓ Boston, ⟨to live⟩ & there the northwest wind with all his snows took me in ⟨his⟩ charge & defended me from all company in winter, & the hills & sand-banks that intervened between me & the city, kept guard in summer.

25 Jan. This evening the heavens afford us the most remarkable spectacle of Aurora Borealis. A deep red plume in the East & west streaming almost from the horizon to the zenith, forming at the zenith a sublime coronet; the stars peep delicately through the ruddy folds & the whole landscape ⟨cover⟩ below covered with snow is crimsoned. The light meantime equal nearly to that of full moon, although the moon was not risen.

[8] 27 Jan. "The best use of money is to pay debts with it."

[17] This paragraph, struck through in pencil with a diagonal use mark, is used in "Religion," *Lectures*, II, 86.
[18] This paragraph, struck through in pencil with a diagonal use mark, is used in "Prudence," *Lectures*, II, 322.
[19] *The London and Westminster Review*, XXVI (Oct. 1836), 30–57, had reviewed five recent publications concerning Shakespeare.

The only aristocracy in this country is the ⟨aristocracy of⟩ editors of newspapers.

As Goethe says that any particular bone that is in one animal may be found in every other, however abridged or obscure, so I am never quite acquainted with my neighbor until I have found somewhat in his nature & life to tally with every thing I know of myself.

The true explanation of "Res nolunt diu male administrari" [20] undoubtedly is that mischief is shortlived, & all things thwart & end it. Napoleon's empire built up amid universal alarm — in how short a space of time vanished out of history like breath into the air: but St Paul, the tent maker, — see what a tent he built.[21]

[January] 29. One has patience with every kind of living thing but not with the dead alive. ⟨I hate⟩ I, at least, hate to see persons of that lumpish class who are here they know not why, & ask not whereto, but live as the larva of the ant or the bee to be lugged into the sun & then lugged back into the cell & then fed. The end of nature for such, is that they should be fatted. If mankind should pass a vote on the subject, I think they would throw them in sacks into the sea.

God set man's eyes in his forehead not in his hindhead; & in like manner,

> "Man's heart the Almighty to the future set
> By secret but inviolable springs" [22]
> [Young, *Night Thoughts*, "Night VII," ll. 119–120, misquoted]

[9] Party. The "Globe" newspaper has its lie for each new emergency ⟨as⟩ to hoodwink its honest millions as we in Massachusetts put a headboard on a cow lest she break fences.

---

[20] Jonathan Swift, Letter XXXVII, to Lord Bolingbroke, April 5, 1729, in *The Poetical Works of Alexander Pope*, 9 vols. (London, 1760), IX, 130. Translated in Emerson's words above, p. [3], as "things refuse to be ill administered"; rendered in "Compensation," *W*, II, 100, as "Things refuse to be mismanaged long," and in "Politics," *W*, III, 205, as "things refuse to be trifled with."

[21] This paragraph is struck through in pencil with a wavy diagonal use mark. The second sentence is used in "Ethics," *Lectures*, II, 156.

[22] This paragraph is struck through in pencil with a vertical use mark; the first clause is used in "The American Scholar," *W*, I, 90.

3 Feb. Whilst Stetson whispered at the Ordination I could not help thinking that next to so notable a wit should always be posted a phlegmatic bolt upright man able to stand without movement of muscle whole broadsides of this Greek fire. And yet the person who has just received this discharge, if in a solemn company, has the air very much of a stout vessel which has just shipped a heavy sea & though it does not split it the poor bark is for the moment critically staggered.[23]

> Nunc non e manibus illis
> Nunc non e tumulo, fortunataque favilla
> Nascuntur violae? [24]   *Persius*. [Satire I, 38–40]

"The reward of a thing well done is to have done it." Seneca [25]

Charles in a conversation I have mentioned in my old Journal expressed much such an opinion as Montaigne who says of himself that "if there is any good in him, it came in by treachery." [26]
[Montaigne, *Essays*, 1700,] Vol. 2   p. 497 —

[10] Let a man behave in his own house as a guest.[27]

Feb. 6. There is one memory of waking, & another of sleep. Certainly in my dreams the same scenes or fancies are associated & a whole crew of boarders at some dream house of which gentlemen & ladies I can trace no shadow of remembrance in any waking experience of mine. ↑In sleep, I also travel certain roads in certain stage coaches, & walk alone in meadows whose archetype I wot not.↓ [28]

---

[23] This paragraph, struck through in pencil with a diagonal use mark, is used in "The Comic," *W*, VIII, 162.

[24] "Will not violets now spring up from those remains, from the tomb and its thrice-blessed ashes?" (The Loeb text reads "nascentur" where Emerson and Montaigne have "Nascuntur".)

[25] The extracts from Persius and Seneca are quoted by Montaigne, "Of Glory," *Essays*, 1700, II, 486, 488 respectively.

[26] Cf. Montaigne, "Of Presumption": "If there be any Glory . . . , 'tis superficially infus'd into me by the treachery of my Complexion, and has no Body that my Judgment can discern."

[27] This sentence, struck through in pencil with a vertical use mark, is used in "Sovereignty of Ethics," *W*, X, 194.

[28] This paragraph, struck through in pencil with a vertical use mark, is used in "Demonology," *W*, X, 5.

In these Lectures which from week to week I read, each on a topic which is a main interest of man, & may be made an object of exclusive interest I seem to vie with the brag of Puck "I can put a girdle round about the world in forty minutes." [29] I take fifty.

"⟨The⟩Than our laws of widowhood will well allow"

[11] A great law, "what we have within, that only can we see without." Only so much of Arabian history can I read, as I am Arabian within, though I should parse & spell Ockley & Abulfeda.[30]

Feb. 20. Undoubtedly it was designed that life, — or rather I would say, — life tends to be picturesque. I think *O'Connell's South sea Islands*[31] the best book we have published in this country this long while.

Warren st Chapel[32] is all a holy hurrah[.]

Old & New put their stamp to every thing in Nature. The snow-flake that is now falling is marked by both. ⟨The⟩ The present moment gives the motion & the color of the flake: Antiquity, its form & properties. All things wear a lustre which is the gift of the present & a tarnish of time.[33]

March 4. I have finished on Thursday evening last, my course of twelve Lectures ⟨at t⟩ on the Philosophy of History. I read the first on the 8 December, 1836 — The audience attending them, might average 350 persons. I acknowledge the Divine Providence which has given me perfect health & smoothed the way unto the end.

---

[29] Cf. *A Midsummer Night's Dream*, II, i, 175–176.

[30] Simon Ockley (1678–1720), English orientalist, author of *The History of the Saracens*, 3 vols., 1708–1757 (cf. *Lectures*, II, 329); abu-al-Fida (1273–1331), Arabian geographer and historian.

[31] Probably *A Residence of Eleven Years in New Holland and the Caroline Islands: Being the Adventures of James F. O'Connell* (Boston, 1836).

[32] Built in 1835 as a "Children's Church." The aim of its founder, Charles F. Barnard, was to bring art, science, and industrial work as well as religion to the sons and daughters of the poor.

[33] This paragraph, struck through in pencil with two diagonal use marks, is used in "The Present Age," *Lectures*, II, 158.

[12] March 14. Edward Taylor came last night & gave us in the old church a Lecture on Temperance. A wonderful man; I had almost said, a perfect orator. The utter want & loss of all method, the ridicule of all method, the bright chaos come again [34] of his bewildering oratory, certainly bereaves it of power but what splendor! what sweetness! what richness what depth! what cheer! How he conciliates[,] how he humanizes! how he exhilarates & ennobles! Beautiful philanthropist! godly poet! the Shakspeare of the sailor & the poor. God has found one harp of divine melody to ring & sigh sweet music amidst caves & cellars.

He spent the night with me. He says "he lives a monarch's life, he has none to control him, or to divide the power with him." His word is law for all his people & his coadjutors. He is a very charming object to me. I delight in his great personality, the way & sweep of the man which like a frigate's way takes up for the time the centre of the ocean, paves it with a white street, & all the lesser craft "do curtsey to him, do him reverence." [34a] Every body ⟨becom⟩ plays a second part in his presence, & takes a deferential & apologetic tone. In the church, likewise, every body, — the rich, the poor, the scoffer, the drunkard, the exquisite, & the populace, acknowledge the Man, & feel that to be right & lordly which he doth, — so that his prayer is a winged ship in which all are floated forward.[n] [13] The wonderful & laughing life of his illustration keeps us broad awake. A string of rockets all night. He described his bar-room gentry as "hanging like a half dead bird over a counter." He describes Helen Loring as out on her errands of charity, & "running through the rain like a beech-bird." He speaks of poor ministers coming out of divinity schools, &c. as "poor fellows hobbling out of Jerusalem." [35] "We'll give you hypocrites for honest men, two for one, & trade all night." "The world is just large enough for the people. There is no room for a partition wall."

March 1⟨6⟩↑8↓. A strong South wind today set all the hills &

---

[34] Cf. *Othello*, III, iii, 92; see *JMN*, III, 102.
[34a] Cf. *The Merchant of Venice*, I, i, 13.
[35] Under "illustration keeps . . . Jerusalem.' " are written in pencil the quotations concerning Captain Cook rewritten in ink on p. [15] below.

fields afloat under melting snow banks. Tempted out by the new brown of the hill-sides, I climbed for the first time since autumn the opposite hill to see if the snows were abated & my wood alleys open but there was too much winter left, & I retreated.

[March] 19. Today at Waltham I talked of the potential invention of all men. Caroline Sturgis[36] can sketch with invention; others can draw as well, but cannot design. I call it self-distrust, — a fear to launch away into the deep which they might freely & safely do. It is as if the dolphins should float on rafts or creep & squirm along the shore in fear to trust themselves to the element which is really native to them.[37]

I read not long ago in the newspapers that the School Committee in Boston had sustained the Master of one of the public schools in his forbiddal of the practice of the girls to come to school occasionally[n] [14] with their hair in papers.

[15] "I who had ambition not only to go farther than any one had been before, but as far as it was possible for man to go, was not sorry at meeting this interruption," says Capt. Cook when he came to impenetrable ice in lat. S. 71.10 long. W. 106.54.[38] In the Friendly islands when "the nobles no longer pilfered in person, depredations were continued by their slaves on whom a flogging appeared to make no more impression than it would have done on the mainmast." [Cf. *An Historical Account of the*] *Circumnavigation* p. 410

[March] 19. Yesterday I read many of C.C.E.'s letters to E.H. I find them noble but sad. Their effect is painful. I withdrew myself from the influence. So much contrition, so much questioning, so little hope, so much sorrow, harrowed me. I could not stay to see my noble brother tortured even by himself. No good or useful air goes out of

---

[36] A young Bostonian, known to the Emersons since before their marriage and later a frequent visitor in Concord.

[37] "others can draw . . . them.", struck through in pencil with a diagonal use mark, is used in "Being and Seeming," *Lectures*, II, 308.

[38] See *An Historical Account of the Circumnavigation of the Globe, and of the Progress of Discovery in the Pacific Ocean, from the Voyage of Magellan to the Death of Cook*, 2nd ed. (Edinburgh, 1837), p. 367.

such scriptures, but cramp & incapacity only. I shall never believe
that any book is so good to read as that which sets the reader into
a working mood, makes him feel his strength, & inspires hilarity.
Such are Plutarch, & Montaigne & Wordsworth.

But also Charles would say this, & his conversation was of this character; but when he shut his closet door, "a quality of darkness"
haunted him.[39]

[1⟨5⟩↑6↓][40] Salem March 22. Dr Jarvis said he had seen in a
New Orleans paper an advertisement of coffins in nests for sale,[n]
and told the story of F.'s going to Mrs G. & describing his visit at a
house in Concord, where the people were so poor, or so odd, that they
had no table, & held their tea cups in their laps. And he ⟨told ⟨th⟩of
the sailor who asked his mess mate "What do you suppose the land-
lubbers do with dead folks?" "Why I suppose they bring 'em down
to the dock & throw 'em over." "Oh no they boxes 'em up & directs
'em."⟩ [41]

Every man has hydrophobia the first time in summer he goes
into the salt water baths. Life. As you sit in the tavern & see the
stage passengers come in to warm them, a new generation each hour,
men seem to be on the confines of uncontrollable laughter all the time,
& always too on the edge of the sublime. We are up to anything
Ligariuslike,[42] [—] godlike, or devilish.

Our carpets & paper hangings & fluted & moulded wood work,
in every house show the existence of fine taste somewhere, which,
like the blue of the s⟨ky⟩un or the gaiety of the clouds blesses every
eye without being noticed by hardly one.

The popularity of Thom's statues of Old Mortality, & Tam
O'Shanter,[43] is a good problem. So the experiments on Living. The

[39] For the quoted phrase, cf. *Institutes of Hindu Law*, trans. Sir William Jones,
1825, as quoted in "Religion," *Lectures*, II, 88.

[40] The four paragraphs on this page are struck through in pencil with two intersecting diagonal lines, possibly use marks.

[41] This last anecdote is canceled with heavy ink lines.

[42] Cf. Emerson's letter to Margaret Fuller, July 18, 1837 (*L*, II, 88): Ligarius
"would fain be well if there were anything for a man to do." The allusion is to
Julius Caesar, II, i, 316–317, or to "The Life of Marcus Brutus," *Plutarch's Lives*,
1822, IV, 138.

[43] James Thom (1802–1850), self-taught Scottish sculptor noted for his figures
of Scott's "Old Mortality" and Burns's "Tam o'Shanter."

papers say that 10,000 copies of "Living without means" were sold in less than ten days — twelve editions in eleven days. I doubt they lie. And 20000 copies of The Three Experiments have been sold.[44]

[1⟨6⟩↑7↓] "Lively feeling of the circumstance, & faculty to express it, makes the poet." *Goethe*

"They say much of the study of the ancients, but what else does that signify, than, Direct your attention to the real world, & seek to express it, *since that did*[45] the ancients whilst they lived." *Goethe*[46]

The country people say of the bad roads today, that "the bottom is taken out." Wifey says, 'as proud as the child that has sewed her first stitch[.]'

March 29. Noble paper of Carlyle on Mirabeau.[47] This piece will establish his kingdom, I forebode, in the mind of his countrymen. How he gropes with giant fingers into the dark of man! into the obscure recesses of power in human will, and we are encouraged by his word to feel the might that is in a man. "Come the ruggedest hour that time & fate dare bring to frown upon the enraged Northumberland."[48] ⟨T⟩Indeed this piece is all thunder[,] ↑gigantic portrait painting↓.
The "Diamond Necklace"[49] too, I doubt not, is the sifted story, the veritable fact, as it fell out, yet so strangely told by a series of pictures, cloud upon cloud, that the eye of the exact men is speedily confused

[44] Hannah Farnham Sawyer Lee, *Three Experiments of Living: Living within the Means, Living up to the Means, Living beyond the Means* (Boston, 1837), ultimately achieved thirty American and ten English editions. Emerson's second reference may be to an anonymous work entitled *Three Experiments in Drinking, or Three Eras in the Life of an Inebriate*, also published in Boston in 1837.

[45] Underlined in pencil.

[46] Emerson translated the two comments by Goethe from Johann Peter Eckermann, *Gespräche mit Goethe in den letzen Jahren seines Lebens 1823–1832*, 2 vols. (Leipzig, 1837), I, 223, 240, respectively. He had borrowed Margaret Fuller's copy of this work (*L*, II, 64).

[47] "Memoirs of Mirabeau," *London and Westminster Review*, XXVI (Jan. 1837), 382–439.

[48] *II Henry IV*, I, i, 150–152, misquoted; see *JMN*, III, 252.

[49] Published in *Fraser's Magazine*, XV (Jan., Feb. 1837), 1–9, 172–189.

& annoyed. It seems to me, his genius is the redolence of London "the Great Metropolis." So vast, enormous, with endless details, & so related to all the world, is he. It would seem as if no baker's shop, no mutton stall, no Academy, no church, no placard, no coronation, but he saw & sympathized with all, & took all up into his omnivorous /fancy/memory/, & hence his panoramic style, & this encyclopediacal allusion to [18] all knowables.

Then he is a worshipper of strength, heedless much whether its present phase be divine or diabolic. Burns, Geo. Fox, Luther, and those unclean beasts Diderot, Danton, Mirabeau, whose sinews are their own & who trample on the tutoring & conventions of society he loves. For he believes that every noble nature was made by God, & contains — if savage ⟨stre⟩ passions, — also fit checks & grand impulses within it, hath its own resources, &, however erring, will return from far. ↑Then he writes English & crowds meaning into all the nooks & corners of his sentences. Once read he is but half read.↓ [50]

I rode well. My horse took hold of the road as if he loved it. I saw in Boston my fair young L. but so rashly grown that her sweet face was like a violet on the top of a pole.

A disaster at Lowell. The powder mill blew up & two men so shattered that their remains were gathered in a basket.

Carlyle again. I think he has seen as no other in our time how inexhaustible ⟨th⟩a mine ⟨was⟩ ↑is↓ the language of Conversation. He does not use the *written* dialect of the time in which scholars, pamphleteers, & the clergy write, nor the parliamentary dialect, in which the lawyer, the statesman, & the better newspapers write, but draws strength & motherwit out of a poetic use of the *spoken* vocabulary, so that his paragraphs are all a sort of splendid conversation.

[19]   The Antique

"The Lacedemonians entering into battle sacrificed to the Muses to the end that their actions might be well & worthily writ[.]" *Montaigne* [51]

[50] A line drawn from the end of this paragraph down the left margin past intervening entries directs attention to the discussion as resumed under the heading "*Carlyle again.*" below.
[51] Cf. "Of Glory," *Essays*, 1700, II, 487.

"The ancient Romans kept their youth always standing, & taught them nothing that they were to learn sitting." *Seneca* — apud Montaigne [52]

I learn from Montaigne, a master of antiquity, also, that when the ancient Greeks would accuse any one of extreme insufficiency, they would say, that he could neither read nor swim.

"Much is said of the study of the ancients. But what else does it signify than this: Direct your attention upon the real world, & seek to express it, since that did the ancients whilst they lived." *Goethe.*[53]

The Peloponnesian league ⟨enjoined⟩ ↑stipulated↓ that "whatever was agreed on by a majority of the confederates should be binding on all, unless some god or hero enjoined a dissent." Thucyd. Vol II   p 81 [54]

The ethical writings of the Ancients are without cant.

The ancients are no transcendentalists: they rest always in the spontaneous consciousness.
See also [Journal] B. p. 297

[20]–[21] [blank]
    [22] April 1.[55] Yesterday I received from Carlyle a letter, a copy of "Mirabeau", of the Diamond necklace, & a proofsheet of the Fr[ench]. Revolution. Blessings on the friend! Today I finished a letter to him.

    [April] 7. My baby's lovely drama still goes forward though he

---

[52] "Against Idleness," *ibid.*, II, 561. The quotation is used in "Manners," *Lectures*, II, 135.
    [53] Eckermann, *Gespräche mit Goethe*, 1837, I, 240; cf. p. [17] above.
    [54] Thucydides, *History of the Peloponnesian War*, trans. William Smith, 2 vols. (New York, 1836).
    [55] Having studied the dates and headings of Emerson's letters to Carlyle during this period, Rusk concluded that the date of this entry should be April 2 (*L*, II, 63, n. 39).

catches sad colds, & wheezes, & grieves. Yet again he sputters, &
spurs, & puts on his little important faces, & looks dignified, & frets,
& sleeps again. We call him little pharisee who when he fasts, sounds
a trumpet before him.[56]

The man of genius — Swedenborg or Carlyle, or Alcott, is ever,
as Shelley says of his skylark,

> "Like a poet hidden
> In the light of thought
> Singing hymns unbidden
> Till the world is wrought
> To sympathy with hopes & fears it heeded not." [57]
> *Shelley.* ["To a Skylark," ll. 36–40]

[April] 8. Ah! my darling boy, so lately received out of heaven leave
me not now! Please God, this sweet symbol of love & wisdom may
be spared to rejoice, teach, & accompany me.

People expect to read a lesson of the Divine Providence in a
death or a lunacy as they would read a paragraph in a newspaper, &
when they cannot, they say like my Irishman Roger Herring to the
Probate Court, "Well, I am not satisfied." But one lesson we are
to learn is the course or *genius* of the Divine Providence, which a
malady or any fact cannot teach, but a sober view of the events of
years, the action & reaction of character & events, may. ↑See p. 183↓

[23] 9 April. ⟨An extraordinary young man is sure to defeat
expectation.⟩ How many extraordinary young men we have seen or
heard of who never ripened or whose performance in actual life was
not extraordinary. When we see their air & expression, when we hear
them speak of society, of books, of religion, we admire their superiority, — they seem to throw contempt on the whole state — of the
world; it is the tone of a youthful giant who is sent to work revolutions. But the moment they enter an active profession, the forming
colossus shrinks to the common size of man. The power & the charm
they possessed was the ideal tendencies which always make the

[56] This paragraph, struck through in pencil with a diagonal use mark, is used
in "Domestic Life," *W*, VII, 104. Cf. Matt. 6:2: "sound a trumpet before thee."

[57] This paragraph is struck through in pencil with a diagonal use mark.

actual ridiculous; but the tough world had its revenge when once they put their horses of the sun to plough in its furrow.[58] Then, if they die, we lose our admiration another way, for we say this superiority was not healthy, was not just, or it would have enabled the body to work.

[April] 10. Very just are the views of Goethe in Eckermann that the poet stands too high than that he should be a partisan.[59] I thought as I rode through the sloughs yesterday that nothing is more untrue as well as unfavorable to power than that the thinker should open his mind to fear of the people among whom he works. Rather let him exult in his force. Whichever way he turns, he sees the pleasure & deference which these faculties of writing & speaking excite. The people call them out; the people delight in them; the better ⟨half⟩ part of every man feels, 'This is my Music'; [60] surely therefore the poet should [24] respond & say, 'the people & not solitude is my home.' Never my lands, my stocks, my salary, but this power to help & to charm the disguised soul that sits veiled under this whiskered & that smooth visage, this is my rent & ration. ↑See ⟨below,⟩ p. 37.↓

==

10 April.　　　　　　　Love an eye-water.

==

Love is fabled to be blind, but to me it seems that kindness is necessary to perception, that love is not an ophthalmia but an electuary. Let us never argue disputed points. The poet should never ⟨with⟩ know an antagonist. Few men can be trusted, almost no man has temper enough to argue with an adversary. But meet joyfully on what common ground they can, & extend in love that area, and ere they know it the boundary mountains on which the eye had fastened have melted into air.[61]

[58] "⟨An extraordinary . . . furrow." is struck through in pencil with a diagonal use mark and in ink with vertical use marks. "How many . . . furrow." is used in "Heroism," Lectures, II, 335–336, and "Heroism," W, II, 258–259.

[59] Eckermann, Gespräche mit Goethe, 1837, II, 356–357.

[60] "The people call . . . Music';", struck through in ink with a vertical use mark, is used in "The American Scholar," W, I, 103.

[61] "Love an eye-water. . . . air.", struck through in both pencil and ink with

Slavery is an institution for converting men into monkeys. ⟨So call it the monkey manufactory.⟩

All the professions are timid and incomplete agencies. The priest has some reference to the exigences of the parish, some to his own, & much regard to the faculty & course of his own thought. He says his prayers & his sermon, & is very glad if they answer to the case of any one individual, — if they bring the smallest spiritual aid to any soul; if to two, if to ten, it is a signal success. But he walked to the church without any assurance that he knew the distemper or could heal it. [25] ⟨t⟩The physician prescribes hesitatingly out of his few resources the same stimulus or sedative to this new & peculiar constitution which he has applied with various success to a thousand men before. If the patient mends, he is glad & surprised, but to himself he could not predict it. The lawyer advises the client and tells his story to the jury and leaves it with them & is as gay & as much relieved as the client, if it turns out that he has a verdict. He could not predict it. The judge weighs the arguments & puts a brave face on the matter, ↑&↓ since there must be a decision, decides as he can, & hopes he has done justice, & given satisfaction to the community but is only an advocate after all. And so is all life a timid & unskilful spectator. "If God to build the house deny, the builders work in vain." [62]

As smooth as a cat came W.

[April] 11. I wrote G[eorge]. P. B[radford]. that Eckermann was full of fine things & helps one much in the study of Goethe. Always the man of genius dwells alone, ⟨in solitude⟩ & like the mountain pays the tax of snows & silence for elevation. It would seem as if he hunted out this poor Dutch Boswell for a thing to talk to, that his thoughts might not pass in smother. His thinking, as far as I read him, is of great altitude & *all level*. Dramatic power I think he has very little. The great felicities, the miracles of Poetry, he has never.

---

two vertical use marks, is used in "Prudence," *Lectures*, II, 320–321, and "Prudence," *W*, II, 238.

[62] Ps. 127:1, paraphrased.

It is all design with him, just thought, & instructed expression, analogies, allusion, illustration, which knowledge & correct thinking supply;[n] [26] but of Shakspeare & the transcendant muse no syllable.[63] But he is a pledge that the antique force of nature is not spent & 'tis gay to think what men shall be. —

Is not life a puny unprofitable discipline whose direct advantage may be fairly represented by the direct education that is got at Harvard College? As is the real learning gained there, such is the proportion of the lesson in life.[64]

[April] 12. I find it the worst thing in life that I can put it to no better use.[65] One would say that he can have little to do with his time who sits down to ⟨to⟩ so slow labor & of such doubtful return as studying Greek or German; as he must be an unskilful merchant who should invest his money at three per cent. Yet I know not how better to employ a good many hours in the year. If there were not a general as well as a direct advantage herein we might shoot ourselves[.][66]

Where I see anything done, I behold the presence of the Creator. Peter Howe knows what to do in the garden, & Sullivan at a ball, & Webster in the Senate, & I over my page. Exchange any of our works, & we should be to seek. And any work looks wonderful to me except that one which I can do.

How little of the man see we in his person. The man Minot who busies himself all the year round under my windows[67] writes out his nature in a hundred works, in drawing water, hewing wood, building fence, ⟨providing for⟩ ↑feeding↓ his cows, haymaking & a few times in the year he goes into the woods. Thus his human spirit unites itself with nature. Why need I ever hear him speak articulate words?

[27] I listen by night I gaze by day at the endless procession of

[63] "His thinking . . . syllable.", struck through in ink on p. [25] with a vertical use mark, is used in "Thoughts on Modern Literature," W, XII, 326–327.

[64] There is a vertical line in ink along the left margin of this paragraph.

[65] This sentence, struck through in ink with a vertical use mark, is used in "Being and Seeming," Lectures, II, 296.

[66] This paragraph is struck through in pencil with a diagonal use mark.

[67] George Minott, Emerson's neighbor to the west.

wagons loaded with the wealth of all regions of England, of China, of Turkey, of the Indies which from Boston creep by my gate to all the towns of New Hampshire & Vermont. ⟨Creaking⟩ With creaking wheels at midsummer & crunching the snows on huge sledges in January, the train goes forward at all hours, bearing this cargo of inexhaustible comfort & luxury to every cabin in the hills.

In life all finding is not that thing we sought, but something else. The lover on being accepted, misses the wildest charm of the maid he dared not hope to call his own. The husband loses the wife in the cares of the household. ⟨He⟩ ↑Later, he↓ cannot rejoice with her in the babe for by becoming a mother she ceases yet more to be a wife.[68] With the growth of children the relation of the pair becomes yet feebler from the demands children make, until at last nothing remains of the original passion out of which all these parricidal fruits proceeded; and they die because they are superfluous.

16 April. How little think the youth & maiden who are glancing at each other across a mixed company with eyes so full of mutual intelligence — how little think they of the precious fruit long hereafter to proceed from this now quite external stimulus. The work of vegetation begins first in the irritability of the bark & leaf buds. From exchanging glances they proceed to acts of courtesy & gallantry, then to fiery passion, then [28] to plighting troth & to marriage. Immediately they begin to discover incongruities[,] defects. Thence comes surprise, regret, strife. But that which drew them at first was signs of loveliness[,] signs of virtue. These virtues appear & reappear & continue to draw, but the regard changes, quits the sign & attaches to the substance. This comes in to mitigate the disaffection. Meantime as life wears on it proves to be nothing but a game of permutation & combination of all possible positions of the parties to extort all the resources of each & acquaint each with the whole strength & weakness

[68] Cf. Emerson's poems "Each and All," ll. 29–36, W, IX, 5, and "Holidays," W, IX, 136, stanza 4:

"Whither went the lovely hoyden?
Disappeared in blessed wife;
Servant to a wooden cradle,
Living in a baby's life."

of the other. All the angels that inhabit this temple of a human form show themselves at the doors & all the gnomes also.[69] By all the virtues that appear[,] by so much kindness, justice, fortitude &c[,] by so much are they made one. But all the vices are negations on either part & they are by so much two. At last they discover that all that at first drew them together was wholly caducous[,] had merely a prospective end like the scaffolding by which a ⟨building⟩ house is built[,] & the unsuspected & wholly unconscious growth of principles from year to year is the real marriage foreseen & prepared from the first but wholly above their consciousness. This is the boardingschool & God.[70]

[29] Retzch is a Gothic genius [—] not the Greek simplicity but the Gothic redundancy of meaning & elaboration of details. His pictures are like Herbert's poems hard to read[,] for every word is to be emphasized.

The Newspapers persecute Alcott. I have never more regretted my inefficiency to practical ends. I was born a seeing eye not a helping hand.[71] I can only comfort my friends by thought, & not by love or aid. But they naturally look for this other also, & thereby vitiate our relation, throughout.

The pure in heart shall see God.[72] The pure in heart shall be God. Only God can see God.

19 April. We live with those who help us not & so degrade us. We do not know it until a clear soul passes by & the incongruity betwixt our good & our bad angel is manifest. Best amputate.

20 April. I read in a letter of William Tischbein to Merck (Rome 1785) that pictures are there made for the eye & not for the

[69] This sentence is used in "The Heart," *Lectures*, II, 283.

[70] This paragraph, struck through in both pencil and ink with vertical use marks, is used in "Love," *W*, II, 184–187.

[71] Cf. Emerson's letter to Alcott, April 14, 1837: "But I was created a seeing eye and not a useful hand" (quoted in *The Journals of Bronson Alcott*, 1938, p. 87). With this letter, incidentally, Emerson returned the first portion of Alcott's journal for 1837.

[72] Cf. Matt. 5:8.

soul. But he says matters mend. "*How* they should paint, they already know but *what* to paint, still fails them. Since Painting is for significance, & pleasure is but its secondary aim." p. 465 [73]

Poverty is the ornament of a philosopher.

[30] Camper [74] complains to Merck that "what happened in regard to petrifications has happened to him in regard to his collection of diseased bones, to wit, that he created the taste in Holland, in France, in Germany, & now is not able to get any specimen, — no not for money." [*Briefe an . . . Merck*,] p. 484

"I have been employed for six weeks upon the Cetacea. I dare say I understand ⟨the⟩ actually the osteology of the head of all these monsters. I have made the combination with the human head so well that ⟨al⟩ every body appears to me narwhale, marsonin, or cachalot. Women considered as pretty by their youth and those whom I find ugly they are all marsonins or cachalots to my eyes." Camper to Merck. [75]

↑See p 139↓

Sommering possessed ↑in his cabinet↓ the hand of a certain Paule de Viguier nearly 300 years old. This beautiful person was such an object of universal wonder to her contemporaries for her enchanting form, virtue, & accomplishments that according to the assurances of one of them the citizens of her native city Tholouse obtained the aid of the civil authorities to compel her to appear publicly on the balcony at least twice a week & as often as she showed herself ⟨a mul⟩ the crowd was dangerous to life.   ↑So Lady Hamilton was a modern Helen.↓ [76]

[73] Emerson is translating from *Briefe an Johann Heinrich Merck von Göthe, Herder, Wieland und andern bedeutenden Zeitgenossen* (Darmstadt, 1835), which he had borrowed from Margaret Fuller (*L*, I, 70–71). Both Merck (1741–1791), a writer and literary critic, and Johann Heinrich Wilhelm Tischbein (1751–1829), the painter whose letter is cited here, were friends of Goethe.

[74] Pieter Camper (1722–1789), Dutch anatomist and naturalist.

[75] *Briefe an . . . Merck*, 1835, p. 485; Emerson's translation abridges Camper's original French. This paragraph, struck through in pencil with a vertical use mark, is used in "The Comic," *W*, VIII, 167.

[76] For Paule de Viguier, see *Briefe an . . . Merck*, 1835, p. 494 and note. This paragraph, struck through in pencil with one vertical and one diagonal use mark,

↑In vino veritas↓[77]

↑Mine↓ Asia grudges the time she is called away from her babe because he grows so fast that each look is new & each is never to be repeated.

[31] Dr R[ipley]. told us of the clergyman in Marlborough who in the revolution prayed the Lord to look on us in these very peaked times.

Good letter from Tischbein to Merck describing Michel Angelo's last Judgment which he had the opportunity of seeing very near, & was astonished at the minute finish of muscles & nerves. Finished like a miniature. "A group of the damned whom the devils drive into hell made me so much distress that I feared I should fall from the ladder. I was forced to hold on with both hands & to banish the shuddering thoughts[.]" [78]

Wieland says Goethe read to them his account of their (Granduke & G.) passage through /Valois/*Wallis*/ over the Furka & St Gothard & it was as good as Xenophon's Anabasis. "It was also a true fieldmarch against all the elements which opposed them. The piece is one of his most masterly productions & thought & written with the great mind peculiar to him. The fair hearers were enthusiastic at the Nature in this piece; ⟨to me was⟩ ↑I liked↓ the sly Art in the composition whereof they saw nothing still better. It is a true poem so concealed is the art also. But ⟨the⟩ what most remarkably in this, as in all his other Works distinguishes him from Homer & Shakspear, is, that to *ME* the *Ille ego* everywhere glimmers through, although without any boasting, & with an infinite fineness." [79] [*Briefe an . . .*] *Merck* p[p. 235–]236

"I have sometimes (says the Grand duke) remarked before great

is used in "The Eye and Ear," *Lectures*, II, 276, and "Beauty," *W*, VI, 296–297; the latter passage adds an account of Lady Hamilton, née Elizabeth Gunning (1734–1790), the celebrated Scottish beauty who married James Douglas, 6th Duke of Hamilton.

[77] "In wine is truth" (Ed.).

[78] *Briefe an . . . Merck*, 1835, pp. 260–261.

[79] This paragraph, struck through in ink with a vertical use mark, is used in "Thoughts on Modern Literature," *W*, XII, 325–326.

works of art, & just now especially in Dresden, how much a certain property contributes to the lively effect which thrills our hearts, & makes us fall down upon our faces to worship, which gives life [32] to the figures & to the life an irresistible truth. This property is the hitting in all the figures we draw the right centre of gravity. I mean the placing the people firm upon their feet, making the hands grasp, & fastening the eyes ⟨up⟩on the spot where they should look. Even ⟨in⟩ lifeless figures as in geschlossenen[80] pictures, vessels, stools, let them be ↑drawn &↓ painted ever so fine, lose all effect so soon as they lack the resting upon their centre of gravity, & have ⟨something —⟩ ↑a certain↓ swimming & oscillating appearance. The Raphael in the Dresden Gallery[,] the only ⟨really⟩ greatly affecting picture which I have seen[,] is the quietest & ⟨p⟩ most passionless picture you can imagine. A couple of saints who worship the Virgin & child. Nevertheless it makes a deeper impression than the contorsions of ten crucified martyrs. ⟨"&c &c Letter from the Granduke of Saxe Weimar to Merck p. 362⟩ But it possesses besides all the resistless & instreaming beauty of form, in the highest degree the property of the perpendicularity of all the figures.[81] The Virgin Mary walks the cloud so lightly & notwithstanding, you have no fear of a mis-step." Letter to Merck p[p]. 362[–363]

[33] New England
     21 April. It has been to me a sensible relief to learn that the destiny of New England is to be the manufacturing country of America. I no longer suffer in the cold out of morbid sympathy with the farmer. The love of the farmer shall spoil no more days for me. Climate touches not my own work. The foulest or the coldest wind is as dear to the muses as the sweet southwest, & so to the manufacturer & the merchant. Where they have the sun, let them plant; we who have it not, will drive our pens & waterwheels.[82] I am gay as a canary bird with this ⟨thought⟩ new knowledge. ↑In the Tyrolese mountains they do not plant corn, but every man & woman carves

---

     [80] "geschlossenen" is written in pencil.
     [81] " 'I have sometimes . . . figures.'", struck through in both pencil and ink with vertical use marks, is used in "Prudence," *Lectures*, II, 315, and "Prudence," *W*, II, 229–230.
     [82] "It has been . . . waterwheels.'", struck through in pencil with a diagonal use mark, is used in "Doctrine of the Hands," *Lectures*, II, 237.

wooden foxes, wolves, & smoking Dutchmen or tends goats. I will write & so teach my countrymen their office as Johan Mez did his by carving. ^{x}p 34$^{\downarrow83}$

An opinion is seldom given; & every one we have heard of, weighs with us. Let an opinion be given upon a book, the *vis inertiae* [84] of the general mind is proved by the circulation this sentence has. It runs through a round of newspapers, & of social circles, & finds mere acquiescence in ⟨hundreds⟩ thousands. If the subject is one which has a political or commercial bearing, it commonly happens that another individual protests against the opinion, & affirms his own to be just the reverse. In that case still I should think is there but one opinion ↑affirmed & denied↓: there is yet no new *quality* shown.[85]

⟨An⟩ ↑Wo unto you, critics! for an↓ opinion is indeed not the safest ware to deal in. It is a ⟨stone⟩ cotton-ball thrown at an object, but the thread at the other end remains in the thrower's bag. Or rather it is the harpoon ^{n} [34] thrown at the whale & if the harpoon is not good, or not well thrown, it will go nigh to cut the steersman in twain, or drown the boat.[86]

---

^{x}↑p 33↓ In the Tyrol they carved & whittled until one morning they went to the mountain & behold there was not one pine tree left standing.[87]

I learn evermore. In smooth water I discover the motion of my boat by the motion of trees & houses on shore, so the progress of my mind is proved by the perpetual change in the persons & things I daily behold.

Beauty is ever that divine thing the ancients esteemed it. It is, as

[83] "In the Tyrolese . . . ^{x}p 34", struck through in ink with a vertical use mark, is used in "The American Scholar," *W*, I, 97.

[84] "Power of inertia" (Ed.), or "indolence," as Emerson rendered the phrase in "Being and Seeming."

[85] This paragraph, struck through in pencil with a diagonal use mark, is used in "Being and Seeming," *Lectures*, II, 304.

[86] This paragraph, struck through in ink with vertical use marks, is used in "Compensation," *W*, II, 110.

[87] This sentence, struck through in ink with a vertical use mark, is used in "The American Scholar," *W*, I, 97.

they said "the flowering of Virtue." [88] I see one & another, & another fair girl, about whose form or face glances a nameless charm. I am immediately touched with an emotion of tenderness or complacency. They pass on, and I stop to consider at what this dainty emotion, this wandering gleam points. It is no poor animal instinct, for this charm is destroyed for the imagination by any reference to animalism. It points neither to any relations of friendship or love that society knows & has, but as it seems to me to a quite other & now unattainable sphere, relations of transcendant delicacy & sweetness, a true faerie-land to what roses & violets hint & foreshow. We cannot *get at* beauty. Its nature is evanescent.[89]

[35] "The alphabet is a work of the mouth, Metre a work of the pulse" says Zelter.[90]

Napoleon said, "L'Empereur ne connoit autre maladie que la mort."

22 April. Culture — how much meaning the Germans affix to the word & how unlike to the English sense. The Englishman goes to see a museum or a mountain for itself; the German for himself; the Englishman for entertainment, the German for culture. The German is conscious, & his aims are great. The Englishman lives from his eyes, & immersed in the apparent world ——

Our culture comes not alone from the grand & beautiful, but also from the trivial & sordid. We wash & cleanse out every day for sixty years, this temple of the human body. We buy wood & ⟨make fires⟩ tend our fires, & deal with the baker & fisherman & grocer, & take a world of pains which nothing but concealed moral & intellectual ends of great worth can exalt to an ideal level.[91] If we knew we were in a purgatory, if we knew of crimes, & ⟨were⟩ ↑are↓ now in hell,

---

[88] Cf. "Of Love," *Plutarch's Morals*, 1718, IV, 297: "But some say that Beauty is the Flower of Virtue." See *JMN*, III, 147, and "The Eye and Ear," *Lectures*, II, 264, 275.

[89] This paragraph, struck through in pencil and ink with vertical use marks, is used in "Love," *W*, II, 179.

[90] *Briefwechsel zwischen Goethe und Zelter in den Jahren 1796 bis 1832*, 6 vols. in 3 (Berlin, 1833–1834), II, 91. The first double volume had been sent to Emerson by Margaret Fuller (*L*, II, 68, n. 48; 71).

[91] "Our culture . . . level.", struck through in pencil with a vertical use mark, is used in Human Culture: "Introductory," *Lectures*, II, 221.

the lowness & filths of life were then explained. But we are void of such consciousness.

Polarity is a law of all being. Superinduce the magnetism at one end of a needle, the opposite magnetism takes place at the other end. If the south attracts, the north repels. To empty here, you must condense there. Light, shade; heat, cold; centrifugal, centripetal; action, reaction.[n 92] If the mind idealizes at one end perfect goodness into God [36] coexistently it ⟨forms at⟩ abhors at the other end, a Devil.

Cold April; hard times; men breaking who ought not to break; ⟨desperate specul⟩ banks bullied into the bolstering of desperate speculators; all the newspapers a chorus of owls. 'Tobacco, cotton, teas, indigo, & timber all at tremendous discount & the end not yet.' Eight firms in London gave the bank a round robin bond for £3 800 000 of discounts. — Such things I read in the papers specially "London Age" of March 12. Loud cracks in the social edifice. — Sixty thousand laborers, says rumor, to be presently thrown out of work, and these make a formidable mob to break open banks & rob the rich & brave⟨,⟩ the domestic government. ↑May 5↓ ↑In New York the president (Fleming) of the Mechanics Bank resigns, & the next morning is found dead in his bed "by mental excitement," according to the verdict of the Coroner. Added bitterness from the burning of the Exchange in New Orleans by an incendiary; the Park mobs, & the running on banks for specie in N.Y.↓

[37] There is a crack in every thing God has made.[93] Fine weather! — yes but cold. Warm day! — 'yes but dry.' — 'You look well' — 'I am very well except a little cold.' The case of damaged hats — one a broken brim; the other perfect in the rim, but rubbed on the side; the third whole in the cylinder, but bruised on the crown.

I say to L[idian]. that in composition the *What* is of no impor-

[92] "Polarity is . . . reaction", struck through in ink with a vertical use mark, is used in "Compensation," *W*, II, 96–97.
[93] Cf. *JMN*, IV, 362. This sentence, struck through in pencil with a horizontal line plus a diagonal use mark in ink, is used in "Compensation," *W*, II, 107.

tance compared with the *How*. The most tedious of all discourses are
⟨often⟩ on the subject of the Supreme Being.

23 April. How much benefit in the common well-meaning private
person. I was at Wayland today & could not help feeling & expressing
a gratitude to that worthy R. Heard as to a main column on which
their municipal & ecclesiastical wellbeing leans; & again ⟨seeing⟩ what
a benefactress to the place is the beautiful singer Mrs M[ellen]. only
by ⟨the⟩ her voice in the church. ↑See p 150↓[94]

Trust your nature[,] the common mind. Fear not to sound its
depths to ejaculate its grander emotions. Fear not how men shall
take it. See you not they are following your thought & emotion because it leads them deeper into their own? I see with joy I am speaking their word[,] fulfilling their nature when I thought the word &
nature most my own. ↑See p 24.↓

All good writing might be called Occasional Poems as it is only
a composition of many visions in the writer's private experience.

[38] ⟨It is remarkable that⟩ The[n] young find a keener pleasure
in the riot of the imagination than any which nature has in store. & by
means of natural pleasures in later life they are cured of their delicious madness. Meantime what a dupe is the libertine! He thinks he
has the sparkle & the color of the cup & the chaste married pair only
the lees. They see that he stays always in the base court & never has
one glimpse of the high joys of a perfect wedlock.

"What you love not, you cannot do."[95] *Zelter.*
What pleases me, will please many.

April 26. More conversation about the German Man. I perceived that he differed from all the great in a total want of frankness.
Whoso saw Milton[,] whoso saw Shakspeare saw them do their best &

[94] "How much . . . wellbeing leans;", struck through in pencil with two diagonal use marks, is used in "Being and Seeming," *Lectures*, II, 305. "See p 150" is
added in pencil.
[95] "the young find . . . cannot do.' " is struck through in pencil with a vertical
use mark. The quotation from Zelter is used in "Doctrine of the Hands," *Lectures*,
II, 236.

utter their whole heart manlike among their brethren. No man was permitted to call Goethe brother. He hid himself & worked always to astonish, which is an egotism & therefore little.[96]

⟨He thought⟩ Furthermore as he describes the Devil as the great Negation [97] [—] or as Carlyle says the Lie is the Second Best[,] God & truth being the first [—] so it would appear as if he aimed himself to be the Third Term or the Universal Quiz[,] a sort of Bridge from the truth to the Lie. He thought it necessary therefore to dot round as it were the entire sphere of knowables & for many of his stories this seems [39] the only reason: viz. Here is a piece of humanity I had hitherto omitted to sketch — take this. This, to be sure, he never expresses in words. Yet a sort of incumbency to be up to the Universe is the best account of many of them.[98]

On the whole What have these German Weimarish Art friends done? They have rejected all the traditions & conventions[,] have sought to come thereby one step nearer to absolute truth. But still they are not nearer than others. I do not draw from them great influence. The heroic, the holy, I lack. They are contemptuous. They fail in sympathy with humanity. The voice of Nature they bring me to hear is not divine, but ghastly hard & ironical. They do not illuminate me: they do not edify me. Plutarch's heroes cheer[,] exalt. The old bloodwarm Miltons & Sidneys & Pauls help & aggrandize me. The roots of what is great & high must still be in the common life.

[40] Christianity. To those fundamental natures that lie as the basis of the soul[,] truth, justice, love, &c[,] the idea of eternity is essentially associated. Jesus a pure intellect exclusively devoted to this class of abstractions (the ethical) ⟨felt⟩ did never yet utter one syllable about the naked immortality of the soul[,] never spoke of simple duration. His disciples felt as all must the coexisting perception of eternity & separated it & taught it as a doctrine & maintained

---

[96] This paragraph, struck through in ink with a vertical use mark, is used in "Thoughts on Modern Literature," W, XII, 326.

[97] In *Faust*, Part I, Mephistopheles identifies himself to Faust as "der Geist der stets verneint!" (*Werke*, 1828–1833, XII, 70).

[98] "He thought it . . . them.", struck through in ink with vertical use marks, is used in "Thoughts on Modern Literature," W, XII, 323–324.

it by evidences.[99] It ought never to be. It is an impertinence to struggle up for the immortality. It is inevitable to believe it if you come down upon the conviction from the seeing these primary natures in the mind.

29 April. Warm & welcome blows the southwind at last, & the sun & moon shine again to raise the desponding hearts of the people in these black times. Yet our idle dallying tentative conversation goes on, sunshine still lying kindly on my hearthstone. Therefor be lowly interceding praise from me & mine.

Mrs Lee gave me beautiful flowers. These gay natures contrast with the somewhat stern countenance of the world in these latitudes. They are like music heard out of a workhouse or jail. Nature does not cocker us. We are children, not pets. She is not fond. Everything is dealt to us without fear or favor after serene severe Universal laws. Yet these delicate flowers look [41] like the frolic & interference of love & beauty. They use to tell us that we love flattery even which we see through because it shows that we are of importance enow to be courted. Something like that pleasure the star, the flower, & the tinted cloud give us. Well[,] what am I to whom these sweet & sublime hints are addressed! [100]

How wild & mysterious our position as ⟨me⟩ individuals to the Universe! Here is always a certain amount of truth lodged as intrinsic foundation in the depths of the soul, a certain perception of absolute being, as justice, love, & the like, ⟨which⟩ natures which must be the God of God, and this is our capital stock. This is our centripetal ⟨gravity⟩ force. We can never quite doubt, we can never be adrift; we can never be nothing, because of this Holy of Holies, out of sight of which we cannot go. Then on the other side all is to seek. We understand nothing; our ignorance is abysmal, — the overhanging immensity staggers us, whither we go, what we do, who we are, we cannot even so much as guess. We stagger & grope.

[99] "Jesus a pure . . . evidences.", struck through in ink with a vertical use mark, is used in "The Over-Soul," W, II, 283–284.
[100] This paragraph, struck through in ink with vertical use marks, is used in "Gifts," W, III, 159–160.

[42] Fine manners present themselves first as formidable; they are primarily useful as the noble science of defence is, merely to parry & ward & intimidate, but once matched by our own skill they drop the point of the sword — points & shields all disappear & you find yourself in a perfectly transparent medium wherein life is a finer vehicle & not a cloud like that which Beckendorf's [101] keen eye detected in his glass, is visible between man & man. They aim at good certainly. They aim to facilitate life; to get rid of chaff & husks & to bring the ⟨pure⟩ man pure to operate. They aid society as a railway aids travelling by getting rid of all the details of the road & leaving nothing to be conquered but pure space[.] [102]

Miss Fuller read Vivian Gray & made me very merry. Beckendorf is a fine teaching that he who can once conquer his own face, can have no farther difficulty. Nothing in the world is to him impossible. As Napoleon who discharged his face of all expression whilst Mme de Stael gazed at him.[103]

↑The existence of↓ aⁿ 'Paradise Lost'[,] a Dante's 'Inferno' argu⟨e⟩es a half disbelief of the immortality of the Soul.

If with a lowly mind you elect writing for your task in life, I believe you must renounce all pretensions to reading.

[43] I will add it to my distinctive marks of man & woman — the man loves hard wood the woman loves pitch pine.

The merchant fails. He has put more than labor[,] he has put character & ambition into his fortune & cannot lose it without bitter mortification. It is not clear to the recluse the ambition of a merchant. It seems that he could & should have been content with safe wealth & not so ventured & so fallen. But the merchant in every conversation in the Insurance Office, feels the weight of ⟨the⟩ his neighbor a greater capitalist; in every transaction of business he feels his own & his

[101] Beckendorff is the Grand Duke's minister in Disraeli's *Vivian Grey* (1826), Bk. VI.
[102] This paragraph, struck through in pencil with a diagonal use mark, is used in "Prudence," *Lectures*, II, 325, and "Manners," *W*, III, 126–127.
[103] This sentence is used in "Manners," *W*, III, 135–136.

neighbor's measure. He sees that he can augment his own consideration & wield as enviable power. He sees moreover that a great fortune has not ⟨a wo⟩ an evil[,] a dishonorable influence, that is, its influence is very far from being built on the weakness & sycophancy of men, but it is a certificate of great faculty of virtues of a certain sort. Moral considerations give currency every day to notes of hand. Success & credit depend on enterprize, on accurate perceptions, on honesty, on steadiness of mind. This man in the land-fever ⟨w⟩ bought no acre in Maine or Michigan. His notes of hand have a better currency as long as he lives. That man is a commission merchant & in the midst of a vast business, does not trade on his own account to the amount of a dollar. Every body gladly buys his paper.[104]
Steady Steady!

[44]   France
In France, one who hisses is called 'de l'avis de l'aspic[.]'

" 'Adieu Société!' was the dying speech of one of the fellow conspirators of Berton when about submitting his neck to the guillotine."
                                    Ed[inburgh]. Rev[iew].

" 'The French,' said Goethe 'have understanding & talent but no Foundation & no piety. What serves them for the moment, what can benefit their party, is to them the Right. They praise us, therefore, not out of recognition of our merit, but only when they can strengthen their party through our views.' "
                    Eckermann [Gespräche mit Goethe, 1837,]
                                    Vol. 1 p[p.] 168[–169]
"The French esprit said Goethe comes near that which we Germans name Witz. Our Geist would the French perhaps express through esprit and ame. There lies in the word the import of productiveness which the French esprit has not[.]" Eckermann Vol. 2, p. 323.

It is true ⟨however⟩ ↑'tis↓ incredible the condition of art here (in Paris) at this time (Apr. 1781). M. Wille said to me that ⟨now⟩ no

---

[104] This paragraph, struck through in pencil with a vertical use mark, is used in "Doctrine of the Hands," *Lectures*, II, 238–239.

painter, if he would resist hunger, can now undertake to paint any other subject than a *gallant* one.

Letter from L[eonhard] Zeutner in Correspondence of Mer[c]k

p. 288 [105]

"A tragedy a poem with Voltaire is not to be 'a manifestation of Man's Reason in forms suitable to his Sense,' but rather a highly complex egg dance, to be danced before the King, to a given tune, & without breaking a single egg." *Carlyle.* [Cf.] For[eign]. Review vol III [April 1829,] p 464

No Frenchman could ever sing[.]

"The French Nation have predominant in them la vanità, la leggerezza, l'independenza ed il capriccio, with an unconquerable passion for glory. They will as soon do without [45] bread as without glory⟨. A⟩; & a proclamation will lead them (*les entrainer*)" said Napoleon to O.'meara.[106]

"The drawing rooms of Paris are indeed tremendous with their jokes;" said Napoleon, "they always assail the enemy at the breach, & a total defeat is the consequence."

Las Cases [107]

⟨In Paris there was masked gambling, until Napoleon prohibited it.⟩[108]

As a specimen of these Paris jokes I quote from the F.Q.R. ↑July 1838↓ article on Queen Hortense, that Madame Alf.... de N. had given the Countess Dulauloy the nickname of 'Le Grénadier tricolore' in allusion to her tall fine figure as well as to her republican opinions. She again retaliated by calling Madame Alf.... de N., who was very lean, the "Venus of the Père la Chaise." [109]

---

[105] *Briefe an . . . Merck*, 1835.

[106] Cf. Barry Edward O'Meara, *Napoleon in Exile: or, A Voice from St. Helena*, 2 vols. (Boston, 1823), I, 286–287.

[107] Cf. Count Emmanuel Augustin Dieudonné de Las Cases, *Mémorial de Sainte Hélène. Journal of the Private Life and Conversations of the Emperor Napoleon at Saint Helena*, 4 vols. (Boston, 1823), II, iii, 61.

[108] Cf. Las Cases, *Journal*, 1823, IV, vii, 113.

[109] Cf. *Foreign Quarterly Review*, XXX (July 1838), 306. This paragraph, struck through in pencil with a diagonal use mark and in ink with a vertical use mark, is used in "The Comic," W, VIII, 171. Note that this paragraph (reading

In Paris there was masked gambling until Napoleon prohibited it.

The French seem to have somewhat negrofine in their taste. How much rhodomontade in Napoleon's & Las Cases' conversation. How much about glory & principles that is not glory & that are not principles. Sophomorical [—] repudiated by the stern English sense[.]

[46] [blank]
[47]   *Thomas Carlyle's Writings.*[110]
        German Romance, 4 Volumes.   Life of Schiller. 1 vol.
        Translation of Wilhelm Meister,   3 Volumes

"July 1838"), the last entry on p. [45] (copied from p. [318] below), and perhaps other entries under "France" must have been written no earlier than 1838.

[110] The works listed are the following: *German Romance*, 4 vols. (Edinburgh and London, 1827); *The Life of Friedrich Schiller* (London, 1825); *Wilhelm Meister's Apprenticeship*, 3 vols. (Edinburgh and London, 1824); "Corn-Law Rhymes," *Edinburgh Review*, LV (July 1832), 338–361; "State of German Literature," *ibid.*, XLVI (Oct. 1827), 304–351; "Burns," *ibid.*, XLVIII (Dec. 1828), 267–312; "Characteristics," *ibid.*, LIV (Dec. 1831), 351–383; "Signs of the Times," *ibid.*, XLIX (June 1829), 439–459; "Taylor's Historic Survey of German Poetry," *ibid.*, LIII (March 1831), 151–180; "Jean Paul Friedrich Richter Again," *Foreign Review*, V (Jan. 1830), 1–52; "Life and Writings of Werner," *ibid.*, I (Jan. 1828), 95–141; "Diderot," *Foreign Quarterly Review*, XI (April 1833), 261–315; "Novalis," *Foreign Review*, IV (July 1829), 97–141; "Goethe's Helena," *ibid.*, I (April 1828), 429–468; "Goethe," *ibid.*, II (July 1828), 80–127; "Voltaire," *ibid.*, III (April 1829), 419–475; "German Literature of the Fourteenth and Fifteenth Centuries," *Foreign Quarterly Review*, VIII (Oct. 1831), 347–391; "Goethe's Works," *ibid.*, X (Aug. 1832), 1–44; "German Playwrights," *Foreign Review*, III (Jan. 1829), 94–125; "Schiller," *Fraser's Magazine*, III (March 1831), 127 152, "Boswell's Life of Johnson," *ibid.*, V (May 1832), 379–413; "Thoughts on History," *ibid.*, II (Nov. 1830), 413–418; "Luther's Psalm," *ibid.*, II (Jan. 1831), 743–744; "Sartor Resartus," *ibid.*, VIII (Nov., Dec. 1833), 581–592, 669–684; IX (Feb., March, April, June 1834), 177–195, 301–313, 443–455, 664–674; X (July, Aug. 1834), 77–87, 182–193; "Count Cagliostro," *ibid.*, VIII (July, Aug. 1833), 19–28, 132–155; "The Diamond Necklace," *ibid.*, XV (Jan., Feb. 1837), 1–19, 172–189; "Biography," *ibid.*, V (April 1832), 253–260; "Tragedy of the Night Moth," *ibid.*, IV (Aug. 1831), 64; "Memoirs of Mirabeau," *London and Westminster Review*, XXVI (Jan. 1837), 382–439; "Parliamentary History of the French Revolution," *ibid.*, XXVII (April 1837), 233–247; "Memoirs of the Life of Scott," *ibid.*, XXVIII (Jan. 1838), 293–345; "Varnhagen von Ense's Memoirs," *ibid.*, XXXII (Dec. 1838), 60–84; *The French Revolution: A History*, 3 vols. (London, 1837).

In Edinburgh Review No

CX	Cornlaw Rhymes
XCII	German Literature
XCVI	Burns
CVIII	Characteristics
XCVIII	Signs of the Times
CV	Taylor's Historic Survey

In Foreign Review Vol. 5   Richter

In Foreign ⟨Q.⟩ Review   Vol 1   Werner

  Foreign [Quarterly] Rev

   Vol II [XI]   Diderot

  Foreign Rev   Vol 4   Novalis

  Foreign Review   Vol 1   Goethe's Helena

  Foreign Rev.   Vol II   Goethe

  Foreign Review   Vol VI   Voltaire

Foreign Q. Review, Vol. VIII   German Literature in 14 & 15 Centuries

F.   Q. R.   Vol X   Goethe's Works

  Foreign Review   Vol 3   German Playwrights

In Fraser's Magazine   Vol 3   Schiller

   Vol 5. p. 379   Samuel Johnson

   Vol 2 p. 413   Thoughts on History

   Vol 2   Luther's Hymn

   [Vol. 8]   Sartor Resartus

   Vol. 8   Count Cagliostro

    Diamond Necklace

   Vol. 5   Biography

   Vol 4   Night Moth

In Westminster Review, No   Mirabeau

    French Parliamentary History

    Lockhart's Life of Scott

    Varnhagen von Ense

[48]   The French Revolution, A history; 3 vols.

[49] [blank]
[50]   Goethe.
"We then spoke of the many years of his Theatre-management &
what amount of time he had thereby lost from composition. 'Certainly,' said Goethe, 'I had in the meantime been able to write many
good pieces yet when I rightly bethink it I regret it not. I have ever
regarded all my working & performance only ↑as↓ symbolical and at
bottom it seems to me quite immaterial whether I make cups or
platters.' " [111]
                    Eckermann. [*Gespräche mit Goethe*, 1837,]
                         Vol 1. p[p]. 155[–156]
"I will tell you something & you will often find it confirmed in your
lifetime. All Epochs considered in their receding & dissolution are
subjective; but on the contrary all advancing Epochs have an objective direction. Our whole present Epoch is a receding since it is a
subjective period. This you see not only in poetry but also in painting
& many other⟨s⟩ ↑things↓. Every great Effort, on the other hand, tends
from within out upon the world, as you see in all great Epochs which
really were conceived in Endeavor & ⟨adv⟩ progress, & all objective
Natures[.]" V. Eckermann Vol 1, 240[–241]

"Homer's poem," he said, "had the wonderful virtue of the heroes
of Valhalla which in the morning were hewed in pieces & at evening
sat down safe & sound to table." Eckermann — [I, 339–340]

"If you think justly of Art from within outward you must wish
that it should treat worthy & significant objects. Since after the last
artistic perfection comes to us (morally considered) the Gehalt immer
als hochste Einheit wieder entgegen. ⟨w⟩Wherefore we W. K. F. in
the Propylaea [112] whilst [51] genetically, ↑we had the notion that it
should work on Men↓ expressed ourselves so truly upon the Object
& directed our prize question thereto. But this is all become of no use,

---

[111] This paragraph, struck through in pencil with a diagonal use mark, is used in
"Prudence," *Lectures*, II, 326.
[112] A periodical, organ of the "Weimarischen Kunstfreunde" ("W. K. F.").

since, immediately afterwards, the Saints & Legends-Fever has in-
fected all, & has driven all true ⟨& genial⟩ ↑love of↓ life out of the
plastic Arts. Yet I complain of this only, in passing, since in addition
to my first Essay, would I only say that Art, as it represents itself in
the highest Artist, creates a so powerful form, that it ennobles &
⟨cha⟩ transforms every material." To Zelter — Vol II   p 66 —[113]

A characteristic of Goethe is his choice of topics. What an eye for
the measure of things! Perhaps he is out in regard to Byron, but not
of Shakspear; & in Byron he has grasped all the peculiarities. Paper-
money; Periods of belief; Cheerfulness of the poet; French Revolution; how just are his views of these trite things! What a multitude
of opinions & how few blunders! The estimate of Sterne, I suppose
to be one.[114]

"I send you," writes he to Zelter, "the Metamorphosis of Plants.
When thou again readest it in quieter time, take it symbolically, &
account thyself the while another creature which progressively unfolds itself out of itself. I have again today examined Linnaeus's
writings in which he treats of the foundations of botany, & I see
clearly that I have only used them symbolically, that is, I have endeavored to convert this method & treatment to other objects &
woven me thereby an organ wherewith much may be done."
[*Briefwechsel zwischen Goethe und*] Zelter
Vol 2   p. 326 [abridged]

[52][115] It is to me very plain that no recent genius can work
with equal effect upon mankind as Goethe, for no intelligent young
man can read him without finding that his own compositions are immediately modified by his new knowledge.
I do not remember a joke or aught laughable in all Goethe
except Philina cracking nuts upon the trunk & perhaps Friedrich's gibe
at Natalia.[116]

---

[113] *Briefwechsel zwischen Goethe und Zelter*, 1833–1834.

[114] Emerson may have been thinking of "Lorenz Sterne," *Werke*, 1828–1833,
XLV, 300–301, or of incidental references in Goethe's conversations and correspondence — e.g., in *Briefwechsel zwischen Goethe und Zelter*, 1833–1834, VI, 30, 207.

[115] "Goethe" is centered above "very plain" at the top of the page.

[116] See *Wilhelm Meister's Apprenticeship*, Bk. IV, ch. 8; Bk. VIII, ch. 7.

For the new Faust and the "classick Carnival," as Margaret Fuller calls it, I seem to see some explanation in the man's desire that every word should be a thing. These figures[,] he would say these Chirons, Sphinxes & Peneus, Helen & Leda[,] are somewhat & do exert a specific influence on the mind. So far they are eternal entities as real today as in the first Olympiad. Much revolving them he writes out freely his humor & having given them by successive efforts body to his own imagination he thinks they have humanity to other men to whom they are wholly fantastic.[117]

[53] (ART, by Plotinus.)
"Whilst we are convinced that those who behold the intellectual world & the beauty of true intellect can also well behold their Father who is exalted over all sense[,] so ↑let us↓ attempt ⟨us⟩ then to inquire after the powers, & ⟨for⟩ ourselves to express, ⟨in⟩so far as things of this kind can be ⟨m⟩ explained, in what manner we can apprehend the beauty of the Soul & of the World.

"Let two stone ⟨masses⟩ ↑blocks↓ be placed together whereof one ↑is↓ rough & without artificial labor, but the other is formed by art to a human or divine statue. Were it of a god, so might it represent a ⟨g⟩Grace or a Muse. Were it of a man, so is it not a ⟨remarkable⟩ ↑historical↓[118] man but rather of some one whom art has collected out of all beauties.

"But to you will the Stone which is brought by art into a beautiful form appear altogether beautiful, yet not because it is stone, since ⟨otherwise⟩ ↑then↓ will the other ⟨mass⟩ ↑block↓ also pass for beautiful, but because it has a form which Art has imparted to it.

"But Matter has no such form; but this was in the thinker before it came to the stone. It was already in the Artist, not because he had eyes & hands but because he was endowed with art.

"Also was in art a far greater beauty, since not that form which resides in Art came to the stone but that remains where it was, & there went out into the stone another inferior which does not abide pure in itself nor quite as the Artist wishes but only as far as the material would obey Art.

[117] This paragraph, struck through in ink with a vertical use mark, is used in "History," *W*, II, 33.
[118] The cancellation and insertion are in pencil.

"But ⟨when⟩ ↑if↓ Art ↑should↓ also produce⟨s⟩ what it is & possesses & produce the beautiful after Reason according to which it evermore [54] worketh, yet would ⟨this⟩ ↑the Reason↓ the more & truer ↑possess↓ a greater & more conspicuous beauty of Art, ⟨possess⟩ perfecter than all which exists outwardly.

"Since whilst the Form proceeding into matter is already extended, so is it weaker than that which abides in Unity. Since what in itself endures a removal departs away from itself[,] strength from strength, heat from heat, force from force, so also beauty from beauty. Therefore must the workman be more excellent than the work, since[n] not the Unmusic makes the Musician but the Music & the Supersensual music produces the music in sensuous sound.

"But would any one despise Art because it imitates Nature? Let us reply that the natures also ↑imitate↓ many others ⟨imitate⟩; that moreover Art does not directly imitate that which eyes can see, but goes back upon the R⟨easonable⟩↑ational↓ out of which Nature consists & after which Nature worketh.

"Furthermore ↑the↓ Arts produce many things out of themselves & add on the other hand many things hereto which lack perfectness whilst yet they have beauty in themselves. So could Phidias form the God although he imitated nothing perceptible to the senses, but made himself in his mind such a form as Jove himself would appear if he should become obvious to our eyes."

Plotinus translated by Goethe in Letters to Zelter [*Briefwechsel zwischen Goethe und Zelter*, 1833–1834,] vol. I, p. 190

[55] "The faults" writes Goethe to Schiller (Briefe[119] p. 66) "which you rightly indicate, come out of my inmost nature, out of a certain realistic whim, through which I find it pleasing to withdraw my existence, my actions, my writings out of the eyes of men. So ⟨will⟩ I ↑like↓ ever ↑to↓ travel incognito, choose worse rather than better clothes & in intercourse with strangers or half strangers, prefer a trifling subject & common expressions, /behave/seem/ myself more /capricious/light minded/ than I am, & place myself so to speak between me & my appearance."

---

[119] *Goethe's Briefe in den jahren 1768 bis 1832*, ed. Heinrich Döring (Leipzig, 1837). This volume, rather than Döring's *Göthe's Leben*, is evidently the "Doring" borrowed from Margaret Fuller (*L*, II, 77, 87–88, 202, 205).

Goethe prefers to drop a profound observation incidentally to stating it circumstantially[:] for example "Seneca sees nature as an uncultivated man; since not it, but its events interest him."

Nachg[elassene]. W[erke].[120] vol. 13   p 68.

So, speaking of Bacon he says, "Revolutionary thoughts arise in individual men rather ⟨through⟩ ↑from↓ single occasions than ⟨through⟩ ↑from↓ ⟨universal⟩ the general state of affairs & so we meet in Bacon's writings some such axioms which he with special stress harps upon; e.g. the doctrine of final causes is particularly odious to him." Nachg. W. [i.e., *Werke*,] vol. 13. p. 157

"Yet was Tycho Brahe with all his merits one of those limited minds who feel themselves to be in some measure in contradiction with nature, & on that account love complex paradoxes more than simple truth, & enjoy themselves in error because it gives them occasion to show the sharpness of their wit; whilst ⟨those⟩ he who recognizes the True seems ever to honor God & nature, but not himself, & of this last sort was Kepler." [*Werke*,] Vol 13   p[p.] 171[–172]

[56] I owe the presentation of a book to N[athaniel]. L. F[rothingham]., [Mrs. ?] S. A. D[ewey?]., C[harles]. W. U[pham]., B. Do[?], Dr. E. H., Mrs A. D. A[dams]. (Waltham), Dr J[ohn]. Ware[.][121]

May 1. I do not forgive in any man this forlorn pride as if he were an Ultimus Romanorum.[122] I am more American in my feeling. This country is full of people whose fathers were judges, generals, & bank presidents & if all their boys should give themselves airs thereon & rest henceforth on the oars of their fathers' merit, we should be a sad[,] hungry generation. ⟨But I am more philosophical also⟩ Moreover I esteem it my best birthright that our people are not crippled by family & official pride, that the best ⟨coat⟩ broadcloth coat in the country

[120] Not *Nachgelassene Werke*, but *Werke*: see p. 127 above, n. 390.

[121] The identifications are by E. W. Emerson, who in the manuscript penciled "Dr. E[dward]. H[ooper]." but in *J*, III, 222, n. 1, specified "Dr. Ebenezer Hobbs." Dr. Ware, a physician who had been among Emerson's parishioners at the Second Church in Boston, attended both Emerson and his brother Charles during their residence in the city.

[122] "Last of the Romans" (Ed.).

is ⟨hung on a peg &⟩ ↑put off to put on↓ a blue frock ⟨put on⟩, that the
best man in town may steer his plough tail or may drive a milk cart.
⟨The quality⟩ There is a great deal of work in our men & a false
pride has not yet made them idle or ashamed. Moreover I am more
philosophical than to love this retrospect. I believe in the being God
not in the God that has been. I work; my fathers may have wrought
or rested. What have I to do with them or with the Fellatahs or the
great Khan! [123] I know a worthy man who walks the streets [57]
with silent indignation as a last of his race quite contemptuously eye-
ing the passing multitude as if none of them were for him & he for
none of them, as if he belonged to the club & age of Shakspear, Bacon,
Milton, but by some untoward slip in old spiritual causes had been
left behind by the etherial boat that ferried them into life & came
now scornful an age too late. But what a foolish spirit to pout & sneer.
That did not these able persons; & if some good natured angel should
transport him into their serene company they would say unto him
'We know you not.' [123a] What if a man has great tastes & tendencies.
Is not that the charm & wonder of time, the oil of life that in common
men every where gleam out these majestical traits so wildly contrasting with their trivial employments, ⟨elevating⟩ ↑decking↓ their narrow patch of black loam with sunshine & violets so that the lowest
being, intimately seen, never suffers you to lose sight of his relations
to the highest & to all? [n] [124] ↑See p 160↓

Character is higher than intellect. And Character is what the
German means when he speaks of the Daimonisches. A strong monad
is strong to live as well as to think, & this is the last resource. Do I
lack organ or medium to ⟨commun⟩ impart my truths? I can still re-
treat on this elemental force of living them. This is a total act; all [n]
thinking is a partial act. Webster in his speech does but half engage
himself.[125] ↑I feel that there is a great deal of waste strength.↓ Therefore I say let me not meet a great man in a drawing room or [58] in

---

[123] "This country is . . . Khan!", struck through in pencil with a vertical use
mark, is used in "Doctrine of the Hands," *Lectures*, II, 244–245.

[123a] Cf. Job 36:26; Matt. 25:12; Luke 22:57.

[124] "What if a . . . all?", struck through in pencil with two diagonal use marks,
is used in "Doctrine of the Hands," *Lectures*, II, 245.

[125] "Character is higher . . . himself.", struck through in ink with a vertical
use mark, is used in "The American Scholar," *W*, I, 99.

an Academy or even in my own ⟨study⟩ ↑library↓ but let him ⟨intent⟩ bound on his private errand meet me bound on mine in the stage coach our road being the same for two or three hundred miles[,] then will a right natural conversation grow out of our ↑mutual↓ want of relief & entertainment. Or better yet, put us into the cabin of a little coasting merchantman to roll & welter in the gulf Stream for a fortnight towards Savannah ⟨S⟩or St Croix. Then will two persons feel each the force of the other's constitution[,] the weight of each other's metal far better than it can be estimated from a speech or an Essay.[126]

I went to see Mr Jonathan Phillips once & he said to me "when you come into the room, I endeavor to present humanity to you in a lovely & worthy form to put away every thing that can mar the beauty of the image." He also said that "life appeared to him very long; his existence had stretched over a vast experience."

May 4. I have copied into p. 33 of my Transcript, an account of the founding of an Alpine Hospital for travellers in 1386 by Heinrich the Foundling as a specimen of active beneficence. ⟨Here⟩ In this instance doing good is as clear & respectable as sunshine or self respect or aught else which the fastidious philosopher can still revere.

[59] Margaret Fuller left us yesterday morning. Among many things that make her visit valuable & memorable, this is not the least that she gave me five or six lessons in German pronunciation never by my offer and rather against my will, each time, so that now spite of myself I shall always have to thank her for a great convenience — which she foresaw.

[60][127] Economy does not consist in saving the coal but in using the time whilst it burns.

In conversation there are tides, and the visiter of a few days will see the ebb & the succeeding mud, but *living* is the channel which upbears ships & boats at ⟨the⟩ all hours.

---

[126] This sentence is struck through in ink with a vertical use mark. Emerson is apparently recalling his conversations at sea with Achille Murat in 1827 (*JMN*, III, 77).

[127] "Be & Seem" is written above "Economy" at the top of the page.

Day before yesterday (2 May) Dr Hobbs, Dr Adams, & Mr Ripley, sent me from Waltham 31 trees which I have planted by my house. What shall I render to my benefactors?

———

↑Be & Seem↓

Creation is genius, however, whenever. There are few actions. Almost all is appetite & custom. A new action commands us & is the Napoleon or Luther of the hour. So with manners. They are sometimes a perpetual creation & so do charm & govern us. So with opinions (as above, p. 33.). Miss Edgeworth has not *genius*, nor Miss Fuller; but the one has genius-in-narrative, & the other has genius-in-conversation. At Palermo I remember how shabby & pitiable seemed the poor opera company to me until the prima donna appeared & spoke. Presently she uttered cries of passion and the mimic scene becomes instantly real & vies at once with whatever is human & heroic. ↑I have recorded an action p. 59↓[.] [128]

[61] The lady told me that she had never seen heroic manners. I think she has, in fragments, or the word would not be significant to her. I know them well yet am the least heroic of persons & I see well that my types of them are not one but many. Murat, Wordsworth. Sweet tempered ability & a scientific estimate of ↑popular↓ opinion, are essential.

The law of communication is this: Here am I a complex human being — Welcome to me all creatures; Welcome each of you to your part in me; St Paul to his; the eagle to his; the horse & the bat to theirs.[129]

Vivian Gray is a bible to a class of young persons.

5 May.[130] It is curious to observe how strangely experience becomes thought or life, truth. The conversion is hourly going on. Will & Necessity, or, if you please character & condition beget an act. It is a

[128] This paragraph, struck through in pencil with a vertical use mark, is used in "Being and Seeming," *Lectures*, II, 308–309.

[129] This paragraph, struck through in pencil with a vertical use mark, is used in "The Heart," *Lectures*, II, 291.

[130] Note also the addition to p. [36] above, made as of "May 5".

part of life & remains for a time immersed in our unconscious life being more or less a source of pleasure & pain. In some intellectual hour it detaches itself like a ⟨fr⟩ ripe fruit from the life to become a treasure of the mind. Instantly it is raised & transfigured. The corruptible has put on incorruption.[131] Always now it is an object of beauty however base its origin & neighborhood. But what is strange is the impossibility of antedating this act. In its grub state it cannot fly, it cannot shine, it is a loathsome maggot. But suddenly, without observation, the selfsame thing unfurls beautiful [62] wings and is an angel of wisdom. So is there no fact, no event, how intimate[,] how great soever in our history, which shall not sooner or later lose its adhesive inert form, & astonish & rejoice us by soaring from our body into the Empyrean. Cradle & infancy, school & playground, the fear of boys & dogs, the love of little maids & berries, & many another once absorbing fact are gone already; friend & relative, party & profession, Boston & Concord, country, wife, child, & world must also soar & sing.[132]

To make the Omnipresence of God a fact & not a name to the mind, we must look at spiritual laws. The history of the mind is a constant creation. It sleeps on a past law no moment. Let me make a few notes towards a Report of the decisions of this Supreme Court. It is strange that I find no such attempt in all the ages as a digest or even a catalogue of ⟨S⟩ them.

[63] 6 May. I see with joy the visits of heat & moisture to my trees & please myself with this new property. I strangely mix myself with Nature & the Universal God works, buds, & blooms in my ↑grove &↓ parterre. I seem to myself an enchanter who by some rune or dumb gesture compels the service of superior beings. But the instant I separate my *own* from the tree & the potato field, it loses this piquancy. I presently see that I also am but an instrument like the tree, a reagent. The tree was to grow; I was to transplant & water it, not for me, not for it, but for all.[133]

---

[131] Cf. I Cor. 15:53.

[132] This paragraph, struck through in ink with a vertical use mark, is used in "The American Scholar," *W*, I, 96–97.

[133] "I strangely mix . . . all." is struck through in pencil with a diagonal use mark.

⟨The⟩ A lesson learned late in life is that every line that one can draw on paper has expression. A boy making his first attempts at drawing thinks a neck is a neck, and that there is one ↑right↓ way for that part to be sketched. By & by he learns that every variation of the outline has meaning.[134]

It occurred today how slowly we learn to trust ourselves as adepts of the common Nature. When a fashionable man, when a great judge or Engineer performs a charity, it gives us pause, it seems strange & admirable, we fear it will not last. Yet the same thing would appear not strange in me but quite natural. Slowly ⟨m⟩I learn with amazement that in my wildest dream, in my softest emotion, in my tear of contrition, I but repeat moment for moment the impulses [64] & ⟨thoughts⟩ ↑experience↓ of the fashionist, the buccaneer, the slave, or whatever other Variety may be of the generic man.

The words "I am on the eve of a revelation," & such like, when applied to the influx of truth in ordinary life, sound sad & insane in my ear.[135]

Sad is this continual postponement of life. I refuse sympathy & intimacy with people as if in view of some better sympathy & intimacy to come. But whence & when? I am already thirtyfour years old. Already my friends & fellow workers are dying from me. Scarcely can I say that I see any new men or women approaching me; I am too old to regard fashion; too old to expect patronage of any greater or more powerful. Let me suck the sweetness of those affections & consuetudes that grow near me, — that the Divine Providence offers me. These old shoes are easy to the feet.[136] But no, not for mine, if they have an ill savor. I was made a hermit & am content with my lot. I pluck golden fruit from rare meetings with wise men. I can well

---

[134] This paragraph, struck through in pencil with a diagonal use mark and in ink with a vertical use mark, is used in "The Eye and Ear," *Lectures*, II, 264–265.

[135] This sentence is used in "Culture," *W*, VI, 133.

[136] "Sad is this . . . feet.", struck through in pencil with a diagonal use mark and in ink with a vertical use mark, is used in "Prudence," *Lectures*, II, 321, and "Prudence," *W*, II, 240. For "old shoes" — a phrase of King James I — see *JMN*, IV, 19.

abide alone in the intervals, and the fruit of my own tree shall have a better flavor.

[65] 7 May. The Sabbath reminds me of an advantage which education may give[,] namely a normal piety[,] a certain levitical education which only rarely devout genius could countervail. I cannot hear the young men whose theological instruction is exclusively owed to Cambridge & to public institution, without feeling how much happier was my star which rained on me ⟨ancestral⟩ influences of ancestral religion. The depth of the religious sentiment which I knew in my Aunt Mary imbuing all her genius & derived to her from such hoarded family traditions[,] from so many godly lives & godly deaths of sainted kindred at Concord, Malden, York, was itself a⟨n⟩ culture[,] an education. I heard with awe her tales of the pale stranger who at the time her grandfather lay on his death bed tapped at the window & asked to come in. The dying man said, 'Open the door;' but the timid family did not; & ⟨pres⟩ immediately he breathed his last, & they said one to another It was the angel of death. Another of her ancestors when near his end had lost the power of speech & his minister came to him & said, 'If the Lord Christ is with you, hold up your hand'; and he stretched up both hands & died. With these I heard the anecdotes of the charities of Father Moody & his commanding administration of his holy office. When the offended parishioners would rise to go out of the church he cried "Come back, you graceless sinner, come [66] back!" And when his parishioners ventured into the ale house on a Saturday night, the valiant pastor went in, collared them, & dragged them forth & sent them home. Charity then went hand in hand with zeal. They gave alms profusely & the barrel of meal wasted not.[137] Who was it among this venerable line who whilst his house was burning, stood apart with some of his church & sang "There is a house not made with hands." [138] Another was wont to go into the road whenever a traveller past on Sunday & entreat him to tarry with him during holy time, himself furnishing food for man & beast. In my childhood Aunt Mary herself wrote the prayers which first

[137] Cf. I Kings 17:14. "Father Moody" was the Reverend Samuel Moody of York, Maine.
[138] Emerson's great-grandfather, Reverend Joseph Emerson of Malden, who married Samuel Moody's daughter Mary. See *JMN*, III, 352, and n. 6.

my brother William & when he went to college I read aloud morning & evening at the family devotions, & they still sound in my ear with their prophetic & apocalyptic ejaculations.[139] Religion was her occupation, and when years after, I came to write sermons for my own church I could not find any examples or treasuries of piety so high-toned, so profound, or promising such rich influence as my remembrances of her conversation & letters.

This day my boy was baptized in the old church by Dr Ripley. They dressed him in the selfsame robe in which twentyseven years ago my brother Charles was baptised. Lidian has a group of departed Spirits in her eye who hovered [67] around the patriarch & the babe.

↑Where there is no vision, the people perish.↓[140]

⟨I ‖ . . . ‖⟩ I could ill dissemble my impatience at the show of instruction without one single real & penetrating word. Here is a young man who has not yet learned the capital secret of his profession namely to convert life into truth. Not one single fact in all his experience has he yet imported into his doctrine. & there he stands pitiable & magisterial, & without nausea reads page after page of mouth-filling words & seems to himself to be doing a deed. This man has ploughed & rode & talked & bought & sold[.] He has read books, & eaten & drunk; his cow calves; his bull genders; he smiles & suffers & loves. ↑See p. 68↓ Yet, all this experience is still aloof from his intellect; he has not converted one jot of it all into wisdom.[141] I thought we might well propose that as the end of education to teach the pupil the symbolical character of life. Let him know that a people can well afford to settle large incomes on a man that he may marry, buy, & sell and administer his own goods if the practical lesson that he thus learns he can translate into general terms & yield them its poetry from week to week. Truly they will find their account in it. It would elevate their life also which is contemporary & homogeneous & that

---

[139] "The Sabbath reminds . . . ejaculations." is struck through in pencil on pp. [65] and [66] with first a diagonal and then a vertical use mark.

[140] Prov. 29:18. Quoted in "The Method of Nature," *W*, I, 191.

[141] "I could ill . . . wisdom.", struck through in ink with a vertical use mark, is used in the Divinity School Address, *W*, I, 138.

is what the priest is for.[142] Mr Flint & Mr Buttrick can well afford to come to church to hear Edward Taylor, & will feel that it is [68][143] the best day in the week and that they are abler & nobler men for the hearing; but sooner or later they must find out their mistake, & with indignation, when they have nothing for their time & their pew-tax but a houseful of words. Indeed[,] indeed the bitter rebuke which such a preacher has is the attentive face & drinking ear of the poor farmer.

Turns   "Each dog"[144]

One thing experience teaches, the variety of men. The recluse thinks of men as having his manner or not having his manner; and as having degrees of it, more & less. But when he comes into a public assembly then he sees with surprise that men have very different manners from his own & in their way admirable.[145]

Moreover perhaps he thinks he has got the whole secret of manner when he has learned that disengaged manners are commanding. But if he see J. Q Adams then he learns that a man may have extreme irritability of face, voice, & bearing & yet underneath so puissant a will as to lose no advantage thereby. A steady mind[,] a believing mind wins the world.[146]

———

↑See p ⟨7⟩67. — All this has my man done yet was there not a surmise[,] a hint in all the discourse that he had ever lived at all. Not one line did he draw out of real history.↓[147]

———

[69] ↑8 May↓. It ought to have been more distinctly stated in "Nature" than it is that life is our inexhaustible treasure of language

[142] "Where there is . . . priest is for." is used in Address on Education, *Lectures,* II, 202–203.
[143] "Nature will not drill." is written above "day in the week" at the top of the page.
[144] Cf. "Every dog has his day, and every man his hour," in Fielding, *Select Proverbs,* 1825, p. 26.
[145] This paragraph, struck through in ink with a diagonal use mark, is used in "Nominalist and Realist," *W,* III, 238.
[146] This paragraph is used in "Behavior," *W,* VI, 175–176.
[147] This paragraph, struck through in ink with a vertical use mark, is used in the Divinity School Address, *W,* I, 138.

for thought. Years are well spent in the country in country labors, in towns, in the insight into trades & manufactures, in intimate intercourse with many men & women, in science, in art, to the one end of mastering in all their facts a language by which to illustrate & speak out our emotions & perceptions. I learn immediately from any speaker how much he has really learned, through the poverty or the splendor of his speech.

↑⟨Nature⟩ My garden is my dictionary.↓[148]

There are three degrees of proficiency in this lesson of life. The one class live to the utility of the symbol as the majority of men do, regarding health & wealth as the chief good. Another class live above this mark, to the beauty of the symbol; as the poet & artist, and the Sensual school in philosophy. A third class live above the beauty of the symbol, to the beauty of the thing signified; and these are wise men. The first ⟨is the⟩ class have common sense; the second, taste; and the third spiritual perception.

I see in society the neophytes of all these classes, the class especially of ⟨thos⟩ young men who in their best knowledge of the sign have a misgiving[n] that there is yet an unattained substance & they grope & sigh & aspire long in dissatisfaction, the sand-blind adorers of the symbol meantime chirping & scoffing & trampling them down. I see moreover that the perfect man — one to a millenium, — if so many, traverses the whole scale & sees & enjoys the symbol solidly; then also has a clear eye for its beauty; & lastly wears it lightly as a robe which he can easily throw off, for he sees the [70] reality & divine splendor of the inmost nature bursting through each chink & cranny.[149] ↑(See p 81)↓

Dr R[ipley]. has lived so long that he says things every now & then, with the most laudable impatience; but he idealizes nothing: out he comes with literal facts & does not dream among words. Homely & dry his things are because they ⟨fr⟩ are traditions accepted

[148] "It ought to . . . dictionary.", struck through in ink with a vertical use mark, is used in "The American Scholar," *W*, I, 69.

[149] This and the preceding paragraph, struck through in ink on p. [69] with a diagonal use mark, are used in "Prudence," *Lectures*, II, 311–312, and "Prudence," *W*, II, 222–223.

for nature & facts out of life crude & unassimilated[,] in short just as he found them. But you do not feel cheated & ⟨inane⟩ empty as when fed by the grammarians.

C.C.E. said when his friend was engaged, "At such times it is a comfort to feel that you are something to offer."

↑May 9↓. Two babies Willie & Wallie and excellent cousins they prove. Willie conscious of seniority in all the dignity of twentytwo months; Wallie ↑six & a fortnight↓ any thing but indifferent to his handsome cousin, whom he regards as a capital plaything, & his hair is divine to pull. So says Wallie's mamma, & moreover that he accounts her a porridgepot, & papa a prime horse.

Yesterday in the woods I followed the fine humble bee with rhymes & fancies fine.[150]

May 14. Harder times. Two days since the suspension of specie payments by the [New York &] Boston Banks. William and his wife & child have spent a little time with us. F.H.Hedge was here ⟨to⟩ day before yesterday. We walked in the wood & sat down there to discuss why I was I. Yesterday came Dr Channing & Mr Jonathan [71] Phillips & honored our house with a call. But sages of the crowd are like kings so environed with deference & ceremony, that a call like this gives no true word for the mind & heart.
The true medicine for hard times seems to be sleep. Use so much bodily labor as shall ensure sleep, then you arise refreshed and in good spirits and in Hope. That have I this morn. Yesterday afternoon I stirred the earth about my shrubs & trees & quarreled with the piper-grass and now I have slept, & no longer am morose ⟨with⟩ nor feel twitchings in the muscles of my face when a visiter is by. The humblebee & the pine warbler seem to me the proper objects of attention in these disastrous times*. I am less inclined to ethics, to history, to aught wise & grave & practick, & feel a new joy in nature. I am glad it is not my duty to preach these few sundays & I would

* The hollowness so sad we feel after too much talking is an expressive hint[.]

[150] See Emerson's poem "The Humble-Bee," W, IX, 38–40.

invite the sufferers by this screwing panic to recover peace through these fantastic amusements during the tornado.

Our age is ocular.

[72] May 19. Yesterday Alcott left me after three days spent here. I had "lain down a man & waked up a bruise" by reason of a bad cold, & was lumpish, tardy, & cold. Yet could I see plainly that I conversed with the most extraordinary man and the highest genius of the time. He is a Man. He is erect: he sees: let who ever be overthrown or parasitic or blind. Life he would have & enact, & not nestle into any cast off shell & form of the old time and now proposes to preach to the people or to take his staff & walk through the country conversing with the school teachers, & holding conversations in the villages. And so he ought to ⟨off⟩ go publishing through the land his gospel like them of old time. Wonderful is his vision. The steadiness & scope of his eye at once rebukes all before it, and we little men creep about ashamed. It is amusing even to see how this great visual orb rolls round upon object after object, & threatens them all with annihilation, seemeth to wither & scorch.

Coldly he asks 'whether Milton is to continue to meet the wants of the mind?' & so Bacon, & so of all.

He is, to be sure, monotonous: you may say, one gets tired of the uniformity, — he will not be amused, he never cares for the pleasant side of things, but always truth & their origin he seeketh after.

[73] [151] Is it not pathetic that the action of men on men is so partial? We never touch but at points. The most that I can have or be to my fellow man, is it the reading of his book, or the hearing of his project in conversation? I approach some Carlyle with desire & joy. I am led on from month to month with an expectation of some total embrace & oneness ⟨of⟩ with a noble mind, & learn at last that it is only so feeble & remote & hiant action as reading a Mirabeau or a Diderot paper, & a few the like. This is all that can be looked for. More we shall not be to each other. Baulked soul! It is not that the

[151] "Society an imperfect Union." is written above "Is it not pathetic" at the top of the page.

sea & poverty & pursuit separate us. Here is Alcott by my door, —
yet is the union more profound? No, the Sea, vocation, poverty, are
seeming fences, but Man is insular, and cannot be touched. Every
man is an infinitely repellent orb, & holds his individual being on that
condition.[152]

Conversation among the witty & well-informed hops about from
spot to spot around the surface of life. Like the bird, we peck at this
moss, & that bud, & that leaf upon the bark & the interior of the tree
seems to us inedible, stringy, uniform, uninteresting. But the philosopher comes like the soul of vegetation itself & manifests great
indifference at these excrescences, & the pretty colors & pretty organizations we magnify, & insists upon entering the sap that bubbles[n]
[74][153] up from the root & accompanying it upward & outward, forms
the ⟨the⟩ bough, the bud, the leaf, the excrements & configur⟨ing⟩es
the rough rind as a mere superficial effect of its interior arrangements.[154]

George Bradford compares the happiness of Gore R[ipley].[155]
riding the horse to plow, with boys in Boston of his age, who are too
old to play on the common, and who can only dress & fix straps to their
pantaloons.

Men are continually separating & not nearing by acquaintance.
⟨o⟩Once Dr Channing filled our sky. Now we become so conscious of
his limits & of the difficulty attending any effort to show him our
point of view, that we doubt if it be worth while. Best amputate. Then
we come to speak with those who most fully accord in life & doctrine
with ourselves, and lo! what mountains high & rivers wide. How still
the word is to seek which can like a ferryman transport either into
the point of view of the other. Invisible repulsions take effect also.
The conversation is tentative, groping, only partially successful; and

[152] This paragraph, struck through in pencil with a diagonal use mark, is used
in "The Heart," *Lectures*, II, 279.
    [153] "Association separates" is written above "up from the" at the top of the page.
    [154] This paragraph, struck through in pencil on p. [73] with a diagonal use
mark, is used in "The Heart," *Lectures*, II, 292.
    [155] Christopher Gore Ripley, son of Reverend Samuel Ripley.

although real gratification arises out of it, both parties are relieved by solitude. I more. I hug the absolute being unbroken[,] undefined of my desart.[156]

[75][157] I bask in beauty. But I may be ⟨made⟩ inspired with a greater ambition & taught to conquer in my own person every calamity by understanding it & its cause. When I see an evil, it is unmanly to hide my head in the flowering bushes & say I will hunt the humble bee & behold the stars & leave this sorrow for those whom it concerns. I ought rather to live towards it, grasping firm in one hand the hand of the Invisible Guide until gradually a perfect insight of the disaster is an everlasting deliverance from its fear.[158]

Yes it is true there are no men. Men hang upon things. They are overcrowed by their own creation. A man is not able to subdue the world. He is a Greek grammar. He is a money machine. He is an appendage to a great fortune, or to a legislative majority or to the Massachusetts Revised Statutes or to some barking & bellowing Institution, Association, or Church. But the deep & high & entire man, not parasitic upon time & space, upon traditions, upon his senses, or his organs, but who utters out of a central hope an eternal voice of Sovereignty, we are not, & when he comes, we hoot at him. Behold this dreamer cometh! [159]

⟨Where⟩ It is very true that Society presents fair game to the censure of the Ideal⟨ist⟩ Reformer. Harvard College, the Latin Schools, the Schools everywhere, the city life, the devotion of human life to trade — these are sorry [76] things & are tenderly treated by us only because we see no better actual life. We contrast so vast an Actual with the remote unembodied Ideal, & despair. We say it is impossible that we should realize our ideal & frigidly dismiss the Reformer. But if it indeed be that God ⟨h⟩opens himself so ⟨m⟩deeply

---

[156] This paragraph is struck through in pencil with two broken diagonal use marks. All but the last two sentences are used in "The Heart," *Lectures*, II, 279–280.

[157] "No men." is written above "beauty. But" at the top of the page.

[158] This paragraph is struck through in ink with a vertical use mark. Cf. "The American Scholar," *W*, I, 104.

[159] "Behold . . . cometh!": Gen. 37:19. This paragraph is used in Address on Education, *Lectures*, II, 196–197.

It is essential to a true theory of nature & man, that it
should contain somewhat progressive, should ascribe free
dom to the will, or benevolent designs to the Deity.
And the effect of the ideal theory truly seen is this;
Nature is not stable but fluid. Spirit alters, moulds,
makes it. The immobility or bruteness of nature
is the absence of spirit; to pure spirit it is fluid,
it is volatile, it is obedient. Believe that the
world exists for you. for you is the phenomenon perfect
what we are, that only we see. All that Adam
had, all that Caesar could, you have & can do.
Adam called it the earth, Caesar called life Rome;
you perhaps call it a cobler's trade, yet line for
line & point for point, you have the whole circle.
As fast as your spirit quits its earth, disagreeable
appearances, prisons, spiders, snakes, pests, madhouses,
vanish. they are temporary & shall be no more seen
The sordor & filths of nature, the sun shall dry
up & the wind exhale. As before
the Summer, the snow banks melt and the
face of the earth becomes green so shall
the spirit shall create its ornament
along its path & carry with it the beauty it
visits & the forms which enchant it. creates in
telligent faces & warm hearts and sweet discourse
around its way, until evil is no more seen
This kingdom of man over nature which
shall not come with observation, a dominion
in such as now is beyond his dream of God,
he shall enter without more wonder than
the blind man feels who is gradually
restored to perfect sight.

Plate I   Journal B, page 215   Text, pages 182–183
Draft of the concluding paragraph of Nature

332 Dec. 10. Pleasant walk yesterday, the most pleasant-
of days. At Walden Pond, I found a new musical
instrument which I call the ice-harp. A thin
coat of ice covered a part of the pond, but melted
around the edge of the shore. I threw a stone
upon the ice which rebounded with a shrill
sound, & falling again & again, repeated
the note with pleasing modulation.
I was so taken with the music that I threw
down my stick & spent twenty minutes in
throwing stones single or in handfuls on
this crystal drum.

At night, with other friends came Shack-
ford with a good heart & inquisitive mind. He broached
the question, out of Brownson's book, of the
positiveness or entity of moral evil; which I
gladly & strenuously denied, — as a Corollary
to my last night's discourse on the Unity
of Mind 'There is one mind in many individuals'.
I maintained that evil is merely privative
not absolute. It is like Cold the privation of heat.
All evil is death. Benevolence is absolute &
real. So much benevolence & justice as a
man hath, so much life hath he. For all
things proceed out of this same spirit
whose attributes are love justice &c
& all things conspire with them. Whilst
a man seeks these ends he is strong by
the whole strength of the Universe. In so
far as he roves from these ends, he bereaves
himself of power, of auxiliaries; his being
shrinks out of all remote channels &
he disuniversalizes & individualizes himself
& becomes all the time less & less — a mote,
a point. Until absolute badness

Plate II   Journal B, page 332   Text, pages 265–266
Genesis of a passage in the Divinity School Address

these hard times. Yet ~~I know~~ how can I lament, when I see the resources of this Continent in which three months will anywhere ~~yet~~ yield a crop of wheat or potatoes. On the bosom of this vast plenty, the blight of trade & manufactures seems to me a momentary mischance.

26 May. Who shall define to me an Individual? I behold with awe & delight many illustrations of the One Universal Mind. I see my being imbedded in it. As a plant in the earth so I grow in God. I am only a form of him. He is the soul of me. I can even with a mountainous aspiring say, I am God, by transferring my me out of the flimsy & unclean precincts of my body, my fortunes, my private will, & meekly retiring upon the holy austerities of the Just & the loving — upon the foundations of Nature. That thin & difficult ether, I also can breathe. The mortal lungs & nostrils burst & shrivel, but the soul itself needeth no organs it is all element & all organ. Yet why not always so? How came the Individual thus accomplished to parricide thus murderously inclined ever to traverse & kill the divine life. Oh wicked Manichee! Into that dim problem I cannot enter. A believer in Unity, a seer of Unity, I yet behold two. Whilst I feel myself in sympathy with Nature & rejoice with ~~divine~~ greatly beating heart in the course of Justice & Benevolence overpowering me, I yet find little access to this Me of Me. I fear what shall befal: I am not enough a party to the Great Order as to be tranquil. I hope & I fear, I do not see: At one time, I am a Doer. A divine life I create scenes & persons around & for me & unfold my thought by a perpetual successive projection. At least I so say, I so feel. But presently I return to the habitual attitude of suffering.

Plate III   Journal C, page 84   Text, pages 336–337
". . . a seer of Unity, I yet behold two."

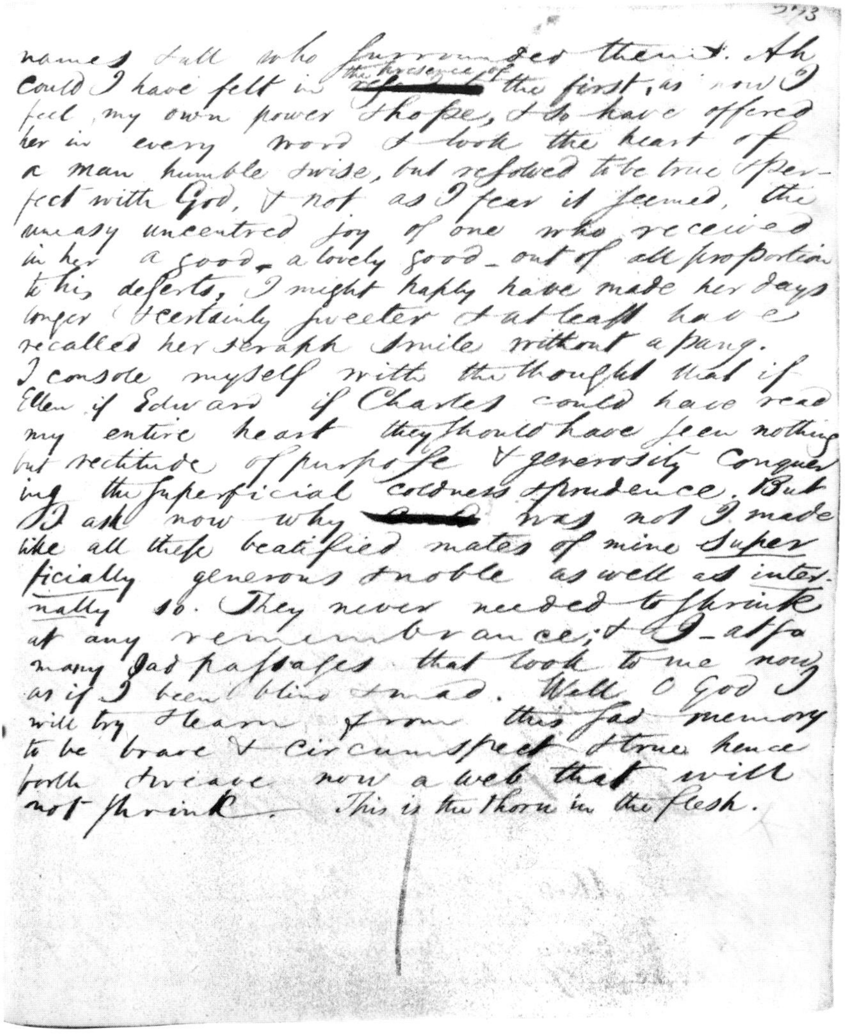

273

names all who surround them. Ah could I have felt in the presence of the first, as now I feel, my own power & hopes, & to have offered her in every word & look the heart of a man humble & wise, but resolved to be true & perfect with God, & not as I fear it seemed, the uneasy uncentred joy of one who received in her a good, a lovely good, out of all proportion to his deserts, I might haply have made her days longer & certainly sweeter & at least have recalled her seraph smile without a pang. I console myself with the thought that if Ellen, if Edward, if Charles could have read my entire heart they should have seen nothing but rectitude of purpose & generosity conquering the superficial coldness & prudence. But I ask now why ——— was not I made like all these beatified mates of mine superficially generous & noble as well as internally so. They never needed to shrink at any remembrance, & I — alas a many sad passages that look to me now as if I been blind & mad. Well O God I will try & learn from this sad memory to be brave & circumspect & true hence forth & weave now a web that will not shrink. This is the thorn in the flesh.

Plate IV   Journal C, page 273   *Text, page 456*
Self-criticism: "This is the thorn in the flesh."

in one mind as that his ⟨deep⟩ ↑far↓ insight sees the Whole Actual as somewhat ephemeral & caducous he has ⟨every⟩ right to stand up & testify & predict the downfal of the great Babylon, and we ought instantly to be inspired with his soul & open our minds to him until we see. Then has Babylon the great fallen.

Symbols on symbols, riddles, phantoms, lo! how they rise. Idealism may be held. Steadily ⟨as Berkeley⟩ & ethically. I see a certain obstruction as a depreciation of my property. The Creative Me is then to energize & countercreate which it does in certain wills & affections whose external signs and termini are lucrative labors, property stocks, & the like[.] ↑See D p 322↓ [160]

May 20. The man of strong Understanding always acts unfavorably upon the Man of Reason, disconcerts, and makes him less than he is.

Is the world sick? Bankruptcy in England & America: Tardy rainy season; snow in France; plague in Asia & Africa; these are the morning's news[.]

[77] Ill nature, peevishness, is a cutaneous matter. It is seated no deeper than Temperament & inflamed or allayed by Weather, quantity of food, of sleep, and the news. ↑See p. 166↓

21 May. He judgeth every man, yet is judged of no man.[161]

I see a good in such emphatic & universal calamity as the times bring, that they dissatisfy me with society. Under common burdens we say there is much virtue in the world & what evil coexists is inevitable. I am not aroused to say, 'I have sinned; I am in the gall of bitterness, & bond of iniquity';[162] but when these full measures come, it then stands confessed — Society has played out its last stake; it is checkmated. Young men have no hope. Adults stand like daylaborers idle

---

[160] Journal D will be printed in *JMN*, VII.
[161] Cf. I Cor. 2:15.
[162] Cf. Acts 8:23.

in the streets. None calleth us to labor. The old wear no crown of warm light on their grey hairs.[163] The present generation is bankrupt of principles & hope, as of property. I see man is not what man should be. He is the treadle of a wheel. He is a tassel at the apron string of Society. He is a money chest.[164] He is the servant of his belly.[165] This is the causal bankruptcy — this the cruel oppression that the ideal should serve the actual; that the head should serve the feet. Then first I am forced to inquire if the Ideal might not also be tried. Is it to be taken for granted that it is impracticable? Behold the boasted world has come to nothing. Prudence itself is at her wits' end. [78] Pride, and Thrift, & Expediency, who jeered and chirped and were so well pleased with themselves and made merry with the dream as they termed it of philosophy & love[:] Behold they are all flat and here is the Soul erect and Unconquered still. What answer is it ⟨to⟩ now to say — it has always been so. — I acknowledge that as far back as I can see the winding procession of humanity the⟨y⟩ marchers are lame & blind & deaf; but, to the soul, that whole past is but the finite series in its infinite scope. Deteriorating ever and now desperate. Let me begin anew. Let me teach the finite to know its Master. Let me ascend above my fate and work down upon my world.

↑May 22.↓ Let us not sit like snarling dogs ⟨snapping at those who work ill⟩ working not at all, but snapping at those who work ill.

I told the Sunday School yesterday that the misfortunes of the adult generation give a new interest to childhood as born to a new state of things[,] born to better fortunes. Let them learn that what we live to know is Ourselves. That out of every school-lesson, game, errand, friendship, quarrel, they come forth different persons from that they went in, with a new faculty unlocked. So let them behold themselves and their exercises with awe & hope.

[79] The black times have a great scientific value. It is an epoch so critical a philosopher would not miss. As I would willingly carry

---

[163] "Young men . . . hairs." is used in Address on Education, *Lectures*, II, 198.
[164] "He is the treadle . . . chest." is used in Address on Education, *Lectures*, II, 196.
[165] Cf. Rom. 16:18.

myself to be played upon at Faneuil Hall by the stormy winds & strong fingers of the enraged Boston so is this era more rich in the central tones than many languid centuries. What was, ever since my memory, solid continent, now yawns apart and discloses its composition and genesis. I learn geology the morning after an earthquake. I learn fast on the ghastly diagrams of the cloven mountain & upheaved plain and the ⟨bare bed⟩ ↑dry bottom↓ of the Sea. The roots of orchards and the cellars of palaces and the cornerstones of cities are dragged into melancholy sunshine. I see the natural fracture of the stone. I see the tearing of the tree & learn its fibre & its rooting. The Artificial is rent from the eternal.[166]

The world has failed. The pretended teachers who have scoffed at the Idealist, have failed utterly. The very adulation they offer to the name of Christ, the epithets with which they encumber his name, the ragged half screaming bass with which they deepen the sentences of sermons on purity, martyrdom, & spiritual life, do preach their hollowness & recoil upon them. They lash themselves with their satire.

[80] The kingdom of the involuntary, of the not me. See they not how when the unfit guest comes in, the master of the house goes out? He is not at home, he cannot be at home whilst the guest stays. His body is there and a singular inconvenience to ⟨g⟩ any family. Men & women should not contend with the laws of human nature. They sit at one board, but a cloud falleth upon their faces, that hinders them from seeing one another.

People are stung by a pregnant saying and will continue to repeat it without seeing its meaning. I said 'If you sleep, you show character' — ⟨and⟩ and the young girls asked what it could mean. I will tell you. You think that because you have spoken nothing when others spoke and have given no opinion upon the times, upon Wilhelm Meister, upon Abolition, upon Harvard College, that your

---

[166] "The black times . . . of the Sea." is used in "Considerations by the Way," *W*, VI, 262. "I learn geology . . . eternal." is used in Address on Education, *Lectures*, II, 196.

verdict is still expected with curiosity as a reserved wisdom. Far otherwise; it is known that you have no opinion: You are measured by your silence & found wanting. You have no oracle to utter, & your fellowmen have learned that you cannot help them; for oracles speak. Doth not wisdom cry & understanding put forth her voice[?] [167]

Among provocatives, the next best thing to good preaching is bad preaching. I have even more thoughts during or enduring it than at other times.

[81] I wrote above that life wants worthy objects: the game is not worth the candle: It is not that ↑not↓ I, — it is that *nobody* employs it well. The ⟨earth⟩ land stinks with suicide.

It is easy for the philosophic class to be poor. Poverty is their ornament. [168] They wear with it a sort of ⟨pride⟩ ⟨prote⟩ silent protest & challenge admiration. They need not immerse themselves in sense[;] they ⟨contemn the knowledge⟩ ↑scorn to knit their brows on the merits↓ of a sauce & a soup because they are haunted with the thought that matter has higher uses, namely, its poetical use, or language. But not so easy is it to the unphilosophical class to be poor. My ⟨neighbor⟩ ↑friend↓ has no books, no conversation, no fine insight, in short no certificate that he is a↑ny↓ better man than his thousand neighbors except his great house & marble mantelpieces ↑his ↑superb↓ centre table and the portfolio of engravings lying on it.↓ These realize to him his inward merit. These are tough medals of his honesty & labor & the regard of fellow men. It is very cruel of you to insist because you can very well forego them that he shall.

I wrote p. 70 that men classed themselves by their perception of the symbolical character of life. As a steppingstone to this perception they have certain translations to be made intellectually in their common life. Thus every object of convenience whether food or dress or utensil, is readily & habitually considered as property & immedi-

---

[167] "Doth not . . . voice[?]": Prov. 8:1. "You think that . . . voice", struck through in ink with a vertical use mark, is used in "Spiritual Laws," *W*, II, 156.
[168] Cf. p. [29] above: "Poverty is the ornament of a philosopher."

ately appraised in money. And the master of a family learns to translate every article that passes before him as household commodity into
a money value which he measures ⟨in⟩ a proportion ⁿ [82]¹⁶⁹ to ⟨his⟩
the income of his estate.

May 23. You may regret calamities if you can thereby help the sufferer, but if you cannot, mind your own business. Then instantly you
are comforted, then instantly the evil begins to be repaired.

May 25. "My dear Sir, clear your mind of cant," said Dr Johnson.¹⁷⁰
Wordsworth, whom I read last night, is garrulous & weak often, but
quite free from cant. I think I could easily make a small selection
from his volumes which should contain all their poetry. It would
take Fidelity, Tintern Abbey, Cumberland Beggar, Ode to Duty,
↑September, The force of prayer, Lycoris, Lines on the death of Fox,
Dion, Happy Warrior, Laodamia, the Ode↓

Philosophical poetry. The extract at the close of the New volume[.] ¹⁷¹

[83] There is still the Universal beyond and above. There is
still room to say "What light shall be vouchsafed" as A[lcott]. writes
me today.¹⁷² I am never so much party as I am receiver.

Composition
Let not a man decline being an artist under any greenhorn notion
of ⟨m⟩ intermeddling with sacred thought. It is surely foolish to
adhere rigidly to the order of time in putting down one's thoughts
& ↑to↓ neglect⟨ing⟩ the order of thought. I put like things together.
↑See D p 325↓

---

¹⁶⁹ "Wordsworth" is written above "to ⟨his⟩" at the top of the page.
¹⁷⁰ In conversation with Boswell, May 15, 1783. See *Boswell's Life of Johnson*,
ed. G. B. Hill, revised and enlarged edition by L. F. Powell, 6 vols. (Oxford, 1934),
IV, 221.
¹⁷¹ *Yarrow Revisited*, 1835; see Journal B, p. [182].
¹⁷² In his letter of May 24, 1837 (Harvard College Library), Alcott had written
of his "waiting for light as this shall be vouchsafed."

Let a man be a guest in his own house.[173] Let him be a spectator of his own life. Let him heal himself not by drugs but by sleep.[174] Let him not only do but be. Let him not vaticinate but hear. Let him bask in beauty [175] & not always carry on a farm. I wrote at sea, Jan. 1833, "I am well pleased, yet I have nothing to record; I have read little; I have done nothing. What then? Need we be such barren dogs that the whole beauty of heaven, the main, & man, cannot entertain us unless we too must needs hold a candle & daub God's world with a smutch of our own insignificance? Not I, for one. I will be pleased though I do not deserve it. &c." [176]

A young man told Edmund Hosmer that he had come for the honeysuckles because his father liked them but for his own part he would rather see a hill of potatoes. Hillman [177] could not see in the yellow warbler on the fir tree, any more beauty than in a rat.

[84][178] Still hard times. Yet ⟨I lament⟩ how can I lament, when I see the resources of this continent in which three months will anywhere ⟨fur⟩ yield a crop of wheat or potatoes. On the bosom of this vast plenty, the blight of trade & manufactures seems to me a momentary mischance.

26 May. Who shall define to me an Individual? I behold with awe & delight many illustrations of the One Universal Mind. I see my being imbedded in it. As a plant in the earth so I grow in God. I am only a form of him. He is the soul of Me. I can even with a mountainous aspiring say, *I am God*, by transferring my *Me* out of the flimsy & unclean precincts of my body, my fortunes, my private will, & meekly retiring upon the holy austerities of the Just & the Loving — upon the secret fountains of Nature. That thin & difficult ether, I also can

---

[173] Cf. p. [10] above: "Let a man behave in his own house as a guest."

[174] Cf. p. [71] above: "The true medicine for hard times seems to be sleep."

[175] Cf. p. [75] above: "I bask in beauty."

[176] See *JMN*, IV, 105. Most of the foregoing paragraph (from "vaticinate but hear") is struck through in pencil with a diagonal use mark; the entire paragraph is used in "Being and Seeming," *Lectures*, II, 303.

[177] The late George Sampson's young son Hillman, who lived for a short time with the Emersons (*J*, IV, 247, n. 1).

[178] "The times.   The Individual" is written above "hard times . . . how can" at the top of the page. See Plate III.

breathe. The mortal lungs & nostrils ⟨die⟩ burst & shrivel, but the soul itself needeth no organs [—] it is all element & all organ. Yet why not always so? How came the Individual thus ⟨accomplished⟩ ↑armed & impassioned↓ to parricide thus murderously inclined ever to traverse & kill the divine life? Ah wicked Manichee! Into that dim problem I cannot enter. A believer in Unity, a seer of Unity, I yet behold two. Whilst I feel myself in sympathy with Nature & re-joice with ⟨divine⟩ greatly beating heart in the course of Justice & Benevolence overpowering me, I yet find little access to this Me of Me. I fear what shall befal: I am not enough a party to the great order ⟨as⟩ to be tranquil. I hope & I fear[;] I do not see.   At one time, I am a Doer. A divine life I create[,] scenes & persons around & for me[,] & unfold my thought by a perpetual successive projection. At least I so say, I so feel. But presently I return to the habitual atti-tude of suffering.

[85]¹⁷⁹ I behold; I bask in beauty; I await; I wonder; Where is my Godhead now? This is the Male & Female principle in Nature. One Man, male & female created he him.¹⁸⁰ Hard as it is to describe God, it is harder to describe the Individual[.]

A certain wandering light comes to me which I instantly perceive to be the Cause of Causes. It transcends all proving. It is itself the ground of being; and I see that it is not one & I another, ⟨but⟩ but this is the life of my life. That is one fact, then; that in certain moments I have known that I existed directly from God, and am, as it were, his organ. And in my ultimate consciousness Am He. Then, secondly, the ⟨se⟩ contradictory fact is familiar, that I am a surprised spectator & learner of all my life. This is the habitual posture of the mind, — beholding. But whenever the day dawns[,] the great day of truth on the soul, it comes with awful invitation to me to accept it, to blend with its aurora[.]

Cannot I conceive the Universe without a contradiction[?]

[86] Why rake up old MSS to find therein a man's soul? You do not ⟨ex⟩ look for conversation in a corpse.

¹⁷⁹ "The Individual" is written above "I bask in" at the top of the page.
¹⁸⁰ For "bask in beauty" see pp. [75], [83] above; with "male & female created he" cf. Gen. 1:27.

To behold the great in the small, the law in one fact, the vegetation of all the forests on the globe in the sprouting of one acorn, this is the vision of genius.

I hail with glad augury from afar that kindred emotion which the grand work of genius awakens kindred with that awakened by works of Nature. The identity of their origin at the fountain head, I augur with a thrill of joy. Nature is too thin a screen; the glory of the One breaks through everywhere.[181]

To run after one's hat is ludicrous.

May 30. Yesterday I attended in Boston, Hedge's Club. ⟨Twelve⟩ ↑Eleven↓ persons were present, Messrs Francis, Stetson, Ripley, Hedge, Brownson, Alcott, Bartoll, Putnam, Dwight, Osgood, Emerson. We met at Mr Ripley's house[.] [182]

[87] The other day talking with Hedge of the deference paid to talent I said there was a pathetic sentiment in receiving such for it showed how little wit was in the world when an individual pittance is so much accounted. Hedge applied Wordsworth's line

> "Alas the gratitude of man
> Hath oftener left me mourning" [183]

It occurred to me again that another instance of this sentiment was a fact that chanced lately & gave me pain when the good N[ancy].[184] apologised for going out of the front door to church. —

31 May. We have had two peerless summer days after all our cold winds & rains. I have weeded corn & strawberries, intent ⟨to⟩on being fat & have forborne study. The Maryland yellow-throat pipes to me all day long, seeming to say extacy! Extacy! and the Bobo'-lincoln flies & sings.

---

[181] This sentence, followed by "Printed" in blue crayon, is used in "The Preacher," *W*, X, 223.

[182] Of the newcomers, George Putnam was minister of the First Church at Roxbury; Samuel Osgood, a protegé of James Walker, had taken his divinity degree in 1835; John Sullivan Dwight, a divinity school graduate in the following year, later left the ministry and became a noted music teacher and critic.

[183] Cf. Wordsworth, "Simon Lee," ll. 95–96.

[184] The Emersons' housemaid, Deborah Colesworthy, also known as "Nancy" (*L*, II, 131, n. 117).

I read during the heat of the day Beppo & Manfred. What famine of meaning! Manfred is ridiculous for its purposeless raving. Not all the genuine love of nature nor all the skill of utterance can save it. It is all one circular proposition[.]

29 June. Almost one month lost to study by bodily weakness & disease.

Lately I have been reading with much exhilaration Boswell's life of Johnson and was glad I had remembered such a book was. Then by easy steps I came to his Journey to the Western Islands then to the Life of Pope[,] of Cowley. Strong good sense has Johnson but he no philosopher, as likewise he says *philosophical*[n] [88] when he means *scientific*. "Judgement is forced upon us by experience" — "Of his (Pope's) intellectual character, the constituent & fundamental principle was good sense[,] a prompt & intuitive perception of consonance & propriety." — "Of genius that power which constitutes a poet that quality without which judgment is cold & knowledge is inert; that energy which collects, combines, amplifies, & animates, the superiority must," &c. — "The true genius is a mind of large general powers accidentally determined to some particular direction." (Life of Cowley.) — [185]

Such are the Doctor's poor definitions. His best is that of Wit in Cowley's life.[186] Vol 9   p. 20
Yet he is a Muttonhead at a definition. Before Coleridge he would be dumb. Much of his fame is doubtless owing to the fact that he concentrates the traits of the English character. He is a glorified John Bull[,] so downright, so honest, so strongminded & so headstrong.

[89] Εν και παν

"If men be worlds there is in every one
Something to answer in some proportion
All the world's riches: and in good men, this
Virtue, our form's form, & our soul's soul, is."
                    Donne p. 154 [187] ["To Mr. R. W.," ll. 29–32]

[185] See *The Works of Samuel Johnson*, 1806: "Pope," XII, 163, 169; "Cowley," IX, 2.
[186] Johnson terms wit "a kind of *discordia concors*; a combination of dissimilar images, or discovery of occult resemblances in things apparently unlike."
[187] John Donne, *Poems on Several Occasions* (London, 1719).

⟨The person Love to us does fit⟩

"The person Love does to us fit,
Like manna, has the taste of all in it."
                        Cowley ["Resolve to be Beloved," ll. 23–24]

I must quote a few lines from Donne's elegy on Elizabeth
Drury [188]

— "We understood
Her by her sight; her pure & eloquent blood
Spoke in her cheeks & so distinctly wrought
That one might almost say her body thought.[189]
        x x x x   [ll. 243–246] p. 204
What hope have we to know ourselves when we
Know not the least things which for our use be
        x x x x x   [ll. 279–280, p. 205]
Why grass is green & why our blood is red
Are mysteries which none have reach'd unto
In this low form poor soul what wilt thou do[?]
O when wilt thou shake off this pedantry
Of being taught by Sense & Fantasy?
Thou look'st through Spectacles; small things seem great
Below; but up unto the watch tower get
And see all things despoiled of fallacies
Thou shalt not peep thro' lattices of eyes
Nor hear thro' labyrinths of ears nor learn
By circuit or collections to discern
In heaven, thou straight know'st all concerning it
[90]   And what concerns it not, shall straight forget
There thou (but in no other school) may'st be
Perchance as learned & as full as she;
She who all libraries had thoroughly read
At home in her own thoughts; and practised
So much good as would make as many more;"
&c &c &c   [ll. 288–305, p. 205]

"O how feeble is man's power,
That if good fortune fall
Cannot add another hour,
        Nor a last hour recall.
But come bad chance,

[188] Cf. "Of the Progress of the Soul: The Second Anniversary," in *Poems*, 1719.
[189] " 'The person Love . . . thought.", struck through in pencil with a diagonal
use mark, is used in "Love," *W*, II, 186, 184.

>   And we join to it our strength,
>   And we teach it art & length,
>   Itself o'er us to advance." [190]
>   [Cf. "Song" ("Sweetest Love . . ."),
>   ll. 17–24] p. 12
>   x [191] And Virtue's whole sum is but Know and Dare.
>   Donne p. 160 ["To the Countess of Bedford," l. 23]

[91] July 17. Did I read somewhere lately that the sum of Virtue was to know & dare? x The analogy is always perfect between Virtue & genius. One is ethical the other intellectual creation. To create, to create is the proof of a Divine presence. Whoever creates is God, and whatever talents are, ⟨exhibited⟩ if the man create not, the pure efflux of Deity is not his. I read these Donnes & Cowleys & Marvells with the most modern joy; — with a pleasure, I mean, which is in great part caused by the abstraction of all *time* from their verses. What pleases most, is what is next to my Soul; what I also had well nigh thought & said. But for my faith in the oneness of Mind, I should find it necessary to suppose some preestablished harmony, some foresight of souls that were to be & some preparation of stores for their future wants like the fact observed in insects who lay up food before their death for the young grub they shall never see. Here are things just hinted which not one reader in a hundred would take, but which lie so near to the favorite walks of my imagination and [192] to the facts of my experience that I read them with a surprise & delight as if I were finding very good things in ⟨an⟩ a forgotten manuscript of my own.

Creation is always the style & act of these minds. You shall not predict what the poet shall say and ⟨you⟩ whilst ephemeral poetry hath its form, its contents, & almost its phrase out of the books & is only a skilful paraphrase or permutation of good authors, [92][193] in these the good human soul speaks because it has something new to

---

[190] " 'O how feeble . . . advance.' " is struck through in pencil with a diagonal use mark.

[191] See the following entry, p. [91].

[192] "To create . . . imagination and" is struck through in ink with a heavy diagonal use mark. This passage through "shall never see." is used in "The American Scholar," *W*, I, 90, 91–92.

[193] "Be & Seem" is written above "in these the" at the top of the page.

say. It is only another face of the same fact to denominate them sincere. The way to avoid mannerism, the way to write what shall not go out of fashion is to write sincerely[,] to transcribe your doubt or regret or whatever state of mind, without the airs of a fine gentleman or great philosopher, without timidity or display, just as they lie in your consciousness, casting on God the responsibility of the facts. This is to dare.[194]

Cowley & Donne are philosophers. To their insight there is no trifle. But philosophy or insight is so much the habit of their minds that they can hardly see as a poet should the beautiful forms & colors of things,[n] as a chemist may be less alive to the picturesque. At the same time their poems like life afford the chance of richest instruction amid frivolous & familiar objects; the loose & the grand, religion & mirth stand in surprising neighborhood and, like the words of great men, without cant.

[93] Two proverbs I found lately; one; "He who would bring home the wealth of the Indies, must carry out the wealth of the Indies."[195] The other may serve as foil to this magnificent sentence, "Small pot, soon hot." Then again I found in "the Phenix", the Persian sentence, "Remember always that the gods are good" which for genius equals any other golden saying.[196]

[July 18 or 19, 1837.][197] At Plymouth which is one of the most

---

[194] "It is only . . . consciousness," is struck through in pencil with a vertical use mark. "The way to avoid . . . dare." is used in "Being and Seeming," *Lectures*, II, 300–301; "The way to avoid . . . sincerely" is used in "Spiritual Laws," *W*, II, 153.

[195] Cf. "the Spanish proverb" cited by Samuel Johnson in conversation of April 17, 1778; see *Boswell's Life of Johnson*, 1934, II, 302. " 'He who would . . . Indies.' ", struck through in ink with three diagonal use marks, is used in "The American Scholar," *W*, I, 92–93.

[196] Variants of "Small pot, soon hot" occur in both Ray, *A Complete Collection of English Proverbs*, 1817, p. 90, and Fielding, *Select Proverbs*, 1825, p. 20. For "the Persian sentence," cf. *The Phenix; A Collection of Old and Rare Fragments* (New York, 1835), p. 170: "Not knowing that every god is good, you are fruitlessly vigilant."

[197] Like two other entries below, pp. [94] and [96], this paragraph corresponds in phrasing to portions of Emerson's letter of July 18 to Margaret Fuller (*L*, II,

picturesque of towns with its two hundred ponds, its hills and the great sea-line always visible from their tops I enjoyed the repose that seems native to the place. On the shore of Halfway Pond our party ate their gipsy dinner[;] the next day we rolled on the beach in the sun & dipped our spread fingers in the warm sand and peeped after bugs & botanized & rode & walked & so yielded ourselves to the Italian genius of the town[,] the dolce far niente. It is even so that the population of the historical town is on its back presently after dinner[.]

[94] Lidian says that they who have only seen her baby well, do not know but half of his perfections; they do not [know] how patient he is, & suffers just like a little angel⟨.⟩↑: they must see him sick↓.[198] If he should flap his little wings & fly straight up to heaven, he would not find there anything purer than himself. ↑He coos like a pigeon house↓[.] [199]

[July] 19. If you go into the garden & hoe corn or kill bugs on the vines or pick pease, when you come into the house you shall still for some time see simulacra of weeds, vines, or peapods as you see the image of the sun sometime after looking at the sun. Both are disagreeable phenomena, as bad as laughing.

The office of reading is wholly subordinate. I am certainly benefitted by each new mechanical or agricultural process. I see & do, chiefly as it affords me new language, & power of illustration. Precisely so am I gainer by reading history, by knowing the geography & civil annals of Arabia, of Germany; by knowing the systems of philosophy that have flourished under the names of Heraclitus, Zoroaster, Plato, Kant; by knowing the life & conversation of Jesus, of Napoleon, of Shakspear & Dante; by knowing chemistry & commerce; that I get thereby a vocabulary for my ideas. I get no ideas.

87–89), which it possibly antedates; the other entries, however, were evidently written after the letter.

[198] Waldo "caught cold" in Plymouth "& made the end of the visit & the return anxious" (*L*, II, 87).

[199] "He coos like a pigeon house" is used in "Domestic Life," *W*, VII, 104.

There is however one other service of good books. They provoke thoughts[.] [200]

[95] [blank]
[96] G. P. B. thought at Plymouth that the finest gifts for music yet always needed culture.

[July 18, 1837.] [201] I wrote this P.M. to Miss Fuller, that Power & Aim seldom meet in one soul. The wit of our time is sick for an object. Genius is homesick. I cannot but think that our age is somewhat distinguished hereby, for you cannot talk with any intelligent company without finding ↑expressions of↓ regret⟨s⟩ & impatience that attack the whole structure of our Worship, Education, & Social Manners. We all undoubtedly expect that time will bring amelioration but whilst the grass grows, the noble steed starves [202] — we die of the numb palsy.

But Ethics stand when wit fails. Fall back on the simplest sentiment, be heroic, deal justly, walk humbly,[203] & you do something and do invest the capital of your being in a bank that cannot break & that will surely yield ample rents —

[July] 21. Abide by your spontaneous impression with good humoured inflexibility then most when the whole cry of voices is on the other side. ⟨The⟩↑Else↓, tomorrow ⟨the voice of⟩ a stranger will say with masterly good sense precisely what you have thought & felt all the time, & ⟨with⟩ you will be forced to take with shame your own opinion from another.[204]

Courage consists in the conviction that they with whom you contend, are no more than you. If we believed in the existence of strict

[200] Material of this and the preceding paragraph recurs in "The American Scholar," *W*, I, 91, 89.

[201] The letter of "this P.M." to Margaret Fuller (*L*, II, 87–89) is so dated. What follows here is an abridgment.

[202] Cf. Ray, *A Complete Collection of English Proverbs*, 1817, p. 79; see *L*, II, 88.

[203] Cf. Micah 6:8.

[204] This paragraph, struck through in ink with a vertical use mark, is used in "Self-Reliance," *W*, II, 46.

individuals, natures, that is, not radically identical but unknown immeasureable, we should never dare to fight.[205] ↑See p. 119↓

———

[97] Crabbe knew men, but to read one of his poems seems to me all one with taking a dose of medicine.

Aristides was made "General Receiver of Greece" to collect the tribute which each state was to furnish Athens against the Barbarian. "Poor" says Plutarch, "when he set about it, ↑but↓ poorer when he had finished it." [206]

Deb [207] sent out little Faya into the garden to gather gooseberries & bade her pick the reddest & bring them in. Faya did as she was bid; but Deb knit her brows & drove her back to the ⟨garden⟩ bushes and told her to do as she had commanded her. Did I not tell you to pick the reddest? So now Faya gathered all the pink ones,[n] and went in as before. But old Deb sent her again into the garden angrily with the like words. So now she picked those that were red on one side.

We are begirt with spiritual laws[.]

Epitaph

"Behold all you who now pass by!
As you are now, so once was I;
As I am now, so you shall be;
Prepare for death, and follow me."

[98] July 26. Yesterday I went to the Atheneum, & looked thro' Journals & books — for wit, for excitement, — to awake in me the muse. In vain and in vain. And am I yet to learn that the God dwells within? that books are but crutches, the resorts of the feeble & lame, which if used by the strong, weaken the muscular power, & become necessary aids? I return home. Nature still solicits me. Over-

---

[205] This paragraph, struck through in pencil with a vertical use mark, is used in "The Heart," *Lectures*, II, 285.

[206] Cf. "The Life of Aristides," *Plutarch's Lives*, 1822, II, 127. This paragraph is used in "Domestic Life," *W*, VII, 116.

[207] Probably the maid, Deborah Colesworthy.

head the sanctities of the stars shine forevermore & to me also, pouring satire on the pompous ⟨bustle⟩ business of the day which they
close & making the generations of men show slight & evanescent. A
man is but a bug, the earth but a boat a cockle drifting under their
old ⟨lamps⟩ light.

27 July. A letter today from Carlyle rejoiced me. Pleasant would
life be with such companions. But if you cannot have them on good
mutual terms, you cannot have them. If not the Deity but ⟨yo⟩ our
wilfulness hews & shapes the new relations their sweetness escapes as
⟨garden⟩ strawberries lose their flavor by cultivation.[208]

The sublime envelopes us like air enters into every thing &
recommends Peter Howe's employment as much to him as Webster's
or Wordsworth's to them. Who can doubt that the clerk enjoys in the
balance of his ledger the grandeur of the law of Compensation as
really as the poet enjoys the same element in the ebb & flow of the
sea, in the law of light & darkness, heat & cold? [209] This is the tolerable-
ness of servile or disagreeable ⟨duties⟩ vocations.
Every object in nature is a private door that lets in the wise to ⟨the⟩
profound mystery, the music of numbers.[n]

[99][210] Richter said to Music, "Away! away! thou speakest of
things which throughout my endless life I have found not & shall
not find." [211] The ancient British Bards had for the title of their
order "Those who are free throughout the world," [212] and their
motto was "The truth against the world." "Poets are the natural
guardians of admiration in the hearts of the people." "Es ist alles

---

[208] "Pleasant would . . . cultivation.", struck through in ink with a vertical
use mark, is used in "Prudence," *Lectures*, II, 321, and "Prudence," *W*, II, 240.

[209] See Journal B, p. [297]. The second sentence, struck through in ink with a
vertical use mark, is used in "Compensation," *W*, II, 115.

[210] The material on this page, with the exception of the final paragraph, was first
written in pencil and then copied in ink, though in a different order. The version in
pencil is omitted here.

[211] This sentence, struck through in ink with a vertical use mark, is used in
"Love," *W*, II, 179.

[212] The sentence to this point is used in "The Poet," *W*, III, 32.

wahr wodurch du besser wirst." "An Epicure is a man that can eat anything[.]"

"I turned from all she brought to all she could not bring[.]"
Byron [Cf. *Childe Harold's Pilgrimage*, III, xxx, 270]

I find these scraps in Chorley's Mrs Hemans.[213]

[100] Many trees bear only in alternate years. Why should you write a book every year[?]

29 July. If the Allwise would give me light, I should write for the Cambridge men a theory of the Scholar's office.[214] It is not all books which it behooves him to know[,] least of all to be a bookworshipper[,] but he must be able to read in all books that which alone gives value to books — in all to read one[,] the one incorruptible text of truth. That alone of their style is intelligible[,] acceptable to him. ⟨in Shakspear or Plato all else he rejects were it never so many — times Shakspear's & Plato's⟩

Books are for the scholar's idle times. When he can read God directly, the hour is too precious to be wasted on other men's transcripts of their readings. ⟨It is⟩ The poet, the prophet is caught up into the mount of vision, & thereafter is constrained to declare what he has seen. As the hour of vision is short & rare among heavy days & months so is its record perchance the least part of his volume. But the reverence which attaches to the record spreads itself soon over all his books especially for the bulk of mankind. Hence the book learned class who value books as such not as related to Nature & the human constitution but as making themselves a Third Estate. But the discerning man reads in his Shakspear or Plato only that least part, only the authentic utterances of the oracle, and all the rest he rejects were it never so many times Shakspear's & Plato's.[215]

[213] Cf. Henry F. Chorley, *Memorials of Mrs. Hemans* (Philadelphia, 1836), pp. 116, 40, 238–239, 118, 107, 215.

[214] On June 22, 1837, C. C. Felton, then professor of Greek literature at Harvard, had written Emerson asking him to deliver the Phi Beta Kappa address at Cambridge on August 31, as a substitute for the Reverend Dr. Wainwright (*L*, II, 94, n. 150).

[215] This paragraph, struck through in ink with a diagonal use mark, is used in "The American Scholar," *W*, I, 91, 93, 89, 93.

[101] Books may be read too much. Genius is the enemy of genius by overinfluence.[216] Pope and Johnson and Addison write as if they had never seen the face of the country but had only read of trees & rivers in books. The striped fly that eats our squash & melon vines, the rosebug, the cornworm, the red old-leaf of the ⟨strawberry⟩ ↑vines↓ that ⟨stimulates⟩ ↑entices↓ the eye to new search for the lurking strawberry, the thicket and little bowers of the pea vine, the signs of ripeness and all the hints of the garden [—] these grave city writers never knew. The towers of white blossoms which the chestnut tree uplifts in the landscape ↑in July↓; the angle of strength (almost a right angle) at which the oak puts out its iron arms; the botany of the meadows & watersides — what had Queen Ann's wits to do with these creatures? Did they ever prick their fingers with the thorn of a gooseberry? Did they ever hear the squeak of a bat, or see his flitting[?]

↑I Aug.↓ I should think Water the best of inventions if I were not acquainted also with air & fire[.] [217]

There are graces in the demeanour of a polished & noble person which are lost upon the eye of a churl. These are like the stars whose light has not yet reached us.[218]

Jesus seems to me to be the only person who ever entertained a just estimate of the worth of a man.[219]

[102] 2 August. The farmer's rule for making hay is to keep the rake as nigh the scythe as you can, & the cart as nigh the rake.[220]

A beauty overpowering all analysis or comparison & putting us

[216] See Journal B, pp. [232], [252]. This sentence is used in "The American Scholar," *W*, I, 91.

[217] Following this sentence are eight large X's, in pencil.

[218] This paragraph, struck through in ink with a vertical use mark, is used in "Spiritual Laws," *W*, II, 147.

[219] This sentence, struck through in ink with a diagonal use mark, is used in the Divinity School Address, *W*, I, 130.

[220] This sentence is struck through in ink with a diagonal use mark.

quite beside ourselves we can seldom see after thirty. Gertrude had a cheek like a sunset.[221]

I find it to be a mischievous notion of our times that men think we are come late into nature, that the world is finished & sealed, that the world is of a constitution unalterable, and see not that in the hands of genius old things are passed away & all things become new.[222] Not he is great that can alter matter, but he that can alter my state of mind. But they are the kings of the world who give the color of their present thought to all nature & all art, & persuade men by the cheerful serenity of their carrying the matter that this ⟨it⟩ is ↑the apple↓ which ages have aspired ⟨after⟩ ↑to pluck↓ now at last ripe and inviting nations to the harvest. The great man makes the great thing. Linnaeus makes Botany the most attractive of studies & wins it from the farmer & the herbwoman. Genius makes the ⟨golden⟩ ↑stony↓ hours sing & shine for me ⟨which were of lead & of stone⟩. The day is always his who works in it with serenity. Wherever Macdonald sits, there is the head of the table.[223] The pale young men diffident & complaisant who ride & walk into town in search of a place to fix themselves ought to feel that the differences between them & their [103] proud patrons is slightest[,] that as infancy conforms to nobody, but all conform to it; so that one babe commonly makes four or five ↑out of the adults who↓ prattle & play to it; so God has armed ⟨adolescence⟩ ↑youth↓ & puberty and manhood with its own piquancy & charm & made it enviable & gracious and its claims not to be put by if it will stand by itself. The nonchalance of boys who are sure of a dinner & would disdain as much as a lord to do or say aught to ⟨deserve it⟩ conciliate ⟨it⟩ one[,] is the healthy attitude of ⟨most[?]⟩ human nature[,] and the good youth & the good man though their pockets were empty would not bate one jot of assurance that ⟨it⟩ ↑bread↓ was their due[.] [224]

The two most noble things in the world are Learning & Virtue.

[221] This sentence is struck through in pencil with two diagonal use marks.
[222] Cf. II Cor. 5:17.
[223] "I find it . . . table.", struck through in ink with a vertical use mark, is used in "The American Scholar," *W*, I, 105.
[224] "as infancy conforms . . . due", struck through in pencil with a diagonal use mark, is used in "Self-Reliance," *W*, II, 48.

The latter is ⟨for⟩ health, the former is power; the latter is Being, the former Action. But let them go erect evermore & strike sail to none.

An enchanting night of southwind & clouds; mercury at 73°. All the trees are windharps. Blessed be light & darkness, ebb & flow, cold & heat, ⟨for⟩ these restless pulsations of Nature which by & by will throb no more. Poetry I augur shall revive and stamp a new age as the astronomers assure us that the star in the constellation Harp shall be, in its turn, the Pole Star for a thousand years.[225]

I knew a man scared by the rustle of his own hatband[.]
Scholars; who being poor made many rich. ↑Eyes were they to the blind[,] feet were they to the lame.↓ [225a]

[104] When the narrowminded & unworthy shall knock at my gate, I will say 'Come now will I sacrifice to the gods below;' then will I entertain my guests heartily & handsomely. Besides is it for thee to choose what shadows shall pass over thy magical mirror[?]

↑Aug. 3↓. Hannah H[askins].[226] tells well the story of Aunt Mary's watcher whilst she had a fellen on her thumb. She had never a watcher in her life & was resolved to have one once. So seized the chance. All day she was making preparations for her coming & requiring the family to have things in readiness[.] Twice or thrice she sent messages over to the woman's house to tell her to sleep & to ⟨settle⟩ ↑fix↓ the hour of her coming. When at last she came she first put ⟨her⟩ ↑the watcher↓ to bed that she might be ready & watched ↑her↓ herself. But presently woke her because she thought her head did not lie comfortably; then again because she snored, to forbid her making such a shocking noise. At last she became anxious lest her watcher should spend the night, & day break before she had

[225] "An enchanting . . . new age" is struck through in pencil with a diagonal use mark; "Poetry I . . . years." is struck through in ink with a diagonal use mark. The first three sentences are used in "The Eye and Ear," *Lectures*, II, 274; the fourth sentence is used in "The American Scholar," *W*, I, 82.
[225a] Cf. Job 29:15.
[226] Emerson's double cousin, later Mrs. Augustus Parsons, who "during her youth, and occasionally after her marriage, took care of Miss Mary Moody Emerson" (*J*, IV, 262, n. 2).

got any service from her, so she determined to get up & have her own bed made, for the sake of giving her something to do. But at last growing very impatient of her attendant, she dismissed her before light, declaring she never would have a watcher again, she had passed the worst night she remembered. On the other part [105] Miss ————, the Watcher declared that no consideration would tempt her to watch with Miss Emerson again.

"By the shadow of the stone of hours."

It is ignorance only which complains of a trite subject. Every subject is new to the wise & trite to the incapable.

It was a just sentiment of Clarendon's which induces him to stop the thread of his narrative when Falkland dies, that he may describe the perfections of ⟨his⟩ that eminent person saying that "the celebrating the memory of eminent & extraordinary persons & transmitting their great virtues for the imitation of posterity is one of the principal ends & duties of history." Vol. 3 p. 1518 [227] — ———— Falkland who "cared only that his actions should be just, not that they should be acceptable." [*Ibid.*, p. 1523]

↑Plutarch I esteem a greater benefactor than Aristotle. To him we owe the Brasidases, the Dions, the Phocions, & the other men.↓ [228]

A Scholar is one ⟨s⟩ attuned to nature & life so that heaven & earth traverse freely with their influences his heart and meet in him. He is one who strives to raise himself from private considerations & to breathe & live on public & illustrious thoughts. [229]

Always great thoughts are dancing before us. We all but apprehend — we vaticinate the laws of human life. We say — 'I will walk abroad & the truth will take form & clearness to me.' We go forth

[227] Edward Hyde, 1st Earl of Clarendon, *The History of the Rebellion and Civil Wars in England*, 6 vols. (Boston, 1827). "It was a just . . . of history.' " is struck through in pencil with a diagonal use mark.

[228] These two sentences are used in "Heroism," *Lectures*, II, 329, and "Heroism," *W*, II, 248.

[229] This sentence, struck through in ink with two diagonal use marks, is used in "The American Scholar," *W*, I, 101.

but cannot find it. It seems as if we [106] only needed the stillness & composed attitude of the study to seize the thought. But we come in & still are as far from it as at first.[230]

↑Aug. 4↓. I ask not for the great, the remote, the romantic, for Italy or Arabia, for the Greek Art or Provencal Minstrelsy; I embrace the common; I explore and sit at the feet of the familiar, the low; give me insight into today, and you may have the antique & the future worlds; the meal in the firkin, the milk in the pan, the beggar and the insane man, aunts & cousins[.] [231]

[107] Punishment grows out of the same stem as crime like the Hedysarum Nudicaulis[.] [232]

Eloquence washes the ears into which it flows[.]

The grass is mown; the corn is ripe; autumnal stars arise. After raffling all day in Plutarch's Morals, ⟨‖ . . . ‖⟩ or shall I say angling there for such fish as I might find, I sallied out this fine afternoon through the woods to Walden Water. The Woods were too full of musquitoes to offer any hospitality to the muse & when I came to the blackberry vines the plucking the crude berries at the risk of splintering my hand and with a musquito mounting guard over every particular berry seemed a little too emblematical of general life whose shining & glossy fruits are very hard beset with thorns & very sour & good for nothing when gathered. But the pond was all blue & beautiful in the bosom of the woods and under the amber sky — like an ⟨amethyst⟩ ↑sapphire↓ lying in the moss. I sat down a long time on the shore to see the show. The variety ↑& density↓ of the foliage at the eastern end of the pond is worth seeing, then the extreme softness & holiday beauty of the summer clouds floating feathery overhead enjoying as I fancied their height & privilege

---

[230] "Always great thoughts . . . as if we" is struck through in pencil on p. [105] with a diagonal use mark. This paragraph is used in "The Head," *Lectures*, II, 251–252, and "Intellect," *W*, II, 331–332.

[231] This paragraph, struck through in ink with a vertical use mark, is used in "The American Scholar," *W*, I, 111.

[232] In species of Hedysarum (perennial herbs), a common stem puts forth both leaf-bearing and pod-bearing branches.

of motion & yet & yet not seeming so much the drapery of this place & hour as forelooking to some pavilions & gardens of festivity beyond. I rejected this fancy with a becoming spirit & insisted that clouds, woods, & waters were all there for me. [108] The waterflies were full of happiness. The frogs that ⟨start⟩ ↑shoot↓ from the ⟨shore⟩ ↑land↓ as fast as you walk along, a yard ahead of you, are a meritorious beastie. For their cowardice is only greater than their curiosity & desire of acquaintance with you. Three strokes from the shore the little swimmer turns short round, spreads his webbed paddles, & hangs at the ⟨water's⟩ surface, ⟨&⟩ looks you ⟨full⟩ in the face & so continues as long as you do not assault him.

I sometimes fear that like those Savoyards who went out one day to find stock for their wooden images and discovered that they had whittled up the last of their pinetrees, so I careless of action, intent on composition, have exhausted already all my stock of experience, have fairly written it out.[233]

Language
      As Boscovich taught that two particles of matter never touch, so it seems true that nothing can be described as it is. The most accurate picture is only symbols & suggestions of ⟨i⟩the thing but from the nature of language all remote[.]

[109] 5 August. A man should behave himself as a guest of Nature[234] but not as a drone.

God never cants. And the charm of Plutarch & Plato & Thucydides for me I believe, is that there I get ethics without cant.

I am struck with the splendor of the sentences I meet in books, especially in Plutarch taken from Pindar, Plato, & Heraclitus, these three.
      It was Menander who said, "Whom the gods love die young[.]"[235]

---

[233] See pp. [33], [34] above. This paragraph, struck through in ink with a vertical use mark, is used in "The American Scholar," W, I, 97.
      [234] See p. [10] above: "Let a man behave in his own house as a guest."
      [235] Menander, *The Double Deceiver*, Fragment 125.

The English dramatic poets all Shakspearize.[236]

He lives for us. Men behold in the hero or the poet their own being ripened and are content to be less so that may attain to its full stature. They are content that they themselves shall be brushed like flies from the path of a great person so that ⟨their inward⟩ justice shall be done by him to that ⟨great⟩ common nature which it is the dearest desire of all to see enlarged & glorified. They sun themselves in the great man's light & feel it to be their own element. This is the principle of Aristocracy in history, its foundation in human nature that the poor & low find some amends to their immense moral capacity in their acquiescence to a political & social inferiority. They cast the dignity of man upon the shoulders of a hero & will perish to add one drop of blood to make that great heart beat[,] those giant [110] sinews fight.[237]

8 August. I have read Miss Martineau's first volume[238] with great pleasure. I growled at first at the difference betwixt it & the Plutarch I had just left. The sailors ⟨esche⟩ refuse lemonade & ⟨s⟩ cake & sugarplums and ask for pork & biscuit "something to line their ribs with"; and pleasant and exhilarating as the book is, I lacked the solids. It pleases like a novel[,] the brilliant pictures of scenery & of towns & things which she sketches, but I feel as I read I enrich myself not at all. Yet better pleased as I read on, I honored the courage & rectitude of the woman. How ⟨will she⟩ faithful is she found where to be faithful is praise enough. She gives that pleasure which I have felt before, when a good cause which has been trampled on is freshly & cheerily maintained by some undaunted ↑man of↓ good sense & good principle, and we are all contrite that we had not done it. As if we could have done it! This attribute of genius she has, that she talks so copiously & elegantly of ⟨things⟩ ↑subjects↓ so familiar that they seemed desperate and writes evermore from one point of view. The *woman* is manifest, as she seems quite willing, in the

[236] This sentence, struck through in ink with two diagonal use marks, is used in "The American Scholar," *W*, I, 91.
[237] This paragraph, struck through in ink with a diagonal use mark, is used in "The American Scholar," *W*, I, 106–107.
[238] Harriet Martineau, *Society in America*, 2 vols. (New York, 1837).

superfluous tenderness for the fine boy & the snug farmhouse & other privacies. But the respect for principles is the genius of the book & teaches a noble lesson through every page. I will thank those who teach me not to be easily depressed[.]

[111] An excellent specimen of poetry of its kind is the epitaph on the criminal who was killed by a fall from his horse[:]

Epitaph

>   "Between the stirrup & the ground
>   I mercy asked, I mercy found."
>   V. Boswell's Johnson [239]

Which word can you spare? What word can you add?

>   "En peu d'heure Dieu labeure" [240]

A proud man should not wear shoes nor eat sugar in his tea, nor walk ↑in the road↓ nor ride, no, nor eat or drink or wear anything. If he is so good that he cannot associate with men, let him not creep about their debtor for every thing. We are so helplessly mendicant in our relation to each other that pride is dishonest. Robinson Crusoe may be as proud as he pleases.

The ⟨object⟩ aim of churches & colleges & parties is to drill; the aim of Reason & of God to ⟨inspire⟩ create.

I read with pleasure in Miss Martineau's book the lines of Brutus in Shakspear

>   Countrymen
>   My heart doth joy that yet in all my life
>   I found no man but he was true to me.* [241]

* Shakspeare knew better than to put the coxcomb speech that has been reported of old in Brutus' mouth at his death "that he had worshipped Virtue all his life & found it but a shadow." [242]

---

[239] Conversation of April 28, 1783. See *Boswell's Life of Johnson*, 1934, IV, 212.
[240] See Journal B, p. [225].
[241] *Julius Caesar*, V, v, 33–35, quoted in Harriet Martineau, *Society in America*, 1837, p. 31. Used in "Prudence," *Lectures*, II, 319.
[242] In "Heroism," *Lectures*, II, 333, and "Heroism," *W*, II, 255, Emerson observes that Brutus "is slandered" by the report that he died with this line on his lips; in "The Fugitive Slave Law," *W*, XI, 226, he declares the speech to be "falsely

& for quite different reason, the vivacious expression that the western emigrants were "the perspiration of ⟨New England⟩ the Eastern States." ⟨She⟩

[112] 9 August. Clarendon alone among the English authors (though I think I see the love of Clarendon in Burke) has successfully transplanted the Italian superlative style.

Nec intersit deus dignus nisi vindice nodus.[243] This rule of rhetoric is a rule of conversation also. ⟨Let God be always supposed.⟩ Always suppose God. And do not cant upon interpositions here & there, as if anywhere he were absent or you were any thing. What is man but God impure?

The world seems very simple & easily dispatched — to the theorist. There are but two things, or but one thing & its shadow — Cause & Effect, and Effect is itself worthless if separated from Cause. It is Cause still that must be worshipped in Effect; so that it is only one thing. The worship of Effect is Idolatry. The Church including under the name, Doctrine, Forms, Discipline, Members, is the instant Effect: Weak man adheres to the Effect & lets God go. The Iliad, the Porch, the Academy is the Effect admirable,[n] adorable in the moment of their appearance & their spontaneous working on the mind; but when, as speedily happens, ⟨sequestere⟩ severed from the Cause & regarded as having a perfection per se, they spawn with rules, prescriptions, observances, they ⟨are⟩ ↑become↓ noxious idols. The indisposition of ⟨the mind⟩ men to go back to the source & mix with Deity is the reason of degradation[n] [113] & decay. Education is expended in the measurement & imitation of effects[:] in the study of Shakspear for example as itself a perfect being instead of using Shakspeare merely as an effect of which the Cause is with ⟨eac the⟩ every scholar. Thus the College becomes idolatrous — a temple full of

---

ascribed" to Brutus. Edward Emerson's note to the latter passage cites Dio Cassius, xlvii, 49–52, where Brutus is said to have uttered "this sentiment of Herakles"; cf. Wordsworth, "The Excursion," III, 775–777.

[243] "And let no god intervene, unless a knot [come] worthy of such a deliverer." Cf. Horace, *Ars Poetica*, l. 191; see *JMN*, III, 135.

idols. Shakspear will never be made by the study of Shakspear.[244] I know not how directions for greatness can be given. Yet greatness may be inspired[.]

Always cast back the child, the man on himself. Teach him to treat things & books & sovereign genius[,] as himself also a sovereign[;] that he is porous to principles[,] by nature a perfect conductor of that electricity[,] and when ↑he↓ is in the circuit, divine; when not, dead.[245]

As the world was plastic & fluid in the hands of God, so it always is. To ignorance, to sin, it is ever flint. They say 'Nolumus leges Angliae mutare', — The old nest is good enough;[246] but in proportion as a man ⟨becomes⟩ ↑is↓ divine, the ⟨elements⟩ ↑firmament↓ ⟨flee⟩ ↑flows↓ before him, & take his signet & form[.][247]

My garden is a mat of vines, herbs, corn, & shrubs. One must pick strawberries & pease before he can know that there are as many to glean as to gather. I like the fragrance that floats by from I know not what weeds or plants as I stand in the pea vines & pluck the little pendulums. Every time I pull one, his neighbors make a gentle rattle in their pod to invite the hand to them.

[114] ⟨It is found⟩ Man can live upon any food & attain old age under the line or in the polar circle, in ⟨the⟩ ↑a ship's↓ forecastle ⟨of⟩, in a salt mine, in ditches or on the Andes. So it seems his mind can be nourished on any food and if he have not many events & ⟨powerful⟩ urgent motives of hope or fear he can find exercise & thought in barren idleness with books which tell of events. Beforehand, we should have said A man must act to know; but experience teaches us that character as forcible as Johnson's can be built up in a pedant's garret.[248]

[244] This sentence is used in "Self-Reliance," *W*, II, 83. The thought of this paragraph is also reflected in "The American Scholar," *W*, I, 88–89, and the Divinity School Address, *W*, I, 126–127.

[245] This paragraph, struck through in pencil with three diagonal use marks, is used in "The Head," *Lectures*, II, 260.

[246] Literally, "We decline to alter the laws of the English" (Ed.).

[247] This paragraph, struck through in ink with two diagonal use marks, is used in "The American Scholar," *W*, I, 105.

[248] This paragraph is used in "The American Scholar," *W*, I, 92.

I sit and have nothing to say. In the great calm my ship can do nothing. I have confidence that if the winds arise & the waves toss, I have rigging & rudder & hands to sail my ship. But when the sea is full there is no whirlpool, when the river is flooded no falls, ⟨when⟩ in the Stoical Plenum no motion.

[115] I had a letter from Dr Frothingham today. The sight of that man's handwriting is parnassian. Nothing vulgar is connected with his name but on the contrary every remembrance of wit & learning & contempt of cant. In our Olympic Games we love his fame. But that fame was bought by ↑many↓ years' steady rejection of all that is popular with our saints & and as persevering study of books which none else reads & which he can convert to no temporary purpose. There is a Scholar doing a Scholar's office.

Carlyle: how the sight of his handwriting warms my heart at the little post window. How noble it seems to me that his words should run out of Nithsdale or London over land & sea, to ⟨Germany⟩ ↑Weimar↓, to Rome, to America, to Watertown, to Concord, to Louisville, that they should cheer & delight & invigorate me: A man seeking no reward, warping his genius, filing his mind[249] to no dull public but content with the splendors of Nature & Art as he beholds them & resolute to announce them if his voice is orotund & shrill, in his own proper accents — please or displease the World, how noble that he should trust his eye & ear above all London & know that in all England is no man that can see so far behind or forward; how good & just that amid the hootings of malignant men he should hear this & that whispered qualification of praise of Schiller, Burns, Diderot, &c the commended papers being more every year & the commendation [116] louder. How noble that alone & unpraised he should still write for he knew not who, & find at last his readers in the valley of the Missisippi, and they should brood on the pictures he had painted & ⟨unwind the⟩ ↑un↓twist the many colored meanings which he had spun & woven into so rich a web of sentences and domesticate in so many & remote heads the humor, the learning, and the philosophy which year by year in summer & in frost this lonely man had lived in the moors of Scotland. This man ⟨propels⟩ upholds & propels

[249] Cf. *Macbeth*, III, i, 65.

civilization. For every wooden post he knocks away he replaces one of stone. He cleanses and exalts men & leaves the world better. He knows & loves the heavenly stars and sees fields below with trees & animals; he sees towered cities; royal houses; & poor men's chambers & reports the good he sees ↑God thro' him↓ telling this generation also that he has beholden his work & sees that it is good.[250] He discharges his duty as one of the World's Scholars.

[117] The farmer turns his capital once a year. The merchant many times oftener. The scholar cannot. The knowledge which he acquires will not become bread or reputation to him in a year or two years or ten. There is no doublespeeder, no railroad, no mechanical multiplication. He gives himself to the slow & unhonored task of observation. Flamsteed & Herschel in their glazed observatory may catalogue the stars with the good will of all men & the results being conspicuous, splendid, & useful ⟨their⟩ honor is sure. But he in his private observatory cataloguing obscure & nebulous stars of the human mind which as yet no man has thought of as such; & watching days & months sometimes for a few facts; correcting still his old records must sacrifice display & immediate fame; more than that, he must accept, often, a certain ignorance & shiftlessness in ordinary business ⟨whe⟩ incurring the disdain of the able who shoulder him aside[.] He must stammer in his speech, he must forego the living for the dead, he must accept poverty, obscurity, & solitude. For robust health he becomes a valetudinarian; for the ease & pleasure of treading the beaten track accepting the fashions, the religion, the education of society he ⟨inc[?]⟩ assumes the bold responsibility of making his own, & of course the self accusation, the faint heart, the frequent uncertainty & loss of time which are thorns & nettles in the way of the self relying & self-directed; and the [118] state of ⟨apparent⟩ ↑virtual↓ hostility in which he seems to stand to ⟨all who⟩ society & especially ↑to↓ educated society. For all this ⟨privation⟩ ↑loss & scorn↓ he is to find consolation in exercising the highest functions of human nature. He is to resist the prosperity that retrogrades ever to barbarism by preserving & communicating heroic sentiments, noble biographies, melodious verse, & the conclusions of history; whatsoever oracles the

[250] Cf. Gen. 1:4 ff.

human heart in all emergences[,] in all solemn hours has uttered as its commentary on the ⟨whirling⟩ storm of actions.[251] The wisdom that he painfully gathers sweetens his own life. He is made gentle, noble, & self centred and who is so becomes in the heart of all clearseeing men venerable & salutary & oracular. He preserves for another generation the knowledge of what is noble & good.

The Southerner asks ⟨of⟩concerning any man "How does he fight?" The Northerner asks, "What can he do?"[252]

[119] Aug. 12. It is a sublime thing to oversee oneself as we do in Memory.

⟨From p. 96⟩ In addition to what was said, p. 96, I observe that the general has only to stimulate the mind of his troop to that degree that they ascend to the perception that they are men & the enemy is no more, and they are bold & the Victory is already won. In like manner when a man fears the tiger, the lion, it is because he thinks they draw their savageness from an infinitude of malignity, but let a man see that their nature is limitary because it is bad, that he knows them, for their nature lies ↑far↓ within the /ambitious/spacious/ circle of his own, and is a mean spot therein, and he overawes & looks down the lion. How foolish is war. Let the injured party speak to the injurer until their minds meet, & the artillery is discharged and the forced marches of the army that were clambering in six weeks over mountains & rivers are too slow & cumberous, the blow is already struck, the Victory gained, the Peace sworn. I fear the Cochran rifle or the Perkins steam battery will never do. These are wrath & wrong embodied but unhappily for their patentees they are finite and the force opposed to them is infinite and if they could contrive ↑an engine↓ to rain cannon-balls[n] ↑all day↓ over an acre as we water a garden bed it would prove nothing but ingenious & speedy transporta-

---

[251] "He gives himself . . . actions.", struck through in ink with diagonal use marks, is used in "The American Scholar," *W*, I, 100–102.

[252] This paragraph is struck through in pencil with a diagonal use mark. The passage, repeated on p. [161] below, is used in "Doctrine of the Hands," *Lectures*, II, 244.

tion of iron, a pretty toy but for tyranny or anger [120] quite useless.[253]

If you gather apples in the sunshine or make hay or hoe corn and then retire within doors & strain your body or squeeze your eyes *six hours after* ⟨and⟩ you shall still see apples hanging in the bright light with leaves & boughs thereto.[254] There lie the impressions still on the retentive organ though I knew it not. So lies the whole series of natural images with which my life has made me acquainted in my memory, though I know it not and a thrill of passion, a sudden ⟨thought⟩ emotion flashes light upon their dark chamber & the Active power seizes instantly the fit image as the word of his momentary thought.[255] So lies all the life I have lived as my dictionary from which to extract the word which I want to dress the new perception of this moment. This is the way to learn Grammar. God never meant that we should learn Language by Colleges or Books. That only can we say which we have lived.
Life lies behind us as the quarry from whence we get tiles & copestones for the masonry of today.[256]

14 August. The preacher enumerates his classes of men and I do not find my place therein. I suspect then that no man does. Every thing is my cousin, and when he speaks things, I immediately feel he is touching some of my relations, & I am uneasy, but whilst [121] he deals in words I can ⟨safely⟩ ↑slumber and↓ sleep.

All Literature writes the character of the wise man. Is a man a bigot, a chemist, a shopman, he will only find his biography treated at long intervals in a short notice but all books, monuments, conversation, are portraits in which the wise man finds the lineaments he is forming,

---

[253] This paragraph, struck through in pencil with a vertical use mark, is used in "The Heart," *Lectures*, II, 285–286.

[254] Cf. p. [94] above.

[255] "If you gather . . . thought.", struck through in pencil with two diagonal use marks, is used in "The Head," *Lectures*, II, 254, and "Intellect," *W*, II, 333–334.

[256] "So lies all . . . today.", struck through in pencil with one, and in ink with two, diagonal use marks, is used in "The American Scholar," *W*, I, 95 ("Only so much do I know, as I have lived."), 98.

he has formed⟨,⟩. The silent and the loud praise him and accost him and he is stimulated wherever he moves as by personal allusions. The flowering weed and sere stubble, gay facts or grave facts alike confirm his thought not less than if there were a voice "As thou hast said." [257] ↑See D, p. 211↓

If Jesus came now into the world, he would say — You, YOU! He said to his age, I.

He that perceives that the Moral Sentiment is the highest in God's order, rights himself, he stands in the erect position, and therefore is strong⟨er⟩, ⟨work⟩ uses his hands, works miracles just as a man who stands on his feet is stronger than a man who stands on his head.[258]

There never was a saint but was pleased to be accused of pride, and this because pride is a form of self-trust.

[122] I like not to have the day hurry away under me whilst I sit at my desk; I wish not reveries; I like to taste my time & spread myself through all the hour.

Do they think the composition too highly wrought? A poem should be a blade of Damascus steel ⟨of⟩ made up a mass of knife blades & nails & parts every one of which has had its whole surface hammered & wrought before it was welded into the Sword to be wrought over anew.

The least effect of the oration is on the orator. Yet it is something; a faint recoil; a kicking of the gun.

17 August. This morng. Mr Alcott & Mr Hedge left me. Four or five days full of discourse & much was seen. I ↑incline to↓ withdraw

---

[257] Cf. Ezra, 10:12: "As thou hast said, so must we do." The first three sentences of this paragraph, struck through in ink with diagonal use marks, are used in "History," *W*, II, 7.

[258] This paragraph, struck through in ink with a vertical use mark, is used in "Self-Reliance," *W*, II, 89. Another vertical use mark in pencil extends through this and the following paragraph.

continually as from a surfeit, but the stomach of my wise guests being stronger, I strain my courtesy to sit by though drowsy. In able conversation we have glimpses of the Universe, perceptions of the soul's omnipotence but not much to record. I who enjoin on Alcott records, can attain to none myself, — ⟨of⟩ to no register of these far darting lights & shadows or any sketch of the mountain landscape which has opened itself to the eye. It would be a valuable piece of literature, could a Report of these extended & desultory but occasionally profound, often ornamented, often sprightly & comic dialogues, be made, sinking some parts, fulfilling others, and chiefly, putting [123] together things that belong together. I would rather have a perfect recollection of all this, ⟨than⟩ of all that I have thought & felt in the last week, than any book that can now be published.

> Arboreous nature
> pertinence & impertinence
> Feeding on Nature. Water
> Iteration
> Euphuism [259]

[124] [260] 17 August. These caducous relations are in the soul as leaves, flowers, & fruits are in the arboreous nature, and wherever it is put & how often soever they are lopped off, yet still it renews them ever.[261]

Infancy, Coleridge says, is body & spirit in unity, the body is all animated. ↑If↓ this[n] state should be perpetuated we should have men like the ⟨figures⟩ ↑gods & heroes↓ carved on the friezes of the Parthenon.[262] Now the adult figure is ugly, & we are thankful it is clothed to save our eyes from offence. But Phidias's men are as lovely & majestic in their nakedness as is the child.

The oeillade (in Journal B p. [[5]]) is to be explained on the principle of community or oneness of Nature. It is the body's percep-

---

[259] "Arboreous nature . . . Euphuism" is written in pencil. These notes are expanded on p. [125].

[260] "Society" is written above "August. These" at the top of the page.

[261] This sentence is struck through in pencil with a diagonal use mark.

[262] "Infancy, Coleridge . . . Parthenon.", struck through in pencil with a diagonal use mark, is used in "Domestic Life," *W*, VII, 103–104.

tion of difference based on radical oneness. Strange that any body who ever met another person's eyes, should doubt that all men have one soul.[263]

[125]   gleams of beauty
                Upham
                glance
                demonology moaning
                arboreous nature
                pertinence & impertinence
                feeding on nature. water
                Iteration
                Euphuism
                ground your points depress your shears
                coffin & queue
                cumber the forest floor
                Criticism of Alcott's writing
                Goethe modern of moderns ancient of ancients
                Fatalism affirms a truth. Your atmosphere repels the
                    snake
                Infancy & Phidias's friezes
                Gothic architecture in German text
                The missionary ship
                Sandwich Islander my fringes
                fear & knowledge
                limboes & paradises clumsy [264]

[126] *A good style.* Nothing can be added to it neither can anything be taken from it.

August 18. The hope to arouse young men at Cambridge to a worthier view of their literary duties ⟨teach⟩ prompts me to offer the theory of the Scholar's function. He has an office to perform in society. What

---

[263] This paragraph, struck through in pencil with a diagonal use mark, is used in "The Heart," *Lectures*, II, 283.

[264] These penciled notes, an expansion of those on p. [123] above, draw on various entries from p. [124] to p. [138] which must have been already written when the notes were made.

is it? To arouse the intellect; to keep it erect & sound; to keep admiration in the hearts of the people; to keep the eye open upon its spiritual aims.

How shall he render this service? By being a Soul among those things with which he deals. Let us look at the world as it aids his function.

One thing is plain he must have a training by himself — then training of another age will not fit him. He himself & not others must judge what is good for him. Now the young are oppressed by their instructors. Bacon or Locke saw and thought, & inspired by their thinking a generation & now all must be pinned to their thinking which ⟨the⟩ a year after was already too narrow for them. The coverlet is too narrow & too short. They were born heirs of the dome of God [265] thereunder or therein to move unshackled & unbounded and we would confine them under a coverlet. Meek young men grow up in colleges & believe it is their duty to accept the views which ⟨others ha⟩ books have given & grow up slaves.[266] Some good angel in the shape of a turnkey bids them demand a habeas corpus and the moment they come out of durance the heaven opens & the earth smiles.

[127] The human mind thinks and records its thought. The sacredness of the act is instantly transferred to the record and they think to pin down the Soul in eternising the thought. This is obvious in Church, in State, in Schools, in Arts, in Books, in Marriage.[267]

They say, the insane like a master; so always does the human heart hunger after a leader[,] a master through truth.

19 Aug. It is true that in our age the common & near have been explored & poetised. Burns, Goldsmith, Cowper, Goethe, Wordsworth, Carlyle, have differently done this & with various success. ⟨The⟩ ↑This writing is bloodwarm↓. ⟨man⟩Man is surprised to find that things near are not less beautiful & wondrous than things ⟨far⟩

[265] Cf. "the bending dome of day" in "The American Scholar," *W*, I, 86.

[266] This sentence is used in "The American Scholar," *W*, I, 89; cf. "Bacon or Locke" above.

[267] Cf. pp. [112]–[113] above. This paragraph, struck through in ink with two diagonal use marks, is used in "The American Scholar," *W*, I, 88.

remote. The secret of the scholar or intellectual man is that all nature is only the foliage, the flowering, & the fruit of the Soul and that every part therefore exists as emblem & sign, of some fact in the soul. Instantly rags & offal are elevated into hieroglyphics; as the chemist sees nothing unclean so the poet does not. This needed the Reflective Age. The near explains the far; a drop of water tells all that is true of the ocean; a family will reveal the state & one man the All. The Reflective Age should make the greatest discoveries. Thus Goethe ⟨is⟩ the most modern of the moderns has ⁿ shown us ↑as none ever did↓ the genius of the Ancients.²⁶⁸ Let me once go behind any material fact & see its cause in an affection[,] an idea & the fact assumes at once a scientific value. Facts are disagreeable or loathsome to me so long as I have no clue to [128] them; persons are formidable or tedious. But give me the chain that connects them to the Universal consciousness & I shall see them to be Necessary & see them to be convenient & enlarge my charity one circle more & let them in. Let me see how the man not "is tyrannised over by his members" but by his thoughts, and these, — thoughts of mine, — thoughts that I have also though qualified in me by other thoughts not yet ripened in him, and I can pardon & rejoice in him also. Community, Identity of Nature, is the ground of that boundless trust in men which always has its reward in reciprocal trust.

Emanuel Swedenborg has a literary value which has scarcely yet been estimated as he is chiefly known as the teacher of a sect. He saw & showed the connexion between the lower parts of nature & the ⟨the⟩ affections of the Soul & may be said to have given us a theory of Beasts, of Insanity, of bogs, & sinks. He has also given the agreeable forms of creation in connexion with virtue but has done the first part best.²⁶⁹

He who sees in the human mind the necessity of a French Revolution, the necessity of a generation of vain & selfish soldiers enamored

---

²⁶⁸ "It is true . . . things remote." is struck through in ink with a diagonal use mark; "The Reflective Age . . . Ancients." is struck through in ink with three vertical use marks. "The American Scholar," *W*, I, 110, 112, draws on the entire paragraph to this point.

²⁶⁹ "Emanuel Swedenborg . . . best.", struck through in ink with a vertical use mark, is used in "The American Scholar," *W*, I, 112–113.

of show & conquest, & of course that the most selfish, most showy, & most conquering man shall be the general & Napoleon of them, can outspeed in his intelligence newspapers & telegraphs[.]

[129] I please myself with getting my nail box set in the snuggest corner of the barn chamber & well filled with ⟨conv⟩ nails & gimlet pincers, ⟨&⟩ screw driver↑, & chisel↓. Herein I find an old joy of youth[,] of childhood which perhaps all domestic children share, — the cat-like love of garrets, barns, & corn chambers and of the conveniences of long housekeeping.[270] It is quite genuine. When it occurs today, I ask — Have others the same? Once I should not have thought of such a question. ⟨I⟩What I loved, I supposed all children loved & knew, & therefore I did not name them. We were at accord. But much conversation[,] much comparison apprises us of difference. The first effect of this new learning is to ⟨tempt⟩ incline us to hide our tastes. As they differ, we must be wrong. Afterwards some person comes & wins eclat by simply describing this old but concealed fancy of ours. Then we immediately learn to value all the parts of our nature, to rely on them as Self-authorised and that to publish them is to please others. So now the nailbox figures for its value ⟨in my Journal⟩.[271]

We are indeed discriminated from each other by very slight inequalities which by their accumulation constitute at last broad contrasts. Genius surprises us with every word. It does not surprise itself. It is moving by the selfsame law as you obey in your daily cogitation & one day you will tread without wonder the same steps[.]

[130] *Plutarch*

> Man serried close to Man in dangerous field
> Whilst morions morions touched, & shield to shield
> <div style="text-align:right">Homer in Plutarch <i>Of Love</i> [272]</div>

"the glory at Marathon the honor gained over the Curymedontes, and the Dianium,

---

[270] "I please . . . housekeeping.", struck through in pencil with two diagonal use marks, is used in "Prudence," *Lectures*, II, 314, and "Prudence," *W*, II, 227.
[271] "in my Journal" is canceled in pencil.
[272] Cf. *Plutarch's Morals*, 1718, IV, 284.

———— When the Athenian Youth
The famed foundations of their Freedom laid" [273]
Plut. ["Concerning such whom God is slow to punish,"] Morals
Vol 4. p. 154 ——

Hesiod says

"Bad counsel so the gods ordain
Is most of all the adviser's bane" [274]
Plut. ["Concerning such whom God is slow to punish,"] M[orals].
Vol. 4   p 158

The Delphic Oracle said to Coraz the Naxian

It sounds profane impiety
To teach that human souls e'er die.[275]
["Concerning such whom God is slow to punish,"] Ib[id]. p. 174

"They should have left every one in those sentiments which they had from
the laws & custom concerning the Divinity;
Since neither now nor yesterday began
These thoughts, that have been ever, nor yet can
A man be found who their first entrance knew" [276]
["Of Common Conception against the Stoics," *ibid.*,] p. 391

"Dost thou behold the vast & azure sky
How in its liquid arms the earth doth lie."
["A discourse to an unlearned Prince," *ibid.*,] p. 320

"Truth being the greatest good that man can receive, and the goodliest
blessing that God can give," [277]
["Of Isis and Osiris," *ibid.*,] p. 60

"There is no greater benefit that men can enjoy from God than by the
imitation & pursuit of those perfections & that sanctity which is in him,
to be excited to the study of virtue."
["Concerning such whom God is slow to punish, *ibid.*,] p. 151

[273] See *JMN*, IV, 437; Emerson's letter to William Emerson, June 30, 1837 (*L*,
II, 84).
[274] Cf. "Compensation," *W*, II, 109.
[275] Quoted in "Plutarch," *W*, X, 313.
[276] Quoted in "Experience," *W*, III, 72, and "Plutarch," *W*, X, 313.
[277] Quoted in "Plutarch," *W*, X, 312–313.

"Nature sent us out free & loose, we bend & straiten & pin up ourselves in houses & reduce ourselves into a scant [131] & little room." [278]
["Of Banishment," *ibid.,*] Vol 3   p. 51

"Not on the store of sprightly Wine
Nor plenty of delicious meats
Though generous Nature should design
To court us with perpetual treats,
'Tis not on these we for content depend
So much as on the shadow of a friend." [279]
Menander ap. Plut. ["Of Brotherly Love,"]
Mor[als]. Vol. 3. p. 69

"Stern Jove has in some angry mood
Bereft us of his solitude." Telemachus in Homer ap Plut
["Of Brotherly Love," *ibid.,*] Vol 3   p 73

"Unvanquished love! whatever else deceives
Our trust, 'tis this our very selves outlives."
["Of Brotherly Love," *ibid.,*] p. 74

"Plato will have a man to be a heavenly tree growing with his root, which is his head, upward." [280]   ["Why the Pythian Priestess Ceases her
Oracles in Verse," *ibid.,*] p. 111

"Men cannot exercise their rhetoric unless they speak but may their philosophy even whilst they are silent or jest merrily; for 'tis not only, as Plato says, the highest degree of injustice not to be just & yet seem so; but the top of wisdom to philosophize yet not appear to do it, & in mirth to do the same with those that are serious & seem in earnest; for, as in Euripides, the Bacchae, though unprovided of iron weapons and unarmed, wounded their invaders with their boughs, thus the very jests & merry talk of true philosophers move those that are not altogether insensible & unusually reform" [281]   ["Symposiacs," *ibid.,*] p. 229

↑"&↓ if ⁿ the greater part consists of such who can better endure the noise of any bird, fiddlestring, or piece of wood than the voice of a philosopher, ——— "   ["Symposiacs," *ibid.,* p.] ↑229↓

---

[278] Cf. "Nature," *W*, III, 170.

[279] Quoted in "Domestic Life," *W*, VII, 128.

[280] See Journal B, p. [112].

[281] This paragraph, struck through in pencil with a diagonal use mark, is used in "Plutarch," *W*, X, 312 ("the top of wisdom . . . to do it").

[132]   "The Isthmian garland I will sell as cheap
           As common wreaths of parsley may be sold"
                              ["Symposiacs," *ibid*.,] p. 348

Evenus said that Fire was the sweetest of all the sauces in the world.[282]   ["Symposiacs," *ibid*.,] p 391

"It is an expression of Pindar, that we tread the dark bottom of hell with necessities as hard as iron." [283]   Plut. ["Consolations to Apollonius,"]
                              Mor[als]. Vol I   p 288

After a festival you may see "the dirt of Wine." [284] "To reap corn with slings." [285]

"The sea was the tear of Saturn" [286]

"A walk near the sea, and a sail near the shore are best" [287]

[133][288] [blank]

[134] 20 August. Many persons take pleasure in showing the ⟨s⟩ differences that will never blend, the strong individualities of men. For these two years back, I incline more to show the insignificance of these differences as they melt into the Unity which is the base of them all. Aristotle & Plato are reckoned the respective heads of schools between which a yawning gulf lies. I like to see that Aristotle Platonizes[.] [289]

Carlyle & Wordsworth now act out of England on us, — Coleridge also.

[282] This sentence, struck through in pencil with a vertical use mark, is used in "Prudence," *Lectures*, II, 324. Cf. Journal B, p. [320], where the saying is attributed to Prodicus.
[283] Used in "New England Reformers," *W*, III, 274; "Uses of Great Men," *W*, IV, 17; and "Progress of Culture," *W*, VIII, 231–232.
[284] "Of Anger," *Plutarch's Morals*, 1718, I, 56.
[285] "Of Banishment," *ibid*., III, 53 ("they reap down their Figs with Slings").
[286] "Of Isis and Osiris," *ibid*., IV, 93. See "Poetry and Imagination," *W*, VIII, 14.
[287] Cf. "Symposiacs," *Plutarch's Morals*, 1718, III, 244 ("That a Voyage near the Land, and a Walk near the Sea, is the best Recreation"); see "Inspiration," *W*, VIII, 289.
[288] The page number has been supplied.
[289] This paragraph, struck through in pencil with a diagonal use mark, is used in "The Head," *Lectures*, II, 255, and "Circles," *W*, II, 308.

Lidian remembers the religious terrors of her childhood when *Young* tinged her day & night thoughts, and the doubts of *Cowper* were her own; when every lightning seemed the beginning of conflagration, & every ⟨explosion⟩ ↑noise in the street↓ the crack of doom. I have some parallel recollections at the Latin School ⟨&⟩ when I lived in Beacon street. Afterwards ⟨th⟩ what remained for me to learn was cleansed by books & poetry & philosophy & came in purer forms ⟨at⟩ of literature at College. These spiritual crises no doubt are periods of as certain occurrence in some form of agitation to every mind as dentition or puberty. Lidian was at that time alarmed by the lines on the gravestones quoted ⟨pa⟩ above p. 97[.]

The babe cheers me with his hearty & protracted laugh which sounds to me like thunder in the woods.[290]

Aug. 21. A dream of a duel. Dreams may explain the magnetic *directed dream*. Dreams are the sequel of waking knowledge. Awake I know the character of Andrew, but do not think what he may do. In dream [135] I turn that knowledge into a fact; and it proves a prophecy. In like manner the Soul contains in itself the event that shall presently befal it for the event is only the actualization of its thoughts. Why then should not symptoms, auguries, forebodings also be, and, as Hedge said, "the moanings of the spirit"[?][291]

What means all the monitory tone of the world of life, of literature, of tradition? Man is fallen Man is banished; an exile; he is in earth whilst there is a heaven. What do these apologues mean? ⟨We c⟩ⁿ These seem to him traditions of memory. But they are the whispers of hope and Hope is the voice of the Supreme Being to the Individual[.]

We say Paradise was; Adam fell; the Golden Age; & the like. We mean man is not as he ought to be; but our way of painting this is on Time, and we say *Was*.

I believe that I shall some time cease to be an Individual, that

---

[290] Cf. Emerson's "Threnody," *W*, IX, 155: "Laughter rich as woodland thunder".
[291] "Dreams are the sequel . . . spirit' " is used in "Demonology," *W*, X, 8–9.

the eternal tendency of the soul is to become Universal to animate the last extremities of organization.

[August] 22. ↑I↓ received ⁿ this morning *"The French Revolution a History* by Thomas Carlyle" from him.

[August] ↑26↓. Draw circles. The man finishes his story how good! how final! He fills the sky. ⟨Hark⟩ ↑Lo↓! on the other side rises also a man and draws a circle around the circle which we had just pronounced the outline of the sphere; then already is our first speaker not Man, but only a first speaker. His only [136] ⟨Hi⟩ redress is forthwith to draw a circle outside of his antagonist.ⁿ   And so on.[292]

Sept. 6. Not a word inscribed for ten days.
And now we bask in warm & yellow light of three pearly days — corn, beans, & squashes ripening every hour,ⁿ the garden, the field an Indian paradise.
It seemed the other day a fact of some moment that the project of our companion be he who he may, & that what it may, is always entitled in courteous society to deference and superiority[.] [293]

[September] 13. We need Nature, & cities give the human ⟨body⟩ senses not room enough. I go out daily & nightly to feed my eyes on the horizon & the sky and come to feel the want of this scope as I do of water for my washing.[294]
Yesterday as I watched the flight of some crows I suddenly discovered a hawk high over head & then directly four others at such a height they seemed smallest sparrows. There, on high, they swooped & circled in the pure heaven. After watching them for a time, I turned my eye to my path, & was struck with the dim & leaden color all unattractive & shorn of beams [295] of this earth to him whose eye has conversed with heaven.

[292] This paragraph, struck through in pencil with diagonal use marks, is used in "The Head," *Lectures*, II, 254–255, and "Circles," *W*, II, 304–305.
[293] This sentence, struck through in pencil with a vertical use mark, is used in "The Heart," *Lectures*, II, 287.
[294] This paragraph, struck through in pencil with a vertical use mark, is used in "The Eye and Ear," *Lectures*, II, 275, and "Nature," *W*, III, 171.
[295] Cf. Milton, *Paradise Lost*, I, 596.

Today I wrote a letter to Carlyle.[296]

↑On the 1 September, The Club spent the day with me; present Alcott, Barlow, Bradford, Clark, Dwight, Emerson, Francis, Hedge, Osgood, Peabody, Putnam, Ripley, Robbins, Stetson　　　　　Elizabeth Hoar, Mrs Ripley, & Margaret Fuller also honoured our séance.↓[297]

[137] The American artist who would carve a wood-god and who was familiar with the forest in Maine where enormous fallen pine trees "cumber the forest floor"[,] where huge mosses depending from the trees and the mass of the timber give a savage ⟨app⟩ & haggard strength to the grove — would produce a very different statue from the sculptor who only knew an European woodland, — the tasteful Greek, for example.

The German printed type resembles the Gothic architecture[.]

It occurred the other day in hearing some clapping of hands after a speech, that the orator's value might be measured by every additional round after the three first claps, just as jockeys are wont to pay ten dollars for every additional roll of a horse who rolls himself on the ground. For in both cases the first & second roll come very easily off, but it gets beyond the third very hardly.

Sept. ⟨20⟩18. In the woods today I heard a pattering like rain & looking up I beheld the air over & about the tops of the trees full of insects (the winged ant) in violent motion & gyrations and some of them continually dropping out of the flying or fighting swarm & causing the rain-like sound as they fell upon the ⟨le⟩ oakleaves. The fallers consisted of little knots of two or three insects apparently biting each other & so twisted or holden together as to encumber the wings.[298]

[296] September 13, 1837.
[297] Barlow, George P. Bradford, Peabody, Robbins, and the three women were newcomers to the club. David Hatch Barlow was a minister in Lynn and later in Worcester; Ephraim Peabody had been occupying the pulpit of Federal Street Church in Boston and was shortly to serve in New Bedford; Chandler Robbins had succeeded Emerson at the Second Church in Boston.
[298] This paragraph is used in "Literary Ethics," *W*, I, 168.

[138]²⁹⁹ Sept. 19. There are few experiences in common life more mortifying & disagreeable than "the foolish face of praise" ³⁰⁰ — the forced smile which we put on in company where we do not feel at ease in answer to conversation which does not interest us. The muscles not spontaneously moved but moved by a low usurping wilfulness, grow tight about the outline of the face & make the most disagreeable sensation — a sensation of rebuke & warning which no young man ought to suffer more than once.³⁰¹

Society is needed to the generation of Man; Society is needed to diagrammatize our consciousness; and now the experiments of Animal Magnetism tend to show that we can do that by deputy in the *other self* which we *cannot* do in our own.

I should like very well to get the data of the good story which Lidian tells of the stout soldier who persisted in wearing his military queue when the reforming major ordered all queues to be cut off in the regiment; the soldier held fast to his own & dying required that a hole should be made underneath his head in his coffin and the dear queue should project decent & honorable thereout.

[139] C.C.E talking of Mrs   , said that she had two faces, and when conversing with her, you looked up & would suddenly find that instead of talking with the beautiful Mrs   , you were talking with a ghoul. ↑See p. 30↓

The hand is needed to teach the use of the eye.

We can hardly speak of our own experience & the names of our family sparingly enough. The rule seems to be that we should not use these dangerous personalities any more than we are sure the sympathies of the interlocutors will go along with us. In good company the individuals at once merge their egotism into a social soul exactly coextensive with the ⟨cons⟩ several consciousnesses there pres-

---

²⁹⁹ "Be true" is written above "Sept. 19   There" at the top of the page.

³⁰⁰ Pope, "Epistle to Dr. Arbuthnot," l. 212. See *JMN*, II, 365.

³⁰¹ This paragraph, struck through in ink with a vertical use mark, is used in "Self-Reliance," *W*, II, 55.

ent. No partialities of friend to friend[,] no fondnesses of husband to wife are then pertinent, but quite otherwise. Only he may then speak who can sail as it were on the common thought of the party, & not poorly limited to his own[.] [302]

Sept. 6.   The Aesthetic Club met at Mr Clarke's in Newton. Present — Alcott, Clarke, Dwight, Emerson, Francis, Hedge, Osgood, Ripley, Stetson.
Miss Clarke,[303] Miss Fuller, & Miss Peabody were also present.

[140] Our spontaneous action is always our best. Come out of the study & walk abroad & you shall get suddenly a spontaneous glance of the soul at your subject more searching & just than any the hours of labor had given. Yet was the labor a needful preamble. So the first retrospect on yesterday's thought which we have on waking: Mark, keep, & deepen that.[304]

I have among my kinsmen a man to whom more than any one I have known I may apply the phrase 'an afternoon man'.[305] He rolls & riots in delays. His wife & daughters beseech him to plant his corn early, that it may not be killed by frost as it was last year. "Pooh" he says, "I hate to have all the corn ripe; I like to see some of it cut in the stalk for fodder." The horse I bought of him was very small; — "O yes" he says, "None of those great overgrown creatures that eat all before them." Mr Lamb complained of the ⟨terri⟩ very bad roads in Maine which had racked his chaise badly; "Why Mr Lamb," said my friend, "I always think that it does a chaise good to come down into this country, it drives in the spokes of the wheels, and makes all tight & strong."

---

[302] "In good company . . . own", struck through with two diagonal use marks, one in pencil and one in ink, is used in "The Heart," *Lectures*, II, 289, and "Friendship," *W*, II, 207.

[303] Sarah Freeman Clarke, sister of James Freeman Clarke, was a close friend of Margaret Fuller (*L*, II, 76, n. 78).

[304] This paragraph is used in "The Head," *Lectures*, II, 250, and "Intellect," *W*, II, 328.

[305] This phrase occurs in Journal B, p. [218]; Human Culture: "Introductory," *Lectures*, II, 229; "Prudence," *Lectures*, II, 315; and "Prudence," *W*, II, 229.

[141] On the 29 August, I received a letter from the Salem Lyceum signed I.F Worcester, requesting me to lecture before the institution next winter and adding "The subject is of course discretionary with yourself 'provided no allusions are made to religious controversy, or other exciting topics upon which the public mind is honestly divided.'" I replied on the same day to Mr W. by quoting these words & adding "I am really sorry that any person in Salem should think me capable of accepting an invitation so encumbered."

"The motto on all palace gates is *Hush*."
Lady Louisa Stuart Anecdotes of Lady
Mary Wortley Montagu.[306]

Mr Lee said "Miss F. remembers; it is very ill bred to remember."

Nothing is more carefully secured in our constitution than that we shall not systematize or integrate too fast. Carry it how we will, always something refuses to be subordinated & to drill. It will not toe the line. The facts of Animal Magnetism are now extravagant. We can make nothing of them. What then? Why, own that you are a tyro. We make a dear little cosmogony of our own that makes the world & tucks in all ⟨history⟩ ↑nations↓ like cherries into a tart, & 'tis all finished & rounded into compass & shape, but unluckily we find that it will not explain the existence of the African Race[.] [307]

[142] It was the happiest turn to my old thrum which Charles H Warren [308] gave as a toast at the ΦBK Dinner. "Mr President," he said, "I suppose all know where the orator comes from; and I suppose all know what he has said. I give you *The Spirit of Concord. It makes us all of One Mind.*"

[143] That a man appears scornful & claims to belong to another age & race is only affirmation of weakness. A true man belongs to no other time or place but is the centre of things. He measures you & all

---

[306] *The Letters and Works of Lady Mary Wortley Montagu*, ed. Lord Wharncliffe, 3 vols. (London, 1837), I, 39.
[307] This paragraph, struck through in pencil with a diagonal use mark, is used in "The Head," *Lectures*, II, 253.
[308] Of Plymouth, later of Boston (*J*, IV, 294, n. 1).

men & all events. You are constrained to accept his standard.[309] ↑See
p. 56↓

Lidian's Aunt Sarah Cotton when washing clothes with her
sisters was addressed by her father who passed thro' the kitchen
"Girls, who that saw you now would think you the descendants of
Robert Bruce?" "Father," said she, "if I knew in which of my veins
his blood ⟨was⟩ ↑flowed↓, I would instantly let it out into the wash-
tub."

20 Sept. I read this morning some lines written by Mr Allston
to M⟨iss⟩rs Jameson, on the Diary of the Ennuyée,[310] very good &
entirely self-taught, original — not conventional. And always we
hear a sublime admonition in any such line. But the verses celebrate
Italy not as it is, but as it is imagined. *That* ⟨"⟩Earth fills her lap with
pleasures not her own,[311] but supplied from selfdeceived imaginations.
I must think the man is not yet married to nature who sighs ever for
some foreign land. Italy can never show me a better earth & heaven
than many a time have intoxicated my senses within a mile of my
house. Then I must think the man is not yet ripe who is not yet
domesticated in his native spot, who has not yet domesticated Art &
Nature, grandeur & beauty, Hope & fear, friendship, angels, & God,
in the chamber where he sits[,] in the half acre where his chimney
rises. Epaminondas brave & affectionate[n] [144] does not seem to us
to need Olympus to die upon, nor the Syrian sunshine. He lies very
well where he is. The Jerseys were handsome grounds enough for
Washington to tread, and London streets for the feet of Milton. As
soon as he is an adult man he shall see that he illustrates the place,
he burnishes his skies; he makes his climate splendid in the imagination of men, and its air the beloved element of all delicate

[309] "A true man . . . standard.", struck through in pencil with one diagonal
and one vertical use mark, is used in "Self-Reliance," *W*, II, 60–61.
[310] See "To the Author of 'The Diary of an Ennuyée,'" *Lectures on Art, and
Poems*, by Washington Allston, ed. Richard Henry Dana, Jr. (New York, 1850), pp.
377–380.
[311] Cf. Wordsworth, "Ode: Intimations of Immortality," l. 77, adapted as above,
p. [1]. The first two sentences of this paragraph are used in "Self-Reliance," *W*, II,
45.

Spirits.   The passion for travelling is a mark of our age & of this country & indicates youth, noviciate, & not yet the reign of heroic instincts. It is like the conjugating French verbs which has in some families been called Education. Some people are curious about reliques, Shakspeare's Mulberry, & the houses in which Milton lived; about removing from city to city or country to country the remains of a dead friend. He who has indeed a friend, who has found an unity of consciousness with his brother, & seen into the glorious goal of right & great with him will think little of bringing home his shoes or his body.[312]

21 September. The autumnal equinox comes with sparkling stars and thoughtful days. I think the principles of the Peace party sublime and that the opposers of this philanthropy ⟨have⟩ do not sufficiently consider the positive side of the spiritualist ⟨&⟩ but only see his negative or abstaining side.[313] But if a nation of men is exalted to that ⟨pitch⟩ height of morals as to refuse to fight & choose rather to suffer [145] loss of goods & loss of life than to use violence, they must be not helpless but most effective and great men; they would overawe their invader, & make him ridiculous; they would communicate the contagion of their virtue & inoculate all mankind.

22 Sept. Fonblanque said that the reason of Sir James Scarlett's extraordinary success with juries was that "there were twelve Scarletts in the jurybox."[314]

[September] 23. I wrote long since thus. — When phrenology came, men listened with alarm to the adept who seemed to insinuate with knowing look that they had let out their Secret, that, maugre themselves, he was reading them to the bone & marrow. They were presently comforted by learning that their human incognito would be

---

[312] "I must think the man . . . body." is struck through in pencil with diagonal use marks. The passage "I must think . . . delicate Spirits." is used in "Heroism," *Lectures*, II, 335, and "Heroism," *W*, II, 257–258. On "The passion for travelling" see "Self-Reliance," *W*, II, 82.

[313] Emerson was to emphasize "the positive side" in his lecture before the American Peace Society in Boston on March 12, 1838. See "War," *W*, XI, 151–176.

[314] This paragraph is struck through in pencil with a diagonal use mark.

indulged to them a short time longer, until the artists had settled what allowance was to be made for temperament, & what for counteracting organs, which trifling circumstances hindered the most exact observation from being of any value.

28 Sept. I hope New England will come to boast itself in being a nation of servants, & leave to the planters the misery of being a nation of served.[315]

30 September. The child delights in shadows on the wall. The child prattles in the house, but if you carry him out of doors, he is overpowered by the light & extent of natural objects & is silent.[316] But there was never child so lovely but his mother was glad to get him asleep.

[146] 30 Sept. I get no further than my old doctrine that the Whole is in each man, & that a man may if he will as truly & fully illustrate the laws of Nature in his own experience as in the History of Rome or Palestine or England. A great deal of pregnant business is done daily before our eyes, of which we take very little note. Sift, for instance, what people say in reference to property, when the character of any man is considered. It will appear that it is an essential element to our knowledge of the man what was his opinion, practice, & success, in ⟨life⟩ regard to the institution of property. It tells a great deal of his spiritual history, this part. He was no whole man until he knew how to earn a blameless livelihood. Society is barbarous until every industrious man can get his living without dishonest customs.[317] When Eli Robbins insists that rules of trade apply to clergy as well as shopkeepers, he means no insult but a recognition only that there is a just law of humanity now hid under the canting of society.

[315] This paragraph, struck through in pencil with a vertical use mark, is used in "Doctrine of the Hands," *Lectures*, II, 244, and "The Fortune of the Republic," *W*, XI, 541–542.
[316] "The child delights . . . silent.", struck through in pencil with a vertical use mark, is used in "Domestic Life," *W*, VII, 104.
[317] "Sift, for instance . . . customs.", struck through in pencil with a vertical use mark, is used in "Doctrine of the Hands," *Lectures*, II, 239–240.

[147] October 1. I thought again today how much it needs to preach the doctrine of Being against Seeming. Especially to young women ⟨whose⟩ the tendency of example, of precept, of constitution, & of their first experience ⟨might teach⟩ is almost irresistible in favor of preferring appearances. Let them know that ⟨to⟩ whatever they may think they know to the Contrary, it is not the pretty form, face, or fair hair that wins, much less the skill of dress, but that faces are but urns into which they may infuse an inexpressible loveliness and that every thing they do, every noble choice they make, every forbearance, every virtue beautifies them with a charm to all beholders. Let them know, that, as God liveth, they that be shall have, & not they that seem. One class win now, glitter, & disappear; the other class begins & grows & becomes for ever. Already I see an early old age creeping over faces that were yesterday rosebuds, — because they aimed to seem: I see again the Divinity of hope & power beaming out of eyes that never sparkled with gratified vanity.[318]

[148] The young preacher preached from his ears & his memory, & never a word from his soul. His sermon was loud & hollow. It was not the report so much as the rimbombo, the reverberation of Calvinism. A solemn conclusion of a Calvinistic discourse imitated at the end of a Unitarian sermon, is purely ludicrous like grandfather's hat & spectacles on a rogue of six years. Alas, I could not help thinking how few prophets are left: There are five or six seers & sayers in the land: all the rest of the preaching is the reverberation of theirs. The good hearer is sure he has been touched sometimes, is sure there is somewhat to be reached & some word that can reach it. When he listens to the sanctimonious sounds he comforts himself by their relation to his remembrance of better hours & so they clatter & echo unchallenged.[319]

[149] The young man relying on his instincts who has only a good intention is apt to feel ashamed of his inaction & the slightness

[318] This paragraph, struck through in pencil with a curved diagonal use mark, is used in "Being and Seeming," *Lectures*, II, 302.

[319] "The good hearer . . . unchallenged.", struck through in ink with a vertical use mark, is used in the Divinity School Address, *W*, I, 139.

of his virtue when in the presence of the active & zealous leaders of the philanthropic enterprizes of Universal Temperance, Peace, & Abolition of Slavery. He only loves like Cordelia after his duty.[320] Trust it nevertheless. A man's income is not sufficient for all things. If he spend⟨s⟩ here, he must save there. If he choose to build a solid hearth, he must postpone painting his house. Let each follow his taste, but let not him that loves fine porticoes & avenues, reprove him that chooses to have all weathertight & solid within. It is a grandeur of character which must have unity, & reviews & pries ever into its domestic truth & justice, loving quiet honor better than a proclaiming zeal. I think the zealot goes abroad from ignorance of the riches of his home.

But this good intention which seems so cheap beside this brave zeal is the backbone of the world: ⟨T⟩When the ⟨outworks of the Societies⟩ ↑trumpeters &↓ Heralds have been ⟨won⟩ ↑scattered↓, it is this which must bear the brunt of the fight. This is the martyrable stuff. Let it, for God's sake, grow free & wild, under wind under sun to be solid heart of oak and last forever.[321]

[150] Every day is new; every glance I throw upon nature ought to bring me new information: the gains of each day ought to bestow a new vision on tomorrow's eyes[,] a new melody on tomorrow's ears.

It is very shallow to think the world full of vice because the conventions of Society are little worth. Henry & James & Jane & Anna are generous, tenderhearted, & of scrupulous conscience whilst they are entirely immersed in these poor forms & conventions. Only they are not critical. They may make very great growth too before they shall become critical. By & by, that unfolding must be also & then they will snap asunder the Social cords like green withs. ↑See p 37↓[322]

---

[320] Cf. *King Lear*, I, i, 93 ff:

> "I cannot heave
> My heart into my mouth, I love your Majesty
> According to my bond; no more nor less . . . ."

[321] This and the preceding paragraph, struck through in pencil with a diagonal use mark, are used in "Being and Seeming," *Lectures*, II, 299.

[322] "See p 37" is written in pencil. This paragraph, struck through in pencil with a diagonal use mark, is used in "Being and Seeming," *Lectures*, II, 305.

We put nothing on positive but all on moral obligation[,] nothing on authority all on expediency. This is in strict accord with the ⟨law of the⟩ doctrine we are constrained to preach that God exists entire to the believer today as to Adam & is as good a judge now of what is fit as in the beginning. Say then "Speak Lord thy servant heareth." [323]

[151] Lidian grieves aloud about the wretched negro in the horrors of the middle passage; and they are bad enough. But to such as she, these crucifixions do not come. They come to the obtuse & barbarous to whom they are not horrid but only a little worse than the old sufferings. They exchange a cannibal war for a stinking hold. They have gratifications which would be none to Lidian. The grocer never damned L. because she had not paid her bill; but the good Irish woman has that to suffer once a month. She in return never feels weakness in her back because of the slave-trade. [324] The horrors of the middle passage are the wens & ulcers that admonish us that a violation of nature has ⟨been made⟩ ↑preceded↓. I should not — the nations would not know of the extremity of the wrong but for the terrors of the retribution. [325]

[152] October 2. My classmate Turnbull said of some praised belle that he had seen her on a certain day & did not think her handsome. Gourdin replied that it was a rainy day & she was not well drest. [326] Turnbull insisted that was fudge, that beauty was that which looked well wet days & dry, in silks or flannel.

Whatsoever the mind doth or saith is after a law. Hence the most random word can be set in a place by a philosopher. Why then should we think it strange that critics of today should find wonderful ideal truth in Shakspeare's Tempest, or, much more, in the Homeric mythology[?]

---

[323] Cf. I Sam. 3:9.
[324] "Lidian grieves . . . slave-trade.", struck through in pencil with a diagonal use mark, is used in "The Tragic," W, XII, 415.
[325] "The horrors . . . retribution." is struck through in pencil with a double vertical use mark.
[326] Andrew Turnbull, of Charleston, S. C., and John Gourdin of Pineville, S. C.; Gourdin roomed with Emerson during their junior year at Harvard.

Consumption kills the Speakers. Speaking is apt to engender a worse consumption within. Blessed are they that hear.

I must think that every analogical hint is to our science precious,[327] however odious at first sight its tendency may be. Knowledge is undoubtedly lodged in the affinity betwixt man & ape; in equivocal generation;

[153] I have read the second volume of Bancroft's History of U.S.[328] It is very pleasing. He does not I think ever originate his views, but he imports very good views into his book, & parades his facts by the brave light of his principles. A very pleasant book, for here lo! the huge world has at last come round[329] to Roger Williams, George Fox, & William Penn; & time-honored John Locke receives kicks. ⟨My⟩ An objection to the book is the insertion of a boyish hurra every now & then for each State in turn,[n] which resembles the fortune of the good Professor of Mathematics in a Southern College who was not permitted to go on with his exercise on Election day without interposing in his demonstration A B F equal G H I (Hurra for Jackson!) and so on.

One would think the right use of words is almost lost who reads such a sentence as that of Lord Jefferies[330] to Richard Baxter & compares it with our Latinized formulas. "Richard, thou art an old knave; thou hast written books enough to load a cart, every one as full of sedition as an egg is full of meat. I know thou hast a mighty party, & a great many of the brotherhood are waiting in corners to see what will become of their mighty Don; but by the grace of Almighty God, I'll crush you all."

Bancroft [History of the United States,]
Vol. II   p[p.] 441[–442].

[327] See "The Head," *Lectures*, II, 253: "Every analogical hint is precious."
[328] George Bancroft, *A History of the United States, from the Discovery of the American Continent*, 10 vols. (Boston, 1834–1875).
[329] Cf. "The American Scholar," *W*, I, 115: "the huge world will come round to him."
[330] George Jeffreys, 1st Baron Jeffreys of Wem.

[154] The pagan theology of our churches treats Heaven as an inevitable evil which as there is no help against, the best way is to put the best face on the matter we can. "From whence," said the good preacher yesterday in his prayer, "we shall not be able to return". Truth will out.

We have vastly more kindness than is ever spoken. Maugre all the selfishness, the whole human family is bathed with an element of love like a fine ether. How many persons I meet in houses whom I scarcely speak to, who yet honor me & I them. How many I see in the street or sit with in the Church whom I warmly rejoice to be with. The heart knoweth.[331]

We owe much illustration of moral truth to such teaching as the *composition of forces* which was also mechanically shown us in the College Apparatus. The virtue of society is really the basis of its stability and all the showmen deceive themselves in thinking that their trumpeting does aught.[332]

I think it would be easy to show the great analogical value of most of our natural science. The chemical production of a *new* substance by the combination of old;

[155] Progress of the species. Every soul has to learn the whole lesson for itself. It ⟨has⟩ must go over the whole ground. What it does not see[,] what it does not live it will not know. What the former age has epitomized into a formula or rule for manipular convenience, it will lose all the good of verifying for itself by means of the wall of that Rule. Sometime or other, somewhere or other, it will demand & find compensation for that loss by doing the work itself. How then, since each must go over every line of the ground can there be any progress of the Species? ↑Ferguson discovered many things which had long been very well known. The better for him that he did not know.↓[333]

---

[331] Cf. Prov. 14:10. This paragraph, struck through in pencil and in ink with two diagonal use marks, is used in "The Heart," *Lectures*, II, 282, and "Friendship," *W*, II, 191.

[332] This sentence is struck through in pencil with a diagonal use mark; the first clause is used in "Being and Seeming," *Lectures*, II, 305.

[333] The reference is presumably to James Ferguson (1710–1776), the Scottish

Is it not a reason & a topic for discoursing that the Soul is not admired? Let me say with Plotinus, "Since therefore you admire soul in another thing, admire yourself." [334] Admire the world and admire the more true world of which this is the image —
The beauty of the Soul is immense. [335]

[156] 3 October. The very naming of a subject by a man of genius is the beginning of insight. [336]

We do not love the ⟨strong[?]⟩ man who gives us thoughts in conversation. We do not love that act. Why? does it violate our thinking? does it accuse our unthinking? We like the company of him whose manners or unconscious talk set[s] our own minds in action & we take occasions of rich opinions from him as we take apples off a tree without any thanks. How seldom we meet a man who gives us thoughts directly. It seems as if I could name all my benefactors, though I remember them as I do the lady who made me shirts. Say Dr G[amaliel]. B[radford].; A.B.A[lcott]; [n] M[ary]. M[oody]. E[merson]; C[harles]. C. E[merson]; H[enry]. H[edge]; G[eorge]. P. B[radford]; O[rville]. D[ewey]; [337]   and now that I name them, ⟨&⟩ I see that what I have said is not true for these, & needs much sharp qualification. But we ⟨may⟩ feel towards a person who gives us beforehand what should be one of our thoughts, as we do to one who ⟨t⟩[n] insists on telling us a conundrum we had all but guessed; he has defrauded us of a pleasant labor & a just honor. ↑See p. 283↓

[157] October 5. I was glad to learn that the tree gets only one twentieth of its nourishment from the ground; the rest it drinks in by its aerial roots the leaves from the air. The advantage of a tree-

---

astronomer. This paragraph, struck through in pencil with a diagonal use mark, is used in "History," *W*, II, 10.

[334] *Select Works of Plotinus*, trans. Thomas Taylor (London, 1817), p. 259.

[335] Cf. *ibid.*, p. 116. The sentence, struck through in pencil with two diagonal use marks, is used in "Holiness," *Lectures*, II, 356, and "The Over-Soul," *W*, II, 297.

[336] This sentence is struck through in pencil with a diagonal use mark.

[337] Orville Dewey, then minister of the Second Unitarian Church of New York and formerly of New Bedford, had married a cousin of Emerson, Louisa Farnham, in 1820.

covered country over bald hills & fields in attracting electricity & rain, was also alluded to in the most ridiculous discourse of yesterday's Cattle Show.

Rest is only in principles. Keep the valve open & let them in; the conversation bobs up & down uneasy, immethodical, unsatisfying, heartless, until at last some one opens the soul to it; then the waters without mix with the Great Deep, & equilibrium & peace ensue. ↑As long as you name persons ⟨& parties⟩there can be parties; when you speak of the human soul, there can be none.↓

I gladly see in the last F[oreign]. Q[uarterly]. Review the same doctrine preached in reference to Architecture which I preach in literature & life.[338]

The list of ships' names in the newspaper is worth considering. ⟨It seems⟩ Like[n] the moon[,] the sea seems the refuge of things lost on earth. Fairy, Sylph, Neptune, Britomart, Ivanhoe, Rob Roy.

A great man must always be willing to be little. Captain Pitts was the most important person by his own account of any in the world. No man had ever the advantage of him. But the speculative man has not the temper of the world's man & his voice becomes husky & his eyes look down as the conversation wakens the partisan [158][339] in him. Instantly the changed tone alters the tone of the other speakers, invites attack, scrutiny; lowers their respect & throws him at once into a new position where he can no longer fight at arms' length, but must fight hand to hand with dirk & short sword. Then he has a chance to learn something. Then his memory serves him no longer[.] Now he is put on his wits, — on his manhood; if[n] he is defeated, ⟨so⟩ all the better: he has gained facts; knowledge of himself; of his ignorance; of the strength of others; is cured of some insanity of conceit; & got some moderation & real skill in defence instead. Never sit on the cushion of your advantages. Do not like a coward fly to sanctuary either of place, profession, or manners at the first onset. You must

[338] "Influence of Construction on Style in Architecture," a review of four recent German publications, *Foreign Quarterly Review*, XIX (April 1837), 62–91.
[339] "Defeats" is written above "Instantly" at the top of the page.

pay dearly for the momentary shelter. Thereby you ⟨put⟩ ↑set to a↓ seal & put under lock & key your acquisitions thus far, & enrol yourself Emeritus, & forego the prerogative of humanity — of using your acquisitions as seed wheat & of ⟨going⟩ acquiring the All. Go rather & court defeat, mortification, & disgrace. Nothing venture, Nothing have.[340]

You might as well expect the cannon on ⟨one⟩ ↑the north↓ side of a fort to fire also south & east, as look for victory from the same man in every crisis. There is a time when common sense is impertinent[,] for foresight & philosophy are wanted; ⟨some⟩ a time when arithmetic is vain, for wit & imagination are in request; a time when philosophy & imagination are absurd, for [159] one must act, ↑count, measure,↓ plunge, strike, & die.[341]

I suppose there was seldom a person of my age & advantages whom so little people could pull down & overcrow. The least people do most entirely demolish me. I always find some quarter, & some orts of respect from the mediocre. But a snippersnapper eats me whole.

There is no activity but accomplishes somewhat. A man is sometimes offended at the superfluous supererogatory order & nicety of a woman who is the good housewife. But he must bear with little extremities & flourishes of a quality that makes comfort for all his senses throughout his house. He must look at a virtue *whole*, & not only at the skirt of its garment where it gathers up a little dust.[342]

In the days in which there is no vision we learn that instructive negative.

There are other advantages to be won besides money in the trading of every man. I covet the genuine conversation of my workmen. Where money is the main object in view, it is the least thing gained in the transaction[.]

[160] 6 October. A great man must not grumble at his contemporaries. God saith to him what the poet said,

[340] Cf. Ray, *A Complete Collection of English Proverbs*, 1817, p. 114. The expression is used in "Compensation," *W*, II, 109.

[341] This and the preceding paragraph, struck through in pencil on p. [158] with a diagonal and a vertical use mark, are used in "The Head," *Lectures*, II, 258–259.

[342] This paragraph is struck through in pencil with a diagonal use mark.

The piece, you say, is incorrect; — why, take it,
I'm all submission, What you'd have it, make it.
[Pope, "Epistle to Dr. Arbuthnot," ll. 45–46, misquoted]

If you don't like the world, make it to suit you. All true men
have done so before you. Mr Allston heroically says "His art must
be sufficient to the Artist." But the Danas grumble like sick women.[343]
↑See p. 56↓

I wonder at the interest that Animal Magnetism inspires in fine
persons. Not at all that it startles the thoughtless. I feel no strong
interest in it. I do not doubt the wonder, but there is wonder enough
in my thumbnail already. Its phenomena belong to the copious chapter of Demonology under which category I suppose every body's experience might write a few facts. These obscure facts are only to suggest that our being is richer than we knew; & we are now only in the
fore court or portico. The hints we have, the dreams, the coinci-
dences, do make each man stare once or twice in a lifetime. But Animal
Magnetism seems the phenomena of Disease & too fuliginous &
typhoid in their character to attract any but the physician. I suppose
that as the marketplace & the alleys need to be stimulated by the raw
head & bloody bones of a murder or piracy with wood-cuts so our
wise cotemporaries are glad to be made to wonder by something that
is wonderful to the *senses*. ⟨It is lik⟩ Animal magnetism is the shovel
put under the feet to show how poor [161] our foundations are.[344]
Laban Turner told me that the musicians of the Brigade Band
are paid six dollars a day, & their expenses ⟨paid⟩, & that some of them
are employed almost every day of the year. Several of them are men
of good estate; & they are not dissipated.

8 October. Last evening, I had a good hour with Mrs Ripley.
⟨I think⟩
The young Southerner comes here a spoiled child with graceful
manners, excellent self command, very good to be spoiled more, but

[343] In 1830 Allston, then a widower, married a daughter of Francis Dana, who
had been Chief Justice of the Massachusetts Supreme Court.
[344] Some of the phrasing of the foregoing paragraph is incorporated in "Demonology," *W*, X, 3, 10.

good for nothing else, a mere parader. He has conversed so ⟨long⟩ ↑much↓ with rifles, horses, & dogs that he is become himself a rifle, a horse, & a dog and in civil educated company where anything human is going forward he is dumb & unhappy; like an Indian in a church. Treat them with great deference as we often do, and they accept it all as their due without misgiving. Give them an inch & they take a mile. They are mere bladders of conceit. Each snippersnapper of them all undertakes to speak for the entire Southern states. "At the South, the reputation of Cambridge" &c. &c. which being interpreted, is, In my negro village of Tuscaloosa or Cheraw or St Marks I supposed so & so. "We, at the South," forsooth. They are more civilized than the Seminoles, however, in my opinion; a little more. Their question respecting any man is like a Seminole's, How can he fight? In this country, we ask, What can he do? [345] His pugnacity is all they prize, in man, dog, or turkey. The proper way of treating them is not deference but to say as Mr Ripley [162] does "Fiddle faddle"[n] ⟨In⟩in answer to each solemn remark about "The South." "It must be confessed" said the young man, "that in Alabama, we are dead to every thing, as respects politics." "Very true," replied Mr Ripley, "leaving out the last clause."

[163] I scarce ever see young women who are not remarkably attractive without a wish an impulse to preach to them the doctrine of character. I have sad foresight of the mortifications that await them when I see what they look on. Could once their eye be turned on the beauty of being as it outshines the beauty of seeming, they would be saved.

[164] When C.C E was newly engaged Aug 1833 he writes to E.H.   Do you know there seems to me a rose light shed on the very pages of my law-books.

How is a man wise? by the perception of a principle[.]
    The immortality is as legitimately preached from the intellections as from the moral volitions. Every intellection is prospective. Its present value is its least. It is a little seed. Each principle that a man

[345] See p. [118] above; "Doctrine of the Hands," *Lectures*, II, 244.

acquires is a lanthorn which he instantly turns full on what facts &
thoughts l⟨ie⟩ay already in his mind and instantly all the ⟨clutter &⟩
rubbish that had littered his garret become precious. Every old &
trivial fact in his private biography becomes illustration of this new
principle & is recalled into day & delights all men by its piquancy &
new charm. Men say where did he get this? & think there was something divine in his life. But no; they have myriads of facts just as
good, would they only get a lamp to ransack their attics withal.[346]

[165] Insist that the Schelling, Schleiermacher, Ackermann or
whoever propounds to you an Ontology, is only a more or less awkward translator of entities in your consciousness which you have
also[,] your own way of seeing, perhaps of denominating. Say then,
instead of too timidly pouring into his obscure sense that he has not
succeeded in rendering back to you your consciousness: he has not
succeeded, now let another try. If Spinosa cannot, perhaps Kant will:
If Kant cannot, then perhaps Alcott. Any how, when at last it is done,
you will find it no recondite but a simple common state which the
writer restores to you.[347]   ↑See C. p. 120↓[130?]

[166][348] A good coat is always respected, they say, in the stage coach.
⟨Reason⟩ Good reason; a good coat stands for Something, implies a
small history: it shows that the wearer had some kind of a coat before, probably a good one & will have another when this is worn out;
it shows that the wearer lives among people who wear good coats.
Beside a man's coat money is usually only a small proportion to his
food & ↑fire &↓ house & travelling money & by the ⟨goodness⟩ outlay
he can afford in the coat, ⟨they⟩ ↑we↓ infer what outlay he can make
in all.

The common complaint is of the dulness of life. I do not know
but it must be confessed that the glance we give at the world in a

---

[346] This paragraph, struck through in ink with a curved vertical use mark, is
used in "The Head," *Lectures*, II, 253–254, and "Intellect," *W*, II, 332.

[347] This paragraph, struck through in pencil with a diagonal use mark and in
ink with a vertical use mark, is used in "The Head," *Lectures*, II, 260–261, and "Intellect," *W*, II, 344–345.

[348] "A coat" and "Who loses wins" are written respectively above "A good" and
"always respected" at the top of the page as index headings for the two entries below.

leisure hour is melancholy: that melancholy cleaves to the English mind as to the Aeolian harp. But I maintain that all melancholy belongs to the exterior of man [349] * [*See above p. 77]; I claim to be a part of the All. All exterior life declares interior life. I could not be but that absolute life circulated in me & I could not think this without being that absolute life. The constant ⟨strife in⟩ warfare in each heart is betwixt Reason & Commodity. The victory is won as soon as any soul has learned always to take sides with Reason against himself; to transfer his *Me* from his person, his name, his interests, back upon Truth & Justice, so that when he is disgraced & defeated & fretted & disheartened [167] & wasted by nothings, he bears it well, never one instant relaxing his watchfulness, & as soon as he can get a respite from the insults or the sadness, records all these phenomena, pierces their beauty as phenomena, and like a god oversees himself ⟨as a valley⟩. Thus he harvests his losses & turns the dust of his shoes to gems.[350]

Keep the habit of the observer & as fast as you can, break off your association with your personality & identify yourself with the Universe. Be a football to time & chance[,] the more kicks the better so that you inspect the whole game & know its uttermost law. As true is this ethics for trivial as for calamitous days.   ↑See p 158 & p. 240.↓

———

It is better to hear than to speak. As long as I hear truth, I am bathed by a beautiful element & am not conscious of any limits to my nature. The suggestions are thousandfold that I hear & see. The waters of the great Deep have ingress & eggress [egress] to the soul. But if I speak, then I define, confine, ⟨& amless⟩ & am less. Silence is a menstruum that dissolves personality & gives us leave to be great & universal.[351]

———

Let me add of the winning loser described above, that a wise

[349] For "melancholy cleaves . . . Aeolian harp." see Journal B, p. [117]. The paragraph to this point, struck through in pencil with a diagonal use mark, is used in "The Tragic," W, XII, 406.

[350] "The victory is won . . . gems.", struck through in pencil with diagonal use marks, is used in "The Head," *Lectures*, II, 259.

[351] For the first sentence of this paragraph, see Journal B, p. [108], and cf. p. [152] above: "Blessed are they that hear." The paragraph, struck through in pen-

man will come to see the truth & wit of all the ⟨reproaches⟩ censures
he received during his nonage and to apply the very same with better
wit & skill to the same faults as they reappear elsewhere like the
defenders of a besieged town who gather up the ⟨bullets⟩ dead balls
that have been discharged at them & launch them at the enemy.

[168] We are carried by destiny along our life's course looking
as grave & knowing as little as the infant who is carried in his wicker
coach thro' the street.

[October] 12. I learn from the Westminster Review (July
1837) that the French make better gloves than the English because
they have a better knowledge of the shape of the hand. That they
also are never guilty of the inaccuracy of printing with a flower on
silks or papers, leaves not belonging to that flower, as the English
are. Also that the most beautiful scroll ornaments & indeed designs
of every kind on a Cashmere shawl[,] on all upholstery[,] & furniture may be traced to the walls of Egyptian palaces & tombs whence
first the Greeks borrowed them[.] [352]

[169]   "Stir not my bones
             Which are laid in clay
             For I must rise at
             The Resurrection day."

             Woman, from Calidasa's Megha Duta [stanza 81]
                          translated by Professor Wilson
             There in the fane a beauteous creature stands
             The first best work of the Creator's hands
             Whose slender limbs inadequately bear
             A full orbed bosom and a weight of care
             Whose teeth like pearls whose lips like cherries show
             And fawn-like eyes still tremble as they glow.
                    [Cf. "A Familiar Analysis of Sanskrit Poetry,"
                    No. II,] Asiatic Journal Aug. 1837 [XXIII, 243]

---

cil with a diagonal use mark, is used in "The Head," *Lectures,* II, 257–258, and
"Intellect," *W,* II, 342, 343.

   [352] From an article on arts, manufactures, and public taste, *The London and
Westminster Review,* XXVII (July 1837), 135, 134, 128.

The words entered not the grieving heart but returned to him that spoke them.

"He that taketh off weights advantageth motion as much as he that addeth wings;" said Pym, when he proposed to remove grievances *before* granting subsidies.[353]

"Principle is a passion for truth." *Hazlitt* [354]

"It is not permitted to a man to corrupt himself for the sake of mankind."
                                                              Rousseau

Character is the only Rank[.]

[170] October 13. With much to say I put off writing until perhaps I shall have nothing in my memory. Now too soon then too late. I must try the pen & make a beginning[.]
At Boston Thursday I found myself nearly alone in the Athenaeum & so dropt my book to gaze at the Laocoon. The main figure is great: the two youths work harmoniously ⟨with the man⟩ on the eye producing great admiration, so long as the eye is directed at the old man, but look at them & they are slight & unaffecting statues. No miniature copy ↑and no single busts↓ can do justice to this work. Its mass & its integrity are essential. At the Athenaeum, you cannot see it unless the room is nearly empty. For you must stand at the distance of nearly the whole hall to see it and interposing bystanders ⟨break⟩ eclipse the statue. How is time abolished by the delight I have in this old work and without a name I receive it as a gift from the Universal Mind.

[171] Then I read with great content the ⟨July⟩ ↑August↓ number of the Asiatic Journal. Herein is always the piquancy of the meeting of civilization & barbarism. Calcutta or Canton are twilights where Night & Day contend. A very good paper is the Narrative of Lord Napier's mission to China (who arrived at Macao 15 July 1834 and

[353] Cf. John Forster, "John Pym," in Dionysius Lardner, ed., *Cabinet Cyclopædia: Lives of Eminent British Statesmen* (London, 1831–1839), III (1837), 90; see *L*, II, 100.
[354] William Hazlitt, "On Good Nature," *The Round Table: A Collection of Essays on Literature, Men, and Manners*, 2 vols. (Edinburgh, 1817), II, 17.

died 11 October.) There stand in close contrast the brief wise English despatches with the mountainous nonsense of the Chinese diplomacy. The "red permit" writ by the vermilion pencil of the emperor, the superafrican ignorance with which England is disdained as out of the bounds of civilization, & her king called "reverently submissive" &c, &c.[355] There is no farce in fiction better than this historical one of John Bull & the Yellow Man: albeit it ends tragically, as Lord Napier died of vexation apparently. I must get that book again.

Then I read an ascent of the Himmaleh mounts and the terror of the cold & the river seen bursting through caves of snow, and the traveller finding all over the desolate mountains bears' dung. Then, a duel: pistols for two and coffee for the survivor. Then an escape from a tiger in a cane-brake.

Then thinking of the trees which draw out of the air their food by their aerial roots the leaves, I mused on the strange versatility of the mind's appetite & food. Here were in the Reading Room some four or five men besides me, feeding on newspapers & Journals[,] unfolding our being thereby. Secluded from War, from trade, & from tillage, we were making amends to ourselves by [172] devouring the descriptions of these things & atoning for the thinness by the quantity of our fare.

C.C.E. said that any man could be a great lawyer who would stoop to be so.

[173] I can easily persuade myself — can I not persuade others that ⟨Caesar⟩ kingdom & lordship[,] power & estate are only a more pompous vocabulary than private John & Edward in a small house & common day's work? But the things of life are the same to both. The sum total of both is the same. Yet I read with joy the life of Hampden, Pym, or Penn, of men conversant with governments & Revolutions and dilate in the swelling scene. Is not the delight I there find an intimation that not always in speculation[,] not always by the poetic imagination alone, shall the scholar[,] the private soul be great, but one day ⟨by⟩ ↑in↓ action also? When private men shall

---

[355] "A Sketch of Lord Napier's Negociations with the Authorities at Canton," *Asiatic Journal*, N. S. XXIII (Aug. 1837), 267–279.

act with vast views, the lustre will be transferred from the actions of kings to those of gentlemen. It made my heart beat quicker to think that the gorgeous pictures which fill my imagination in reading the actions of Hampden, Pym, Falkland are only a revelation to me how needlessly mean our life is, that we by the depth of our living should deck it with more than regal or national splendor.[356]   Very coarse, very abhorrent to the imagination is the American White House. Because it has no historic lustre & natural growth out of feudalism &c like theirs, & is not on the other hand a new creation out of the soul, out of virtue & truth, outshining theirs but is an imitation of their gaudiness like a negro gay with cast off epaulettes & gold laced hat of his master. ↑See p. 178↓

[174][357] How very significant are things. How few lines tell how complex a story. A man whose coat has lost the haunch button. A man with a ragged coat. A man with a good coat. A neck is a neck, we say; but the limner knows better, — knows that ⟨one outline⟩ if the pencil swerve this way, it draws a beast; if that way, a god. The addition of a little capacity of attention would change a fool into a Shakspeare. Do manners tell no story? Did you ever see a poor child to whom if you offered a piece of cake it would grab it with a scream & put it behind its back, *as a Broad-Street child will do*.
    See B

[175][358] Oct. 14. A house wants a good hat & a good pair of shoes.

A fact like the lacking haunch button: which so pricks attention, is ever worth recording. We do not yet understand the fact, but may trust that it would not so draw our eye but for some significant truth which it covers.

---

[356] The paragraph to this point is struck through in pencil with a diagonal use mark and in ink with a vertical use mark. The last sentence is used in "Heroism," *Lectures*, II, 335, and "Heroism," *W*, II, 258; the preceding sentences are used in "Self-Reliance," *W*, II, 62–63.

[357] "Expression" is written above "How very significant" at the top of the page.

[358] "Eyetraps", "Boys know", "All new" are written above "Oct 14 . . . hat" at the top of the page as index headings for the second, third, and fourth entries below.

Therefore I will not omit what caught my ear the other day[:] the certainty there is, that every boy among boys will find his exact place as surely as a potato in a waterpail its specific gravity. The foreign boy comes to the school with airs & pretensions: an old boy sniffs thereat & says to himself It is of no use; we shall find ⟨them⟩ ↑him↓ out tomorrow.[359]

When a soul has set forth on its career of Culture it learns that the number of novel objects for its study is coextensive with the number of objects in the world. Each one it is to challenge & see anew. Not an old church bell but it is anew to hear as for the first time & weigh its sense. Not a baker's score, not a lamppost, not a stagecoach, but he is to explore its value in absolute being & interrogate mainly its relation to him. What does Sardanapalus mean to me? Answer. It means the love of self indulgence which shrinks & cowers over the fire & will not stretch itself to get what it exceedingly covets, conscious albeit the while that when it has once manned itself & drawn on coat & hat & rubbers, it will be just as pleasant to face the blast & laugh at the fireside. —

[176][360] Go out to walk with a painter and you shall see for the first time groups, colors, clouds, & keepings,[n] and shall have the pleasure of discovering resources in a hitherto barren ground[,] of finding as good as a new sense in such skill to use an old one. Gentilhomme Bourgeois was really right in being glad to know that he was talking prose.[361] When the telescope turns on our own barn & chimney we like the new old sight better than the finest foreign turrets.

October 15. Mr Hoar says he would not give one cent for the effect upon a jury of a lawyer who does not believe in his heart that his client ought to have a verdict. If he does not believe it, ⟨the⟩ his belief will appear to the jury & become their belief. This is that law, — is it not? — whereby a work of art of whatever kind sets

[359] This paragraph, struck through in pencil with a diagonal use mark, is used in "Being and Seeming," *Lectures*, II, 302, and "Spiritual Laws," *W*, II, 157–158. For the potato image, see Journal B, p. [84].

[360] "New Eyes." and "What is, appears." are written above "Go out . . . painter" at the top of the page as index headings for the two entries below.

[361] M. Jourdain in Molière, *Le Bourgeois gentilhomme*, II, vi.

us in the same state of mind as the artist was in when he made it. So said Swedenborg[:] in the spiritual world no person can pronounce a word which he does not believe though he try never so hard & fold his lips to indignation.[362]

[177][363] October 16. Scholastic fancies — which I account to be at least as good as those of my financial fathers whom I encountered in solemn session in the Bank parlor. I was caught by the name of "Fuller's Worthies of England," & tempted like some great Columbus or Ledyard instantly to get to horse & travel to Cambridge Library & spend a day with Fuller. The same emotions take different directions & of course clothe themselves at last in strangest varied acts as the same drop that fell on the ridge of Mount Washington goes ↑half↓ to New York & half to Canada.

The grandeurs of England[,] the sepulchral monuments of old families came up in my imagination as I read Ben Jonson. Those marble scrolls & heraldic pomps that so cold & dim deck the tombs in churches were not meant to project on the eye like the blue slate stone of John Crosby which yesterday I saw *outside* of Billerica graveyard[;] their Office is not to shine like a rocket but to be aloof[,] a faint departing vision to fill up as tassel or fringe the hollow places of the memory of the name they bear.

It is well to study the necessary cause of the marble tomb in the religion & culture of the society. The Rom⟨ish⟩↑an↓ Church built tombs; the theology of the verse I have copied above p. 169, was ⟨careful⟩ ↑saving↓ of the dust: A philosophic period would build anything but tombs.

[178] Oct. 16. The babe stands alone today for the first time.

In History, our imagination makes fools of us, plays us false. Why all this deference to Sidney & Hampden[,] to Pym & Vane? Suppose

---

[362] For the allusion to Swedenborg, see *The Apocalypse Revealed*, 1836, I, 255; *JMN*, IV, 343; Journal B, pp. [4] and [127]. This paragraph, struck through in pencil with a diagonal use mark, is used in "Being and Seeming," *Lectures*, II, 300, and "Spiritual Laws," *W*, II, 156–157. Cf. also the "maxim in art" cited in "The Eye and Ear," *Lectures*, II, 270.

[363] "Fuller's Worthies" and "Tombs" are written above "October 16 . . . which" at the top of the page as index headings for the two entries below.

they were virtuous, did they wear out virtue? As great a stake depends ↑upon↓[,] as mighty Motives move your private act today, as
touched their public & renowned steps.[364]   ↑See p. 173↓

Knowledge alters every thing & makes every thing fit for use.
The vocabulary of two omniscient men would embrace words &
images now excluded from all polite conversation.[365] The wise will
⟨pro⟩ use the language which once he rejected. Wisdom is free.
↑See p. 181↓

Culture inspects our dreams also. The pictures of the night will
always bear some proportion to the visions of the day.[366]

I looked over the few books in the young clergyman's study
yesterday till I shivered with cold. Priestley; Noyes; Rosenmuller;
Joseph Allen, & other Sunday School books; Schleusner; Norton; &
the Saturday Night of Taylor; [367] the dirty comfort of the farmer
could easily seem preferable to the elegant poverty of the young
clergyman.

[179] What a dream our Boston is, and New York will one day be
an ancient illustration.

The great poets are content with truth. They use the positive

[364] "In History . . . steps.", struck through in pencil and ink with two vertical
use marks, is used in "Self-Reliance," *W*, II, 62, 63.

[365] "Knowledge alters . . . conversation.", struck through in ink with a vertical
use mark, is used in "The Poet," *W*, III, 17.

[366] This sentence is used in "Spiritual Laws," *W*, II, 148; cf. "Memory," *W*, IX,
295: "Night-dreams trace on Memory's wall / Shadows of the thoughts of
day . . . ."

[367] The authors are Joseph Priestley, chemist and clergyman, who wrote *Unitarianism Explained and Defended* (1796) and *A General History of the Christian
Church* (1802); George Rapall Noyes, translator of Job, Psalms, and Proverbs and
writer of various Unitarian tracts; Johann Georg Rosenmüller, German theologian,
or his son Ernst Friedrich Karl Rosenmüller, Orientalist and biblical scholar; Joseph
Allen, minister of the First Church at Northboro, Mass., and conductor of a noted
school in its parsonage; Johann Friedrich Schleusner, German biblical scholar; and
Andrews Norton, of Cambridge, author of *The Evidences of the Genuineness of the
Gospels*, 3 vols. (1837–1844). "Saturday Night" is evidently Isaac Taylor's *Saturday Evening* (1832).

degree. They seem frigid & phlegmatic to those who have been spiced with the frantic passion and violent coloring of the modern Byrons & Hemanses & Shelleys. But it is like taking a walk or drinking cold water, to the simple who read them.[368] Such is Ben Jonson whose Epistles to Wroth & others; & Penshurst & a Masque in Vol 3 of Nature & Prometheus &c I read this morn.[369] I call this their Humanity. ↑See p 222↓

A lovely afternoon and I went to Walden Water & read Goethe on the bank.

↑In↓ the ⁿ present moment all the past is ever represented. The strong roots of ancient trees still bind the soil. The Provencal literature is not obsolete for me, for I have Spenser's Faerie Queen to read and all that faded splendor revives again in him for some centuries yet. Nor will Homer or Sophocles let me go though I read them not for they have formed those whom I read. Nor will the Egyptian designer die to me[;] my chair & tables forget him not[.] [370] ↑(See above p. 168)↓

[180] Time is the principle of levity dissipating solidest things like exhalations. The monasteries of the Middle Ages were builded of timber, brick, & stone, so were the temples of Jove & those of Osiris[,] yet they dance now before me late come into their globe like words or less.

Oct. 17. The character of the ancient English gentleman as I gather it from Hampden's remark concerning Sir Edward Vere, was, "All summer in the field, all winter in his study." Of this man he adds — "in whose fall, fame makes this kingdom a great loser."

                              Life of Pym [Hampden] [371]

[368] "The great poets . . . them." is struck through in pencil with a diagonal use mark.
[369] Emerson's references are to "The Forest," Bk. II, ii, iii ff, and to the masque "Mercury Vindicated from the Alchymists," in *The Works of Ben. Johnson*, 6 vols. (London, 1716), III, 177 ff, 470–478.
[370] This paragraph is struck through in pencil and in ink with two diagonal use marks.
[371] Cf. John Forster, "John Hampden," in Lardner, *Cabinet Cyclopædia: Lives*

October 18. Custom is the Circe whose cup makes fool & beast of us. Would you know how abhorrent to all right reason is War, see what horrid spectres it creates, when it locks up the beauty of Man in one of those brass or iron lobsters that we so wisely admire in the Tower of London[.]

In the fine day we despise the house.

[181] Every man is weak himself but strong in relation to others. I am afraid of Mr Bacon, but Mr Bacon also is afraid of me. I am solicitous of the goodwill of the meanest person, afraid of his ill will. But the sturdiest offender of my peace & of society's, if you rip up his claims is as thin & timid as any. And the peace of Society is kept because as children say, one is afraid & the other dares not. Far off, men swell & bully & threaten, bring them hand to hand, and they are a feeble folk.[372]

I am willing to know in my bosom these palpitations for a time that I may learn their law.

The *brize* of Io Æschylus mentions again & again. This is another sense to the saying that "intense light will make anything beautiful."[373] What would be base even obscene to the obscene said in a great connexion of thought by the great becomes illustrious. So the oft marked grossnesses of the Hebrew prophets.[374] ↑See above p 178↓

Again see how fleeting is form. Io ⟨changed⟩ ↑transformed↓ into a cow offends the imagination; but how changed when as Isis in Egypt she meets Jove[,] a beautiful woman with nothing of the metamorphosis left but the lunar horns as the splendid ornament of her brows.[375]

---

of *Eminent British Statesmen*, III (1837), 318. The "remark" is used in "Prudence," *Lectures*, II, 324.

[372] This paragraph, struck through in pencil and ink with two diagonal use marks, is used in "Prudence," *Lectures*, II, 320, and "Prudence," *W*, I, 238.

[373] See *JMN*, IV, 376; *Nature, W*, I, 15.

[374] This paragraph, struck through in ink with a vertical use mark, is used in "The Poet," *W*, III, 17.

[375] This paragraph, struck through in ink with a vertical use mark, is used in "History," *W*, II, 14.

One of the last secrets we learn as scholars is to confide in our own impressions of a book. If Æschylus is that man he is taken for, he has not yet done his office when he has educated the learned of Europe for a thousand years[;] [182][376] he is now to approve himself a master of delight to me also. If he cannot do that, all his fame shall avail him nothing. I were a fool not to sacrifice a thousand Aeschyluses to my intellectual integrity.[377]

Skill in writing ⟨(if not general Culture)⟩[378] consists in ⟨substi⟩ making every word cover a thing. In the tragedies of Æschylus the thing is tragic and all the fine names of gods & goddesses stand for something in the reader's mind. ⟨It is remarkable⟩ The human mind is impatient of falsehood & drops all words that do not stand for verities: this by its instinct. Thus the Greeks called Jove, Supreme God, but having traditionally ascribed to him very bad & false actions, they involuntarily made amends to Reason by tying up the hands of so bad a god. He is like a king of England so helpless alone. Prometheus knows one secret which he is obliged to bargain for. He cannot get his own thunders. Minerva keeps the key of them,

> "Of all the Gods I only know the keys
> That ope the solid doors within whose vaults
> His thunders sleep."
> > *The Furies* of Aeschylus
> > [tr. R. Potter, ll. 894–896, misquoted]

A plain confession of the endless inworking of the All. & of its moral aim.[379]

[183] I went thro' the wood to Sleepy Hollow & sat down to hear the harmless roarings of the sunny Southwind. Into the narrow throat of the vale flew dust & leaves from the fields, & straggling leaves mounted & mounted to great heights. The shining boughs

---

[376] "Truth will out" is written above "himself a master" at the top of the page.

[377] This paragraph, struck through in ink with vertical use marks, is used in "The Head," *Lectures*, II, 260, and "Intellect," *W*, II, 344.

[378] "if not general Culture" is enclosed in penciled parentheses and canceled in pencil.

[379] "Thus the Greeks . . . aim.", struck through in ink with a diagonal use mark, is used in "Compensation," *W*, II, 106.

of the trees in the sun, the swift sailing clouds, & the warm air made me think a man is a fool to be mean & unhappy when every day is made illustrious by these splendid shows.[380] If Nature relented at all from her transcending laws, if there were any traces in the daily Obituary that the yellow fever spared this doctor or that Sunday School teacher, if any sign were that a "good man" was governing, we should lose all our confidence, the world all its sublimity. ↑See p. 22↓

Oct. 19. We demand the sufficient reason for every fact. The Greek marbles amaze us until ⟨we⟩ our knowledge or our reflection has supplied every step from the common human consciousness to such peculiar excellence, as, e.g. a^n religion asking Statues; Pentelican quarries; the Egyptian arts; the happy climate & presence of perfect naked forms in the games; the ⟨unreflecting⟩ unchained imagination now experimenting in a new direction & so unfettered by any conventions; the unreflecting genius of the people which permitted them to surrender themselves to the instincts of taste.

In skating over thin ice your safety is in your speed and a critical judgment would have checked & so broken the invention of Phidias, & his fellows.[381]

[184] A gothic cathedral affirms that it was done by us and not done by us. Surely it was by Man but we find it not in our man. Then we remember the forest dwellers, the first temples, the ⟨imitation & idealisation of⟩ adherence to ⟨&⟩ the first type, & the decoration of it as the wealth of the nation increased. The value which is given to wood by carving led to the carving over the whole mountain of stone of a cathedral. When we have gone through this process and added thereto the Catholic Church its Cross, its music, its processions, its Saints' days & image worship, we have, as it were, ⟨made⟩ been the man that made the minster, we have seen how it could & must be, we have the sufficient reason.[382]

---

[380] "I went thro' . . . shows.", struck through in pencil with a vertical use mark, is used in "The Eye and Ear," *Lectures*, II, 273–274.

[381] This sentence, struck through in pencil with a diagonal use mark, is recast on p. [200] below.

[382] This paragraph, struck through in pencil with a diagonal use mark, is used in "The Eye and Ear," *Lectures*, II, 268, and "History," *W*, II, 11–12.

So stand we before every public every private work; before an oration of Webster, before a victory of Napoleon; before a martyrdom of Sir Thomas More, of Sidney, of Marmaduke Robinson[;] [383] ⟨We⟩ before a French Reign of Terror and a Salem hanging of Witches; before a fanatic revival, and the Animal Magnetism ⟨of⟩ ↑in Paris or in↓ Providence. We assume that we in like influence should be like affected & should achieve the like, & we aim to master intellectually the steps & reach the same height or the same degradation that our fellow our proxy has done. [384]

[185]   The Appeal to the Future.

The appeal to the future is a great part of life. The boy is allowed to be ignorant & helpless because of the tacit appeal to what he shall be & do. Then comes the young man, the young woman; they have studied much latin and german, but do not know the meaning of this sentence, and are ashamed to use the dictionary, or to say 'I do not know.' Consent to be despised as ignorant now, and boldly appeal to the Future, still. You are old if you reckon the short human life but if you compare your years with the eternity into which you advance, ⟨yo the⟩ to your extreme youth this unskilfulness will seem very reasonable. And this I think is the reason why Genius is said to retain the feelings & freshness of Childhood, because to it the horizon does not shut down a short way before the eye, but opens indefinitely.

Trust the Future & it shall not betray you. The young man finds the present hostile & cold, it pays him no dividend, it bakes him no bread. He takes this to be unequivocal hint that he should abandon his poetic thoughts & all his higher culture & should accept the ⟨popular⟩ vulgar maxims of thrift as the only trustworthy truth.

But let him, on the contrary, according to the Spartan maxim of fighting better in the shade, /use/thank God for/ this cold eclipse as happiest leisure which he shall not always have & bend himself with nimble vigor to laying up the stores of rare knowledge, court

[383] As Charles Eliot Norton pointed out to Edward Emerson, Emerson probably compounded "Marmaduke Robinson" out of "the names of the two Quakers hung on Boston Common in 1659, Marmaduke Stevenson and William Robinson" (W, II, 382, n. 1 to W, II, 10).

[384] This paragraph, struck through in pencil with diagonal use marks, is used in "History," W, II, 10–11.

the sublime muse, and if his lodging is narrow & his fare the Pytha-
gorean bean,[385] regale himself with the august society of all the
bards & philosophers, verily he has chosen well, he shall never be
ashamed.[386]

[186][387] A great step is made before the soul can feel itself
not a charity boy, not a bastard, not an interloper in its own world.
To most men a palace, a statue, or a costly book have an alien air
much like a gay equipage, and seem to say like that, ⟨w⟩Who are you,
Sir? A man is to know that they all are his, suing his notice, petitioners to his faculties, that they will come out & take possession, born
thralls to his sovereignty, conundrums he alone can guess, chaos
until he come like a Creator & give them light & order. My position
in the world is wholly changed as soon as I see that a picture waits
for my verdict & is not to command me but I am to settle its claims
to praise. The arts are appeals to my Taste; the laws, to my Understanding; Religion to my Reason. Indeed it is a changed position.
Now I come meek but well assured as a Youth who comes to the
College to be matriculated not like an interloper who gets in at an
open door to gaze at some thing that caught his eye in the street.
⟨It seems as if⟩ That ⁿ popular fable of the sot who was picked up dead
drunk in the street, carried to the duke's house, washed & dressed &
put in the duke's bed, and then on his waking treated with all ⟨cere-
mony⟩ obsequious ceremony like the duke & assured that he had
been insane, owes its popularity to the fact that it symbolizes so well
the state of man in the world who is actually a sot & a vagabond but
now & then wakes up & finds himself ⁿ [187] a true prince.[388]   This
is the discipline of the mind in the degrees of property. He learns

[385] As Edward Emerson points out, Pythagoras forbade use of the bean rather
than prescribing it (*J*, IV, 329, n. 1).

[386] The three paragraphs headed "The Appeal to the Future." are struck through
in pencil with a diagonal use mark; the first is used in "Being and Seeming," *Lectures*, II, 303.

[387] "Taking possession." is written above "A great step" at the top of the page.

[388] Cf. *The Taming of the Shrew*, Induction; Warton, *The History of English
Poetry*, 1824, IV, 118–121, quotes other versions of the same tale. "A great step
. . . prince.", struck through in both pencil and ink with vertical use marks, is
used in Human Culture: "Introductory," *Lectures*, II, 223, and "Self-Reliance," *W*,
II, 61–62.

that above the merely external rights to the picture, to the equipage, — which the law protects, — is, a spiritual property which is Insight. The Kingdom of the Soul transcendeth all the walls & muniments of possession & taketh higher rights not only in the possession but in the possessor, & with this royal reservation can very well afford to leave the so-called proprietor undisturbed as ⟨h⟩i⟨s⟩ts keeper or trustee.

Therefore the wise soul cares little to whom belongs the legal ownership of the Grand Monadnoc, of the Cataract of Niagara, or of the Belvedere Apollo, or whatever else it prizes. It soon finds that no cabinet though decorated with colonnades miles long were large enough to hold the beautiful wonders it has made its own. It has found the beauty & the wonder progressive; the street is not without its charm; the blacksmith's shop is a picture; the motion & the sound[,] the play of living light on things it cannot spare. At last it discovers that the whole world is a museum & that things are more glorious in their order & home than when a few are carried away to ⟨shine⟩ glitter alone.[389]

Let us be honest. Selection is beautiful also. A ⟨nosegay of⟩ well chosen nosegay has its own charm ⟨which⟩ ↑& affects the eye as↓ fields of the same flowers cannot.

[188][390] When you are sincerely pleased without any misgiving, you are nourished.[391]

Nature softens & harmonizes: she curls the hair where it terminates above the neck; ⟨the waves break into loveliest forms &⟩ ↑as↓ she curves the ⟨borders⟩ ↑margin↓ of lakes & ponds, & breaks the waves into loveliest forms & paints shadows on the ground & the wall.

October 20. As the contemporaries of Columbus hungered to see the wild man so undoubtedly we should have the liveliest in-

---

[389] "This is the discipline . . . alone.", struck through in pencil with a diagonal use mark and in ink with a vertical use mark, is used in Human Culture: "Introductory," *Lectures*, II, 223–224.

[390] "Wild man attracts" is written above "When you are" at the top of the page.

[391] This sentence is marked in pencil with a marginal line; "without any misgiving" is enclosed in pencil parentheses, possibly Emerson's.

terest in a wild man but men in society do not interest us because they are tame. We know all they will do and man is like man as one steamboat is like another. Tame men are inexpressibly tedious like the talking with a young Southerner who says "Yes ↑Sir"↓, indifferently to every sort of thing you say, thinking *Yes sir*, to mean nothing.

From every man even from great men as the world goes, a large deduction is to be made on account of this taming, or Conventions. His going to church does not interest me because all men go to church. His staying at home would, until I see why he stays at home; ⁿ if from vulgar reasons, — it is dulness still. But he falls desperately in love. ⟨a⟩Ah ha! does he? now I am wide awake[.] This is not conventional but the great epoch of the revelation of Beauty to his soul. Now let me see every line he writes, every step he makes, every kiss which makes him immortal; let those laugh who never were worthy to love; [392] to me each act of [189][393] his in these golden hours is holy & beautiful. The eternal beauty of this passion is sufficiently shown from the interest which attaches to every sort of love-tale in verse or prose which the press spawns from January to December.

We are eager to know what Shakspeare said at the Boar's Head in Eastcheap. We should like to see him bring wood to his fire or walking in his /yard/field/ but rather would we see what book he chose to entertain a solitary evening or refusing all books what he did. Rather would I know how he looked at the Supreme Being in some lonely hour of fear or gratitude, hear what he said, or know what he forbore to say.

Boswellism scrapes all together & would know how the hero did what every body does & what he did as every body does it. But the philosopher drops all the conventional part & only studies the new & voluntary part of each man. As far as Sir Walter Scott aspired to be known for a fine gentleman so far our sympathies leave him. We know very well the height of that doll & do not suppose he was any finer gentleman than Beau Brummel or Lord Chesterfield. Our

[392] "As the contemporaries . . . love;", struck through in pencil with a vertical use mark, is used in "Being and Seeming," *Lectures*, II, 306.
[393] "Selfhood attracts" is written above "his . . . golden" at the top of the page.

concern is only with the residue where the Man Scott was warmed with a divine ray that clad with beauty every sheet of water[,] every bald hill in the country he looked upon & so reanimated the well nigh obsolete feudal ⁿ [190] history & illustrated every trivial corner of a barren & disagreeable territory.[394]

In our times, a good example was set by the members of the New Jerusalem Church in London. Somebody at great pains violated the tomb of Swedenborg & brought away the skull from the body. It was then offered at a great price to his disciples. Not one of them ⟨would⟩ cared to look at it. The Roman Church exhibits & sells the hair of St Paul & the shoes of St Luke. Luther & Calvin ↑who↓ wore out their life upon the epistles of one & the Gospel of the other made all jokes upon the old hair & the mouldy leather. ↑See p. 144↓

Margaret Fuller talking of Women, said, "Who would be a goody that could be a genius?"

[191] We are of that sympathetic nature that ⟨an open⟩ a half open trunk or snuff box disposes us to gape.

When I commended the adroit New York broker to Alcott he replied that he saw he had more austerity than I, and ↑that he↓ gave his hand with some reluctance to a mere merchant or banker. What is so comic, I pray, as the mutual condescension with which Alcott & Col. Perkins [395] would give the hand to each other?

What a cry about adapting your word to the comprehension of people. The newspaper and Maria Monk [396] I suppose are the only things adapted to their comprehension.

The same complaint I have heard is made against the Boston Medical College as against the Cambridge Divinity School that those

[394] This and the preceding paragraph, struck through in pencil on p. [189] with a diagonal use mark, are used in "Being and Seeming," Lectures, II, 306–307.

[395] Colonel Thomas Handasyd Perkins of Boston.

[396] Awful Disclosures of Maria Monk . . . , the notorious anti-Catholic narrative since adjudged a hoax, had been published in 1836, provoking much discussion.

who there receive their education, want faith, & so are not as successful as practitioners from the country schools who believe in the power of medicine. ↑See p. 207↓

[192] October 21. One of the facts which I contemplate with awe because it is the beneficence of the circumambient Soul & no way a benefit of Consciousness is the aid we get from alien events. I fully intended to have done a deed which I esteemed not unfit nor unnecessary. I was hindered by the absence of the parties concerned. Now I see that the deed is far better undone and thankfully owe the hint for my future guidance to the God.

A valuable fact is that mutual teaching which went on in Pestalozzi's School at [Yverdon] ⟨short⟩ where the tutors quitted their chair at the end of an hour to go ⟨with⟩ and become with their scholars a class to receive instruction of another teacher each being thus in turn teacher & pupil.[397] This is natural & wise and every Man is for his hour, or for his minute, my tutor. Can I teach him something? as surely, can he me. The boy in the road of whom I ask my way is my tutor; knows that I do not, & cannot forego his tuition.[398] But this relation is instantly vitiated the moment there is the least affectation. If an old ⟨baldhead⟩ ↑man↓ runs & sits down ↑on the same bench↓ with rosycheeked boys to hear some formal not real teaching, ↑for the sake of example[,]↓ he is a fool for his pains and they may well cry, Go up, thou baldhead go.[399] "Solus docet qui dat, ⟨&⟩et discit qui recipit." [400]

[193] I said when I awoke, After some more sleepings & wakings I shall lie on this mattrass sick; then, dead; and through my gay entry they will carry these bones. Where shall I be then? I lifted my head and beheld the spotless orange light of the morning beaming up from the dark hills into the wide Universe.

---

[397] Edward Biber, *Henry Pestalozzi and His Plan of Education*, 1831, p. 58.

[398] "This is natural . . . tuition." is struck through in pencil with two diagonal use marks.

[399] Cf. II Kings 2:23.

[400] "He alone teaches who gives, and he who receives, learns." *The Select Works of Robert Leighton*, 2 vols. (London, 1823), I, 444.

[194]⁴⁰¹ It is well & truly said that proportion is beauty. That no ornament in the details can compensate for want of this, nay that ornamented details only make disproportion more unsightly; and that proportion charms us even more perhaps when the materials are coarse & unadorned[.] ⁴⁰²

I see these truths chiefly in that species of architecture which I study & practice, namely, Rhetoric or the Building of Discourse. Profoundest thoughts, sublime images, dazzling figures are squandered & lost in an immethodical harangue. We are fatigued, & glad when it is done. We say of the writer, 'Nobody understood him: he does not understand himself.' But let the same number of thoughts be dealt with by a natural rhetoric, let the question be asked — What is said? How many things? Which are they? Count & number them: put together those that belong together. Now say *what your subject is*, for now first you know: and now state your inference or peroration in what calm or inflammatory temper you must, and behold! out of the quarry you have erected a temple, soaring in due gradation, turret over tower to heaven, cheerful with thorough-lights, majestic with strength, desired of all eyes ⟨visited by all ages.⟩. You will find the matter less cumbersome, it even seems less when put in order, and the discourse as fresh & agreeable at the conclusion as at the commencement. Moreover, if a natural order is obediently followed, the composition will have an abiding charm to your self as well as to others; you will [195] see that you were the scribe of a higher wisdom than your own, and it will remain to you like one of nature's works pleasant & wholesome, & not as our books so often are, a disagreeable remembrance to the author.

A man may find his words mean more than he thought when he uttered them & be glad to employ them again in a new sense.
↑Of Proportion in Character, see p. 238↓

October 23. It is very hard to be simple enough to be good.
An Individual is the All subordinated to a Peculium.
Montaigne, Alcott, M.M.E., and I, have written Journals; beside these, I did not last night think of another.

⁴⁰¹ "PROPORTION" is written above "It is . . . truly" at the top of the page.
⁴⁰² This paragraph is used in "The Eye and Ear," *Lectures*, II, 265.

In conversing with a lady it sometimes seems a bitterness & unnecessary wound to insist as I incline to, on this self sufficiency of man. There is no society say I; there can be none. 'Very true but very mournful,' replies my friend; we ⁿ talk of ⟨m⟩ courses of action. But to women my paths are shut up and the fine women I think of who have had genius & cultivation who have not been wives but muses have something tragic in their lot & I shun to name them. Then I say Despondency bears no fruit. We do nothing whilst we distrust. It is ignoble ⟨to owe⟩ also to owe our success to the coaxing & clapping of Society, to be told by the incapable, "That's capital. Do some more." That only is great that is thoroughly so and from the egg, a god.[403]

[196] Therefore I think a woman does herself injustice who likens herself to any historical woman, who thinks because Corinna or De Stael or M.M.E. do not satisfy the imagination and the serene Themis, none can, certainly not she. It needs that she feel that a new woman has a new as yet inviolate problem to solve[:] perchance the happiest nature that yet has bloomed is hers[;] let it not [be] ruined beforehand on despair grounded on their failure; but let the maiden with erect soul walk serenely on her way, accept the hint of each new pleasure she finds, try in turn all the known resources, experiments, pleasures that she may learn ↑from↓ what she cannot as well as what she can do, the power & the charm that — like a new dawn radiating out of the Deep of Space, — her new born being is.[404]

Tears are never far from a woman's eye. The loveliest maiden on whom every grace sits, who is followed by all eyes, & never knew anything but admiration weeps much and if unexpected changes should blast her hopes then the tears fall so naturally as nothing but grief seems ↑her↓ native element.

[197] It seems to me as if the high idea of Culture as the end of existence, does not pervade the mind of the thinking people of our community[;] the conviction that a discovering of human power to which the trades & occupations they follow, the connexions they form,

---

[403] "But to women . . . god." is struck through in pencil with a diagonal use mark.

[404] This paragraph, struck through in pencil with a vertical use mark, is used in "Heroism," *Lectures*, II, 336, and "Heroism," *W*, II, 259.

and the motley tissue of their common experience are quite subordinate & auxiliary: ⟨is the main interest of history.↓ Could this be properly taught, I think it must provoke and overmaster the young & ambitious, & ⟨pr⟩ yield rich fruits.

Culture in the high sense does not consist in polishing or varnishing but in so presenting the attractions of Nature that the slumbering attributes of man may burst their iron sleep & rush full grown into day. Culture is not the trimming & turfing of gardens, but the showing the true harmony of the unshorn landscape with horrid thickets & bald mountains & the balance of the land & sea.[405]

[198] The Heart in a cultivated nature is the emotion of delight which is awakened by any manifestation of goodness. The heart in a cultivated nature is the unerring measure of genuine goodness in any person & is not betrayed by *penchants* or passions to honor the semblance of goodness. The Heart in a cultivated nature knows its own. Nobody need tell it what its friend said or did, it thoroughly knows its friend. Those who are still in any degree under the influence of *penchants* may be curious to know of third persons what a friend thinks of them; whether a friend really loves them. But the Heart, as I said, knows its own,[n] knows that such & such persons are constitutionally its friends because they are ⟨like it⟩ lovers of the same things with it. The Heart alike in a conscious or an unconscious mind is the reverence for moral beauty. That is its God. Meekly as a maiden when that appears, it bows itself & worships.[406]

[October] 24. I find in town the Φ.B.K. Oration, of which 500 copies were printed, all sold, in ⟨about⟩ ⟨just↓⟩ one month.

[199] The habitual attitude of the wise mind must be Adoration.

October 27. I suppose it must be true that each man ⟨ought⟩ is able in a right state of society to maintain five or six persons beside himself & still have leisure for self cultivation or rather maintain

---

[405] This and the preceding paragraph are struck through in pencil with a vertical use mark. This paragraph is used in Human Culture: "Introductory," *Lectures*, II, 216.

[406] This paragraph, struck through in pencil with a vertical use mark, is used in "The Heart," *Lectures*, II, 293–294.

them by such labor as might be called all leisure, all being the species
of employment most agreeable to his constitution. Yet now if some
persons are credible, a man cannot honestly get a livelihood by trade
in the city. His integrity would be a disqualification. He might however, they agree, if he had sufficient time to build up a credit for
honesty but no poor man proceeding on borrowed capital can afford
to wait so long. What does this show? Why, that the true way now
of beginning is to play the hero in commerce, as it has been done
in war, in church, in school, in state, not begin with a borrowed capital but ⟨must begin with the Se⟩ must raise an estate from the seed,
must begin with his hands, and earn one cent; then two; then a
dollar; then stock a basket; then a barrow; then a booth; then a
shop; & then a warehouse, & not on this dangerous balloon of a credit,
make his first structure. Franklin, William Hutton, & many New
England merchant princes are men of this merit.[407]

[200] Iron if kept at the ironmonger's, will rust. Beer if not made
in right state of the atmosphere will sour. Timber of ships will rot
at sea, or if laid up high & dry, will strain, warp, & dry rot. ⟨Money
if invested in⟩ Money if ⟨un⟩ kept by us ⟨is⟩yields no rent & is liable
to risk of loss; if invested, is liable to the depreciation of the particular kind of stock into which it is exchanged. Our New England
trade is much of it on the extreme of this prudence. It saves itself
by extreme activity. It takes banknotes good, bad, clean, ragged &
saves itself by the speed with which it passes them off. Iron cannot
rust nor beer sour nor timber rot nor calico⟨s⟩es go out of vogue nor
money stocks depreciate in the ↑few↓ swift moments which the Yankee
allows any one of them to remain in his possession. In skating over
thin ice, our safety is in our speed.[408]

Dr Bartlett[409] has reclaimed a bog at the bottom of his garden
ditching & earthing it for $27.08. A quarter of an acre.

[407] William Hutton (1723–1814) was an antiquarian known as "the English
Franklin." This paragraph is struck through in pencil with two diagonal use marks.
"I suppose . . . to his constitution." and "Yet now . . . of this merit." are used in
"Doctrine of the Hands," *Lectures*, II, 240, 242, respectively.

[408] For the concluding sentence, see p. [183] above. This paragraph, struck
through in pencil with a diagonal use mark, is used in "Doctrine of the Hands,"
Lectures, II, 243, and "Prudence," *W*, II, 234–235.

[409] Josiah Bartlett, the Emerson family doctor.

[201] When Monti's mother removed to Majano where the charitable habits of the family were unknown she complained in a sort of alarm that they were no longer visited by the poor.[410]

How short is the distance from the two alarms. The ready hand is too frequently put under contribution until the man becomes prudent & refuses to give. Instantly pride, resentment, & inexpectancy hinder all petitioners from asking at his gate. Then the man self-reproached is alarmed on the other side, and saith, the curse of the poor is falling on my roof. This is progress. As it is progress from ⟨self distrust to⟩ pride to humility[.] [411]

[202] *Places.* Foscolo lived at the Villa Pliniana by the lake of Como. "And perhaps in all the varied earth no spot affords such a combination of the picturesque, the beautiful, the rich, the balmy & the sublime".[412]

Then how noble was the picture in Davy's Consolations ⟨in⟩of Travel, of the country of Austrian Alps; Styria.[413]

Then Alfieri said that "Italy & England are the only countries in which it is desireable to live; the former, because there Nature vindicates her rights, & rises triumphant over the evils inflicted by the governments; the latter, because art conquers nature, & transforms a rude ungenial land into a paradise of comfort & laughing abundance." [414]

Charles V said that Florence was a city only fit to be seen on holidays[.]

[203] We understand exceeding well in America the charm of English manners, and as we by age, cultivation, & leisure, refine &

[410] Cf. James Montgomery, "Monti," in Dionysius Lardner, ed., *Cabinet Cyclopædia: Lives of the Most Eminent Literary and Scientific Men of Italy, Spain, and Portugal,* 3 vols. (London, 1835–1837), II, 306.

[411] This and the preceding paragraph, struck through in pencil with a diagonal use mark, are used in "The Heart," *Lectures,* II, 293.

[412] Cf. James Montgomery, "Foscolo," in Lardner, *Cabinet Cyclopædia: Lives of the Most Eminent Literary and Scientific Men,* 1835–1837, II, 379.

[413] Sir Humphry Davy, *Consolations in Travel* (London, 1830), pp. 171–174.

[414] Cf. James Montgomery, "Alfieri," in Lardner, *Cabinet Cyclopædia: Lives of the Most Eminent Literary and Scientific Men,* 1835–1837, II, 266. This paragraph is struck through in pencil with a diagonal use mark. Cf. "Land," *W,* V, 34.

ripen, come to set a very high value on that very species of breeding which foreigners from a more sanguine temperament & we too
from our democratic wantonness ⟨d⟩usually blame in the English, —
the mild exact decorum, the cool recognition of all & any facts by a
steadiness of temper which hates all starts, screams, faintings, sneez-
ings, laughter, and all violence of any kind. The English & we also
are a commercial people, great readers of newspapers & journals &
books, and are therefore familiar with all the variety of tragic comic
political tidings from all parts of the world, are not to be astonished
or thrown off their balance by any accident near by like villagers,[n]
whom the overturn of a coach or a robbery or a dog with a kettle sets
agape & furnishes with gossip for a week.[415]

———

Beauty is a ticket of admission to all spectacles, to all hospitality. Beauty is welcome as the sun wherever it pleases to shine, &
pleases every body with it & with themselves.[416]

[204] The Heroic cannot be the common nor the common the
heroic. Yet we have the weakness to expect the sympathy of people
in those actions whose very excellence is that they outrun all sympathy & appeal to a tardy justice. If you would serve your brother
because it is fit for *you* to serve him, do not take back your words or
falter in your purpose & discountenance your brother, when you
find that prudent people do not commend you. Be still true to your
own act. And leap for joy if you have simply done something strange
& extravagant & broken the leaden monotony of the decorous Age.
Alfieri lived after his way & so counts One. Metastasio was a gentleman[,] Goldoni was ⟨a⟩none. Who are you, sir? Do you feed very
nicely & sleep very warm? [417]

A friendship is good which begins on sentiment & proceeds into
all mutual convenience and alternation of great benefits. Less good
that which begins in commodity & proceeds to sentiment.

[415] This paragraph, struck through in pencil with a diagonal use mark, is used
in "Prudence," *Lectures*, II, 325.

[416] This paragraph is struck through in pencil with a diagonal use mark.

[417] This paragraph is struck through in pencil with a vertical use mark. The first
five sentences are used in "Heroism," *Lectures*, II, 336–337, and "Heroism," *W*, II,
260.

[205] I suppose Goethe's Tasso may be a pretty fair historical portrait and that is true tragedy. It does not seem to me so genuine grief when some tyrannous Richard III oppresses & slays a score of innocent persons as when Antonio & Tasso both right, wrong each other. That is a grief we all feel, a knot we cannot untie & refer it to the absolute & eternal. Tasso's is a common case. A man of genius, of an ardent temperament, careless of prudence, & reckless of physical laws, self-indulgent, presently becomes unfortunate, querulous, a "discomfortable cousin," a displeasure to himself & to others. Such was Burns, Savage, Cowper,[418]

Montaigne was an unbuttoned sloven.
A.H.E[verett]. & writers of his stamp, like Bolingbroke patronise Providence[.]

Let the air in. The Advertising is one of the signs of our times: the hanging out a showy sign with the hitherto unheard of name of the huckster flourished in letters more gorgeous than ever the name of Pericles or of Jove was writ in. They do wisely who do thus. It is a petty title of nobility. The man is made one of the public in a small way. What he doth is of some more importance; he is more responsible. His gay sign & far flying advertisement hold him at least to decency. So the publishing names of boys who have won school medals illustrates them, & bringing a petty ⟨caus⟩ Broad street scuffle into court lets the air in, & purges blind alleys.

[206] October 28. The event of death is always astounding; our philosophy never reaches, never possesses it; we are always at the beginning of our catechism; always the definition is yet to be made, What is Death? ⟨Death⟩ I see nothing to help ⟨fu⟩ beyond observing what the mind's habit is in regard to that crisis. Simply, I have nothing to do with it. It is nothing to me. After I have made my will & set my house in order, I shall do in ⟨regard⟩ the immediate expectation of death the same things I should do without it.

[418] This uncompleted paragraph, struck through in pencil with a diagonal use mark and in ink with a vertical use mark, is used in "Prudence," *Lectures*, II, 315–316, and "Prudence," *W*, II, 232–233. For "discomfortable cousin" see *Richard II*, III, ii, 36.

But more difficult is it to know the death of another. Mrs Ripley says that her little Sophia told the Mantuamaker this morning that "in heaven she was going to ask Dod to let her sit by Mother,⟨"⟩ all the time." And if this little darling should die, Mrs R thinks she could not live. So with the expectation of the death of persons who are conveniently situated, who have all they desire, & to whom death is fearful, she looks in vain for a consolation. In us there ought to be remedy. There ought to be, there can be nothing, to which the soul is called, to which the soul is not equal. And I suppose that the roots of my relation to every individual are in my own constitution & not less the causes of his disappearance from me.

[207] Why should we lie so? A question is asked of the Understanding which lies in the province of the Reason and we foolishly try to make an answer. Our constructiveness ⟨is⟩ overpowers our love of truth. How noble is it when the mourner looks for comfort in your face to give only sympathy & confession; confession that it is great grief & the greater because the apprehension of its nature still loiters.

Who set you up for Professor of omniscience? & cicerone to the Universe? Why teach? Learn rather.[419]

When the conversation soars to principles, Unitarianism is boyish.[420]

[208] Nov. 2. I learn from my wise masters that Art does not love imitation, does not propose to make grapes that birds will peck, nor a cow that the gadfly will alight upon, but proposes to show the Mind of Nature in the work, and is therefore equally or better pleased with miniatures or colossal images, as with the size of life. Myron's Cow, according to Goethe, was so made as entirely to paint to the eye the beautiful instinct of the sucking calf & the sucked cow; and they mispraise it who ⟨thi⟩ say the herdman threw a stone at the cow to make her move.[421]

---

[419] "A question is asked . . . rather.", struck through in pencil with a diagonal use mark, is used in "Being and Seeming," *Lectures*, II, 302–303.

[420] This sentence, struck through in pencil with a diagonal use mark, is used in "Holiness," *Lectures*, II, 346.

[421] Cf. Goethe, *Werke*, 1828–1833, XXXIX, 290. "I learn . . . sucking calf" is

Goethe says "The mind & the endeavor of the Greeks ⟨was⟩is to deify man not to humanize the Godhead. Here is a theomorphism not anthropomorphism. Moreover the Bestial should not be ennobled to the Human, but the Human of the Beast be raised, that ⟨t⟩so we may therein enjoy a higher pleasure of Art as we already do following an irresistible impulse of Nature in choosing so gladly the Animals to be our companions & servants." [*Werke*, 1828–1833,] Vol 39 p[p]. 289[–290]

One more thought is that ⟨in "this as in other fine works of Art &⟩ "the Artist ⁿ concentrates the look, the thought, the interest of the ⟨spectator⟩ beholder, and he can think of nothing without, nothing near, nothing else; as truly a masterpiece of Art should exclude & for the time ⟨as it were⟩ annihilate everything else[.]"

Art seeks not nature but the ideal which nature herself strives after.[422]

[209] Immense curiosity in Boston to see the delegation of the Sacs & Foxes, of the Sioux & the Ioways. I saw the Sacs & Foxes at the Statehouse on Monday, — about 30 in number. Edward Everett addressed them & they replied. One chief said "They had no land to put their words upon, but they were nevertheless true." One chief wore the skin of a buffaloe's head with the horns attached, on his head↑, others birds with outspread wings↓. Immense breadth of shoulder & very muscular persons. ⟨They were so⟩ Our Picts were so savage in their headdress & nakedness that it seemed as if the bears & catamounts had sent a deputation. They danced a war-dance on the Common, in the centre of the greatest crowd ever seen on that area. The Governor cautioned us of the gravity of the tribe & that we should beware of any expression of the ridiculous; and the people all seemed to treat their guests gingerly as the keepers of lions & jaguars do those creatures whose taming is not quite yet trustworthy.

Certainly it is right & natural that the Indian should come &

---

struck through in pencil with a diagonal use mark. The first sentence of this paragraph is used in "The Eye and Ear," *Lectures*, II, 266.

[422] This and the preceding paragraph are struck through in pencil with a vertical use mark. The first sentence is used in "The Eye and Ear," *Lectures*, II, 267.

see the civil White man, but this was hardly genuine but a show so we were not parties but spectators[.]

Therefore a man looks up & laughs & meets the eyes of some bystander who also laughs. Keokuk, Black Hawk, Roaring Thunder,

At Faneuil Hall they built a partition between the two tribes because the tribes are at war.

[210] Nov. 3. Last night I wrote to Carlyle to inform him of the new edition of his history: and to Mr Landor I sent Nature & the Oration ΦBK by Charles Sumner Esq.

Our Calendar. New Year's day   4th March.   April Fools.
May Day.   ↑Election.↓   Fourth of July: Independence.
Commencement.   Phi Beta Kappa.   Cattle Show.
Muster.ⁿ   Thanksgiving.   Christmas.

[211] It is the right economy of time to do nothing by halves, nothing for show, nothing perfunctorily. If you write a letter, put your earnest meaning in, & God shall reward you by enlarging your sight. But save your thought & you shall find it worthless & your wordy letter worthless also. In writing a review, put in only that you have to say, only the things, & leave the consideration of the Greeks & Romans & the Universal History quite out. Stop when you have done. And stop when you have begun if it is not something to you.[423]

Poetry precedes prose as the child sings all his words before he speaks them.

People are not the better for the sun & moon, the horizon & the trees, as it is not observed that the keepers of Roman galleries or the valets of painters have any elevation of thought, or that librarians are wise men.[424]

[423] This paragraph, struck through in pencil with a diagonal use mark, is used in "The Head," *Lectures*, II, 257.

[424] This sentence, struck through in ink with a diagonal and a vertical use mark, is used in "Spiritual Laws," *W*, II, 147.

How idle this curiosity about other people's estimate of you: how idle this discontent at remaining unknown. If a man knows that he can do any thing[,] that he can do it better than any one else[,] he has a perfect assurance before him of an acknowledgement of that fact by all persons as surely as his shadow follows his body.[425]

[212] November 6. M.M.E. says, "I hate to be expecting a cat." So universal ought culture to be as to make no part of a man seem to be made in vain. Yet, I have seen men certainly who did not seem to use their legs, their hips, shoulders, & got the least service out of their eyes. So ⟨d⟩ concentrated to some focal point was their vitality, that the limbs & constitution appeared supernumerary. Much oftener have I seen men whose emotive, whose intellectual, whose moral faculties lay dormant.[426]

Fuller at Providence [427] explained to me his plans, "that he was to keep the school 5 years — income so much; outlay so much; then he should be able to go to Europe; &c, &c." When I repeated all this to Alcott, he expressed chagrin & contempt. For Alcott holds the School in so high regard that he would scorn to exchange it for the Presidency of the United States. The School is his Europe. And this is a just example of the true rule of Choice of Pursuit. You may do nothing to get money which is not worth your doing on its own account. This is the sense of "he that serves at the altar shall live by it." [428] Every vocation is an altar. There must be injury to the constitution from all false[,] from all half-action. Nor will the plainly expressed wishes of other people be a reason why [213] you should do to oblige them what violates your sense, what breaks your integrity & shows you falsely not the man you are.

---

[425] This paragraph, struck through in pencil with a vertical use mark and in ink with two diagonal use marks, is used in "Being and Seeming," *Lectures*, II, 301, and "Spiritual Laws," *W*, II, 157.

[426] This paragraph, struck through in pencil with a vertical use mark, is used in Human Culture: "Introductory," *Lectures*, II, 215.

[427] Hiram Fuller, whose Greene Street School Emerson had helped to dedicate in June, 1837.

[428] Cf. "He that serves at the altar ought to live by the altar," no. 2294 in Thomas Fuller, *Gnomologia: Adages and Proverbs* (London, 1816), p. 68.

They do not know yet what ⟨y⟩ their importunity hinders you from being. Resist their windy requests[;] give leave to Great Nature to unbind fold after fold, the tough integuments in which your secret character lies, & let it open its proud flower & fruitage to the day, and when they see what costly and ⟨as⟩ hitherto unknown ⟨bea⟩ blessing they had well nigh defrauded the world,ⁿ they will thank you for denying their prayer & will say, we would have used you as a handy tool, Now we worship you as a Redeemer. The difficulty in each particular case is the greater that the recusant himself seldom sees clearly enough what he wants, whither he tends, to be able to justify himself for shoving by gilded invitations & seems to his friends & sometimes to himself a tedious refiner & windy talker.

Here serves however the Spartan in us, the grit, the terror, the indomitable will. Let them denounce, let them laugh, let them scold, let them hint extreme measures & take extreme measures & if it come to that let the best friends you have shut the door in your face. And now under the cold heaven with literal grim poverty to meet as you can is something for a man to do[;] here is need for your pluck & kings for your competitors.

Poverty is commonly lamentable because there [214] is no soul[;] the poor are chickenhearted people who desire to save appearances, to eat roast meat & dress in a gentlemanlike manner & be thought to have business in State Street and all the charity & all the sighing of his friends is directed to that end to new paint him. If poverty is merely culinary it is very sad, because it is very helpless. But if his poverty is want of bread to eat & clothes to wear simply because he will not sell his Will, his tastes, his honor for that pottage,[429] & he keeps of course his will, his tastes, & his honor, it is very remediable & nowise lamentable poverty. It is a time, as Burke said, for a man to act in. ⟨A few shillings⟩ˣ[430] He is now to convert the warlike part of ⟨our⟩ his nature, always the attractive, always the salient; the almighty part, ⟨to resist⟩ and which lies in the lukewarm milky dog days of common village life quite stupid, & so leaves common life so unattractive, he is to ⟨co⟩ bring this artillery to bear, he is to ↑"↓cry ⟨"⟩Havoc, & let slip the dogs of war."[431]

[429] See Gen. 25:29–34.
[430] See p. [215], for Emerson's intended addition at this point.
[431] *Julius Caesar*, III, i, 273.

⟨He is to show⟩ He has now field & hour & judges & is to fight out (with all gods to friend) his just cause with a resolution & address like Alexander's at Arbela. Caesar, Bonaparte, Alexander had not just cause[;] even Tell, Washington, & Miltiades in the judgment of William Penn & William Ladd had not just cause but he has.

[215] In the common life a man feels hampered & bandaged: he cannot play the hero: there would be affectation in it: he must fight like poor   with his pump head. But if he is once rejected by all patrons & all relatives, ⟨then he⟩ is fairly ⟨af⟩ set adrift, why then let him thank his gods that he has sea-room, & use his freedom so as never to lose it again. ⟨A few⟩ It is an immense gain if he reckon it well to have no longer false feelings & conventional appearances to consult. A few shillings a day will keep out cold & hunger & he will not need to study long how to get a few shillings a day honestly.[432]

Why yes perhaps he said wisely who said that war is the natural state of man & the nurse of all virtues. I will not say man is to man a wolf,[433] but man should be to man a hero.

ˣ Now is the time to set the teeth, to plant the foot[.] [434]

"Two cubes placed together are considered a good proportion." (for a concert room) ⟨"Music of Nature"⟩
↑Quarterly Rev
No. 88↓ [435]

[432] "And this is a just example" [p. [212]] . . . honestly." is struck through in pencil with curved vertical use marks. This passage is used in "Doctrine of the Hands," *Lectures*, II, 240–242, which supplies the name omitted in the final paragraph: Oliver Proudfute in Sir Walter Scott, *The Fair Maid of Perth*, ch. VIII.

[433] See *Philosophical Rudiments Concerning Government and Society*, in *The English Works of Thomas Hobbes*, 11 vols. (London, 1839–1845), II, 11: "the natural state of men, before they entered into society, was a mere war"; II, ii: *"man to man is an arrant wolf."*

[434] This sentence, marked for insertion on p. [214], is struck through in pencil with a vertical use mark.

[435] Emerson's original reference, though incomplete, was correct: William Gardiner, *The Music of Nature* (London, 1832), p. 299, note. The erroneous revision apparently derives from another note by Gardiner, p. 300, which cites experiments by French astronomers on the velocity of sound discussed in "the *Quarterly Review*, No.

[216] It is a question of Culture which is best[,] a fair or a blotted page?

The ultra benevolence of mine Asia reminds me of the pretty fable of the seven cedar birds sitting on the bough who passed the morsel which one had taken from bird to bird with courtesy until it returned again to the first. None cared for the morsel: All are fed with love. Asia makes my gods hers.

Perhaps in the village we have manners to paint which the city life does not know. Here we have Mr S. who is man enough to turn away the butcher who cheats in weight & introduce another butcher into town. The other neighbors ⟨w⟩could not take such a step. Here is Mr. E. who when the ⟨Chairman of the Selectmen⟩ ↑Moderator of the Townmeeting↓ is candidate for representative & so stands in the centre of the box inspecting each vote & each voter dares carry up a vote for the opposite candidate & put it in. There is the hero who will not subscribe to the flag staff or the engine though all say it is mean. There is the man who gives his dollar but refuses to give his name though all other contributors are set down. There is Mr H. who never loses his spirits though always in the minority & though the⟨y⟩ people behave as bad as if they were ⟨half⟩ drunk, he is just as determined in opposition & just as cheerful as ever. [217] Here is Mr C. who says "Honor bright" & keeps it so. Here is Mr S. who warmly assents to what ever proposition you ↑please to↓ make & Mr M. who roundly tells you he will have nothing to do with the thing. The high people in the village are timid[,] the low people are bold & nonchalant; negligent too of each other's opposition for they see the amount of it & know its uttermost limits which the more remote proprietor does not. Here too are not to be forgotten our two companies[,] the Light Infantry & the Artillery who brought up one the Brigade Band & one the Brass Band from Boston, set the musicians side by side under the ⟨same⟩ ↑great↓ tree on the common, & let them play two tunes & jangle & drown each other & presently got the companies into actual hustling & kicking.

To show ⟨what pluck you have⟩ the force that is in you, (whether

---

88" — i.e., a review of J. F. W. Herschel's *Treatise on Sound*, in *The Quarterly Review*, XLIV (Feb. 1831), 475–511.

you are a philosopher & call it heroism, or are a farmer & call it pluck,) you need not go beyond the tinman's shop or the first corner; nay, the first man you meet who bows to you, may look you in the eye & call it out.

↑The stealthy Mr E. stealthiest of faces & forms. Here is J. M. not so much a citizen as a part of nature in perfect rapport with the trout in the stream, the bird in the wood or pond side, & the plant in the garden; whatsoever is early or rare or nocturnal; game or agriculture; he knows being awake when others sleep & asleep when others wake. Snipe, pelican, or breed of hogs; or grafting, or cutting; woodcraft; or bees.↓

[218] ⟨The⟩ "⟨m⟩Miracles have ceased." Have they indeed? When? They had not ceased this afternoon when I walked into the wood & got into bright miraculous sunshine in shelter from the roaring wind. Who sees a pine cone or the ⟨exuding⟩ turpentine exuding from the tree, or a leaf the unit of vegetation fall from its bough ⟨saying⟩ ↑as if it said↓ 'The Year is finished,' or hears in the quiet piny glen the /Chickadee/titmouse/ chirping his cheerful note, or walks along the lofty promontory-like ridges which like natural causeways traverse the morass, or gazes upward at the rushing clouds or downward at a moss or a stone & says to himself 'Miracles have ceased'? [n]

Tell me good friend when this hillock on which your foot stands, swelled from the level ⟨by vo⟩ of the sphere by volcanic force.[n] ⟨Look at⟩ ↑Pick up↓ that pebble at your feet, look at its gray sides, its sharp crystal, & tell me what fiery inundation of the world melted the minerals like wax & as if the globe were one glowing crucible gave this stone its shape. There ⟨are⟩ is the truth[-]speaking pebble itself to affirm to endless ages the thing was so. Tell me where is the manufactory of this air so thin, so blue, so restless which eddies around you, ↑in↓ which your life floats, of which your lungs are but an organ, and which you coin into musical words. I am agitated with curiosity to know the secret of Nature. Why cannot Geology, why cannot [219] Botany speak & tell me what has been[,] what is, as I run along the forest promontory & ask when it rose like a blister on heated steel? Then I looked up & saw the Sun shining in the vast Sky & heard the wind bellow above & the water glistened in the vale. These were the forces that wrought then & work now. ↑Yes there they grandly speak to all plainly in proportion as we are quick to apprehend.↓ [436]

A dangler is a man out of place and every man is sometimes a dangler.

Go into a botanical garden: is not that a place of some delight? Go to a muster-field where four regiments are marching with flags, music, & artillery: is not that a moving spectacle? Go to a dance & watch the forms & movement of the youths & maidens: have they nothing of you in keeping? Go to a church where gray old men & matrons & children bend & sit still in pious frames. Go to the top of Monadnoc; to the Vatican; to the unburied Pompeii; [437]

[220] The world needs a missionary to denounce its conventions. Why should each new soul that is launched out of God into Nature be wrecked at ⟨its⟩ the beginning of the voyage by following the charts of its mates instead the compass, the stars, & the continents? Young men go to parties & feel when they come back as if they had been at insane asylums. Hollow ashamed compunctions[,] the doom of the false & of the Halves[,] lies heavy on them.

Nov. 7. Mr Graeter could not draw a geological sketch of a ledge of rocks until the formation had been explained to him.[438]

It needs a well read variously informed man to read Carlyle, from his infinite allusion. He knows every joke that ever was cracked.

Thersites, in Troilus & Cressida, says that the Greeks have not "circumvention enough to deliver a fly from a spider without drawing their massy irons & cutting the web." [439]

[436] This paragraph, struck through in pencil with vertical use marks, is used in "The Eye and Ear," *Lectures*, II, 274.

[437] This uncompleted paragraph, struck through in pencil with a vertical use mark, is used in Human Culture: "Introductory," *Lectures*, II, 222.

[438] This and the preceding paragraph are struck through in pencil with a curved diagonal use mark. Francis Graeter taught drawing at Alcott's Temple School.

[439] Cf. *Troilus and Cressida*, II, iii, 17.

[221] November 8. Yesterday William Channing & J.S. Dwight came here & found me just ready to go to Lowell to read the first Lecture of my Course. As they seemed to be bearers of the right Promethean fire I hated the contretem[p]s. To Lowell also went wife & child. It seems to be worthy to be set down as a general rule of manners, In conversation never intimate that you ever was sick or ever shall be. So few people have dexterity enough to touch this dangerous topic without instantly becoming tedious, that I think the rule ought to stand without loopholes. If the unsavory ⟨attributes⟩ corruption of lungs & stomach are alluded to[,] instantaneously change the conversation.

I believe the man & the writer should be one & not diverse, as they say Bancroft, as we know Bulwer is. ⟨Mr⟩ Wordsworth gives us the image of the truehearted man, as Milton, Chaucer, Herbert do; not ruffled fine gentlemen who condescend to write like Shaftes-bury, Congreve, & greater far, Walter Scott. Let not the author eat up the man, so that he shall be a balcony & no house. Let him not be turned into a dapper clerical anatomy to be assisted like a lady over a gutter or a stone wall. In meeting Milton, I feel that I should en-counter a real man but Coleridge is a writer, & Pope, Waller, Addison & Swift & Gibbon though with attributes are too modish. It is not Man but the fashionable wit they would be. Yet Swift has properties. Allston is respectable to me. Novalis, Schiller are only voices, no men. Dr Johnson was a man though he lived in unfavorable [222] solitude & society of one sort so that he was an unleavened lump at last on which a genial unfolding had only begun. Humanity cannot be the attribute of these people's writing. Humanity which smiles in Homer, in Chaucer, in Shakspear, in Milton, in Wordsworth. Montaigne is a Man.   ↑See what is written in B p. 225 on the Humanity of Milton.↓

Hag

[223] Lidian made a very just remark today that certainly she gave clothes, bedding, or money to her sick & poor neighbors lately with the greater confidence because ↑of↓ the written verse, "Give to him

425

that asketh of thee & from him that would borrow of thee turn not thou away." [440] It is true that the inclination to bestow gets edge from the time-honoured text in which it is embodied. As good a commentary as need be on ↑the↓ power of a sentence. ↑As good a commentary on Christianity as is often to be found.↓

The eyes of men converse as much as their ⟨lips⟩ tongues, and the eyes often say one thing, & the tongues, another. A practised man relies always on the language of the first as it is very hard to counterfeit. [441] And to what end all the forms of society, all these meetings & partings, these professions, invitations, courtesies if by them all a man cannot learn something vastly more weighty than the mere formal occasion & pretext of the hour. In every company into which a man goes there is he guaged[,] there he feels himself tried, assayed, & stamped with his right number. So long as there is about him any thing unreal anything factitious so long he feels unworthy & uneasy & afraid. However plausible & applauded his performance, he feels that he practises a degree of imposition upon men & stands on ticklish terms with them[.] [442]

[224][443] Milton's expression of "Music smoothing the raven down of darkness till it smiled" [444] has great beauty. Nothing in nature has the softness of darkness. Ride in the night through a wood, and the overhanging boughs shall become to the eye lumps of darkness and of an unutterable gentleness to the sense.

[225] To talk from the memory is the talk of display & you impress, you shine, & you lose all your time, for you have not had a thought, you have been playing a trick. A forfeit too which this sort of talk has often to pay is the agreeable fact of finding that

[440] Cf. Matt. 5:42.

[441] "The eyes of men . . . counterfeit.", struck through in pencil with a vertical use mark, is used in "The Heart," *Lectures*, II, 285, and "Behavior," *W*, VI, 179–180.

[442] "In every company . . . them" is used in "The Heart," *Lectures*, II, 285; the first sentence ("In every company . . . number."), struck through in ink with a vertical use mark, is also used in "Being and Seeming," *Lectures*, II, 301–302.

[443] "DARKNESS" is written above "Milton's expression" at the top of the page.

[444] Cf. *Comus*, ll. 250–251.

you have repeated the same series of remarks to the same company before. But talk from the moment & do not shine but lie low in the Lord's power, wait & follow with endeavoring thoughts the incidents of the conversation, & you shall come away wiser than you went. You shall be uplifted into new perceptions[.] [445]

↑Nov. 9.↓ Differences. Take any collection of young men as West Point Academy or Harvard College: Do they all one thing? Or will you find one straggling off into remote pastures & to slaughter-houses for bones to make phosphorus with; ⟨in his chamber,⟩ & one scouring the woods with dog & rifle or down in the marsh for yellow-legs; and one tooting all day on a flute & one forever dressing & trimming himself for a party or a dance; & one with knife & gimlet making traps & boxes; & one with crayons & brushes sketching land-scapes & caricatures; & one trading books, ⟨&⟩ pictures, cloaks; & one always declaiming & acting plays where any ⟨are⟩ can be found to listen? [n 446]

[226] How graceful & lively a spectacle is a squirrel on a bough cracking a nut! how sylvan beautiful a stag bounding through Plymouth Woods! how like a smile of the earth is the first violet we meet in spring! Well, it was meant that I should see these & partake this agreeable emotion. Was it not? And was it not further designed that I should thereby be prompted to ask the relation of these natures to my own, & so the great word Comparative Anatomy has now leaped out of the womb of the Unconscious. I feel ⟨my mind a closet in my⟩ a cabinet in my mind unlocked by each of these new interests. Wherever I go, the related objects crowd on my Sense & I explore backward & wonder how the same things looked to me before my attention had been aroused.

Goethe remarks that the face ⟨viewed⟩ much magnified in a concave mirror, loses its expression.

[445] This paragraph, struck through in pencil with a diagonal use mark, is used in "The Heart," *Lectures*, II, 292–293, where Emerson correctly attributes the expression "Lie low in the Lord's power" to George Fox.
[446] This paragraph, struck through in pencil with a diagonal use mark, is used in "Doctrine of the Hands," *Lectures*, II, 235–236.

Rightminded men have recently been called to decide for Abolition[.]

[227] It is long ere we discover how rich we are. Our history we are sure is quite tame. We have nothing to write, nothing to infer. ⟨No⟩ But our wiser years still run back to the before despised recollections of childhood & always we are fishing up some wonderful article out of that pond. Until by & by we begin to suspect that the foolish biography of the one foolish person we know is in reality nothing less than a miniature paraphrase of the ⟨Universal History in a⟩ Hundred Volumes of the Universal History[.] [447]

11 November. In Boston yesterday heard Governor Everett read a Lecture to the Diffusion Society [448] & thence went to Faneuil Hall where Webster presided at the caucus & heard [John] Bell of Tenessee; [William J.] Graves, & [Joseph R.] Underwood, of Kentucky; & [Josiah O.] Hoffmann, of New York. [449] The speaking was slovenly, small, & tiresome, but the crowd exciting & the sound of the cheering extraordinarily fine. Webster said, when Bell ended, that "it was not a festive occasion, yet he ⟨thought the⟩ would venture to propose a sentiment to the Meeting.⟨"⟩ The Health of Mr Bell & the Whigs of Tenessee and three times three." Then was heard the splendid voice of 4 or 5 000 men in full cry together. Such voice might well predominate over brute beasts. It was merely a spectacle to me. But the *Genius loci* [450] is more commanding at Faneuil Hall than at any other spot in America. The air is electric. Every man thinks he can speak whilst he hears, — lifted off his feet oftentimes, — the multitude swaying alternately this side & that. In such crowds few old men[,] mostly young & middle aged, with shining heads & swoln veins. The mob is all the time interlocutor & the [228] bucket goes up & down according to the success of the speaker. The pinched,

[447] This paragraph, struck through in pencil with two diagonal use marks, is used in "The Head," *Lectures*, II, 254, and "Intellect," *W*, II, 334.

[448] The Society for the Diffusion of Useful Knowledge.

[449] According to the Boston *Daily Advertiser*, Representative Edward Curtis of New York also addressed the Whig rally of November 10 that Emerson describes. All five speakers were congressmen.

[450] "Spirit of the place" (Ed.).

⟨crowded⟩ ↑wedged↓, elbowed, sweltering multitude as soon as the speaker loses their ear by tameness of his harangue feel all sorely how ill accommodated they are & begin to attend only to themselves & the coarse outcries made all around them. Then they push, resist, swear, & fill the hall with cries of tumult. The speaker stops[;] the moderator persuades, commands, entreats, "Order"[;] the speaker gets breath & a new hint & resumes, goes to the right place, his voice alters, vibrates, pierces the private ear of every one, the mob quiets itself somehow, every one being magnetized, & the hall hangs suspended on the lips of one man. ⟨If the speak⟩ A happy deliverance of common sentiments charms them. Never the fineness or depth of the thought but the good saying of the very few & very poor particulars which lie uppermost in every man's mind at the meeting. All appear struck with wonder & delight at this cheap & mediocre faculty. So rarely is it found. If the speaker become dull again[,] instantly our poor wedges begin to feel their pains & strive & cry.[451]

[229] A few kernels of corn will support life as well as tables groaning with meats & sauces from every zone of the globe. In the profusion of our books, we ⟨look up⟩ slightly turn over the leaves of a journal & ⟨seize⟩ ↑pass to↓ a new one; but in the barroom of a country tavern, we find information, & suggestion in every shipping-list & auctioneer's advertisement in a newspaper. A few coals to kindle the fire are as good as a ton.

A musical tone out of Judæa makes itself heard farther on time than the mad hurlyburly of the Reign of Terror.[452]

[230] November 16. Day before yesterday the Board of Education sent their Secretary hither to form a County Association, & ⟨mr⟩Mr [Horace] Mann spent his time in the intervals at my house. Hither came too Dr Walker & Mr Stetson. Prudence is a virtue also, & when you are tempted out to expound your deeper mind, it is as disagreeable to have the conversation instantaneously changed as to

---

[451] Within this paragraph "Then was heard . . . of one man." and the concluding sentence are struck through in pencil with diagonal use marks.

[452] This sentence is struck through in pencil with a curved vertical use mark.

find the stair much longer than you have stepped for. One of the fine things said by Mr Mann was, that "we should think on oath."

In these days I Sardanapalize, being sick[,] and sit by the fire,[453] & read three new Reviews. A Review is a stage coach or an /omnibus/ferryboat/ for the incongruity of the company it assorts. I pass from Ciceronian splendor to hand-bill writers. I am glad to have poor Puckler Muskau however so butchered as he is in the Quarterly with all kinds of rotten eggs & spit balls pelted, — the "dragon of the chambermaids" they call him, & sneer at his title, & expose his poverty, & hiss at his nation ⟨& s call him lousy,⟩ & bastinado his vices; nor stick to call him lousy, & to say he stinketh.[454] Very sweet words these must be to a German fop who rates England so high, & would so gladly pass for an Englishman. But he seems to be such a mischievous scamp that I give him up.

More gladly I read of Bradley & his beautiful discovery of the Aberration of light guided thereto by the striking analogy of the shifting of the vane on a boat's mast[.] [455]

[231][456] A fine scholar may appear very silly to every one ⟨of th⟩ in succession of the audience whom he delights with his eloquence. He is a lens that has no power but at its focus: at any other distance it gives all blur & dislocation. He is a cannon that destroys at a distance but ⟨run up to the touch hole⟩ ↑bring the battle hand to hand↓ & the weapon is cumbrous & useless & ⟨not to be compared with⟩ ↑no match for↓ a knife.

It occurred yesterday in reading of Lord Bacon that every one of the twenty individuals we best know rightly represents to us a vast multitude of men, a class. So that always you walk as a king with a train of deputies about you[,] one bringing the claims of Massachu-

[453] Cf. "Prudence," *Lectures*, II, 324.
[454] Review of *Semilasso in Africa* By Prince Pückler-Muskau (London, 1837), in *The Quarterly Review*, LIX (July 1837), 134–164, *passim*.
[455] The incident, dating from 1728, is commonly reported in notices of Bradley and his work. Emerson may have read of it in a periodical review of S. P. Rigaud, *Miscellaneous Works and Correspondence of James Bradley* (Oxford, 1832); there is no record of his consulting the volume itself.
[456] "Turns" is written above "A fine" at the top of the page.

setts, another of New York, another of Carolina or one of England, one of Africa; one of Learning; one of Finance; one the Hand; one of Historical Religion, or the Church; one, of the Fine Arts &c. &c. And so of the various properties of the Actual. These all in turn are represented & must be somehow answered & satisfied by compliance or by compensation.[457] Again as a man rises in turn above one & another of the ⟨nati⟩ accidental companions of his day & journey he rises not above them only, but over the vast multitude which they represent. I think every philosopher may find in his own connexion a proxy to answer to the various characters he has seen drawn in good fiction or good prose which do not ordinarily draw their classes so subtilely but any other figure will stand for them as well.

[232] In the common progress of life ⟨your a⟩ we feel that our acquaintance with a few lawyers, with a few political men, with a few merchants has fitted us adequately to converse with all others of those classes, that is, when we are conscious of having mastered the difficulties which once made our talk with either of these tribes useless or embarrassing, when we no longer fear or hate them, then we are quite assured in the expectation of meeting any new individuals of the same class. So according to our success in talk with our score, would be our chance with ten score. Can you justify your secretest thought to another man & find that with him it still tells as with you for somewhat important, so will it seem to the human race[.]

Nov. 23. This morn.g. I sent to Dr Walker a critical notice of Carlyle, but I doubt it will return to me.[458]

———

↑Tone.↓

A fine paper ascribed to Parsons in the Daily Advertiser, not so much for the things said, as for the masterly tone. It is as hard to get the right tone as to say good things. One indicates character the other intellect.

[457] "It occurred yesterday . . . compensation." is struck through in pencil with a diagonal use mark.
[458] Walker printed only a portion of Emerson's article: as "Carlyle's French Revolution," *The Christian Examiner*, XXIII (Jan. 1838), 386–387. (See *L*, II, 108.)

[233][459] Music.   Beethoven sat upon a stile near Vienna one hot summer's day & caught the tone of the choral flies whose hum filled the air & introduced it with charming effect into his Pastoral Sinfony.[460]

"In brightness of tone the flute so transcends the other instruments that the composer reserves it for particular occasions. In the song which describes the creation of man, 'In his eyes brightness' how beautifully is it introduced. The few pointed notes impart the same brilliancy as the spots of light upon the eyes given by the painter" *Music of Nature.* p. 310

"Probably the greatest good effected by the Thirty Years' War was the improvement of the wind-instruments" Music of Nature p. 352 [461]

The Trumpet. "Its splendid tone is heard at a greater distance than that of any other instrument; hence it is pressed into the service of arms. No one has felt its powerful clang like the soldier. Amidst the thunder of the war its lancet tone cuts through the air and drives the cohorts to battle."

[*Ibid.*,] p. 364 [misquoted]

Tone   *Tone.*

"It is a curious fact that musical sounds fly farther & are heard at a greater distance than those which are more loud & noisy. When Barthelemon led, the opera connoisseurs would go into the gallery to hear the effect of his Cremona violin which at this distance predominated greatly above all the other instruments. though in the orchestra it was not perceptibly louder than any of the rest." [*Ibid.*,] p. 12[; p. 13, note]

[234][462] "A probably represented the figure of the mouth when open and the bar across it the line which the teeth would form while uttering this sound.

"The upper part of the small letter e would represent the figure of the mouth as but just opened & which would give the true sound of this vowel.

"The vowel O accurately represents the circular form of the mouth for that sound

[459] "MUSIC" is written above "Music.   Beethoven" at the top of the page.

[460] Cf. William Gardiner, *The Music of Nature*, 1832, pp. 421–422.

[461] "Oneideaed" is written diagonally in the right margin following this page reference; it is partly circled.

[462] "MUSIC" is written above "represented the" at the top of the page.

"The letter **U** probably in its original form was an exact representation of the scooped figure of the tongue in uttering that sound

"The two semicircles in **B** represent the lips as closely pressed together in the act of forcing that explosive sound & the consonant **P** having but one curve would intimate a slighter effect of the same kind."

Music of Nature p. 33 [abbreviated]

↑Character↓ [463]

"Lord Chatham's eloquence was attended with this important effect, that it impressed every hearer with the conviction that there was something in him finer even than his words; that the man was infinitely greater than the orator." [464] ap. M[usic]. of N[ature]. p. 48

Haydn, Mozart, Beethoven introduced sounds of nature & of the human voice into music[.]

"The Pastoralla of Beethoven pourtrays the serene landscape of a retired village near Vienna. In it we may fancy that we hear the song of birds, the hum of insects in the noontide sun, the tinkling rills & murmuring brooks forming a picture of tranquil beauty never before attempted in sounds" [*Ibid.*, p]p. [421–]422. [abridged]

[235] "The strains of the Irish & Welch may be referred to the harp. The dance tunes of Spain to the guitar; the mountain airs of the swiss to the hunting horn; & the music of the Turks to the rhythmical clangor of the ancient Greeks." [*Ibid.*,] p. 460

Musical instruments do not love the cold. They are injured & ruined by leaning against a cold wall in winter [*Ibid.*, p. 458]

[236] Nov. 24. The selfsubsistent shakes like a reed before a sneering paragraph in the Newspaper or even at a difference of opinion concerning something to be done expressed in a private letter from just such another shaking ⟨reed⟩ bulrush as himself. He sits expecting a dinner guest with a⟨n⟩ suspense which paralyses his inventive or his acquiring faculties. He finds the solitude of two or three entire days when mother, wife, & child are gone, tedious & dispiriting. Let him not wrong the truth & his own experience by too stiffly standing on the cold & proud doctrine of self sufficiency. [465]

[463] "Character" is inserted in pencil, possibly by Edward Emerson.

[464] This paragraph, struck through in ink with a vertical use mark, is used in "Character," *W*, III, 89.

[465] This entry, struck through in pencil with a diagonal use mark, is used in "The Heart," *Lectures*, II, 280.

CULTURE

To what end existed those gods of Olympus or the tradition so irresistibly embodied in sculpture, architecture, & a perdurable literature, that the names Jupiter, Apollo, Venus, still haunt us in this cold Christian ⟨English⟩ ↑Saxon↓ America, & will not be shaken off? To what end the ethical revelation which we call Christianity with all its history, its corruption, its Reformation; the Revivals of Letters; the Press; the planting of America; the conversion of the powers of nature to the domestic service of man, so that the ocean is but a water wheel & the ⟨moon &⟩ solar system but a clock? To what end are we distributed into electoral nations made to know & do; half subject still to England through the dominion of British intellect, [237] & in common with England, not yet recovered from the astonishing infusions of the Hebrew soul in the beginning of the world? Why is never a pencil moved in the hand of Raphael or Rembrandt & never a pen in that of Moses or Shakspeare but it communicates emotion & thought to me at the end of 500 years and across the breadth of half a globe? And whilst thus the prolific powers of Nature over a period of 3 or 4 000 years to yield spiritual aliment are epitomized & brought to a focus on the stripling now at school, why does yet his relation to a few men & women close by him outweigh in intensity the entire congregated attractions of worlds & ages[?] [466]

John Bunyan

"He that is down needs fear no fall
    He that is low no pride
He that is humble ever shall
    Have God to be his guide
Fulness to such a burden is
    That go on pilgrimage
Here little & hereafter bliss
    Is best from age to age."
                "The dunghill-raker, spider, hen
                The chicken too, to me
                Have taught a lesson; let me then
                Conformed to it be.

[466] This paragraph, struck through in pencil with vertical use marks, is used through "stripling now at school" in Human Culture: "Introductory," *Lectures*, II, 224–225.

> The butcher, garden, & the field,
> The ⟨r⟩Robin & his bait,
> Also the rotten tree, doth yield
> Me argument of weight." [467]

[238] A page which is tedious to me today, tomorrow becomes precious because I read in a book that it is precious to another man. This vexes me, that I should be of that infirm temper as to owe my ebbs & flows of estimation to any thing extrinsic. Patience and the memory of these humiliations & the calm abstraction which detects at a distance the different depth of successive states of mind & of course the different authority of these, will gradually invigorate the constitution of the mind to a more prompt & genuine judgment, so that all men shall say, There spoke the Truth.

Proportion certainly is a great ⟨part⟩ ↑end↓ of Culture. A man should ask God morning & evening with the philosopher that he might be instructed to give to every being & thing in the Universe its just measure of importance; but let not any say that the only remedy against the idols of the cave is conversation with many men & a knowledge of the world. This is also distorting: State street or the Boulevards of Paris are no truer pictures of the world than is a Monastery or a laboratory. The brokers & attornies are quite as far wide of the mark on one side, as monks & academicians on the other. Their multitude is no argument even to themselves. There are two ways of cultivating the Proportion of Character[:] 1. The habit of attending to all sensations & putting ourselves in a way to receive a variety as by attending spectacles, visiting theatres, prisons, senates, factories, ships, [239] museums, churches, & hells; a thing impossible to many & except in merest superficiality impossible to any, for a man is not in the place to which he goes unless his mind is there; and moreover let him go to all such places as I have named, What does he know about the miners of Cornwall? Is he sure to allow all that is due to that phase of human nature disclosed in the Thugs of the Desert? Does he appreciate Insanity? or know the military life of Russia? or that of the Italian lazzaroni? or the aspirations & ten-

---

[467] See John Bunyan, *The Pilgrim's Progress from this World to That which is to Come* (Oxford, 1960), pp. 238, 208–209.

dencies of the Sacs & Foxes?   2. The other mode of cultivating Gradation & forming a just Scale is to ⟨observe⟩ ↑compare↓ the depth of thought to which different objects appeal. Nature & the course of life furnish every man the most recluse with a sufficient variety of objects to ⟨fur⟩ supply him with the elements & divisions of a Scale. Let him look back upon any portion of his life[;] he will see that things have entirely lost the relative proportions which they wore to the eye at the moment when they transpired. The dearest aims of his ambition have sunk out of sight & some transient shade of thought looms up out of forgotten years.

Proportion is not the effect of circumstances but a habit of mind. The truth is the Mind is a perfect measure of all things & the only measure.[468]

[240][469] In the woods this afternoon, the bud on the dry twig appeared to reach out unto & prophesy an eternity to come.

———

The wise man always throws himself on the side of his assailants. It is more his interest than it is theirs to find out his weak point[;] it falls from him like a dead skin & he passes on invulnerable.[470]

———

He is not a skeptic who denies a miracle, who denies both angel & resurrection, who does not believe in the existence of such a city as ancient Rome or Thebes, but he is a skeptic & attacks the constitution of human society who does not think it always an absolute duty to speak the truth[;] who pretends not to know how to discriminate between a duty & an inclination; & who thinks the mind is not itself a perfect measure.[471]

———

[468] This and the preceding paragraph, struck through in pencil with vertical use marks, are used in Human Culture: "Introductory," *Lectures*, II, 226–227.

[469] "BUDS" is written above "In the words" at the top of the page.

[470] This paragraph, struck through in pencil and in ink with two vertical use marks, is used in "The Head," *Lectures*, II, 259–260, and "Compensation," *W*, II, 118.

[471] This paragraph, struck through in pencil with a vertical use mark, is used in Human Culture: "Introductory," *Lectures*, II, 228.

When a zealot comes to me & represents the importance of this Temperance Reform my hands drop — I have no excuse — I honor him with shame at my own inaction.

Then a friend of the slave shows me the ⟨g⟩ horrors of Southern slavery — I cry guilty guilty! Then a philanthropist tells me the shameful neglect of the Schools by the Citizens. I feel guilty again.

Then I hear of Byron or Milton who drank soda water & ate a crust whilst others fed fat & I take the confessional anew.

[241] Then I hear that my friend has finished Aristophanes, Plato, Cicero, & Grotius, and I take shame to myself[.]
Then I hear of the generous ↑Morton↓[472] who offers a thousand dollars to the cause of Socialism, and I applaud & envy[.]
Then of a brave man who resists a wrong to the death and I sacrifice anew[.]
I cannot do all these things but these my shames are illustrious tokens that I have strict relations to them all. None of these causes are foreigners to me.[n] My Universal Nature is thus marked. These accusations are parts of me too. They are not for nothing.[473]

———

It seems to me that Circumstances of man are historically somewhat better here & now than ever. That more freedom exists for Culture. It will not now run against an axe at the first step. In other places it is not so: the brave Lovejoy has given his breast to the bullet for his part and has died when it was better not to live.[474] He is absolved. There are always men enough ready to die for the silliest punctilio; to die like dogs who fall down under each other's teeth, but I sternly rejoice, that one was found to die for humanity & the rights of free speech & opinion.[475]

[472] Possibly Ichabod Morton of Plymouth, who later gave financial support to the Brook Farm experiment.
[473] "When a zealot [p. [240]] . . . nothing.", struck through in pencil with vertical use marks, is used in "The Heart," Lectures, II, 287.
[474] On the night of November 7, 1837, Reverend Elijah P. Lovejoy had been shot dead, in Alton, Illinois, by a mob angered by his journalistic crusade against slavery.
[475] This paragraph is struck through in pencil and ink with two vertical use marks. The first four sentences are used in "Heroism," Lectures, II, 337–338, and "Heroism," W, II, 262.

[242] The highest culture asks no costly apparatus, neither telescope nor observatory nor College; everywhere its apparatus is where are human beings & necessity & love.

It is

Nov. 25. What is that society which ⟨presents⟩ ↑unites↓ the most advantages to the culture of each? The poor but educated family. The eager blushing boys discharging as they can their little chares, & hastening into the little parlor to the study of tomorrow's merciless lesson yet stealing time to read a novel hardly smuggled in to the tolerance of father & mother & atoning for the same by some pages of Plutarch or Goldsmith; the warm sympathy with which they kindle each other in the yard & woodshed with scraps of Everett's Oration, or mimicry of Webster; the youthful criticism on Sunday of the Sermons; the School declamation faithfully rehearsed at home ↑to the vexation somewhat oftener than to the admiration of sisters;↓ the first solitary joys of literary vanity when the poem or the theme has been completed sitting alone near the top of the house; the cautious comparison of the attractive advertisement of the arrival of Kean or Kemble or the Lecture of the well known orator, with the expense of attending the same; the warm affectionate delight with which they behold & greet the return of each after the early separation of School or business require; the foresight with which [243] during such absences they hive the honey which opportunity offers for the ear & imagination of the others, & the unrestrained glee with which they profusely disburden themselves of their early mental treasures when the holidays bring them together again. What is the hoop that holds them staunch? It is the iron band of Poverty, of Necessity, of Austerity which excluding them from the sensual enjoyments that make other boys too early old, has directed their activity into safe & right channels, & made them spite of themselves reverers of the grand, the beautiful, & the good. ↑Ah!↓ Shortsighted students of books, of nature, & of man; too happy could they know their advantages! they pine for freedom from that mild parental yoke; they sigh for ⟨th⟩ fine clothes; ⟨the⟩ ↑for↓ rides; ↑for↓ the theatre & premature freedom & dissipation which others possess; wo^n to them if their wishes were crowned. The angels that dwell with them and are weaving laurels of life for their youthful brows are Toil & Want & Truth & Mutual Faith.[476]

[244][477] Primi in prœliis oculi vincuntur.[478] ⟨Extreme⟩ ↑Entire↓ self-possession may make a battle very little more dangerous to life than a game at football. The terrors of a storm are known only to those within the house: the drover[,] the teamster buffets it all day, & finds his health renews itself at as vigorous a pulse under the pelting snow as in the sun of June.[479] Dr Bartlett who rode with me from Lexington in a driving snowstorm, said he had as lief be sitting so as ⟨at⟩ with his legs over his fender.

I supposed that it was only ⟨for⟩ soldiers & Emperors that slept but four hours in the twenty four: but David Buttrick told me that since he had followed Teaming, he had not ⟨slept⟩ averaged more than this. And further, that it sometimes happened that he would be so overcome with drowsiness on the road that he could not proceed. Then he stops his team, turns into a bush at the roadside, & sleeps for five minutes. This satisfies him & he goes on as wakeful as after a night's sleep.[480]

I do not like to see a sword at man's side. If it threaten man, it threatens me. A company of soldiers is an ⟨naughty⟩ offensive spectacle[.]

---

[476] "Printed." is written in ink and partly encircled at the end of this paragraph, which is struck through in ink with use marks: three vertical lines on p. [242], three intersecting lines on p. [243]. This passage is used in "Domestic Life," W, VII, 119–121.

[477] "Self possession" is written above "in prœliis" and "sleep." appears above "vincuntur" at the top of the page as index headings for the two paragraphs immediately following.

[478] Cf. Tacitus, Germania, 43: "nam primi in omnibus proeliis oculi vincuntur." — "In every battle after all the eye is conquered first." See "On the Relation of Man to the Globe," Lectures, I, 38.

[479] "Primi in . . . June.", struck through in pencil and in ink with two vertical use marks, is used in "Prudence," Lectures, II, 319–320, and "Prudence," W, II, 237.

[480] This paragraph, struck through in pencil with a diagonal use mark, is used in "Prudence," Lectures, II, 323.

[245] 26 November. How can such a question as the Slave⟨ry⟩ Trade be agitated for forty years by the most enlightened nations of the world without throwing great light on ethics into the general mind? The fury with which the slaveholder & the slavetrader defend every inch of their plunder[,] of their bloody deck, & howling Auction, only serves as a Trump of Doom to alarum the ear of Mankind, to wake the sleepers, & drag all neutrals to take sides & listen to the argument & to the Verdict ↑which Justice shall finally pronounce↓. The ⟨frightful⟩ loathsome details of the kidnapping; of the middle passage; six hundred living bodies sit for thirty days betwixt death & life ⟨in the posture of statues⟩ in a posture of stone & when brought on deck for air cast themselves into the sea — were these details merely produced to harrow the nerves of the susceptible & humane or for the purpose of engraving the question on the memory that it should not be dodged or obliterated & securing to it the concentration of the whole conscience of Christendom? [n]

The Temperance question is that of no use[,] a question which rides the conversation of ten thousand circles, of every Lyceum, of every stage coach, of every church meeting, of every county caucus, which divides the whole community as accurately as if one party wore Blue coats & the other Red, which is tacitly present to every bystander in a bar room when liquor is drunk & is tacitly heeded by every visiter at a private table drawing with it all the curious ethics of the Pledge, of the Wine Question, [246] of the equity of the Manufacture & of the Trade.

The question of Antimasonry has a deep right & wrong which gradually emerge to sight out of the turbid controversy[.]

The political questions as of Banks; of the limits of Executive power; of the right of the people to instruct their representative; ↑of↓ the Tariff; of the treatment of Indians; are pregnant with doctrine. Can a War pass over a Nation without leaving some ethical conclusions laid up in the mind of all intelligent citizens? Can an Election? An appeal for the Greeks, an appeal for the Poles, an appeal for the ↑little↓ islands of Cape de Verd? [481]

---

[481] This and the three preceding paragraphs (from "How can such", p. [245]),

The Visit of a stranger like Lafayette; Spurzheim, Hall, Martineau; has great uses of thought & culture.

The Sunday School, the Charitable societies, the School Committees

The Crisis of Trade contrasting with the flowing sheet that just before was wafting us over illimitable spaces[,] the Crisis of Trade which always teaches political economy & constrains every man to explore the process involving the labors of so many by which a loaf of bread comes from the seed wheat ⟨in⟩to his table.

↑All these get epitomized into a song, a proverb, a byword, & so their spirit stays↓[.]

All these instructive slides in our lantern show us something of ethics & something of practicks. Whom do they teach? Do not ask Who. They teach you and if you [247] then tens of thousands. They settle what is & what ought to be. The gloomy catastrophe of a bankruptcy, of a revolution, of a war, which wrap cities & nations in black, is only an emphatic exposition of the natural results of given courses of action as we look at a pod to learn the virtues of a plant[.]

Does any say that it does no good for those who have learned by mistakes of policy which extend over fifteen or twenty years, what is right, ⟨& will⟩ die, & their wisdom dies with them,[482] for Time or Saturn is always devouring his children[?]

With that death I have no concern — the soul in us gives us no anticipation of any such fate[;] on the contrary, never looks that way; says, What have I to do with it? & craves always this nectar of the gods, knowledge, ambrosia. The earth is not a place of results, but a place of lessons and it doth not yet appear what we shall be.[483]

It does not exactly fit the thing to say *it was designed* that these ⟨event⟩ transactions should so teach us as t⟨o⟩hey have, but ⟨the soul⟩ this effect & this ⟨f[?]⟩action meet as accurately as the splendid lights of morning & evening meet the configuration of the human eye, and the more interior eye of Taste.[484]

---

struck through in ink with vertical use marks, are used in "Lecture on the Times," *W*, I, 269–270.

[482] Cf. Job 12:2. Under "which" is worked out a problem in division: 20/340

[483] I John 3:2.   17

[484] This paragraph is used in Human Culture: "Introductory," *Lectures*, II, 225.

[248] Nov. 27.   What is culture? The chief end of man
                 What is the apparatus? His related nature
                 What is the scale? Himself
                 What are my advantages? The total New England.

Condition

I fancy at times that I do not attribute importance enough to my external position; to Christianity, to Boston, to the laws, & the books. I do not think it any man's merit, the security or the light I enjoy from abroad, — I do not think it proceeds from any man's conscious action, — but is a composite force indicating the exact amount of conviction of the necessity of self control existing in the total mind of the community. For every individual who scorns it, it descends; for every individual who passionately attaches himself to it, it ascends. It indicates only the amount of acquaintance with those laws of Nature which it respects, in the body of the people. The reflecting educated population are temperate, pacific, & well read. ↑Look in B for the pendant.↓ [485]

[249][486] I magnify instincts. I believe that those facts & words & persons which dwell in a man's memory without his being able to say why, remain because they have a relation to him not less real for being as yet unapprehended. They are symbols of value to him as they can interpret parts of his consciousness which he would vainly seek words for in the conventional images of books & other minds. What therefore attracts my attention shall have it, as I will go to the man who knocks at my door, & a thousand persons as worthy go by it, to whom I give no heed.[487]

Dec. 3. Lidian says, it is wicked to go to church Sundays.[488]
Dec. 3. Waldo walks alone.

Whilst meditating on the Ideal, I hear today from the pulpit,

[485] This sentence is added in pencil.
[486] "Expressiveness" is written above "I magnify" at the top of the page.
[487] "I believe that . . . heed." is used in "Spiritual Laws," *W*, II, 144.
[488] This sentence is used in the Divinity School Address, *W*, I, 143.

"The friendship of the world is enmity with God," [489] which thus translates itself into the language of philosophy; Harmony with the Actual is discord with the Ideal.

[250]   ↑Ends meet or the Modern Use of Antiquity.↓

The progress of science is to bring the remote near. The kelp which grew neglected on the roaring sea beach of the Orkneys, now comes to the shops; the seal, the otter, the ermine, that none saw but the Esquimaux in the Rocky Mountains, they must come to Long Wharf also: the shells; the strombus, the turbo, the pearl, that hid six hundred fathoms down in the warm waters of the Gulf, they must take the bait & leave their silent houses & come to Long Wharf also: even the birds of Labrador that laid their eggs for ages on the rocky coast must send their green eggs now to Long Wharf whilst this happens[.]

So I think will it be the effect of insight to show nearer relations than are yet known between ⟨history⟩ remote periods of history & the present moment. The Assyrian, the Persian, the Egyptian era now fading ↑fast↓ into twilight must reappear to day and as a varnish brings out the original colors of an antique picture, so a better knowledge of our own time will ⟨pour⟩ ↑be a sunbeam to↓ search ⟨with floods of light⟩ the faintest traces of character in ⟨f⟩the foundations of the world. So I think Olympus & Memphis & Moses & Zoroaster & Tubal Cain have not done all their duty yet.

Homer, Greece, Rome, & Egypt certainly have come nearer to us for Bentley, Wolf,ⁿ Niebuhr, Muller, ⟨& Ch⟩ Win[c]kelmann, & Champollion[.] [490]

[251] You do not doubt that the same book, the same history yields different light to a boy & ↑to↓ a man. Last year you were a boy[;] now you are a man. Again; today you are a boy, & next year you shall be a man.

It is remarkable that we know so well the ideal of the human

---

[489] James 4:4.

[490] This and the preceding paragraph are struck through in pencil with a vertical use mark. The first paragraph is used in Human Culture: "Introductory," *Lectures*, II, 225–226.

form. A child knows at once if an arm or leg be distorted in a picture, if the attitude be natural, be grand or mean, though he has never received any instruction in drawing, nor heard any conversation on the subject nor can himself draw with correctness a single feature in the body. A good form strikes all eyes pleasantly long before they have any science on the subject.[491]

"Look from West to East along;
Father, old Himala weakens, Caucasus is bold & strong."

[252] [blank]

[253] I read in Mc Clelland's Geology of Kemaon that the villages affected with goitre in that part of India are disposed in lines parallel to the direction of the strata of the earth indicating that these contain the source of the contagion. Limestone always present. A village of Cretins.

The city of Chompawut was erected on Gneiss at the northern side of Choura Pany & was totally destroyed by the decomposition of the ⟨eminence⟩ rock on which it stood. This is supposed to have happened 500 years ago. A few vestiges remain (sculptured fragments of granite of great magnificence) owing to the accidental circumstance of their having been erected on the more durable beds of rock.[492]

Base of the Himalaya — "Nature has bestowed on the gigantic elephant & savage tiger the perpetual inheritance of this most awful landscape & to make one spot secure from the tyranny of Man, has bestowed on this part of the Tarai a climate which the human constitution could not endure even for a day at certain seasons. On the one hand, we have plains extending almost to the African Continent & to the Indian Ocean, with hardly an undulation to relieve the monotony of space. On the other, an almost interminable succession of mountains ascend one above another until they penetrate ⟨above⟩ beyond the regions of animal existence & conceal themselves

---

[491] This paragraph, struck through in pencil with a diagonal use mark, is used in "Intellect," *W*, II, 337.

[492] Cf. John McClelland, *Some Inquiries in the Province of Kemaon, Relative to Geology and Other Branches of Natural Science* (Calcutta, 1835), pp. 287 ff, 48.

in the clouds. Nor is there here as in most countries any of softening of parts — any blending of extremes. A foot of earth — a single line marks the awful contrast." [493]

[254] Dec. 4. How much waste strength is in the World since no man works with half or a quarter or a tithe of his strength, considering his profession or office not his proper work, but only perfunctorily done. [494]

Dec. 8. The fair girl whom I saw in town expressing so decided & proud ⟨a⟩ choice of influences, so careless of pleasing, so wilful & so lofty a will, inspires the wish to come nearer to & speak to this nobleness: So shall we be ennobled also. I wish to say to her, Never strike sail to any. Come into port greatly, or sail with God the seas. ⟨The⟩ Not in vain you live, for the passing stranger is cheered, refined, & raised by the vision. [495]
"Understanding"
    The small man's part in the conversation seems to be to keep by him an ⟨s⟩ewer containing cold water, and as fast as in different parts of the room a little blaze is generated, he applies a little cold water with his hand to the place[.]

    Sunday [December 10, 1837]. I could not help remarking at church how much humanity was in the preaching of my good Uncle, Mr ↑S.↓ R↑ipley.↓ The rough farmers had their hands at their eyes repeatedly. But the old hardened sinners, the arid educated men, ministers & others, were dry as stones.

[255] Dec. 9. Truth is our element & life, yet if a man fasten his attention upon a single aspect of truth, & apply himself to that alone for a long time, the truth itself becomes distorted, &, as it were, false.

---

[493] The source of this quotation has not been located; the passage is not from McClelland's book on Kemaon.

[494] This paragraph, struck through in pencil with a diagonal use mark, is used in "Doctrine of the Hands," *Lectures*, II, 236.

[495] This paragraph, struck through in pencil with a vertical use mark, is used in "Heroism," *Lectures*, II, 336, and "Heroism," *W*, II, 259–260.

Herein resembling the air which is our natural element & the breath of the nostrils, but if a stream of air be directed upon the body for a time it causes cold, fever, and even death.[496] *The lie of One Idea.*

E[lizabeth]. H[oar] made a just remark the other evening about the fair girl I spake of, that among grown up or married women she knew no one who fulfilled the promise of that one. But there were idealizing girls when these women were young. She said she never knew a woman excepting M.M.E. who gave high counsels.

In the sunset against the sky, the stone wall looked like a locket of black beads.

[256] Dec. 18. Ah that we had power to trace the parentage & the high distinctions of the Intellect[.] [497]
God is pure Intellect. Where it becomes one with Truth. Or is it bipolar there also & to be called Reason subjectively, Truth objectively? Of this deity the old sage might well say, Its beauty is immense.[498] As it enters our lower sphere, the Vision, that high power which perceives the excellence of Truth & Justice — is called Reason; the perception of the relations of the Apparent world is called Common Sense, and we apply the term Understanding to the activity of the mind upon the apparent objects, comparing, reasoning, constructing.

But Intellect & Intellection signify to the common ear something else, the consideration of abstract truth. It implies the power always to separate the fact from yourself, from all personality, & look at it [n] as if it existed for itself alone. It is entirely void of all affection, & sees an object, a thought, as it stands there in the light of the mind quite cool & disengaged. The Intellect goes out of the Individual, & floats over its own being, & regards its own being always as a foreign fact, & not as I & mine. *I & mine* cannot see the

---

[496] This paragraph is used in "Intellect," *W*, II, 339.
[497] Cf. "The Head," *Lectures*, II, 246–247, and "Intellect," *W*, II, 325.
[498] Plotinus: see p. [155] above.

Wonder of their existence. This the Intellect always ponders. It is never a partisan. It is always an observer.

God shows all things bound & formed. The subtle intellect detects the secret intrinsic likeness between remotest things, &, as a menstruum dissolves all things into a few principles. This power ⟨differs entirely⟩ does not appear in beasts. They ⟨do not⟩ are [257] wholly immersed in the Apparent, & do never, as we say, float over it, ↑& see↓ themselves also as facts.[499]

The order of the Universe seems always one, not diverse, but more & less. Thus over all the brute creation seems to brood⟨,⟩ — a common soul, the same in all, & never individualized. Each ox, each sheep is not an individual as a man is, but only one piece more of the ox ⟨nature⟩ ↑kind↓[,] of the sheep kind. Their life which ⟨gives⟩ contains their instincts is over them, according to the ancient saying, God is the soul of brutes.[500] In a higher sphere ⟨the⟩ of rational life dwells the infant man. The child is pervaded by an element of reason, but does not individualize himself, or say I. The child lives with God, but as a dweller in this higher sphere, that of Absolute Truth; this infinite nature bursts through at last into the affirmation of real being, I am. ⟨Only littl⟩ Feebly it enters into him; his life is the life of the senses, of the Apparent, of the Actual.[n]

But he is continually impelled by the influx of the higher principle to abstract himself from effects, & dwell with causes. This is ⟨Th⟩the region of laws, the ⟨regi⟩ sphere of the Intellect, the native air of the human soul. ↑Few men enter it, but all men belong there↓[.] [501]

[258] Dec. 30. Remarkable weather for these many days past, mild, clear, & in the morning hoar frost. Mercury at noon today 44° in

[499] From "As it enters" in the second paragraph to this point, the entry for December 18 is struck through in pencil with diagonal use marks. The second, third, and fourth paragraphs are used in "The Head," *Lectures,* II, 248–249, 249–250; the third and fourth, in "Intellect," *W,* II, 325–326.
[500] The saying is found in John Abernethy's *Physiological Lectures . . . delivered before the Royal College of Surgeons in the year 1817* (London, 1817), p. 272; see *JMN,* IV, 9.
[501] This and the preceding paragraph, struck through in pencil with diagonal use marks, are used in "The Head," *Lectures,* II, 247–248.

447

the shade. ↑Jan 5; 9 P.M. mercury 42°↓ ↑7th Mercury at 52 in shade.↓ ↑So on for seventeen days until 12 Jan.↓

Napoleon during his coronation, the whole time did nothing but gape.[502]

1838 [503]

Jan. 26. All this mild winter, Hygeia & the Muse befriend with the elements the poor driven scribe. Eight lectures have been read on eight fine evenings; and today the mercury stands at 52° (3 o'clock P.M.) in the shade.
Today I send the Oration to press again.

———

Sleep & dreams. The landscape & scenery of dreams seem not to fit us but like ⟨somebody's⟩ a cloak or coat of some other person to overlap & encumber the wearer. So is the ground, the road, the house ⟨of dre⟩ in dreams. Too long or too short. & if it served no other purpose would at least show us how accurately Nature fits man ⟨by day⟩ awake.[504]

[259] Jan. 27. How much superstition in the learned & the un-learned! All take for granted that a great deal, — nay, almost all — is known & forever settled. That which a man now says he merely throws in as confirmatory of this Corpse or Corporation Universal of Science.

Whilst the fact is, ↑that↓ nothing is known: And every new mind ought to take the attitude of Columbus, — launch out from the ignorant gaping World, & sail west for a new world.[505] Very, very few thoughts in an age. Now; Wordsworth has thought, & more truly Goethe has thought. Both have perceived the extreme poverty of literature. But all the rest of the learned were men of talents merely, who had some feat which each could do with words; Moore, Campbell, Scott, Mackintosh, Niebuhr; & the rest.

[502] This sentence is struck through in pencil with a diagonal use mark.
[503] "1838" is written in pencil — possibly not by Emerson.
[504] This paragraph, struck through in pencil with a diagonal use mark, is used in "Demonology," W, X, 5.
[505] The entry to this point is used in "General Views," Lectures, II, 359.

I think too that if there were philosophers, orators, men, to think boldly, there would be no difficulty in carrying with you the mind of any mixed audience. As soon as you become yourself dilated with a thought, you carry men with you as by miraculous uplifting; you lose them by your own want of thought, of which impotence they become instantly aware; simply as long as there is magnetism they are attracted [—] when there is no magnetism they are not.[506]

[260] Feb. 3. Five days ago came Carlyle's letter & has kept me warm ever since with its affection & praise. It seems his friend John Sterling loves Waldo Emerson also, by reason of reading the book "Nature." I am quite bewitched maugre all my unamiableness with so dainty a relation as a friendship for a scholar & poet I have never seen, and he Carlyle's friend. I read his papers immediately in Blackwood & see a thinker if not a poet. Thought he has & right in every line, but Music he cares not for. I had certainly supposed that a lover of Carlyle & of me must needs love rhythm & music of ⟨speech⟩ style.

So pleasant a piece of sentiment as this new relation, it does not seem very probable that any harsh experience will be allowed to disturb. It is not very probable that we shall meet bodily to put the ætherial web we weave to the test of any rending or straining. And yet God knows I dare & I will boldly impawn his temper that he dares meet & cooperate until we are assayed & proven. I am not a sickly sentimentalist though the name of a friend warms my heart & makes me feel as a girl, but must & will have in my companion sense & virtue.

[261] Feb. 5. But the Lecture must be writ — friend or no friend. And it seems as if Condition might be treated. Fate, fortune, Love, Demonology, Sleep; Death — what deities or demons environ man; Nothing but aids him.[507]

Then the ⟨circ⟩ fact that we lie open to God, & what may he not do!

---

[506] "As soon as . . . not." is struck through in pencil with a vertical use mark.
[507] "Nothing" is printed rather than written out. This paragraph apparently anticipates Emerson's lecture "General Views": see headnote, *Lectures*, II, 357.

But no; we can predict very well that though new thoughts may come & cheer & gild, they shall not transport us. There are limits to our mutability. Time seems to make these shadows that we are tough & peaked.

Yet remember that the hunger of people for truth is immense. The reason why they yawn, is because you have it not. Consider too how Shakspear & Milton are formed. They are just such men as we all are to their cotemporaries, and none suspected their superiority, — but after all were dead & a generation or two besides, it is discovered that they surpass all. ⟨You⟩ Each of us then take the same moral to himself[.]

True greatness will preach its own contentment. It will not sneer: it will not scold, — it will smile at the pomp-encumbered king, it will pity those who harness themselves with cares, but will persist itself in wearing a simpler & lighter costume. It will reckon All its own.

There are merits we cannot estimate, — the military, & the arithmetical, & the intellectual, [262] ↑we can but scarce any others. Observe our defective names for character.↓

But piety transcends. And there may be many elements of character that we want skill now to detect as we cannot find any virus in the air of a plague hospital, but the air of Alps & the air of the Dead ⟨Chamber⟩ Room give the same result. ↑We walk with Angels unawares.↓ [507a]

Fame is not the result we seek. Fame to my man shall be as the tinkle of a passing sleigh-bell[.] [508] ↑But he shall have the Past in the Present[,] he shall foresee himself in scanning the genius of Divine Providence↓[.]

[263] Feb. 9, 1838. In Boston, Wednesday Night, I read at the Masonic Temple the tenth & last lecture of my Course on Human Culture[.]

[507a] Cf. Heb. 13:2.
[508] See Journal B, pp. [149], [182].

Lecture I   Introductory
        II   The Hands
        III   The Head
        IV   The Eye & the Ear
        V   The Heart
        VI   The Heart   Continued
        VII   Prudence
        VIII   Heroism
        IX   Holiness
        X   General Views.

The pecuniary advantage of the Course has been considerable[.]
    Season tickets sold 319   for $620
    Single tickets sold 373   for   186
                                   ——
                                    806
        deduct error somewhere   13
                                   ——
                                    793
    deduct expenses   225
                                   ——
                        $568. net profit

The attendance on this course adding to the above list 85 tickets distributed by me to friends, will ⟨mak⟩ be about 439 persons on the average of an evening — & as it was much larger at the close than at the beginning I think 500 persons at the closing lectures.

A very gratifying interest on the part of the audience was evinced in the views offered — which were drawn chiefly out of the materials already collected in this Journal. The ten lectures were read on ten pleasant winter evenings on consecutive Wednesdays. Thanks to the Teacher [264] of me & of all, the Upholder, the Health giver; thanks & lowliest wondering acknowledgment.

⟨The opinion⟩ Opinion is our secondary or outward conscience, — very unworthy to be compared with the primary, but when that is seared this becomes of great importance. A man whose legs are sound may play with his cane or throw it away, but if his legs are gouty he must lean on his cane.

⟨The drawing rooms of Paris are indeed tre⟩

You must love me as I am. Do not tell me how much I should love you. I am content. I find my satisfactions in a calm considerate reverence measured by the virtues which provoke it. So love me as I am. When I am virtuous, love me; when I am vicious, ⟨slight⟩ hate me; when I am lukewarm, neither good nor bad, care not for me.

But do not by your sorrow or your affection solicit me to be somewhat else than I by nature am.[508a]

[265] Love men, and do what you will with them.

Mrs W. lived with my wife as chambermaid & received nine shillings a week for wages. She boarded her two children with her sister in the neighborhood for eight shillings. She did not go to church for six weeks because she said her sister would be very much hurt if she should go to church without a black ribbon on account of the death of the sister's little son, and my wife could not for a week or two find a ribbon to lend her. The best of it was, ⟨the⟩ Mrs W. is a total stranger in the town of Concord & not a soul would know whether she wore black ribbons or spangles, and the sister poor woman is struggling all the time with sickness & extreme poverty & a sot of a husband.

[266] 11 February. At the "teachers' meeting" last night my good Edmund after disclaiming any wish to difference Jesus from a human mind suddenly seemed to alter his tone & said that Jesus made the world & was the Eternal God. Henry Thoreau merely remarked that "Mr Hosmer had kicked the pail over." I delight much in my young friend, who seems to have as free & erect a mind as any I have ever met. He told as we walked this afternoon a good story about a boy who went to school with him, Wentworth, who resisted the school mistress' command that the children should bow to Dr Heywood & other gentlemen as they went by, and when Dr Heywood stood waiting & cleared his throat with a Hem! Wentworth said, "You need not hem, Doctor; I shan't bow."

[508a] The thought of this and the preceding paragraph anticipates Emerson's lines beginning "You shall not love me . . . ," printed among "Fragments on Nature and Life" in *Poems, W*, IX, 352.

16 February. And what can you say for Milton, the king of song in the last ages, Milton the heroic, the continuator of the series of the Bards[,] the Representative of the Immortal Band with fillet & harp & soul all melody? To me he is associated with my family[,] with my two glorious dead — Edward & Charles, — whose ear tingled with his melodies — with Charles especially, who I think knew the delight of that man's genius as well or better than any one who ever loved it. It was worth Milton's labor on his poems to give so much [267][509] clear joy & manly satisfaction to a noble soul in this distant time. ⟨I think⟩ Of this I am very sure, that Milton ⟨would⟩ himself would more prize the admiration ⟨& almost⟩ ↑nay↓ that is almost too strong a word, I may ⟨surel[?]⟩ dare to say rather tho' even love of Charles than of any other person who has written about him. For Charles's severe delicate discriminating taste read in Milton what seemed ⟨his own⟩ I doubt not ⟨rot⟩ rather his own writing than another man's. Charles could not write as he could read and Milton wrote for Charles. My ⟨ea⟩own ear still rings with the diamond sharpness of his poetic recitations of Samson Agonistes —

> "Is this he
> The renowned, the irresistible Samson
> Who tore the lion as the lion tears the kid"
> &c &c

and "the tame villatic fowl" [510]
and "Held up their pearled wrists & took /them/him/ in." [511]

And so does Milton seem to me a ⟨man⟩poet who had a majestic ear & an ear for all the delicacies of ⟨sound &⟩ rhythm   not at all squeamish[.]

[268] 17 February. My good Henry Thoreau made this else solitary afternoon sunny with his simplicity & clear perception. How comic is simplicity in this doubledealing quacking world. Every thing that boy says makes merry with society though nothing can be graver than his meaning. I told him he should write out the history of his

[509] "267" is written in pencil.
[510] Cf. Milton, *Samson Agonistes*, ll. 124–128, 1695, respectively.
[511] Misquoted from Milton, *Comus*, l. 833.

College life as Carlyle has his tutoring. We agreed that the seeing the stars through a telescope would be worth all the Astronomical lectures. Then he described Mr Quimby's electrical lecture here & the experiment of the shock & added that "College Corporations are very blind to the fact that that twinge in the elbow is worth all the lecturing."

Tonight I walked under the stars through the snow & stopped & looked at my far sparklers & heard the voice of the wind so slight & pure & deep as if it were the sound of the stars themselves revolving.

[269] How much self reliance it implies to write a true description of anything[.] For example Wordsworth's picture of skating; that leaning back on your heels & stopping in mid career.[512] So simple a fact no common man would have trusted himself to detach as a thought.[513]

19 February. Solitude is fearsome & heavy hearted. I have never known a man who had so much good accumulated upon him as I have. Reason, health, wife, child, friends, competence, reputation, the power to inspire, & the power to please. Yet leave me alone a few days, & I creep about as if in expectation of a calamity. My mother, my brother are at New York. A little farther, — across the sea, — is my friend Thomas Carlyle. In the islands I have another friend, it seems. I will love you all & be happy in your ⟨adm[?]⟩ love. My gentle wife has an angel's heart; & for my boy, his grief is more beautiful than other people's joy.
Carlyle too: ⟨a⟩Ah my friend! I thought as I looked at your book today which all the brilliant so admire, that you have spoiled it for me. Why, I say, should I read this book? the man himself is mine: he can sit under trees of Paradise & tell me a hundred histories deeper, truer, dearer than this, all the eternal days of God. I shall not tire, I shall not shame him: We shall be children in heart, & men

---

[512] Wordsworth, "Influence of Natural Objects . . . ," ll. 56 ff (*The Prelude*, I, 456 ff).
[513] This paragraph is struck through in pencil with a vertical use mark.

in counsel & in act. The pages which to others look so rich & alluring, to me have a frigid [270] & marrowless air for the warm hand & heart I have an estate in & the living eye of which I can almost discern across the sea some sparkles. I think my affection to that man really incapacitates me from reading his book. In the windy night, in the sordid day, out of banks & bargains & disagreeable business, ⟨I espy⟩ I espy you, & run to my pleasant thoughts.

[271] 23 February. Abel Adams told me that [Dwight] Boyden the late landlord of the Tremont House told him that he made forty five thousand dollars in one year in that establishment and was frightened at his success. Another year he made nearly so much. But it nearly killed him with care & confinement. He kept it eight years.

March 2. "Society," said M.M.E. in speaking of the ⟨sever⟩ malignity & meanness of conversation, "Society is like a corpse that purges at the mouth."

[272] March 4. I told Alcott that in the city, Cousin & Jouffroy & the opinion of this & that Doctor ⟨famed⟩ showed very large; a fame of the bookstores seemed commanding; but as soon as we got ten miles out of town, in the bushes we whistled at such matters, cared little for Societies, systémes, or bookstores. God & the world return again to mind, sole problem,[n] and we value an observation upon a brass knob, a genuine observation on a button, more than whole Encyclopaedias. It is even so; as I read this new book of Ripley's [514] it looks to me, neat, elegant, accurate as it is, a mere superficiality: in my Jack Cade way of counting by number & weight, counting the things, I find nothing worth in the accomplished Cousin & the mild Jouffroy. The most unexceptionable cleanness, precision, & good sense, — never a slip, never an ignorance, but unluckily, never an inspiration. One page of Milton's poorest tract is worth the whole. ↑See p. 276↓

[514] *Philosophical Miscellanies, Translated from the French of Cousin, Jouffroy, and B. Constant. With Introductory and Critical Notices.* By George Ripley (Boston, 1838), 2 vols. (Specimens of Foreign Standard Literature, vols. I–II). On p. [276] below, Emerson refers to this work as "G. Ripley's Specimens &c".

Last night a remembering & remembering talk with Lidian. I went back to the first smile of Ellen on the door stone at Concord. I went back to all that delicious relation to feel as ever how many shades, how much reproach. Strange is it that I can go back to no part of youth[,] no past relation without shrinking & shrinking. Not Ellen, not Edward, not Charles. Infinite compunctions embitter each of those dear [273] names & all who surrounded them.[515] Ah could I have felt in ⟨regard to⟩ ↑the presence of↓ the first, as now I feel my own power & hope, & so have offered her in every word & look the heart of a man humble & wise, but resolved to be true & perfect with God, & not as I fear it seemed, the uneasy uncentred joy of one who received in her a good — a lovely good — out of all proportion to his deserts, I might haply have made her days longer & certainly sweeter & at least have recalled her seraph smile without a pang. I console myself with the thought that if Ellen, if Edward, if Charles could have read my entire heart they should have seen nothing but rectitude of purpose & generosity conquering the superficial coldness & prudence. But I ask now why ⟨could⟩ was not I made like all these beatified mates of mine *superficially* generous & noble as well as *internally* so. They never needed to shrink at any remembrance; & I — at so many sad passages that look to me now as if I been blind & mad. Well O God I will try & learn, from this sad memory to be brave & circumspect & true henceforth & weave now a web that will not shrink.   ↑This is the thorn in the flesh.↓[516]

[274] At Church I saw ⟨nothing⟩that beautiful child A.P. & my fine natural manly neighbor who bore the bread & wine to the communicants with so clear an eye & excellent face & manners. That was all I saw that looked like God, at church: Let the clergy beware when the well disposed scholar begins to say, 'I cannot go to Church, time is too precious.'

That which was once a circumstance merely — that the best & the worst men in the parish met one day as fellows in one house, the eminent & the plain men, — has come to be a paramount motive for

---

[515] "I went back . . . them." is used in "Love," *W*, II, 171. Plate IV reproduces the conclusion of this passage on p. [273].

[516] Cf. II Cor. 12:7.

going to Church, — that one should not shun the one opportunity of equal meeting with all citizens that is left!!! [517] ↑I go to be of one counsel, to own the sentiment of Holiness with Carr & Wright & Buttrick.↓

Bad to see a row of children looking old[.]

5 March. Yesterday (Sunday) was a beautiful day, mild, calm, & though the earth is covered with snow, somewheres two feet deep, yet the day & the night moonlit were as good for thought, if the man were rested & peaceful, as any in the year. The meteorology of thought I like to note.

They say of Alcott, & I have sometimes assented, that he is onetoned & hearkens with no interest to books or conversation out of the scope of his one commanding [275] idea. May be so, but very different is his centralism from that of vulgar monomaniacs. For he looks with wise love at all real facts [—] at street faces, at the broad-shouldered long haired farmer, at the domestic woman, at the kitchen, at the furniture, at the season, [—] as related to Man, & so on. He can hear the voice which said to George Fox, "That which others trample on, must be thy food." [518]

What shall I answer to these friendly Youths who ask of me an account of Theism & think the views I have expressed of the impersonality of God desolating & ghastly? [519] I say that I cannot find when I explore my own consciousness any truth in saying that God is a Person, but the reverse. I feel that there is some profanation in saying He is personal. To represent him as an individual is to shut him out of my consciousness. He is then but a great man such as the crowd worships. Yet, yet, Cor purgat oratio. [520]

---

[517] "That which was . . . left!!!", struck through in ink with a vertical use mark, is used in the Divinity School Address, *W*, I, 143.

[518] Quoted from William Sewel, *The History of the Rise, Increase, and Progress of the Christian People Called Quakers*, 3rd ed., 2 vols. (Philadelphia, 1823), I, 44, in *JMN*, IV, 32; in "George Fox," *Lectures*, I, 171; and in "Holiness," *Lectures*, II, 351.

[519] Evidently students in the Divinity School at Cambridge: see *L*, II, 129, n. 109.

[520] "Prayer purifies the heart" (Ed.). Abbreviated from Robert Leighton, *Select*

[276] Of the French Eclecticism & what Cousin ⟨s⟩thinks so conclusive (See G. Ripley's Specimens &c vol 1. p. 45) [521] I would say there is an optical illusion in it. It looks as if they had got all truth in taking all the systems & had nothing to do but to sift & wash & strain, & the gold & diamonds would remain in the last cullinder. But in fact this is not so. For Truth is ⟨of⟩ such a flyaway, such a slyboots, so untransportable & unbarrelable a commodity that it is as bad ↑to catch↓ as light. Shut the shutters never so quick to keep all the light in, 'tis all in vain[,] 'tis gone before you can say Jack. Well how is it with our philosophy? Translate ⟨compare⟩, collate, distil all the systems, it steads you nothing, for truth will not be compelled in any mechanical manner. But the first observation you make in the sincere act of your nature, though on the veriest trifle may immediately open a new view of nature & of men that like a menstruum shall dissolve all systems in it; shall take up Greece, Rome, Stoicism, Eclecticism, & what not, as mere data & food for analysis and dispose of your world-containing system as a very little unit, (a kissed finger cannot write)   Take Cousin's Philosophy.[522] Well this book (if the pretension they make be good) ought to be wisdom's wisdom, & we can hug the volume to our heart & ⟨let⟩ make a bonfire of all the libraries. But here are people who have read it & still survive, [277] nor is it at once perceptible in their future reasonings that they have talked with God face to face. Indeed ⟨we⟩ ↑I↓ have read it ⟨ourselves⟩ ↑myself↓ as ⟨we⟩ ↑I↓ have read any other book. ⟨We⟩I found in it a few memorable thoughts, for philosophy does not absolutely hinder people from having thoughts, but by no means so many memorable thoughts as ⟨we⟩I have got out of many another ⟨work⟩ book, say, for example, Montaigne's Essays. A profound thought anywhere classifies all things. A profound thought will lift Olympus. ⟨The fact is⟩ ⟨t⟩The book of philosophy is only a fact, &

Works, 1823, I, 274, note: *"Cor serenat et purgat oratio, capaciusque efficit ad excipienda divina munera.* S[aint]. Aug[ustine]."

[521] *Philosophical Miscellanies,* trans. George Ripley, 1838. Cousin would "finally disengage what is true in [other] systems, and thus construct a philosophy superior to all systems, which shall govern them all by being above them all, which shall be . . . philosophy itself in its essence and in its unity."

[522] "Of the French . . . Cousin's Philosophy", struck through in ink with a vertical use mark, is used in "Literary Ethics," *W,* I, 171–172.

no more inspiring fact than another, & no less; but a wise man will never esteem it anything final or transcending. ↑Go & talk with a man of genius & the first word he utters sets all your so called knowledge afloat & at large.↓ ↑Plato, Bacon, & Cousin condescend instantly to be men & mere facts.↓ [523]

I have read with astonishment & unabated curiosity & pleasure Carlyle's Revolution again half through the second volume. I cannot help feeling that he squanders his genius. Why should an imagination such as never rejoiced before the face of God since Shakspear be content to play? Why should he trifle & joke? I cannot see; I cannot praise. It seems to me, he should have writ in such deep earnest that he should have trembled to his fingers' ends with the terror & the beauty of his visions. Is it not true that with all his majestic toleration[,] his infinite superiority as a man to the flocks of clean & unclean creatures [278] he describes, that yet he takes a point of view somewhat higher than his insight or any human insight can profitably use & maintain, that there is therefore some inequality between his power of painting which is matchless & his power of explaining which satisfies not.   ↑Somewhere you must let out all the length of all the reins. There is somewhat real; there is God.↓

We acquire courage by our success daily & have a daring from experience which we had not from genius. I regret one thing omitted in my late Course of Lectures; that I did not state with distinctness & conspicuously the great error of modern Society in respect to religion & say, You can never come to any peace or power until you put your whole reliance in the moral constitution of man & not at all in a historical Christianity. ⟨The unbelief of man⟩ The Belief in Christianity that now prevails is the Unbelief of men. They will have Christ for a lord & not for a brother. Christ preache⟨d⟩s the greatness of Man but we hear only the greatness of Christ.

↑6 March.↓ Read in Montaigne's chapter on Seneca & Plutarch Vol [II] p. [624] a very good critique on the Systems & Methods on

[523] "The book of philosophy . . . facts." is struck through in ink with vertical use marks. "A profound thought . . . facts." is used in "Literary Ethics," W, I, 172.

which I expended my petulance in these pages yesterday.[524] Montaigne is spiced throughout with rebellion as much as Alcott or my young Henry T.

[279] It is a mystery of numbers that in loss & gain, whether of finances or of political majorities, the transfer of one counts not one but two. Well in magnanimities it is not otherwise. I have generous purposes & go on benefitting somebody, wellpleased with myself. Presently I listen to the prudences, & say this person is heedless & ungrateful — I withhold my hand. Instantly the new coldness awakens resentment in the other party & all the feelings that naturally respond to selfishness. I who pleased myself with my generosity & am still the same person find no sort of complacency toward myself in the supposed beneficiary but only hard thoughts. And the difference of cost betwixt munificence & meanness may amount to one dollar fifty three cents.

I like, to be sure, Mrs Hoar's good saying that when that transcendant beggar Ma'am Bliss received the beefsteaks she had sent her, saying, "Yes, you can leave it; Mrs D. has sent me some turkey, but this will do for the cat;" Mrs H. told Elizabeth, that, "it would do her as much good as if she thanked us". ⟨M⟩Very true & noble, Mrs H! and yet I grudged the dollar & a half paid to my stupid beggar-mannered thankless, Mrs W. because all that I gave to this lump of tallow was so much taken from my friend & brother whom I ought to go labor on daywages to help.

[280] 9 March. There was a simple man grew so suddenly rich that coming one day into his own stately door & hall in a reverie, he felt on his mind the accustomed burden of fear that now he should see a great person, & was making up his mouth to ask firmly if ———— was at home, when he bethought himself, Who is ————? who is it I should ask for?, & on second thought, he saw it was his own house, & he was ————.

[524] *Essays*, 1700. Writing to Hedge on March 27, Emerson again applied to "Cousin's pompous plea for Eclecticism" the strictures on Cicero in Montaigne's essay (*L*, II, 123).

There was a lady who planted a parlor full of bulbs, & they all came up onions.

We take great pleasure in meeting a cultivated peasant, and think his inde⟨n⟩pendence of thought & his power of language surprising, but it is soon tedious to talk with him, for there is no progress in his conversation, no speed, no prompt intelligence, but a steady ox-team portage that you can see from where you stand where it will have got half an hour hence. The scholar is a comfort to your heart for he leaves all the details of the way & will jump with you over a few centuries when we have got into a bog.

Of droll word blunders Lidian could never cure Mrs W. of calling mashed, *smashed.* "↑Oh↓ yes ⁿ she had fed Baby with a smashed potato."   ↑Snowed *snew*   Hintz
"You fired the scissors at me."↓ [525]

[281] 11 March. The advantage of riches seems to be in the skin ↑or↓ not much deeper. I wake up in the morning & think, Well, I need not go to Boston or New York: I need not purse my mouth in expectation of any great man to descend into the parlor. I need not consult any worse man's or odd man's humor[;] I am no man's man. I am quite free to go to my work, the work which is my joy to do. This makes a state of perfect preparation for the work.ⁿ   If I wake up in another man's house or in a hotel or place of constraint, where I have come to do a forced work, come not with ideal freedom but with external compulsion of some sort, then I feel an irritability as much in the skin as in the soul, that pesters & hinders me. If I were master of Millions I should not feel such vexation but should control the circumstances & inasmuch as I am master of hundreds or thousands, I do. And such & no other seems the advantage of riches. If a man have more soul, more will, less *skin*, — he can do without riches. [526]

"Love is the sole title-deed to property in the spiritual world." C.C.E.

[282] 14 March. Read a lecture on Peace at the Odeon on Monday

[525] "Snowed . . . at me." is added in pencil.
[526] This paragraph is struck through in pencil with a succession of five diagonal use marks.

evening, 12th.[527] Yesterday saw Margaret Fuller and the Tremont Pictures & talked of Carlyle & Cousin & at the soiree saw Bancroft, & Ripley, & Loring,[528] & so had a pleasant Boston visit. Bancroft talked of the foolish Globe Newspaper. It has ⟨30 000⟩ a circulation of 30 000. & as he said each copy is read by ten persons so that an editorial article is read by 300 000 persons which he pronounced with all deepmouthed elocution. I only told him then I wished they would write better if they wrote for so many. I ought to have said What utter nonsense to name in *my* ear this *number*, as if that were anything. 3,000 000 such people as can read the Globe with interest are as yet in too crude a state of nonage to deserve any regard. I ought to have expressed a sincere contempt for the Scramble newspaper.

18 March. I was so ungrateful in reading & finishing Carlyle's History yesterday as to say But Philosophes must not write history for me. They know too much. I read some Plutarch or even dull Belknap or Williamson[529] & in their dry dead annals I get thought which they never put there. I hear a voice of great nature through these wooden pipes. But my wise poet sees himself all that I can see of the divine in events & however slightly says that he sees it. So is my subject exhausted & my end as an artist not furthered [283] for do they not say that the highest joy is the creator's not the receiver's[?]
↑See what is said above p. 156↓

Yet wiser I have been & am whenever I sit & hear & wiser I am in this reading when my poet soars highest. It is strange how little moral sentence[,] how few moral sentences there are in literature. They affect us deeper[,] greatlier than all else. Yet how rare! ⟨t⟩The whole praise of Wordsworth is based on some ten pages or less of such matter. Herbert's is that; Shakspeare has spoken a little: & Carlyle has uttered both before & again in this book some immortal accents.

---

[527] See "War," *W*, XI, 151–176. The Odeon Hall was in Boston.
[528] The historian George Bancroft, George Ripley, and the lawyer-philanthropist Ellis Gray Loring (1803–1858); Loring, who had been Emerson's classmate at the Boston Latin School, wrote to him on March 16 (*L*, VI, 505).
[529] Jeremy Belknap, *History of New Hampshire*, 3 vols. (1784–1792); William Durkee Williamson, *History of the State of Maine*, 2 vols. (1832).

Thus what[n] is said of De Launay who could not fire the Bastille Magazine; what[n] is said of Danton the realist & of the moral to go & do otherwise issuing from this era; abide in my memory with vital heat.[530]   ↑See p. 301↓

I have read the second volume of Poems by Tennyson with like delight to that I found in the first & with like criticism. Drenched he is in Shakspeare, born baptised & bred in Shakspear, yet has his own humor & original rhythm, music, & images. How ring his humorsome lines in the ear[:]

> "In the afternoon they came unto a land
> In which it seemed always afternoon."
>   ["The Lotos-Eaters," ll. 3–4]

The ⟨new⟩Old year's Death pleases me most.[531] But why I speak of him now is because he had a line or two that looked like the moral strain amaranthine I spake of.

[284] At Church all day but almost tempted to say I would go no more. Men go where they are wont to go else had no soul gone this afternoon. The snowstorm was real[,] the preacher merely spectral.[532] Vast contrast to look at him & then out of the window. Yet no fault in the good man. Evidently he thought himself a faithful searching preacher, mentioned that he thought so several times; & seemed to be one of that large class, *sincere persons based on shams; sincere persons who are bred & do live in shams.* He had lived in vain. He had no one word intimating that ever he had laughed or wept, was married or enamoured, had been cheated, or voted for, or chagrined. If he had ever lived & acted we were none the wiser for it. It seemed strange they should come to church. It seemed as if

---

[530] On the Marquis de Launay, see *The French Revolution: A History*, vol. I, Bk. V, ch. VI ("Wo to thee, De Launay, in such an hour, if thou canst not, taking some one firm decision, *rule* circumstances!"); on Danton, vol. III, Bk. I, ch. IV (". . . a Reality and not a Formula"; "it is on the Earth and on Realities that he rests."). See *The Works of Thomas Carlyle*, 1896–1901, II, 190; IV, 23, respectively.

[531] "The Death of the Old Year," *Poems by Alfred Tennyson*, 2 vols. (London, 1833 [1832]), II, 154–157.

[532] The preacher was Reverend Barzillai Frost, Dr. Ripley's assistant in Concord. See Kenneth W. Cameron, "Emerson, Thoreau, Parson Frost, and 'The Problem,'" *Emerson Society Quarterly*, No. 6 (I Quarter, 1957), p. 16.

their own houses were very unentertaining that they should prefer this thoughtless clamorous young person. I think it shows what I said on the last page to be true, that there is commanding attraction in the moral sentiment that can lend a faint tint of light to such dulness & ignorance as this coming in its place & name. What a cruel injustice it is to moral nature to be thus behooted & behowled, & not a law, not a word of it articulated.[533]

But why do I blame the preachers? What is so rare among men may be rare among preachers: All men are bound to articulate speaking as well as they. I doubt I shall never hear the august laws of morals as I am [285] capable of them. No pronouncer of them shall fill my ear.

Carlyle has too much reason for his insisting so oft on articulate speech as opposed to hysterics. There is but little. Even the few speeches he quotes from his great men in his History after the first or second sentence, do merely verb it. Verbs & not thoughts.

The Church is a good place to study Theism by comparing the things said with your Consciousness.

There is no better subject for effective writing than the Clergy. I ought to sit & think & then write a discourse to the American clergy showing them the ugliness & unprofitableness of theology & churches at this day & the glory & sweetness of the Moral Nature out of whose pale they are almost wholly shut.

Present Realism as the front face. & remind them of the fact that I shrink & wince as soon as the prayers begin & am very glad if my tailor has given me a large velvet collar to my wrapper or cloak, the prayers are so bad.[534] A good subject, because we can see always the good ideal, the noble Ethics of Nature, as contrast to the poverty stricken pulpit. Tell them that a true preacher can always be known by this, that he deals them out his life, life metamorphosed;

---

[533] "At Church all day . . . articulated." and "*sincere persons* . . . articulated.", struck through in ink with vertical use marks, are used in the Divinity School Address, *W*, I, 137–138, 138–139, 141–142.

[534] "Present Realism . . . prayers begin" is struck through in ink with a diagonal use mark. The paragraph to this point is used in the Divinity School Address, *W*, I, 137.

as Taylor, Webster, Scott, Carlyle ↑do↓. But of the bad preacher, it could not be told from his sermon, what age of the world he fell in, [286] whether he had a father or a child, whether he was a freeholder or a pauper, whether he was a citizen or a countryman, or any other fact of his biography. But a man's sermon should be rammed with life.[535]

The men I have spoken of above — sincere persons who live in shams, are those who accept another man's consciousness for their own, & are in the state of ⟨one⟩ ↑a son↓ who should ⟨grow up⟩ always suck at his mother's teat. I think Swedenborg ought so to represent them or still more properly, as permanent embryos wh⟨o⟩ich received all their nourishment through the umbilical cord & never arrived at a conscious & independent existence.

Once leave your own knowledge of God, your own sentiment, & take a secondary knowledge as St Paul's, or George Fox's, or Swedenborg's, and you get wider from God with every year this secondary form lasts; & if, as now, eighteen centuries; why, the chasm ⟨is very wide⟩ yawns to that breadth that men can scarcely be convinced there is in them anything divine.[536]

See how easily these old worships of Moses, of Socrates, of Zoroaster, of Jesus, domesticate themselves in my mind.[537] It will be admitted I have great susceptibility to such. Will it not be as easy to say they are other Waldos? n

[287] A man comes now into the world a slave, he comes saddled with twenty or forty centuries. Asia has arrearages & Egypt arrearages; not to mention all the subsequent history of Europe & America. But he is not his own man but the hapless ⟨servant⟩ bond-

---

[535] "Tell them . . . life.", struck through in ink with one diagonal use mark on p. [285] and two vertical use marks on p. [286], is used in the Divinity School Address, W, I, 138.

[536] This paragraph, struck through in ink with two vertical use marks, is used in the Divinity School Address, W, I, 145.

[537] This sentence is used in "History," W, II, 28; cf. also the Divinity School Address, W, I, 145: ". . . one good soul shall make the name of Moses, or of Zeno, or of Zoroaster, reverend forever."

man ↑of Time↓ with these continents & aeons of prejudice to carry on his back. It is now grown so bad that he cannot carry the mountain any longer & be a man. There must be a Revolution. Let the revolution come & let ⟨o⟩One come breathing free into the earth to walk by hope alone. It were a new World & perhaps the Ideal would seem possible.[538] ↑But now it seems to me they are cheated out of themselves, & live on another's sleeve.↓

Astronomy is sedative to the human mind. In skeptical hours, when things go whirling, & we doubt if all is not an extemporary dream: the calm, remote,[n] & secular character of astronomical facts composes us to a sublime peace.[539]

19 March. Yesterday a snowstorm; lying today as in January banks; & the bluebirds have disappeared. If the best people I know, say, A. & B, & C, & L, & S, should meet with highest aims, should meet for worship I think they would say, Come, now let us join in ⟨|| ... ||⟩ Aspirations to the Soul — How little a portion is known of Him! What needs but lowly utter sincerity? And let us say together what we feel; then, let each if he be so happy as to have any moral sentiment[,] any moral law to announce, tell it, that we may animate each other's love & courage & hope.

[288] To absolute mind, a person is but a fact, but consciousness is God.

Of the new testament the supreme value is the charm I wrote of yesterday which attaches ⟨highest⟩ to moral sentences, to the Veda, to Seneca, to all the Vaticinations, & highest to the Hebrew Muse: But it is true of the N[ew]. T[estament]. as of them all, that it has no epical integrity. I look for some moral Bard who shall see so far those shining laws that he shall see them come full circle & shall show them for their Beauty & not alone as Good. I call it fragmentary; & aver that the thought which can see their rounding complete grace & the identity of the law of gravitation with purity of heart

---

[538] "A man comes . . . possible." is struck through in pencil with a vertical use mark.

[539] This paragraph is struck through in pencil with a vertical use mark.

has not yet come. God send me that Bard, Auspicious Babe be born! [540]   ↑V[ide]. p. 301 & p. 283↓

21 March. Last night, George Minot says, he heard in his bed the screaming & squalling of the wild geese flying over ⟨at⟩ between 9 & 10 o'clock. The newspaper notices the same thing. I riding from Framingham at the same hour heard nothing. The collar of my wrapper did shut out Nature.

[289] 24 March. The natural motions of the Soul are so much better than the voluntary ones that you will never do yourself justice in dispute. The thought is not then taken hold of by the "right handle"[,] [541] does not ⟨ext⟩ show itself ⟨in its⟩ proportioned & in its true bearings. It bears extorted, hoarse, & half witness.

I have been led yesterday in to a rambling exculpatory talk on Theism. I say that here we feel at once that we have no language; that words are only auxiliary & not adequate; are suggestions and not copies of our cogitation. I deny Personality to God because it is too little not too much. Life, personal life is faint & cold to the energy of God. For Reason & Love & Beauty, or, that which is all these, is the life of life, the reason of reason, the love of love.

In the highest moments, we are a vision. There is nothing that can be called gratitude nor properly joy. The soul is raised over passion. It seeth nothing so much as Identity. It is a Perceiving that Truth & Right ARE. Hence it becomes a perfect Peace out of the knowing that all things will go well. Vast spaces of Nature [—] the Atlantic ocean, the South Sea; vast intervals of time [—] years, centuries, are annihilated to it; this[n] which I think & feel underlay that former state of life & circumstances, as it does underlie my present, & will always all circumstance, and what is called life & what is called death ⟨are superficial to this⟩.[542]

[540] "But it is true . . . born!", struck through in ink with a vertical use mark, is used in the conclusion of the Divinity School Address, W, I, 151.

[541] Cf. Epictetus, Encheiridion, 43: "Everything has two handles, by one of which it ought to be carried and the other not." See "The American Scholar," W, I, 84, and "Art and Criticism," W, XII, 300–301, 302.

[542] This paragraph, struck through in pencil with a vertical use mark, is used in "Self-Reliance," W, II, 69.

[290]⁵⁴³ March 26. Thought is only to be answered by thought not by authority[,] not by wishes. I tell men what I find in my consciousness. They answer me. ["]It is wrong; it is false; for we wish otherwise.["] I report to them from my thought how little we know of God, and they reply "We think you have no Father. We love to address the Father." Yes, I say, ⟨but⟩ the Father is a convenient name & image to the affections; but drop all images if you wish to come at the elements of your thought & use as mathematical words as you can. We must not be so wise. We must not affect as all mankind do, to know all things & to have quite finished & done God & Heaven. We must come back to our real initial state & see & own that we have yet beheld but the first ray of Being. In strict speech it seems fittest to say, *I Become* rather than *I am*. I am a *Becoming*. So do I less sever or divide the One. I am now nothing but a prophecy of that I shall be. To me sing & chant sun & stars & persons[;] they all manifest to me my far off rights. They foreshow or they are the first ⟨b⟩ⁿ ripples & wavelets of that vast inundation of the All which is beyond & which I tend & labor to be.

[291] March 27. This is one of the chilly white days⁵⁴⁴ that deform my spring.

It ⟨is⟩ seems as if we owed to literature certain impressions concerning nature which nature did not justify[.]

By Latin & English poetry, I was born & bred in an oratorio of praises of nature, flowers, birds, mountains, sun & moon, and now I find I know nothing of any of these fine things[,] ⟨an⟩that I have conversed with the merest surface & show of them all; & of their essence or of their history know nothing. Now furthermore I melancholy discover that nobody, — that not these chanting poets themselves know anything sincere of these handsome natures they so commended[;] that ⟨if I go into⟩ they contented themselves with the passing chirp of a bird or saw his spread wing in the sun as he fluttered by, they saw one morning or two in their lives & listlessly looked

⁵⁴³ "Law of Conversation" is written above "March . . . only" at the top of the page.
⁵⁴⁴ According to Edward Emerson, his father "always objected to 'white days,' when there was a slight film over the sun, but rejoiced in a 'yellow day,' with its splendor of color" (*J*, IV, 417, n. 1).

at sunsets, & repeated idly these few glimpses in their song. But if
I go into the forest, I find all new & undescribed. Nothing has been
told me. The screaming of wild geese was ⟨overlooked⟩ never heard;
the thin note of the titmouse & his bold ignoring of the bystander;
the fall of the flies that patter on the leaves like rain; [545] the angry
hiss of some bird that crepitated at me yesterday. The formation of
turpentine & indeed any vegetation, any animation, any & all, are
alike undescribed. Every man that goes into the wood seems to be
the first man that ever went into a wood. His sensations & his World
are new. You really think [292] that nothing new can be said about
morning & evening. And the fact is morning & evening have not yet
begun to be described. When I see them I am not reminded of these
Homeric or Miltonic or Shakspearian or Chaucerian pictures, but I
feel a pain of an alien world or I am cheered with the moist, warm,
glittering, budding, & melodious hour that takes down the narrow
walls of my soul & extends its life & pulsation [n] to the very horizon.
↑That is Morning. To cease for a bright hour to be a prisoner of this
sickly body & to become as large as the World.↓ [546]

Somewhere, as I have often said, not only every orator but every
man should let out all the length of all the reins[,] [547] should find or
make a frank & hearty expression of himself. If G[eorge]. P. B[rad-
ford]. keeps school & in the details of his week loses himself or fails
to communicate himself to the minds of his scholars in his full stature
& proportion as a wise & good man, he does not yet find his vocation:
he must find in that an outlet for his ⟨tho⟩ character, so that he may
justify himself to their minds for doing what he does. He must take
some trivial exercise or lesson, & make it liberal. Whatever he knows
& thinks[,] whatever in his apprehension is worth his doing, — that
let him communicate, or they will never know him & honor him
aright.[548] G[eorge]. B. E[merson]. is more interested in his trees
& cabinet of shells than in books; ⟨a⟩ he has not then given his lesson
to his school until he has shown them the shells & the shrubs.

[545] See p. [137] above.
[546] This paragraph, struck through in ink with vertical use marks, is used in
"Literary Ethics," W, I, 167–169.
[547] See p. [278] above.
[548] The paragraph to this point is used in "Spiritual Laws," W, II, 141–142.

[293] I thought as I rode to Acton that we all betray God to the devil, Being to Negation. I know well the value of a sentiment & of sincerity yet how easily will any fop, any coat-&-boots draw me to an appearance of sympathy with him & to an air of patronising the sentiments; the ⁿ commonest person of condition & fashion affects me more than is right, & I am mute, passive, & let their world wag; let them make the world, I being but a block of the same. I ought to go upright & vital & say the truth in all ways. When the stiff, hard, proud, clenched Calvinist takes up Abolition & comes to me with his last news from Montserrat; ⟨w⟩Why should I not say to him, Out upon this nonsense; hush. Go learn to love your infant, your woodcutter; be good natured & modest; have that gleam of grace & not varnish over your hard uncharitable ambition with this incredible tenderness for black folks a thousand miles off. Why should all small, poor, disappointed bigots be so fierce in this philanthropy as languages, Frenchmen, & the cholera follow the watercourses? Rough & graceless would be such greeting nor ⟨betray || . . . ||⟩ indicate much love. Yet do not ⟨l⟩ carry love to affectation & slaver.[549]

Plain it is that our culture is not come[,] that none are cultivated. That it could not be said by the traveller — I met in that country one highsouled & prevailing man. Foolish whenever you take the meanness & formality of what thing you do as a lecture, a preaching, a school, a teachers' meeting & do not rather [294] ⟨enlarge⟩ magnify it to be the unwilling spiracle of all your character & aims. Let their ears tingle, let them say, 'we never saw it in this manner.'[550]

The effeminate rich man says in his shrug[,] in his gloves & surtout on the cold spring day[,] that he fears the earth will not yield to man bread this year. The hard visaged farmer looks contented & fearless. He has fronted the year cold & grim. He has embraced the shovel & the ox yoke & ploughtail long ago & knows well that the hardest year that ever blew afforded to such straining & sweating as his, milk, rye, potatoes[;] at least pork & cattle[;] & he does not think of famine. Any more than a sailor rowing to a ship doubts any-

---

[549] "I ought to go . . . slaver." is used in "Self-Reliance," *W*, II, 51.

[550] "Foolish whenever . . . manner.' " is struck through in pencil with vertical use marks.

thing about sinking before he gets there; he rows & goes; ⟨there⟩ landsmen may do the doubting & fearing, if they like it.[551]

It seemed when I described the possible church the other day as if very hardly could any such sincerity & singleness be retained as was needful to a Worship: very hardly even by such saints & philosophers as I could name. This morbid delicacy of the religious sentiment, this thin existence fluttering on the very verge of nonexistence, accuses our poverty[,] jejune life. It will be better by & by, will it not? Will it not when habitual be more solid, & admit of the action of the Will without deceasing[?]

[295] 1 April. Cool or cold windy clear day. The Divinity School youths wished to talk with me concerning theism. I went rather heavy-hearted for I always find that my views chill or shock people at the first opening. But the conversation went well & I came away cheered. I told them that the preacher should be a poet smit with ⟨the⟩ love[552] of the harmonies of moral nature: and yet look at the Unitarian Association & see if its aspect is poetic. They all smiled No. A minister nowadays is plainest prose, the prose of prose. He is a Warming-pan, a Night-chair at sick beds & rheumatic souls; and the fire of the minstrel's eye & the vivacity of his word is exchanged for intense grumbling enunciation of the Cambridge sort, & for scripture phraseology.

Lidian said as I awoke this morning a lively verse enough of some hymn of Bunyan. There is no fanaticism as long as there is the creative muse. Genius is a character of illimitable freedom. And as long as I hear one ↑graceful↓ modulation of wit I know the genial soul & do not smell fagots. The Bunyan[,] the Boehmen is nearer far to Rabelais & Montaigne than to Bloody Mary & Becket & Inquisitions.[553]

[296] How ⟨f⟩ⁿ well the newspapers illustrate the truth that only biography[,] not nations interest. The Reporters tell us nothing but of

---

[551] This paragraph is struck through in pencil with a vertical use mark.
[552] Cf. Milton, *Paradise Lost*, III, 29: "smit with the love of sacred song."
[553] This paragraph is struck through in pencil with a diagonal use mark.

Calhoun, Clay, & Webster[,] not the Sub Treasury Bill but the personal controversy absorbs them.

I thought as I read of Napoleon yesterday in O'meara that the growths of genius, ⟨|| . . . ||⟩ even of the nocturnal sort like his, (or Will without love) are of a certain voluminous secular, federal, cosmic, cyclic unfolding that does not advance the elect individual first over John, then Adam, then Richard, & give to each the pain of discovered inferiority, but by every pulsation he expands there where he works passing at each pulsation classes[,] populations of men as the plumule of the oak passes the proportions of the plumule of the whortleberry.[554] He was plebeian. When Emperor he felt that a baron[,] a count of the old noblesse had certain advantages of him not felt whilst his Genius was in place & could justify its upstart growth by his prodigious energy fashioning Italy, fashioning Spain, but visible to both when he ⟨was[?]⟩ sat discrowned in a paltry house at St Helena. ↑See ⟨p⟩above p.231↓

I like the man in O'⟨m⟩Meara's picture. He is goodnatured as greatness always is & not pompous. He liked well to talk of the Bourbons & noblesse as a hereditary race of asses.[555] Ample good nature. Able men are moral. "A man of my stamp" said N. "does not commit a crime from a caprice." [556]

[297] "Tell him" (Sir H. Lowe) said Bonaparte, "that when a man has lost his word, he has lost every thing which distinguishes him from the brute." O'meara.[557]

Nothing said Napoleon has been more simple than my elevation. It was not the result of intrigue or crime. It was owing to the peculiar circumstances of the times & because I fought successfully against the enemies of my country [558]

"Massena was a man of superior talent. He generally however made bad dispositions previous to a battle; & it was not until the dead began to fall about him that he began to act with that judgment which he ought to have

---

[554] "the growths of genius . . . whortleberry." is struck through in ink with a vertical use mark.

[555] Cf. "Napoleon," *W*, IV, 239: Napoleon "made no secret of his contempt for the born kings, and for 'the hereditary asses,' as he coarsely styled the Bourbons."

[556] This sentence, struck through in ink with a diagonal use mark, is used in "Napoleon," *W*, IV, 231.

[557] *Napoleon in Exile*, 1823, I, 265.

[558] Cf. *ibid.*, I, 272–273. This paragraph, struck through in both pencil and ink with vertical use marks, is used in "Napoleon," *W*, IV, 231.

displayed before. In the midst of the dying & the dead, of balls sweeping away those who encircled him then Massena was himself; gave his orders & made his dispositions with the greatest sangfroid & judgment. This is *la vera nobilità di sangue.* It was truly said of Massena that he never began to act with judgment until the battle was going against him.[559] He was however a robber. He went halves with the contractors & commissaries of the army." O'meara [*Napoleon in Exile*, I, p]p. 183[-184] Boston Edit. 182⟨1⟩3

"Josephine was the most accomplished lady in France. She was the goddess of the toilette: all the fashions originated with her: everything she put on appeared elegant. & she was so kind, so humane, she was the best woman in France" [*Ibid.*,] p. 174.

"The Bourbons have learned nothing they have forgotten nothing. They would make generals out of these imbeciles *de la grande naissance.* I made most of mine *de la boue.* The king of Spain is a friar." [560]

"They will say, mais pour y arriver il commit beaucoup de crimes. Now the fact is that I not only never committed any crimes but I never even thought of doing so." [561]

turn to p. 299.

[298] Consider that it is a refreshment to the eyes to look at a poultry-yard. I hear the hen cluck & see her stepping round with perfect complacency, but if a man goes by, I have a sorrowful feeling. But if a friend, if a man of genius, if a hero passes, then I rejoice & can no longer see hens.

Why, since a babe is beautiful, should a man, almost every man, be ugly? [562]

Consider also the fact stated somewhere above, that ⟨I⟩ at church I look through the window at the snowstorm as more beautiful than the speaking man in the house.[563]   ↑See p. 300↓

In conversation, women *run on,* as it is called. A great vice. A fine woman keeps her purpose & maintains her ground with integrity of

---

[559] " 'Massena was a man . . . him." is struck through in both pencil and ink with vertical use marks. The comment on Massena as adapted on p. [322] below is used in the Divinity School Address, *W*, I, 149.

[560] Cf. *Napoleon in Exile*, 1823, I, 88, 164. " 'The Bourbons . . . boue.", struck through in ink with a vertical use mark, is used in "Napoleon," *W*, IV, 239.

[561] Cf. *Napoleon in Exile*, 1823, I, 297.

[562] "Consider that it . . . ugly?" is struck through in pencil with a diagonal use mark.

[563] See p. [284] above. This sentence, struck through in ink with two diagonal use marks, is used in the Divinity School Address, *W*, I, 137.

manner whilst you censure or rally her. If she is disconcerted & grieved the game is up & society a gloom.[564]

Preaching especially false preaching is for able men a sickly employment. Study of books is also sickly & the garden & the family, wife, mother, son, & brother are a balsam. There is health in table talk & nursery play. We must wear old shoes & have aunts & cousins.

"Napoleon directed particular attention to the improvement & embellishment of the markets of the Capital. He used to say 'The market place is the Louvre of the common people' " Las Cases.[565]
[299][566] "J'ai toujours marché avec l'opinion de grandes masses et les evenemens." Of what use then would crime have been to me   J'ai marché toujours avec l'opinion de cinq ou six millions d'hommes; of what use would crime have been to me
My ambition was great I admit but it was of a cold nature, d'une nature froide & caused by events & the opinion of great bodies.[567]
    la morgue aristocratique [568]

Las Cases Journal Boston Ed. 1823 ⟨v⟩Vol [I, part] 2.p.9[:] "The fate of a battle" said Napoleon "is the result of a moment, of a thought: the hostile forces advance with various combinations, they attack each other & fight for a certain time; the critical moment arrives, a mental flash decides, & the least reserve accomplishes the object."
    "As to moral courage, I have rarely met with the *two o'clock in the morning kind*. I mean unprepared courage that which is necessary on an unexpected occasion & which in spite of the most unforeseen events leaves full freedom of judgment & decision." He did not hesitate to declare that he was himself eminently gifted with this two o'clock in the morning courage & that in this respect he had met with few persons who were equal to him.[569]
"Generals are rarely found eager to give battle." [570]

[564] This paragraph is struck through in pencil with a vertical use mark.
[565] Cf. *Mémorial de Sainte-Hélène. Journal of . . . Napoleon at Saint Helena*, 1823, IV, vii, 120. This paragraph, struck through in pencil and in ink with two vertical use marks, is used in "Napoleon," *W*, IV, 240.
[566] "Bonaparte" is written above "J'ai . . . marché" at the top of the page.
[567] Cf. O'Meara, *Napoleon in Exile*, 1823, I, 297–298. This paragraph, struck through in ink with two vertical use marks, is used in "Napoleon," *W*, IV, 231, 237.
[568] In O'Meara, *Napoleon in Exile*, 1823, II, 265, Napoleon applies the phrase to the English aristocracy.
[569] Cf. Las Cases, *Journal*, 1823, I, ii, 10. " 'The fate of a battle . . . him.'", struck through in ink with a vertical use mark, is used in "Napoleon," *W*, IV, 237.
[570] Las Cases, *Journal*, 1823, I, ii, 11.

"I know the depth or what I call the draught of water of all my generals."
In one general named "judgment was superior to courage; it could not be
denied that he was ↑a↓ brave man; but he calculated the chance of the
cannon ball, like so many others." [571]

Napoleon during his military career fought sixty battles. [572]

[300] 19 April. I have been to New York & seen Bryant & Dewey,
& at home seen young Jones Very, & two youthful philosophers ⟨on⟩
who came here from Cambridge, Edward Washburn & Renouf, &
who told me fine hopeful things of their mates in the senior class.
And now young Eustis has been here & tells me of more aspiring
& heroical young men, & I begin to conceive hopes of the Republic. [573]
Then is this disaster of Cherokees [574] brought to me by a sad friend
to blacken my days & nights. I can do nothing. Why shriek? Why
strike ineffectual blows?

20 April. Last night, ill dreams. Dreams are true to nature & like
monstrous formations (e.g. the horsehoof divided into toes) show the
law. Their double consciousness[,] their sub- & ob-jectiveness is the
wonder. I call the phantoms that rise the creation of my fancy but
they act like volunteers & counteract my inclination. They make me
feel that every act, every thought, every cause, is bipolar & in the
act is contained the counteract. If I strike, I am struck. If I chase, I
am pursued. If I push, I am resisted. [575]

[571] Cf. Las Cases, *Journal*, 1823, I, ii, 11. " 'I know . . . my generals.' ",
struck through in ink with a vertical use mark, is used in "Napoleon," *W*, IV, 244–
245.

[572] Cf. Las Cases, *Journal*, 1823, IV, vii, 119. This sentence, struck through in
ink with two vertical use marks, is used in "Napoleon," *W*, IV, 236.

[573] Emerson's first references here are to William Cullen Bryant and Orville
Dewey. Jones Very, currently a tutor in Greek at Harvard and a divinity student,
had been sent to Emerson by Elizabeth Peabody. Of the other "Divinity School
youths," Washburn but not Renouf appears among Emerson's correspondents; Frederic Augustus Eustis became a minister in Philadelphia after his graduation in 1839
(*L*, II, 444).

[574] The Cherokee Indians were to be removed from Georgia and resettled beyond
the Mississippi in accordance with a treaty of 1835. A majority of the tribe protested that they had never approved the treaty.

[575] "Dreams are true . . . resisted.", struck through in pencil with vertical use
marks, is used in "Demonology," *W*, X, 7–8.

I have mentioned the fine persons I have seen but I must add human nature's postscript that persons unless they be of commanding excellence do not rejoice heads as old as mine like thoughts. Persons I labor at & grope after & experiment[n] [301] upon — make continual effort at sympathy which sometimes is found & sometimes is missed, but I tire at last & the fruit they bring to my intellect or affection is oft ⟨slend⟩ small & poor. But a thought has its own proper motion which it communicates to me not borrows of me, & on its Pegasus back I override & overlook the world.[576]   ↑See p 298↓

I sa⟨y⟩id to Bryant & to these young people that the high poetry of the world from the beginning has been ethical & it is the tendency of the ripe modern mind to produce it. Wordsworth's merit is that he saw the truly great across the perverting influences of society & of English literature & though he lacks executive power yet his poetry is of the right kind. He shows & is the Tendency. As I think no man could be better occupied than in making up his own bible by hearkening to all those sentences which now here, now there, now in nursery rhymes, now in Hebrew, now in English bards thrill him like the sound of a trumpet.[576a] So I think the true poetry which mankind craves is that Moral Poem of which Jesus chanted to the Ages stanzas so celestial yet only stanzas. The Epos is not yet sung. That is the gospel of glad tidings kings & prophets wait for. Cudworth is a Magazine or album of such. [302] Herbert is its lyrist. Milton, Marvell, Shakspeare, Orpheus, Hesiod, the dramatists, Zoroaster, Vedas, Confucius, Plato. See above ↑p 28⟨5⟩3↓

Always pay. I am praised by some half seeing friends for punctuality & common sense. They see not as I see, that for just that seemliness & passableness I fail so much to think & live in the right Olympian loftiness. Better be a guest in thine own house [577] than too shrewd a world's man.

---

[576] "I have mentioned . . . world.", struck through in pencil with vertical use marks, is used in "The School" (in Emerson's lecture series on Human Life, 1838–1839).

[576a] See Journal B, p. [220].

[577] See pp. [10] and [83] above.

21 April. The condition of influence by virtue is time. To convert a congregation in a four days' meeting is possible to a Calvinistic sermon: but to convert one man by the persuasion of your character needs time[.]

23 April. This tragic Cherokee business which we stirred at a meeting in the church yesterday will look to me degrading & injurious do what I can. It is like dead cats around one's neck. It is like School Committees & Sunday School classes & Teachers' meetings & the Warren street chapel & all the other holy hurrahs.[578] I stir in it for the sad reason that no other mortal will move & if I do not, why it is left undone.

The amount of it, be sure, is merely a Scream but sometimes a scream is better than ⟨an argument⟩ a thesis.

[303] Last night the old question of miracles was broached again at the Teachers' meeting & shown up & torn up in the usual manners. They think that God causes a miracle to make men Stare & then says, Here is truth. They do not & will not perceive that it is to distrust the deity of truth — its invincible beauty — to do God a high dishonor, — so to depict him. They represent the old trumpery of ⟨g⟩God sending a messenger to raise man from his low estate. Well then he must have credentials & miracle is the credentials. I answer God sends me messengers alway. I am surrounded by messengers of God who show me credentials day by day. Jesus is not a solitary but still a lovely herald.

But beware of making the gospel unlovely & of shearing him of the locks of beauty & the attributes of heaven. When I see a majestic Washington, a worshipped orator, or a maiden of transcendant beauty; when I vibrate all over to the rhythm & images of a poem; I see beauty that is to be desired. Now do not degrade the life & dialogues of Christ out of the circle of this charm by insulation & peculiarity. Let them lie as they befel, alive & warm, part of human life & of the landscape & the cheerful day.[579]

---

[578] See p. [11] above.

[579] This paragraph, struck through in ink with a diagonal use mark, is used in the Divinity School Address, *W*, I, 133.

Once more: There is no miracle to the believing soul. When I ascend to the Spiritual state of a holy Soul[,] enter into the rapture of a Christ[,] the miracle seems fit drapery enough of such a man & such a thought. When I do not so ascend [304] I cannot be said to believe the miracle. There it lies a lump. Any annotator may show the text to be spurious & I shall thank him. Any ⟨philosopher may⟩ caviller may suggest the profusion of testimony to this sort of marvel & I shall not care to refute him. Any philosopher may have my ear who offers me other truth in her own native lineament & proportion. It is idle to represent the historical glories of Christianity as we do. There are no Christians now but two or three or six or ten. There never were at any time but a few. The accepted Christianity ↑of↓ the mob of Churches is now as always a caricature of the real. The heart of Christianity is the heart of all philosophy. It is the sentiment of piety which Stoic & Chinese[,] Mahometan & Hindoo labor to awaken. The miracles if you please add proselytes of the thousand & thousand to Xy as ⟨they do⟩ in other climates other miracles (reputed) do to the Shaster & Koran & Mass Book. But converts to the soul of Xy[,] sympathisers with the man Jesus[,] are as rare as lovers of Socrates & are added by the same means [—] the reception of beautiful sentiments [—] never by miracle.

[305] Young Eustis[n] slightly said he had not read Bacon except the Apothegms, he had seen those, &c. So pass the Essays that were meat & drink to plodding me in early years over the gay brain of the juniors. Yet is this the right way for a Thinker to speak of them, slightingly — the apothegms, — Yes but ⟨the⟩ after their value has been probed & settled by microscopic loving study then to be able to throw them into ⟨righ⟩ due perspective, & sternly refuse them for all our labor & old love any higher place than belongs to them in God & call them apothegms, & pass on [—] that were well. The glance of the ↑ignorant↓ gentleman has justice in it; and the sincere knowledge of the scholar has disproportion in it.

[April] 24. This cold, dreary, desponding weather seems to threaten the farmer who sourly follows his plough or drops pea seed in the garden. I like to think that instinct[,] impulse ⟨will carry⟩

478

would carry on the world,[n] that nature gives hints when to plant & when to stick poles & when to gather. But the turning out of the farmers in this ⟨Jan⟩ November sky with coats & mittens to spring work, seems to show that calculation as well as instinct must be or that calculation must contravene instinct. Yesterday Peter Howe planted pease for me, & the garden was ploughed the 21st. Lidian says that when she gives any new direction in the kitchen she feels like a boy who throws a stone & runs.

[306] 26 April. The "Sirius" & the "Great Western," Steam packets, have arrived at New York from England, and so England is a thousand or 1500 miles nearer than it was to me, & to all.

Yesterday went the letter to V[an]. B[uren]. a letter hated of me.[580] A deliverance that does not deliver the soul. What I do, be sure, is all that concerns my majesty & not what men great or small think of it.[580a] Yet I accept the Dartmouth college invitation to speak to the boys with great delight.[581] I write my journal, I read my lecture with joy — but this stirring in the philanthropic mud, gives me no peace. I will let the republic alone until the republic comes to me.

I fully sympathise, be sure, with the sentiment I write, but I accept it rather from my friends than dictate it. It is not my impulse to say it & therefore my genius deserts me, no muse befriends, no music of thought or of word accompanies. Bah!

As far as I notice what passes in philanthropic meetings & holy hurrahs,[582] there is very little depth of interest. The speakers warm each other's skin & lubricate each other's tongue & the words flow, & the

[580] See Emerson's "Letter to President Van Buren," W, XI, 87–96, written on the subject of the Cherokee question as Emerson had agreed, with reluctance, to do when the matter was discussed at the public meeting in Concord on April 23 (p. [302] above). Rusk, L, II, 126–127, notes that the letter was sent to Congressman John Reed of Massachusetts, who arranged for its publication in the Daily National Intelligencer of Washington on May 14 (see p. [358] below, n. 657); it may never have been given directly to Van Buren. A variant version appeared in the Yeoman's Gazette of Concord on May 19.

[580a] Cf. "Self-Reliance," W, II, 53.

[581] Emerson had received an invitation on April 20 from two Dartmouth literary associations (L, II, 144, n. 162); for his Dartmouth address of July 24, "Literary Ethics," see W, I, 153–187.

[582] See pp. [11] and [302] above.

superlatives thicken, & the lips quiver, & the eyes moisten, & an observer new to such scenes would say, here was true fire; the ⟨Audience⟩ assembly were all ready to be martyred, & the effect of such a spirit on the community would be irresistible. But they separate & go to the shop, to a dance, to bed, & an hour afterwards they ⟨care⟩ ↑care↓ so little [307] for the matter that on slightest temptation each one would disclaim the meeting. "Yes, he went, but they were for carrying it too far, &c. &c."
The lesson is to know that men are superficially very inflammable but that these fervors do not strike down & ⟨end⟩ reach the action & habit of the man[.]

Yesterday P.M. I went to the Cliff with Henry Thoreau. Warm, pleasant, misty weather which the great mountain amphitheatre seemed to drink in with gladness. A crow's voice filled all the miles of air with sound. A bird's voice[,] even a piping frog enlivens a solitude & makes world enough for us. At night I went out into the dark & saw a glimmering star & heard a frog & Nature seemed to say Well do not these suffice? Here is a new scene[,] a new experience. Ponder it, Emerson, & not like the foolish world hanker after thunders & multitudes & vast landscapes[,] the sea or Niagara.   ↑See ↑p.↓ 310↓

Have I said it before in these pages, then I will say it again, that it is a curious commentary on society that the expression of a devout sentiment by any young man who lives in society strikes me with surprise & has all the air & effect of genius; as when J. Very spoke of "sin" & of "love" & so on.[583]

[308] [584] In spite of all we can do, every moment is new.[585]
[April 29?] [586] Lidian came into the study this afternoon & found the

---

[583] This paragraph is struck through in pencil with a diagonal use mark.

[584] "Limitation" is written beneath "mind by one" at the bottom of the page.

[585] Cf. "Literary Ethics," W, I, 167: "The perpetual admonition of nature to us, is, 'The world is new . . . .' "

[586] The paragraph following is copied, with date "1838 29 April", on the first leaf of a fragment among Emerson's lecture manuscripts headed "Waldo"; on the second leaf is found the sentence written as of May 12 on p. [330] below. The anecdote is used in "Domestic Life," W, VII, 104.

towerlet that Wallie had built half an hour before, of two spools, a card, an awl-case, & a flourbox top — each perpendicularly balanced on the other, & could scarce believe that her boy had built the pyramid, & then fell into such a fit of affection that she lay down by the structure & kissed it down, & declared she could possibly stay no longer with papa, but must go off to the nursery to see with eyes the lovely creature; & so departed.

30 April. Saturday, Cyrus Warren set out 41 white pines, 2 hemlocks, 1 white maple & 2 apple trees, in my lot.

Yesterday at Waltham. The kindness & genius that blend their light in the eyes of Mrs. Ripley inspire me with some feeling of unworthiness at least with impatience of doing so little to deserve so much confidence.

Could not the natural history of the Reason or Universal Sentiment be written? One trait would be that all that is alive & genial in thought must come out of that. Here is friend B[arzillai]. F[rost]. grinds & grinds in the mill of a truism & nothing comes out but what was put in. But the moment he or I desert the tradition & speak a spontaneous thought, instantly poetry, wit, hope, virtue, learning, anecdote, all flock to our aid.[587] This topic were no bad one for the Dartmouth College boys whom I am to address in July. Let them know how prompt the *limiting* instinct is in our constitution so that the moment the mind by one bold leap (an impulse from [309] the Universal) has set itself free of the old church and of a thousand years of dogma & seen the light of moral nature, say *with Swedenborg*, on the instant the defining lockjaw shuts down his fetters & cramps all round us, & we must needs think in the genius & speak in the phraseology of Swedenborg, & the last slavery is even worse than the first. Even the disciples of the new unnamed or misnamed Transcendentalism that now is, vain of the same, do already dogmatise & rail at such as hold it not, & can not see the worth of the antagonism also. The great common sense (using the word in ⟨a[?]⟩its higher sense) is the umpire that holds the balance of these kingdoms. We come from the college or the coterie to the village & the farm &

---

[587] "all that is alive . . . aid.", struck through in ink with a diagonal use mark, is used in "Literary Ethics," *W*, I, 165–166.

find the natural sentiment in the shrewd yet religious farmer, we see the manly beauty in his life[,] the tenderness (even) of his sense of right & wrong[,] of wise & silly, & we are ashamed of our pedantries & pitiful Chinese estimates. "Friends, sit low in the Lord's power". Precipitandus est liber spiritus.[588]

It is perfectly legitimate to generalize in the common way & call Jesus a poet & his labor a poem. People very significantly distinguish betwixt Plato a thinker & Jesus a doer, & suppose that the former ⟨infl⟩ acts upon a few, the latter (through the difference of doing) upon millions & all history. The difference is in the thought still. The moral sentiment affects men omnipotently & instantly ⟨cl⟩ raises the receiving mind to the level of the supernatural & miraculous and it has upon all receivers [310] abiding effect. Jesus taught that. But he was in love with his thought & quitted all for it. Any mind that *thought so* would have *acted so.* He must live somehow & his life can be discerned through the fragmentary & distorted story to have been just the life of a soul enamoured of moral truth. The difference betwixt the thinker & doer ⟨is that⟩ when it appears is that of the man of talents & of genius[.]

Write the Nat[ural]. Hist[ory]. of Reason. Recognize the inextinguishable dualism. Show that after the broadest assertions ⟨proclamation⟩ of the One nature we must yet admit always the co-presence of a superior influx, must pray, must hope (and what is hope but affirmation of two?), must doubt. &c. But also show that to seek the Unity is a /law/necessity/ of the mind[,] that we do not *choose* to resist duality[,] complexity. Show that Will is absurd in the matter[.] Napoleon in Las Casas has an admirable candor which belongs to philosophy, rails at no enemy, puts every crime down to the ignorance of the agent, & stands ready to make a marshal of him one day. ↑See p. 349.↓

↑Εν και παν↓

Two or three events[,] two or three objects large or small suffice

---

[588] "The free spirit of genius must plunge headlong." Quoted from Petronius Arbiter, *Satyricon*, 118, in Coleridge, *Biographia Literaria*, 1834, p. 178. For the preceding quotation, from George Fox, see p. [225] above and n. 445.

to genius. Let Dulness work with multitudes & magnitudes. The poor Pickwick stuff (into which I have only looked & with no wish for more) [589] teaches this[,] that prose & parlors & shops & city, widows, the tradesman's dinner, & such matters are as good materials in a skilful hand for interest & art as palaces & revolutions.

↑See p 307↓

[311]   Over me branched a tree of buds
          And over the tree was the moon
          And over the moon were the starry studs
          That drop from the angels' shoon.[590]

1 May. Distinction gives freedom to the wise man. It gives him leave to speak the truth & act with spirit. Forevermore, let him say what he thinks, instead of being a brute echo, as Webster is Webster in passing conversation. If people say the Spring is beautiful, let him think whether it is or is not, before he ducks to the remark with a paraphrastic Yes. So in all estimates, most are foolish. The parts of hospitality, the connexion of families, the impressiveness of death, & a thousand other things royalty makes its own new estimate of, & a royal mind will. We defer all along to the great importance of family events, which are really of none, would we but see & act anew. Napoleon pleases me in Las Cas⟨a⟩es by the new estimate he makes habitually. This is elevation. The *name* of goodness is not a barrier to him.[591]

Las Cases pleases me by describing Napoleon thus. "The Emperor is eminently gifted with two excellent qualities; a vast fund of justice & a disposition naturally open to attachment. Amidst all his fits of petulance or anger, a sentiment of justice still predominates." &c see the whole passage ([*Journal of . . . Napoleon at*

---

[589] The Boston *Daily Advertiser* had published extracts from Dickens' *The Posthumous Papers of the Pickwick Club* during the preceding winter.

[590] The quatrain is struck through in ink with a diagonal use mark. See Emerson's "Excelsior," *W*, IX, 293: "Over his head were the maple buds . . . ."

[591] "So in all estimates . . . him.", struck through in pencil with two diagonal use marks, is used in "Spiritual Laws," *W*, II, 143.

Saint Helena,] Vol [I, part] 2 p. 25 Boston Ed. 1823). Elsewhere the Admiral Cockburn admits that "Napoleon is the most good-natured [312] & reasonable of the whole set." [592] Able men generally have this vast fund of justice & good dispositions because an able man is nothing else than a good free vascular organization whereinto the Universal spirit freely flows; so that his fund of justice is not only vast but infinite. All men in the abstract are just & good — What hinders them in the particular, is, the momentary predominance of the finite & individual over the General truth.

The Condition of our incarnation seems to be a perpetual tendency to prefer its law, to obey its impulse to the exclusion of the law of Universal being. The great man is great by means of the predominance of the Universal nature: he has only to open his mouth & it speaks: he has only to be forced to act & it acts. All men catch the word or embrace the ⟨act⟩ deed with the heart, for it is theirs by emphasis as much as his, — but in them this disease of an excess of organization cheats them of equal issues. Nothing is more simple than greatness; indeed to be simple is to be great[,] [593] yet always it astonishes because ⟨it⟩ matter, appetite, & individuality always exist & rule from the earth upward six feet. Or hat high.

The severity with which we judge other men's derelictions & pardon our own is a part of the amabilis insania [594] of Individuality. We admit the Universal obligation of the law & prefer only a single private good to it, viz. our own. No other exception whatever. [313] And the reason why we admit this one exception, is, ↑that↓ our perfect consciousness of the Universal law, even in the hour of our transgression warrants us, we think, from a total dereliction.

The spontaneous sentiment is therefore the panacea for this disease. Utter the great sentiment of the world against your own private one. All men are judges, when the matter concerns not them.

---

[592] Although the words Emerson puts within quotation marks do not appear in Sir George Cockburn, *Buonaparte's Voyage to St. Helena* (Boston, 1833), the observation squares with the remark attributed to Cockburn, without citation of source, in Archibald Philip Primrose, 5th Earl of Rosebery, *Napoleon, The Last Phase* (London, 1900), p. 64: "'he [Napoleon] has throughout shown far less impatience about the wind and the weather, and made less difficulties, than any of the rest of the party'."

[593] "Able men generally . . . great", struck through in ink with a diagonal use mark, is used in "Literary Ethics," *W*, I, 164–165.

[594] See Journal B, pp. [120] and [172].

The Universal ⟨mind⟩ ↑tide↓ rises in our cellar, — in every man's, heart high; but the little private puddle of the Blood ⟨usurps⟩ ↑trickles to↓ the tongue & the finger ends. We are in thought wise & sublime, in word & deed silly & selfish.[595]

The advantage of the Napoleon temperament[,] impassive[,] unimpressible by others[,] is a signal convenience over this other tender one which every aunt & every gossipping girl can daunt & tether. This weakness be sure is merely cutaneous, & the sufferer gets his revenge by the sharpened observation ⟨‖ ... ‖⟩that belongs to such sympathetic fibre. As ⟨onc⟩ even in college I was already content to be *"screwed"* in the recitation room, if, on my return, I could accurately paint the fact in my youthful Journal.

[314][596] Las Cases [*Journal of . . . Napoleon at Saint Helena,*] Vol [I, part] 2 p. 171[:] "I have a lucky hand, Sir; those on whom I lay it are fit for ⟨any⟩ ↑every↓ thing"
"When Josephine succeeded under the sanction of my name in acquiring some masterpieces, though they were in my palace, under my eyes, in my family apartments, they offended me; I thought myself robbed; they were not in the Museum." [*Ibid.,* I, ii, 159]

↑Cultivated Class↓ [597]
In the year III after Napoleon had reduced the Sections of Paris under the Convention "Napoleon had frequently to harangue at the markets, in the streets, in the sections, in the faubo↑u↓rgs; & it is worthy to remark that he always found the faubourg St Antoine the most ready to listen to reason ⟨the⟩& the most susceptible of a generous impulse." [598] [Las Cases, *Journal,*] Vol [I, part] II p 95
When Napoleon was walking abroad & met Mrs Balcombe & Mrs Stuart; some slaves carrying heavy boxes passed by us on the road; Mrs Balcombe desired them in rather an angry tone to keep back; but the emperor interfered, saying: "Respect the burden, Madam!" [599] [Las Cases, *Journal,*] Vol. [I, part] 1 p[p.] 161[−162]

---

[595] "And the reason . . . selfish." is struck through in pencil with a vertical use mark.
[596] "Napoleon" is written above "Las Cases . . . p. 171" at the top of the page.
[597] Possibly intended as an index heading rather than a caption.
[598] This paragraph is struck through in ink with a vertical use mark.
[599] This paragraph, struck through in ink with a vertical use mark, is used in "Napoleon," *W,* IV, 240.

"We can do nothing," said Pitt, "against a man who carries a whole invasion in his own head." [Cf. *ibid.*, II, iv, 114]

Napoleon said, "that he had been like a block of marble during all the great events of his life; that they had slipped over him without producing any impression on his moral or physical nature[.]" [600] [Las Cases, *Journal,*] Vol [II, part] 3 [p]. 133

"Sir" said Napoleon to Sir H. Lowe who wished to in[vite] N. to be accompanied by one of the Gov.'s staff instead of the officer at Longwood, "when soldiers have been christened by the fire of the battle field, they have all one rank in my eyes." [601]

M. de Narbonne was the only ambassador who had really fulfilled the duties of his office; "And that by the peculiar [315] advantages not only of his talent but of his old fashioned morals, his manners, & his name." It is indispensable to send to the old aristocracy of the Courts of Europe only the elements of that aristocracy which in fact constitutes a sort of free masonry. A Narbonne possessed the advantages of affinity, sympathy, identity, and in less than a fortnight penetrated all the secrets of the Vienna cabinet. [602] Las Cases [*Journal,*] Vol [II, part] 3 p 42

"All the great captains of antiquity" said Napoleon "& those who in modern times have successfully retraced their footsteps performed vast achievements only by conforming with the rules & principles of the art; that is to say by correct combinations & by justly comparing the relation between means & consequences efforts & obstacles. [603] They succeeded only by the strict observance of these rules whatever may have been the boldness of their enterprises or the extent of the advantages gained. . . My greatest successes have been ascribed merely to good fortune; & my reverses will no doubt be imputed to my faults. But if I should write an account of my campaigns, it will be seen, that, in both cases, my reason & faculties were exercised in conformity with principles". *Las Cases [Journal,]* Vol 4 [part vii,] p 95

"The vulgar call good fortune that which, on the contrary, is produced by the calculations of genius." [604] [*Ibid.,*] p 96

[600] The material of this paragraph is used in "The Tragic," *W*, XII, 416.

[601] Las Cases, *Journal,* 1823, II, iii, 147. This paragraph, struck through in ink with a vertical use mark, is used in "Napoleon," *W*, IV, 245.

[602] This paragraph, struck through in ink with vertical use marks, is used in "Spiritual Laws," *W*, II, 145.

[603] " 'All the great . . . obstacles." is struck through in ink with a vertical use mark.

[604] This sentence is struck through in ink with a vertical use mark.

"The Emperor conceived that it would be impossible to form a perfect army without abolishing our arms magazines commissaries & carriages. until in imitation of the Roman custom the soldier should receive his supply of corn, grind it in his hand-mill, & bake his bread himself.[605] We must abolish all our monstrous train of civil attendants & commissaries"   [Las Cases, *Journal,*] IV. p. 97   Part VII

See further p. 348 of
this MS.[606]

[316] May 1. I sat in sunshine this P.M. ⟨in the⟩ beside my little pond in the woods & thought how wide are my works & my plays from those of the great men I read of or think of. And yet the solution of Napoleon whose life I have been reading, lies in my feelings & fancies as I loiter by this rippling water. I am curious concerning his day. ⟨The soul⟩ What filled it? the crowded orders, the stern determinations, the manifold etiquette?[n] The soul answers. Behold his day! In the sighing of these woods, in the quiet of these gray fields, in the cool breeze that sings out of those northwestern mountains, in the workmen, the boys, the girls you meet, in the hopes of the morning, the ennui of noon, & sauntering of the afternoon, in the disquieting comparisons, in the regrets at want of vigor, in the great idea & the puny execution, behold Napoleon's day; another yet the same; behold Byron's, Webster's, Canning's, Milton's, Scipio's, Pericles's day — Day of all that are born of woman. I am tasting the selfsame life, its sweetness, its greatness, its pain, which I so admire in other men. Do not foolishly ask of the inscrutable obliterated Past, what it cannot tell, the details of that nature, of that Day called Byron, or Burke, but ask it of the Enveloping Now; the more quaintly you inspect its evanescent beauties, its wonderful details, its astounding whole, its spiritual causes, so much the more you master the biography of this hero, & that, & every hero. Be lord of a day through wisdom & justice & you can put up your history books: they can teach you nothing.[607]

---

[605] This sentence is used in "Self-Reliance," *W*, II, 87.

[606] Further quotations from Las Cases appear on p. [348] below.

[607] "I am curious . . . nothing.", struck through in ink with a vertical use mark, is used in "Literary Ethics," *W*, I, 162–163.

[317] The first men had no glory. They did necessary actions, & all actions were alike creditable. Presently, peculiar vigor would somewhere appear. A man would yield himself to great Natural influences, & all would see that the act was admirable, & of course also would be deceived into the belief that the only divinity of action lay in just that species of works in which this individual labored. Whether lawmaking, music, war, colonies, arts, or whatever else. New impulses would however come to others & to many in different ⟨parts of life⟩ sorts of activity, genius in eloquence, in affairs, in agriculture, in inventions. & yet at this day the first opinion seems to hold still. We think greatness entailed or organized in some places or duties[,] in certain offices or occasions[,] & do not see that Paganini will draw celestial beauty out of a fiddle & a nimble Billings boy out of shreds of paper with his scissors & Landseer out of swine & the hero out of the pitiful habitation & company in which they have tried to eclipse him forever. So keep your school[,] eat your porridge in what is called vulgar society [—] in society that is whose poetry is not yet written [—] & be great.[608]

Beautiful leaping of the squirrel up the long bough of a pine then instantly on to the stem of an oak & on again to another tree. This motion & the motion of a bird is the right perfection for foresters as these creatures are. They taste the forest joy. [318] [609] Man creeps along so slowly through the woods that he is annoyed by all the details & loses the floating exhaling evanescent beauty which these speedy movers find.

May 2. Homer's is the only Epic. How great a deduction do all the rest suffer from the fact of their imitated form. It is especially fatal to poetry, thought's chosen & beloved form, — the encroachment of these traditions.

May 4. Walter Scott says, that, "at night, the kind are savage[.]" The French seem to have somewhat negrofine in their taste. How

---

[608] "We think greatness . . . great.", struck through in pencil and in ink with two vertical use marks, is used in "Spiritual Laws," *W*, II, 142–143.

[609] "Limitation" is written above "creeps along" at the top of the page.

much rhodomontade in Napoleon's & Las Cases's conversation. How much about glory & principles that is not glory & that are not principles. Sophomorical — repudiated by the stern English sense. Yet Napoleon now & then speaks with memorable vivacity. He was nicknamed *cent mille hommes*.[610] ↑See D p. 2⟨7⟩1,↓

How painful to give a gift to any person of sensibility or of equality! It is next worse to receiving one. The new remembrance of either is a scorpion.

To keep a party conveniently small is the trick of our local politics.

May 5. Last night E.H described the apathy from which she suffers. I own I was at a loss to prescribe as I did not sufficiently understand the state of mind she paints. It seems to me as if what we mainly need, is the power of recurring to the sublime at pleasure. And this we possess. If the splendid function of seeing should lose its interest I can still flee to the sanctity of my moral nature [319] & trust, renounce, suffer, bleed.

I complain in my own experience of the feeble influence of thought on life, a ray as pale & ineffectual as that of the sun in our cold & bleak spring. ⟨It ta⟩ They seem to lie — the actual life, & the intellectual⟨,⟩ intervals, in parallel lines & never meet. ↑[See p. 340]↓ Yet we doubt not they act & react ever, that one is even cause of the other; that one is causal, & one servile, a mere vesture. Yet it takes a great deal of elevation of thought to produce a very little elevation of life. How slowly the highest raptures of the intellect break through the trivial forms of habit. Yet ⟨yet⟩ imperceptibly they do. Gradually in long years we bend our living towards our idea. But we serve seven years & twice seven for Rachel.[611] If Mr G that old gander (I owned) should now stop at my gate I should duck to him as to an angel & waste all my time for him &c. &c instead of telling him, as truth seems to require, that his visit & his babble was an impertinence, &

[610] "The French . . . sense." is copied on p. [45] above. In "Considerations by the Way," *W*, VI, 250, Emerson notes: "Napoleon was called by his men *Cent Mille*."

[611] Gen. 29:20. "I complain . . . Rachel." is struck through in pencil with a vertical use mark.

bidding him Begone. Just so, when Miss W. & Mrs G. & Miss M. come, I straightway sit glued to my chair all thought, all action, all play departed & paralysed, & acquiesce & become less than they are, instead of nodding slightly to them & treating them like shadows & persisting in the whim of pathos or the whim of fun or the whim of poetry in which they found me & constraining them to accept the law of this higher thought (also theirs) instead of kneeling to their triviality[.]

I'll tell you what to do. Try to make Humanity lovely unto them.[612]

[320] The prayers in houses are like the zodiack of Denderah, & the ⟨other[?]⟩ astronomical monuments of the Hindoos, wholly insulated from any thing now extant in the life & business of the people. They show the height of some old tide a century ago. They are like thinking *versus* habit.[613]

↑Limitation↓ [614]

Sad is sleep. What a satire to behold the man who has been astonishing a company with his assurances of the infinite faculties & destiny of man, nodding in his chair.

On Anniversaries

May 6. Not without some remnant of its old radiance dawns yet the Sabbath on the heart. Any holiday communicates to me its color. I wear its cockade in my feelings were it the Christmas which by the way has lent its poetry to the hemlock-pine with the boughs ↑of↓ which in my infancy I ⟨first⟩ saw the Roman & Episcopal churches decorated, to the Commencement Day whose light tho' in a swamp would be to me festive & its air faintly echoing with plausive academic thunders; the Fourth of July red with artillery, the Common full of children, the woods full of gunners and ⟨the⟩ at night the sky crackling with rockets even down to the ⟨Artillery⟩ Election ↑mis-↓ called by wanton boys "Nigger 'Lection." I have kindly vision out

---

[612] These two sentences are written in faint pencil — very possibly by Mrs. Emerson, as Edward Emerson suggests (*J*, IV, 442, n. 1).

[613] This paragraph, struck through in ink with two diagonal use marks, is used in the Divinity School Address, *W*, I, 139.

[614] Apparently an index heading, as at the top of p. [318].

in these lone fields of marching ranks with red fa⟨cein⟩cings & white shoes; of boys in vacation; & on such a no day as that, I still feel a gayer air. But when this hallowed hour [321] dawns out of the Deep a white page which the wise may inscribe with truth, whilst the savage scrawls with fetishes[,] the cathedral music of all history breathes through it a psalm to my solitude.[615]

At Church, the slender occupation of the minds of so many persons & the willingness with which it is borne, seem to show that the people have a plenty of time. Yet though the patience seems Turkish I still think it safe to argue from one to all, from me to the congregation, & to infer a preference of realities. In the dead pond which our church is, no life appear↑s↓. Yet who can doubt it to be a treasury of all fine & all sublime faculties if their objects appeared or if an electric atmosphere of thought & heroism enveloped them. How grand are ⟨fr⟩traits of which all are capable[:] for example the independence of those who love & flatter you[,] the ability to disappoint the feelings of kindness in their freest flow & appealing to sympathies far in advance. A solidity of virtue which is above praise & which is so essentially & manifestly virtue that it is taken for granted that the right, the brave, the generous step will be taken by it and nobody thinks of commending it. You would ⟨praise⟩ ↑compliment↓ a coxcomb doing a good act, but you would not praise an angel. This silence, then, that accepts merit as the most natural thing in the world, is the highest applause. The people that I speak of are like the [322] ⟨i⟩Imperial guard of Napoleon, the perpetual reserve, the dictators of fortune, one needs not praise their courage, they are the heart & soul of Nature. I designed to have said above when speaking of the latent virtue that slumbers in these lazy times in a church[,] in a college that one ought to remember that many men rise refreshed ⟨by h⟩ on hearing a threat[,] that a crisis which intimidates & paralyzes the majority of an ⟨popular⟩ assembly demanding faculties that neither sell tape, nor calculate the rise of stocks, nor dig, nor weigh,

[615] Three passages within the paragraph — "Any holiday communicates . . . my feelings"; "the Commencement Day . . . academic thunders"; and "dawns out of . . . solitude." — are struck through in ink with groups of three vertical use marks. These passages are used in "Works and Days," *W*, VII, 168–169.

nor eat, nor ride, but comprehension, immoveableness, & the readiness of sacrifice is snuffed from afar with dilated nostril by others before weary & discontented. So I dare not question the masculine faculties of a quiet multitude but shall await the revolutions that shall show me their terror & their beauty. Napoleon said of Massena that he was not himself until the battle began to go against him[;] then awoke his powers of combination & he put on determination & Victory as a robe.[616]

I hear in the church with joy the Music of two or three delicious Voices. There, in Music is the world idealized in poor men's parlors, in the washroom, & the kitchen. Every strain of a rich voice does instantly imparadise the ear. I cannot wonder that it is the popular heaven.

[323] The antagonism of goodies. — Sir, sir, did you speak of the S[unday]. S[chool].? — Pardon me, sir, I did. — Sir you are an antinomian.

Wherever a man comes, there comes revolution. The old is for slaves. When a man comes, all books are legible, all things transparent, all religions are forms. He is religious. Man is the wonder worker. He is seen amid miracles. All men bless & curse. He saith yea & nay only.[617] The stationariness of religion, the assumption that the age of inspiration is past, that the bible is closed; the fear of degrading ⟨or⟩ the character of Jesus by representing him as a man, indicate with sufficient clearness the falsehood of our theology.[618] The inexhaustible soul is insulted by this low paltering superstition no more commendable in us than the mythology of other heathens. We would speak the words of Jesus & use his name only, as if we would play the tunes of Handel only, or learn Handel's music, instead of be-

---

[616] For Napoleon's remark, see p. [297] above. "How grand are [p. [321]] . . . robe.", struck through in ink with vertical use marks, is used in the Divinity School Address, W, I, 148–149. What Emerson terms a "continuation" of the present discussion occurs on p. [330] below.

[617] Cf. Matt. 5:37: "let your conversation be yea, yea; Nay, nay . . . ."

[618] "Wherever a man . . . theology.", struck through in ink with a vertical use mark, is used in the Divinity School Address, W, I, 144.

coming Handels ourselves by expressing the beauty that enamours the soul through the modulations of the air.

We are apt to feel defrauded of the retribution due to evil acts because the bad man goes his way[,] adheres to his vice & contumacy[;] you adhere to your virtue, but he does not come to a crisis or judgment anywhere in visible nature. There is no ⟨thunderous⟩ ↑stunning↓ confutation[n] [324] of his nonsense before men & angels.[619] Well. Learn to make the witness of the Spirit in us, what it is, a Verdict of the Universe. ↑Find the punishment in the act.↓ Learn that the malignity & ⟨folly⟩ lie of the wrongdoer are the shadows of death creeping over him; that so far is he deceasing from nature; that in a virtuous action I properly *am*; in a virtuous act I extend myself into real nature, & see the darkness ⟨on⟩ ↑receding↓ the limits of the horizon.[620]

Do not charge me with egotism & presumption. I see with awe the attributes of the farmers & villagers whom you despise. A man saluted me today in a manner which at once stamped him for a theist, a selfrespecting gentleman, a lover of truth & virtue. How venerable are the manners often of the poor.

A great man escapes out of the kingdom of time; he puts time under his feet. He does not look at his performance & say I am 20, I am 30, I am 40 years old, & I must therefore accomplish somewhat conspicuous. See Napoleon at 25. See what he had done at 40. He says rather, Is this that I do genuine & fit? Then it contributes no doubt to immortal & sublime results; no doubt it partakes of the same lustre itself. Dark though the hour be, & dull the wit, no flood of thoughts, no lovely pictures in memory or in hope, only heavy weary duty moving on cart-wheels along the old ruts of life; I will still trust. Was not Luther's Bible, Shakspear's Hamlet, [325] Paul's letter, a deed as notable & farreaching as Marengo or the dike of Arcola? Yet these were written by dint of flagging spirits. Sobs of

[619] "We are apt . . . angels." is used in "Compensation," *W*, II, 121.
[620] "of his nonsense . . . horizon." is struck through in pencil with a vertical use mark; "in a virtuous . . . horizon." is used in "Compensation," *W*, II, 122.

the heart & dull, waste, unprofitable hours taught the master how to write to apprehensive thousands the tragedy of these same.[621]

May 7. Aunt Mary said of a sermon she had heard, "If they say it's good, then 'tis good; if they say it's bad, then 'tis bad." It is even so. ⟨W⟩In all that we hear & read, there ⟨is⟩ ever is so much of nature that a trifle hath some majesty, and the mediocre production may be cracked up by the affectionate into a sort of Olympian merit, & find allowance from us though not its spontaneous praisers. Bowles's sonnets, Southey's Roderick, Wordsworth's Wagoner, may come to be esteemed very fine, such latitude of aboriginal worth[n] Nature yields to everything not contrarious.

May 9. A letter this morning from T. Carlyle. How should he be so poor? It is the most creditable poverty I know of.

[May] ↑9.↓ It seems as if a wise man would be an incarnated Veneration. He would revere everything, even folly, crime, ignorance, not as far as they were these, but as also demonstrations of the dazzling beauty of the Cause. How shallow is Contempt! I will never scorn a man again. To a difference of opinion I will kneel as to an unrevealed face of God. Anciently friends exchanged names in sign of love. Henceforth I [326] will call my enemy by my own name, for he is serving me with his might, exposing my errors, stigmatising my faults.

It seems to me that we should load our shoulders with love till we bend, kneel, & lie down under the burden. Why need you think afar off of one or two acts of virtue as you pay thirty dollars to constitute you a life member of the Charities? Go to it man! Set down your shoulder with a *yeo heave O!* & understand well without mincing the matter, there are you to sweat & drudge & toil forever & ever. Condition, your private condition of riches or talents or seclusion [—] What difference does that make? [622] As a man that once came to summon my brother ⟨&⟩ William & me to *train*, replied to the excuse that we were instructors of youth, "Well & I am a watch-

---

[621] This paragraph is struck through in pencil with vertical use marks.

[622] Page [326] is struck through in pencil with a diagonal use mark to this point.

maker." [623] It is not other people's wants, but your own wants that crave your devotion. You will find[,] be your condition what it may[,] that the world[,] your native world is a poor beggar, naked, cold, starving, sick, whom you must clothe, warm, feed, & restore. Unless you kill yourself you cannot get out of the sight of its wants nor out of the hearing⟨s⟩ of its piteous moanings. You are rich, you are literary, you lament you have not the helping hand. I think no wise man will ever be rich; none, that is, will have any thing at his disposal, for unless he had the riches of nature at hand he could not supply all the needs that look to him for ⟨fo⟩ relief. Friends near, & friends afar, brothers, cousins, parents, [327] virtuous men unkindly used by the world, bereaved women & children, beside that ⟨inventive⟩ creative charity which will never let us be, but as if out of the wantonness & ingenuity of goodness is ⟨carving out⟩ contriving objects & inventing new subscription papers. The richest man needs to economize his clothes, his hay, his house labor, & ⟨show⟩ ↑wear↓ the ⟨se⟩ white seam[,] the soiled hat of his fellow's need, if not of his own. I must regard the ⟨thrift⟩ old ⟨hat⟩ ↑coat↓, the dusty shoes, the weary limbs of the man frugal from benevolence as luminous points that ray out glory to all the sundered friends he loves & serves. The call comes. Death & rates ↑men say↓ are sure.[624] ⟨Love's⟩ ↑These Poor-↓rates are surest of all. They knock at every door. They go to every room; they levy a poll-tax. Fool[,] you will not decline it. Then look ahead a little, & see that this ugly beggar is the Deity in disguise, this sturdy beggar that takes substance & time & pleasures and peace, is enriching you by every thing he seems to take; he has given you learning & wit & sympathy & insight & noble manners, & the blessing of every eye that sees & ear that hears you. How came that great heart to such a ↑huge↓ compass of love? How but because it has loved & served so many that it is now charged with the life of thousands, of countries, of races.[625]

[328] Another thought of like color has affected me. You have good

---

[623] This sentence is marked in ink with a marginal line.

[624] See Journal B, p. [268].

[625] "It is not other people's [p. [326]] . . . races." is struck through in pencil with diagonal use marks.

philosophy & disdain the feeble routine & mere verbal learning ⟨of⟩ & ritual virtue of the School & the Church. Well beware of Antinomianism. All men have a slight distrust of your novelties & think you do not esteem the old laws of true witness, just dealing, chaste conversing as much as they. They have some reason. For as they make a bad use of their old truths so we make a bad use of our new ones. They know that we have brought with us the clinging temptations that whisper so softly by night & by day in lonely places[,] in seductive company[,] & they query whether the loss of the old checks will not sometimes be a temptation which the unripeness of the new will not countervail. Therefore if you hear or read a word which galls you, which accuses you, be to it all ear. If it pricks your ear it is for something. It points at a weak side, at a peccant humor, at a spiritual defect. Expose freely the place to the thorn[,] to the knife[.] You have no interest like your own health. The sanctity of a Soul ⟨is⟩ secure⟨d⟩s its equipoise & so its reason.

[May] 10. Wrote a letter today to T. Carlyle[.]

[329] Caricatures are often the truest history of the time for they only express in a pointed unequivocal action what really lies at the bottom of a great many plausible, public, hypocritical Manoeuvres.

The Bivouac or rest without lodging, is a trait of modern war. What are the bivouacs of literature? the Newspaper? & of the social economy?

11 May. Last night the moon rose behind four distinct pine tree tops in the distant woods & the night at ten was so bright that I walked abroad. But the sublime light of night is unsatisfying, provoking, it astonishes but explains not. Its charm floats, dances, disappears, comes & goes, but palls in five minutes after you have left the house. Come out of your warm angular house resounding with few voices into the chill grand instantaneous night, with such a Presence as a full moon in the clouds, & you are struck with poetic wonder. In the instant you leave far behind all human relations[,] wife, mother, & child, & live only with the savages — water, air, light, carbon, lime,

& granite. I think of Kuhleborn.[626] I become a moist cold element. "Nature grows over me." Frogs pipe; waters far off tinkle; dry leaves hiss; grass bends & rustles; & ⟨‖ . . . ‖⟩I have died out of the human world & come to feel a strange cold, aqueous, terraqueous, aerial, ethereal sympathy & existence. I sow the sun & moon for seeds.[627]

[330] May 12. Baby warbles quite irresistibly as if telling a secret too to all the house, "Mamma ky, Mamma ky!" thus blabbing Mamma's flebile tendencies.[628]

[May] ↑13↓. In continuation of what was written above, (p[p]. 321[–322]) — ⟨t⟩There are sublime merits, persons who are not actors not speakers but influences: persons too great for fame, for display, who disdain eloquence, to whom all we call Art & Artist seems too nearly allied to show & by-ends, to the exaggeration of the finite & selfish & loss of the Universal such as Wordsworth describes in his Classes of Men, such as Confucius points at when he disparages eloquence. Such as the rapture of piety is even in the obscure & ignorant. The orators[,] the poets are great only as beautiful women are by our allowance & homage. Slight them by preoccupation of mind, slight them as you can well afford to do by high & universal aims, & they instantly feel that you have right & that it is in lower places that they must shine. They also feel your right for they with you are open to the /deluges of[629] /inundation of/ the Spirit which sweeps away before it all our little architecture of wit & memory as straws & straw huts before the torrent. These are great only by comparison with each other, Ivanhoe & Waverley compared with Castle Radcliff & Porter novels[,] but nothing is great [—]not mighty Homer & Milton[—]beside the Infinite Reason. It carries /all/ them/ away as a flood. They are as a sleep.[630]

---

[626] The water-spirit, uncle of Undine, in La Motte-Fouqué's *Undine* (1811).

[627] Cf. Emerson's "The Poet," *W*, IX, 310: "He sowed the sun and moon for seeds."

[628] See n. 586 above.

[629] "deluges of" is circled in ink, probably for revision (*W*, I, 148, reads "influx of").

[630] This paragraph, struck through in ink with vertical use marks, is used in the Divinity School Address, *W*, I, 147–148.

[331] Last night walking under the pleasant cloud-strown dim-starred sky, I sought for topics for the young men at D[artmouth]. & could only think one thing, namely, that the cure for bigotry & for all partiality is the recurrence to the experience, that we have been in our proper person Robinson Crusoe, & Saint John, Dr Pedant & Sardanapalus. In the hour of spiritual pride when, unsuspecting, &, as it were, of course, we don the judgment robes, let it qualify the sentence that damns my brother, that I have been him & presently shall very naturally become him again.

May 14. What do we chiefly recommend to the student? Solitude — Silence. Why? — ⟨t⟩That he may become acquainted with his thoughts. If he is in a lonely place hankering for the crowd, for display, to make a figure, — he is not in the lonely place, he does not see, he does not hear, he does not think. O go alone, cherish your soul, expel companions, go set your habits to a life of solitude[;] then will the faculties rise fair & full within like growing grass & budding flowers[;] then will you have results which, when you meet your fellow men, you can communicate & they will gladly receive. But do not go into solitude only that you may presently come into public. Such solitude denies itself, is public & stale. The Public can get public experiences but they wish the scholar to replace to them those private, sincere, divine experiences of which they have [332] been defrauded by dwelling in the street.
It is the noble, manlike, just thought which is the superiority demanded of you & not crowds but solitude confers this elevation. Be an artist superior to tricks of art. Show frankly as a saint would do all your tools & means & modes. Welcome all comers to the freest use of the same. And out of this superior frankness & charity you shall learn higher secrets of your nature which gods will bend & aid you to communicate.[631] It is yourself which is the self of all, whereof all wish to know, & it is solitude & Virtue which can furnish farther informations.
Another example of the Entsagen (see above p. 321) is the fine admonition in Sprague's Centennial Ode in Boston in which the

---

[631] "What do we [p. [331]] . . . communicate.", struck through in ink with vertical use marks, is used in "Literary Ethics," W, I, 173–174, 184.

present generation are told that their part in history is not to shine like their fathers but to be obscurely good.[632]

[333]   ↑Put in a little heat.↓

How simple the causes of how various effects! A little heat, that is, a little motion, is all that differences the bald, dazzling white, deadly cold poles of the earth from the golden ↑tropical↓ climates, the cumbrous gigantic vegetation, the air loaded to sickness with aromatics, the sky full of birds, the huge animals that browse, leap, or glide, the young lions playing in the sand & Man with a dilated flexible elegant form with gentle & majestic manners.

↑A Bird-while.↓

In a natural chronometer, a Birdwhile may be admitted as one of the metres since the space most of the wild birds will allow you to ⟨se⟩make your observations on them when they alight near you in the woods, is a pretty equal & familiar measure.

↑Life & Death ↑are↓ apparitions.↓

Last night the Teachers' S[unday]. S[chool]. met here & the theme was Judgment. I affirmed that we were Spirits now incarnated & should always be Spirits incarnated. Our thought is the income of God. I taste therefore of eternity & pronounce of eternal law now & not hereafter. Space & time are but forms of thought. I proceed from God now & ever shall so proceed. Death is but an appearance. Yes & life's circumstances are but an appearance through which the firm virtue of this God-law penetrates & which it moulds. The inertia of matter & of fortune & of our employment is the feebleness of our spirit.[633]

[632] Charles Sprague, *An Ode: Pronounced before the Inhabitants of Boston, September the Seventeenth, 1830, at the Centennial Celebration of the Settlement of the City* (Boston, 1830), stanzas xxv–xxvi, p. 19:

"'Tis yours to do unknown,
    And then to die unsung.
To other days, to other men belong
The penman's plaudit and the poet's song;

. . . .

    Be ye by goodness crowned,
    Revered, though not renowned . . . . "

[633] "Death is but . . . spirit." is struck through in pencil with a diagonal use mark.

[334] May 17. It is as easy to speak extempore as to be silent.   A man sitting silent admires the miracle of free, impassioned, picturesque speech in the man addressing the assembly[,] a state of being & of power how unlike his own. Presently his ↑own↓ emotion rises to his lips & overflows in speech. He must also rise & say somewhat. Once embarked, once having overcome the novelty of the situation he finds it just as easy & natural to speak, to speak with thoughts, with pictures, with rhythmical balance of sentences — as it was to sit silent for it needs ⟨now but to⟩ not to do but to suffer[;] he only adjusts himself to the free spirit which gladly utters itself through him. This is a practical lesson in the doctrine that there is but one Mind. Motion is as easy as rest.[634]

We talked yesterday of Alcott's school. J. S. Dwight thought he should not feel the less certain of the good influence of his teaching on the boys though he never recognised it. — Yes, that is right. The unspoken influence of nature we know is greatest, yet we do not recognize & specify it in the man, & Alcott's aim is to ⟨creat⟩ make a spoken teaching that shall blend perfectly therewith.

[335] May 18. The ⟨theological schools⟩ ↑public↓ necessarily pick out for the emulation of the young men the Oberlins, the Wesleys, Dr Lowell & Dr Ware. But with worst effect. All this excellence kills beforehand their own. They ought to come out to their work ignorant that ever another had wrought. Imitation cannot go above its model. The imitator dooms himself to mediocrity. The inventor did it, because it was natural to him & so in him it has a charm. In the imitator something else is natural, & so he bereaves himself of his own beauty, to come short of another man's. The young preacher comes to his parish & learns there are 300 families which he must visit each once in a year. In stead of groping to get exactly the old threads of relation to bind him to the people that bound his venerable predecessor, let him quit all leather & twine[,] let him so highly & gladly entertain his most poetic & exhilarating office as to cast all this nonsense of false expectation & drivelling Chinese secondariness

---

[634] This paragraph, struck through in ink with a diagonal use mark, is used in "Literary Ethics," *W*, I, 166.

behind him, & acquaint them at first hand with Deity. ⟨When he⟩ Let him be a man. Let him see to it first & only that he is a man, that fashion, custom, authority, pleasure, & money, are nothing to him, — are not bandages over his eyes that he cannot see, but that he seeth as Adam saw, & liveth on with the privilege of God[,] with a hope as broad as the ⟨expanding walls of the⟩ ↑unbounded↓ Universe[.]

[336] Let him not be anxious to get out to see in civil sort his 300 families with tablebook to know the times how oft & when. Perhaps it is mere folly for him to visit one. But let him when he meets one of these men or women be to them divine man, be to them thought & virtue, let their timid aspirations find in him a friend, let their trampled instincts be genially ⟨dra⟩ tempted out in the mellow atmosphere of his society, let their doubts know that he hath doubted and their wonder feel that he has wondered. Despite all our pennywisdom, despite all our piddling & quiddling, despite all our pompous plans of life & pompous executions of the same[,] it is not to be doubted that all men do value the ↑few↓ real hours of life; they love to be heard; they love to be caught up into the vision of principles & they mark with light in their memory the few interviews they have had in the dreary years of routine & of sin with souls that made our souls wiser, that spoke what we thought, that told us what we knew, that gave us leave to be what we inly were. Discharge to them the priestly office, & ↑absent or present↓ you shall be followed with their veneration & grappled to them by love [635] ⟨as much absent as present⟩. Scorn trifles. Leave to the man-milliners the question of coat & hat & gown, the color of your dress, the mode of riding, of the question of dancing, of parties, & all the jackstraws on which Doctors have debated. The sailor damns the proprieties. It is the only good sense on the subject tho' coarse the expression." [337] It is an infallible sign of the torpidity of the priest & poet soul when the minor faculties of taste & of decorum emerge into distinct consideration.

---

[635] Within the entry for May 18, pp. [335]–[336], the following passages are struck through in ink with diagonal use marks: "Imitation cannot . . . another man's."; "behind him, & acquaint . . . unbounded Universe"; and "But let him . . . to them by love". The Divinity School Address, W, I, 145–147, draws on both marked and unmarked passages.

May 19. The Cologne was so good it bit his nose. Stetson talking the other day of the exceeding trouble of carrying any large sum in specie, ↑in travelling,↓ said, "I had as lief carry a child".

20 May. Met at Medford at Mr Stetson's, Messrs Francis, Hedge, G. Ripley, Alcott, T. Parker, G. Briggs, J. Very, C. Bartol, J. S Dwight; Emerson; [636] & discussed the question of Mysticism. But I am a bad associate, since for all the wit & talent that was there, I had not one thought nor one aspiration. It is true I had not slept the night before. Yet I am a bad associate.[637]

[337]–[338] [Letter omitted] [638]
[338] 26 May. Nettled again & nervous (as much as sometimes by flatulency or piddling things) by the wretched Sunday's preaching of Mr H. You Cambridge men affect to think it desireable that there should be light in the people. But the elevation of the people by one degree of thought would blow to shreds all this nightmare preaching. How miserable is that which stands only in the wooden ignorance of villages. As the dull man droned & droned & wound his stertorous horn upon the main doctrine of Xty the resurrection, namely, & how little it was remembered in modern preaching, & modern prayers, I could not help thinking that there are two emphases that distinguish [n] [339] the two sorts of teachers[:] 1. *Human life*. 2. *Thought*. Those who remain fast in the first, respect facts ⟨mainly⟩ supremely; & thought is but a⟨n⟩ tool for them. Those who dwell in the second, respect principles; — & facts & persons & themselves they regard only as slovenly unperfect manifestations of these; they care not for Christ, nor for Death, nor for resurrection, except as illustrations[.]

I found Hedge the other day fully disposed to agree with me in regard to the social position of domestics.

[636] Newcomers at this meeting of the club were the Reverend Theodore Parker, then of West Roxbury, the Reverend George Ware Briggs of Plymouth, and Jones Very.

[637] An entry for May 22 begins on p. [340] below.

[638] The first paragraph only of Emerson's letter to Margaret Fuller, May 23, 1838; printed complete in *L*, II, 134–136, which reads "Dwight came with him [Hedge] & staid longer" for "Dwight came here", "you once" for "you", "Carlyle Cambridge Dr Channing" for "Carlyle, Channing, Cambridge", "spout that is to be." for "spout ⟨that is to be).", "forty four pine trees" for "44 pinetrees", and "do you think" for "⟨do you think)"; there are minor variations in punctuation.

[340] ↑22 May.↓ Dr Jackson once said that the laws of disease were as beautiful as the laws of health. Our good Dr Hurd [639] came to me yesterday before I had yet seen Dr Ripley (yesterday represented as in a dying condition) — with joy sparkling in his eyes. "And how is the Doctor, sir," I said. "I have not seen him today," he replied, "but it is the most correct apoplexy I have ever seen, face & hands livid, breathing sonorous, & all the symptoms perfect" & he rubbed his hands with delight.[640]

The little village newspapers, I observe, stick in regularly every week paragraphs about the value of newspapers, which are true of the great newspapers as the National Gazette or Boston Advertiser but ludicrously untrue of these pert little country sheets. So Wordsworth, for a great man, has a great deal too much to say about what he the poet writes or does.

How noble a trait does Miss Sedgwick draw in her Mrs Hyde, when Lucy Lee says, "It makes people civil to speak to her." [641]
How we glow ⟨under⟩ over these novels! How we drivel & calculate & shuffle & lie & skulk, in life! ↑See above p. 319↓ ↑Democrat.↓
"My blood was not ditch water," said Napoleon in allusion to Duc d'Enghien[.] [642]

[341] In the wood, God was ⟨very⟩ manifest as he ⟨surely⟩ was not in the sermon. In the cathedralled larches the ⟨wild⟩ ground pine crept him, the thrush sung him, the robin complained him, the catbird mewed him, the anemone vibrated him, the wild apple bloomed him; the ants built their little Timbuctoo wide abroad; the wild grape budded; the rye was in the blade; high overhead[,] high over cloud the faint sharphorned moon sailed steadily west through fleets

[639] Dr. Charles T. Jackson, brother of Mrs. Emerson, was a geologist of note and a rival of W. T. G. Morton and Horace Wells in the discovery of ether as an anesthetic.

[640] This paragraph, struck through in ink with a vertical use mark, is used in "The Comic," W, VIII, 167.

[641] Catherine Maria Sedgwick, *Live and Let Live; or, Domestic Service Illustrated* (New York, 1837), p. 212.

[642] Cf. Las Cases, *Journal*, 1823, IV, vii, 133. This sentence, struck through in ink with a diagonal use mark, is used in "Napoleon," W, IV, 241–242.

of little clouds; the sheaves of the birch brightened into green below. The pines kneaded their aromatics in the sun. All prepared itself for the warm thunderdays of July. Riding with Dwight the other day I saw a broad cloud a quarter of a mile parallel to the horizon quite accurately in the form of the cherub as painted over churches[,] a round block in the centre which it was easy to animate with eyes & mouth supported on either side by widestretched symmetrical wings. I told D. who pointed it out that undoubtedly it was the archetype of that familiar ornament. In like manner I have myself seen in the sky a thunderbolt which satisfied me that the Greeks drew from nature when they painted that image in the hand of Jove. And I have seen a snowdrift along the wallsides that [342] obviously gave the idea of a common architectural scroll to support a tower.[643]

Realist seems the true name for the movement party among our scholars here. I at least endeavor to make the exchange evermore of a reality for a name. I say there is no teaching until the child is brought into the same place, state, principle in which you are[;] a perfect transfusion takes place[:] he is you & you are he[;] then is a perfect teaching & ⟨by per⟩ by no chance, unfriendly, or ↑bad↓ company can he ever quite lose the benefit[.] But your propositions run out of one ear as they ran in at the other. So it seems to me that Christianity is the famous name, the moral sentiment, the nut of truth[.] [644]

[343] A valuable teaching was that interference of Napoleon with the British file of soldiers on board the Bellerophon who were exercising in honor of their guest.[645]

Do not put yourself in a false position in regard to your co-temporaries. If your views are in straight antagonism to theirs, nevertheless assume ⟨the⟩ an identity of sentiment, — that you are saying

[643] "I saw a broad cloud . . . tower.", struck through in ink with vertical use marks, is used in "History," W, II, 18–19.
[644] "I say . . . truth", struck through in pencil with a diagonal use mark and in ink with a curved diagonal use mark, is used in "Spiritual Laws," W, II, 152.
[645] Las Cases, Journal, 1823, I, i, 26. This sentence is struck through in ink with a vertical use mark. See "Literary Ethics," W, I, 178–179, which gives details taken directly from Las Cases.

precisely that they all think, & in the flow of wit & love roll out your
ultra paradoxes in solid column with not the infirmity of a doubt,
knowing that really & underneath all their external denials & diver-
sities, they are of one heart & mind.[646]   ↑See p. 344.↓

At dinner, today we wickedly roasted the martyrs. I say that
nothing is so disgusting in our days as nothing is so dog-cheap as
martyrdom. Dr A or Mr M the Messieurs Bookmakers should be
requested to prepare a work immediately on the Duties of Martyrs
↑of all sizes & sexes.↓ Q., the Abolitionist, came here to Concord
where every third man lectures on Slavery & being welcomed by
some gentleman at the church to Concord replied "Yes we that turn
the world upside down have come hither also." It reminds one of a
sophomore's exclamation during a college rebellion, "Come, Bowers!
let us go join these noble fellows." Next worst to the Martyrs are
the officers of the philanthropic societies who have just got letters
from Antigua & so on. These martyrs are such vermin that it needs
to have a man of brawn & of virtue die, to put an end [344] to them.
These are dead already, & can as well be stoned or shot as not. But
now let a man that is alive, laughing with life, all action, all power,
who scorneth death, & who cannot die, let him meet the Axe's edge
& thrill them with the conviction of immortality. Slay a gentleman,
& put this gibbering rabble of ghosts out of countenance & out of
misery forever ⁿ↑ — martyrs whose skin was never scratched, who
have not a hang nail to show.↓

[A woman's strength is not masculine but is the unresistable
might of weakness.] ↑To the pseudo-martyrs also belong the Elec-
tioneers Curtis, Hoffman, Prentiss, &c↓[.]

June 2. Hostility, bitterness to persons or to the age indicate infirm
sense, unacquaintance with men who are really at top selfish & really
at bottom fraternal, alike, identical;   ↑See p 343↓

[345] There is somewhat ⟨greatl⟩ inconvenient & injurious in the
position of the Scholar. They whom his thoughts have entertained

---

[646] This paragraph is struck through in ink with a vertical use mark.

or inflamed seek him before yet they have learned the ⟨laws⟩ hard conditions of thought. They seek him ⟨to⟩ that he may turn his lamp upon the dark riddles whose solution they think is scrawled on the Walls of their being. They find that he is a poor ignorant man in a seamed rusty coat like themselves nowise emitting a continuous stream of light but now & then a jet of luminous thought ⟨then⟩ followed by total darkness[,] that he cannot make of his infrequent illumination a portable taper to carry whither he would, & explain now this dark riddle, then that Sorrow ensues. The scholar ⟨is⟩ regrets to damp the hope of ingenuous boys. The boy has lost a star out of his new flaming firmament. Hence the temptation to the scholar to mystify; to hear the question, to sit upon it, to give an answer of words in lieu of the ⟨w⟩ lacking things.[647]

[346] June 6. Every body, I think, has sublime thoughts sometimes. At times they lie parallel with the world ↑or↓ the axes coincide so that you can see through them the great laws. *Then* be of their side. Let your influence be so true & simple as to bring them into these frames.

Another thing:[n] We resent all criticism which denies us any thing that lies in our line of advance. Say that I cannot paint a Transfiguration or build a steamboat, or be a grand marshal, & I shall not seem to me depreciated. But deny me any quality of metaphysical or literary power, & I am piqued. What does this mean? Why, simply that the soul has assurance by instincts & presentiments of *all* power in the direction of its ray, as well as the special skills it has already got.* [648]

---

* When I told Alcott, that, I would not criticise his compositions; that it would be as absurd to require them to conform to my way of writing & aiming, as it would be to reject Wordsworth because he was wholly unlike Campbell; that here was a new mind & it was welcome to a new style; — he replied, well pleased, "That is criticism."

[647] This paragraph, struck through in ink with a vertical use mark, is used in "Literary Ethics," *W*, I, 183.

[648] "We resent . . . got.", struck through in ink with a vertical use mark, is used in "Literary Ethics," *W*, I, 164.

Another thing:[n] A man that can speak well belongs to the new era as well as to the old. A revolution is welcome to him & oriental stability is friendly to him. I look with pity upon the young preachers who float into the profession thinking all is safe. But as soon as I hear one of them uttering out of the old velveted tub manly poetic words I see him to be Janus-faced & well to do in past or future.

[347] 7 June. I wish a church to worship in, where all the people are better than I am, & not spotted souls. ⟨The⟩Nothing shows more plainly the bad state of society than the ⟨im⟩difficulty or impossibility of representing to the mind any fit church or cultus.

↑Martyrs again   See p. 343↓

Take care oh ye martyrs! who like St Ursula & her choir, number Eleven Thousand[,] if of all one of you, one single soul is true take care not to snap in petulance instead of jetting out in spouts of true flame. Reserve your fire. Keep your temper. Render soft answers. Bear & forbear. Do not dream of suffering for ten years yet. Do not let the word *martyrdom* ever escape out of the white fence of your teeth. Be sweet & courtly & merry these many long summers & autumns yet, & husband your strength so that when an authentic inevitable crisis comes, & you are fairly driven to the wall, cornered up in your Utica, you may then at last turn fairly round on the baying dogs, all steel — with all Heaven in your eye & die for love, with all heroes & angels to friend.

[348] *Napoleon.* "In Napoleon's eyes Merit was single by itself. & he recompensed it in one manner. Thus the same titles the same decorations were awarded equally to the ecclesiastic, the soldier, the artist, the philosopher & the man of letters."[649] [Cf.] *Las Cases* [*Journal,* 1823, IV, vii, 120]

At St Helena, he said, "Nature seems to have calculated that I should have to endure great reverses; for she has given me a mind of marble. Thunder cannot ruffle it, the shaft merely glides along."[650] Las C[ases, *Journal,* IV, vii, 121]

[649] This paragraph is used in "Spiritual Laws," *W,* II, 165.
[650] This paragraph is struck through in pencil with a diagonal use mark.

When reviewing a regiment of horse chasseurs at Lobenstein two days before the battle of Jena Napoleon addressing the Colonel said, "How many men are there here?" — "Five hundred" replied the Colonel "but there are many raw troops among them" — "What signifies that," said the Emperor in a tone which denoted surprise at the observation, "Are they not all Frenchmen!" Then turning to the regiment "My lads, you must not fear death. When soldiers brave death, they drive him into the enemy's ranks." [651] At these words a sudden movement among the troops accompanied by a murmur of enthusiasm seemed to foretell the memorable victory of Rosbach which took place fortyeight hours after[.] [652] [Cf. *ibid.*, IV, vii, 121–122]

Napoleon struck in the Russian campaign by the courage & strength of mind displayed by Ney was often heard to say, "I have two hundred millions in my coffers & I would give them all for Ney." [653] [*Ibid.*, IV, vii, 123]

[349][654] It was observed that the Emperor was not fond of setting forward his own merits. "That is" said he, "because with me morality & generosity are not in my mouth but in my nerves. My hand of iron was not at the extremity of my arm, it was immediately connected with ⟨the⟩my head. I did not receive it from nature; calculation alone has enabled me to employ it." [655]

"What," said he, "is the truth of history? A fable agreed upon." [656]

Napoleon like all men of genius is greatly impersonal in his

[651] "When reviewing . . . ranks.' ", struck through in pencil with a vertical use mark, is used in "Napoleon," *W*, IV, 236.

[652] The entire paragraph is struck through in ink with a curved vertical use mark.

[653] This paragraph, struck through in ink with a vertical use mark, is used in "Napoleon," *W*, IV, 244.

[654] "NAPOLEON" is printed above "It was observed" at the top of the page.

[655] Las Cases, *Journal*, 1823, IV, vii, 123. "My hand of iron . . . my head.", struck through in pencil with three vertical use marks and in ink with a single vertical use mark, is used in "Napoleon," *W*, IV, 231.

[656] Cf. Las Cases, *Journal*, 1823, IV, vii, 124. This remark is used in "History," *W*, II, 9.

habit of thought. He sees the sublime Laws & not the individual men. Men are to him but illustrations & hence a magnanimous tolerance.

[350]–[351] [blank]

[352]–[357] [Index material omitted]

[358] [Clipping omitted] [657]

[359] [Index material omitted]

[657] Emerson's letter on the Cherokee question (p. [306] above), as printed in the *National Intelligencer* of Washington, May 14, 1838, captioned "COMMUNICATION. TO MARTIN VAN BUREN, President of the United States." and signed RALPH WALDO EMERSON."

B

17 connexions, | They **19** Taylors' **21** into . . . damned$_2$ will . . . respect$_1$ | liar; **22** peoples'. **25** from, **30** junction, **33** candle. **35** fairy, tale | Robbins. | Lexington, **39** instruments, **40** up. **41** His . . . it$_2$ He . . . wheels$_1$: and **48** eat; | has . . . back$_2$ in . . . act.$_1$ **61** truth; **62** companies. **63** alleged; **67** com-[71]municate **69** revo-[74]lutions, **73** shown, **75** a⟨n⟩ | As[82]trology **76** sense. **78** summer | cotempora[85]neous **80** arbitrary[89]ness **82** R's. **83** Love **88** When | which **89** Ravenswod; | Taste, **90** it | man. **96** does **98** piety, **112** One, **115** faces. **125** give **130** in ⟨us | in-lieu **133** what | mortals. **134** Goethe. **135** worst. **136** Mind. **137** there[153]fore **143** 2$_3$4, **146** ⟨true Order⟩ of **147** superior; **149** Every **150** Iliad, **152** persons. **153** mind; **154** life, **166** aim. | bar. | luxury. **176** an a **177** was, **180** causing$_2$ in-streaming$_1$ **183** vanish. | shall ⟨the | it. creates | observation. **186** azote; **187** me"; | You **192** things. **196** observed.) | words, **197** what$_2$ is often$_1$ | away. . . . body. **198** And **205** head. | nose. | state **207** tint$_2$ . . . spine$_1$ | The | The | cities$_2$ & families$_1$ **208** it. **212** avoid. | panoram[255]ic **213** "There **214** might. **215** &c, &c, **217** Berserkirs$_2$ & Druids$_1$ | synthesis. | therewith. **218** others. **220** nature.' | law — [?] | blossom. **222** just. **225** jewels, **228** mine," **229** the | Man. **231** In **232** elements. — | lessened. **233** But **235** This **243** week. **245** Shakspear, | naivetê **246** than than[them?] that **250** Euxine. | under-[312]took **252** hour. **253** cellar,. **255** hope, by | him. who **256** [The most attractive . . . things]$_2$ is [the . . . stale]$_1$ **259** laws. | fruits$_2$ & flowers$_1$ **262** good." **267** propo[334]-sitions

RO Mind

274 Yet

C

280 has **283** do **287** for-[13]ward **288** occasion-[14]ally **289** sale. **296** sup-[26]ply; **302** har[34]poon **304** reaction; **305** the **308** A **316** Since **318** all. | All **326** [have a misgiving]$_2$ [in . . . sign]$_1$ **329** bub-[74]bles **335** pro[82]portion **339** philosoph[88]ical **342** things. **345** ones. **346** numbers, **356** adorable$_2$ admirable$_1$ | degrada[113]tion **360** rain-cannon balls **363** This **365** The **366** and has **369** "if **371** We c **372** Received | antagonist; | hour. **377** af-[144]fectionate **383** turn. **385** A;B;A; | t **386** like | If **389** faddle." **396** keepings. **399** The **402** A **404** that | him[187]self **406** home, **407** feu-[190]dal **410** We **411** own. **414** villagers. **417** & the Artist⟩ **418** Cattle Show Muster, **420** world & **423** ceased.' | force; **427** listen. **437** foreigners. to me **438** Wo **440** Christendom. **443** Wolf$_2$ Bentley$_1$ **446** as it **447** Actual, **455** problem. **461** oh Yes | work; **463** What | What **465** Waldos:[?] **466** remote$_2$ calm$_1$ **467** This **468** b **469** pulsation$_2$ & life$_1$ **470** The **471** f **476** experi-[301]ment **478** ⟨Eustis⟩ **479** world. **487** it. . . . etiquette. **493** confu[324]-tation **494** worth, **501** ex-[337]pression **502** dis[339]tinguish **505** forever. **506** thing; **507** thing;

Index

This Index includes Emerson's own index material omitted from the text. His index topics, including long phrases, are listed under "Emerson, Ralph Waldo, INDEX HEADINGS AND TOPICS." If Emerson did not specify a manuscript page or a date to which his index topic referred, the editor has chosen the most probable passage(s) and added "(?)" to the printed page number(s). If Emerson's own manuscript page number is an obvious error, it has been silently corrected.

References to materials included in *Lectures* are grouped under "Emerson, Ralph Waldo, LECTURES." References to drafts of poems occurring in these journals are under "Emerson, Ralph Waldo, POEMS." Under "Emerson, Ralph Waldo, WORKS" are references to later printed versions of these and other poems, to lectures and addresses included in *W* but not in *Lectures*, and to Emerson's essays and miscellaneous publications.

INDEX

Dryden, John, 83
Dualism, 30, 336–337, 482
Dulauloy, Countess, 310
Dunbar, William, *The Goldyn Targe*, 84
Duty, 28, 72, 87, 150, 172
Dwight, John Sullivan, 338, 373, 375, 425, 500, 502, 504

E., Mr. (of Concord), 422, 423
Eckermann, Johann Peter, 294, 295, 309; *Gespräche mit Goethe . . .*, 290n, 292n, 294, 313
Eclecticism, 458
Economy, 89, 319; economy of time, 6, 48, 133, 225, 418
Edgeworth, Maria, 320
Edinburgh Review, The, 309, 311n, 312
Education, 50, 98, 163, 175, 203, 222, 234, 324, 378, 408
Egotism, 493
Egypt, 400, 443, 465; arts of, 402; palaces of, 392
Egyptian, the, 399, 443
Electromagnetism, 42
Eleusinian Mysteries, 265
Eliot, John, 155, 257
Elliot, James, 45 (?), 78 (?)
Elliott, Ebenezer, 45 (?); "The Village Patriarch," 45n, 134n
Eloquence, 44, 88, 143, 210, 219, 243, 352, 449, 463–465
Emerson, Charles Chauncy (brother), 14n, 16n, 20, 21n, 24, 32, 33, 38, 45, 51n, 52, 54, 56, 76, 77, 81, 83, 84n, 86, 87, 88, 89, 90, 97, 99, 102n, 107, 108, 109–110, 125–126, 135, 140, 141, 144, 149, 150, 150–155, 158, 165, 171, 174–175 (?), 237n, 239–240, 244, 255, 285, 288–289, 324, 327, 374, 385, 389, 394, 453, 456, 461; letters to Elizabeth Hoar, 155–160, 161
Emerson, Edward Bliss (brother), 20, 102, 144, 151, 239, 240, 453, 456; "The Last Farewell," 17
Emerson, Ellen Tucker (first wife), 8–9, 19, 85, 108 (?), 119 (?), 216, 456
Emerson, George Barrell, 239, 264, 469
Emerson, Joseph (of Malden), 323
Emerson, Joseph (of Mendon), 56n
Emerson, Lidian (Lydia) Jackson (second wife), 14, 48, 52, 87, 138, 139n, 149, 234, 263n, 280, 290, 300, 304, 321, 324, 327, 343, 371, 374, 382, 422, 425, 442, 452,

454, 456, 461, 471, 474, 479, 480–481, 490n, 497
Emerson, Mary Moody (aunt), 16, 19, 36, 46, 52, 64, 65n, 80, 89, 102, 144, 190, 244, 264, 323, 350–351, 385, 409, 410, 419, 446, 455, 495
Emerson, Ralph Waldo, Account Book (1828–1835), 36n; Encyclopedia, 45n, 141n; Index Minor [A], 7n; Journal A ("1833", "1833–1834", "1834", "my last Blotting Book"), 7, 24, 103, 117, 219, 258, 275n; Journal B ("1835"), 121, 256n, 258, 270n, 272n, 273n, 274n, 276n, 282n, 292, 335n, 346n, 348n, 355n, 363, 369n, 370n, 375n, 391n, 395, 396n, 397n, 425, 450n, 476n, 484n, 495n; Journal C, 103n, 127n, 205n, 258n, 390; Journal D, 331, 335, 362; Journal Italy ("Italian Journal", "Journal at Naples"), 40–41, 205; Journal Q ("1832"), 227, 271n; Journal RO Mind, 23n, 38n, 50n, 136n; Journal T ("Transcript"), 45n, 47, 112, 130, 319; lecture series on Biography, 12n; lecture series on Human Culture, 274n, 425, 448, 450–451, 459; lecture series on Philosophy of History, 218, 221–222, 233, 266, 286; Notebook Composition, 84; Notebook L Concord, 55n; Notebook Σ Anecdotes, 76. *See also* "Chronology," xvii–xviii, *and* "self," *under* DISCUSSIONS *below*
    DISCUSSIONS: A. Bronson Alcott, 170, 178, 328, 457; architecture, 198, 206–207, 215; art and the age, 150, 195–196, 210–211; being and seeming, 46, 380, 389; biography, 11; benefactors, 160–161, 385; Napoleon Bonaparte, 472, 483–484, 485, 487, 488–489; books and reading, 72, 345, 347–348; Thomas Carlyle, 111–112, 173–174, 290–291, 358–359, 454–455, 459, 462–463; Christianity, 15, 90–91, 126, 135, 267, 459; composition and rhetoric, 25–26, 39–40, 92–93, 197, 198, 291, 335, 401, 409; conversation, 10–11, 23, 54, 329, 362–363, 374, 385; dreams, 27, 371, 475; dualism, 30, 336–337, 482; education, 408; Charles Emerson, 150–155, 239–240; Waldo Emerson, 234–235, 292–293; evil, 266, 330; experience, 188, 324–325, 361, 463–464, 464–465; expression, 322; extempore speaking, 500; the French Revolution, 15–16; friendship, 174–175; Margaret Fuller, 188, 319, 320; God, 6,

520